GOSPEL
DOCTRINE

GOSPEL DOCTRINE

SELECTIONS FROM

THE SERMONS AND WRITINGS

OF

JOSEPH F. SMITH

Sixth President of the Church of Jesus Christ
of Latter-day Saints

DESERET BOOK COMPANY
SALT LAKE CITY, UTAH

Library of Congress Catalog Card Number 99-70625

ISBN 1-57345-532-6

Printed in the United States of America   18961-6469

10   9   8   7   6   5   4   3   2   1

PREFACE

President Joseph F. Smith was so long in the public service of the Church that his published sermons and writings would fill many volumes. The difficult problem of the compilers of this volume has been to make a collection of extracts that would do full justice to the man and that, at the same time, could be contained in a volume of moderate size. Every reader who knows Church literature will note the shortcomings of the work; and none more than the compilers. However, incomplete as it may be, this collection is well worth while, for it contains a wealth of gospel wisdom, to instruct, comfort, and inspire the Saints.

The literature of the Church has been carefully and systematically searched to discover all of President Smith's public writings and sermons. Those of a historical nature have not been used in this collection, as they may well be made into another volume.

The compilers give their thanks to the many who, with hearts full of love for President Smith, have helped in the work.

The work has reaffirmed to us that prophets, speaking for God, are with us.

THE COMPILERS.

INTRODUCTION

President Joseph F. Smith incidentally stated on one occasion that when he should pass away, unlike many of his brethren, he would leave no written work, by which he might be remembered. It was his modest way of viewing his own ministry and literary labors, for President Smith would live in the hearts of the people even if he had said nothing for the printed page; but on the contrary, it was discovered that there are volumes in print, though at that time it had not been gathered and was therefore not so well known.

One of the compilers of this volume, Dr. John A. Widtsoe, listening to his remark, thought to himself, "certainly it cannot be true that he has left no written work." He then decided to look into his published writings and sermons, conceived the idea of making extracts from them and arranging these extracts by subjects and in chapters, in the form of a book. The result is this splendid volume now presented to the public under the title GOSPEL DOCTRINE.

Doctor John A. Widtsoe interested his brother, Prof. Osborne J. P. Widtsoe, also Albert E. Bowen, Doctor F. S. Harris, and Joseph Quinney, in the work of compiling and classifying from the voluminous writings and sermons of President Smith, such extracts as would bear upon the subjects chosen for consideration—subjects covering a wide range in gospel doctrine and philosophy, as taught by the Latter-day Saints. Lorenzo N. Stohl generously paid the expenses of the work.

Without price, and as a matter of love for the work in hand, these brethren proceeded with the compilation, had four typewritten copies prepared, nicely bound and titled, and were privileged, sometime before the death of the President, to offer him the first typewritten copy of the work, with their love and gratitude for his life, his example, and his inspired teachings, as well as for his gentle kindness and constant helpfulness to each of them.

Needless to say, the presentation and the work were gladly accepted and gave President Smith great delight.

The Committee on Study for the Priesthood Quorums, being apprised by the compilers of the work, conceived the idea, under the initiative of Elder David O. McKay, of the Council of the Twelve, of making it a text book for the Priesthood. The volume is now presented to the Melchizedek Priesthood Quorums of the Church for their study and consideration. To accompany it is "A GUIDE" for the direction of teachers and students, and adopted tor convenience in reference and study.

The sermons and writings of President Joseph F. Smith teach, in wisdom and moderation, practically every essential doctrine of the Latter-day Saints concerning the present life and the life hereafter. Not only that, but they abound in helpful counsel and advice on everyday practices in right living, stated in simple and persuasive language. President Smith's sermons and writings breathe the true spirit of the Gospel, are sound as gold in tenet and precept, and express the will of the Master in every word. Gathered, classified, arranged, and printed as in this volume, they constitute a compendium of the doctrine and teachings of the Church that we believe will stand as a safe guide for its members for generations to come.

In presenting this compilation to the public, we are confident that every reader will be fully repaid in its perusal, containing, as it does, rich and vital selections from the sayings, teachings and sermons of one of the foremost prophets of the Lord in the Dispensation of the Fulness of Times.

COMMITTEE ON COURSES OF STUDY FOR THE PRIESTHOOD, SALT LAKE CITY, MAY, 1919.

PUBLISHER'S PREFACE

The greatest things in this world are the greatest truths, and there are no truths of greater worth than the truths of salvation. To know and live those truths which bring us again into the presence of God is the crowning achievement of man. Among men, none ought be more honored than those chosen of God to teach his gospel and to be special witnesses of the divinity of his Son. Endowed with power from on high, ordained in celestial councils, schooled in the academies of heaven from eternities past, these humble yet noble souls are our guides through the deserts of Sinai as we seek the Lord in his holy mountain. Their words are to us as manna from heaven.

Among the noble and great ones so called and ordained was Joseph F. Smith, sixth president of The Church of Jesus Chirst of Latter-day Saints (1901-1918). President Smith presided over the Church during a period of intense anti-Mormon sentiment on both a local and national scale. Speaking at a general conference in April 1907, President Smith said: "Never were our principles or our purposes more widely misrepresented, more seriously misunderstood. Our doctrines are distorted, the sacred ordinances of our religion ridiculed, our Christianity questioned, our history falsified, our character traduced and questioned, and our course of conduct as a people reprobated and condemned."

The times demanded strong men and doctrines to match. Joseph F. Smith was more than equal to the challenge. He knew the gospel and the scriptures; what he did not know was fear or doubt where principles of truth were involved. To contend against Mormonism, President Smith declared, was to contend against the Bible; it was to contend against God,

Christ, and all that was true. No one, he affirmed, could contend against Mormonism on scriptural grounds. "Why? Because we believe in the scripture; we are established upon the scriptures of divine truth; we are built upon the foundations of apostles and prophets, Jesus Christ himself being the chief cornerstone. They cannot uproot us nor overturn us by the scriptures; it can't be done. . . . The moment that men attempt to fight this Church they fight God, they fight the principles of His gospel and His truth; they fight faith in God, faith in Jesus Christ, faith in righteousness, faith in the resurrection of the Lord Jesus Christ, faith in every principle that exalts and uplifts and ameliorates the condition of man in the world. If they undertake to fight us they fight these principles, because we have espoused these principles. They are our principles, and they are not principles of error, of injustice, or unvirtue, or of ungodliness. We do not espouse any such doctrine as that, neither do we teach it, when we are in the faith and fellowship of the Lord." (*Conference Report,* October 1910, pp. 128-29.)

It is a cardinal principle in the kingdom of the adversary that if you cannot refute doctrine, you impugn character. During these years, the Church in general and Joseph F. Smith in particular were attacked mercilessly in the press and at the pulpit. This was but a teaching moment for President Smith. He desired that Mormons not partake of the spirit of their enemies on the one hand, yet that they not be naive on the other. "I feel in my heart to forgive all men in the broad sense that God requires of me to forgive all men," he said, "and I desire to love my neighbor as myself; and to this extent I bear no malice toward any of the children of my Father. But there are enemies to the work of the Lord, as there were enemies to the Son of God. There are those who speak only evil of the Latter-day Saints. There are those—and they abound largely in our midst—who will shut their eyes to every virtue and to every good thing connected with this latter-day work, and will pour out floods of falsehood and misrepresentation against the people of God. I forgive them for this. I leave them in the hands of the just Judge. Let him deal with them as seemeth him good, but they are not and cannot become my bosom companions. I cannot condescend to that. While I would not harm a hair of their heads, while I would not throw a straw in their path, to hinder them from turning from the error of their way to the light of truth; I would as soon think of taking a centipede or a scorpion, or any poisonous reptile, and putting it into my bosom, as I would think of becoming a companion or an associate of such men." (See *Gospel Doctrine*, p. 337.)

From birth Joseph F. Smith was a seed cast on rocky soil. He entered mortality in 1838, the most strife-torn year in the Church's history. His mother, Mary Fielding Smith, a legend of faith in her own right, gave birth to this child of destiny on November 13 at Far West, Missouri. That same day a mock trial commenced in Richmond, Missouri, where his father, Hyrum, stood trial with Joseph Smith and other leaders of the Church. Though the trial was a sham, it offered some relief from the chains with which they had been shackled and the dungeon in which they were being held captive. A few days after Joseph F. Smith's birth, he almost suffocated when a mattress was thrown over him by a mob ransacking the little home in which he was born. Before his sixth birthday, his father would lean from his saddle, pick him up, hug him, and ride off with his prophet brother to Carthage and martyrdom.

Joseph F. Smith was the last of our prophets to have personally known Joseph Smith. As an older man he visited Nauvoo and could remember the very spot where he had stood when he bid that final farewell to his father. At eight years of age he was chased by hostile Indians at Winter Quarters. By his tenth year he was a seasoned teamster, having driven his mother's covered wagon across the plains and through the Rockies to the Salt Lake Valley. Before he turned fourteen his mother died. At fifteen he was expelled from school. The schoolmaster was going to use a leather strap on Joseph's little sister Martha. Joseph objected. The teacher mistakenly turned his wrath on the upstart, gangly youth and in the process learned quite a lesson himself. Joseph gave him a good licking and with it ended his formal schooling. Not knowing what to do with him, the brethren sent him on a mission. Thus at the age of fifteen, Joseph F. was ordained an elder and sent as a missionary to what we know today as the Hawaiian Islands. The fierce winds of sorrow and hardship caused the roots of his testimony to grow deep, while his innate love of justice and truth forced the branches of his understanding to reach upward in search of heaven's light.

Though left without father at the age of six and his mother at the tender age of thirteen, Joseph F. Smith was not without the protecting hand of Providence. While a young missionary in Hawaii, during a period of excessive loneliness and discouragement because of his indigent circumstances and his lack of education, he was granted a very remarkable dream, one in which he was invited to stand in the presence of the Prophet Joseph, his father, Brigham Young, Heber C. Kimball, and Willard Richards as they gave a special blessing to a baby—presumably himself as a child. (See *Gospel Doctrine*, pp. 541-43.) Of that experience he said, "To me it is a reality. There never could be anything more real to me. I felt the hand of Joseph Smith. I felth the warmth of his stomach, when I put my hand against him. I saw the smile upon his face." And in that experience he learned that he had been blessed by those great apostles of the Restoration. Some six decades later, as an aged prophet presiding over the general conference of the Church, he said, "I have a feeling in my heart that I stand in the presence not only of the Father and of the Son, but in the presence of those whom God commissioned, raised up and inspired to lay the foundations of the work in which we are engaged. I believe we move and have our being in the presence of heavenly messengers and of heavenly beings. We are not separate from them. . . . I stand also in the presence of Joseph and Hyrum and Brigham and John, and those who have been valiant in the testimony of Jesus Christ and faithful to their mission in the world, who have gone before." (*Conference Report,* April 1916, pp. 2-3.)

During the final years of his life, there were a number of occasions in which the veil became very thin for President Smith and in which marvelous visions were manifest to him. One of the most remarkable and instructive is now known to Latter-day Saints as the Vision of the Redemption of the Dead (D&C 138), which was added to our canon of scripture at general conference in April 1976. That revelation and the host of truths it contains, though new to many Latter-day Saints, had been available to them in *Gospel Doctrine* since its publication in 1919. (See pp. 472-76.) There is much else within the covers of this volume that could properly be considered scriptural and prophetic. (See D&C 68:4.) For instance, President Smith's warning about the three great dangers that threaten the Church from within—the flattery of those of prominence in the world, false educational ideas, and sexual impurity. (See pp. 312-13.) Similarly, his identification of the two primary sources of false doctrine among Latter-day Saints—"the hopelessly ignorant, whose lack of intelligence is due to their indolence and sloth," and the proud and self-vaunting . . . who read by the lamp of their own conceit." (See p. 373.)

Gospel Doctrine stands in a class of its own as a reference book and as a source of edification to the Latter-day Saint reader. Within the covers of this book one will find scripture, prophecy, wise counsel, and good doctrine. Truly it is a book that edifies. As President of the Church, Harold B. Lee said: "When I want to seek for a more clear definition of doctrinal subjects, I have usually turned to the writing and sermons of President Joseph F. Smith." (*Conference Report,* October 1972,

p. 18.) Likewise, Joseph Fielding Smith, the son and namesake of Joseph F. Smith, observed while he presided over the Church that the words and teachings of no man had influenced him like those of his father. "It was marvelous how the words of living light and fire flowed from him," he said. Joseph Fielding added that he had greater confidence in his father and his teachings than any other man he had ever known. Notwithstanding the fact that Joseph F. Smith never wrote a book, he is still one of the most often quoted of our Latter-day Saint leaders. Truly his was a voice of authority—he was a prophet's prophet.

If the measure of a man is the life he lived and the doctrine he taught, few men stand taller than Joseph F. Smith. Like his uncle, the Prophet Joseph Smith, whose name he bore, though cut from rough stone he became a polished shaft in the quiver of the Almighty. His formal education consisted of little more than that received by the Prophet Joseph, and yet his speech was refined, his vocabulary expansive, and his expression strong and colorful. His was an eloquence born of the Spirit. Wilford Woodruff had him stand before congregations of the Saints and would tell them that Joseph F. Smith looked more like the Prophet Joseph Smith than any man living, and that someday he would lead the Church. His spirit, too, was a reflection of the Prophet Joseph. In all that he taught, he was true to the message of the Restoration and true to those faithful brethren who blessed him as an infant.

Within this volume the reader will find the wisdom and spirit of a prophet.

JOSEPH FIELDING MCCONKIE
Associate Professor of Ancient Scripture
Brigham Young University

CONTENTS

CHAPTER VI

The Purpose and the Mission of the Church

CHAPTER VII

The First Principles of the Gospel

CHAPTER VIII

The Church and the Man

CHAPTER IX

PRIESTHOOD

CHAPTER X

SPIRITUAL GIFTS

CHAPTER XI

OBEDIENCE

CHAPTER XII

PRAYER

CHAPTER XIII

TITHING; THE POOR; INDUSTRY

CHAPTER XIV

TEMPERANCE; THE SABBATH

CHAPTER XV

MANY DUTIES OF MAN

CHAPTER XVI

MARRIAGE, THE HOME AND THE FAMILY

CHAPTER XVII

AMUSEMENTS AND FASHIONS

CHAPTER XVIII

LOVE YOUR ENEMIES

CHAPTER XIX

EDUCATION AND INDUSTRIAL PURSUITS

CHAPTER XX

MISSIONARIES

CHAPTER XXI

FALSE TEACHINGS

CHAPTER XXII

AUXILIARY ORGANIZATIONS

CHAPTER XXIII

POLITICAL GOVERNMENT

GOSPEL DOCTRINE

CHAPTER I

TRUTH, THE FOUNDATION

OUR HOPE FOUNDED ON TRUTH. Our hope of salvation must be founded upon the truth, the whole truth, and nothing but the truth, for we cannot build upon error and ascend into the courts of eternal truth and enjoy the glory and exaltation of the kingdom of our God. That cannot be done.—Oct. C. R.,* 1917, p. 3.

THE GOSPEL FOUNDED IN TRUTH. I have no fears in my heart, or mind, that that which is called "Mormonism"—which is indeed the gospel of Jesus Christ—will not bear the scrutiny of science and the researches of the learned and literate into all truth. The gospel of Jesus is founded in truth. Every principle of it is susceptible of demonstration beyond any just reason for contradiction. The Lord is doing his work and will do it, and no power can stay it.—Oct. C. R., 1908, p. 127.

TRUTH, THE FOUNDATION. We believe in righteousness. We believe in all truth, no matter to what subject it may refer. No sect or religious denomination in the world possesses a single principle of truth that we do not accept or that we will reject. We are willing to receive all truth, from whatever source it may come; for truth will stand, truth will endure. No man's faith, no man's religion, no religious organization in all the world, can ever rise above the truth. The truth must be at the foundation of religion, or it is in vain and it will fail of its purpose. I say that the truth is at the foundation, at the bottom and top of, and it entirely permeates this great work of the Lord that was established through the instrumentality of Joseph Smith, the prophet. God is with it; it is his work, not that of man; and it will succeed, no matter what the opposition may be. We look now at the opposition arrayed against the Church of Jesus Christ of Latter-day Saints, and smile, so to speak, with feelings of confidence, doubly assured by the experience of the past, in comparison to the feelings that possessed the souls of our fathers and mothers in the early days of the Church, when they were but a

*October Conference Report.

handful, with all the world arrayed against them; just a few poor, homeless people, driven from their possessions, cast out from the communities in which they sought to establish themselves and build their homes. When I think of our people, thrust into the wilderness, wandering and seeking for a place where the soles of their feet might rest, and see, then, the world arrayed against them, and think of the little chance that appeared before them, for success and the accomplishment of their purposes, I wonder that more of them did not tremble and falter than did; but some of them were true in the midst of it all, even unto death. If it had been necessary for them to have been martyred for the truth, willingly would they have given their lives, as they gave all else that they possessed in the world, for the knowledge they had of the divinity of the work in which they were engaged. Are we as faithful today? Are we as devout as our fathers were? Oh, my God, help me to be as true as they were! Help me to stand as they stood, upon the pedestal of eternal truth, that no power on earth, or in hell, may remove me from that foundation. This is my prayer to the Lord for my own sake, and it is my prayer to him for every Latter-day Saint throughout the length and breadth of the world.—Apr. C. R.,* 1909, p. 7.

MAN SAVED BY TRUTH. We have no ill feelings in our hearts toward any living creature. We forgive those who trespass against us. Those who have spoken evil of us, and who have misrepresented us before the world, we have no malice in our hearts toward them. We say, let God judge between them and us; let him recompense them for their work. We will not raise a hand against them; but we will extend the hand of fellowship and friendship to them, if they will repent of their sins and come unto the Lord and live. No matter how malicious they may have been, or how foolish they may have acted, if they will repent of it we will receive them with open arms and we will do all we can to help them to save themselves. I cannot save you; you cannot save me; we cannot save each other, only so far as we can persuade each other to receive the truth, by teaching it. When a man receives the truth he will be saved by it. He will not be saved merely because some one talks to him, but because he received and acted upon it. The gospel is consistent, it is common sense, reason, revelation; it is almighty truth from the heavens made known to man.—Apr. C. R., 1902, p. 86.

April Conference Report.

GOSPEL TRUTH CAN NOT BE SUPERSEDED. There is no science, nor philosophy, that can supersede God Almighty's truth. The Lord has said, "My word is truth," and indeed it is; and I believe that the Latter-day Saints know enough about the word of God to know it is his word when they see it and shun whatever is not; and that they will abide by the word of God, for it is truth. As the Savior said, "If ye continue in my word, then are ye my disciples indeed; and ye shall know the truth, and the truth shall make you free." I believe that the Latter-day Saints, and especially the leading men in Israel, have sufficient knowledge and understanding of the principles of the gospel that they know the truth, and they are made free by its possession—free from sin, free from error, free from darkness, from the traditions of men, from vain philosophy, and from the untried, unproven theories of scientists, that need demonstration beyond the possibility of a doubt. We have had science and philosophy through all the ages, and they have undergone change after change. Scarcely a century has passed but they have introduced new theories of science and of philosophy that supersede the old traditions and the old faith and the old doctrines entertained by philosophers and scientists. These things may undergo continuous changes, but the word of God is always true, is always right. I want to say to you that the principles of the gospel are always true—the principles of faith in God, of repentance from sin, of baptism for the remission of sins by authority of God, and the laying on of hands for the gift of the Holy Ghost; these principles are always true and are always absolutely necessary for the salvation of the children of men, no matter who they are or where they are. These principles are always true, and you cannot get away from them. No other name, under heaven, is given, but that of Jesus Christ, by which you can be saved or exalted in the Kingdom of God. No man can enter into the kingdom of heaven except he be born again of the water and of the Spirit. These principles are indispensable, for God has declared them. Not only has Christ declared them by his own voice, and his disciples from generation to generation, in the olden time, but in these latter days, they have taken up the same testimony and declared these things to the world. They are true today as they were true then, and we must obey these things.—Apr. C. R., 1911, pp. 7, 8.

MAN'S GREATEST ACHIEVEMENT. The greatest achievement mankind can make in this world is to familiarize themselves with divine truth, so thoroughly, so perfectly, that the example or conduct of no

creature living in the world can ever turn them away from the knowledge that they have obtained. "In the footsteps of the Master," the
greatest of all the teachers that this world has ever received, is the
safest and surest course to pursue that I know of in the world. We
can absorb the precepts, the doctrines and the divine word of the
Master, without any fear that the exemplar will fail of carrying out
and executing his own precepts and fulfilling his own doctrines and
requirements.

From my boyhood I have desired to learn the principles of the
gospel in such a way and to such an extent that it would matter not
to me who might fall from the truth, who might make a mistake, who
might fail to continue to follow the example of the Master, my foundation would be sure and certain in the truths that I have learned,
though all men else go astray and fail of obedience to them. We all
have heard of people who have pinned their faith to the arm of flesh,
who have felt that their belief, their confidence and their love for the
principles of the gospel of Jesus Christ would be shattered, if their
ideals—those possibly who first taught them the principles of the
gospel—should make a mistake, falter or fall.

I know of but One in all the world who can be taken as the
first and only perfect standard for us to follow, and he is the Only
Begotten Son of God. I would feel sorry indeed, if I had a friend
or an associate in this life who would turn away from the plan of
life and salvation because I might stumble or make a failure of my
life. I want no man to lean upon me nor to follow me, only so far
as I am a consistent follower in the footsteps of the Master.—*Juvenile
Instructor*, 1915, Vol. 50, pp. 738, 739.

TRUTH AND RIGHTEOUSNESS WILL PREVAIL. I do not expect
any victory, any triumph, anything to boast of, to come to the Latter-
day Saints, except upon the principles of righteousness and of truth.
Truth and righteousness will prevail and endure. If we will only
continue to build upon the principles of righteousness, of truth, of
justice, and of honor, I say to you there is no power beneath the
celestial kingdom that can stay the progress of this work. And as
this work shall progress, and shall gain power and influence among
men, so the powers of the adversary and of darkness will diminish
before the advancement and growth of this kingdom, until the kingdom of God, and not of men, will triumph.—*Apr. C. R.*, 1914, p. 4.

REALITY OF THE FAITH OF THE SAINTS. There is no doubt in
the minds of Latter-day Saints in relation to the existence and per-

sonage of the Lord God Almighty, who is the Father of our Lord
and Savior Jesus Christ. There is no doubt in the minds of Latter-day
Saints that Jesus is the Son of God, being begotten of the Father in
the flesh. And there is no Latter-day Saint in all the world but
knows as truly and as fully as God can impart that knowledge to the
soul of man, that he shall live again after death, and that men and
women shall be associated together as God has ordained, and they
have been united by his power, to dwell together forever and forever;
and they shall know as they are known, they shall see as they are
seen, and they shall understand as God understands; for they are
his children.—Apr. C. R., 1907, p. 39.

MEANING OF SCIENCE. True science is that system of reasoning
which brings to the fore the simple, plain truth. The Savior of the
world was pre-eminently the Scientist of this earth, and the truths
he uttered 1900 years ago have withstood the assaults of science and
prejudice and hate.—Logan Journal, Logan, February 6, 1912.

ALL TRUTH FROM GOD. Let us sustain the cause of Zion. Let
no man speak lightly of the principles of the gospel. Let no one
treat lightly the ordinances of the house of God. Let no one hold
in derision the Priesthood that the Lord has restored to the earth,
which is the authority that he has given unto men. Let no man
look contemptuously upon the organization of the Church of Jesus
Christ of Latter-day Saints as it has been established in the earth
through the instrumentality of the Prophet Joseph Smith, whom the
Lord raised up when he was but a child to lay the foundation of the
same. Let no man treat these things lightly or doubtingly; but let
every man seek earnestly to understand the truth and teach his children to become familiar with those truths of heaven that have been
restored to the earth in the latter-days. I believe with all my soul
in God the Father and our Lord and Savior Jesus Christ. I believe
with all my might, mind and strength in the Savior of the world,
and in the principle of redemption from death and sin. I believe
in the divine mission of the Prophet Joseph Smith. I believe in all
the truth that I know, and I believe that there are many principles
of eternal truth that still lie hidden from me and from the understanding of men, which will yet be revealed by the power of God unto
his faithful servants. I believe that the Lord has revealed to the
children of men all that they know. I do not believe that any man
has discovered any principle of science, or art, in mechanism, or
mathematics, or anything else, that God did not know before man

did. Man is indebted to the Source of all intelligence and truth, for the knowledge that he possesses; and all who will yield obedience to the promptings of the Spirit, which lead to virtue, to honor, to the love of God and man, and to the love of truth and that which is ennobling and enlarging to the soul, will get a cleaner, a more expansive, and a more direct and conclusive knowledge of God's truths than anyone else can obtain. I tell you this, because I know it is true. The Lord Almighty lives; he made the heavens and the earth, and the fountains of water; and we are his children, his offspring, and we are not here by chance. The Lord designed our coming, and the object of our being. He designs that we shall accomplish our mission, to become conformed to the likness and image of Jesus Christ, that, like him, we may be without sin unto salvation, like him we may be filled with pure intelligence, and like him we may be exalted to the right hand of the Father, to sit upon thrones and have dominion and power in the sphere in which we shall be called to act. I testify to this doctrine, for the Lord has made me to know and feel the truth of it from the crown of my head to the soles of my feet. I love good, honorable men—even men who may be mistaken, as far as their judgment is concerned, but who try to do right; I love them for the reason that they are my brethren, the sons of my Father, and I would that they might all see the truth as it is in Christ Jesus, and accept it, and receive all the benefits of it, in time and throughout all eternity. If the Lord has revealed to the world the plan of salvation and redemption from sin, by which men may be exalted again into his presence and partake of eternal life with him, I submit, as a proposition that cannot be controverted, that no man can be exalted in the presence of God and attain to a fulness of glory and happiness in his kingdom and presence, save and except he will obey the plan that God has devised and revealed.—*Apr. C. R.*, 1902, pp. 85, 86.

THE SAINTS MAY KNOW THE TRUTH. To the faithful Latter-day Saint is given the right to know the truth, as God knows it; and no power beneath the celestial kingdom can lead him astray, darken his understanding, becloud his mind or dim his faith or his knowledge of the principles of the gospel of Jesus Christ. It can't be done, for the light of God shines brighter than the illumination of a falsehood and error; therefore, those who possess the light of Christ, the spirit of revelation and the knowledge of God, rise above all these vagaries in the world; they know of this doctrine, that it is of God and not of man.—*Oct. C. R.*, 1909, p. 9.

How the Truth May Be Known. It is a wicked and adulterous generation that seeketh after a sign. Show me Latter-day Saints who have to feed upon miracles, signs and visions in order to keep them steadfast in the Church, and I will show you members of the Church who are not in good standing before God, and who are walking in slippery paths. It is not by marvelous manifestations unto us that we shall be established in the truth, but it is by humility and faithful obedience to the commandments and laws of God. When I as a boy first started out in the ministry, I would frequently go out and ask the Lord to show me some marvelous thing, in order that I might receive a testimony. But the Lord withheld marvels from me, and showed me the truth, line upon line, precept upon precept, here a little and there a little, until he made me to know the truth from the crown of my head to the soles of my feet, and until doubt and fear had been absolutely purged from me. He did not have to send an angel from the heavens to do this, nor did he have to speak with the trump of an archangel. By the whisperings of the still small voice of the Spirit of the living God, he gave to me the testimony I possess. And by this principle and power he will give to all the children of men a knowledge of the truth that will stay with them, and it will make them to know the truth, as God knows it, and to do the will of the Father as Christ does it. And no amount of marvelous manifestations will ever accomplish this. It is obedience, humility, and submission to the requirements of heaven and to the order established in the kingdom of God upon the earth, that will establish men in the truth. Men may receive the visitation of angels; they may speak in tongues; they may heal the sick by the laying on of hands; they may have visions and dreams; but except they are faithful and pure in heart, they become an easy prey to the adversary of their souls, and he will lead them into darkness and unbelief more easily than others.—Apr. C. R., 1900, pp. 40, 41.

How Man Lays an Imperishable Foundation of Truth. But the men and the women who are honest before God, who humbly plod along, doing their duty, paying their tithing, and exercising that pure religion and undefiled before God and the Father, which is to visit the fatherless and the widows in their afflictions and to keep oneself unspotted from the world, and who help look after the poor; and who honor the holy Priesthood, who do not run into excesses, who are prayerful in their families, and who acknowledge the Lord in their hearts, they will build up a foundation that the gates of hell

cannot prevail against; and if the floods come and the storms beat
upon their house, it shall not fall, for it will be built upon the rock of
eternal truth. I pray that this vast congregation will build upon this
imperishable foundation, upon the principle expressed by the words
of Joshua, "as for me and my house, we will serve God," and as also
expressed by Job, "though he slay me, yet will I trust in him." If
you have that spirit toward God and his work in these latter days,
you will build steadily and slowly, it may be, but surely, upon a foundation that will endure throughout the countless ages of eternity. And
if you do not get any great manifestations, you need not worry about
it. You will get the testimony of Jesus Christ in your hearts, and you
will know God and Jesus whom he has sent, whom to know is life
eternal, just as well as those who receive visions. For those who do
receive visions, the devil will try to make them believe that they were
delusions, and if they commit sin, he will be sure to make them
believe it. God bless you, is my prayer. Amen.—Apr. C. R., 1900,
p. 42.

REWARD OF ALL HONEST PEOPLE. In some instances you will
find examples of people out in the world who do not know as much
as you do of the gospel of Jesus Christ, who have not the testimony
of the Spirit in their hearts, as you have, of the divinity of Christ and
of Joseph Smith, who are just as devout, just as humble, just as
contrite in spirit, and as devoted to what they know, as some of us
are, and they will be rewarded according to their works, every one
of them, and will receive reward far surpassing anything that they
dream of.—Apr. C. R., 1912, p. 8.

THE GOSPEL IS SIMPLE. Some subjects are in themselves, perhaps, perfectly harmless, and any amount of discussion over them
would not be injurious to the faith of our young people. We are
told, for example, that the theory of gravitation is at best a hypothesis,
and that such is the atomic theory. These theories help to explain
certain things about nature. Whether they are ultimately true can
not make much difference to the religious convictions of our young
people. On the other hand, there are speculations which touch
the origin of life and the relationship of God to his children. In a
very limited degree that relationship has been defined by revelation,
and until we receive more light upon the subject we deem it best to
refrain from the discussion of certain philosophical theories which
rather destroy than build up the faith of our young people. One thing
about this so-called philosophy of religion that is very undesirable

lies in the fact that as soon as we convert our religion into a system of philosophy, none but philosophers can understand, appreciate, or enjoy it. God, in his revelation to man, has made his word so simple that the humblest of men, without special training, may enjoy great faith, comprehend the teachings of the gospel, and enjoy undisturbed their religious convictions. For that reason we are averse to the discussion of certain philosophical theories in our religious instructions.—*Juvenile Instructor*, Vol. 46, pp. 208, 209, April, 1911.

OUR KNOWLEDGE IS LIMITED. Our methods in speculation and reasoning about the things of God may often be harmless; but if we depart from the simplicity of God's word into a spirit of rationalism, we become the victims of vanity, which endangers the true spirit of worship in the human heart. It is not easy for men to give up their vanities, to overcome their preconceived notions, and surrender themselves heart and soul to the will of God which is always higher than their own. The dangers of religious speculations are as great today as they were in the days of Christ, and if we would avoid these dangers we must adhere to the simplicity of our religious beliefs and practices. When men and women realize they are getting into deep water where their footing is insecure, they should retreat, for they may be sure that the course they have been taking will lead them more and more away from their bearings which are not always easy to regain. The religion of the heart, the unaffected and simple communion which we should hold with God, is the highest safeguard of the Latter-day Saints. It is no discredit to our intelligence or to our integrity to say frankly in he face of a hundred speculative questions, "I do not know."

One thing is certain, and that is, God has revealed enough to our understanding for our exaltation and for our happiness. Let the Saints, then, utilize what they already have; be simple and unaffected in their religion, both in thought and word, and they will not easily lose their bearings and be subjected to the vain philosophies of man. —*Juvenile Instructor*, Vol. 46, p. 269, May, 1911.

BLESSINGS FOR THE LOVE OF TRUTH. If you love the truth, if you have received the gospel in your hearts, and love it, your intelligence will be added upon, your understanding of truth will be expanded, become larger than in any other way. Truth is the thing, above all other things in the world, that makes men free—free from indolence and carelessness, free from the fearful consequences of neglect, for it will be a fearful consequence, if we neglect our duty before the living God. If you will learn the truth and walk in the light of truth, you shall be made free from the errors of men and of crafts; you will be above suspicion and above wrong-doing of every description. God will approve of you and bless you and your inheritances, and make you prosper and flourish like a green bay tree.—*Improvement Era*, Vol. 21, p. 102, December, 1917.

Chapter II

THE ETERNAL NATURE OF THE CHURCH, THE PRIESTHOOD, AND MAN

ETERNAL NATURE OF THE PLAN OF SALVATION. I feel this morning as I have felt all my life, but I feel it stronger this morning, perhaps, than ever before, that there is nothing under the heavens of so much importance to me or to the children of men as the great plan of life and salvation which was devised in the heavens in the beginning, and which has been handed down from period to period through the inspiration of holy men called of God until the day of the coming of the Son of Man, for this gospel and this plan of salvation was revealed to our first parents. The angel of God carried to them the plan of redemption, and of salvation from death and sin that has been revealed from time to time by divine authority to the children of men, and it has undergone no change. There was nothing in it, in the beginning, that was superfluous or unnecessary; nothing in it that could be dispensed with; it was a complete plan devised in the beginning by the wisdom of the Father and the holy ones for the redemption of the human race and for their salvation and exaltation in the presence of God. It was taught more fully, and exemplified more perfectly in the being, the life and mission, the instruction and doctrine, of the Son of God, than ever before, unless there may be an exception in the days of Enoch; but through all the generations of time, the same gospel, the same plan of life and salvation, the same ordinances, burial with Christ, remembrance of the great sacrifice to be offered for the sins of the world and for man's redemption, have been handed down from time to time, from the time of the creation. —Oct. C. R., 1913, p. 2.

GOSPEL PRINCIPLES ARE ETERNAL. Faith in God is an irrevocable principle, just as much as "thou shalt not kill;" "thou shalt not steal;" "thou shalt not commit adultery." Repentance of a sin is an eternal principle, and is as essential in its place, and is as much an integral part of the gospel of Jesus Christ as: "thou shalt not kill," or, "thou shalt have no other gods before me."

Baptism for the remission of sin, by one having authority, is an eternal principle, for God devised it, and commanded it, and Christ himself was not above obeying it; he had to obey it in order to fulfil the law of righteousness.

And then the rites of the Priesthood of the Church, as the Lord has revealed them, and the principles that underlie the organization of the Church of Jesus Christ, are irrevocable, unchanging and unchangeable. We talk of the "everlasting gospel of Jesus Christ," which "is the power of God unto salvation," and these principles in and of themselves are eternal principles, and will last while life, or thought, or being last, or immortality endures.—Oct. C. R., 1912, p. 11.

PRE-EXISTING STATES.

Mrs. Martha H. Tingey,
      President, Y. L. M. I. A.

DEAR SISTER: The First Presidency have nothing to advance concerning pre-existing states but that which is contained in the revelations to the Church. The written standards of scripture show that all people who come to this earth and are born in mortality had a pre-existent, spiritual personality as the sons or daughters of the Eternal Father. (See *Pearl of Great Price*, Chap. 3, verses 5-7.) Jesus Christ was the Firstborn. A spirit born of God is an immortal being. When the body dies the spirit does not die. In the resurrected state the body will be immortal as well as the spirit. Speculations as to the career of Adam before he came to the earth are of no real value. We learn by revelation that he was Michael, the Archangel, and that he stands at the head of his posterity on earth (*Doctrine and Covenants*, Sec. 107:53-56.) Dogmatic assertions do not take the place of revelation, and we should be satisfied with that which is accepted as doctrine, and not discuss matters that, after all disputes, are merely matters of theory.

Your brethren,
      JOSEPH F. SMITH,
      ANTHON H. LUND,
      CHARLES W. PENROSE,
                  First Presidency.

—*Young Woman's Journal*, Vol. 23, pp. 162, 163, 1912.

SPIRIT MEMORIES. (Letter written to Elder O. F. Whitney who was a missionary in England.) I heartily endorse your sentiments respecting congeniality of spirits. Our knowledge of persons and things before we came here, combined with the divinity awakened within our souls through obedience to the gospel, powerfully affects, in my opinion, all our likes and dislikes, and guides our preferences in the course of this life, provided we give careful heed to the admonitions of the Spirit.

All those salient truths which come home so forcibly to the head and heart seem but the awakening of the memories of the spirit. Can we know anything here that we did not know before we came? Are not the means of knowledge in the first estate equal to those of this? I think that the spirit, before and after this probation, possesses greater facilities, aye, manifold greater, for the acquisition of knowledge, than while manacled and shut up in the prison-house of mortality.

Had we not known before we came the necessity of our coming, the importance of obtaining tabernacles, the glory to be achieved in posterity, the grand object to be attained by being tried and tested—weighed in the balance, in the exercise of the divine attributes, god-like powers and free agency with which we are endowed; whereby, after descending below all things, Christ-like, we might ascend above all things, and become like our Father, Mother and Elder Brother, Almighty and Eternal!—we never would have come; that is, if we could have stayed away.

I believe that our Savior is the ever-living example to all flesh in all these things. He no doubt possessed a foreknowledge of all the vicissitudes through which he would have to pass in the mortal tabernacle, when the foundations of this earth were laid, "when the morning stars sang together, and all the sons of God shouted for joy." When he conversed with the brother of Jared, on the Mount, in his spiritual body, he understood his mission, and knew the work he had to do, as thoroughly as when he ascended from the Mount of Olives before the wondering gaze of the Jewish disciples, with his resurrected, glorious and immortal body.

And yet, to accomplish the ultimatum of his previous existence, and consummate the grand and glorious object of his being, and the salvation of his infinite brotherhood, he had to come and take upon him flesh. He is our example. The works he did, we are commanded to do. We are enjoined to follow him, as he followed his Head; that where he is, we may be also; and being with him, may be like him. If Christ knew beforehand, so did we. But in coming here, we forgot all, that our agency might be free indeed, to choose good or evil, that we might merit the reward of our own choice and

conduct. But by the power of the Spirit, in the redemption of
Christ, through obedience, we often catch a spark from the awakened
memories of the immortal soul, which lights up our whole being as
with the glory of our former home.—*Contributor*, 1883, Vol. 4, pp.
114, 115.

THE IMMORTALITY OF MAN. We are called mortal beings because in us are seeds of death, but in reality we are immortal beings,
because there is also within us the germ of eternal life. Man is a
dual being, composed of the spirit which gives life, force, intelligence
and capacity to man, and the body which is the tenement of the
spirit and is suited to its form, adapted to its necessities, and acts in
harmony with it, and to its utmost capacity yields obedience to the
will of the spirit. The two combined constitute the soul. The body
is dependent upon the spirit, and the spirit during its natural occupancy of the body is subject to the laws which apply to and govern
it in the mortal state. In this natural body are the seeds of weakness
and decay, which, when fully ripened or untimely plucked up, in the
language of scripture, is called "the temporal death." The spirit is
also subject to what is termed in the scriptures and revelations from
God, "spiritual death." The same as that which befell our first
parents, when, through disobedience and transgression, they became
subject to the will of Satan, and were thrust out from the presence
of the Lord and became spiritually dead, which the Lord says, "is
the first death, even that same death which is the last death, which
is spiritual, which shall be pronounced upon the wicked when I shall
say, Depart, ye cursed!" And the Lord further says, "But behold, I
say unto you, that I the Lord God gave unto Adam and unto his
seed that they should not die as to the temporal death, until I the
Lord God should send forth angels to declare unto them repentance
and redemption (from the first death), through faith on the name
of mine Only Begotten Son. And thus did I, the Lord God, appoint
unto man the days of his probation; that by his natural death he
might be raised in immortality unto eternal life, even as many as would
believe; and they that believe not, unto eternal damnation, for they
cannot be redeemed from their spiritual fall, because they repent not."
From the natural death, that is the death of the body, and also from
the first death, "which is spiritual," there is redemption through
belief on the name of the Only Begotten Son, in connection with
repentance and obedience to the ordinances of the gospel, declared
by holy angels, for if one "believe," he must also obey; but from

the "second death," even that same death which is the first death, "which is spiritual," and from which man may be redeemed through faith and obedience, and which will again be pronounced upon the wicked when God shall say, "depart, ye cursed," there is no redemption, so far as light on this matter has been revealed. (See *Doc. and Cov.* 29:41-44.)

It is written that "all manner of sin and blasphemy shall be forgiven unto men" who receive me and repent; "but the blasphemy against the Holy Ghost, it shall not be forgiven unto men." If men will not repent and come unto Christ, through the ordinances of his gospel, they cannot be redeemed from their spiritual fall, but must remain forever subject to the will of Satan and the consequent spiritual darkness or death unto which our first parents fell, subjecting all their posterity thereto, and from which none can be redeemed but by belief or faith on the name of the Only Begotten Son and obedience to the laws of God. But, thanks be to the eternal Father, through the merciful provisions of the gospel, all mankind will have the opportunity of escape, or deliverance, from this spiritual death, either in time or in eternity, for not until they are freed from the first can they become subject unto the second death, still if they repent not "they cannot be redeemed from their spiritual fall," and will continue subject to the will of Satan, the first spiritual death, so long as "they repent not, and thereby reject Christ and his gospel;" but what of those who do believe, repent of their sins, obey the gospel, enter into its covenants, receive the keys of the Priesthood and the knowledge of the truth by revelation and the gift of the Holy Ghost, and afterwards turn away wholly from that light and knowledge? They "become a law unto themselves," and "will to abide in sin;" of such it is written, "whoso breaketh this covenant, after he hath received it, and altogether turneth therefrom, shall not have forgiveness in this world nor in the world to come." And again, "Thus saith the Lord, concerning all those who know my power, and have been made partakers thereof, and suffered themselves, through the power of the devil, to be overcome, and to deny the truth and defy my power—they are they who are the sons of perdition, of whom I say that it had been better for them never to have been born, for they are vessels of wrath, doomed to suffer the wrath of God, with the devil and his angels in eternity; concerning whom I have said there is no forgiveness in this world nor in the world to come, having denied the Holy Spirit after having received it, and having denied the Only

Begotten Son of the Father—having crucified him unto themselves, and put him to an open shame."—*Doc. and Cov.* 76:31-35.

Now, there is a difference between this class and those who simply repent not and reject the gospel in the flesh. Of these latter it is written, "they shall be brought forth by the resurrection of the dead, through the triumph and the glory of the Lamb," and "shall be redeemed in the due time of the Lord after the sufferings of his wrath." But of the others it is said, "they shall not be redeemed," for "they are the only ones on whom the second death shall have any power." The others, never having been redeemed from the first, cannot be doomed to the second death, or in other words cannot be made to suffer eternally the wrath of God, without hope of redemption through repentance, but must continue to suffer the first death until they repent, and are redeemed therefrom through the power of the atonement and the gospel of salvation, thereby being brought to the possession of all the keys and blessings to which they will be capable of attaining or to which they may be entitled, through the mercy, justice and power of the everlasting God; or, on the other hand, forever remain bound in the chains of spiritual darkness, bondage and banishment from his presence, kingdom and glory. The "temporal death" is one thing, and the "spiritual death" is another thing. The body may be dissolved and become extinct as an organism, although the elements of which it is composed are indestructible or eternal, but I hold it as self-evident that the spiritual organism is an eternal, immortal being, destined to enjoy eternal happiness and a fulness of joy, or suffer the wrath of God, and misery—a just condemnation, eternally. Adam became spiritually dead, yet he lived to endure it until freed therefrom by the power of the atonement, through repentance, etc. Those upon whom the second death shall fall will live to suffer and endure it, but without hope of redemption. The death of the body, or natural death, is but a temporary circumstance to which all were subjected through the fall, and from which all will be restored or resurrected by the power of God, through the atonement of Christ.

Man existed before he came to this earth, and he will exist after he passes from it; and will continue to live throughout the countless ages of eternity.

There are three classes of beings; or rather, man exists in three separate conditions, before and after his probation upon this earth—first, in the spirit or pre-existent state; second, in the disembodied state, the condition which exists after the dissolution of the body and spirit until the resurrection take place; and third, in the resurrected state. For instance, some two thousand years before the coming of Christ into the world to sojourn in the flesh, he showed himself to the brother of Jared and said, "Behold, this body, which ye now behold, is the body of my spirit; and man have I created after the body of my spirit; and even as I appear unto thee to be in the spirit, will I appear unto my people in the flesh." He further declared, "Behold, I am he who was prepared from the foundation of the world to redeem my people. Behold, I am Jesus Christ." (Ether 3:16, 14.)

Here Jesus showed himself unto this man in the spirit, even after the manner and in the likeness of the same body, even as he showed himself unto the Nephites—that is, prior to his coming in the flesh. This I consider typical of the first condition of all spirits. Again it is written, "For Christ also hath once suffered for sins, the just for the unjust, that he might bring us to God, being put to death in the flesh, but quickened by the Spirit: by which also he went and preached unto the spirits in prison: which sometime were disobedient, when once the longsuffering of God waited in the days of Noah, while the ark was a preparing, wherein few, that is, eight souls were saved by water," etc. Thus we see that while the body of our Savior slept in the tomb, he went in the spirit and preached his glorious gospel to "the spirits in prison," who were disobedient in the days of Noah, and were destroyed in the flesh by the flood. This was their second condition or state in the spirit, awaiting the resurrection of their bodies which were slumbering in death. "Marvel not at this:" saith Jesus, "for the hour is coming, in the which all that are in the graves shall hear his [the Redeemer's] voice, and shall come forth; they that have done good, unto the resurrection of life; and they that have done evil, unto the resurrection of damnation." In reference to the third condition or state, we will refer to the account given of the risen Redeemer before his ascension. John tells us that he appeared unto his disciples three times after his resurrection, on which occasions he ate bread, broiled fish and honeycomb, and opened the eyes of their understanding, that they began to comprehend the Scriptures and the prophecies concerning Christ. But when he appeared unto them they were terrified and affrighted, and supposed that they had seen a spirit. "And he said unto them, Why are ye troubled? and why do thoughts arise in your hearts? Behold my hands and my feet, that it is I myself: handle me, and see; for a spirit hath not flesh

and bones, as ye see me have." (Luke 24:38-9.) Here is presented
the true type of the resurrected being. And after this manner are all
those who have their resurrected bodies, and there are many of these,
for we are told in the scriptures that "the graves were opened, and
many bodies of the Saints which slept arose and came out of the
graves, after his resurrection, and went into the holy city and appeared
unto many." This class of beings dwell in heaven, or in the paradise
of the just, having been counted worthy to come forth in the first
resurrection, even with Christ, to dwell with him and to be associated
with the members of the kingdom of God and his Christ. These
comprise the three conditions or estates of man in heaven. Not all,
however, of the disembodied spirits enjoy the same privileges, exaltation and glory. The spirits of the wicked, disobedient, and unbelieving, are denied the privileges, joys and glory of the spirits of the just
and good. The bodies of the Saints will come forth in the first
resurrection, and those of the unbelieving, etc., in the second, or last.
In other words, the Saints will rise first, and those who are not
Saints will not rise until afterwards, according to the wisdom, justice
and mercy of God.

Christ is the great example for all mankind, and I believe that
mankind were as much foreordained to become like him, as that
he was foreordained to be the Redeemer of man. "Whom
God did foreknow" — and whom did he not foreknow? — "he
also did predestinate to be conformed to the image of his Son,
that he might be the firstborn among many brethren." It is very
plain that mankind are very far from being like Christ, as the world is
today, only in form of person. In this we are like him, or in the
form of his person, as he is the express image of his Father's person.
We are therefore in the form of God, physically, and may become
like him spiritually, and like him in the possession of knowledge,
intelligence, wisdom and power.

The grand object of our coming to this earth is that we may
become like Christ, for if we are not like him, we cannot become the
sons of God, and be joint heirs with Christ.

The man who passes through this probation, and is faithful, being
redeemed from sin by the blood of Christ, through the ordinances
of the gospel, and attains to exaltation in the kingdom of God, is not
less but greater than the angels, and if you doubt it, read your Bible,
for there it is written that the Saints shall "judge angels," and also
they shall "judge the world." And why? Because the resurrected,

righteous man has progressed beyond the pre-existent or disembodied spirits, and has risen above them, having both spirit and body as Christ has, having gained the victory over death and the grave, and having power over sin and Satan; in fact, having passed from the condition of the angels to that of a God. He possesses keys of power, dominion and glory that the angel does not possess—and cannot possess without gaining them in the same way that he gained them, which will be by passing through the same ordeals and proving equally faithful. It was so ordained when the morning stars sang together, before the foundations of this earth were laid. Man in his pre-existent condition is not perfect, neither is he in the disembodied estate. There is no perfect estate but that of the risen Redeemer, which is God's estate, and no man can become perfect except he become like the Gods. And what are they like? I have shown what Christ is like, and he is like his Father, but I will refer to an undoubted authority to this people, on this point: "The Father has a body of flesh and bones as tangible as man's; the Son also; but the Holy Ghost has not a body of flesh and bones, but is a personage of Spirit, were it not so, the Holy Ghost could not dwell in us." (Doc. and Cov., Sec. 130.) There is not time to refer to the many scriptural passages which might be cited in proof of these important facts, enough already have been referred to, to place the matter beyond a doubt.

It is believed by many, in the Christian world, that our Savior finished his mission when he expired upon the cross, and his last words on the cross, as given by the Apostle John—"It is finished," are frequently quoted as evidence of the fact; but this is an error. Christ did not complete his mission upon the earth until after his body was raised from the dead. Had his mission been completed when he died, his disciples would have continued fishermen, carpenters, etc., for they returned to their several occupations soon after the crucifixion, not yet knowing the force of their holy calling, nor understanding the mission assigned them by their Master, whose name would soon have been buried with his body in the grave to perish and be forgotten, "for as yet they knew not the scripture, that he must rise again from the dead." But the most glorious part of his mission had to be accomplished after the crucifixion and death of his body. When on the first day of the week some of the disciples went to the tomb with certain preparations for the body of their Lord, they were met there by two men clothed in "shining garments," who said unto them, "Why seek ye the living among the dead?

He is not here, but is risen. Remember how he spoke unto you when he was yet in Galilee, saying, The Son of Man must be delivered into the hands of sinful men and be crucified, and the third day rise again." And not until then did the disciples remember these words of the Savior, or begin to understand their meaning. Why were they thus forgetful and seemingly ignorant of all they had been taught by the Savior respecting the objects of his mission to the earth? Because they lacked one important qualification, they had not yet been "endowed with power from on high." They had not yet obtained the gift of the Holy Ghost. And the presumption is, they never would have received this important and essential endowment had Christ's mission been completed at the time of his death.

It may seem strange to some who may not have reflected on this matter fully, that the disciples of Christ were without the gift of the Holy Ghost until after his resurrection. But so it is written, notwithstanding the Savior on one occasion declared, "blessed art thou Simon, etc., for flesh and blood hath not revealed this unto thee, but my Father which is in heaven." While Jesus was with them he was their light and their inspiration. They followed him by sight, and felt the majestic power of his presence, and when these were gone they returned to their nets and to their various occupations and to their homes saying, "we trusted that it had been he which should have redeemed Israel, but the chief priests and our rulers have delivered him to be condemned to death, and have crucified him." No wonder that Jesus exclaimed unto some of them, "O fools, and slow of heart to believe all that the prophets have spoken."

If the disciples had been endowed with the "gift of the Holy Ghost," or "with power from on high," at this time, their course would have been altogether different from this, as the sequel abundantly proved. If Peter, who was the chief apostle, had received the gift of the Holy Ghost, and the power and testimony thereof prior to the terrible night on which he cursed and swore and denied his Lord, the result would have been very different with him, for then he would have sinned against "light and knowledge," and "against the Holy Ghost," for which there is no forgiveness. The fact, therefore, that he was forgiven, after bitter tears of repentance, is an evidence that he was without the witness of the Holy Ghost, never having received it. The other disciples or apostles of Christ were precisely in the same condition, and it was not until the evening of the day on which Jesus came out of the grave that he bestowed upon them this inestimable gift. John gives a careful description of this important event which concludes as follows: "Then said Jesus to them again, Peace be unto you: as my Father hath sent me, even so send I you. And when he had said this, he breathed on them, and saith unto them, Receive ye the Holy Ghost: whose soever sins ye remit, they are remitted unto them," etc. This was their glorious commission, and now were they prepared to receive the witness of the Spirit—even the testimony of Jesus Christ. Yet they were told to tarry in Jerusalem, until they were endued with power from on high, which they did. Jesus further told them that if he went not away the "Comforter"—that is, the Holy Ghost—would not come unto them, but if he went away he would "send him," and he it was who should testify of Christ, and of the Father, and bring to their remembrance "all things whatsoever" he had commanded or taught them, and it should "lead them into all truth." Thus we see that the resurrection from the dead, not only of Christ, but of all mankind, in the due time of the Lord; the endowment of the apostles with the Holy Ghost, and their glorious commission from Christ, being sent out by him as he was sent by the Father; the opening of the eyes of the disciples to understand the prophecies of the Scriptures, and many other things did Jesus after he cried out upon the cross, "It is finished." Further, the mission of Jesus will be unfinished until he redeems the whole human family, except the sons of perdition, and also this earth from the curse that is upon it and both the earth and its inhabitants can be presented to the Father redeemed, sanctified and glorious.

Things upon the earth, so far as they have not been perverted by wickedness, are typical of things in heaven. Heaven was the prototype of this beautiful creation when it came from the hand of the Creator, and was pronounced "good."—*Journal of Discourses,* Vol. 23 (1883), pp. 169-175, delivered June 18, 1882.

MAN ETERNALLY RESPONSIBLE. Man will be held responsible in the life to come for the deeds that he has done in this life, and will have to answer for the stewardships entrusted to his care here, before the Judge of the quick and the dead, the Father of our spirits, and of our Lord and Master. This is the design of God, a part of his great purpose. We are not here to live a few months or years, to eat, drink and sleep, then to die, pass away and perish. The Lord Almighty never designed man to be so ephemeral, useless and imperfect as this. I would pity the being who had such a conception as this of the Creator of the starry heavens, the planets, and the world on which we dwell, poor as it is in glory in comparison to the many others created. Is it conceivable that one possessing such power, majesty, intelligence, light and knowledge would create a world like this and people it with beings in his own image and likeness only to live and grovel through a short, miserable existence, then die and perish? No such thing! There is no death here, but there is life!

God is the God of the living, and not of the dead. He is the God of Abraham, Isaac and Jacob, and of the ancient prophets. They live! They live not only in the words they spoke, the predictions they made, and in the promises handed down from generation to generation to the children of men; they live not only in the record they made, in the doctrines that they taught, and in the hope that they held out for redemption, atonement and salvation, but they live in spirit, in entity, as they lived here. They are prophets, as they were prophets here, the chosen of God; patriarchs, as they were here; possessing the same identity, the same entity; and by and by, if not already, they will possess the same bodies they possessed while journeying in mortality. Those bodies will become purified, cleansed, and made perfect; and the spirit and the body will be reunited, never more to be separated, never again to taste of death. This is the law and the promise of God, and the words spoken to his ancient prophets, come down to us through the generations that have followed.—*Improvement Era*, Vol. 21, p. 357, Feb., 1918.

OUR INDESTRUCTIBLE, IMMORTAL IDENTITY. What a glorious thing it is to know and be true to that which has been revealed in these latter times through the instrumentality of the Prophet Joseph Smith. It was revealed anciently by the Savior himself, and he exemplified that glorious principle of which I wish to say a few words, and which has been renewed and emphasized more especially in these latter days through Joseph Smith—I refer to our identity, our indestructible, immortal identity. As in Christ we have the example, he was born of woman, he lived, he died, and he lived again in his own person and being, bearing even the marks of the wounds in his flesh, after his resurrection from the dead—so also a testimony has been given to you, in later days, through the Prophet Joseph Smith, and others who have been blessed with knowledge, that the same individual Being still lives and will always live. Jesus is possessed of immortality, and eternal life; and in evidence of his existence and his immortality, and in evidence of the great and glorious truths of the gospel which he taught, the death which he died, and the resurrection that he wrought from the dead, he has revealed himself and borne his own record and testimony to those who have lived and still live in this day and age. What a glorious thought it is, to me at least, and it must be to all who have conceived of the truth or received it in their hearts, that those from whom we have to part here, we will meet again and see as they are. We will meet the same identical being that we associated with here in the flesh—not some other soul, some other being, or the same being in some other form, but the same identity and the same form and likeness, the same person we knew and were associated with in our mortal existence, even to the wounds in the flesh. Not that a person will always be marred by scars, wounds, deformities, defects or infirmities, for these will be removed in their course, in their proper time, according to the merciful providence of God. Deformity will be removed; defects will be eliminated, and men and women shall attain to the perfection of their spirits, to the perfection that God designed in the beginning. It is his purpose that men and women, his children, born to become heirs of God, and joint heirs with Jesus Christ, shall be made perfect, physically as well as spiritually, through obedience to the law by which he has provided the means that perfection shall come to all his children. Therefore, I look for the time when our dear Brother William C. Staines, whom we all knew so well, and with whom we were familiar for years—I was familiar with him, all my life, just as I was familiar with Aunt Rachel here all my life, and do not remember the time when I did not know her—I look for the time, I say, when Brother Staines will be restored. He will not remain the crippled and deformed William C. Staines that we knew, but he will be restored to his perfect frame—every limb, every joint, every part of his physical being will be restored to its perfect frame. This is the law and the word of God to us, as it is contained in the revelations that have come to us, through the Prophet Joseph Smith. The point in my mind which I desire to speak of particularly is this: When we shall have the privilege to meet our mother, our aunt, our sister, this noble woman whose mortal remains lie here now, but whose immortal spirit has ascended to God from whence it came, when that spirit shall return to take up this tabernacle again, she will be Aunt Rachel in her perfection. She will not always remain just as she will appear

when she is restored again to life, but she will go on to perfection.
Under that law of restoration that God has provided, she will regain
her perfection, the perfection of her youth, the perfection of her
glory and of her being, until her resurrected body shall assume the
exact stature of the spirit that possessed it here in its perfection,
and thus we shall see the glorified, redeemed, exalted, perfected Aunt
Rachel, mother, sister, saint and daughter of the living God, her
identity being unchanged, as a child may grow to manhood or womanhood and still be the same being.

I want to say to my friends, my brethren and sisters, and to the
kindred, that the Lord Almighty has revealed these truths to us in
these days. We not only have it in the written word, we have it in
the testimony of the spirit of God in the heart of every soul who has
drunk from the fountain of truth and light, and that witness bears
record of these words to us. What else would satisfy us? What else
would satisfy the desire of the immortal soul? Would we be satisfied
to be imperfect? Would we be satisfied to be decrepit? Would we
be satisfied to remain forever and ever in the form of infirmity
incident to age? No! Would we be satisfied to see the children
we bury in their infancy remain as children only, throughout the
countless ages of eternity? No! Neither would the spirits that did
possess the tabernacles of our children be satisfied to remain in that
condition. But we know our children will not be compelled to
remain as a child in stature always, for it was revealed from God, the
fountain of truth, through Joseph Smith the prophet, in this dispensation, that in the resurrection of the dead the child that was buried
in its infancy will come up in the form of the child that it was when
it was laid down; then it will begin to develop. From the day of
the resurrection, the body will develop until it reaches the full
measure of the stature of its spirit, whether it be male or female. If
the spirit possessed the intelligence of God and the aspirations of
mortal souls, it could not be satisfied with anything less than this.
You will remember we are told that the spirit of Jesus Christ visited
one of the ancient prophets and revealed himself to him, and he
declared his identity, that he was the same Son of God that was to
come in the meridian of time. He said he would appear in the flesh
just as he appeared to that prophet. He was not an infant; he was
a grown, developed spirit; possessing the form of man and the form
of God, the same form as when he came and took upon him a tabernacle and developed it to the full stature of his spirit. These are

truths that have been revealed to us. What for? To give us intelligent hope; to give us intelligent aspiration; to lead us to think, to hope, to labor and accomplish what God has aimed and does aim and design that we should accomplish, not only in this life, but in the life to come.

I rejoice exceedingly that I know and have known nearly all my life such a noble woman. I do not remember the first time that I saw Aunt Rachel, I can't recall it; it seems to me I always knew her, just as I knew my mother in my childhood and all the way through life; and I rejoice exceedingly in this testimony of the Spirit of the Lord that has come to us through revelation in the latter days. Through this testimony I am confident that I shall see Aunt Rachel, by and by; and when I go—and I expect to go, perhaps, long before she shall recover this tabernacle—I expect to meet her there. I expect to meet the same individual that I knew here. I expect to be able to recognize her, just as I could recognize her tomorrow, if she were living. I believe I will know just exactly who she is and what she is, and I will remember all I knew about her; and enjoy her association in the spirit as I did in the flesh; because her identity is fixed and indestructible, just as fixed and indestructible as the identity of God the Father and Jesus Christ the Son. They cannot be any other than themselves. They cannot be changed; they are from everlasting to everlasting, eternally the same; so it will be with us. We will progress and develop and grow in wisdom and understanding, but our identity can never change. We did not spring from spawn. Our spirits existed from the beginning, have existed always, and will continue forever. We did not pass through the ordeals of embodiment in the lesser animals in order to reach the perfection to which we have attained in manhood and womanhood, in the image and likeness of God. God was and is our Father, and his children were begotten in the flesh of his own image and likeness, male and female. There may have been times when they did not possess the same intelligence that they possessed at other times. There are periods in the history of the world when men have dwindled into ignorance and barbarism, and then there were other times when they have grown in intelligence, developed in understanding, enlarged in spirit and comprehension, approaching nearer to the condition and likness of their Father and God, and then losing faith, losing the love of God, losing the light of the Spirit and returning again to semi-barbarism. Then again, they have been restored, by the power and operation of the Spirit of the Lord upon their minds, until they again reached a degree of intelligence. We have reached a degree of intelligence in our dispensation. Will this same degree of intelligence, that now exists throughout the world, continue to exist? Yes; if the world continue to abide in the light that has been shed-abroad in the world by the Father of light, with whom there is no variableness nor shadow of turning. But let them deny God, let them deny truth, let them depart from righteousness, let them begin again to wallow in wickedness and transgression of the laws of God, and what will be the result? They will degenerate; they will again recede possibly into absolute barbarism, unless they repent, and the power of God will be again restored to them and they be again lifted up by that light which shines and is never dim, except to men who shut their hearts and eyes and ears against it and will not receive it.

I did not expect to enter into any lengthy discourse. I thank God for my relationship and acquaintance with this noble, good mother. I expect to be associated with her throughout all the ages to come, if I can be as faithful as she has been. I desire to be, and that isn't all—with the help of God, I intend to be faithful, as she has been faithful, that in the end I may be worthy to dwell where she will dwell, with the Prophet Joseph Smith, with her husband with whom she was associated here in the flesh, with her son and her children, from generation to generation. I expect to be associated with them in the mansions that are prepared for the righteous, where God and Christ are, where those shall be who believe in his name, who receive his work and abide in his law! Oh! that I could be instrumental in the hands of the Lord in bringing every loved soul unto him, for there are souls that are still lacking, whom I love, and if it were possible, how I would love to be instrumental in the hand of the Lord in bringing those loved souls to a knowledge of this truth, that they might receive of its glory, benefits and blessings, in this life and in the life to come. From my childhood, I have always tried to be a savior on Mount Zion, a savior among men. I have that desire in my heart. I may not have been very successful in my ambition to accomplish this work, but I have desired it, and I still desire that I may be instrumental in helping to spread this truth to the earth's remotest bounds and the testimony of it to the children of men in every land. I know it is true. It appeals to my judgment, to my desires, and to the aspirations of my soul; I want my family; I want those the Lord has given to me; I want them now; I want them forever! I want to be associated with them forever. I do not want them to change their identity. I do not want them to be somebody else. This idea of theosophy, which is gaining ground even among so-called Christians, in these latter days, is a fallacy of the deepest kind. It is absolutely repugnant to the very soul of man to think that a civilized, intelligent being might become a dog, a cow, a cat; that he might be transformed into another shape, another kind of being. It is absolutely repulsive and so opposed to the great truth of God, that has been revealed from the beginning, that he is from the beginning always the same, that he cannot change, and that his children cannot change. They may change from worse to better; they may change from evil to good, from unrighteousness to righteousness, from humanity to immortality, from death to life everlasting. They may progress in the manner in which God has progressed; they may grow and advance, but their identity can never be changed, worlds without end—remember that; God has revealed these principles, and I know they are true. They assert their truth upon the intelligent mind and soul of man. They embrace or embody that which the Lord has planted in our hearts and souls to desire, and to give it unto us. They put us in the way of receiving that which we most desire and most love, that which is most necessary and essential to our happiness and exaltation. They take of the things of God and give them to us, and they prepare us for the future, for exaltation and for eternal happiness, a reward which all the souls in the world desire, if they are correct in their lives and thoughts. It is only the vicious and the truly wicked who do not desire purity; they do not love purity and truth. I do not know whether it is possible for any soul to become so debased as to lose all regard for that which is pure and chaste, good and true and godlike. I believe that there still lingers in the heart of the most vicious and wicked, at times at least, a spark of that divinity that has been planted in the souls of all the sons of God. Men may become so corrupt that they do not have more than mere glimpses of that divine inspiration that strives to lead them toward and to love good; but I do not believe there is a soul in the world that has absolutely lost all conception and admiration of that which is good and pure, when he sees it. It is hard to believe that a human being may become so depraved that he has lost all desire that he might also be good and pure, if it were possible; but many people have abandoned themselves to evil and have come to the conclusion that there is no chance for them. While there is life there is hope, and while there is repentance there is a chance for forgiveness; and if there is forgiveness, there is a chance for growth and development until we acquire the full knowledge of these principles that will exalt and save us and prepare us to enter into the presence of God the Father, who is the Father of our spirits, and who is the Father in the flesh, of his Only Begotten Son, Jesus Christ, who joined divine immortality with the mortal, welded the link between God and man, made it possible for mortal souls, on whom the sentence of death had been placed, to acquire eternal life, through obedience to his laws. Let us, therefore, seek the truth and walk in the light as Christ is in the light, that we may have fellowship with him, and with each other, that his blood may cleanse us from all sin.

May the Lord comfort my brother Heber, and I know he will. Brother Heber does not feel that there is any death here. I don't think I could weep for sorrow. I could give way to tears just now, but they would not be tears of sorrow, of mourning, or of grief, for this good soul. They would only express the love I have for her; they would only indicate my feelings toward her, for the noble and pure example she set before me and all who have known her. I could weep for joy in the knowledge that I possess that she, in her spirit life and being, is and will be associated with all those who have been endeared to her by the persecutions, the experiences and the trials through which she has had to pass in this world. With them she is rejoicing today, as one born of death into life everlasting. She is not dead; she lives! What greater proof do you want of that fact than to see her lifeless form? Who is she? This is her casket. This is her mortal tenement; this is but the clay that enveloped the immortal, living Aunt Rachel, the living spirit. The spirit has fled. Her spirit, the immortal part, has departed from this tabernacle; hence, this tabernacle lies here lifeless and ready to return to mother earth from whence it came, but to be restored again, every element to be recalled and re-formed in its perfect frame, when Aunt Rachel will come and take possession of it and inherit it forever, just as Christ came and took up his body that was not suffered to see corruption, and inherited it in its immortal state, never to be separated again; so it will be with her.—*Improvement Era*, Vol. 12, p. 591, June, 1909. Speech at the funeral services of Rachel Grant, mother of President Heber J. Grant.

No New Principles in the Gospel. We have no new principle to advocate; but we have come to preach the gospel of life and salvation, to testify to the divinity of our Lord and Savior, Jesus

Christ, and of the divine mission of the Prophet Joseph Smith, through whose instrumentality the truth was restored in this dispensation.—*Improvement Era*, Vol. 21, p. 98, December, 1917.

FOUNTAIN OF TRUTH. We hear frequently of men who throw discredit on the doctrine of Jesus Christ, our Savior and Redeemer, because some of the principles, doctrines, and philosophy which he taught are said to have been spoken before his day by heathen philosophers.

A variety of examples are sometimes quoted to show that the ideals which have grown from the doctrines of Christ are a direct development of what is found in the teachings of the Old Testament, particularly, in the Psalms and in the second part of Isaiah. But, on the other hand, it is just as certain that these ideals receive a finish and an enrichment, by the touch of the Savior, vastly beyond and above what they possessed before, and also they are placed on deeper and firmer foundations. This, let it be said to begin with, is because they were his before they were ever uttered by man.

Even in the five distinctive and characteristic topics generally considered by commentators original in the teachings of Jesus, we find little if anything new, except the enlargement. These are named as, the Fatherhood of God, the Kingdom of God; subjects or members of the Kingdom; the Messiah, the Holy Ghost; and the Trinity of God.

But the idea of the Fatherhood of God was not unknown either to the Pagans or to Israel. Zeus, from the time of Homer, had borne the name "father of gods and men." But, both in Jewish and Pagan literature, the idea was superficial and meant little more than "originator" (Genesis 1:26); and in the old Jewish scripture God is more particularly called the "Father of his people, Israel" (Deut. 14:1; Isaiah 63:16). But in the teachings of Christ there is a fuller embodiment of revelation in the word Father, and the application which he makes of the Fatherhood of God invests his life with supreme tenderness and beauty. As an example: In the old scripture, we are told, "Like as a father pitieth his children, so the Lord pitieth them that fear him" (Psalms 103:13); but by the interpretation of Jesus, the love of God as Father extends beyond these limitations even to those who are unthankful and evil: "But I say unto you, Love your enemies, bless them that curse you, do good to them that hate you, and pray for them which despitefully use you and persecute you; that ye may be the children of your Father which is in heaven; for he maketh his sun to rise on the evil and on the good, and sendeth rain on the just and on the unjust" (Matthew 5:45). "But love ye your enemies, and do good, and lend, hoping for nothing again; and your reward shall be great, and ye shall be the children of the Highest; for he is kind unto the unthankful and to the evil" (Luke 6:35).

And so with other doctrines of Christ; while perhaps not new they are enriched by the addition of fuller, broader, more loving conceptions of God and his purposes; in which compulsion was eliminated, and lowly service, love, and self-sacrifice were substituted and made the true forces of an acceptable life. Even the answer to the lawyer's question, often called the eleventh commandment: "Master, which is the great commandment in the law?" had been given to the children of Israel (Lev. 19:18), over two thousand years before its perfected meaning was impressed upon the learned Pharisee (Matt. 22:34, 40).

But what of all this? Are we therefore to discredit the teachings of the Savior? Verily no. Let it be remembered that Christ was with the Father from the beginning, that the gospel of truth and light existed from the beginning and is from everlasting to everlasting. The Father, Son and Holy Ghost, as one God, are the fountain of truth. From this fountain all the ancient learned philosophers have received their inspiration and wisdom—from it they have received all their knowledge. If we find truth in broken fragments through the ages, it may be set down as an incontrovertible fact that it originated at the fountain, and was given to philosophers, inventors, patriots, reformers, and prophets by the inspiration of God. It came from him through his Son Jesus Christ and the Holy Ghost, in the first place, and from no other source. It is eternal.

Christ, therefore, being the fountain of truth, is no imitator. He taught the truth first; it was his before it was given to man. When he came to the earth he not only proclaimed new thought, but repeated some of the everlasting principles which had been heretofore only partly understood and enunciated by the wisest of men. And in so doing he enlarged in every instance upon the wisdom which they had originally received from him, because of his superior abilities and wisdom and his association with the Father and the Holy Ghost. He did not imitate men. They made known in their imperfect way what the inspiration of Jesus Christ had taught them, for they obtained their enlightenment first from him.

Christ taught the gospel to Adam, and made known his truths to Abraham and the prophets. He was the inspirer of the ancient philosophers, Pagan or Israelite, as well as of the great characters of modern times. Columbus, in discovery; Washington, in the struggle for freedom; Lincoln, in emancipation and union; Bacon, in philosophy; Franklin, in statesmanship and diplomacy; Stephenson, in steam; Watts, in song; Edison, in electricity, and Joseph Smith, in theology and religion, found in Christ the source of their wisdom and the marvelous truths which they advocated.

Calvin, Luther, Melanchthon, and all the reformers, were inspired in thoughts, words, and actions, to accomplish what they did for the amelioration, liberty and advancement of the human race. They paved the way for the more perfect gospel of truth to come. Their inspiration, as with that of the ancients, came from the Father, his Son Jesus Christ, and the Holy Ghost, the one true and living God. This may also truthfully be said concerning the Revolutionary fathers of this nation, and all who have in the ages past contributed to the progress of civil and religious freedom. There is no light nor truth which did not come to them first from him. Men are mere repeaters of what he has taught them. He has voiced no thoughts originating with man. The teachings of Jesus did not begin with his incarnation; for, like truth, he is eternal. He not only inspired the ancients, from the beginning, but when he came to earth he reiterated eternal, original truth, and added gloriously to the revelations men had uttered. When he returned to the Father he still took and does take an interest in his children and people, by revealing to them new truths, and by inspiring their actions; and, as men grow in the knowledge of God, they shall become more and more like him unto the perfect day, when his knowledge shall cover the earth as the waters cover the deep.

It is folly, therefore, to discredit the Savior on the grounds that he has uttered nothing new; for, with the Father and the Spirit, he is the author of that which persists—the truth—that which has been, that which is, and that which will continue forever.—*Improvement Era*, Vol. 10, pp. 627-630, 1906-7.

ETERNITY OF THE SPIRIT OF MAN. Again, where are we going?

We come here and sojourn in the flesh a little season and then we pass away. Every soul that is born into the world will die. There is not a soul that has escaped death, except those upon whom God has passed, by the power of his Spirit, that they should live in the flesh until the second coming of the Son of Man; but they will eventually have to pass through the ordeal called death; it may be in the twinkling of an eye, and without pain or suffering; but they will pass through the change, because it is an irrevocable edict of the Almighty. "In the day that thou eatest thereof thou shalt surely die." This was the edict of the Almighty and it pertains to Adam—that is, all the human race; for Adam is many, and it means you and me and every soul that lives and that bears the image of the Father. We shall all die. But is that the end of our being? If we had an existence before we came here we certainly shall continue that existence when we leave here. The spirit will continue to exist as it did before, with the additional advantages derived from having passed through this probation. It is absolutely necessary that we should come to the earth and take upon us tabernacles; because if we did not have tabernacles we could not be like God, or like Jesus Christ. God has a tabernacle of flesh and bone. He is an organized being just as we are who are now in the flesh. Jesus Christ was born of his mother, Mary. He had a fleshly tabernacle; he was crucified on the cross, and his body was raised from the dead. He burst the bonds of the grave and came forth to newness of life, a living soul, living being, a man with a body, and with parts and with spirit—the spirit and the body becoming a living and immortal soul. You and I have got to do the same thing. We must go through the same ordeal in order to attain to the glory and exaltation which God designed we should enjoy with him in the eternal worlds. In other words, we must become like him; peradventure to sit upon thrones, to have dominion, power and eternal increase. God designed this in the beginning. We are the children of God. He is an eternal being, without beginning of days or end of years. He always was, he is, he always will be. We are precisely in the same condition and under the same circumstances that God our heavenly Father was when he was passing through this or a similar ordeal. We are destined to come forth out of the grave as Jesus did, and to obtain immortal bodies as he did—that is, that our tabernacles are to become immortal as his became immortal, that the spirit and the body may be joined together and become one living being, indivisible, inseparable, eternal.—Deseret Weekly News, Vol. 33, pp. 130, 131.

PURPOSE OF THE ALMIGHTY UNCHANGEABLE. The purposes of the Almighty are unchanged and unchangeable. His laws endure, and he is the same yesterday, today and forever. His purposes will ripen and be consummated and his designs be completed. Therefore, if we do not conform to his will, obey his laws and yield to his requirements in this world, we will be consigned to the "prison house," where we will remain until we pay the debt to the uttermost farthing.—Deseret Weekly News, Vol. 24, 1875, p. 708.

CHAPTER III

REVELATION

VALUE OF THE SPIRIT OF REVELATION. The man who possesses the spirit of revelation can realize whether he is a sinner, whether he is prone to evil, whether he is magnifying his standing before the Lord, or not, better than a man who has not the Spirit of the Lord in him, can he not?—Apr. C. R., 1912, p. 7.

THE SPIRIT OF INSPIRATION—OF REVELATION—BY WHOM ENJOYED. And the spirit of inspiration, the gift of revelation, does not belong to one man solely; it is not a gift that pertains to the Presidency of the Church and the Twelve apostles alone. It is not confined to the presiding authorities of the Church, it belongs to every individual member of the Church; and it is the right and privilege of every man, every woman, and every child who has reached the years of accountability, to enjoy the spirit of revelation, and to be possessed of the spirit of inspiration in the discharge of their duties as members of the Church. It is the privilege of every individual member of the Church to have revelation for his own guidance, for the direction of his life and conduct; and therefore I aver—and I believe I may do so without any reasonable chance for it being gainsaid or opposed—that there is not another church in the world, or an organization of religious people, who are so universally spiritual in their lives, and who are so universally entitled to the gifts of the Spirit of God as are the members of the Church of Jesus Christ of Latter-day Saints. You are all entitled to revelation. It is your privilege to have it revealed to you whether I am a servant of God or a servant of men; whether I am in the discharge of my duty or not; whether I, as a presiding officer in the Church, am acting in the discharge of my duty acceptable to you and the Lord. It is your privilege to have revelation in regard to this, and to know the truth yourselves. And it is my privilege to have revelation from God, as an individual, for my own temporal guidance, and I repeat again that there never was a time on the earth, since the Church was organized, when the spirituality of the people of God was greater than it is today.—Apr. C. R., 1912, p. 5.

THE SPIRIT OF REVELATION ENJOYED BY ALL. I believe that every individual in the Church has just as much right to enjoy the spirit of revelation and the understanding from God which that spirit of revelation gives him, for his own good, as the bishop has to enable him to preside over his ward. Every man has the privilege to exercise these gifts and these privileges in the conduct of his own affairs, in bringing up his children in the way they should go, and in the management of his farm, his flocks, his herds, and in the management of his business, if he has business of other kinds to do; it is his right to enjoy the spirit of revelation and of inspiration to do the right thing, to be wise and prudent, just and good in everything that he does. I know that this is a true principle, and I know that I know it, too; and that is the thing that I would like the Latter-day Saints to know.—Apr. C. R., 1912, pp. 9, 10.

NEW REVELATION. So far as I know there is not an ordinance of the Church now enjoyed or practiced that was not revealed to the Church by the Prophet Joseph Smith. I know of no new doctrine that has been revealed. Principles that were revealed to the Prophet Joseph have grown and developed more fully and clearly to the under-standing; but we have received nothing new that I know of. Yet, if we should receive something new, through the proper channels of the Church, we should be as ready and willing to receive it as we were, or would be, to receive the same at the hands of the Prophet Joseph himself.—Oct. C. R., 1900, p. 47.

WHEN TO EXPECT NEW REVELATION. We have nothing that is not in common with the Latter-day Saints. We know nothing, and we will preach nothing to the people except that which the Lord God has revealed, and we advise and counsel those who are in au-thority, and whose duty and business it is to teach and preach the principles of the gospel to the world and to the Latter-day Saints, to confine their teachings and their instructions to the word of God that has been revealed. There is a great deal that has been revealed that has not yet been lived up to, I assure you. There is a great deal yet remaining to be learned. There is a great deal that is yet to be taught in the spirit of instruction, and there is a great deal that has been revealed through the Prophet Joseph and his associates that the people have not yet received in their hearts, and have not yet become converted to as they should. When we obey and are capable of observing the precepts of the gospel and the laws of God and the requirements of heaven, which have already been revealed, we will be far better off and nearer the goal of perfection in wisdom, knowledge and power than we are today. When that time comes, then there are other things still greater yet to be revealed to the people of God. Until we do our duty, however, in that which we have received, until we are faithful over the things that are now committed into our hands, until we live our religion as we have it now, as the Lord has given it to us, to add commandments, to add light and intelligence to us over that which we have already received, which we have not yet fully obeyed, would be to add condemnation upon our heads. It is enough for us to live in the light of present inspiration and present revelation and for each individual member of the Church to keep the commandments of the Lord and labor in the Church as the Spirit may give him and her guidance in the performance of duty. Every soul of us is entitled to inspiration from God to know what is our duty and how we are to do it. We have not learned it yet, not all of us, but we are in a fair way to learn. The Lord is still patient; he is long-suffering; he is full of love and graciousness towards all, and we are doing a little better all the time. I believe we are a little more faithful in the performance of our duties than we have been in the past; yet there is great room for improvement.—Oct. C. R., 1917, p. 5.

How the Lord Reveals His Purposes Concerning the Church. And I know this, that God has organized his Church in the earth, and I know that when he designs or purposes to make any change in the matter of governing or controlling or presiding over the affairs of his Church, that he will make the change, and he will make it in such a way that the whole people of the Church, who are doing right, will understand and accept it. I know that the Lord will not raise up "Tom, Dick, or Harry," here, there and everywhere, claiming to be Christ, or "one mighty and strong," claiming to be inspired and called to do some wonderful thing. The Lord will not deal with men in that way; that while the organization of the Church exists, while quorums and councils of the Priesthood are intact in the Church, the Lord will reveal his purposes through them, and not through "Tom, Dick, or Harry." Put that in your little note books now, and remember it; it is true.—Apr. C. R., 1912, p. 10.

Modern Revelation is Necessary. Are we to understand, then, that God does not, and will not further make known his will to men; that what he has said suffices? His will to Moses and Isaiah and John is abundant for modern followers of Christ? The Latter-day Saints take issue with this doctrine, and pronounce it illogical, inconsistent, and untrue, and bear testimony to all the world that God lives and that he reveals his will to men who believe in him and who obey his commandments, as much in our day as at any time in the history of nations. The canon of scripture is not full. God has never revealed at any time that he would cease to speak forever to men. If we are permitted to believe that he has spoken, we must and do believe that he continues to speak, because he is unchangeable.

His will to Abraham did not suffice for Moses, neither did his will to Moses suffice for Isaiah. Why? Because their different missions required different instructions; and logically, that is also true of the prophets and people of today. A progressive world will never discover all truth until its inhabitants become familiar with all the knowledge of the Perfect One. How shall men become acquainted with the knowledge of the Father? Only as he reveals it to them. Now if we are permitted to believe that the Lord revealed himself to the ancients of whose deeds we read in the Holy Scriptures, it seems to me that there is no good reason for believing that it is not necessary that he should reveal himself in this day to others who desire to be guided by his Spirit and inspiration. Every new truth which grows into living action in the lives of men is a revelation in itself from God, and without the revelation of additional truth, men would not progress in this world, but, left to themselves, would retrograde, being cut off from the light and life of the great fountain of all intelligence, the Father of all.

What is revelation but the uncovering of new truths, by him who is the Fountain of all Truth? To say that there is no need of new revelation, is equivalent to saying that we have no need of new truths—a ridiculous assertion.

Now, as to the usefulness of modern revelation, that has been referred to above, in the brief treatment of its need, and it is no sign that revelation is useless because it is not proper that it should be accepted in the courts. "Render unto Caesar the things that are Caesar's, and unto God the things that are God's." Revelation given for the personal knowledge or guidance of any person should not be given to the public, either in a civil or religious capacity; but because it might be (and in such cases is) considered improper for public use, it is no sign that even such revelation is useless to the person for whom it is intended. It might be said in passing, however, that the revelation which the ministers were so troubled about, turned out to be correct and in conformity with the evidence, and the decision of the court and jury.

Our testimony is that God lives, and that he speaks by his power to men who seek him and believe in him, thus making known his will to them in matters that pertain, not only to his true Church, but in matters that pertain to each individual who seeks him.—*Improvement Era*, Vol. 5, p. 805.

THEORY AND DIVINE REVELATION. Our young people are diligent students. They reach out after truth and knowledge with commendable zeal, and in so doing they must necessarily adopt for temporary use, many theories of men. As long, however, as they recognize them as scaffolding useful for research purposes, there can be no special harm in them. It is when these theories are settled upon as basic truth that trouble appears, and the searcher then stands in grave danger of being led hopelessly from the right way. * * *

The Church holds to the definite authority of divine revelation which must be the standard; and that, as so-called "Science" has changed from age to age in its deductions, and as divine revelation is truth, and must abide forever, views as to the lesser should conform to the positive statements of the greater, and, further, that in institutions founded by the Church for the teaching of theology, as well as other branches of education, its instructors must be in harmony in their teachings with its principles and doctrines. * * *

There are so many demonstrated, practical, material truths, so many spiritual certainties, with which the youth of Zion should become familiar, that it appears a waste of time and means, and detrimental to faith and religion to enter too extensively into the undemonstrated theories of men on philosophies relating to the origin of life, or the methods adopted by an Allwise Creator in peopling the earth with the bodies of men, birds and beasts. Let us rather turn our abilities to the practical analysis of the soil, the study of the elements, the productions of the earth, the invention of useful machinery, the social welfare of the race, and its material amelioration; and for the rest cultivate an abiding faith in the revealed word of God and the saving principles of the gospel of Jesus Christ, which give joy in this world and in the world to come eternal life and salvation.

Philosophic theories of life have their place and use, but it is not in the classes of the Church schools, and particularly are they out of place here or anywhere else, when they seek to supplant the revelations of God. The ordinary student cannot delve into these subjects deep enough to make them of any practical use to him, and a smattering of knowledge in this line only tends to upset his simple faith in the gospel, which is of more value to him in life than all the learning of the world without it.

The religion of the Latter-day Saints is not hostile to any truth, nor to scientific search for truth. "That which is demonstrated, we accept with joy," said the First Presidency in their Christmas greeting to the Saints, "but vain philosophy, human theory and mere speculations of men we do not accept, nor do we adopt anything contrary to divine revelation or to good common sense, but everything that tends to right conduct, that harmonizes with sound morality and increases faith in Deity, finds favor with us, no matter where it may be found."

A good motto for young people to adopt, who are determined to delve into philosophic theories, is to search all things, but be careful to hold on only to that which is true. The truth persists, but the theories of philosophers change and are overthrown. What men use today as a scaffolding for scientific purposes from which to reach out into the unknown for truth, may be torn down tomorrow, having served its purpose; but faith is an eternal principle through which the humble believer may secure everlasting solace. It is the only way to find God.—*Improvement Era*, Vol. 14, p. 548.

Science and philosophy through all the ages have undergone change after change. Scarcely a century has passed but they have introduced new theories of science and philosophy, that supersede the old traditions and the old faith and the old doctrines entertained by philosophers and scientists. These things may undergo continuous changes, but the word of God is always true, is always right. The principles of the gospel are always true, the principles of faith in God, repentance from sin, baptism for the remission of sins by authority of God, and the laying on of hands for the gift of the Holy Ghost—these principles are always true, and are always absolutely necessary for the salvation of the children of men, no matter who they are and where they are. No other name under heaven is given but that of Jesus Christ, by which you can be saved or exalted in the kingdom of God. Not only has God declared them, not only has Christ declared these principles, by his voice to his disciples, from generation to generation, in the old time, but in these latter days, they have taken up the same testimony and declared these things to the world. They are true today as they were then, and we must obey these things.—*Improve-ment Era*, Vol. 14, p. 641.

REVELATION AND LEGAL EVIDENCE. Recently a man charged with the murder of another man was examined before a committing magistrate in Salt Lake City. The father-in-law of the murdered man, during the examination on the part of the State, related a con-versation had between himself and the accused soon after the com-mission of the crime. During the conversation, according to news-paper report, the father-in-law of the murdered man laid the crime at the door of the accused. In the cross-examination the attorney for the defendant pressed the witness as to how he knew that the accused was guilty of the crime. The reply, as given in the press, was, because God had revealed it to him. It does not appear from the further proceedings in the case that the testimony was excepted to or withdrawn, or that the magistrate informed the witness that such evidence was incompetent and could not be received. The statement gave rise to comment in the press and has been the subject of discourse from the pulpit. Of course, every person must know that such evidence is not admissible in a court of law, and if it had been in a trial before a jury it would have been the duty of the judge to order the testimony stricken out, and in the charge to the jury, they would have been warned to disregard it altogether. In view of the probability that there are those who may persist in the associa-tion of such evidence with the religious body of which the witness is a member, it may be proper to say, without discrediting in the least the witness' conviction of the revelation he had received, that no member of the Church of Jesus Christ of Latter-day Saints should, for one moment, regard such testimony as admissible in a court of law, and to make the case perfectly clear it may be further stated that such evidence would not be permissible even in a Church court, where rules of evidence, though not so technical, are founded largely upon the same principles that govern the rules of evidence in a court of law. Any attempt, therefore, to make it appear that such evidence is in keeping with the tenets of the "Mormon" faith is wholly un-justified.—*Juvenile Instructor*, p. 114, Feb. 15, 1902, Vol. 37.

PROPER CHANNELS FOR REVELATION. It has sometimes been sorrowful to see respected members of the Church, men who should know better, allow themselves to become the tools of seductive spirits. Such men seem, for the time at least, to lose sight of the fact that the Lord has established on earth the Priesthood in its fulness; and that by direct revelation and commandment from heaven; that he has instituted an order or government that is beyond the capacity, and that is superior to the wisdom and learning and understanding of man, so far, indeed, that it seems impossible for the human mind, unaided by the Spirit of God, to comprehend the beauties, powers, and character of the Holy Priesthood. It seems difficult for men to comprehend the workings of the Priesthood, its legitimate authority, its scope and power; and yet by the light of the Spirit it is easily comprehended, but not understanding it, men are easily deceived by seductive spirits that are abroad in the world. They are led to believe that something is wrong, and the next thing that transpires, they find themselves believing that they are chosen specially to set things right. It is very unfortunate for a man to be taken in this snare; for be it understood by the Latter-day Saints that as long as the servants of God are living pure lives, are honoring the Priesthood conferred upon them, and endeavoring to the best of their knowledge to magnify their offices and callings, to which they have been duly chosen by the voice of the people and the priesthood, and sanctioned by the approval of God, so long as the Lord has any communication to make to the children of men, or any instructions to impart to his Church, he will make such communication through the legally appointed channel of the priesthood; he will never go outside of it, as long, at least, as the Church of Jesus Christ of Latter-day Saints exists in its present form on the earth.

It is not the business of any individual to rise up as a revelator, as a prophet, as a seer, as an inspired man, to give revelation for the guidance of the Church, or to assume to dictate to the presiding authorities of the Church in any part of the world, much less in the midst of Zion, where the organizations of the priesthood are about perfect, where everything is complete, even to the organization of a branch. It is the right of individuals to be inspired and to receive manifestations of the Holy Spirit for their personal guidance to strengthen their faith, and to encourage them in works of righteousness, in being faithful and observing and keeping the commandments which God has given unto them; it is the privilege of every man and woman to receive revelation to this end, but not further. The moment an individual rises up assuming the right to control and to dictate, or to sit in judgment on his brethren, especially upon those who preside, he should be promptly checked, or discord, division and confusion will be the result. Every man and woman in this Church should know better than to yield to such a spirit; the moment that such a feeling presents itself to them they should rebuke it, as it is in direct antagonism to the order of the Priesthood, and to the spirit and genius of this work. We can accept nothing as authoritative but that which comes directly through the appointed channel, the constituted organizations of the priesthood, which is the channel that God has appointed through which to make known his mind and will to the world.

Through Joseph, then, the Lord revealed himself to the world, and through him he chose the first elders of the Church—men who were honest in their hearts; men who he knew would receive the word, and labor in connection with Joseph in this great, important undertaking; and all that have been ordained to the Priesthood, and all that have been appointed to any position whatever in this Church have received their authority and commission through this channel, appointed of God, with Joseph at the head. This is the order, and it could not be otherwise. God will not raise up another prophet and another people to do the work that we have been appointed to do. He will never ignore those who have stood firm and true from the commencement, as it were, of this work, and who are still firm and faithful, inasmuch as they continue faithful to their trust. There is no question in my mind of their ever proving themselves unfaithful, as a body, for if any of them were to become unworthy in his sight, he would remove them out of their place and call others from the ranks to fill their positions. And thus his priesthood will ever be found to be composed of the right men for the place, of men whose backs will be fitted for the burden, men through whom he can work and regulate the affairs of his Church according to the counsels of his own will. And the moment that individuals look to any other source, that moment they throw themselves open to the seductive influences of Satan, and render themselves liable to become servants of the devil; they lose sight of the true order through which the blessings of the Priesthood are to be enjoyed; they step outside of the pale of the kingdom of God, and are on dangerous ground. Whenever you see a man rise up claiming to have received direct revelation from the Lord to the Church, independent of the order and channel of the priesthood, you may set him down as an impostor. God has not called you to go out to the world to be taught, or to receive revelations through apostates or strangers; but he has called and ordained you and sent you forth to teach and lead people in the paths of righteousness and salvation.

Now, how should it be? I will tell you. In the first place every person should know that the gospel is true, as this is everyone's privilege who is baptized and receives the Holy Ghost. A man may be grieved in his feelings because of some difficulty between himself and President Taylor, or Cannon, or myself; he may have feelings in his heart which lead him to think that he could not sustain us in his faith and prayers; but if this should be the case, what is the course for him to pursue? He should say in his heart, "God has established his kingdom, and his priesthood is upon the earth; and notwithstanding my dislike for certain men, I know that the gospel is true, and that God is with his people; and that if I will do my duty and keep his commandments, the clouds will roll by, and the mists will disappear, the Spirit of the Lord will come more fully to my relief, and by and by I will be able to see—if I am in error, wherein I erred, and then I will repent of it, for I know that every wrong thing will yet be made right." I think all men should feel that way.

Never is there but one appointed at a time to hold the keys of the kingdom of God pertaining to the earth. While Christ remained on the earth he held them; but when he departed, he committed them to Peter, he being the president or chief of the apostles; and it was his right to direct and to receive revelation for the Church, and to give counsel to all the brethren. After Satan and wicked men had prevailed against the Church, crucified the Savior and killed the apostles, the keys of the kingdom were taken from the earth. John the Revelator describes it most clearly. And from that time until Joseph Smith was called by the voice of the Almighty, and ordained to hold those keys, no man held them upon the earth that we know of. It is true the Lord did appoint other Twelve upon this continent, and his Church flourished and prospered in this land for many years, but the Lord declared that Peter, James and John, and the Twelve that walked with him at Jerusalem, held the presidency over them. God may reveal himself to different nations, and establish among them the same gospel and ordinances as he did anciently, if necessity require, but if these nations should be joined together there would be one head, and all the rest would be subordinate. So that from the time that the keys of this Priesthood were taken from the earth until they were received by Joseph Smith, no man ever possessed that Priesthood, nor the keys thereof, with

authority to build up the Zion of God, and prepare a church or
people for the second coming of Christ, "as a bride is adorned for
the bridegroom," unless it may have been among the lost tribes,
yet of this we have no knowledge, but if so they would receive those
keys necessary to administer in the ordinances of the gospel for their
salvation. We know not of their existence or the condition in which
they are placed. The gospel that is given to them is suited to their
needs and conditions, and is for their salvation, not ours; and yet, it
will be the same gospel. And God will not call one from them to give
to us the Priesthood, or to give to us the keys and blessings, or to
point out the organizations of the kingdom of God, because he has
established that Priesthood here, and we have it. If he has any
communication to make to us he will send his messengers to us. And
in this way he will deliver his law and give his mind and will to the
people. He will do it through the ordained channels of the priesthood which he acknowledges and which he has established in the
earth. He will go nowhere else to do it, neither will he send us to
them, unless they should be without the Priesthood and it becomes
necessary to take the blessings of the gospel to them, and I presume
that will be the case.

When Joseph received the keys of the Priesthood, he alone on
the earth held them; that is, he was the first, he stood at the head.
It was promised that he should not lose them nor be removed out
of his place, as long as he was faithful. And when he died, President
Young was chosen by the voice of the people, and sanctioned by the
voice of God. He held the Priesthood which was after the order
of the Son of God, with the keys which pertain to the presidency
of that Priesthood upon earth. He received it from the hands of
Joseph, directly from him or by his authority; and he held it until
his death. When he died, that mantle fell upon John Taylor, and
while he lives he will hold that authority, inasmuch as he is faithful.
So it was with President Brigham Young; he held it on condition
of his faithfulness. If any man in that position should become
unfaithful, God would remove him out of his place. I testify in
the name of Israel's God that he will not suffer the head of the
Church, whom he has chosen to stand at the head, to transgress his
laws and apostatize; the moment he should take a course that would
in time lead to it, God would take him away. Why? Because to
suffer a wicked man to occupy that position would be to allow, as it

were, the fountain to become corrupted, which is something he will never permit.

The moment a man says he will not submit to the legally constituted authority of the Church, whether it be the teachers, the bishopric, the high council, his quorum, or the First Presidency, and in his heart confirms it and carries it out, that moment he cuts himself off from the privileges and blessings of the Priesthood and Church, and severs himself from the people of God, for he ignores the authority that the Lord has instituted in his Church. These are the men that generally get crotchets in their heads, that get inspiration (from beneath), and that are often so desirous to guide the Church, and to sit in judgment upon the priesthood. The only safe way for us to do, as individuals, is to live so humbly, so righteously and so faithfully before God that we may possess his Spirit to that extent that we shall be able to judge righteously, and discern between truth and error, between right and wrong; and then we shall know when a decision is rendered against us that in ninety-nine cases out of a hundred, we are in error, and that the decision is right; and although we may, at the time, not be fully able to see and feel its justness, yet will be constrained to say that "inasmuch as there are sixteen chances against one for me to be wrong, I will gracefully and humbly submit." The pith of the matter is: the Lord has established his Church, organized his priesthood, and conferred authority upon certain individuals, councils and quorums, and it is the duty of the people of God to live so that they shall know that these are acceptable unto him. If we begin to cut off this one and that one, and set their authority aside, we may just as well at once set God aside, and say that he has no right to dictate.—*Journal of Discourses,* Vol. 24, pp. 187-194, 1884, Ogden, June 21, 1883.

THE DOCTRINE AND COVENANTS. I say to my brethren that the book of Doctrine and Covenants contains some of the most glorious principles ever revealed to the world, some that have been revealed in greater fulness than they were ever revealed before to the world; and this, in fulfilment of the promise of the ancient prophets that in the latter times the Lord would reveal things to the world that had been kept hidden from the foundation thereof; and the Lord has revealed them through the Prophet Joseph Smith.—Oct. C. R., 1913, p. 9.

HOW TO READ THE BIBLE. That which characterizes above all else the inspiration and divinity of the Scriptures is the spirit in which they are written and the spiritual wealth they convey to those who faithfully and conscientiously read them. Our attitude, therefore, toward the Scriptures should be in harmony with the purposes for which they were written. They are intended to enlarge man's spiritual endowments and to reveal and intensify the bond of relationship between him and his God. The Bible, as all other books of Holy Writ, to be appreciated must be studied by those spiritually inclined and who are in quest of spiritual truths.—*Juvenile Instructor*, Vol. 47, p. 204, April, 1912.

PERSECUTION FOLLOWS REVELATION. I do not believe there ever was a people who were guided by revelation, or acknowledged of the Lord as his people, who were not hated and persecuted by the wicked and the corrupt, and perhaps no people were ever more persecuted than this people would be if it were in the power of the enemy today to persecute us as it was in the power of Nero and the Romans to persecute the Saints in their day. There never was a time when it was more fixed and determined in the heart of the wicked to fight against and destroy the kingdom from the earth than now, and their failure will be due only to the impossibility of the task they have undertaken. And this is an evidence to everyone that God's Priesthood is here, that many of the Saints are magnifying their calling and honoring the Priesthood and also the Lord, both with their lives and with their substance, which are his.—*Deseret Weekly News*, Vol. 24, p. 708, 1875.

Chapter IV

FREE AGENCY

THE LATTER-DAY SAINTS A FREE PEOPLE. We will now present before the conference the names of the general authorities of the Church, with the earnest desire that all the members of the Church present, who by reason of their good standing before the Lord are entitled to the privilege, will express their will according to the God-given agency that every man in the world enjoys, and which is not lessened, but rather increased, in all those who have made covenant with God by sacrifice and through obedience to the principles of the gospel. The freedom of the Latter-day Saints has never been curtailed nor lessened one whit by their becoming members of the Church of Christ. Rather has it been enlarged. There are no freer people upon the face of the earth today than the Latter-day Saints. They are bound to the Church by no ties or strings, but by their own conviction of the truth. And whenever a man makes up his mind that he has had enough of what is called "Mormonism," all he has to do is to make it known, and we will sever the bond that unites him with the body and let him go his own way, only bearing toward him the feeilng of sympathy and true brotherly kindness, and wishing him still the mercies of God. We will cry, "Father, have mercy upon him," because he knows not what he is doing. For when a man denies the truth, when he departs from the right way, when he rejects the right of God to counsel in the affairs of men, he is either ignorant or wilfully wicked, and it only excites our pity for him. As the Savior cried upon the cross, so we will cry in the same spirit, Father, forgive him; have mercy upon him; for he knows not what he does. Therefore, we expect only those to vote at this time who are members of the Church in good standing, but all such we do expect to vote, according to their own free will, whether it be yea or nay. However, we wish it distinctly understood that no question upon these matters will be discussed in this conference; for this is not the place to discuss questions of difference or of feeling that we may possess one towards another. Still we can manifest our approval or our disapproval by the uplifted hand; and if there are any disapprovals, we will have them heard and adjusted later on, but not here.—Oct. C. R., 1903, p. 84.

THE USE OF FREEDOM AND HUMAN JUDGMENT. I think that in the realms of liberty, and the exercise of human judgment, all men should exercise extreme caution, that they do not change nor abolish those things which God has willed and has inspired to be done. It has been in this realm of freedom, and the exercise of human judgment that most of the evils that have occurred in the world have been done—the martyrdom of Saints, the crucifixion of the Son of God himself, and much of the apostasy and departure from the work of righteousness, and from the laws of God, have occurred in this realm of freedom and the exercise of human judgment. God in his boundless wisdom and gracious mercy has provided means, and has shown the way to the children of men whereby, even in the realms of freedom and the exercise of their own judgment, they may individually go unto God in faith and prayer, and find out what should guide and direct their human judgment and wisdom; and I do not want the Latter-day Saints to forget that this is their privilege. I would rather that they should seek God for a counselor and guide, than to follow the wild harangues of political leaders, or leaders of any other cult.—Oct. C. R., 1912, pp. 41-42.

LATTER-DAY SAINTS SHOULD EXERCISE FREE AGENCY. We desire that the Latter-day Saints will exercise the liberty wherewith they have been made free by the gospel of Jesus Christ; for they are entitled to know the right from the wrong, to see the truth and draw the line between it and error; and it is their privilege to judge for themselves and to act upon their own free agency with regard to their choice as to sustaining or otherwise those who should exercise the presiding functions among them. We desire the Latter-day Saints at this conference to exercise their prerogative, which is, to vote as the Spirit of the Lord prompts them on the measures and the men that may be presented unto them.—Apr. C. R., 1904, p. 73.

HOW TO OBTAIN BLESSINGS OF GOD. There are blessings which pertain to the gospel of Jesus Christ and to the world to come, which cannot be secured by personal influence, nor be bought with money, and which no man by his own intelligence or wisdom can obtain except through compliance with certain ordinances, laws and commandments which have been given. And it is well, in my judgment, for the Latter-day Saints to continue to bear in mind that the inestimable blessings of the gospel have been bestowed upon them through their faith, that a remission of sins has been obtained by baptism and repentance, and that it is only through continuing faithful that they can retain the gifts and blessings which pertain to eternal life. There are many blessings, however, which are common to the human family, which all enjoy, without regard to their moral status or religious convictions. God has given to all men an agency and has granted to us the privilege to serve him or serve him not, to do that which is right or that which is wrong, and this privilege is given to all men irrespective of creed, color or condition. The wealthy have this agency, the poor have this agency, and no man is deprived by any power of God from exercising it in the fullest and in the freest manner. This agency has been given to all. This is a blessing that God has bestowed upon the world of mankind, upon all his children alike. But he will hold us strictly to an account for the use that we make of this agency, and as it was said of Cain, so it will be said of us; "If thou doest well, shalt thou not be accepted? and if thou doest not well, sin lieth at the door" (Gen. 4:7). There are, however, certain blessings which God bestows upon the children of men only upon the condition of the rightful exercise of this agency. For instance, no man can obtain a remission of his sins but by repentance, and baptism by one having authority. If we would be free from sin, from its effects, from its power, we must obey this law which God has revealed, or we never can obtain a remission of sins. Therefore, while God has bestowed upon all men, irrespective of condition, this agency to choose good or evil, he has not and will not bestow upon the children of men a remission of sins but by their obedience to law. Therefore, the whole world lies in sin and is under condemnation, inasmuch as light has come unto the world and men will not place themselves in a proper position before the Lord. And this condemnation rests with tenfold force upon all who have yielded obedience to this law, and have once received a remission of their sins, but have returned unto sin, and have forgotten or disregarded the covenants they made in the waters of baptism. All men are blessed with the strength of their bodies, with the use of their minds, and with the right to exercise the faculties with which they are endowed in a way that seemeth good to their sight, without regard to religion. But God has not and will not suffer the gift of the Holy Ghost to be bestowed upon any man or woman, except through compliance with the laws of God. Therefore, no man can obtain a remission of sins; no man can obtain the gift of the Holy Ghost; no man can obtain the revelations of God; no man can obtain the Priesthood, and the rights, powers and privileges thereof; no man can become an heir of God and a joint heir with Jesus Christ, except through compliance with the requirements of heaven. These are universal blessings, they are great and inestimable privileges which pertain to the gospel and to the plan of life and salvation, which are open and free to all on certain conditions, but which no persons beneath the heavens can enjoy, but through walking in the channel that God has marked out by which they can obtain them. And these privileges and blessings when obtained may be forfeited, and perhaps lost for all eternity, unless we continue steadfast in the course that is marked out for us to pursue. It is well, in my judgment, that the Latter-day Saints do not lose sight of the great privilege that has been bestowed upon them. No man can become a citizen of the kingdom of God but by entering in at the door; there are thousands and tens of thousands, aye, millions of people who will never become citizens of the kingdom of God in this world, because they fail to exercise the agency and the power that have been given to them, in the right direction. Nevertheless, they enjoy many of the blessings that are bestowed upon the world in common. The sun shines upon the evil and the good; but the Holy Ghost descends only upon the righteous and upon those who are forgiven of their sins. The rain descends upon the evil and upon the good; but the rights of the Priesthood are conferred, and the doctrine of the Priesthood distils as the dews of heaven upon the souls of those only who receive it in God's own appointed way. The favor of heaven, the acknowledgment of the Almighty of his children upon the earth as his sons and his daughters, can only be secured through obedience to the laws which he has revealed. Riches, or the wealth of the world, cannot purchase these things. Simon Magus desired to purchase the power to bestow the Holy Ghost, but Peter said unto him, "Thy money perish with thee." These blessings, powers and privileges are not to be purchased except by the atonement of Christ; they are not to be obtained by personal influence, wealth, position or power, or in any other way except the direct way in which God has decreed that they should be obtained. Now, so long as the Latter-day Saints are content to obey the commandments of God, to appreciate the privileges and blessings which they enjoy in the Church, and will use their time, their substance, in honor to the name of God, to build up Zion, and to establish truth and righteousness in the earth, so long our heavenly Father is bound by his oath and covenant to protect them from every opposing foe, and to help them to overcome every obstacle that can possibly be arrayed against them, or thrown in their pathway; but the moment a community begin to be wrapt up in themselves, become selfish, become engrossed in the temporalities of life, and put their faith in riches, that moment the power of God begins to withdraw from them, and if they repent not the Holy Spirit will depart from them entirely, and they will be left to themselves. That which was given them will be taken away, they will lose that which they had, for they will not be worthy of it. God is just, as well as merciful, and we need not expect favors at the hand of the Almighty except as we merit them, at least in the honest desires of our hearts; and the desire and intent will not always avail unless our acts correspond. For we are engaged in a literal work, a reality; and we must practice as well as profess. We must be what God requires us to be, or else we are not his people, nor the Zion which he designs to gather together and to build up in the latter days upon the earth.—*Journal of Discourses*, Vol. 24, 1884, pp. 173-178.

CHAPTER V

GOD AND MAN

GOD HAS DIRECTED HIS LATTER-DAY WORK. It has not been by the wisdom of man that this people have been directed in their course until the present; it has been by the wisdom of him who is above man, whose knowledge is greater than that of man, and whose power is above the power of man; for it is unto God, our Father, we are indebted for the mercies we have enjoyed and for the present prosperous condition of the people of God throughout this intermountain region and throughout the world. The hand of the Lord may not be visible to all. There may be many who cannot discern the workings of God's will in the progress and development of this great latter-day work, but there are those who see in every hour and in every moment of the existence of the Church, from its beginning until now, the overruling, almighty hand of him who sent his Only Begotten Son to the world to become a sacrifice for the sin of the world, that as he was lifted up so he, by reason of his righteousness and power and the sacrifice which he has made, might lift up unto God all the children of men who would hearken to his voice, receive his message, and obey his law.—Apr. C. R., 1904, p. 2.

A PERSONAL KNOWLEDGE OF GOD. We are not dependent for this upon the written word, nor upon the knowledge possessed by the ancient prophets and apostles. We depend only upon God as he reveals himself today and administers unto men by the power of his Holy Spirit. And all men in the world, not only the Latter-day Saints, but those who have never embraced the gospel, have the same privilege that we have, if they will take the course which God has marked out. It is their privilege to come to the knowledge of this truth and to understand these things for themselves. We have derived this knowledge from the Lord, not from man. Man cannot give this knowledge. I may tell you what I know, but that is not knowledge to you. If I have learned something through prayer, supplication, and perseverance in seeking to know the truth, and I tell it to you, it will not be knowledge unto you. I can tell you how you obtain it, but I cannot give it to you. If we receive this knowledge, it must come from the Lord. He can touch your understanding and your spirits, so that you shall comprehend perfectly and not be mistaken. But I cannot do that. You can obtain this knowledge through repentance, humility, and seeking the Lord with full purpose of heart until you find him. He is not afar off. It is not difficult to approach him, if we will only do it with a broken heart and a contrite spirit, as did Nephi of old. This was the way in which Joseph Smith, in his boyhood, approached him. He went into the woods, knelt down, and in humility he sought earnestly to know which church was acceptable to God. He received an answer to his prayer which he offered from the depths of his heart, and he received it in a way that he did not expect.—Oct. C. R., 1899, p. 71.

GOD SPEAKS TO THE HONEST IN HEART. Everywhere the Spirit of the Lord whispers to the honest in heart who are faithful, and gives to them the assurance that his hand is stretched out continually over his people; that, as in the past, he has preserved them and delivered them out of the hands of their enemies, so in the future he will continue to preserve and deliver them, and he will make the wrath of the wicked to praise him and to accomplish the more speedily his purposes. We have every evidence to convince us that the work of the Lord is a reality, a living, active, progressive work in the earth.—Oct. C. R., 1905, p. 5.

GOD CONSTANTLY MINDFUL OF US. I desire to express to you, my brethren and sisters, who are here today, my firm and fixed conviction that God, the eternal Father, is constantly mindful of you. He is mindful of his people throughout all this land, and he will reward you according to your faithfulness in observing the laws of righteousness and of truth. No man need fear in his heart when he is conscious of having lived up to the principles of truth and righteousness as God has required it at his hands, according to his best knowledge and understanding.—Apr. C. R., 1904, p. 2.

GOD'S WILL TO EXALT MEN. We believe that God's will is to exalt men; that the liberty that comes through obedience to the gospel of Jesus Christ is the greatest measure of liberty that can come to man. There is no liberty that men enjoy or pretend to enjoy in the world that is not founded in the will and in the law of God, and that does not have truth for its underlying principle and foundation. It is error that makes bondsmen. It is untruth that degrades mankind. It is error and the lack of knowledge of God's laws and God's will that leaves men in the world on a par with the brute creation; for they have no higher instincts, no higher principle, no higher incentive, no higher aspiration, than the brute world, if they have not some inspiration that comes from a higher source than man himself.—*Apr. C. R.,* 1904, p. 4.

GOD'S RIGHT TO RULE IN THE WORLD. I believe in God's law. I believe that it is his right to rule in the world. I believe that no man has or should have any valid objection in his mind to the government of God, and the rule of Jesus Christ, in the earth. Let us suppose, for a moment, that Christ were here and that he was bearing rule in the world. Who would come under his condemnation? Who would be subject to his chastening word? Who would be in disharmony or unfellowship with God? Would the righteous man? Would the virtuous man? The pure and virtuous woman? The pure and honest in heart? The upright? The straightforward? Those who do the will of heaven? Would they be in rebellion to Christ's rule, if he were to come here to rule? No. They would welcome the rule and reign of Jesus Christ in the earth. They would welcome his law and acknowledge his sovereignty, they would hasten to rally to his standard and to uphold the purpose and the perfection of his laws and of his righteousness. Who would, then, be recreant to the rule of Christ? The whoremonger, the adulterer, the liar, the sorcerer, he who bears false witness against his neighbor, he who seeks to take advantage of his brother, and who would overcome and destroy him for his own worldly gain or profit; the murderer, the despiser of that which is good, the unbeliever in the eternities that lie before us, the atheist, perhaps, although I think that he would not be so far from Christ as some who profess to be teachers of his doctrines and advocates of his laws. It would be the rebellious, the wicked, those who would oppress their neighbors and enslave them if they could. Such as these would be the people who would not welcome the reign of Jesus Christ. Are there any who profess to be Latter-day Saints in this class, and would fear to have Christ reign and rule?—*Apr. C. R.,* 1904, p. 4.

THE LESSON IN NATURAL CALAMITIES. There are, in the great world of mankind, much social and civil unrighteousness, religious unfaithfulness, and great insensibility to the majesty, power, and purpose of our eternal Father and God. In order, therefore, that he may bring the sense of himself and his purposes home to the minds of men, his intervention and interposition in nature and in men's affairs, are demanded. His aims will be accomplished even if men must be overwhelmed with the convulsions of nature to bring them to an understanding and realization of his designs. As long as conditions remain as they are in the world, none is exempt from these visitations.

The Latter-day Saints, though they themselves tremble because of their own wickedness and sins, believe that great judgments are coming upon the world because of iniquity; they firmly believe in the statements of the Holy Scriptures, that calamities will befall the nations as signs of the coming of Christ to judgment. They believe that God rules in the fire, the earthquake, the tidal wave, the volcanic eruption, and the storm. Him they recognize as the Master and Ruler of nature and her laws, and freely acknowledge his hand in all things. We believe that his judgments are poured out to bring mankind to a sense of his power and his purposes, that they may repent of their sins and prepare themselves for the second coming of Christ to reign in righteousness upon the earth.

We firmly believe that Zion—which is the pure in heart—shall escape, if she observes to do all things whatsoever God has commanded; but, in the opposite event, even Zion shall be visited "with sore affliction, with pestilence, with plague, with sword, with vengeance, and with devouring fire" (Doctrine and Covenants 97:26). All this that her people may be taught to walk in the light of truth and in the way of the God of their salvation.

We believe that these severe, natural calamities are visited upon men by the Lord for the good of his children, to quicken their devotion to others, and to bring out their better natures, that they may love and serve him. We believe, further, that they are the heralds and tokens of his final judgment, and the schoolmasters to teach the people to prepare themselves by righteous living for the coming of the Savior to reign upon the earth, when every knee shall bow and every tongue confess that Jesus is the Christ.

If these lessons are impressed upon us and upon the people of our country, the anguish, and the loss of life and toil, sad, great and horrifying as they were, will not have been endured in vain.— *Improvement Era,* Vol. 9, 1905-6, pp. 651-654.

EXTENT OF GOD'S POWER. I do not believe in the doctrine held by some that God is only a Spirit and that he is of such a nature that he fills the immensity of space, and is everywhere present in person, or without person, for I can not conceive it possible that God could be a person, if he filled the immensity of space and was everywhere present at the same time. It is unreasonable, a physical, a theological inconsistency, to imagine that even God the eternal Father would be in two places, as an individual, at the same moment. It is impossible. But his power extends throughout the immensity of space. His power extends to all his creations, and his knowledge comprehends them all, and he governs them all and he knows all.—Apr. C. R., 1916, p. 4.

BEWARE OF LIMITING God. Beware of men who come to you with heresies of this kind, who would make you to think or feel that the Lord Almighty, who made heaven and earth and created all things, is limited in his dominion over earthly things to the capacities of mortal men.—Apr. C. R., 1914, p. 4.

MISFORTUNE AND EVIL NOT ATTRIBUTABLE TO THE WILL OF GOD. We have it enunciated in the revelations to Joseph the Prophet, in the Book of Doctrine and Covenants, that the Lord is greatly displeased only with those who do not confess or acknowledge "his hand in all things, and obey not his commandments." Many things occur in the world in which it seems very difficult for most of us to find a solid reason for the acknowledgment of the hand of the Lord. I have come to the belief that the only reason I have been able to discover by which we should acknowledge the hand of God in some occurrences is the fact that the thing which has occurred has been permitted of the Lord. When two men give way to their passions, their selfishness and anger, to contend and quarrel with each other, and this quarrel and contention leads to physical strife and violence between them, it has been difficult for me to discover the hand of the Lord in that transaction; other than that the men who thus disagree, quarrel and contend with each other, have received from God the freedom of their own agency to exercise their own intelligence, to judge between the right and wrong for themselves, and to act according to their own desire. The Lord did not design or purpose that these two men should quarrel, or give way to their anger to such an extent that it would lead to violence between them, and, perhaps, to bloodshed. God has never designed such a thing as that, nor can we charge such things to the Almighty. People become sick, suffer pain, sorrow and anguish. They linger for months, and perhaps for years, in feebleness of body and of mind. The question arises in them: Why does the Lord suffer it? Is the hand of God in that suffering? Has God designed persons to suffer? Has he touched them with his hand of affliction? Has he caused the evil that has come to them? Too many of us are inclined to think, or lean toward the feeble thought, that the illness that comes to us, the afflictions that we suffer, the accidents that we meet with in life, and the troubles that beset us on our way in the journey of life, are attributable either to the mercy or the displeasure of God. Sometimes we are prone to charge God with causing our afflictions and our troubles; but if we could see as God sees, if we could understand as he understands, if we could trace the effects back to the cause, and that truly, by the spirit of correct understanding, we would unquestionably discover that our troubles, or suffering, or affliction are the result of our own indiscretion or lack of knowledge, or of wisdom. It was not the hand of God that put affliction and trouble upon us. The agency that he has given to us left us to act for ourselves—to do things if we will that are not right, that are contrary to the laws of life and health, that are not wise or prudent—and the results may be serious to us, because of our ignorance or of our determination to persist in that which we desire, rather than to yield to the requirements which God makes of us.—*Improvement Era*, Vol. 20, p. 821, July, 1917.

Goo's WARFARE. God is the greatest man of war of all, and his Son is next to him, and their warfare is for the salvation of the souls of men. It would not be necessary for them to use violence or force, nor to permit their children to use violence nor force in order to conquer if they would but humble themselves, and obey the truth. For, after all, nothing will conquer, nothing will win but the truth; and so far as the wars that are going on in the world are concerned, we not only want to see peace established among the children of men, but also justice, but above all things, truth, that justice, peace and righteousness may be built upon this foundation and not depend upon the covetousness, pride, vanity, evil desire, and lust for power in man.—*Oct. C. R.*, 1914, p. 129.

WE ARE IN Goo's IMAGE. When Brother Penrose shall pray, he will pray unto the Father of our Lord and Savior, Jesus Christ, in whose image and likeness we are made, or were born into the world, and in whose likeness and image we are, for we are God's children, and therefore must resemble his Son in person, and also spiritually, so far as we will obey the principles of the gospel of eternal truth. For, we were foreordained and predestined to become conformed to his likeness through the wise and proper use of our free agency.—Oct. C. R., 1914, p. 8.

GOD'S REST. The ancient prophets speak of "entering into God's rest"; what does it mean? To my mind, it means entering into the knowledge and love of God, having faith in his purpose and in his plan, to such an extent that we know we are right, and that we are not hunting for something else, we are not disturbed by every wind of doctrine, or by the cunning and craftiness of men who lie in wait to deceive. We know of the doctrine that it is of God, and we do not ask any questions of anybody about it; they are welcome to their opinions, to their ideas and to their vagaries. The man who has reached that degree of faith in God that all doubt and fear have been cast from him, he has entered into "God's rest," and he need not fear the vagaries of men, nor their cunning and craftiness, by which they seek to deceive and mislead him from the truth. I pray that we may all enter into God's rest—rest from doubt, from fear, from apprehension of danger, rest from the religious turmoil of the world; from the cry that is going forth, here and there—lo, here is Christ; lo, there is Christ; lo, he is in the desert, come ye out to meet him. The man who has found God's rest will not be disturbed by these vagaries of men, for the Lord has told him, and does tell us: Go not out to seek them: Go not out to hunt them; for when Christ shall come, he will come with the army of heaven with him in the clouds of glory, and all eyes shall see him. We do not need to be hunting for Christ here or Christ there, or prophets here and prophets there.—Oct. C. R., 1909, p. 8.

INTELLIGENCE. Christ inherited his intelligence from his Father. There is a difference between knowledge and pure intelligence. Satan possesses knowledge, far more than we have, but he has not intelligence or he would render obedience to the principles of truth and right. I know men who have knowledge, who understand the principles of the Gospel, perhaps as well as you do, who are brilliant, but who lack the essential qualification of pure intelligence. They will not accept and render obedience thereto. Pure intelligence comprises not only knowledge, but also the power to properly apply that knowledge.—Remarks made at a Weber Stake Conference.

IMPORTANCE OF BEING UNDER THE INFLUENCE OF THE HOLY SPIRIT. The one thing now that I desire to impress upon the minds of my brethren bearing the Holy Priesthood is that we should live so near to the Lord, be so humble in our spirits, so tractable and pliable, under the influence of the Holy Spirit, that we will be able to know the mind and will of the Father concerning us as individuals and as officers in the Church of Christ under all circumstances. And when we live so that we can hear and understand the whisperings of the still, small voice of the Spirit of God, let us do whatsoever that Spirit directs without fear of the consequences. It does not make any difference whether it meet the minds of carpers or critics, or of the enemies of the kingdom of God, or not. Is it agreeable to the will of the Lord? Is it compatible with the spirit of the great latter-day work in which we are engaged? Is the end aimed at likely to advance the Church and to strengthen it in the earth? If its trend is in that direction, let us do it, no matter what men may say or think.—Oct. C. R., 1903, p. 86.

OFFICE OF THE HOLY GHOST. It behooves the Latter-day Saints, and all men, to make themselves acquainted with "the only true God, and Jesus Christ whom he has sent." But can we through our own wisdom find out God? Can we by our unaided ingenuity and learning fathom his purposes and comprehend his will? We have, I think, witnessed examples enough of such efforts on the part of the intelligent world, to convince us that it is impossible. The ways and wisdom of God are not as the ways and wisdom of man. How then can we know "the only true and living God, and Jesus Christ whom he has sent?"—for to obtain this knowledge would be to obtain the secret or key to eternal life. It must be through the Holy Ghost, whose office is to reveal the things of the Father to man, and to bear witness in our hearts of Christ, and him crucified and risen from the dead. There is no other way or means of attaining to this knowledge. How shall we obtain the Holy Ghost? The method or manner is clearly marked out. We are told to have faith in God, to believe that he is, and that he is a rewarder of all who diligently seek him; to repent of our sins, subdue our passions, follies, and improprieties; to be virtuous, honest, and upright in all our dealings one with another, and enter into covenant with God that we will from thenceforth abide in the principles of truth, and observe the commandments which he has given us, then to be baptized for the remission of our sins, by one having authority; and when this ordinance of the gospel is complied with, we may receive the gift of the Holy Ghost by the laying on of the hands of those clothed with the authority of the Priesthood.

Thus the Spirit and power of God—the Comforter—may be in us as
a well of water springing up unto everlasting life. We will bear
record of the Father, testifying of Jesus, and "take of the things of
the Father and reveal them unto us," confirming our faith, establishing us in the truth, that we shall be no longer tossed to and fro
by every wind of doctrine; but shall "know of the doctrine" whether
it be of God or of man. This is the course—it is simple, reasonable
and consistent. Who is there with common abilities that can fail
to see, or comprehend it? Indeed, in the language of the Scriptures
it is so plain, that "the wayfaring man, though a fool, need not err
therein."

Having entered into this covenant, being cleansed from sin, and
endowed with the gift of the Holy Ghost, why should we not abide
in the truth, continuing steadfast before God and firm in the great
work he has established on the earth? We should never cease to serve
him, nor thwart his mercy and goodness towards us; but ever live
so that the Holy Ghost may be within us as a living spring, calculated
to lead us to perfection in righteousness, virtue and integrity before
God, until we accomplish our earthly mission, performing every duty
that may be required at our hands.—Discourse at St. George, April
2, 1877. J. of D. 19:20-21.

HOLY GHOST, HOLY SPIRIT, COMFORTER. The Holy Ghost, who
is a member of the Trinity in the Godhead, has not a body of flesh
and bones, like the Father and the Son, but is a personage of Spirit.
(Doc. and Cov., Sec. 130:22.)

The Holy Spirit, or Spirit of God, both of which terms are sometimes used interchangeably with the Holy Ghost, is the influence of
Deity, the light of Christ, or of Truth, which proceeds forth from
the presence of God to fill the immensity of space, and to quicken
the understanding of men. (Doc. and Cov., Sec. 88:6-13.)

If a man is baptized and ordained to the Holy Priesthood, and
is called upon to perform duties which pertain to that Priesthood,
it does not follow that he must always have the Holy Ghost in person
present with him when he performs his duty, but every righteous act
which he may perform legally will be in force and effect, and will
be acknowledged of God, and the more of the Spirit of God he
possesses in his ministrations, the better for himself, and those will
not suffer any loss unto whom he administers.

Therefore, the presentation or "gift" of the Holy Ghost simply confers upon a man the right to receive at any time, when he is worthy of it and desires it, the power and light of truth of the Holy Ghost, although he may often be left to his own spirit and judgment.

The Holy Ghost as a personage of Spirit can no more be omnipresent in person than can the Father or the Son, but by his intelligence, his knowledge, his power and influence, over and through the laws of nature, he is and can be omnipresent throughout all the works of God. It is not the Holy Ghost who in person lighteth every man who is born into the world, but it is the light of Christ, the Spirit of Truth, which proceeds from the source of intelligence, which permeates all nature, which lighteth every man and fills the immensity of space. You may call it the Spirit of God, you may call it the influence of God's intelligence, you may call it the substance of his power, no matter what it is called, it is the spirit of intelligence that permeates the universe and gives to the spirits of men understanding, just as Job has said. (Job 32:8; Doc. and Cov. 88:3-13.)

Every elder of the Church who has received the Holy Ghost by the laying on of hands, by one having authority, has power to confer that gift upon another; it does not follow that a man who has received the presentation or gift of the Holy Ghost shall always receive the recognition and witness and presence of the Holy Ghost himself, or he may receive all these, and yet the Holy Ghost not tarry with him, but visit him from time to time (Doc. and Cov., Sec. 130:23); and neither does it follow that a man must have the Holy Ghost present with him when he confers the Holy Ghost upon another, but he possesses the gift of the Holy Ghost, and it will depend upon the worthiness of him unto whom the gift is bestowed whether he receive the Holy Ghost or not.

Now I repeat—the Holy Ghost is a personage of spirit, he constitutes the third person in the Trinity, the Godhead. The gift or presentation of the Holy Ghost is the authoritative act of conferring him upon man. The Holy Ghost in person may visit men and will visit those who are worthy and bear witness to their spirit of God and Christ, but may not tarry with them. The Spirit of God which emanates from Deity may be likened to electricity, or the universal ether, as explained in our manual, which fills the earth and the air, and is everywhere present. It is the power of God, the influence that he exerts throughout all his works by which he can effect his purposes and execute his will, in consonance with the laws of free agency which he has conferred upon man. By means of this Spirit every man is enlightened, the wicked as well as the good, the intelligent and the ignorant, the high and the low, each in accordance with his capacity to receive the light; and this Spirit or influence which emanates from God may be said to constitute man's consciousness, and will never cease to strive with man, until man is brought to the possession of the higher intelligence which can only come through faith, repentance, baptism for the remission of sins, and the gift or the presentation of the Holy Ghost by one having authority.— *Improvement Era*, Vol. 12, p. 389, March, 1909.

GOD INSPIRES MAN TO KNOW AND TO DO. I am inclined to acknowledge the hand of God in all things. If I see a man inspired with intelligence, with extraordinary ability and wisdom, I say to myself he is indebted to God for that wisdom and ability; and that, without the providence or interposition of the Almighty, he would not have been what he is. He is indebted to the Lord Almighty for his intelligence, and for all that he has; for the earth is the Lord's and the fulness thereof. God originated and designed all things, and all are his children. We are born into the world as his offspring; endowed with the same attributes. The children of men have sprung from the Almighty, whether the world is willing to acknowledge it or not. He is the Father of our spirits. He is the originator of our earthly tabernacles. We live and move and have our being in God our heavenly Father. And having sprung from him with our talents, our ability, our wisdom, we should at least be willing to acknowledge his hand in all the prosperity that may attend us in life, and give to him the honor and glory of all we accomplish in the flesh. We are particularly dependent upon the Almighty for everything we possess of a worldly character. There is not a man on the earth possessed of the wisdom or power of himself to cause even a spear of grass to grow, or to produce a kernel of wheat or of corn, or any fruit, vegetable, or any material whatever which is essential for the sustenance, the happiness and the well-being of a human creature in the world. It is true we can go to the earth, we find it prepared to a certain extent, and we cultivate, plow and plant, and we reap the harvest; but God has ordained that the fruits of our labor shall be in subjection and in obedience to certain laws which he himself controls, and which he has kept out of the power of man. Man may boast of having a great deal of wisdom; of having accomplished a great deal in this nineteenth century; but, if he did but know it, he derives the ability by which he accomplishes these things from God his Father, who is in heaven. He does not possess the power in and of himself.

I read a Scripture something like this: that "there is a spirit in man." Now, if that should stop here, there would not be perhaps anything very remarkable about man; for the spirit of man knoweth only the things of man, and the things of God are discerned by the Spirit of God. But while there is a spirit in man, it is further stated that "the inspiration of the Almighty giveth them understanding." There is not a man born into the world, but has a portion of the Spirit of God, and it is that Spirit of God which gives to his spirit understanding. Without this, he would be but an animal like the rest of the brute creation, without understanding, without judgment, without skill, without ability, except to eat and to drink like the brute beast. But inasmuch as the Spirit of God giveth all men understanding, he is enlightened above the brute beast. He is made in the image of God himself, so that he can reason, reflect, pray, exercise faith; he can use his energies for the accomplishment of the desires of his heart, and inasmuch as he puts forth his efforts in the proper direction, then he is entitled to an increased portion of the Spirit of the Almighty to inspire him to increased intelligence, to increased prosperity and happiness in the world; but in proportion as he prostitutes his energies for evil, the inspiration of the Almighty is withdrawn from him, until he becomes so dark and so benighted, that so far as his knowledge of God is concerned, he is quite as ignorant as a dumb brute.

Again, where are we going? We come here and journey in the flesh a little season, and then we pass away. Every soul that is born into the world will die. There is not a soul that has escaped death, except those upon whom God has passed, by the power of his Spirit, that they should live in the flesh until the second coming of the Son of Man; but they will eventually have to pass through the ordeal called death; it may be in the twinkling of an eye, and without pain or suffering; but they will pass through the change, because it is an irrevocable edict of the Almighty. "In the day thou eatest thereof thou shalt surely die." This was the edict of the Almighty, and it pertains to Adam—that is, all the human race—for Adam is many—and it means you and me, and every soul that lives and that bears the image of the Father. We shall all die. But is that the end of our being? If we had an existence before we came here, we certainly shall continue that existence when we leave here. The spirit will continue to exist as it did before, with the additional advantages derived from having passed through this probation. It is absolutely necessary that we should come to the earth and take upon us tabernacles; because if we did not have tabernacles we could not be like God, nor like Jesus Christ. God has a tabernacle of flesh and bone. He is an organized being just as we are, who are now in the flesh. Jesus Christ was born of his mother, Mary. He had a fleshly tabernacle. He was crucified on the cross; and his body was raised from the dead. He burst the bonds of the grave, and came forth to newness of life, a living soul, a living being, a man with a body, with parts and with spirit—the spirit and the body becoming a living and immortal soul. You and I have to do the same thing. We must go through the same ordeal in order to attain to the glory and exaltation which God designed we should enjoy with him in the eternal worlds. In other words, we must become like him; peradventure to sit upon thrones, to have dominion, power, and eternal increase. God designed this in the beginning. We are the children of God. He is an eternal being, without beginning of days or end of years. He always was, he is, he always will be. We are precisely in the same condition and under the same circumstances that God our heavenly Father was when he was passing through this, or a similar ordeal. We are destined to come forth out of the grave as Jesus did, and to obtain immortal bodies as he did—that is, that our tabernacles are to become immortal as his became immortal, that the spirit and the body may be joined together and become one living being, indivisible, inseparable, eternal. This is the object of our existence in the world; and we can only attain to these things through obedience to certain principles, through walking in certain channels, through obtaining certain information, certain intelligence from God, without which no man can accomplish his work or fulfill the mission he has come upon the earth to fulfill. These principles are the principles of the gospel of eternal truth, the principles of faith, repentance, and baptism for the remission of sins, the principle of obedience to God the eternal Father; for obedience is one of the first principles or laws of heaven. Without obedience, there can be no order, no government, no union, no plan or purpose carried out. And that obedience must be voluntary; it must not be forced, there must be no coercion. Men must not be constrained against their will to obey the will of God; they must obey it because they know it to be right, because they desire to do it, and because it is their pleasure to do it. God delights in the willing heart.

I am looking forward to the time when I shall have passed away from this stage of existence, there I shall be permitted to enjoy more fully every gift and blessing that have contributed to my happiness in this world; everything. I do not believe that there is one thing that was designed or intended to give me joy or make me happy, that I shall be denied here after, provided I continue faithful; otherwise my joy cannot be full. I am not now speaking of that happiness or pleasure that is derived from sin; I refer to the happiness experienced in seeking to do the will of God on earth as it is done in heaven. We expect to have our wives and husbands in eternity. We expect our children will acknowledge us as their fathers and mothers in eternity. I expect this; I look for nothing else. Without it, I could not be happy. The thought or belief that I should be denied this privilege hereafter would make me miserable from this moment. I never could be happy again without the hope that I shall enjoy the society of my wives and children in eternity. If I had not this hope, I should be of all men most unhappy, for "if in this life only we have hope in Christ, we are of all men most miserable." And all who have tasted of the influence of the Spirit of God, and have had awakened within them a hope of eternal life, cannot be happy unless they continue to drink of that fountain until they are satisfied, and it is the only fountain at which they can drink and be satisfied.—*Journal of Discourses*, Vol. 25, 1884, pp. 51-60.

TRUST IN GOD. The need of one's having a keen knowledge of the truth is paramount. So also is it that every Latter-day Saint should have a deep-rooted conviction of the justice of God, and an implicit confidence and faith in his being and mercy. To rightfully understand the gospel and to be able to keep his commandments such knowledge is absolutely necessary. Let each person ask himself if in his soul there is a sharp and immovable conviction of these facts. Could anything that might occur to you, or that might take place in the Church, or with her officers or authorities, change your faith in the purposes, and in the absolute justice and mercy, of the Lord.

or in the saving power of his gospel, the message of his salvation? If so, your faith is not deep-rooted, and there is strong need of your becoming convinced. * * *

No person can realize the fulness of the blessings of God, unless he can approach, in some degree, at least, the standard of faith in God's justice, exemplified in the examples quoted. He must have founded in his own soul belief and confidence in the justice and mercy of God. It must be individual, no man can act for another. Lessons of this class need be taught and held up before the youth of Zion, to bring forcibly to their minds the truth which alone will make them free and able to stand firm in the faith. Let them, as they are called together in their assemblies, present themselves before God, and be reminded of his gracious benefits, in bringing forth the Book of Mormon, in the scenes of Kirtland, in Zion, in Nauvoo, in the trying days of the exodus, and in the wilderness. This that they might count the mercies of God in his promises, and behold how past affliction and sore trial have been turned to the well-being of his people; and so renew their covenants, filled with a deep-rooted, immovable conviction of the goodness and mercy of the Lord. Each individual must learn this lesson, it must be impressed upon his soul, so deep, and be so well-founded that nothing can separate him from a knowledge of the love of God, though death and hell stand in the way.

God is good; his promises never fail; to trust implicitly his goodness and mercy is a correct principle. Let us, therefore, put our trust in him.—*Improvement Era*, Vol. 7, p. 53, Nov., 1904.

I Know that My Redeemer Lives. It is by the power of God that all things are made that have been made. It is by the power of Christ that all things are governed and kept in place that are governed and kept in place in the universe. It is the power which proceeds from the presence of the Son of God throughout all the works of his hands, that giveth light, energy, understanding, knowledge, and a degree of intelligence to all the children of men, strictly in accordance with the words in the Book of Job: "There is a spirit in man; and the inspiration of the Almighty giveth them understanding." It is this inspiration from God, proceeding throughout all his creations, that enlighteneth the children of men; and it is nothing more nor less than the spirit of Christ that enlighteneth the mind, that quickeneth the understanding, and that prompteth the children of men to do that which is good and to eschew that which is evil; which quickens the conscience of man and gives him intelligence to judge between good and evil, light and darkness, right and wrong.

But the Holy Ghost, who bears record of the Father and the Son, who takes of the things of the Father and shows them unto men, who testifies of Jesus Christ, and of the everliving God, the Father of Jesus Christ, and who bears witness of the truth—this Spirit, this Intelligence, is not given unto all men until they repent of their sins and come into a state of worthiness before the Lord. Then they receive the gift of the Holy Ghost by the laying on of the hands of those who are authorized of God to bestow his blessings upon the heads of the children of men. The Spirit spoken of in that which I have read is that Spirit which will not cease to strive with the children of men until they are brought to the possession of the greater light and intelligence. Though a man may commit all manner of sin and blasphemy, if he has not received the testimony of the Holy Ghost, he may be forgiven by repenting of his sins, humbling himself before the Lord, and obeying in sincerity the commandments of God. As it is stated, "Every soul who forsaketh his sins and cometh unto me, and calleth on my name, and obeyeth my voice, and keepeth my commandments shall see my face and know that I am." He shall be forgiven, and receive of the greater light; he will enter into a solemn covenant with God, into a compact with the Almighty, through the Only Begotten Son, whereby he becomes a son of God, an heir of God, and a joint heir with Jesus Christ. Then if he shall sin against the light and knowledge he has received, the light that was within him shall become darkness, and oh, how great will be that darkness! Then, and not till then, will this Spirit of Christ that lighteth every man that cometh into the world cease to strive with him, and he shall be left to his own destruction.

The question is often asked, Is there any difference between the Spirit of the Lord and the Holy Ghost? The terms are frequently used synonymously. We often say the Spirit of God when we mean the Holy Ghost; we likewise say the Holy Ghost when we mean the Spirit of God. The Holy Ghost is a personage in the Godhead, and is not that which lighteth every man that cometh into the world. It is the Spirit of God which proceeds through Christ to the world, that enlightens every man that comes into the world, and that strives with the children of men, and will continue to strive with them, until it brings them to a knowledge of the truth and the possession of the greater light and testimony of the Holy Ghost. If, however, he receive that greater light, and then sin against it, the Spirit of God will cease to strive with him, and the Holy Ghost will wholly depart from him. Then will he persecute the truth; then will he seek the blood of the innocent; then will he not scruple at the commission of any crime, except so far as he may fear the penalties of the law, in consequence of the crime upon himself.

"And that I am in the Father, and the Father in me, and the Father and I are one." I do not apprehend that any intelligent person will construe these words to mean that Jesus and his Father are one person, but merely that they are one in knowledge, in truth, in wisdom, in understanding, and in purpose; just as the Lord Jesus himself admonished his disciples to be one with him, and to be in him, that he might be in them. It is in this sense that I understand this language, and not as it is construed by some people, that Christ and his Father are one person. I declare to you that they are not one person, but that they are two persons, two bodies, separate and apart, and as distinct as are any father and son within the sound of my voice. Yet, Jesus is the Father of this world, because it was by him that the world was made.

Even Christ himself was not perfect at first; he received not a fulness at first, but he received grace for grace, and he continued to receive more and more until he received a fulness. Is not this to be so with the children of men? Is any man perfect? Has any man received a fulness at once? Have we reached a point wherein we may receive the fulness of God, of his glory, and his intelligence? No; and yet, if Jesus, the Son of God, and the Father of the heavens and the earth in which we dwell, received not a fulness at the first, but increased in faith, knowledge, understanding and grace until he received a fulness, is it not possible for all men who are born of women to receive little by little, line upon line, precept upon precept, until they shall receive a fulness, as he has received a fulness, and be exalted with him in the presence of the Father?

The spirit without the body is not perfect, and the body without the spirit is dead. Man was ordained in the beginning to become like Jesus Christ, to become conformed unto his image. As Jesus was born of woman, lived and grew to manhood, was put to death and raised from the dead to immortality and eternal life, so it was decreed in the beginning that man should be, and will be, through the atonement of

Jesus, in spite of himself, resurrected from the dead. Death came upon us without the exercise of our agency; we had no hand in bringing it originally upon ourselves; it came because of the transgression of our first parents. Therefore, man, who had no hand in bringing death upon himself, shall have no hand in bringing again life unto himself; for as he dies in consequence of the sin of Adam, so shall he live again, whether he will or not, by the righteousness of Jesus Christ, and the power of his resurrection. Every man that dies shall live again, and shall stand before the bar of God, to be judged according to his works, whether they be good or evil. It is then that all will have to give an account for their stewardship in this mortal life.

Now, my brethren and sisters, I know that my Redeemer lives. I feel it in every fiber of my being. I am just as satisfied of it as I am of my own existence. I cannot feel more sure of my own being than I do that my Redeemer lives, and that my God lives, the Father of my Savior. I feel it in my soul; I am converted to it in my whole being. I bear testimony to you that this is the doctrine of Christ, the gospel of Jesus, which is the power of God unto salvation. It is "Mormonism."—*Sermon in Tabernacle*, Salt Lake City, March 16, 1902.

OUR PERSONAL RESPONSIBILITY. If there is one principle of the gospel of Jesus Christ that goes directly to the very foundation of justice and righteousness, it is that great and glorious and God-like principle that every man will have to render an account for that which he does, and every man will be rewarded for his works, whether they be good or evil.—*Improvement Era*, Vol. 21, p. 104.

THE CHURCH A DEMOCRATIC INSTITUTION. The Church of Jesus Christ of Latter-day Saints is the most democratic institution in the world.—*Improvement Era*, Vol. 21, p. 100.

HOW TO SECURE GOD'S BLESSING. If we desire a continuation of the blessings of the Lord, we must do his will and obey the laws on which his blessings are predicated. There is no other way to obtain his blessings.—*Improvement Era*. Vol. 21, p. 99, December, 1917.

JESUS IS THE SON. Jesus Christ is not the Father of the spirits who have taken or yet shall take bodies upon this earth, for he is one of them. He is the Son, as they are sons or daughters of Elohim. So far as the stages of eternal progression and attainment have been made known through divine revelation, we are to understand that only resurrected and glorified beings can become parents of spirit offspring. Only such exalted souls have reached maturity in the appointed course of eternal life; and the spirits born to them in the eternal worlds will pass in due sequence through the several stages or estates by which the glorified parents have attained exaltation.—*Improvement Era*, Vol. 19, p. 942.

JEHOVAH, THE FIRSTBORN. Among the spirit children of Elohim, the first-born was and is Jehovah, or Jesus Christ, to whom all others are juniors.—*Improvement Era*, Vol. 19, p. 940.

NOTHING TEMPORAL WITH GOD. We ought to be united in all things temporal as well as spiritual. With God all things are spiritual. There is nothing temporal with him at all, and there ought to be no distinction with us in regard to these matters. Our earthly or temporal existence is merely a continuance of that which is spiritual. Every step we take in the great journey of life, the great journey of eternity, is a step in advance or in retrogression. We are here in mortality, it is true; but we are ahead of that condition we occupied before we came here and took upon us mortality. We are a step in advance of our former state. What is the body without the spirit? It is lifeless clay. What is it that affects this lifeless clay? It is the spirit, it is the immortal part, the eternal being, that existed before it came here, that exists within us, and that will continue to exist that by and by will redeem these tabernacles and bring them forth out of the graves. The whole mission of ours is spiritual. The work we have to do here, although we call it temporal, pertains alike to our spiritual and our temporal salvation. And the Lord has just as much right to dictate, to counsel, to direct and guide us in the manipulation and management of our temporal affairs, as we call them, as he has to say one word in relation to our spiritual affairs. So far as he is concerned there is no difference in this regard. He looks upon us as immortal beings. Our bodies are designed to become eternal and spiritual. God is spiritual himself, although he has a body of flesh and bone as Christ has. Yet he is spiritual, and those who worship him must do so in spirit and truth. And when you come to separate the spiritual from the temporal, see that you do not make a mistake.— *Deseret Weekly News*, Vol. 23, July 16, 1884, p. 466.

THE IMPORTANT CONSIDERATION. The important consideration is not how long we can live, but how well we can learn the lessons of life, and discharge our duties and obligations to God and to each other. One of the main purposes of our existence is that we might conform to the image and likeness of Him who sojourned in the flesh without blemish—immaculate, pure, and spotless! Christ came not only to atone for the sins of the world, but to set an example before all men, and to establish the standard of God's perfection, of God's law, and of obedience to the Father.—*Improvement Era, Vol. 21, 1917, p. 104.*

Chapter VI

THE PURPOSE AND THE MISSION OF THE CHURCH

THE KINGDOM OF GOD DEFINED. What I mean by the kingdom of God is the organization of the Church of Jesus Christ of Latter-day Saints, over which the Son of God presides, and not man. That is what I mean. I mean the kingdom of which Christ is the King and not man. If any man object to Christ, the Son of God, being King of Israel, let him object, and go to hell just as quick as he please.— Oct. C. R., 1906, p. 9.

"MORMONISM" DEFINED. I desire to say that "Mormonism," as it is called, is still, as always, nothing more and nothing less than the power of God unto salvation, unto every soul that will receive it honestly and will obey it. I say to you, my brethren, sisters and friends, that all Latter-day Saints, wherever you find them, provided they are true to their name, to their calling and to their understanding of the gospel, are people who stand for truth and for honor, for virtue and for purity of life, for honesty in business and in religion; people who stand for God and for his righteousness, for God's truth and his work in the earth, which aims, for the salvation of the children of men, for their salvation from the evils of the world, from the pernicious habits of wicked men and from all those things that degrade, dishonor or destroy; or tend to lessen the vitality and life, the honor and godliness among the people of the earth.—Apr. C. R., 1910, p. 5.

THE MISSION OF THE CHURCH. Our mission has been to save men. We have been laboring all these eighty-odd years of the Church to bring men to a knowledge of the gospel of Jesus Christ, to bring them to repentance, to obedience to the requirements of God's law. We have been striving to save men from error, to persuade them to turn away from evil and to learn to do good. Now if our enemies will only charge us with doing this, all right; and if they wish to oppose us for doing this, that is their business; but when they charge us with doing that which we have not done, believing that which we do not believe, practicing that which we have never practiced, then I pity them. I pity them because they are doing it in ignorance, or because they are wilfully disposed to misrepresent the truth.—Apr. C. R., 1912, pp. 3, 4.

THE PLAN OF LIFE RESTORED. It is the plan of life that the

Almighty has restored to man in the latter days for the salvation of the souls of men, not only in the world to come, but in our present life, for the Lord has instituted his work that his people may enjoy the blessings of this life to the utmost; that they should be saved in this present life, as well as in the life to come, that they should lay the foundation here for immunity from sin and all its effects and consequences, that they may obtain an inheritance in the kingdom of God beyond this vale of tears. The gospel of Jesus Christ is the power of God unto salvation, and it is absolutely necessary for every man and woman in the Church of Christ to work righteousness, to observe the laws of God, and keep the commandments that he has given, in order that they may avail themselves of the power of God unto salvation in this life.—Oct. C. R., 1907, p. 2.

OUR MISSION IS TO SAVE. Our mission is to save, to preserve from evil, to exalt mankind, to bring light and truth into the world, to prevail upon the people of the earth to walk righteously before God, and to honor him in their lives and with the first fruits of all their substance and increase, that their barns may be filled with plenty and, figuratively speaking, that "their presses may burst out with new wine."—Apr. C. R., 1907, p. 118.

THE GOSPEL MESSAGE. I rejoice exceedingly in the truth. I thank God every day of my life for his mercy and kindness, and loving care and protection that have been extended to all his people, and for the many manifestations of his peculiar mercy and blessings that have been extended unto us throughout all the length and breadth of the land and through all the years since the organization of the Church, on the 6th of April, 1830.

The Lord, about that time, or soon after, decreed a decree which he said his people should realize, that they should begin from that very hour to prevail over all their enemies, and, inasmuch as they continued to be faithful in keeping his laws he had given unto them, it was decreed that they should prevail until all enemies were subdued —not subdued by violence, nor the spirit of contention nor of warfare, but subdued by the power of eternal truth, by the majesty and power of Almighty God, but by the increased power of the righteous and of the upright covenanted people of God—should be magnified and increased, until the world shall bow and acknowledge that Jesus is the Christ, and that there is a people preparing for his coming in power and glory to the earth again.

We carry to the world the olive branch of peace. We present to the world the law of God, the word of the Lord, the truth, as it has been revealed in the latter day for the redemption of the dead and for the salvation of the living. We bear no malice nor evil toward the children of men. The spirit of forgiveness pervades the hearts of the Saints of God, and they do not cherish a desire or feeling of revenge toward their enemies or those who hurt or molest them or seek to make them afraid; but on the contrary, the Spirit of the Lord has possession of their spirits, of their souls, and of their thoughts; they forgive all men, and they carry no malice in their hearts toward any, no matter what they have done. They say in their hearts, let God judge between us and our enemies, and as for us, we forgive them, and we bear no malice toward any.—Apr. C. R., 1902, p. 2.

WE ARE AS LEAVEN. While it may be said, and it is in a measure true, that we are but a handful in comparison with our fellowmen in the world, yet we may be compared with the leaven of which the Savior spoke, that will eventually leaven the whole world. We have ample assurance of the fulfilment of this thought in the growth and development of the cause from its incipiency until the present, for it has steadily and increasingly progressed and developed in the earth, from a mere half dozen of men, seventy-nine years ago, until today the members of the Church may be numbered by the hundreds of thousands.—Apr. C. R., 1909, p. 2.

MAN INSIGNIFICANT COMPARED TO CAUSE. We are learning the great truth that man is insignificant in his individuality, in comparison to the mighty cause which involves the salvation of the children of men, living and. dead, and those who will yet live in the earth. Men must set aside their own prejudices, their own personal desires, wishes and preferences, and pay deference to the great cause of truth that is spreading abroad in the world.—Apr C. R., 1909, p. 2.

WHERE THE GOSPEL SPIRIT LEADS. The spirit of the gospel leads men to righteousness; to love their fellowmen and to labor for their salvation and exaltation; it inspires them to do good and not evil, to avoid even the appearance of sin, much more to avoid sin itself. This is indeed the spirit of the gospel, which is the spirit of this latter-day work, and also the spirit that possesses those who have embraced it; and the aim and purpose of this work is the salvation, the exaltation, and the eternal happiness of man, both in this life and in the life to come.—Apr. C. R., 1909, p. 4.

THE FRUITS OF TRUE RELIGION. The fruits of the Spirit of God –the fruits of the spirit of true religion—are peace and love, virtue and honesty, and integrity, and fidelity to every virtue known in the law of God,—while the spirit of the world is vicious. Read the 5th chapter of Galatians, and there you will discover the difference between the fruits of the Spirit of God and the fruits of the spirit of the world. That is one of the great and chief differences between "Mormonism," so-called, and the theology of the world. If "Mormonism" is anything at all more than other religions, it is that it is practical, that the results of obedience to it are practical, that it makes good men better men, and that it takes even bad men and makes good ones of them. That is what "Mormonism" will do, if we will only permit it to do it, if we will bow to its mandates and adopt its precepts in our lives, it will make us the sons and the daughters of God, worthy eventually to dwell in the presence of the Almighty in the heavens.—Apr. C. R., 1905, p. 86.

LATTER-DAY SAINTS POSSESS THE SPIRIT OF SALVATION. The Latter-day Saints possess the spirit of salvation, and not the spirit of destruction; the spirit of life, not the spirit of death; the spirit of peace, not the spirit of disunion; the spirit of love for their fellow beings, not the spirit of hate. And for the enjoyment of this spirit by the Saints of the Most High, we all have great cause to render praise and thanksgiving to him who has so ordered it, and has given to us humility to receive that measure of his Spirit which inclines our hearts to good and not to evil.—Oct. C. R., 1905, p. 2.

MAY ISRAEL FLOURISH. May Israel flourish upon the hills and rejoice upon the mountains, and assemble together unto the place which God has appointed, and there prosper, multiply and replenish the earth, and thence spread abroad throughout the land; for the time will come when we will find it necessary to fulfil the purposes of the Almighty by occupying the land of Zion in all parts of it. We are not destined to be confined to the valleys of the mountains. Zion is destined to grow, and the time will come when we will cry aloud, more than we do today, "Give us room that we may dwell!"—Apr. C. R., 1907, p. 118.

THE WORK OF THE LORD WILL GROW. The kingdom of God and the work of the Lord will spread more and more; it will progress more rapidly in the world in the future than it has done in the past. The Lord has said it, and the Spirit beareth record; and I bear testimony to this, for I do know that it is true.—Apr. C. R., 1909, p. 7.

THE KINGDOM OF GOD TO CONTINUE. The kingdom of God is here to grow, to spread abroad, to take root in the earth, and to abide where the Lord has planted it by his own power and by his own word in the earth, never more to be destroyed nor to cease, but to continue until the purposes of the Almighty shall be accomplished, every whit that has been spoken of it by the mouths of the holy prophets since the world began.—Apr. C. R., 1902, p. 2.

ZION ESTABLISHED TO REMAIN. Zion is established in the midst of the earth to remain. It is God Almighty's work, which he himself, by his own wisdom, and not by the wisdom of man, has restored to the earth in the latter days, and he has established it upon principles of truth and righteousness, of purity of life and revelation from God, that it can no more be thrown down or left to another people, so long as the majority of the Church of Jesus Christ of Latter-day Saints will abide in their covenants with the Lord and keep themselves pure and unspotted from the world, as all members of the Church should keep themselves. Then it will be as God has decreed, perpetual and eternal, until his will is accomplished and his purposes fulfilled among the children of men. No people can ever prosper and flourish very long unless they abide in God's truth. There is nothing, no individuality, no combined influence among men, that can prevail over the truth. The truth is mighty and it will prevail. It may be slow in the consummation of its purpose, in the accomplishment of the work that it has to do, but it is and will be sure; for the truth cannot and will not fail, for the Lord Almighty is behind it. It is his work, and he will see to it that it is accomplished. The kingdom is the Lord's, and the Lord is capable of taking care of it. He has always taken care of it. I want to say to you that there never was a time since the organization of the Church of Jesus Christ of Latter-day Saints, when a man led the Church, not for one moment. It was not so in the days of Joseph; it was not so in the days of Brigham Young; it has not been so since; it never will be so. The direction of this work among the people of the world will never be left to men. It is God's work, let me tell you, and I hope you will put it down in your memoranda, and do not forget that it is the Almighty that is going to do this work, and consummate it, and not man. No man shall have the honor of doing it, nor has any man ever had the power to do it of himself. It is God's work. If it had been the work of man, we would have been like the rest of the world, and it would not have been true of us that God has chosen us out of the world, but we would be a part of it, and "Hail fellow, well met," with it; but it is true that God has chosen us out of the world; therefore we are not of it; therefore they hate us and they will fight us and say all manner of evil against us falsely, as they have ever done from the beginning. And they will continue to seek the destruction of the Latter-day Saints, and to feel towards us in the future, as they have felt in the past. Now, don't you forget it, my brothers and sisters. When you go home, if you have not been in the habit of doing it, or if you have neglected your duty, when you go home today or to your homes in distant settlements, carry this injunction with you: Go into your secret chambers—go into your prayer-rooms —and there by yourselves, or with your family gathered around you, bow your knees before God Almighty in praise and in thanksgiving to him for his merciful providence that has been over you and over all his people from the inception of this work down to the present. Remember that it is the gift of God to man, that it is his power and his guiding influence that have accomplished what we see has been accomplished. It has not been done by the wisdom of men. It is proper we should give honor to those who have been instrumental in bringing to pass much righteousness. They are instruments in God's hands, and we should not ignore that they are such instruments, and we should honor them as such; but when we undertake to give them the honor for accomplishing this work and take the honor from God who qualified the men to do the work, we are doing injustice to God. We are robbing him of the honor that rightfully belongs to him, and giving it to men who are only instrumental in the hands of God in accomplishing his purposes.—Apr. C. R., 1905, pp. 5, 6.

THE PROGRESS OF GOD'S WORK CANNOT BE STOPPED. Now, we are thankful to the Lord that we are counted worthy to be taken notice of by the devil. I would fear very much for our safety if we had fallen into a condition where the devil ceased to be concerned about us. So long as the Spirit of the Lord is enjoyed by you, so long as you are living your religion, and keeping the commandments of the Lord, walking uprightly before him, I assure you that the adversary of souls will not rest easy; he will be discontented with you, will find fault with you, and he will arraign you before his bar; but that will not hurt you very much if you will just keep on doing right. You do not need to worry in the least, the Lord will take care of you and bless you, he will also take care of his servants, and will bless them and help them to accomplish his purposes; and all the powers of darkness combined on earth and in hell cannot prevent it. They may take men's lives; they may slay and destroy, if they will; but they cannot destroy the purposes of God nor stop the progress of his work. He has stretched forth his hand to accomplish his purposes, and the arm of flesh cannot stay it. He will cut his work short in righteousness, and will hasten his purposes in his own time. It is only necessary to try with our might to keep pace with the onward progress of the work of the Lord, then God will preserve and protect us, and will prepare the way before us, that we shall live and multiply and replenish the earth, and always do his will; which may God grant.—Oct. C. R., 1905, pp. 5, 6.

DIVINITY OF THE GOSPEL. Somewhat unexpectedly I am called to stand before you, but I do so with pleasure, as I have a testimony to bear to the work we are engaged in; and it gives me pleasure when an opportunity is afforded to give expression to my feelings in relation to that work. That we have the gospel and have enjoyed its blessings, and that the ordinances of the gospel have been administered to us as Latter-day Saints, there are thousands of witnesses in this territory and in many places in the world can testify. The testimony of the truth of this work is not confined to one or to a few; but there are thousands who can declare that they know it is true, because it has been revealed to them.

We as a people are increasing in numbers, and the Lord Almighty is increasing his blessings upon us, and the people are expanding in their understanding and in the knowledge of the truth. I feel grateful to my heavenly Father that I have been permitted to live in this generation, and have been permitted to become acquainted, somewhat, with the principles of the gospel. I am thankful that I have had the privilege of having a testimony of its truth, and that I am permitted to stand here and elsewhere to bear my testimony to the truth that the gospel has been restored to man.

I have traveled somewhat among the nations preaching the gospel, and have seen something of the conditions of the world, and to a certain extent have become acquainted with the feelings of men, and with the religions of the world. I am aware that the gospel, as revealed in the Bible, cannot be found in the world; the ordinances of that gospel are not administered in any church except the Church of Jesus Christ of Latter-day Saints. If we make ourselves acquainted with the tenets of the religious world we shall find that they have not the gospel nor its ordinances; they have a form of godliness, and I have no doubt, are as sincere as we who have obeyed the gospel as revealed from heaven in these days. But they are devoid of the knowledge which we possess, and it is from the fact that they deny the source by which they might receive this knowledge —namely, revelation from Jesus Christ. In their minds they have closed up the heavens; they declare that God has revealed all that is necessary, that the canon of scripture is full, and that no more will be revealed. Believing thus, they close up the avenue of light and intelligence from heaven; and this will continue so long as they continue in their present course of unbelief. They will not listen to the testimony of men who tell them that the Lord lives and that he is able to reveal his will to man today, as ever. They will not heed this testimony, consequently they close the door of light and revelation. They cannot advance, nor learn the ways of God nor walk in his paths.

We testify that the barriers which separated man from God have been overcome, that the Lord has again communicated his will to man. "But," says one, "how shall we become acquainted with these things? How can we know that you are not deceived?" To all such we say, repent of your sins in all sincerity, then go forth and be baptized, and have hands laid upon you for the gift of the Holy Ghost, and the Spirit will bear record to you of the truth of our testimony, and you will become witnesses of it as we are, and will be able to stand forth boldly and testify to the world as we do. This was the path pointed out by Peter and the apostles on the day of Pentecost, when the Spirit of the Lord Almighty rested upon them with great power to the convincing of the hearts of the people who cried out, "Men and brethren, what shall we do?" And Peter said unto them, "Repent, and be baptized, every one of you, in the name of Jesus Christ, for the remission of sins, and ye shall receive the gift of the Holy Ghost." This was the counsel given them, and inasmuch as they obeyed it, they were entitled to the testimony of the Holy Spirit which would bring peace and happiness, reveal to them their duties, and enable them to understand their relationship to God.

If we look at the condition of the world today, we must come to the conclusion that peace is not likely soon to be established on the earth. There is nothing among the nations that tends to peace. Even among the religious societies the tendency is not to peace and union. They do not bring men to a knowledge of God; they do not possess the "one Lord, one faith, one baptism," and "one hope of their calling" that are spoken of in the Scripture. Every man has gone according to his own notions, independent of revelations, and hence, confusion and division exist; their churches are broken up, and they are quarreling and contending with one another. And as it is in the religious, so it is in the political world; they are all divided, and the more energy they put forth to make proselytes, the greater are their contentions, and the further they go from the mark. This is the condition they have been in, and the course they have been pursuing for almost eighteen hundred years, until today they have become so divided that I think it would puzzle anyone to tell how many religious denominations there are in Christendom. There are thousands, too, who, in consequence of the strife and contention among the religious sects, have become entirely skeptical repecting religion of every kind, and they have concluded that there is no God; at any rate, that there is no God among "Christians"—that all religionists are fanatics and are deceived. The sectarian systems of religion are calculated to lead men of reflection and intelligence into skepticism, to cause them to deny all interference of God with men and their affairs, and to deny even his right to interfere.

The Lord Almighty is the Creator of the earth, he is the Father of all our spirits. He has the right to dictate what we should do, and it is our duty to obey, and to walk according to his requirements. This is natural, and perfectly easy to be comprehended. The gospel has been restored to the earth, and the Priesthood again established, and both are enjoyed by this people; but those unacquainted with the working of the gospel and the Priesthood look upon us with wonder, and are astonished at the union that exists in our midst. We move as a man, almost; we hearken to the voice of our leader; we are united in our faith and in our work. The world can not understand this, and they behold it with wonder.

Let me tell my brethren and friends that this is one of the effects of the gospel of Jesus Christ. We have become united in our faith by one baptism; we know that Jesus Christ lives, we know that he is our Savior and Redeemer; we have a testimony of this, independent of any written books, and we testify of these things to the world. This unison in the midst of the people called Latter-day Saints, and their prosperity, are hard for a great many to understand. I have, however, heard it said, that we boast that we are not so wealthy as our neighbors. But when our circumstances, and the condition of our country when we came here, are considered, I think this statement cannot be sustained. When we. came here we were penniless, and we have not had the advantages of wealth or commerce to help to enrich us, but all we possess is the result of our own physical labor and the blessing of God. We have labored under great disadvantages in freighting our goods and machinery over these vast plains, and besides this we have had a barren soil and drouth to contend with, and when all these things are considered, I think we have been prospered more than any other people. And as it has been in the past so will it be in the future—we will increase, and extend our borders, for this is the work of God; we are his people, and he will continue to bless us as he has done hitherto.

Our business is to learn our duties one towards another and towards our leaders. This is a lesson that we seem rather slow to learn. But it should be with us: when our leaders speak, it is for us to obey; when they direct, we should go; when they call, we should follow. Not as beings who are enslaved or in thraldom; we should not obey blindly, as instruments or tools. No Latter-day Saint acts in this manner; no man or woman who has embraced the gospel has ever acted in this way; but on the contrary men and women have felt to listen cheerfully to the counsels of the servants of God, as far as they were able to comprehend them. The difficulty is not in getting the Latter-day Saints to do right, but in getting them to comprehend what is right. We have obeyed the counsels of our leaders because we have known they have been inspired by the Holy Spirit and because we positively have known that their counsels have been given for our good. We do know and have always known that our leaders have been inspired with wisdom superior to that which we possess. For this reason we take hold of everything they present to us for the good of Zion.

We are engaged in the great latter-day work of preaching the gospel to the nations, gathering the poor, and building up Zion upon the earth. We are working for the triumph of righteousness, for the subjugation of sin and the errors of the age in which we live.

It is a great and glorious work. We believe it is right to love God with all our hearts, and to love our neighbors as ourselves. We believe it is wrong to lie, steal, commit adultery, or do any act forbidden by the gospel of Christ. We believe in all the teachings of the Savior and in everything that is good and moral, and calculated to exalt mankind or to ameliorate their condition, to unite them in doing good. These are among the principles of the gospel, and these principles have been taught to us from the commencement of our career as members of this Church. These principles are carried out among us to an extent not to be found among any other people. We do not believe in worshiping God or being religious on the Sabbath day only; but we believe it is as necessary to be religious on Monday, Tuesday and every day in the week, as it is on the Sabbath day; we believe that it is necessary to do to our neighbors as we would they should do unto us, during the week as it is on the Sabbath. In short, we believe it is necessary to live our religion every day in the week, every hour in the day, and every moment. Believing and acting thus, we become strengthened in our faith, the Spirit of God increases within us, we advance in knowledge, and we are better able to defend the cause we are engaged in.

To be a true representative of this cause a man must live faithful to the light that he has; he must be pure, virtuous and upright. If he comes short of this he is not a fair representative of this work. The gospel of Jesus Christ is the perfect law of liberty. It is calculated to lead man to the highest state of glory, and to exalt him in the presence of our heavenly Father, "with whom is no variableness, neither shadow of turning." If there is any folly to be seen in the midst of this people, it is the folly and weakness of man, and is not because of any failing or lack in the plan of salvation. The gospel is perfect in its organization. It is for us to learn the gospel, and to become acquainted with the principles of truth, to humble ourselves before God that we may bring ourselves into subjection to his laws, and be continually willing to listen to the counsels of those whom the Lord has appointed to guide us.

We know that God has spoken; we testify of this. We stand as witnesses to the world that this is true. We ask no odds of any man, community or nation on the face of the earth in relation to these things. We bear a fearless testimony that they are true. We also bear testimony that Brigham Young is a prophet of the living God, and that he has the revelations of Jesus Christ; that he has guided this people by the power of revelation from the time he became their leader until the present, and he has never failed in his duty or mission. He has been faithful before God, and faithful to this people. We bear this testimony to the world. We fear not, neither do we heed their scorn, contempt, or sneers. We are used to it. We have seen it and heard it, and have become inured to it. We know that the One in whom we trust is God, for it has been revealed to us. We are not in the dark, neither have we obtained our knowledge from any man, synod or collection of men, but through the revelation of Jesus. If there be any who doubt us, let them repent of their sins. Is there any harm in your forsaking your follies and evils, and in bowing in humility before God for his Spirit, and in obedience to the words of the Savior, being baptized for the remission of sins, and having hands laid upon you for the gift of the Holy Ghost, that you may have a witness for yourselves of the truth of the words we speak to you? Do this humbly and honestly, and as sure as the Lord lives, I promise you that you will receive the testimony of this work for yourselves, and will know it as all the Latter-day Saints know it. This is the promise; it is sure and steadfast. It is something tangible; it is in the power of every man to prove for himself whether we speak the truth or whether we lie. We do not come as deceivers or impostors before the world; we do not come with the intention to deceive, but we come with the plain simple truth, and leave it to the world to test it and get a knowledge for themselves. It is the right of every soul that lives—the high, low, rich, poor, great and small, to have this testimony for themselves inasmuch as they will obey the gospel.

Jesus in ancient times sent his disciples forth to preach the gospel to every creature, saying they that believed and were baptized should be saved, but they that believed not should be damned. And said he, "These signs shall follow them that believe: In my name shall they cast out devils; they shall speak with new tongues; they shall take up serpents; and if they drink any deadly thing, it shall not hurt them; they shall lay hands on the sick, and they shall recover." These are the promises made anciently, and there are thousands in this territory and in this congregation who can bear testimony that they have realized the fulfilment of these promises in this day. The healing of the sick among us has become so common that it is apparently but little thought of. We have also seen the lame made to walk, and the blind to receive their sight, the deaf to hear, and the dumb to speak. These things we have seen done by the power of God and not by the cunning or wisdom of men; we know that these signs do follow the preaching of the gospel. Yet these testimonies of its truth are but poor and weak when compared with the whisperings of the still small voice of the Spirit of God. The latter is a testimony that none who enjoy it can deny; it cannot be overcome, for it brings conviction to the heart that cannot be reasoned away or disproved, whether it can be accounted for on philosophical principles or not. This testimony comes from God and convinces all to whom it is given in spite of themselves, and is worth more to men than any sign or gift beside, because it gives peace and happiness, contentment and quiet to my soul. It assures me that God lives, and if I am faithful I shall obtain the blessings of the celestial kingdom.

Is this unscriptural or contrary to reason or to any revealed truth? No, it is in compliance with and in corroboration of all revealed truth known to man. The Lord Almighty lives, and he operates by the power of his Spirit over the hearts of the children of men and holds the nations of the earth in his hands. He created the earth upon which we dwell, and its treasures are his; and he will do with us according as we merit. As we are faithful or unfaithful, so will the Almighty deal with us, for we are his children, and we are heirs of God and joint heirs with Jesus Christ.

We have a glorious destiny before us; we are engaged in a glorious work. It is worth all our attention, it is worth our lives and everything the Lord has put into our possession, and then ten thousand times more. Indeed, there is no comparison, it is all in all, it is incomparable. It is all that is and all that ever will be. The gospel is salvation, and without it there is nothing worth having. We came naked into the world and shall go hence the same. If we were to accumulate half the world, it would avail us nothing so far as prolonging life here, or securing eternal life hereafter. But the gospel teaches men to be humble, faithful, honest and righteous before the Lord and with each other, and in proportion as its principles are carried out so will peace and righteousness extend and be established on the earth, and sin, contention, bloodshed and corruption of all kinds cease to exist, and the earth become purified and be made a fit abode for heavenly beings; and for the Lord our God to come and dwell upon, which he will do during the Millennium.

The principles of the gospel which the Lord has revealed in these days will lead us to eternal life. This is what we are after, what we were created for, what the earth was created for. The reason that we are here is that we may overcome every folly and prepare ourselves for eternal life in the future. I do not think that a principle of salvation is available only as it can be applied in our lives. For instance, if there is a principle calculated in its nature to save me from the penalty of any crime, it will avail me nothing unless I act upon it this moment. If I do this and continue to do so, I act upon the principle of salvation, and I am secure from the penalty of that crime and will be forever, so long as I abide by that principle or law. It is just so with the principles of the gospel—they are a benefit or not, just as they are or are not applied in our lives.

Then let us be faithful and humble; let us live the religion of Christ, put away our follies and sins and the weaknesses of the flesh, and cleave to God and his truth with undivided hearts, and with full determination to fight the good fight of faith and continue steadfast to the end, which may God grant us power to do is my prayer in the name of Jesus. Amen.—Discourse, Nov. 15, 1868, *Journal of Discourses*, Vol. 12, pp. 326-332.

THE GOSPEL ALL COMPREHENSIVE. The gospel of our Lord Jesus Christ embraces all the laws and ordinances necessary for the salvation of man. Paul declared it to be the "power of God unto salvation to everyone that believeth." No man can be saved in opposition to its saving ordinances, but must receive each ordinance in the spirit of humility and faith. Technically, the term "gospel" signifies "good news," and is said to be taken from, or founded on, the annunciation of the angel who appeared to the shepherds at the time of the Savior's birth, declaring, "Behold, I bring you good tidings of great joy, which shall be to all people."

In the theological sense, the gospel means more than just the tidings of good news, with accompanying joy to the souls of men, for it embraces every principle of eternal truth. There is no fundamental principle, or truth, anywhere in the universe, that is not embraced in the gospel of Jesus Christ, and it is not confined to the simple first principles, such as faith in God, repentance from sin, baptism for the remission of sins, and the laying on of hands for the gift of the Holy Ghost, although these are absolutely essential to salvation and exaltation in the kingdom of God.

The laws known to man as the "laws of nature," through which the earth and all things on it are governed, as well as the laws which prevail throughout the entire universe, through which heavenly bodies are controlled and to which they are obedient in all things, are all circumscribed and included in the gospel. Every natural law or scientific principle that man has truly discovered, but which was always known to God, is a part of the gospel truth. There never was and never will be any conflict between truth revealed by the Lord to his servants, the prophets, and truth revealed by him to the scientist, who makes his discoveries through his research and study.

There is a great deal that is taught in the religions of the world as gospel truth that the Lord never did reveal, and which is not in harmony with revealed religion. There is also much that is taught in the world of science that the Lord never did reveal, which is in conflict with the truth. A great deal that man has put forth as scientific theory is founded in error and therefore cannot prevail. The conflict between religion and science is founded in error and therefore cannot prevail. The conflict between religion and science is due to the fact that there are many ideas advanced in false forms of religion and false conclusions reached by men of science. Truth and error can never agree; but truth, no matter where it is found, is consistent and will always harmonize with every other truth. The Lord stated it as follows:

"For intelligence cleaveth unto intelligence; wisdom receiveth wisdom; truth embraceth truth; virtue loveth virtue; light cleaveth unto light; mercy hath compassion on mercy, and claimeth her own." —Doctrine and Covenants 88:40.

The Lord has revealed that man was formed in his image and that we are his offspring. This is a glorious gospel truth. Anything that we may be taught, whether in false forms of religion or in the field of science in conflict with this great truth cannot endure, for it is error. It may be cherished for a season and seem to prevail, as many falsehoods have done in the past when put forth as truth, but the time will come when all theories, ideas and opinions which are not in harmony with that which the Lord has declared, must come to an end; for that which remains and will endure and abide forever, will be the truth, even the gospel of our Lord and Savior Jesus Christ.—*Juvenile Instructor*, Vol. 51, pp. 164, 165, March, 1916.

LET YOUR LIGHT SHINE. Christ, teaching his disciples, called attention to the importance of their position and place in the world. Though poor and despised of men, yet he told them they were the salt of the earth, the light of the world.

Then he encouraged them to effort and achievement by showing them that their exalted position would avail them little, unless they made proper use of their high callings.

These conditions and instructions apply admirably to the Latter-day Saints, who are indeed the salt of the earth, and in whom is vested the gospel light of the world; who, as the apostle said of the Former-day Saints, are a chosen generation, a royal priesthood, an holy nation, a peculiar people; that they should show forth the praises of him who called them out of darkness into his marvelous light.

But all this availeth little or nothing, unless the Saints consider themselves of some consequence, and let their light shine, collectively and individually; unless they are model in their behavior, honest, zealous in the spread of truth, tolerant of their neighbors, "having your conversation honest among the Gentiles; that whereas they speak against you as evil-doers, they may by your good works, which they shall behold, glorify God in the day of visitation."

One fault to be avoided by the Saints, young and old, is the tendency to live on borrowed light, with their own hidden under a bushel; to permit the savor of their salt of knowledge to be lost; and the light within them to be reflected, rather than original.

Every Saint should not only have the light within himself, through the inspiration of the Holy Spirit, but his light should so shine that it may be clearly perceived by others.

Men and women should become settled in the truth, and founded in the knowledge of the gospel, depending upon no person for borrowed or reflected light, but trusting only upon the Holy Spirit, who is ever the same, shining forever and testifying to the individual and the priesthood, who live in harmony with the laws of the gospel, of the glory and the will of the Father. They will then have light everlasting which cannot be obscured. By its shining in their lives, they shall cause others to glorify God; and by their well-doing put to silence the ignorance of foolish men, and show forth the praises of him who hath called them out of darkness into his marvelous light.—*Improvement Era*, Vol. 8, pp. 60-62, 1904-5.

No Cause for Worry. The Saints and their leaders have redeemed the waste places, founded Christian homes, churches, and schools; established industries—because of the very nature of their necessities. Why should they not be permitted to enjoy the fruits of their toils, and why be sneered at and condemned for their energy and enterprise, and especially by men who prove themselves to be hypocrites and liars, who live on what others have produced? Are the Saints to be condemned because they have appropriated the land, paid for it by hard labor, cultivated and made the best out of it by their united strength, under the inspired direction of wise leaders? It will be noted that it is not the people who are complaining, for they have been assisted in many ways to better themselves by such leaders; but it is the ministers, who have no interest whatever, either in our material or spiritual advancement. And then again, are such leaders to be condemned because they have directed and led the way in these things? Had they not done so, whence would our enterprises, our temporal salvation, have come? Never by the help of sectarian ministers, that much is true, at least.

No; young man, you need not be troubled over ministerial accusations against this people, nor over what the people of the world say against us. I have no fears for the Church from these sources, but I confess I have fears when our young men begin to weaken, and to take sides against their fathers; to profess to think that the priesthood is selfish and self-seeking; to follow lies and accusations rather than plain truth; to join in derision against the leaders of the Saints, and to laugh when unfriendly editors and ministers hold them up to ridicule. I fear, when young men deny the truth and follow falsehood; when they become self-sufficient, unvirtuous, worldly and proud; when the sterling qualities of their fathers are derided by them; when they seek the plaudits of men of the world rather than the kingdom of God and his righteousness.

There is no genuine truth in the arraignment of the Church and her officers by the ministers, but much to you, young men, in the way you look upon it, and in your acts and decisions. Especially without careful consideration, should you pay no attention to the accusation of ministers, to whom with force the sentiment of Emerson applies: "We want men and women who shall renovate life and our social state, but we see that most natures are insolvent—cannot satisfy their own wants, have an ambition out of all proportion to their practical force, and so do learn and beg day and night continually."

I say that nothing can bring peace to our young men in this world save the triumphs of the principles of truth which have been revealed of God to the Latter-day Saints, for our doctrines are the practical precepts of the gospel of Jesus Christ, and to behold its triumph should be the overpowering ambition and desire of every righteous soul. This is spiritual salvation which includes the temporal. Seek to know the worth thereof, and let these men's ravings be put under your feet. Remember that "when a man lives with God his voice shall be as sweet as the murmur of the brook and the rustle of the corn." The Saints and their leaders strive diligently to this end. —*Improvement Era*, Vol. 7, p. 303, February, 1904.

THE GOSPEL A SHIELD FROM TERROR. We hear about living in perilous times. We are in perilous times, but I do not feel the pangs of that terror. It is not upon me. I propose to live so that it will not rest upon me. I propose to live so that I shall be immune from the perils of the world, if it be possible for me to so live, by obedience to the commandments of God and to his laws revealed for my guidance. No matter what may come to me, if I am only in the line of my duty, if I am in fellowship with God, if I am worthy of the fellowship of my brethren, if I can stand spotless before the world, without blemish, without transgression of the laws of God, what does it matter to me what may happen to me? I am always ready, if I am in this frame of understanding mind and conduct. It does not matter at all. Therefore I borrow no trouble nor feel the pangs of fear.

The Lord's hand is over all, and therein I acknowledge his hand. Not that men are at war, not that nations are trying to destroy nations, not that men are plotting against the liberties of their fellow creatures, not in those respects at all; but God's hand is not shortened. He will control the results that will follow. He will overrule them in a way that you and I, today, do not comprehend, or do not foresee, for ultimate good. He foresees the end as he foresaw that war should come upon all nations of the world, and as the Prophet has declared it would. The Lord knew it would come. Why? Because he knew what the world was doing. He knew the trend of the spirits of men and of nations. He knew what the results would be, in time. He knew when the time would be, and the results that would be manifest, and so he declared it by the voice of his servants, the prophets; and now we see the fulfilment of the predictions made by the servants of God, as they were inspired to utter them, when they declared that the time would come to pass when war would be poured out upon all nations—not to fulfil the purposes of God, but the purposes of the nations of the earth in consequence of their wickedness. It may be a very difficult thing for me, with the range of words that I possess, to express my thoughts and to explain my full intent; but I repeat to you that the Lord God Almighty is not pleased, nor was it his purpose or design, or intent, to foreordain the condition that the world is in today; nor did he do so. He foresaw what would come, by the conduct of men by their departure from the truth, by their lack of the love of God, and by the course that they should pursue, inimical to the well-being of his children. He foresaw what would be, but he had given them their agency, under which they are bringing it to pass. The results of it, eventually, will be overruled for the good of those who shall live after, not for the good of those who shall destroy themselves because of their wicked propensities and crimes.—*Improvement Era*, Vol. 20, p. 827, July, 1917.

THE GOSPEL TRUMPET. If we are in the line of our duty, we are engaged in a great and glorious cause. It is very essential to our individual welfare that every man and every woman who has entered into the covenants of the gospel, through repentance and baptism, should feel that as individuals it is their bounden duty to use their intelligence, and the agency which the Lord has given them, for the promotion of the interests of Zion and the establishment of her cause in the earth.

It matters not how devout, honest, or sincere we might be in the profession of our faith in God, or in the system of religion we might have adopted, and which we believe to be the everlasting gospel, without repentance and baptism and the reception of the Holy Ghost, which constitute the new birth, we are not of the family of Christ, but are aliens, estranged from God and his laws, and in this fallen condition we shall remain, whether in the body or in the spirit, for time and for eternity, unless we render obedience to the plan devised in the heavens for the redemption and salvation of the human family.

The Latter-day Saints may say, we were taught this doctrine by the elders in our native lands, and we believed it and repented of our sins, and were baptized, and we received the gift of the Holy Ghost, which was a testimony to us that we had done the will of the Father, and since then our testimonies have often been confirmed through the manifestations of the power of God, and the renewal of his Spirit in our hearts. Why, therefore, say they, is it necessary to refer to these things now? We perhaps forget, in consequence of the things of time, which so tempt our fallen nature, that having been born anew, which is the putting away of the old man sin, and putting on of the man Christ Jesus, we have become soldiers of the Cross, having enlisted under the banner of Jehovah for time and for eternity, and that we have entered into the most solemn covenants to serve God and to contend earnestly for the establishment of the principles of truth and righteousness on this earth continually while we live.

In referring to the subject of baptism as essential to salvation, it may be asked by some, what would become of those who heard not the gospel and who therefore had not the opportunity of being baptized, claiming as we do that the gospel was taken from the earth in consequence of its being rejected when proclaimed by Jesus and his apostles? I would say to such, that God has made ample provision for all his children, both the ignorant and the learned; those who have not had the gospel preached to them in the flesh, will hear it in the spirit, for all must have the plan of salvation presented to them for their acceptance or rejection before they can become amenable to the law.

In connection with this work is that spoken of concerning Elijah the prophet, namely, "The turning of the hearts of the children to the fathers, and the hearts of the fathers to the children," which if not done the whole earth will be smitten with a curse.

The kingdom of God must be erected upon the principles which Christ has revealed, upon the foundation of eternal truth; Jesus himself being the chief cornerstone. Those holy and sublime principles must be observed and honored in our lives, in order that we may obtain an exaltation with the sanctified in the kingdom of God.

The beauty of these principles is that they are true, and the satisfaction derived from their adoption is the knowledge which we receive convincing us of this fact. We have not believed a fable, neither are we cherishing a cunningly devised scheme, but we have been inducted into the truth, having Christ for our head, who is our forerunner, our great High Priest and King.

The Holy Ghost is a personage who acts in Christ's stead. Just before the risen Redeemer left the earth he commanded his disciples to tarry in the city of Jerusalem until they should be endowed with power from on high. They did so, and agreeable to promise, the Comforter came whilst they were met together, filling their hearts with unspeakable joy, insomuch that they spake in tongues and prophesied; and the inspiring influence of this holy being accompanied them in all their ministerial duties, enabling them to perform the great mission to which they had been called by the Savior.

I know that God lives and that he has revealed himself. I know that the Holy Ghost has been conferred upon the children of men, and that the gospel has been restored to the inhabitants of the earth in its fulness. I know that the Holy Priesthood, which is the power of God delegated to man, has been restored to the earth. I do know that God has delivered his people and that he will continue to deliver us and lead us on in his own peculiar way from conquest to conquest, from victory to victory, until truth and righteousness gain the ascendency in this his earth, inasmuch as we remain true to him and to one another.

It is the fool who has said in his heart, "There is no God," and it would indeed be a weak and foolish mind that would rest satisfied without knowing beyond a doubt the Author and Source of his religion, when the opportunity of ascertaining the fact is extended to him.

I know the fruits of my religion are good, they are flavored with the sweets of heaven, and they impart health and life to the soul, and I know that God, the Creator of heaven and earth, is its author. No man need wonder whether this be really true or not, for all may know for themselves; all may partake of the fruits of the vine and eat and live; all may drink of the eternal spring, and thirst no more. These things I declare to you to be true and faithful. I have been acquainted with them from my youth, and I have felt their influence from my childhood. I have seen the effect of their opposite, and I know whereof I speak. I cannot deny these things, neither can any man who has ever known them, although he may apostatize from the Church, except he deny himself and his God.

The man who embraces what is called "Mormonism," but which is really the gospel of the Son of God, and lives according to its precepts, will never lie nor steal; he will not dishonor his parents nor despise his poorer brethren; he will never, no never, speak against the Lord's anointed nor be ashamed to own his God, to whom he owes homage and gratitude now and forever; he will never do a dishonorable act, nor fail to acknowledge God in all things, neither will he refuse to render implicit obedience to the revelations of God which are applicable to him. It is true, man may err in judgment, he may be wanting in many things because of his fallen nature, but the system of salvation is perfect. Jesus, the Only Begotten of the Father, in whom there is no blemish, is its author; he is the standard to all the world, and will be forever. He had power to lay down his life and take it up again, and if we keep inviolate the covenants of the gospel, remaining faithful and true to the end, we too, in his name and through his redeeming blood, will have power in due time to resurrect these our bodies after they shall have been committed to the earth.—April 8, 1876, *Journal of Discourses*, Vol. 18, pp. 271-277, 1877.

WHAT CHURCH LEADERS ADVOCATE. We wish to advocate the principle of unity, the love of God and neighbor, the love of a purpose that is great, ennobling, good in itself, and calculated to exalt man and bring him nearer to the likeness of the Son of God.—*Improvement Era*, Vol. 21, p. 98, December, 1917.

OUR MESSAGE ONE OF LOVE. We bring a message of love. We wish to show how much we love you, and to find out how much you love us in return.—*Improvement Era*, Vol. 21, p. 98, December, 1917.

WHENCE? WHITHER? We want to know where we came from, and where we are going. Where did we come from? From God. Our spirits existed before they came to this world. They were in the councils of the heavens before the foundations of the earth were laid. We were there. We sang together with the heavenly hosts for joy when the foundations of the earth were laid, and when the plan of our existence upon this earth and redemption were mapped out. We were there; we were interested, and we took a part in this great preparation. We were unquestionably present in those councils when that wonderful circumstance occurred when Satan offered himself as a savior of the world if he could but receive the honor and glory of the Father for doing it. But Jesus said, "Father, thy will be done, and the glory be thine forever." Wherefore, because Satan rebelled against God, and sought to destroy the agency of man, the Father rejected him and he was cast out, but Jesus was accepted. We were, no doubt, there, and took part in all those scenes, we were vitally concerned in the carrying out of these great plans and purposes, we understood them, and it was for our sakes they were decreed, and are to be consummated. These spirits have been coming to this earth to take upon them tabernacles, that they might become like unto Jesus Christ, being "formed in his likeness and image," from the morn of creation until now, and will continue until the winding up scene, until the spirits who were destined to come to this world shall have come and accomplished their mission in the flesh.—*Deseret Weekly News*, 1884, Vol. 33, p. 130.

LATTER-DAY SAINTS ARE LAW-ABIDING. I wish to enter here my avowal that the people called Latter-day Saints, as has been often repeated from this stand, are the most law-abiding, the most peaceable, long-suffering and patient people that can today be found within the confines of this republic, and perhaps anywhere else upon the face of the earth; and we intend to continue to be law-abiding, so far as the constitutional law of the land is concerned; and we expect to meet the consequences of our obedience to the laws and commandments of God like men. These are my sentiments briefly expressed, upon this subject.—*Deseret Weekly News*, 1882, Vol. 31, p. 226.

Chapter VII

THE FIRST PRINCIPLES OF THE GOSPEL

How the Sinner May be Cleansed. You cannot take a murderer, a suicide, an adulterer, a liar, or one who was or is thoroughly abominable in his life here, and simply by the performance of an ordinance of the gospel, cleanse him from sin and usher him into the presence of God. God has not instituted a plan of that kind, and it cannot be done. He has said you shall repent of your sins. The wicked will have to repent of their wickedness. Those who die without the knowledge of the gospel will have to come to the knowledge of it, and those who sin against light will have to pay the uttermost farthing for their transgression and their departure from the gospel, before they can ever get back to it. Do not forget that. Do not forget it, you elders in Israel, nor you, mothers in Israel, either; and, when you seek to save either the living or the dead, bear it in mind that you can only do it on the principle of their repentance and acceptation of the plan of life. That is the only way in which you can succeed.—Oct. C. R., 1907, pp. 6, 7.

Fallacy of Death-Bed Repentance. I do not believe in the ideas that we hear sometimes advanced in the world, that it matters but little what men do in this life, if they will but confess Christ at the end of their journey in life, and that is all-sufficient, and that by so doing they will receive their passport into heaven. I denounce this doctrine. It is unscriptural, it is unreasonable, it is untrue, and it will not avail any man, no matter by whom this idea may be advocated; it will prove an utter failure unto men. As reasonable beings, as men and women of intelligence, we cannot help but admire and honor the doctrine of Jesus Christ, which is the doctrine of God, and which requires of every man and woman righteousness in their lives, purity in their thoughts, uprightness in their daily walk and conversation, devotion to the Lord, love of truth, love of their fellowman, and above all things in the world the love of God. These were the precepts that were inculcated by the Son of God when he walked among his brethren in the meridian of time. He taught these precepts; he exemplified them in his life, and advocated continually the doing of the will of him that sent him.—Oct. C. R., 1907, p. 3.

THE CHANGE THAT COMES WITH REPENTANCE AND BAPTISM. That change comes today to every son and daughter of God who repents of his or her sins, who humble themselves before the Lord, and who seek forgiveness and remission of sin by baptism by immersion, by one having authority to administer this sacred ordinance of the gospel of Jesus Christ. For it is this new birth that was spoken of by Christ to Nicodemus as absolutely essential that men might see the kingdom of God, and without which no man could enter into the kingdom. Each of us can remember, perhaps, the change that came into our hearts when we were baptized for the remission of our sins. Perhaps it is not proper for one to speak of himself or of his own experiences, because there may be those within the sound of my voice who object to a man speaking of himself, and especially when he shall say any good of himself; yet I speak not of myself, I speak of the influence and power of the Holy Spirit that I experienced when I had been baptized for the remission of my sins. The feeling that came upon me was that of pure peace, of love and of light. I felt in my soul that if I had sinned—and surely I was not without sin—that it had been forgiven me; that I was indeed cleansed from sin; my heart was touched, and I felt that I would not injure the smallest insect beneath my feet. I felt as if I wanted to do good everywhere to everybody and to everything. I felt a newness of life, a newness of desire to do that which was right. There was not one particle of desire for evil left in my soul. I was but a little boy, it is true, when I was baptized; but this was the influence that came upon me, and I know that it was from God, and was and ever has been a living witness to me of my acceptance of the Lord.

Oh! that I could have kept that same spirit and that same earnest desire in my heart every moment of my life from that day to this. Yet many of us who have received that witness, that new birth, that change of heart, while we may have erred in judgment or have made many mistakes, and often perhaps come short of the true standard in our lives, we have repented of the evil, and we have sought from time to time forgiveness at the hand of the Lord; so that until this day the same desire and purpose which pervaded our souls when we were baptized and received a remission of our sins, still holds possession of our hearts, and is still the ruling sentiment and passion of our souls. Though at times we may be stirred to anger, and our wrath move us to say and do things which are not pleasing in the sight of God, yet instantly on regaining our sober senses and recovering from our lapse into the power of darkness, we feel humble, repentant, and to ask forgiveness for the wrong that we have done to ourselves, and perchance to others. The great, earnest, overwhelming desire, which is born of the truth and of the witness of the Holy Spirit in the hearts of the people who obey the truth, assumes sway and again takes possession of our souls, to lead us on in the path of duty. This is my testimony and I know it is true.—Apr. C. R., 1898, pp. 65, 66.

THE NECESSITY OF BAPTISM. "The Light has come to the world, and he who will not see it shall be condemned." The truth is here, and shall men living now be heard to complain hereafter that they have not the truth in their hearts? Certainly not. It is here for all who will seek it, and it shall be to their undoing if they do not obtain it.

The Savior said to Nicodemus, "Except a man be born again, he cannot see the kingdom of God," and that is true today. A man must be born from ignorance into truth, today, before he can expect to see any difference between a Latter-day Saint and another not of the faith. If he is not so born, he is more blind than the one whom Christ healed, for having eyes he sees not, and having ears, hears not.

Is there any difference between the baptized and the unbaptized man? All the difference in the world, I tell you, but it is only discernible through the Spirit. It is a vast difference too great for one not in possession of the Spirit to comprehend. Take two men, they may be equals in point of goodness, they may be equally moral, charitable, honest and just, but one is baptized and the other is not. There is a mighty difference between them, for one is the son of God redeemed by compliance with his laws, and the other remains in darkness.

The Scriptures say that a rich man would hardly enter the kingdom of heaven, but it does not mean that riches will condemn a man, not at all. God is pleased to see us acquire riches, for he intends ultimately to give to us the whole earth as an eternal inheritance, but it is the love of riches that kills. A great gulf separates those who enter the house of the Lord and take wives, and those who do not thus marry—a tremendous gulf, but to the unspiritual eye no difference is apparent.

I thank God for "Mormonism," so-called; it is the power of God unto salvation. It is the duty of every Latter-day Saint to know of its truth and to exemplify it. Its destiny is to overwhelm error and supplant it with righteousness and peace.—*From a sermon, given in Logan, Feb. 2, 1909.*

WHEN TO BAPTIZE CHILDREN. We confess to having been considerably surprised when attending one of our latest Sunday School conventions on learning that in some wards in the Church only once or twice in each year are opportunities given to the children of the Saints to be baptized. We hold the opinion that in every stake of Zion there should be opportunity for baptism every day of every month and every month in every year, for we believe that it is an admirable practice where parents, in conformity with the revelations of God, have taught their children in the first principles of the gospel—faith, repentance and baptism, to have them baptized on their birthdays, when they arrive at the age of eight years. This practice has many advantages. In the first place, when a child is baptized on his birthday, he has no difficulty in remembering the day when that sacred ordinance was performed in his case. Again, it prevents the tendency manifested by some people to delay and postpone duties that are always best performed in their proper time and season. When once a child has passed the eight-year mark, there appears no particular necessity for the immediate performance of the ordinance, and the parents are apt to put it off from day to day and from week to week, until months have passed over, and the matter is not attended to. Should it so happen that in this interval the child is taken by the Lord, then this rite has to be performed in his behalf after his departure from our midst. How much better it is that the child have the opportunity of doing this all-important work for himself or herself!—*Juvenile Instructor, Vol. 40, p. 337, June 1, 1905.*

THROUGH ATONEMENT SINS ARE WASHED AWAY. When we commit sin, it is necessary that we repent of it and make restitution as far as lies in our power. When we cannot make restitution for the wrong we have done, then we must apply for the grace and mercy of God to cleanse us from that iniquity.

Men cannot forgive their own sins; they cannot cleanse themselves from the consequences of their sins. Men can stop sinning and can do right in the future, and so far their acts are acceptable before the Lord and worthy of consideration. But who shall repair the wrongs they have done to themselves and to others, which it seems impossible for them to repair themselves? By the atonement of Jesus

Christ the sins of the repentant shall be washed away; though they be crimson they shall be made white as wool. This is the promise given to you. We who have not paid our tithing in the past, and are therefore under obligations to the Lord, which we are not in position to discharge, the Lord requires that no longer at our hands, but will forgive us for the past if we will observe this law honestly in the future. That is generous and kind, and I feel grateful for it.—Oct. C. R., 1899, p. 42.

CONDITIONS FOR BAPTISM. No person can be properly baptized unless he has faith in the Lord Jesus Christ, and has repented of his sins, with a repentance that need not be repented of. But faith comes by hearing the word of God. This implies that the candidate must be taught. Efficient teaching and preparation must precede the ordinance, so that the candidate may have a proper appreciation and conception of its purposes. The call to baptism, in the mission of our Savior, was always preceded by instructions in the doctrines which he taught.—Improvement Era, Vol. 14, p. 266.

THE FIRST PRINCIPLES OF THE GOSPEL. As Latter-day Saints we have every reason to rejoice in the gospel, and in the testimony we have received concerning its truth. I repeat, we have reason to rejoice and to be exceeding glad, for we possess the testimony of Jesus, the spirit of prophecy, which the people of the world know nothing about, nor can they, without obedience to the gospel.

Jesus thoroughly understood this matter, and fully explained it when he said, "Except a man be born again, he cannot see the kingdom of God." On first reflection, it would seem that anything so clear, reasonable and tangible could be easily made plain to the understanding of all men. Hence the feeling that has prompted many of the Latter-day Saints to believe, after their minds have been enlightened by the Spirit of God—everything being made so plain and clear to them, that they had only to tell their friends and kindred what they had learned and they would gladly receive it. But how disappointed, after they had presented to them the truths of heaven in simplicity and plainness, to hear them say, "We cannot see it!" or, "We do not believe it!" or perhaps bitterly oppose it, which is by far the most common practice of the world. They cannot understand it. Why? Because, as Jesus has said no man can see the kingdom except he is born again. You may preach the gospel to the people but unless they humble themselves as little children before the Lord, acknowledging their dependence upon him for light and wisdom, thy cannot see or sense it, although you may preach to them in as great plainness as it is possible for the truth to be conveyed from one person to another. And should any believe your testimony it would only be belief. They would not see as you see—nor comprehend it, as you do—until they yield obedience to the requirements of the gospel, and through the remission of their sins receive the Holy Ghost. Then they, too, can see as you see, for they have the same spirit; then will they love the truth as you do, and may wonder why they could not comprehend it before or why it is that there can be anybody with common intelligence that cannot understand truth so plain and forcible.

First, then, it is necessary to have faith in God, faith being the first principle in revealed religion, and the foundation of all righteousness.

Faith in God is to believe that he is, and "that he is the only supreme Governor and independent Being, in whom all fulness and perfection and every good gift and principle dwell independently," and in whom the faith of all other rational beings must centre for life and salvation; and further, that he is the great Creator of all things, that he is omnipotent, omniscient, and by his works and the power of his Spirit omnipresent.

Not only is it necessary to have faith in God, but also in Jesus Christ, his Son, the Savior of mankind and the Mediator of the New Covenant; and in the Holy Ghost, who bears record of the Father and the Son, "the same in all ages and forever."

Having this faith, it becomes necessary to repent. Repent of what? Of every sin of which we may have been guilty. How shall we repent of these sins? Does repentance consist of sorrow for wrong doing? Yes, but is this all? By no means. True repentance only is acceptable to God, nothing short of it will answer the purpose. Then what is true repentance? True repentance is not only sorrow for sins, and humble penitence and contrition before God, but it involves the necessity of turning away from them, a discontinuance of all evil practices and deeds, a thorough reformation of life, a vital change from evil to good, from vice to virtue, from darkness to light. Not only so, but to make restitution, so far as it is possible, for all the wrongs we have done, to pay our debts, and restore to God and man their rights—that which is due to them from us. This is true repentance, and the exercise of the will and all the powers of body and mind is demanded, to complete this glorious work of repentance; then God will accept it.

Having thus repented, the next thing requisite is baptism, which is an essential principle of the gospel—no man can enter into the gospel covenant without it. It is the door of the Church of Christ, we cannot get in there in any other way, for Christ hath said it, "sprinkling," or "pouring," is not baptism. Baptism means immersion in water, and is to be administered by one having authority, in the name of the Father, and of the Son, and of the Holy Ghost. Baptism without divine authority is not valid. It is a symbol of the burial and resurrection of Jesus Christ, and must be done in the likeness thereof, by one commissioned of God, in the manner prescribed, otherwise it is illegal and will not be accepted by him, nor will it effect a remission of sins, the object for which it is designed, but whosoever hath faith, truly repents and is "buried with Christ in baptism," by one having divine authority, shall receive a remission of sins, and is entitled to the gift of the Holy Ghost by the laying on of hands.

Only those who are commissioned of Jesus Christ have authority or power to bestow this gift. The office of the Holy Ghost is to bear record of Christ, or to testify of him, and confirm the believer in the truth, by bringing to his recollection things that have passed, and showing or revealing to the mind things present and to come. "But the Comforter, which is the Holy Ghost, whom the Father will send in my name, he shall teach you all things, and bring all things to your remembrance, whatsoever I have said unto you." "He will guide you into all truth." Thus, without the aid of the Holy Ghost no man can know the will of God, or that Jesus is the Christ—the Redeemer of the world, or that the course he pursues, the work he performs, or his faith, are acceptable to God, and such as will secure to him the gift of eternal life, the greatest of all gifts. (John 14:26; 16:13.)

"But," says an objector, "have we not the Bible, and are not the Holy Scriptures able to make us wise unto salvation?" Yes, provided we obey them. "All Scripture is given by inspiration of God, and is profitable for doctrine, for reproof, for correction, for instruction in righteousness; that the man of God may be perfect, thoroughly furnished unto all good works." The "good works" are the great desideratum. The Bible itself is but the dead letter, it is the Spirit that giveth life. The way to obtain the Spirit is that which is here marked out so plainly in the Scriptures. There is no other. Obedience, therefore, to these principles is absolutely necessary, in order to obtain the salvation and exaltation brought to light through the gospel.

As to the question of authority, nearly everything depends upon it. No ordinance can be performed to the acceptance of God without divine authority. No matter how fervently men may believe or pray, unless they are endowed with divine authority they can only act in their own name, and not legally nor acceptably in the name of Jesus Christ, in whose name all these things must be done. Some suppose this authority may be derived from the Bible, but nothing could be more absurd. The Bible is but a book containing the writings of inspired men, "profitable for doctrine, for reproof, for correction, for instruction in righteousness," as such we hold it is sacred; but the Spirit, power and authority by which it is written cannot be found within its lids, nor derived from it. "For prophecy came not in old time by the will of man; but holy men of God spake as they were moved by the Holy Ghost." If by reading and believing the Bible this authority could be obtained, all who read the Bible and believed it would have it—one equally with another. I have read the Bible, and I have as good reason for believing it as any other man, and do believe it with all my heart; but this does not give me authority to teach men in the name of the Lord, nor to officiate in the sacred ordinances of the gospel. Were the Scriptures the only source of knowledge, we would be without knowledge for ourselves, and would have to rest our hopes of salvation upon a simple belief in the testimonies and sayings of others. This will not do for me; I must know for myself, and if I act as a teacher of these things, I must be clothed with the same light, knowledge and authority as those were who acted in a similar calling anciently. Else how could I declare the truth and bear testimony as they did? What right would I have to say, "thus saith the Lord," and call upon man to repent and be baptized in the name of the Lord? or, that "This Jesus hath God raised up [from the dead], whereof we all [the apostles] are witnesses?" And, therefore, let all men "know assuredly that God hath made that same Jesus," who was crucified, "both Lord and Christ." No man, without the Holy Ghost, as enjoyed by the ancient apostles can know these things, therefore cannot declare them by authority, nor teach and prepare mankind for the salvation of God. God Almighty is the only source from whence this knowledge, power and authority can be obtained, and that through the operations of the Holy Ghost. The Scriptures may serve as a guide to lead us to God, and hence to the possession of all things necessary to life and salvation, but they can do no more.

Having profited by this example, and done the works command-ed by both Christ and his apostles, ancient and modern, I am happy of the privilege to declare to the inhabitants of the earth that I have received this testimony and witness for myself. I do know that these things are true. Jesus, my Redeemer, lives, and God hath made him both Lord and Christ. To know and to worship the true God, in the name of Jesus—in spirit and in truth—is the duty of man. To aid and qualify him for this service is the duty and office of the Holy Ghost. Man may fail through faltering and unfaithfulness, but the Spirit of God will never fail, nor abandon the faithful disciple. I can say as one who has tried the experiment—for it may be called an experiment to the beginner—that all who will take the course and accept the doctrine thus marked out will, through faithfulness, become acquainted with the truth, and shall know of the doctrine, whether it be of God or of man, and will rejoice in it as all good, faithful Latter-day Saints do.

Here is an ordinance which we are now administering, the Sacrament of the Lord's supper; it is an ordinance of the gospel, one as necessary to be observed by all believers, as any other ordinance of the gospel. What is the object of it? It is that we may keep in mind continually the Son of God who has redeemed us from eternal death, and brought us to life again through the power of the gospel. Before the coming of Christ to the earth, this was borne in mind by the inhabitants of the earth to whom the gospel was preached, by another ordinance which was a type of the great sacrifice that should take place in the meridian of time. Hence, Adam, after he was cast out of the garden, was commanded to offer sacrifices to God; by this act, he and all who participated in the offerings of sacrifices, were reminded of the Savior who should come to redeem them from death which, were it not for the atonement wrought out by him, would forever exclude them from dwelling in the presence of God again. But in his coming and death, this commandment was fulfilled; and he instituted the Supper and commanded his followers to partake of this in all time to come, in order that they may remember him, bearing in mind that he had redeemed them, also that they had covenanted to keep his commandments and to walk with him in the regeneration. Hence it is necessary to partake of the Sacrament, as a witness to him that we do remember him, are willing to keep the commandments he has given us, that we may have his Spirit to be with us always—even to the end, and also that we may continue in the forgiveness of sins.

In various dispensations there are various differences in regard to certain requirements of the gospel. For instance, in the day of Noah, when he preached the gospel to the antediluvian world, he was given a special commandment to build an ark, that in case the people would reject him and the message sent unto him, that himself and all who believed on him might be saved from the destruction that awaited them. In this dispensation there is a principle or commandment peculiar to it. What is that? It is the gathering of the people unto one place. The gathering of this people is as necessary to be observed by believers, as faith, repentance, baptism, or any other ordinance. It is an essential part of the gospel of this dispensation, as much so as the necessity of building an ark by Noah, for his deliverance, was a part of the gospel of his dispensation. Then the world was destroyed by a flood, now it is to be destroyed by war, pestilence, famine, earthquake, storms and tempest, the sea rolling beyond its bounds, malarious vapors, vermin, disease and by fire and the lightnings of God's wrath poured out for destruction upon Babylon. The cry of the angel unto the righteous of this dispensation is, "Come out of her, my people, that ye be not partakers of her sins, and that ye receive not of her plagues." (Revelation 18:4.)

We believe also in the principle of direct revelation from God to man.

This is a part of the gospel, but it is not peculiar to this dispensation. It is common in all ages and dispensations of the gospel. The gospel cannot be administered, nor the Church of God continue to exist, without it. Christ is the head of his Church and not man, and the connection can only be maintained upon the principle of direct and continuous revelation. It is not a hereditary principle, it cannot be handed down from father to son, nor from generation to generation, but is a living, vital principle to be enjoyed on certain conditions only, namely—through absolute faith in God and obedience to his laws and commandments. The moment this principle is cut off, that moment the Church is adrift, being severed from its ever-living head. In this condition it cannot continue, but must cease to be the Church of God and, like the ship at sea without captain, compass or rudder, is afloat at the mercy of the storms and the waves of ever contending human passions, and worldly interests, pride and folly, finally to be wrecked upon the strand of priestcraft and superstition. The religious world is in this condition today, ripening for the great destruction which awaits them, but there is an ark prepared for such as are worthy of eternal life, in the gathering of the Saints to the chambers of the Almighty, where they shall be preserved until the indignation of God is passed.

Marriage is also a principle or ordinance of the gospel, most vital to the happiness of mankind, however unimportant it may seem, or lightly regarded by many. There is no superfluous or unnecessary principle in the plan of life, but there is no principle of greater importance or more essential to the happiness of man— not only here, but especially hereafter, than that of marriage. Yet all are necessary. What good would it be to one to be baptized and receive not the Holy Ghost? And suppose he went a little further and received the Holy Ghost, thereby obtaining the testimony of Jesus, and then stopped at that, what good would it do him? None whatever, but would add to his condemnation, for it would be as burying his talent in the earth. To secure the fulness of the blessings we must receive the fulness of the gospel. Yet men will be judged and rewarded according to their works. "To him that knoweth to do good and doeth it not, to him it is sin." Those who receive a part of the gospel with light and knowledge to comprehend other principles, and yet do not obey them, will come under this law; hence, condemnation will be added unto such, and that which they did receive may be taken from them and added to those who are more worthy.

Obedience is a requirement of heaven, and is therefore a principle of the gospel. Are all required to be obedient? Yes, all. What, against their will? O, no, not by any means. There is no power given to man, nor means lawful, to be used to compel men to obey the will of God, against their wish, except persuasion and good advice, but there is a penalty attached to disobedience, which all must suffer who will not obey the obvious truths or laws of heaven. I believe in the sentiment of the poet:

"Know this, that every soul is free
To choose his life and what he'll be;
For this eternal truth is given,
That God will force no man to heaven.

"He'll call, persuade, direct aright,
And bless with wisdom, love and light,
In nameless ways be good and kind,
But never force the human mind."

Is it a difficult task to obey the gospel? No. It is an easy matter to those who possess the spirit of it. Most of this congregation can testify that the gospel "yoke is easy, and the burden light." Those who have embraced it will be judged according to their works therein, whether they be good or evil. To such as are untrue to their covenants it may be said, by and by, "Depart from me!" In vain will they plead their former good works and faith. Why? Because the race is not to the swift nor the battle always to the strong, but to him that endures faithful to the end. We must save ourselves from this untoward generation. It is a continual labor, but the strength of the righteous will be sufficient for their day. Jesus said, "In my Father's house are many mansions." There is a glory, or mansion, of which the sun is typical, another of which the moon is typical, and still another like unto the stars, and in this latter the condition of its occupants will differ as the stars differ in appearance. Every man will receive according to his works and knowledge. "These are they who are of Paul, and of Apollos, and of Cephas. These are they who say they are some of one and some of another—some of Christ and some of John, and some of Moses, and some of Elias, and some of Esaias, and some of Isaiah, and some of Enoch; but received not the gospel, neither the testimony of Jesus." (Doc. and Cov. 76:100-101.) Thus, impartial justice will be meted out unto all, and none will be lost but the sons of perdition.—*Journal of Discourses*, Vol. 14, p. 266.

Chapter VIII

THE CHURCH AND THE MAN

THE CHURCH IN ADVANCE OF ITS MEMBERS. "The modern 'Mormon' is far in advance of 'Mormonism.'" The very reverse of this statement is the truth. "Mormonism" is far in advance of the modern or any other class of "Mormons." For not one member of the Church in one hundred, and perhaps not a single member in the whole Church is able to reach the high standards of faith, virtue, honor and truth inculcated in the gospel of Jesus Christ.— *Juvenile Instructor*, Vol. 41, p. 144, March 1, 1906.

THE GOSPEL THE MOST IMPORTANT THING. The religion which we have espoused is not a Sunday religion; it is not a mere profession; it is a most—I was going to say—a most terrible reality—and I believe I would be justified in using that expression, because it savors of life unto life or of death unto death. If it is, and pardon me for using that expression, if it is what we profess it to be, what we have embraced it for, what we believe it to be as members of the Church of Jesus Christ of Latter-day Saints, it is the most important thing in the world to us, and the results to us in this world and in the world to come will depend upon our integrity to the truth and our consistency in observing its precepts, in abiding by its principles, and its requirements.—Apr. C. R., 1916, p. 2.

PERSONAL ADVANCEMENT IS HELP TO THE CHURCH. Whoever will labor for his own welfare, for his own salvation and upbuilding in the knowledge of those principles which draw men nearer to God and make them more like unto him, fitting them better for the performance of the duties required at their hands, is in like manner building up the Church.—Apr. C. R., 1914, p. 2.

COVENANTS OF THE LATTER-DAY SAINTS. Among the covenants are these, that they will cease from sin and from all unrighteousness; that they will work righteousness in their lives; that they will abstain from the use of intoxicants, from the use of strong drinks of every description, from the use of tobacco, from every vile thing, and from extremes in every phase of life; that they will not take the name of God in vain; that they will not bear false witness against their neighbor; that they will seek to love their neighbors as themselves;

to carry out the golden rule of the Lord, do unto others as they
would that others should do unto them. These principles are
involved in the covenants that the people have made in the Church
of Jesus Christ of Latter-day Saints, and it is expected that the
officers and presiding authorities in the Church shall see to it that
the members of the Church of Jesus Christ of Latter-day Saints
will keep these covenants that they have made with the Lord, and
that they will observe these principles and adapt them to their lives
and carry them out, that they may be indeed the salt of the earth;
not salt that has lost its savor and is good for nothing but to be cast
out and trodden under the foot of men, but salt that has its savor
and that is wholesome; that the people of God may be a light unto
this generation and unto the world; that men may see your good
works and glorify your Father which is in heaven; and that, notwithstanding enemies who are filled with the spirit of persecution
and who say all manner of evil things against the Latter-day Saints,
those who have entered into the covenant of the gospel, will keep
the commandments of the Lord, will obey the dictates of the Spirit
of the Lord unto them, will work righteousness in the earth, and
will go right on in the path that Almighty God has marked out for
them to pursue, fulfilling and accomplishing his will and his purposes
concerning them in the latter day.—Oct. C. R., 1904, pp. 4, 5.

A Privilege to be Associated with the Church. I esteem it
a great privilege to be permitted to live and be associated with my
brethren and sisters in the great cause in which we are engaged.
Personally, I have nothing but this cause to live for, for the rest of
my life. It has been very much, almost entirely, the object of life
with me, ever since my childhood; and I am very thankful that I
have had the privilege of being connected with the missionary work
of the Church, and I hope and trust that I may be able to continue
in this ministry the remainder of my days. I feel in my heart that
there is nothing greater for me, or for any other man living than to
be identified with the cause of truth, and I verily believe that we
are engaged in the cause of truth, and not error.—Apr. C. R., 1912, p. 2.

Worth of a Standing in the Church. My standing in the
Church is worth to me more than this life—ten thousand times.
For in this I have life everlasting. In this I have the glorious promise
of the association of my loved ones throughout all eternity. In
obedience to this work, in the gospel of Jesus Christ, I shall gather

around me my family, my children, my children's children, until they become as numerous as the seed of Abraham, or as countless as the sands upon the seashore. For this is my right and privilege, and the right and privilege of every member of the Church of Jesus Christ of Latter-day Saints who holds the Priesthood and will magnify it in the sight of God. Without it, there is death and desolation—disintegration and disinheritance; without it there may be a chance to become a ministering spirit, a servant unto servants throughout the endless ages, but in this gospel there is a chance to become a son of God, in the image and likeness of the Father and of his Only Begotten Son in the flesh. I would rather take my boys and my girls to the grave, while they are innocent, than to see them entrapped in the wickedness, the unbelief and the spirit of apostasy so prevalent in the world, and be led away from the gospel of salvation.—Apr. C. R., 1912, pp. 136, 137.

IMPORTANCE OF HAVING NAMES ON CHURCH RECORDS. Some people may not care very much whether their names are recorded or not but this comes from ignorance of the consequences. If their names are not recorded they will not only be cut off from the assistance which they would be entitled to from the Church, if they needed it, but they will be cut off from the ordinances of the house of God; they will be cut asunder from their dead and from their fathers who have been faithful, or from those who shall come after them who shall be faithful, and they will be appointed their portion with the unbelievers, where there is weeping and gnashing of teeth. It means that you will be cut off from your fathers and mothers, from your husbands, your wives, your children, and that you shall have no portion or lot or inheritance in the kingdom of God, both in time and in eternity. It has a very serious and far-reaching effect.—Oct. C. R., 1899, p. 42.

SECRET ORGANIZATIONS. The Church of Jesus Christ of Latter-day Saints is good enough for me and my family, and I have no time nor means to associate myself with organizations that are not of this Church and which have simply for their objective the laying up of something for my wife to have after I am dead. I cannot afford to do it for this reason: the Lord has seen fit to give me from day to day just sufficient for my needs, and if I were to join these associations for the purpose of looking after the future of my family, I would be compelled to neglect paying my tithing, and present duties, because I would not have means enough to pay my tithing and my dues for these associations. We have known members of the Church, who, when they were asked why they did not pay their tithing, confessed that they were associated with organizations of one kind and another, wherein they were compelled to pay weekly or monthly certain sums of money; they had been associated with these institutions for a number of years, and had put quite a lot of money in them; and now, if they did not continue to pay their dues they would lose all they had put in, then in case of death their families would lose the premium. From this you can see they are in bondage to these secret organizations, and if they want to pay tithing they cannot do it. Well, if they do not, they will be among those whose names will not be found recorded in the books of the law of the Lord and who will not have inheritance in the Zion of God. Furthermore, we have called some of these men to go on missions, but they could not go to preach the gospel to the nations of the earth. Why? Because they belonged to certain secret associations, and they were compelled to be at work all the time in order to pay their dues, or they would lose what they had put in them.—Oct. C. R., 1899, p. 40.

SECRET SOCIETIES. It is a well known truth that the counsel of the First Presidency of the Church, in all cases, has been and is against our brethren joining secret organizations for any purpose whatsoever, and that wherever any of them have already joined, they have bee. and are counseled to withdraw themselves from such organizations, as soon as circumstances permit and wisdom dictates. In taking this position, there has not been, neither is it intended that there shall be, any controversy with the societies, and with their aims and objects. The merits of the various orders are not considered at all; their aims may be ever so worthy and their objects ever so commendable. That matter does not enter into the discussion, so far as a member of our Church is concerned.

The gospel of Jesus Christ is true, and is a power unto salvation, temporal and spiritual. A man who complies in every respect therewith has everything that any society can offer, with countless truths and consolations added: "But seek ye first the kingdom of God, and his righteousness; and all these things shall be added unto you." The Church is divinely organized, and in that organization there is provision for the development and practice of every virtue known, every charity revealed. For this reason and for its promise of eternal life and glory, the gospel, and the Church divinely established for its promulgation, should be nearer and dearer to a follower of Christ than all other things. "No man can serve two masters; for either he will hate the one, and love the other; or else he will hold to the one and despise the other. Ye can not serve God and Mammon."

The members of our Church who have faith to heed the advice of the authorities thereof, will not ally themselves, under any pretense, with any organization not instituted by the Lord for the building up of Zion. Neither will they, for any consideration, allow themselves to imbibe the spirit of the world, or be tempted to lose their faith, which will be the result with those who divide their interests, devoting some to other organizations. This is the testimony of those who have joined and who have later withdrawn. Nothing can be permitted in the members that is calculated to bring division and weakness to the Church, yet those who have been led to join other institutions should not be dealt with harshly, but should be made to understand the position of the Church, and where it is so understood, they should shape their affairs for withdrawal, in humility and repentance, from that which threatens their standing.—*Improvement Era*, Vol. 6, p. 305, February, 1903.

Gossip. The "Mormon" creed: "Mind your own business," is a good motto for young people to adopt who wish to succeed, and who wish to make the best use of their time and lives. And when I say young people, it includes as well aged and middle aged men and women.

Let it be remembered that nothing is quite so contemptible as idle gossip. Byron said a good thing when he put into the mouth of Don Juan these words:

> "In fact there's nothing makes me so much grieve
> As that abominable tittle-tattle,
> Which is the cud eschewed by human cattle."

How idle to go about whispering mysterious words here and there—words often without foundation in fact, but uttered with injurious intent, and perhaps with the idea of creating for the whisperer some imaginary respect, because of his supposed possession of special knowledge! But such action seldom bodes good, or sets upon the round of human lips sentiments of appreciation for the excellent, the beautiful, and the true, in a brother, neighbor, or friend. Such gossip and meddling constantly hold to view the defects of its subjects, and the scandals that are born fly as upon the wings of eagles. To be thus engaged is a positive injury, also, to the person so employed, because, by constantly holding the defects of others in his own mind, he ruins his own ability to see and appreciate the virtues of his fellows, thus stifling his nobler self.

It is so very much better for a person to strive to develop himself by observing all the good points he can find in others, than to strangle the growth of his better self by cherishing a fault-finding, sullen, and intermeddling spirit. The scriptures support this thought. The great Psalmist says in substance in the fifteenth psalm: "He that backbiteth not with his tongue, nor doeth evil to his neighbor, nor taketh up a reproach against his neighbor, shall abide in the tabernacle of the Lord, and never be moved." To abide in the tabernacle of the Lord is to enjoy his Holy Spirit. Now, he that taketh up a reproach against his neighbor is in great danger of losing the Spirit of the Lord. "But my neighbor has done this, that or the other that is forbidden by the law of the Church, or good usage, why should I not set him right?" says one. Let that one ask himself: "Is it my business?" The answer will suggest itself: If it is not my business, let me be wise enough to mind my own business. For "he that refraineth his lips is wise, and he that uttereth a slander is a fool;" and, further, the Lord declares through the Psalmist: "Whoso privily slandereth his neighbor, him will I cut off."

Let it be the aim of the Saints to cultivate the spirit of generosity and good-will, such as was exemplified in the life of Christ, and proclaimed when the angels heralded abroad the message: "Peace on earth, to men good will," and which has been reiterated in the modern restoration of the gospel. Watch constantly for that which is worthy and noble in your fellowman. It makes a person better to see and speak of good in his neighbor; while there is unbounded delight in observing the effect that a few words of appreciation and encouragement have upon men, women, and children with whom we associate. Let those try it who really wish to get the genuine sweets out of life.

The meddler, the gossip, the fault-finder, on the other hand, soon ruin their own capacity for observing the better side of human nature; and, not finding it in others, search in vain for its influence in their own souls.

There is a wonderful field in the organizations of the Church for the cultivation of all the virtues of the human heart. It is the business of every officer and member of the Church, and of her associations and organizations, to lead out in doing good; to stand first in serviceable practices in the gospel's atmosphere of sunshine and peace; to lift up and not cast down; to encourage and not to repress; to dispense joy, and to drown sorrow; to refrain their lips from slander and backbiting, and, by sweet temper and kind words, to unfold the better side of human nature; to mind their own business, and not to unduly criticise, and not to find fault, nor to delight in tale-bearing, scandal, envy, and gossip.

This advice heeded, our social ethics would soon show wonderful improvement; happiness, beauty of disposition, love, and moral cleanliness, would increase among the Saints; the Spirit of God would delight to dwell in their midst, and the best qualities of the people would unfold and develop like the rose in the warm sunshine of June.—*Improvement Era*, Vol. 6, p. 388, March, 1903.

WE WANT TO BE KNOWN AS WE ARE. We want to be known as we are. We want to be seen in our true light. We want the world to become acquainted with us. We want them to learn our doctrine, to understand our faith, our purposes, and the organization of the Church of Jesus Christ of Latter-day Saints. We would like them to know something about the origin of this work, but we desire that they shall see this work in the true spirit of it, and the only way this can be brought about is by the inquiring intelligent world coming in contact with us—those indeed who are disposed to love truth and righteousness, and whose eyes are not so blinded that they can not see the truth when it is presented before them.—Oct. C. R., 1908, p. 3.

TREATMENT OF THOSE WHO WILL NOT OBEY THE LAW OF THE CHURCH. It has occurred to me somewhat in this way: that the body of the Church is likened to the body of a man, and you know men do sometimes get their systems a little deranged—that is to say, sometimes they are flea-bitten. Fleas bite them and mosquitoes bite them and cause little swellings to rise on their face and hands. Sometimes they have boils upon them, and carbuncles, sebaceous tumors and other excrescences, that only need the application of the lance to get out the humor from them or to excise them from the body, or cut them off and let them go, so that the body may be cleansed from their poisonous effect. It is so with the Church. From time to time there are characters who become a law unto themselves and they follow the bent of their own "sweet will" until they get themselves into a condition mentally and spiritually that they become a menace to the body ecclesiastic. In other words, they become like a boil, tumor, or carbuncle on the body, you have to call in the surgeon to apply the knife to cut them out that the body may be cleansed from them; and this has been the case from the beginning.—*Apr. C. R.*, 1905, p. 5.

LATTER-DAY SAINTS MUST BE THINKERS AND WORKERS. To be Latter-day Saints men and women must be thinkers and workers; they must be men and women who weigh matters in their minds; men and women who consider carefully their course of life and the principles that they have espoused. Men cannot be faithful Latter-day Saints unless they study and understand, to some extent at least, the principles of the gospel that they have received. When you hear people, who profess to be Latter-day Saints, running off on tangents, on foolish notions and one-horse, cranky ideas, things that are obviously opposed to reason and to good sense, opposed to principles of righteousness and to the word of the Lord that has been revealed to men, you should know at once that they have not studied the principles of the gospel, and do not know very much about the gospel. When people understand the gospel of Jesus Christ, you will see them walking straightforward, according to the word of the Lord and the law of God, strictly in accordance with that which is consistent, just, righteous, and in every sense acceptable to the Lord who only accepts of that which is right and pleasing in his sight; for only that which is right is pleasing unto him.—*Improvement Era*, Vol. 14, 1910, p. 72.

THE IDENTITY OF THE CHURCH UNCHANGED. We have a double guide and a double assurance in reaching our correct conclusions concerning the perfect identity of the Church now and the Church in the days of its first prophet. The spirit of loyalty and devotion, together with love for the work of building up Zion, characterize the Saints, while the devil rages now in the same manner that he did then. The spirit, on both sides of the controversy, is so identical that it is hard to imagine that any thoughtful Latter-day Saint can be deceived over the situation as it exists today.

By their fruits ye shall know them. The devil caused men to rage over the Nauvoo House, the building of the Nauvoo Temple, the Prophet's Nauvoo brick store, and the material prosperity of the Saints in that beautiful city on the banks of the Mississippi; he causes men to rave over so-called "commercialism" today. Envy was rampant then. It is just as deadly now.—*Juvenile Instructor*, Vol. 40, p. 497, August 15, 1905.

No CLASSES OR NATIONALITIES IN THE CHURCH. The brotherhood and common interests in the Church of Jesus Christ of Latter-day Saints are among the great characteristics of our faith, and whatever, therefore, tends to establish class distinction either in society or nationalities should be discouraged in every way possible. God is no respecter of persons, neither does he glorify one class to the disadvantage of another.

A striking peculiarity of the Saints gathered from all parts of the earth is that they are almost universally of the blood of Ephraim. If they have received the Holy Ghost they are of one spirit, so that whatever creates a discord in the spirit and unity of the Saints is of evil origin. The Spirit of God never begets strife, nor does it set up and insist on distinctions among those who have been its recipients.

There has been in some people's minds the thought that this or that nationality was entitled to certain recognition because of its large numbers or prominence in certain respects. The affairs of the Church are not carried on with respect to what is good or bad policy —there is no policy in the Church, but that of wisdom and truth, and everyone of its members should thoroughly understand that distinctions both in classes and nationalities are odious and out of harmony with the discipline and spirit of Church government. If a man of one or another nationality is honored by any important call, it is because of the spirit in the man, and not because of his nationality, and the Saints may be certain that when any man makes a demand for recognition it is an assumption on his part, and is not in harmony with the life and spirit of our Master.—*Juvenile Instructor*, Vol. 37, p. 658, November 1, 1902.

No NEUTRALS IN THE CHURCH. In Christ's Church we cannot be neutral or inert. We must either progress or retrograde. It is necessary for the Latter-day Saints to keep pushing on in order that they may keep their faith alive and their spirits quickened to the performance of their duties. Let us remember that we are engaged in God's

work—and when I say God's work, I mean that we are engaged in
the work which the Almighty has instituted in the earth for our salvation individually. Every man should be laboring for his own good
and as far as possible for the good of others. There is no such thing
in the science of life as a man laboring exclusively for himself. We
are not intended to be alone in time nor in eternity. Each individual is a unit in the household of faith, and each unit must feel his
or her proportion of the responsibility that devolves upon the whole.
Each individual must be diligent in performing his duty. By doing
this, and keeping himself pure and unspotted from the world, he
assists others to keep themselves pure and unspotted. For instance,
a man who is faithful in observing the Sabbath day and in attending
to the duties of that day will at least set an example unto all with
whom he is associated. The man who is prayerful before the Lord
will set an example before all others who see and know his conduct.
The man who is honest in dealing with his neighbor will set an example
for good. Those who do this are genuine representatives of Zion;
they are the children of God indeed and of a truth, and there rests with
them the spirit of light and the love of God. They are in a saved
condition, and will continue to be in a saved condition so long as they
continue to observe the principles of the gospel. It is useless for us
to mourn over the evils that we ourselves have caused, unless by
repentance we may make restitution for the evils we have done. It
is a terrible thing for men and women to allow themselves to go so far
in the neglect of duty that evils will result from their misconduct
which they will be powerless thereafter to eradicate or to make restitution for.—Sermon, Sunday, June 12, 1898.

DON'T HAVE RELIGIOUS HOBBIES. Brethren and sisters, don't
have hobbies. Hobbies are dangerous in the Church of Christ. They
are dangerous because they give undue prominence to certain principles
or ideas to the detriment and dwarfing of others just as important,
just as binding, just as saving as the favored doctrines or commandments.

Hobbies give to those who encourage them a false aspect of the
gospel of the Redeemer; they distort and place out of harmony its
principles and teachings. The point of view is unnatural. Every principle and practice revealed from God is essential to man's salvation,
and to place any one of them unduly in front, hiding and dimming
all others is unwise and dangerous; it jeopardizes our salvation, for it

darkens our minds and beclouds our understandings. Such a view, no matter to what point directed, narrows the vision, weakens the spiritual perception, and darkens the mind, the result of which is that the person thus afflicted with this perversity and contraction of mental vision places himself in a position to be tempted of the evil one, or, through dimness of sight or distortion of vision, to misjudge his brethren and give way to the spirit of apostasy. He is not square before the Lord.

We have noticed this difficulty: that Saints with hobbies are prone to judge and condemn their brethren and sisters who are not so zealous in the one particular direction of their pet theory as they are. The man with the Word of Wisdom only in his brain, is apt to find unmeasured fault with every other member of the Church who entertains liberal ideas as to the importance of other doctrines of the gospel.

There is another phase of this difficulty—the man with a hobby is apt to assume an "I am holier than thou" position, to feel puffed up and conceited, and to look with distrust, if with no severer feeling, on his brethren and sisters who do not so perfectly live that one particular law. This feeling hurts his fellow-servants and offends the Lord. "Pride goeth before destruction, and an haughty spirit before a fall."—(Prov. 16:18.)

There are some great truths in the plan of redemption that are fundamental. They cannot be ignored; none others can be placed before them. The fatherhood of God, the efficacy of the atonement of our Lord and Savior, the restoration of the gospel in these latter days, must be accepted with our whole hearts. We cannot compensate for a lack of faith in these essential doctrines by the most absolute abstinence from things unhealthful, by the rigid payment of tithing on our "anise and cummin," or by the observance of any other outward ordinance. Baptism itself without faith in God avails nothing.— *Juvenile Instructor*, Vol. 37, pp. 176-177, March, 1902.

WEALTH DOES NOT BRING CHURCH FAVORS. The idea should never gain ground that the rich man in the Church is entitled to any more consideration than the humblest member. Men of superior virtues and powers, whether those virtues and powers be represented in the ability to gain wealth, to acquire education, or to display genius and wisdom, will always occupy a commanding place in the social, the business, and religious world.

It is one thing, however, to respect wealth and its powers, and quite another to become mere sycophants to it. Neither the Church, nor its blessings nor favors, have ever been, from its organization, submissive to or purchasable by the mammon of this world. No man need to hope that he can buy the gifts of God. Those who attempt to buy the treasures of heaven will perish, and their wealth will perish with them. Wealth may wield an undue influence and gain prestige in society, even though its possessor may be greatly wanting in moral worthiness. And being a power in itself, may be a danger through the opportunities for corruption and seduction. Those, therefore, who have listened to the fallacious arguments of the advantages of wealth and its power, independent of virtue, have in store for them a great disappointment if they act upon any such false theories.

The trouble is, that young men are very apt to mistake a friendly and cordial greeting to those in possession of wealth for a genuine friendship and sincere confidence. The unworthy rich should be as much the object of our pity as the unworthy poor. Those who imagine that wealth may be substituted for virtue are certainly doomed to disappointment; and yet men sometimes foolishly and enviously suggest that the highest social recommendation and religious standing as well as the sincere friendship of the pure in heart are subject to the command of the mammon of unrighteousness.

The money offered by Simon the sorcerer to the apostles for the gifts they possessed was spurned by them, and a curse was pronounced both upon him and his wealth. (See Acts 8:14-23)—*Juvenile Instructor*, Vol. 40, pp. 593, 594, October 1, 1905.

THE GOSPEL CAUSES DISTURBANCE. In truth the gospel is carrying us against the stream of passing humanity. We get in the way of purely human affairs and disturb the current of life in many ways and in many places. People who are comfortably located and well provided for, do not like to be disturbed. It angers them, and they would settle things once for all in the most drastic manner. The effects of certain causes are so unlike anything we have ever known that we are not safe in making philosophy our guide; much less are we safe in making those our guide who have some sort of selfish philosophy which they are anxious that others should follow. Those who defend us, do so not infrequently with an apologetic air. The Saints are never safe in following the protests and counsels of those who would have us ever and always in harmony with the world. We have our particular mission to perform; and that we may perform it in consonance with divine purposes, we are running counter to the ways of man. We are made unpopular. The contempt of the world is on us, and we are the unloved child among the peoples of the earth.

"HAVING DONE ALL, STAND." There are people who are courageous in doing all they can to bring about certain results. They will combat evils and resist the wrongs that are inflicted upon them and upon others; but when they have been defeated, when they see a just cause suffer, and evilly disposed men triumphant, they give up. What is the use? That is the question uppermost in their minds. They see wicked men apparently successful. They see men of evil repute honored by their fellowmen until they are almost persuaded that fate has her rewards for wrong doing. With them, what appears to be a lost cause inspires no hope. It is lost, they say, and we shall have to make the best of it, and let it go. They are at heart discouraged. Some almost question the purposes of Providence. They have the courage of men who are brave at heart, but they have not the courage of faith.

How different it was with Paul! He had labored fearlessly, he had delivered a divine message, he had resisted the enemy, and they apparently triumphed over him. He was taken prisoner and subjected to humiliating treatment by the administrators of the law. He was in bonds, and death awaited him, but he was still courageous. His was the courage of faith. Read these stirring words of his sent to the Ephesians, recorded in Ephesians 6:13, sent when most men would have thought their cause lost: "Wherefore take unto you the whole armour of God, that ye may be able to withstand in the evil day, and having done all, to stand."

After we have done all we could do for the cause of truth, and withstood the evil that men have brought upon us, and we have been overwhelmed by their wrongs, it is still our duty to stand. We cannot give up; we must not lie down. Great causes are not won in a single generation. To stand firm in the face of overwhelming opposition, when you have done all you can, is the courage of faith. The courage of faith is the courage of progress. Men who possess that divine quality go on; they are not permitted to stand still if they would. They are not simply the creatures of their own power and wisdom; they are instrumentalities of a higher law and a divine purpose.

Others would quit, they would avoid trouble. When it comes, it is to them most unfortunate. It is really too bad. In their minds,

it might have been avoided. They want to square themselves with
the world. The decree of the world has gone forth, why withstand it?
"We have withstood evil," they say, "and it has overwhelmed us.
Why stand longer?" Such men read history, if at all, only as they
make it; they cannot see the hand of God in the affairs of men, because
they see only with the eye of man and not with the eye of faith.
All resistance is gone out of them—they have left God out of the
question. They have not put on his whole armor. Without it they
are loaded down with fear and apprehension, and they sink. To
such men everything that brings trouble seems necessary. As Saints
of God, it is our duty "to stand," even when we are overwhelmed
by evil.

"And I give unto you a commandment, that ye shall forsake all
evil and cleave unto all good, that ye shall live by every word which
proceedeth forth out of the mouth of God;

"For he will give unto the faithful line upon line, precept upon
precept; and I will try you and prove you herewith;

"And whoso layeth down his life in my cause, for my name's sake
shall find it again, even life eternal;

"Therefore be not afraid of your enemies, for I have decreed in
my heart, saith the Lord, that I will prove you in all things, whether
you will abide in my covenant, even unto death, that you may be
found worthy;

"For if ye will not abide in my covenant, ye are not worthy of
me." (Doc. and Cov. 98:11-15).—*Juvenile Instructor*, Aug. 15, 1904,
Vol. 39, pp. 496, 497.

NOT NATURALLY RELIGIOUS. Some people persist in saying on
occasion that they are not naturally religious. Do they mean by this
that attending meetings, taking part in ward worship, teaching and
preaching, are not congenial to them? Or, do they mean more?
Perhaps the moral restrictions governing an active worker in the
Church are not congenial to them. They reason that it is better to
make no pretensions than to make more than one can live up to;
and so they excuse themselves by declaring they are naturally not
religious.

But religion is not outward show and pretense, and being religious does not altogether consist in compliance with outward forms,
even when these are the ordinances of the gospel. Neither is it an
unfailing sign that a person is conscientious who takes an active part

in organizations of the Church. Evil men may use these for selfish and wicked purposes. I have known men who joined our organizations for such ends, and men who have been baptized who never repented.

Then what is religion? James declares: "Pure religion and undefiled before God and the Father is this: To visit the fatherless and widows in their afflictions, and to keep himself unspotted from the world." This may be interpreted as meaning that a person who is religious is thoughtful to the unfortunate, and has an inner spirit that prompts to deeds of kindness and to the leading of a blameless life; who is just, truthful; who does not, as Paul says, think more highly of himself than he ought to think; who is affectionate, patient in tribulation, diligent, cheerful, fervent in spirit, hospitable, merciful; and who abhors evil and cleaves to that which is good. The possession of such a spirit and feeling is a true sign that a person is naturally religious.

The Church's outward ordinances and requirements are but necessary—yet they are necessary—aids to the inner spiritual life. The Church itself, the organization, meetings, ordinances, requirements, are only helps, but very necessary helps, to the practice of true religion —schoolmasters to direct us in the way of eternal light and truth.

Young men, do not say that you are not naturally religious, and so make that an excuse for evil deeds and forbidden acts, and for not identifying yourselves with the organizations of the Church, and by such course perhaps smothering the Spirit of God within you, possessed as a birthright, or received through the servants of the Lord by the imposition of hands. Be rather religious both in appearance and in reality, remembering what true religion means. Even as the testimony of Jesus is the spirit of prophecy, so is the possession of the knowledge that you love purity, righteousness, honesty, justice and well-doing, an indisputable evidence that you are naturally religious. Search your hearts, and you will find deep down that you possess this knowledge. Then encourage its growth and development to the gaining of your own salvation. The Church and its quorums and organizations will help you, and the living, loving God will add his bounteous blessings.—*Improvement Era*, 1905-6, Vol. 9, pp. 493-495.

STRIVE TO BE AS BROAD AS THE GOSPEL. The gospel of Jesus Christ, properly taught and understood, inculcates broadness, force, and power. It makes intellectually broad and valiant men. It gives to men good, sound judgment in affairs temporal as well as spiritual. There are reasons why it is worth a young man's while to embrace it. Outside of the gospel of Jesus Christ, as taught by the Latter-day Saints, and sometimes within the fold, we frequently look about us and see people who incline to extremes, who are fanatical. We may be sure that this class of people do not understand the gospel. They have forgotten, if they ever knew, that it is very unwise to take a fragment of truth and treat it as if it were the whole thing.

While the first principles of the gospel, faith in God, repentance, baptism for the remission of sins, and the laying on of hands for the reception of the Holy Ghost, the healing of the sick, the resurrection, and for that matter, all the revealed principles of the gospel of Christ are necessary and essential in the plan of salvation, it is neither good policy nor sound doctrine to take any one of these, single it out from the whole plan of gospel truth, make it a special hobby, and depend upon it for our salvation and progress, either in this world or in the world to come. They are all necessary.

It should be the desire of the Latter-day Saints to become as big and broad as the gospel which has been divinely revealed to them. They should, therefore, hold themselves open to the acceptance of all the truths of the gospel that have been revealed, that are now being revealed, and that will be revealed hereafter, and adopt them in the conduct of their daily lives. By honorable and upright living, by obedience to the commandments of God, and by the aid of the Holy Spirit, we shall place ourselves in a position to work out our own salvation here and hereafter, "with fear and trembling," it may be, but with absolute certainty.

This is a work that makes every soul who engages in it big and broad. It is a life-work worth the while of every man in the world.— *Improvement Era*, 1911-12, Vol. 15, pp. 843-845.

SEARCH AND YE SHALL FIND. The fact is that every principle of healing, every principle of the power of the Holy Ghost, and of God, which have been manifested to the Saints in all ages, have been bestowed upon the Latter-day Saints. There is no principle, there is no blessing, there is no advantage, there is no truth in any other religious society or organization, which is not included in the gospel of Jesus Christ as taught by Joseph Smith, the Prophet, and after him by the leaders and elders of this Church; but it requires some effort on our part, some exertion, some devotion, to learn of and to enjoy these things. If we neglect them, we are, of course, not the recipients of the blessings that follow effort, and that come from a thorough understanding of these principles. Hence it is that others may come in among us and advocate their ideas which, though not comparing with ours in plainness, instruction, and truth, are yet listened to by people who are made to believe that all these things are new, and not contained in the gospel of Jesus Christ as taught by the Latter-day Saints. This is a fearful fallacy, and one that should be guarded against by everyone who loves the gospel.

In the Church of Jesus Christ of Latter-day Saints will be found to a greater extent than in any other church, the principles of life and salvation; and if we search them out of our literature and learn them for ourselves, have them confirmed by the Spirit, by right living, and make them a part of ourselves, we shall find greater comfort and richer blessings, greater treasures of everlasting life than in any other teachings that may be given to us by any other organization upon the earth.—*Improvement Era*, May, 1909, Vol. 12, p. 561.

THE SPIRIT OF RELIGION. A serious time will come in every life. There is a parting of the ways. What you indulge in will lead you up or down. I have no hesitancy in declaring in the name of the Lord that the spirit which leads you to complain that you are bored in attending the worshiping assemblies of the Saints has led or will lead you astray; and, on the other hand, that the young people who cultivate the true spirit of worship, and find happiness and pleasure in the associations of the Saints, and who care enough for God and religion to support the Church and attend the meetings, are the people whose moral and spiritual influence will control public sentiment and govern the state and nation. In any conflict with indifference and the spirit of worldly pleasure, moral influence and religious earnestness will always conquer and rule.—*Improvement Era*, October, 1903, Vol. 6, p. 944.

THE MEANING OF SUCCESS. There are daily evidences of a growing tendency among the masses of the civilized world to regard success in life purely from the standpoint of material advancement. The man who has a beautiful home and a large income is looked upon as a successful man. People are constantly talking about the winners of fortune in the contest for wealth. Men who are successful in obtaining the honors bestowed by their fellowmen are envied as among the most fortunate. Everywhere men hear the word success dwelt upon as if success were defined in a word, and as if the highest ambition of men and women was the advancement of some worldly ambition.

All this rage about success simply indicates the gross materialism of the age in which we live. Here is what a State Commissioner of Education says to a graduating class: "You need not expect that people will stand aside because you have come. They are going to crowd you, and you will have to crowd them. They will leave you behind unless you leave them behind." The meaning of such talk is that to be successful you must take advantage of your fellowmen; you must crowd them out and leave them behind; and all because if you do not take advantage of them they will take advantage of you.

After all, what is success, and who are competent to judge? The great masses who lived in the days of Jesus would have said that his life was a stupendous failure, that his life and teachings ended in inglorious defeat. Even his disciples were disappointed in his death; and their efforts to perpetuate his name and teachings were covered with ignominy and contempt. It was centuries before the success of his life became apparent to the world. We can easily comprehend, therefore, how it has taken centuries to accomplish achievements that were set in motion by some obscure or despised personage. The triumph, therefore, of Jesus would have been looked upon by his generation as one of the paradoxes of history.

When the Prophet Joseph Smith was slain, his enemies rejoiced in what they considered the inglorious ending of his life. They were sure that all he had done would end with him, and so they could pronounce his life a burlesque and a failure. It will be seen from these instances that the contemporaries of a man are not always competent to say whether his life has been a success or a failure. A sound judgment must await future generations, perhaps future centuries.

If your neighbor today is a poor widow who rears, amid the greatest struggles and in unbearable poverty, three or four or half a dozen children, perhaps no one would say of her life that it was a success, and yet there may be in her offspring the embryo of future greatness, future generations may cover her motherhood with glory.

After all, one's success must be determined more by the eternal (as well as the present) needs of man, than by temporary standards which men erect in pursuance of the spirit of the age in which they live. Certainly nothing is more fatal to our well being than the notion that our present and eternal welfare is founded upon the wealth and honors of this world.

The great truth enunciated by the Savior seems very generally to be lost sight of in this generation, that it will profit a man nothing though he should gain the whole world, if he lose his own soul.

The standard of success as declared by the word of God, is the salvation of the soul. The greatest gift of God is eternal life.—*Juvenile Instructor*, Sept. 15, 1904, Vol. 39, pp. 561-62.

WHAT IS TO BECOME OF SUCH AS I? That there are many good people in the world who believe the principles of the gospel as taught by the Latter-day Saints and yet, through circumstances and environment, are not prepared publicly to accept the same, is evidenced by the following extract from a letter written by a reverend gentleman:

"What is to become of such as I, who believe this about you, and yet are tied and bound by circumstances such as mine? Here I have been a minister for fifty-five years. I cannot change now if I would."

In answer to the question, "What is to become of such as I?" let it be said that every person will receive his just reward for the good he may do and for his every act. But let it be remembered that all blessings which we shall receive, either here or hereafter, must come to us as a result of our obedience to the laws of God upon which these blessings are predicated. Our friend will not be forgotten for the kindness he has extended to the work and the servants of the Lord, but will be remembered of him and rewarded for his faith and for every good deed and word. But there are many blessings that result from obeying the ordinances of the gospel, and acknowledging the Priesthood authorized of the Father and restored to the Church of Jesus Christ of Latter-day Saints, that cannot be obtained until the person is willing to comply with the ordinances and keep the commandments revealed in our day for the salvation of mankind. The true searcher will see and understand this truth and act upon it, either in this world or in the world to come, and not until then, of course, may he claim all the blessings. The earlier he accepts, the earlier will he obtain the blessings, and if he neglects to accept the laws in this world, knowing them to be true, it is reasonable to suppose that disadvantages will result that will cause him deep regret.—*Improvement Era*, 1912-13, Vol. 16, pp. 70-72.

REST FOR THE PEACEABLE FOLLOWERS OF CHRIST. I desire to call the attention of the Latter-day Saints to the words of the Prophet Moroni, who says, in speaking of his father's instructions to the ancient saints upon this continent:

"Wherefore I would speak unto you that are of the Church, that are the peaceable followers of Christ, and that have obtained a sufficient hope, by which we can enter into the rest of the Lord, from this time henceforth, until ye shall rest with him in heaven."

This is a very significant passage. The rest here referred to is not physical rest, for there is no such thing as physical rest in the Church of Jesus Christ. Reference is made to the spiritual rest and peace which are born from a settled conviction of the truth in the minds of men. We may thus enter into the rest of the Lord today, by coming to an understanding of the truths of the gospel. No people is more entitled to this rest—this peace of the spirit—than are members of the Church. It is true that not all are unsettled. Not all need to seek this rest, for there are many who now possess it, whose minds have become satisfied, and who have set their eyes upon the mark of their high calling with an invincible determination in their hearts to be steadfast in the truth, and who are treading in humility and righteousness the path marked out for the Saints who are complacent followers of Jesus Christ. But there are many who, not having reached this point of determined conviction, are driven about by every wind of doctrine, thus being ill at ease, unsettled, restless. These are they who are discouraged over incidents that occur in the Church, and in the nation, and in the turmoils of men and associations. They harbor a feeling of suspicion, unrest, uncertainty. Their thoughts are disturbed, and they become excited with the least change, like one at sea who has lost his bearings.

Where would you have people go who are unsettled in the truth? The answer is plain. They will not find satisfaction in the doctrines of Men. Let them seek for it in the written word of God; let them pray to him in their secret chambers, where no human ear can hear, and in their closets petition for light; let them obey the doctrines of Jesus, and they will immediately begin to grow in the knowledge of the truth. This course will bring peace to their souls, joy to their hearts, and a settled conviction which no change can disturb. They may be well assured that "he that heareth in secret will reward them openly." Let them seek for strength from the Source of all strength, and he will provide spiritual contentment, a rest which is incomparable w.th the physical rest that cometh after toil. All who seek have a right to, and may enter into, the rest of God, here upon the earth, from this time forth, now, today; and when earth-life is finished, they shall also enjoy his rest in heaven.

I know that Christ is the Only Begotten Son of God, that he is the Redeemer of the world, that he was raised from the dead; and that as he arose, so shall every soul bearing the image of God arise from the dead and be judged according to his works, be they good or evil. In the never-ending eternities of our Father in heaven, the righteous shall rejoice, while the association and love of their families and friends shall glorify them through the ages that are to come. Joy and rest unspeakable will be their reward.

These are some of the doctrines of the gospel of Jesus Christ which the Latter-day Saints believe. I don't wish for anything better; I desire to be satisfied in these, and to possess that peace and joy which spring from the contemplation of the opportunities and truths that are embraced in this gospel. Were I to seek for other truths, where would I go? Not to man. I must know for myself, from the source which provides these blessings and gifts; but what more would I ask for than a knowledge of the resurrection, that I shall be made whole of my sins and become perfect in Christ Jesus, through obedience to his gospel? Is any doctrine more reasonable and more compatible with free agency than this? It is true that ancient philosophers taught us many morals, but where, in all the philosophy of the world, have we better teachings than in the gospel of Christ which has been revealed to us, and which we hold and are made partakers of? No doctrine was ever as perfect as that of Jesus. Christ perfected every principle that had hitherto been taught by the philosophers of the world; he has revealed to us the way of salvation, from the beginning, and through all the meanderings of this life to never-ending exaltation and glory in his kingdom, and to a newness of life therein. He has taught us that man is a dual being, the offspring of God, and that the body and the spirit, blended in one immortal soul, is eventually to stand in the presence of its Maker, and see as it is seen, and know as it is known. Whenever the Lord speaks to man, he speaks to his immortal soul, and satisfaction and unsurpassing peace and joy come to all who listen.

Happy is the man, indeed, who can receive this soul-satisfying testimony, and be at rest, and seek for no other road to peace than by the doctrines of Jesus Christ. His gospel teaches us to love our fellow-men, to do to others as we would have others do to us, to be just, to be merciful, to be forgiving, and to perform every good act calculated to enlarge the soul of man. His perfected philosophy teaches also that it is better to suffer wrong than to do wrong, and to pray for our enemies and for those who despitefully use us. There are no other gospels or systems of philosophy that bear these marks of divinity and immortality. You may hunt the philosophies of the world in vain for any code of ethics that insures the peace and rest that may be found in his comprehensive, yet simple, gospel.

To the young man or the young woman who is at a loss to know what to do, among all the various teachings that are extant in the world, I would say: Search the Scriptures, seek God in prayer, and then read the doctrines that have been proclaimed by Christ in his sermon on the mount, as found in Matthew, and as reiterated to the ancient saints upon this continent (III Nephi). Having studied these splendid standards, and searched deeply the significance of these matchless sentiments, you may defy the philosophies of the world, or any of its ethics to produce their equal. The wisdom of men is not to be compared with them. They lead to the rest of the peaceable followers of Christ, and enable mankind to become perfect as he is perfect. No other philosopher has ever said as Jesus said, "Come unto me." From the beginning of the world until the present time, no other philosopher has ever cried unto the people such words of love, nor guaranteed and declared power within himself to save. "Come unto me, all ye that labor and are heavy laden, and I will give you rest," is his call to all the sons and daughters of men.

The Latter-day Saints have answered the call, and thousands thereby have found rest and peace surpassing all understanding; and this notwithstanding the outward, fiery ordeals, the turmoil and the strife, through which they have passed. They rest in the knowledge that no man could declare or teach such doctrine; it is the truth of God.

I thank our Father that I have come to a knowledge of this truth, that I know that Jesus is the Christ, in whom alone there is rest and salvation. As God lives, they are deceived who follow men and their philosophies; but happy are they who enter into the rest of the peaceable followers of Christ, obtaining sufficient hope from this time henceforth until they shall rest with him in heaven. They depend completely upon the saving power of his gospel, and are therefore at rest in all the tumult of mind and public agitation which besets their way.—*Improvement Era*, 1903-4, Vol. 7, pp. 714-18.

HARMONY. As to harmony, with special reference to the understanding that the Latter-day Saints should have of it, as affecting the membership of the Church, or as subsisting in the quorums of the priesthood, I would say that the harmony that is sought to be established among the Saints, and in the membership of the respective quorums is a harmony that comes from seeing eye to eye in all things; from understanding things alike; a harmony that is born of perfect knowledge, perfect honesty, perfect unselfishness, perfect love. This is the harmony the Church would inculcate among its members, and such the elements from which she would have it arise.

It is with harmony as it is with all the ideals of the gospel. The Saints and elders of the Church may fail in perfect attainment of them, in this life, but they may approximate them. While that is true respecting all the details of the gospel, and as true of the perfect harmony we seek to attain as of other ideal conditions, yet we recognize the fact that a certain degree of harmony is essential in the Church as a working principle. This degree of harmony, essential in the Church, among the members and in the quorums of the priesthood, is neither hard to understand nor difficult of attainment. Neither is it a new principle, nor peculiar to the Church of the Latter-day Saints. It is as old as the society of men. It is common to all men working in community—to parliaments, congresses, conventions, boards, bureaucracies, and conferences of all descriptions. In the Church of Jesus Christ of Latter-day Saints this essential harmony consists of such union or agreement as is necessary to the accomplishment of the purposes of the organization. These purposes, in the main, are accomplished through the several councils of the priesthood, and through the conferences of the Church; hence, the work is done by the combined actions of groups of individuals, and of necessity must be by their agreement or consent. With men of varying intelligence, judgment, and temperament, of course it follows that in the consideration of a given matter there will be a variety of views entertained, and discussion of the subject will nearly always develop a variety of opinions. All this, by the way, is not detrimental to the quality of any purposed action, since the greater the variety in temperament and training, of those in conference, the more varied will be the viewpoints from which the subject in question is considered, until it is likely to be presented in almost every conceivable light, and its strength as well as its weakness developed, resulting in the best possible judgment being formed of it. It is these considerations which doubtless led to the aphorism, "In the midst of counsel there is wisdom." It will sometimes happen, of course, in the experiences of councils or conferences, that all present may not be brought to perfect agreement, with reference to the proposed action; but upon submission of the question to an expression of judgment, it is found that a majority of those having the right to decide a given matter determine it in a certain way. And now the question arises, what shall be the course of those who are in the minority, those not in the agreement perfectly with the decision? Shall they go from the council or conference and contend for their views against the decision rendered and be rebellious and stubborn in adhering to their own judgment, as against the judgment of the majority of the council or conference who had the right to determine what the action should be? The right answer, I think, is obvious. The judgment of the majority must stand. If it is the action of the council or conference having the final word upon the subject, it becomes the decreed action, the rule or law, and must be maintained as such until greater knowledge or changed circumstances shall cause those who rightfully established such decision to modify or abolish it.

Of course, if a member or members of the minority regard the action of the majority as a violation of some fundamental principle, or subversive of the inherent rights of men, against which they conceive it to be a matter of conscience to enter protest or absolute repudiation, I understand it is their right to so proceed; but this, let it be understood, would be revolutionary, it would be rebellion, and if persisted in, could only end in such persons voluntarily withdrawing, or being severed from the organization. They cannot hope to be retained in a fellowship and enjoy the rights and privileges of the Church, and at the same time be making war upon its decisions or its rules and policy. But no power on earth, certainly no power in the Church, can prevent men dissatisfied with the Church, from absolutely withdrawing from it; and such is the disfavor with which the Church is regarded by the world that such withdrawals would in most cases be rewarded by the applause of the world. Or, if the dissatisfaction of the member be only with the quorum or council of the priesthood with which he is connected, he would be at liberty to withdraw from that quorum or council, and still retain his membership in the Church. On the other hand, the harmony which I spoke of as being essential to the Church certainly demands that the Church shall not tolerate, and indeed, if the life of the organization persists, it cannot tolerate such internal conflicts as those just alluded to, as they would lead to confusion, anarchy, disruption, and final abolishment of the organization.

There is one other element to be considered in this matter of harmony, as a doctrine of the Church, which may not operate in other community efforts of men; and that is, the living presence and effective force of the Holy Spirit. That Spirit, it must be remembered, is, by way of preeminence, called "The Spirit of Truth, which proceedeth from the Father." He teaches all things; and brings to the remembrance of the Saints all the instructions of the Master. He guides into all truth, and as in all truth there is unity or harmony, so, it is believed that if the Saints are in possession of this Spirit, the harmony in the Church of Christ will be superior to the harmony that can be looked for or hoped for, in any other organization whatsoever. And because the Saints have free access to the Holy Spirit, and may walk within his light and fellowship and possess the intelligence which he is able to impart, a stricter harmony among the Saints may be insisted upon than in any other organization of men whatsoever. For the same reason, lack of harmony may be more severely censured and persistent opposition and rebellion more justly denounced and swiftly punished.

In all things, however, patience and charity must be exercised— and no less in seeking the perfect harmony we hope for, than in other things. The present state of imperfect knowledge, the struggle it is for all men to live on those spiritual heights where they may be in communion with God, must be taken into account and due allowance made for human weakness and imperfection. So that, while the existence of that degree of harmony essential as a working principle in the Church must always be imperatively demanded, beyond that, the Church, in the manner of harmony, may well afford to exercise forbearance and charity towards all its members until the day of more perfect knowledge shall arise upon the Saints; a day when, through a wider effusion and a deeper penetration of the Holy Spirit they may be brought to stand in perfect harmony with each other and with God.—*Improvement Era*, 1904-5, Vol. 8, pp. 209-215.

CHARACTER, METTLE, AND MISSION OF THE LATTER-DAY SAINTS.

We do not look for absolute perfection in man. Mortal man is not capable of being absolutely perfect. Nevertheless, it is given to us to be as perfect in the sphere in which we are called to be and to act, as it is for the Father in heaven to be pure and righteous in the more exalted sphere in which he acts. We will find in the scriptures the words of the Savior himself to his disciples, in which he required that they should be perfect, even as their Father in heaven is perfect; that they should be righteous, even as he is righteous. I do not expect that we can be as perfect as Christ, that we can be as righteous as God. But I believe that we can strive for that perfection with the intelligence that we possess, and the knowledge that we have of the principles of life and salvation. The duty of the Latter-day Saints, and the paramount duty of those who are leaders in this work of mutual improvement in the Church, is to inculcate in the hearts of the young people these principles of righteousness, of purity of life, of honor, of uprightness and of humility withal, that we may be humble before God and acknowledge his hand in all things. According to his revelations, he is displeased with those who will not acknowledge his hand in all things. When we look at the imperfections of our fellow beings, some of the inclinations of those with whom we are intimately associated in the various organizations of the Church, and discern in them their natural proneness to evil, to sinfulness, to a disregard of sacred things, and sometimes their inclination to disregard and treat lightly, if not with contempt, those things which should be more sacred than life itself, it makes the task seem almost discouraging, and it seems impossible for us to accomplish that which we have in view, and to perform the mission that we have undertaken to our own satisfaction and the acceptance of the Lord.

But what shall we do? Shall we quit because there are those with whom we come in contact who are not willing to rise to the standard to which we seek to exalt them? No! Someone has said that the Lord hates a quitter, and there should be no such thing as quitting when we put our hands to the plow to save men, to save souls, to exalt mankind, to inculcate principles of righteousness and establish them in the hearts of those with whom we are associated, both by precept and by example. There must be no such thing as being discouraged. We may fail over and over again, but if we do, it is in individual cases. Under certain conditions and circumstances, we may fail to accomplish the object we have in view with reference to this individual or the other individual, or a number of individuals that we are seeking to benefit, to uplift, to purify, to get into their hearts the principles of justice, of righteousness, of virtue and of honor, that would fit them to inherit the kingdom of God; to associate with angels, should they come to visit the earth. If you fail, never mind. Go right on; try it again; try it somewhere else. Never say quit. Do not say it cannot be done. Failure is a word that should be unknown to all the workers in the Sunday Schools, in the Mutual Improvement Associations, in our Primary Associations, in the quorums of Priesthood, as well as in all the organizations of the Church everywhere. The word "fail" ought to be expunged from our language and our thoughts. We do not fail when we seek to benefit the erring, and they will not listen to us. We will get the reward for all the good we do. We will get the reward for all the good we desire to do, and labor to do, though we fail to accomplish it, for we will be judged according to our works and our intent and purposes. The victim of evil, or sin, the one whom we seek to benefit, but who will not yield to our endeavors to benefit him, may fail, but we who try to uplift him will not fail, if we do not quit.

If we continue to try, failing, as it were, or missing one mark, should not discourage us; but we should fly to another, keep on in the work, keep on doing, patiently, determinedly doing our duty, seeking to accomplish the purpose we have in view.

It is the duty of the Latter-day Saints, the duty of those auxiliary organizations of the Church, all and each of them, to teach to the children that are brought within our influence and care the divinity of the mission of Joseph Smith, the prophet. Do not forget it. Do not let him perish out of your thoughts and minds. Remember that the Lord God raised him to lay the foundations of this work, and the Lord did what has been done through him, and we see the results of it. Men may scoff at Joseph Smith and at his mission, just as they scoffed at the Savior and his mission. They may ridicule and make light of and condemn the mission of the Christ, and yet with all their condemnation, their scoffing, their ridicule, their contempt and murderous persecution of the Saints of former days, God's name, the name of the lowly Nazarene—he that had not where to lay his head, he that was scoffed at, abused, insulted, persecuted and driven into concealment and into exile, time and again, because they sought his life; he that was charged with doing good, by the power of Satan; he that was charged with violating the Sabbath day, because he permitted his disciples to gather ears of corn and eat them on the Sabbath; he that was called a friend of publicans and sinners, he that was called a friend of winebibbers, and all this sort of thing; and at last was crucified, mocked, crowned with thorns, spat upon, smitten and abused until he was lifted upon the cross, as they shouted: "Now, if thou be the Son of God, come down!"—even the thieves crucified with him mocked and ridiculed him, and asked him, if he were Christ to come down and also deliver them—all this happened to Jesus, the Son of God; but what is the result? Look at the so-called Christian world today. Never has there been a name brought to the intelligence of the human race since the foundations of the world that has accomplished so much, that has been revered and honored so much as the name of Jesus Christ—once so hated and persecuted and crucified. The day will come—and it is not far distant, either—when the name of the Prophet Joseph Smith will be coupled with the name of Jesus Christ of Nazareth, the Son of God, as his representative, as his agent whom he chose, ordained and set apart to lay anew the foundations of the Church of God in the world, which is indeed the Church of Jesus Christ, possessing all the powers of the gospel, all the rites and privileges, the authority of the Holy Priesthood, and every principle necessary to fit and qualify both the living and the dead to inherit eternal life, and to attain to exaltation in the kingdom of God. The day will come when you and I will not be the only ones who will believe this, by a great deal; but there will be millions of people, living and dead, who will proclaim this truth. This gospel revealed by the Prophet Joseph is already being preached to the spirits in prison, to those who have passed away from this stage of action into the spirit world without the knowledge of the gospel. Joseph Smith is preaching the gospel to them, so is Hyrum Smith, so is Brigham Young, and so are all the faithful apostles who lived in this dispensation, under the administration of the Prophet Joseph. They are there, having carried with them from here the holy Priesthood which they received under the hands and by the authority of the Prophet Joseph Smith. With that authority, conferred upon them in the flesh, they are preaching the gospel to the spirits in prison, as Christ directed when his body lay in the tomb, and he went to proclaim liberty to the captives, and to open the prison doors to them that were bound. Not only are these engaged in that work, but hundreds and thousands of others. The elders who have died in the mission field have not finished their missions, but they are continuing them in the spirit world. Possibly the Lord saw it necessary or proper to call them hence, as he did. I am not going to question that thought, at least, not dispute it. I leave it in the hands of God, for I believe that all these things will be overruled for good, for the Lord will suffer nothing to go to his people in the world that he will not overrule eventually for their greater good.—*Improvement Era*, October, 1910, Vol. 13, pp. 1053-1061.

CHAPTER IX

PRIESTHOOD

GOD IS AT THE HELM. We are living in a momentous age. The Lord is hastening his work. He is at the helm; there is no mortal man at the helm of this work. It is true, the Lord uses such instruments as will be obedient to his commandments and laws to assist in accomplishing his purposes in the earth. He has chosen those who, at least, have shown a willingness and a disposition to obey him and keep his laws, and who seek to work righteousness and carry out the purposes of the Lord.—Oct. C. R., 1906, pp. 3, 4.

DISTINCTION BETWEEN KEYS OF THE PRIESTHOOD AND PRIESTHOOD. The Priesthood in general is the authority given to man to act for God. Every man ordained to any degree of the Priesthood, has this authority delegated to him.

But it is necessary that every act performed under this authority shall be done at the proper time and place, in the proper way, and after the proper order. The power of directing these labors constitutes the keys of the Priesthood. In their fulness, the keys are held by only one person at a time, the prophet and president of the Church. He may delegate any portion of this power to another, in which case that person holds the keys of that particular labor. Thus, the president of a temple, the president of a stake, the bishop of a ward, the president of a mission, the president of a quorum, each holds the keys of the labors performed in that particular body or locality. His Priesthood is not increased by this special appointment, for a seventy who presides over a mission has no more Priesthood than a seventy who labors under his direction; and the president of an elders' quorum, for example, has no more Priesthood than any member of that quorum. But he holds the power of directing the official labors performed in the mission or the quorum, or in other words, the keys of that division of that work. So it is throughout all the ramifications of the Priesthood—a distinction must be carefully made between the general authority, and the directing of the labors performed by that authority.—Improvement Era, Vol. 4, p. 230, January, 1901.

CONFERRING THE PRIESTHOOD. The revelation in section 107, Doctrine and Covenants, verses 1, 5, 6, 7, 21, clearly points out that the Priesthood is a general authority or qualification, with certain

offices or authorities appended thereto. Consequently the conferring of the Priesthood should precede and accompany ordination to
office, unless it be possessed by previous bestowal and ordination.
Surely a man cannot possess an appendage to the Priesthood without
possessing the Priesthood itself, which he cannot obtain unless it
be authoritatively conferred upon him.

Take, for instance, the office of a deacon: the person ordained
should have the Aaronic Priesthood conferred upon him in connection with his ordination. He cannot receive a portion or fragment
of the Aaronic Priesthood, because that would be acting on the idea
that either or both of the (Melchizedek and Aaronic) Priesthoods
were subject to subdivision, which is contrary to the revelation.

In ordaining those who have not yet received the Aaronic Priesthood, to any office therein, the words of John the Baptist to Joseph
Smith, Jr., and Oliver Cowdery, would be appropriate to immediately
precede the act of ordination. They are:

"Upon you my fellow servants [servant], in the name of Messiah,
I confer the Priesthood of Aaron."

Of course, it would not necessarily follow that these exact words
should be used, but the language should be consistent with the act
of conferring the Aaronic Priesthood.—*Improvement Era*, Vol. 4, p.
394, March, 1901.*

AN AUTHORITATIVE DECLARATION. The Church of Jesus Christ
of Latter-day Saints is no partisan Church. It is not a sect. It is
The Church of Jesus Christ of Latter-day Saints. It is the only one
today existing in the world that can and does legitimately bear the
name of Jesus Christ and his divine authority. I make this declaration in all simplicity and honesty before you and before all the
world, bitter as the truth may seem to those who are opposed and
who have no reason for that opposition. It is nevertheless true and
will remain true until he who has a right to rule among the nations
of the earth and among the individual children of God throughout
the world shall come and take the reins of government and receive
the bride that shall be prepared for the coming of the Bridegroom.

Many of our great writers have recently been querying and
wondering where the divine authority exists today to command in
the name of the Father and of the Son and of the Holy Ghost, so
that it will be in effect and acceptable at the throne of the Eternal
Father. I will announce here and now, presumptuous as it may

*See addenda at close of volume.

seem to be to those who know not the truth, that the divine authority of Almighty God, to speak in the name of the Father and the Son, is here in the midst of these everlasting hills, in the midst of this intermountain region, and it will abide and will continue, for God is its source, and God is the power by which it has been maintained against all opposition in the world up to the present, and by which it will continue to progress and grow and increase on the earth until it shall cover the earth from sea to sea. This is my testimony to you, my brethren and sisters, and I have a fulness of joy and satisfaction in being able to declare this without regard to, or fear of, all the adversaries of the truth.—This declaration was made on the 88th anniversary of the organization of the Church of Jesus Christ of Latter-day Saints, April 6, 1918.—*Improvement Era*, Vol. 21, p. 639.

THE CHURCH NOT MAN-MADE. We believe in God, the Father of our Lord and Savior Jesus Christ, the Maker of heaven and earth, the Father of our spirits. We believe in him without reserve, we accept him in our heart, in our religious faith, in our very being. We know that he loves us, and we accept him as the Father of our spirits and the Father of our Lord and Savior Jesus Christ. We believe in the Lord Jesus and in his divine, saving mission into the world, and in the redemption, the marvelous, glorious redemption, that he wrought for the salvation of men. We believe in him, and this constitutes the foundation of our faith. He is the foundation and chief cornerstone of our religion. We are his by adoption, by being buried with Christ in baptism, by being born of the water and of the spirit anew into the world, through the ordinances of the gospel of Christ, and we are thereby God's children, heirs of God and joint heirs with Jesus Christ through our adoption and faith.

One of our brethren who spoke today gave out the idea that he knew who was to lead the Church. I also know who will lead this Church, and I tell you that it will be no man who will lead the Church of Jesus Christ of Latter-day Saints; I don't care in what time nor in what generation. No man will lead God's people nor his work. God may choose men and make them instruments in his hands for accomplishing his purposes, but the glory and honor and power will be due to the Father, in whom rests the wisdom and the might to lead his people and take care of his Zion. I am not leading the Church of Jesus Christ, nor the Latter-day Saints, and I want this distinctly understood. No man does. Joseph did not do it; Brigham did not do it; neither did John Taylor. Neither did Wilford

Woodruff, nor Lorenzo Snow; and Joseph F. Smith, least of them all, is not leading the Church of Jesus Christ of Latter-day Saints, and will not lead it. They were instruments in God's hands in accomplishing what they did. God did it through them. The honor and glory is due to the Lord and not to them. We are only instruments whom God may choose and use to do his work. All that we can do we should do to strengthen them in the midst of weaknesses, in the great calling to which they are called. But remember that God leads the work. It is his. It is not man's work. If it had been the work of Joseph Smith, or of Brigham Young, or of John Taylor, Wilford Woodruff, or Lorenzo Snow, it would not have endured the tests to which it has been subjected; it would have been brought to naught long ago. But if it had been merely the work of men, it never would have been subjected to such tests, for the whole world has been arrayed against it. If it had been the work of Brigham Young or Joseph Smith, with such determined opposition as it has met with, it would have come to naught. But it was not theirs; it was God's work. Thank God for that. It is the power of God unto salvation, and I want my boys and girls to take my testimony upon this point. And yet, while we give the honor and glory unto the Lord God Almighty for the accomplishment of his purposes, let us not altogether despise the instrument that he chooses to accomplish the work by. We do not worship him; we worship God, and we call upon his holy name, as we have been directed in the gospel, in the name of his Son. We call for mercy in the name of Jesus; we ask for blessings in the name of Jesus. We are baptized in the name of the Father and of the Son and of the Holy Ghost. We are initiated into the Church and Kingdom of God in the name of the Father and of the Son and of the Holy Ghost, and we worship the Father. We seek to obey the Son and follow in his footsteps. He will lead— no man will ever lead—his Church. If the time or condition should ever come to pass that a man, possessing human weaknesses, shall lead the Church, woe be to the Church, for it will then become like the churches of the world, man-made, and man-led, and have no power of God or of life eternal and salvation connected with it, only the wisdom, the judgment and intelligence of man. I pity the world, because this is their condition.

WHAT IS THE PRIESTHOOD? It is nothing more nor less than the power of God delegated to man by which man can act in the earth for the salvation of the human family, in the name of the Father and the Son and the Holy Ghost, and act legitimately; not assuming that authority, nor borrowing it from generations that are dead and gone, but authority that has been given in this day in which we live by ministering angels and spirits from above, direct from the presence of Almighty God, who have come to the earth in our day and restored the Priesthood to the children of men, by which they may baptize for the remission of sins and lay on hands for the reception of the Holy Ghost, and by which they can remit sin, with the sanction and blessing of Almighty God. It is the same power and Priesthood that was committed to the disciples of Christ while he was upon the earth, that whatsoever they should bind on earth should be bound in heaven, and that whatsoever they should loose on earth should be loosed in heaven, and whosoever they blessed should be blessed, and if they cursed, in the spirit of righteousness and meekness before God, God would confirm that curse; but men are not called upon to curse mankind; that is not our mission; it is our mission to preach righteousness to them. It is our business to love and to bless them, and to redeem them from the fall and from the wickedness of the world. This is our mission and our special calling. God will curse and will exercise his judgment in those matters. "Vengeance is mine," saith the Lord, "and I will repay." We are perfectly willing to leave vengeance in the hands of God and let him judge between us and our enemies, and let him reward them according to his own wisdom and mercy.—Oct. C. R., 1904, p. 5.

THE PRIESTHOOD—DEFINITION, PURPOSE AND POWER. What I mean by the Holy Priesthood is that authority which God has delegated to man, by which he may speak the will of God as if the angels were here to speak it themselves; by which men are empowered to bind on earth and it shall be bound in heaven, and to loose on earth and it shall be loosed in heaven; by which the words of man, spoken in the exercise of that power, become the word of the Lord, and the law of God unto the people, scripture, and divine commands. It is therefore not good that the Latter-day Saints and the children of the Latter-day Saints should treat lightly this sacred principle of authority which has been revealed from the heavens in the dispensation in which we live. It is the authority by which the Lord Almighty governs his people, and by which, in time to come, he will govern the nations of the world. It is sacred, and it must be held sacred by the people. It should be honored and respected by them, in whomsoever it is held, and in whomsoever responsibility is placed in the

Church. The young men and women and the people generally should hold this principle and recognize it as something that is sacred, and that cannot be trifled with nor spoken lightly of with impunity. Disregard of this authority leads to darkness and to apostasy, and severance from all the rights and privileges of the house of God; for it is by virtue of this authority that the ordinances of the gospel are performed throughout the world and in every sacred place, and without it they cannot be performed. Those also who hold this authority should honor it in themselves. They should live so as to be worthy of the authority vested in them and worthy of the gifts that have been bestowed upon them.—Oct. C. R., 1901, p. 2.

MISSION OF THE PRIESTHOOD. We can make advancement only upon the principles of eternal truth. In proportion as we become established upon the foundation of these principles which have been revealed from the heavens in the latter days, and determine to accomplish the purposes of the Lord, will we progress, and the Lord will all the more exalt and magnify us before the world and make us to assume our real position and standing in the midst of the earth. We have been looked upon as interlopers, as fanatics, as believers in a false religion; we have been regarded with contempt, and treated despicably; we have been driven from our homes, maligned and spoken evil of everywhere, until the people of the world have come to believe that we are the offscouring of the earth and scarcely fit to live. There are thousands and thousands of innocent people in the world whose minds have become so darkened by the slanderous reports that have gone forth concerning us, that they would feel they were doing God's service to deprive a member of this Church of life, or of liberty, or the pursuit of happiness, if they could do it.

The Lord designs to change this condition of things, and to make us known to the world in our true light—as true worshipers of God, as those who have become the children of God by repentance; and by the law of adoption have become heirs of God and joint heirs with Jesus Christ; and that our mission in this world is to do good, to put down iniquity under our feet, to exalt righteousness, purity, and holiness in the hearts of the people, and to establish in the minds of our children, above all other things, a love for God and his word, that shall be in them as a fountain of light, strength, faith and power, leading them on from childhood to old age, and making them firm believers in the word of the Lord, in the restored gospel and Priesthood, and in the establishment of Zion, no more to be thrown down or given to another people. If there is anything that I desire above another in this world, it is that my children shall become established in this knowledge and faith, so that they can never be turned aside from it.—Oct. C. R., 1901, p. 70.

WHAT ARE THE KEYS OF THE PRIESTHOOD? The Priesthood that we hold is of the greatest importance, because it is the authority and power of God. It is authority from heaven that has been restored to men upon the earth in the latter days, through the ministration of angels from God, who came with authority to bestow this power and this Priesthood upon men.

I say that the Priesthood, which is the agency of our heavenly Father, holds the keys of the ministering of angels. What is a key? It is the right or privilege which belongs to and comes with the Priesthood, to have communication with God. Is not that a key? Most decidedly. We may not enjoy the blessings, or key, very much, but the key is in the Priesthood. It is the right to enjoy the blessing of communication with the heavens, and the privilege and authority to administer in the ordinances of the gospel of Jesus Christ, to preach the gospel of repentance, and of baptism by immersion for the remission of sins. That is a key. You who hold the Priesthood have the key or the authority, the right, the power or privilege to preach the gospel of Jesus Christ, which is the gospel of repentance and of baptism by immersion for the remission of sins—a mighty important thing, I tell you. There isn't a minister of any church upon all of God's footstool today, so far as we know, except in the Church of Jesus Christ of Latter-day Saints, who has the keys or the authority to enjoy the ministration of angels. There isn't one of them that possesses that Priesthood. But here we ordain boys who are scarcely in their teens, some of them, to that Priesthood which holds the keys of the ministering of angels and of the gospel of repentance and baptism by immersion for the remission of sin. There is not a minister anywhere else in the world, I repeat, who possesses these keys, or this Priesthood or power, or that right. Why? Because they have not received the gospel, nor have they received that Priesthood by the laying on of hands by those having authority to confer it.—Improvement Era, Vol 14, December, 1910, p. 176.

SANCTITY OF THE ORDINANCES OF THE PRIESTHOOD. There appears to be, among some of our people, an inadequate conception of the sanctity attending certain of the ordinances of the Holy Priesthood. True, the ministrations of those in authority among us are not attended with the pomp and worldly ceremony that characterize the procedure in other churches so-called, but the fact that the Church of Jesus Christ of Latter-day Saints is in possession of the Priesthood is sufficient to make any and every ordinance administered by due authority within the Church an event of supreme importance. In performing any such ordinance the one who officiates speaks and acts, not of himself and of his personal authority, but by virtue of his ordination and appointment as a representative of the powers of heaven. We do not set apart bishops and other officers in the Church, with the show and ceremony of a gala day, as do certain sectarians, nor do we make the ordinance of baptism a spectacular display; but the simplicity of the order established in the Church of Christ ought rather to add to than take from the sacred character of the several ordinances.

An illustration of the fact that many do not understand the full sanctity of certain ordinances is found in the desire some evince to have them repeated. Until within a few years, it was a very general custom in the Church to allow a repetition of the baptismal rite to adults before they enter the temples. This custom, first established by due authority, and for good cause (see *Articles of Faith*, by Talmage, 144-148) finally came to be regarded by many members of the Church as essential, and indeed, "re-baptism" was generally looked upon, though wrongly, as separate and different from the first ordinance of the gospel—by which alone one may gain entrance to the Church of Christ. But the most hurtful feature of this misunderstanding was the disposition of some to look upon the repeated baptisms as a sure means of securing forgiveness of sins from time to time, and this might easily have led to the thought that one may sin with comparative impunity if he were baptized at frequent intervals. This condition has been changed in the Church, and at the present time only those who, having been admitted to the fold of Christ by baptism, afterwards stray therefrom, or are disfellowshiped or excommunicated by due process of the Church courts, are considered as fit subjects to receive a repetition of the initiatory ordinance. These remarks, it must be understood, have no reference to the baptisms and other ordinances performed in the temples.—*Juvenile Instructor*, Vol. 38, p. 18, January, 1903.

On Church Government. We are governed by law, because we love one another, and are actuated by long-suffering and charity, and good will; and our whole organization is based upon the idea of

self-control; the principle of give and take, and of rather being willing
to suffer wrong than to do wrong. Our message is peace on earth
and good will towards men; love, charity and forgiveness, which
should actuate all associated with the Church of Jesus Christ of
Latter-day Saints. Ours is a Church where law is dominant, but the
law is the law of love. There are rules which should be observed,
and will be observed if we have the spirit of the work in our hearts;
and if we have not the spirit with us, we have only the form of
godliness which is without strength. It is the Spirit which leads us
to the performance of our duties. There are many who know this
gospel to be true, but have not the least particle of the Spirit, and
therefore are found arrayed against it, and take no part with the
people, simply because they have not the Spirit.

The Priesthood after the order of the Son of God is the ruling,
presiding authority in the Church. It is divided into its various
parts—the Melchizedek and the Aaronic—and all the quorums or
councils are organized in the Church, each with special duties and
special callings; not clashing with one another, but all harmonious
and united. In other words, there is no government in the Church
of Jesus Christ separate and apart, above, or outside of the holy
Priesthood or its authority. We have our Relief Societies, Mutual
Improvement Associations, Primary Associations and Sunday Schools,
and we may organize, if we choose, associations for self-protection
and self-help among ourselves, not subject to our enemies, but for
our good and the good of our people, but these organizations are
not quorums or councils of the Priesthood, but are auxiliary to, and
under it; organized by virtue of the holy Priesthood. They are not
outside of, nor above it, nor beyond its reach. They acknowledge
the principle of the Priesthood. Wherever they are they always
exist with the view of accomplishing some good; some soul's salvation,
temporal or spiritual.

When we have a Relief Society, it is thus organized. It has its
president and other officers, for the complete and perfect accomplishment of the purposes of its organization. When it meets it
proceeds as an independent organization, always mindful of the fact
it is such, by virtue of the authority of the holy Priesthood which
God has instituted. If the president of the stake comes into a meeting of the Relief Society, the sisters, through their president, would
at once pay deference to him, would consult and advise with him,
and receive directions from the presiding head. That head is the

bishop of the ward, the president in the stake, the presidency of the Church, in all the Church. The Young Ladies' and Young Men's Associations, the Primary Associations and the Sunday Schools are the same. All are under the same head, and the same rules apply to each.

When the Young Men's and Young Ladies' Associations meet separately, they each have presiding officers, and they take charge and conduct the business. If the bishop comes in to either the Young Men's or Young Ladies' Association, due deference is paid him. But in joint association of the Young Men's and Young Ladies' officers, there are the two organizations; the two boards are represented. Who shall take the initiative? Who shall exercise the presiding function? Is the sister to take the initiative and exercise the presiding function? Why, no! not so, because that is not in accordance with the order of the Priesthood. If the Young Men's officers are there, they hold the Priesthood, and it is their place to take the initiative. If I were the president of a Young Ladies' Association, and we met in joint meeting, I should expect the president of the Young Men's Association to take the initial step, that he would call the meeting to order, etc., because he holds the Priesthood, and should be the head; then he should not forget that the young ladies have an organization, and are entitled to perfect and complete representation in the conjoint meetings, and, under the Priesthood, should be given charge at least half the time. If he is not in his place, then let the young lady preside as she would in her own meeting. The ladies should not be discriminated against, but should have equal chances. There should be no curtailment nor abridgment of these rights, but every opportunity for their exercise should be given. Gallantry would naturally prompt the young men to give even more, maybe, than they take themselves, but they should direct in all these matters, in the spirit of love and kindness.

There never can be and never will be, under God's direction, two equal heads at the same time. That would not be consistent; it would be irrational and unreasonable; contrary to God's will. There is one head, and he is God, the head of all. Next to him stands the man he puts in nomination to stand at the head on the earth, with his associates; and all the other organizations and heads, from him to the last, are subordinate to the first, otherwise there would be discord, disunion and disorganization.

I am tenacious that all should learn the right and power of the

Priesthood, and recognize it; and if they do it, they will not go far astray. It is wrong to sit in judgment upon the presiding officers. Suppose a bishop does wrong, are we to run away to everyone and backbite and slander him, and tell all we know or think we know, in relation to the matter, and spread it about? Is that the way for Saints to do? If we do so we shall breed destruction to the faith of the young, and others. If I have done wrong, you should come right to me with your complaint, tell me what you know, and not say one word to any other soul on earth; but let us sit down together as brethren and make the matter right; confess, ask forgiveness, shake hands and be at peace. Any other course than this will create a nest of evil, and stir up strife among the Saints.—*Improvement Era*, Vol. 6, July, 1903, pp. 704-708.

A BLESSING AND AN EXPLANATION OF THE PRIESTHOOD. The Lord bless you. From the depths of my soul, I bless you; I hold the right, the keys and the authority of the Patriarchal Priesthood in the Church. I have a right to pronounce patriarchal blessings, because I hold the keys and authority to do it. It is given to me and my associates to ordain patriarchs and set them apart to give blessings to the people, to comfort them by promises made in wisdom and the inspiration of the Spirit of God, of the favor and mercies of the Lord that they may be stronger in good works, and their hopes may be realized and their faith increased. And I bless you, my brethren and sisters, in the cause of Zion, with all my soul and by the authority of the Priesthood that I hold. I hold the Priesthood of the apostleship, I hold the high Priesthood which is after the order of the Son of God, which is at the foundation of all Priesthood and is he greatest of all Priesthoods, because the apostle and the high priest and the seventy derive their authority and their privileges from the Priesthood which is after the Son of God. All authority comes out of that high Priesthood.— Oct. C. R., 1916, p. 7.

THE PRIVILEGE OF THE PRIESTHOOD TO BLESS. We have been told of an incident which occurred a few weeks ago, when a bishop's counselor (and therefore a high priest) from a remote settlement, while visiting Salt Lake City, refused to administer to his sister's child who was dangerously sick, for the reason that he was outside his own ward.

This brother must have had a misunderstanding of the authority of his office, or he was over diffident. Whatever the cause, he was not justified in his refusal. His authority to bless in the name of the Lord was not confined to his ward; no elder's opportunity for doing a purely good deed should be confined to a ward nor to any other limit, and when he went into a house and the head of that household made such a request of him it was clearly not only his privilege and right, but his duty to comply. Indeed, we believe that every man holding the Priesthood, in good standing in the Church, who owns a home, is supreme in his own household, and when another brother enters it, and he requests the latter to perform any duty consistent with his calling, the latter should accede to his wishes; and if there should be anything wrong, he who makes the request as the head of the house into which the brother has come, is responsible therefor. If that head of a household asks anything to be done which for the sake of Church discipline, or to fulfil the revelations of the Lord, should be placed on the records of the Church, he should see to it that the necessary details are supplied and recorded.

We further believe that the rights of fatherhood in all faithful, worthy men are paramount, and should be recognized by all other men holding positions or calling in the Priesthood. To make this idea plainer we will say, as an example of our idea, we do not consider it proper in a bishop or other officer to suggest that the son of such a man (the son himself not being the head of a family, but living with his father) be called upon a mission without first consulting the father. The Priesthood was originally exercised in the patriarchal order; those who held it exercised their powers firstly by right of their fatherhood. It is so with the great Elohim. This first and strongest claim on our love, reverence and obedience is based on the fact that he is the Father, the Creator, of all mankind. Without him we are not, and consequently we owe to him existence and all that flows therefrom— all we have and all that we are. Man possessing the holy Priesthood is typical of him. But as men on earth cannot act in God's stead as his representatives without the authority, appointment and ordina- tion naturally follow. No man has the right to take this honor to himself, except he be called of God through the channels that he recognizes and has empowered.

Returning to the thought expressed in our opening paragraph, we recognize that there is a side to the question that must not be lost sight of, as to ignore that view would be to encourage a condition in the midst of the Saints pregnant with confusion. We have found occasionally that men blessed with some peculiar gift of the spirit have exercised it in an unwise—shall we say, improper—manner. For instance: brethren strongly gifted with the power of healing have visited far and near amongst the Saints (to the neglect sometimes of other duties), until it has almost become a business with them, and their visits to the homes of the Saints have assumed somewhat the character of those of a physician, and the people have come to regard the power so manifested as if coming from man, and he himself has sometimes grown to so feel, and not that he was simply an instrument in the hands of God of bringing blessings to their house. This view is exceedingly unfortunate, when indulged in, and is apt to result in the displeasure of the Lord. It has sometimes ended in the brother possessing this gift, if he encouraged such a feeling, losing his power to bless and heal. Departures from the recognized order and discipline of the Church should therefore be discountenanced and discouraged.—*Juvenile Instructor*, Vol. 37, pp. 50, 51, Jan. 15, 1902.

THE PRIESTHOOD GREATER THAN ANY OF ITS OFFICES. There is no office growing out of this Priesthood that is or can be greater than the Priesthood itself. It is from the Priesthood that the office derives its authority and power. No office gives authority to the Priesthood. No office adds to the power of the Priesthood. But all offices in the Church derive their power, their virtue, their authority, from the Priesthood. If our brethren would get this principle thoroughly established in their minds, there would be less misunderstanding in relation to the functions of government in the Church than there is. Today the question is, which is the greater—the high priest or the seventy— the seventy or the high priest? I tell you that neither of them is the greater, and neither of them is the lesser. Their callings lie in different directions, but they are from the same Priesthood. If it were necessary, the seventy, holding the Melchizedek Priesthood, as he does, I say *if it were necessary*, he could ordain a high priest; and if it were necessary for a high priest to ordain a seventy, he could do that? Why? Because both of them hold the Melchizedek Priesthood. Then again, if it were necessary, though I do not expect the necessity will ever arise, and there was no man left on earth holding the Melchizdek Priesthood, except an elder—that elder, by the inspiration of the Spirit of God and by the direction of the Almighty, could proceed, and should proceed, to organize the Church of Jesus Christ in all its perfection, because he holds the Melchizedek Priesthood. But the house of God is a house of order, and while the other officers remain in the Church, we must observe the order of the priesthood,

and we must perform ordinances and ordinations strictly in accordance with that order, as it has been established in the Church through
the instrumentality of the Prophet Joseph Smith and his successors.
—Oct. C. R., 1903, p. 87.

NECESSITY OF ORGANIZATION. The house of God is a house of
order, and not a house of confusion; and it could not be thus, if there
were not those who had authority to preside, to direct, to counsel,
to lead in the affairs of the Church. No house would be a house of
order if it were not properly organized, as the Church of Jesus Christ
of Latter-day Saints is organized. Take away the organization of the
Church and its power would cease. Every part of its organization
is necessary and essential to its perfect existence. Disregard, ignore,
or omit any part, and you start imperfection in the Church; and if we
should continue in that way we would find ourselves like those of old,
being led by error, superstition, ignorance, and by the cunning and
craftiness of men. We would soon leave out here a little and there a
little, here a line and there a precept, until we would become like the
rest of the world, divided, disorganized, confused and without knowledge; without revelation or inspiration, and without Divine authority
or power.—Apr. C. R., 1915, p. 5.

ACCEPTANCE OF THE PRIESTHOOD A SERIOUS MATTER. This makes
a very serious matter of receiving this covenant and this Priesthood;
for those who receive it must, like God himself, abide in it, and must
not fail, and must not be moved out of the way; for those who receive
this oath and covenant and turn away from it, and cease to do righteously and to honor this covenant, and will to abide in sin and repent
not, there is no forgiveness for them, either in this life or in the world
to come. That is the language of this book, and this is doctrine and
truth which was revealed from God to men through the instrumentality of Joseph Smith the prophet. And this word is reliable. It is
God's word, and God's word is truth; and it becomes necessary for
all those who enter into this covenant to understand this word, that
they may indeed abide in it, and may not be turned out of the way.—
Apr. C. R., 1898, p. 65. See Doc. and Cov. 84:33-41; Book of Mormon,
Mosiah 5.

HOW AUTHORITY SHOULD BE ADMINISTERED. No man should
be oppressed. No authority of the Priesthood can be administered
or exerted in any degree of unrighteousness, without offending God.
Therefore, when we deal with men we should not deal with them
with prejudice in our minds against them. We should dismiss preju-

dice, dispel anger from our hearts, and when we try our brethren for membership or fellowship in the Church we should do it dispassionately, charitably, lovingly, kindly, with a view to save and not destroy. That is our business; our business is to save the world, to save mankind; to bring them into harmony with the laws of God and with principles of righteousness and of justice and truth, that they may be saved in the kingdom of our God, and become, eventually, through obedience to the ordinances of the gospel, heirs of God and joint heirs with Jesus Christ. That is our mission.—Apr. C. R., 1913, p. 6.

AUTHORITY GIVES ENDURING POWER. The Church has two characteristics—the temporal and the spiritual, and one is not without the other. We maintain that both are essential and that one without the other is incomplete and ineffectual. Hence, the Lord instituted in the government of the Church two Priesthoods—the lesser or Aaronic, having special charge of the temporal, and the higher or Melchizedek, looking to the spiritual welfare of the people. In all the history of the Church, there has never been a time when considerable attention was not given to temporal affairs, in the gathering places of the Saints, under all the leaders up to the present time as witness the building of Kirtland, the settlement of Missouri, Nauvoo, and the founding of cities and towns in the far west, our present home. The Saints have lived and helped each other to live, have worked out their temporal salvation with zeal and energy, but withal, have neither neglected nor forgotten the spiritual essence of the great work inaugurated by divine order, as witness their temples, and other houses of worship, that have marked their every abiding place.

And so, while we have devoted much time to temporal affairs, it has always been with a view to better our spiritual condition, it being apparent that the temporal, rightly understood, is a great lever by which spiritual progress may be achieved in this earthly sphere of action. Besides, we have come to understand that all we do is indeed spiritual, for before the Father there is no temporal. Hence, in our labors of redeeming the waste places, a strong spiritual vein underlies the outward temporal covering.—Improvement Era, Vol. 8, pp. 620, 623, 1904-5.

MINISTRY SHOULD KNOW ITS DUTIES AND THE USE OF AUTHORITY. Of course it is very necessary that those who preside in the Church should learn thoroughly their duties. There is not a man holding any position of authority in the Church who can perform his duty as he

should in any other spirit than in the spirit of fatherhood and brotherhood toward those over whom he presides. Those who have authority should not be rulers, nor dictators; they should not be arbitrary;
they should gain the hearts, the confidence and love of those over
whom they preside, by kindness and love unfeigned, by gentleness
of spirit, by persuasion, by an example that is above reproach and
above the reach of unjust criticism. In this way, in the kindness
of their hearts, in their love for their people, they lead them in the
path of righteousness, and teach them the way of salvation, by saying
to them, both by precept and example: Follow me, as I follow our
head. This is the duty of those who preside.—Apr. C. R., 1915, p. 5.

How Officers in the Church are Chosen: A Word to
Bishops. They are faithful men chosen by inspiration. The Lord
has given us the way to do these things. He has revealed to us that
it is the duty of the presiding authorities to appoint and call; and then
those whom they choose for any official position in the Church shall
be presented to the body. If the body reject them, they are responsible
for that rejection. They have the right to reject, if they will, or to
receive them and sustain them by their faith and prayers. That is
strictly in accordance with the rule laid down of the Lord. If any
officer in the Church has my sympathy, it is the bishop. If any
officer in the Church deserves credit for patience, for long-suffering,
kindness, charity, and for love unfeigned, it is the bishop who does
his duty. And we feel to sustain in our faith and love, the bishops
and counselors in Zion. We say to the bishoprics of the various
wards: Be united; see eye to eye, even if you have to go down on
your knees before the Lord and humble yourselves until your spirits
will mingle and your hearts will be united one with the other. When
you see the truth, you will see eye to eye, and you will be united.—
Apr. C. R., 1907, p. 4.

Jurisdiction of Quorums of Priesthood. Now then, we have
our high priests' quorums or councils, and we have our seventies'
councils, and our elders, and then we have the councils of the priests,
teachers and deacons of the lesser Priesthood. These councils each
and all in their organized capacity, have jurisdiction over the fellowship of the members of these councils—if the member is an elder, or
if a man has a standing in the seventies' quorum, or in the high
priests' quorum, and he is misbehaving himself, shows a lack of faith,
a lack of reverence for the position he holds in his council, or quorum,
his fellowship in that quorum to which he belongs, or his standing

should be looked after or inquired into, for he is amenable to his quorum for his good standing and fellowship in it. So that we have the check that the Lord has placed upon members of the Church, and when I say members of the Church, I mean me, I mean the apostles, I mean the high priests and the seventies and elders. I mean everybody who is a member of the Church.—Apr. C. R., 1913, p. 6.

JURISDICTION IN STAKES AND WARDS. Now again, the bishoprics, and the presidents of stakes, have exclusive jurisdiction over the membership or the standing of men and women in their wards and in their stakes. I want to state that pretty plain—that is to say, it is not my duty, it is not the duty of the seven presidents of seventies, nor of the council of the twelve apostles, to go into a stake of Zion and try for membership, or for standing in the Church, any member of a stake or ward. We have no business to do it; it belongs to the local authorities, and they have ample authority to deal with the membership in their wards and in their stakes. The bishops may try an elder for misconduct, for un-Christian-like conduct, for apostasy, or for wickedness of any kind that would disqualify him for membership in the Church, and they may pass upon him their judgment that he is unworthy of fellowship in the Church, and they may withdraw from him their fellowship. Then they may refer his case to the presidency and high council, and it will be the duty of the presidency and high council of the stake to deal with him, even to the extent of excommunication from the Church; and there is no remedy for this, only the right of appeal to the Presidency of the Church. If there may be, perchance, any injustice and partiality, lack of information or understanding on the part of the bishopric, which may not be corrected and therefore might be perpetuated by the decision of the high council, and the party aggrieved does not feel that he has had justice dealt out to him, he then has a right, under the laws of the Church, to appeal to the Presidency of the Church, but not otherwise.—Apr. C. R., 1913, p. 5.

DUTIES OF THOSE ENGAGED IN THE MINISTRY. I need not say to my brethren engaged in the ministry that it is expected of them that one and all will attend to the labors and be true to the responsibilities that rest upon them in the discharge of their duties as officers in the Church. We expect that the presidents of the stakes of Zion will be exemplars to the people. We expect them of a truth to be fathers unto those over whom they preside; men of wisdom, of sound judgment, impartial and just, men who will indeed qualify themselves, or who are indeed qualified by their natural endowments and by the inspiration from God which it is their privilege to enjoy, to preside in righteousness and to sit in righteous judgment over all matters brought to their attention, or that may legitimately belong to their office and calling. We anticipate the same fidelity, the same faithfulness, the same intelligent administration of their duties from the bishops and their counselors, and indeed upon these rests perhaps the greatest possible responsibility, for the reason that they are expected by their presidencies to attend to the various interests and needs of their people. It is expected of a bishop to know all the people in his ward, not only those who are faithful members of the Church, diligent in the performance of their duties and prominent by their good acts, but to know those who are cold and indifferent, those who are lukewarm, those who are inclined to err and to make mistakes; and not only these, but it is expected that the bishops, through their aides in their wards, will become acquainted, not only with their members, male and female, but that they will know also the stranger that is within their gates and be prepared to minister solace, comfort, good counsel, wisdom and every other aid possible to be rendered to those who are in need, whether they are of the household of faith or are strangers to the truth. So that there is a great deal expected of the bishops and their counselors and the elders and lesser priesthood in their wards whom they call to their aid in administering to the people both spiritually and temporally, and I want to remark in this connection that it is the duty of these bishops and of the presidencies of the stakes of Zion, together with their high councils, to administer justice and right judgment to every member of their wards and of their stakes. Included in this are the high priests and the seventies and the elders and the apostles and the patriarchs and the presidency of the Church of Jesus Christ of Latter-day Saints. No man who is a member of the Church of Jesus Christ of Latter-day Saints, or who has a standing in the Church as a member, is exempt from his responsibilities as a member and his allegiance to the bishop of the ward in which he dwells. I am as much bound to acknowledge my bishop as a member of the ward in which I dwell, as the humblest and latest member of the Church. No man, who claims to be a member of the Church in good standing, can rise above or become independent of the authority that the Lord Almighty has established in his Church. This watch-care of the people, of their right living, of their fidelity to their covenants and to the gospel of Jesus Christ, belongs to the presidents of stakes and their counselors and the high councils, or members of the high councils, to the bishop and his counselors and the teachers of his ward.—Apr. C. R., 1913, p. 4.

THE PURPOSE AND THE DUTY OF THE CHURCH: QUALITIES OF LEADERS. The Lord bless you. I see before me the leaders of the Church, the presiding spirits in the capacity of presidents of stakes, counselors to presidents of stakes, high councilors, bishops and their counselors, and those who are engaged in our educational institutions and in other responsible positions in the Church. I honor you all. I love you and your integrity to the cause of Zion. It is the kingdom of God or nothing, so far as I am concerned. I cut no figure personally in this work, and I am nothing except in the humble effort to do my duty as the Lord gives me the ability to do it. But it is the kingdom of God. What I mean by the kingdom of God is the organization of the Church of Jesus Christ of Latter-day Saints, of which Jesus Christ is the king and the head; not as an organization in any wise menacing or jeopardizing the liberties or rights of the people throughout the world, but as an organization calculated to lift up and ameliorate the condition of mankind; to make bad men good, if it is possible for them to repent of their sins, and to make good men better. That is the object and purpose of the Church, that is what it is accomplishing in the world. And it is very strict in regard to these matters. Drunkards, whoremongers, liars, thieves, those who betray the confidence of their fellowmen, those who are unworthy of credence—such, when their character becomes known, are disfellowshiped from the Church, and are not permitted to have a standing in it, if we know it. It is true that there are none of us but have our imperfections and shortcomings. Perfection dwells not with mortal man. We all have our weaknesses. But when a man abandons the truth, virtue, his love for the gospel and for the people of God, and becomes an open, avowed enemy, it becomes the duty of the Church to sever him from the Church, and the Church would be recreant to its duty if it did not sever him from communion, cut him off, and let him go where he pleases. We would do wrong if we hung on to and tried to nurture such evil creatures in our midst, no matter what the relationship may be that exists between us and them. Therefore, I say again, the Church of Jesus Christ stands for virtue, honor, truth, purity of life, and good will to all mankind. It stands for God the eternal Father, and for Jesus Christ, whom the Father sent into the world, and whom to know is life eternal. This is what the Church stands for, and it cannot tolerate abomination, crime and

wickedness, on the part of those who may claim to have some connection with it. We must sever ourselves from them, and let them go.
Not that we want to hurt them. We do not want to hurt anybody.
We never have, and we do not intend to, hurt anybody.   But
we do not intend to be hurt by those who are seeking our destruction, if we can help it. It is our right to protect ourselves.—Apr. C. R.,
1906, pp. 7, 8.

LEADERS MUST BE COURAGEOUS. One of the highest qualities of
all true leadership is a high standard of courage. When we speak of
courage and leadership we are using terms that stand for the quality
of life by which men determine consciously the proper course to
pursue and stand with fidelity to their convictions. There has never
been a time in the Church when its leaders were not required to be
courageous men; not alone courageous in the sense that they were
able to meet physical dangers, but also in the sense that they were
steadfast and true to a clear and upright conviction.

Leaders of the Church, then, should be men not easily discouraged, not without hope, and not given to forebodings of all sorts of evils
to come. Above all things the leaders of the people should never dis-
seminate a spirit of gloom in the hearts of the people. If men standing
in high places sometimes feel the weight and anxiety of momentous
times, they should be all the firmer and all the more resolute in those
convictions which come from a God-fearing conscience and pure lives
Men in their private lives should feel the necessity of extending encouragement to the people by their own hopeful and cheerful intercourse with them, as they do by their utterances in public places. It is
a matter of the greatest importance that the people be educated to
appreciate and cultivate the bright side of life rather than to permit
its darkness and shadows to hover over them.

In order to successfully overcome anxieties in reference to questions that require time for their solution, an absolute faith and confidence in God and in the triumph of his work are essential.

The most momentous questions and the greatest dangers to personal happiness are not always met and solved within oneself, and if
men cannot courageously meet the difficulties, and obstacles of their
own individual lives and natures, how are they to meet successfully
those public questions in which the welfare and happiness of the
public are concerned? Men, then, who are called to leadership should
be alarmed at the possession of a disposition filled with forebodings
and misgivings and doubts and constant wonderments.   Clouds,

threatening storms, frequently rise in the horizon of life and pass by as speedily as they came, so the problems and difficulties and dangers that beset us are not always met and solved, nor overcome by our individual effort nor by our efforts collectively.

It is not discreditable to a man to say, "I don't know," to questions whose solution lies wholly within some divine purpose whose end it is not given man clearly to foresee. It is, however, unfortunate when men and women allow such questions, questions which time and patience alone can solve, to discourage them and to defeat their own efforts in the accomplishment of their chosen lives and professions. In leaders undue impatience and a gloomy mind are almost unpardonable, and it sometimes takes almost as much courage to wait as to act. It is to be hoped, then, that the leaders of God's people, and the people themselves, will not feel that they must have at once a solution of every question that arises to disturb the even tenor of their way.—*Juvenile Instructor*, Vol. 38, p. 339, 1903.

DUTIES OF OFFICERS OF THE CHURCH. The Lord here especially demands of the men who stand at the head of this Church, and who are responsible for the guidance and direction of the people of God, that they shall see to it that the law of God is kept. It is our duty to do this.—*Oct. C. R.*, 1899, p. 41.

TRUTH WILL UNITE US: WORDS TO CHURCH OFFICERS. The truth will never divide councils of the priesthood. It will never divide presidents from their counselors, nor counselors from their presidents, nor members of the Church from one another, nor from the Church. The truth will unite us and cement us together. It will make us strong, for it is a foundation that cannot be destroyed. Therefore, when bishops and their counselors do not see eye to eye, or when presidents and their counselors have any difference whatever in their sentiments or in their policy, it is their duty to get together, to go before the Lord together and humble themselves before him until they get revelation from the Lord and see the truth alike, that they may go before their people unitedly. It is the duty of the presidents of stakes and high councilors to meet often, to pray together, to counsel together, to learn each other's spirit, to understand each other, and unite together, that there may be no dissension nor division among them. The same with the bishops and their counselors. The same may be said of the councils of the priesthood from first to last. Let them get together and become united in their understanding of what

is right, just and true, and then go as one man to the accomplishment
of the purpose they have in view.—*April C. R.*, 1907, pp. 4, 5.

OFFICERS TO SET THE EXAMPLE. The Lord will make a record also
and out of that shall the whole world be judged. And you men bearing the holy Priesthood—you apostles, presidents, bishops, and high
priests in Zion—will be called upon to be the judges of the people.
Therefore, it is expected that you shall set the standard for them to
attain to, and see that they shall live according to the spirit of the
gospel, do their duty, and keep the commandments of the Lord.
You shall make a record of their acts. You shall record when they
are baptized, when they are confirmed, and when they receive the
Holy Ghost by the laying on of hands. You shall record when they
come to Zion, their membership in the Church. You shall record
whether they attend to their duties as priests, teachers or deacons,
as elders, seventies or high priests. You shall write their works, as
the Lord says here. You shall record their tithings and give them
credit for that which they do; and the Lord will determine the difference between the credit which they make for themselves and the
credit which they should make. The Lord will judge between us in
that respect; but we shall judge the people, first requiring them to do
their duty. In order to do that, those who stand at the head must
set the example. They must walk in the right path, and invite the
people to follow them. They should not seek to drive the people;
they should not seek to become rulers; but they should be brethren
and leaders of the people.—*Apr. C. R.*, 1901, p. 72.

DUTY OF THE HOLY PRIESTHOOD. It is the duty of this vast body
of men holding the holy Priesthood, which is after the order of the Son
of God, to exert their influence and exercise their power for good
among the people of Israel and the people of the world. It is their
bounden duty to preach and to work righteousness, both at home and
abroad.—*Oct. C. R.*, 1901, p. 83.

HOW TO VOTE ON CHURCH PROPOSITIONS. We desire that the
brethren and sisters will all feel the responsibility of expressing their
feelings in relation to the propositions that may be put before you.
We do not want any man or woman who is a member of the Church
to violate their conscience. Of course, we are not asking apostates
or non-members of the Church to vote on the authorities of the
Church. We only ask for members of the Church in good standing
to vote on the propositions that shall be put before you, and we

would like all to vote as they feel, whether for or against.—Oct. C. R., 1902, p. 83.

ORDER OF VOTING FOR OFFICERS OF THE CHURCH. The Presidency of the Church will first express their mind, thus indicating, at least in some degree, the mind of the Spirit and the suggestions from the head. Then the proposition will be submitted to the apostles, for them to show their willingness or otherwise to sustain the action of the First Presidency. It will then go to the patriarchs, and they will have the privilege of showing whether they will sustain the action that has been taken; then to the presidents of stakes and counselors and the high councilors; then to the high priests (that office in the Melchizedek Priesthood which holds the keys of presidency); next the traveling elders—the seventies—will be called to express their feelings; and then the elders; then the bishoprics of the Church and the lesser Priesthood, and after them the whole congregation. All the members of the Church present will have the privilege of expressing their views in relation to the matters which shall be proposed, by a rising vote and by the uplifted hand.—Oct. C.R., 1901, p. 73.

OFFICERS DEPENDENT ON VOICE OF PEOPLE. It is well understood that we meet together in general conference twice a year for the purpose of presenting the names of those who have been chosen as presiding officers in the Church, and it is understood that those who occupy these positions are dependent upon the voice of the people for the continuance of the authority, the rights and privileges they exercise. The female members of this Church have the same privilege of voting to sustain their presiding officers as the male members of the Church, and the vote of a sister in good standing counts in every way equal with the vote of a brother.—Apr. C. R., 1904, p. 73.

NEARLY ALL MALE MEMBERS HOLD THE PRIESTHOOD; RESPONSIBILITY. We want the people to understand, and we would like the world to understand, the great fact that it is not the prominent leaders of the Church of Jesus Christ of Latter-day Saints, that wield all the influence among the people of this Church. We want it understood that we have fewer lay members in this Church, in proportion to the number of our membership, than you will find in any other church upon the globe. Nearly every man in the Church of Jesus Christ of Latter-day Saints holds the Melchizedek or the Aaronic Priesthood, and may act in an official capacity by authority of that Priesthood whenever called upon to do so. They are priests and kings, if you please, unto God in righteousness. Out of this vast body of priests we call and ordain or set apart our presidents of stakes, our counselors, our high councilors, our bishops and their counselors, our seventies, our high priests, and our elders, upon whom rests the responsibility of proclaiming the gospel of eternal truth to all the world, and upon whom also rests the great and glorious responsibility of maintaining the dignity, the honor and the sacredness of that calling and Priesthood. So that nearly every male person in the Church, who has reached the years of accountability, is supposed to be, in his sphere, a pillar in Zion, a defender of the faith, an exemplar, a man of righteousness, truth and soberness, a man of virtue and of honor, a good citizen of the state in which he lives, and a staunch and loyal citizen of the great country that we are proud to call our home.—Apr. C. R., 1903, p. 73.

MANY HOLD THE MELCHIZEDEK PRIESTHOOD. Although we may enjoy a little advantage over the rest of the congregation, for my part I could stay here a week longer to hear the testimonies of my brethren, and to give to the world an opportunity to see and know that the Priesthood in the Church of Jesus Christ of Latter-day Saints is not confined to one man, nor to three men, nor to fifteen men, but that there are thousands of men in Zion who hold the Melchizedek Priesthood, which is after the order of the Son of God, and who possess keys of authority and power to minister for life and salvation among the people of the world. I would like to give the world an opportunity to see what we are, to hear what we know, and to understand what our business is, and what we intend to do, by the help of the Lord—Oct. C. R., 1903, p. 73.

PRIESTHOOD QUORUMS' RESPONSIBILITIES. We expect to see the day, if we live long enough (and if some of us do not live long enough to see it, there are others who will), when every council of the Priesthood in the Church of Jesus Christ of Latter-day Saints will understand its duty; will assume its own responsbility, will magnify its calling, and fill its place in the Church, to the uttermost, according to the intelligence and ability possessed by it. When that day shall come, there will not be so much necessity for work that is now being done by the auxiliary organizations, because it will be done by the regular quorums of the Priesthood. The Lord designed and comprehended it from the beginning, and he has made provision in the Church whereby every need may be met and satisfied through the regular organizations of the Priesthood. It has truly been said that the Church is perfectly organized. The only trouble is that these organizations are not fully alive to the obligations that rest upon them. When they become thoroughly awakened to the requirements made of them, they will fulfil their duties more faithfully, and the work of the Lord will be all the stronger and more powerful and influential in the world.—*Apr. C. R.*, 1906, p. 3.

WHAT IS PRIESTHOOD? Honor that power and authority which we call the Holy Priesthood, which is after the order of the Son of God, and which has been conferred upon man by God himself. Honor that Priesthood. What is that Priesthood? It is nothing more and nothing less than divine authority committed unto man from God. That is the principle that we should honor. We hold the keys of that authority and Priesthood ourselves; it has been conferred upon the great masses of the Latter-day Saints. It has, indeed, I may say, been bestowed upon many who were not worthy to receive it and who have not magnified it, and who have brought disgrace upon themselves and upon the Priesthood which was conferred upon them. The Priesthood of the Son of God cannot be exercised in any degree of unrighteousness; neither will its power, its virtue and authority abide with him who is corrupt, who is treacherous in his soul toward God and toward his fellowmen. It will not abide in force and power with him who does not honor it in his life by complying with the requirements of heaven.—*Apr. C. R.*, 1904, p. 3.

WHERE AND HOW COUNSEL SHOULD BE SOUGHT. The attention of the young men in the Church is called to the need of conforming to the order of the Church in matters of difficulty that may arise between brethren, and members and officers, and also in other things where counsel is sought.

The youth of Zion should remember that the foundation principle in settling difficulties lies in the persons themselves who are in difficulty making the adjustments and settlements. If those who vary cannot adjust their differences, it is infinitely more difficult, if not impossible, for a third or fourth party to create harmony between them. In any event, such outside parties can only aid the contending persons to come to an understanding.

But, in case it is necessary to call in the priesthood as a third party, there is a proper order in which this should be done. If no conclusion can be arrived at, in a difficulty or difference between two members of the Church, the ward teachers should be called to assist; failing then, appeal may be made to the bishop, then to the high council of the stake, and only after the difficulty has been tried before that body should the matter ever come before the general presiding quorum of the Church. It is wrong to disregard any of these authorized steps, or authorities.

This matter is generally understood in cases of difficulty, but does not seem to be so well understood in what may be termed smaller, but nevertheless quite as weighty subjects. We often find instances where the counsel and advice and judgment of the priesthood next in order is entirely overlooked, or completely disregarded. Men go to the president of the stake for counsel when in reality, they should consult their teachers or bishop; and often come to the First Presidency, apostles or seventies, when the president of their stake has never been spoken to. This is wrong, and not at all in compliance with the order of the Church. The priesthood of the ward should never be overlooked in any case where the stake authorities are consulted; nor should the stake authorities be disregarded, that the counsel of the general authorities may be obtained. Such a course of disregarding the proper local officers is neither in conformity with the Church instructions and organization, nor conducive to good order. It creates confusion. Every officer in the Church has been placed in his position to magnify the same, to be a guardian and counselor of the people. All should be consulted and respected in their positions, and never overlooked in their places.

In this way only can prevail that harmony and unity which are characteristic of the Church of Christ. The responsibility also of this great work is thus placed upon the laboring priesthood, who share it with the general authorities; and thus likewise, the perfection, strength and power of Church organization shine forth with clearer lustre.—*Improvement Era*, Vol. 5, p. 230; Jan. 1902.

PARENTS SHOULD BE CONSULTED. One of the first duties that a young man owes in the world is his duty to his father and mother. The commandment which God gave early in the history of the Israelites: "Honor thy father and thy mother," was accompanied with a promise that holds good to this day; namely: "That thy days may be long upon the land which the Lord thy God giveth thee."

With obedience naturally comes that respect and consideration for his parents that should characterize a noble youth. They stand as the head of the family, the patriarch, the mother, the rulers; and no child should fail to consult them and obtain counsel from them throughout his whole career under the parental roof.

This feeling should be respected by the Church. Hence, officers who desire to use the services of a young man in any capacity for the business of the Church, should not fail to consult the father before the call is made. We have instances where young men have even been called to fulfil important missions; their names having been suggested to the Church by bishops of wards, or by presidents of quorums, without the father having been consulted whatever. The parents have been entirely overlooked. This is neither desirable nor right, nor is it in conformity with the order of the Church, or the laws that God instituted from the early times. The Church is patriarchal in its character and nature, and it is highly proper and right that the head of the family, the father, should be consulted by officers in all things that pertain to the calling of his children to any of the duties in the Church. No one understands as well as the father, the conditions that surround the family, and what is best for his children; his wishes should therefore be consulted and respected.

Our elders would justly think it wrong to baptize a wife without the consent of her husband, and children without the consent of the parents. So also, it is improper for any officer in the Church to call the children in any family, as long as they are under the care and keeping of the parents, to receive any ordination, or to perform any calling in the Church, without first consulting the parents.

The family organization lies at the basis of all true government, and too much stress cannot be placed upon the importance of the government in the family being as perfect as possible, nor upon the fact that in all instances respect therefor should be upheld.

Young men should be scrupulously careful to impress upon their minds the necessity of consulting with father and mother in all that pertains to their actions in life. Respect and veneration for parents should be inculcated into the hearts of the young people of the Church—father and mother to be respected, their wishes to be regarded—and in the heart of every child should be implanted this thought of esteem and consideration for parents which characterized the families of the ancient patriarchs.

God is at the head of the human race; we look up to him as the Father of all. We cannot please him more than by regarding and respecting and honoring our fathers and our mothers, who are the means of our existence here upon the earth.

I desire, therefore, to impress upon the officers of the Church the necessity of consulting fathers in all things that pertain to the calling of their sons to the Priesthood, and to the labors of the

Church, that the respect and veneration which children should show for parents may not be disturbed by the Church, nor overstepped by its officers. In this way harmony and good will are made to prevail; and the sanction of the families and the family life, on which the government of the Church is based and perpetuated, will thus be added to the calls of the holy Priesthood, insuring unity, strength and power in its every action.—*Improvement Era*, Vol. 5, p. 307, Feb., 1902.

PROPER USE OF TITLES OF THE PRIESTHOOD. There is also another point in this connection to which attention may profitably be drawn. It is the too frequent use in the ordinary conversation of the Saints of the titles "Prophet, Seer and Revelator," "Apostles," etc. These titles are too sacred to be used indiscriminately in our common talk. There are occasions when they are quite proper and in place, but in our every-day conversations it is sufficient honor to address any brother holding the Melchizedek Priesthood as elder. The term elder is a general one, applying to all those who hold the higher Priesthood, whether they be apostles, patriarchs, high priests or seventies; and to address a brother as Apostle So-and-So, or Patriarch Such-a-One, in the common talk of business, and the like, is using titles too sacred to be in place on such occasions. It, in a lesser degree, partakes of the character of that evil of which we are so often warned —the too frequent use of the name of that Holy Being whom we worship, and of his Son, our Redeemer. To avoid this evil the Saints in ancient days called the holy Priesthood after the great high priest Melchizedek, while the royal and correct title is, "The Priesthood after the order of the Son of God." The use of all these titles continuously and indiscriminately savors somewhat of blasphemy, and is not pleasing to our heavenly Father.—*Juvenile Instructor*, Vol. 38, p. 20; Jan. 1, 1903.

ALL OFFICERS OF THE PRIESTHOOD NECESSARY AND SHOULD BE RESPECTED. I believe it to be the duty of the Church to recognize and acknowledge every man who holds an official position in it, in his sphere and in his calling. I hold to the doctrine that the duty of a teacher is as sacred as the duty of an apostle, in the sphere in which he is called to act, and that every member of the Church is as much in duty bound to honor the teacher who visits him in his home, as he is to honor the office and counsel of the presiding quorum of the Church. They all have the Priesthood; they are all acting in their callings, and they are all essential in their places, because the Lord has appointed them and set them in his Church. We cannot ignore them; or, if we do, the sin will be upon our heads.—*Oct. C. R.,* 1902, p. 86.

CHECKS UPON CHURCH MEMBERS. I say that when these members of the Church are in error or doing wrong, we have the check on them in the first place in the wards; bishops look after them; then their quorums to which they belong have jurisdiction and they are required to look after them, too, and then after the quorums look after them the presidencies of the stakes look after them and see that they are helped; that they are strengthened; that they are admonished; that they are warned, and that they are applauded when they do their duties and keep the commandments of the Lord. So the Lord has placed a great many checks upon the members of the Church with a view to teaching them right principles, to help them to do right, to live right and to be pure and clean from the sins of the world, that the body of the Church may be perfected, that it may be free from disease, from all contagious evils, just as the body of the man Jesus Christ is free from all taint, evil and sin. So God has placed these safeguards in the Church, from the deacons to the apostles, and to the presidency of the Church, with a view of persuading men and women to keep themselves pure and unspotted from the world and to help them to be faithful to their covenants entered into with one another and with their God.—*Apr. C. R.,* 1913, pp. 6, 7.

THE PRIESTHOOD SHOULD KNOW SECTION 107 OF THE DOCTRINE AND COVENANTS. I now say to the brethren holding the Priesthood —the high priests, the seventies, the elders and the lesser priesthood— magnify your callings; study the scriptures; read the 107th section of the Doctrine and Covenants on Priesthood; learn that revelation, which was given through the Prophet Joseph Smith, and live by its precepts and doctrine, and you will gain power and intelligence to straighten out many kinks that have heretofore existed in your minds, and to clear up many doubts and uncertainties in relation to the rights of the Priesthood. God gave that word to us. It is in force today in the Church and in the world, and it contains instruction to the priesthood and the people in relation to their duties, which every elder should know.—*Oct. C. R.,* 1902, p. 88.

WHO IS FIT TO PRESIDE? Every man should be willing to be presided over; and he is not fit to preside over others until he can submit sufficiently to the presidency of his brethren.—*Improvement Era,* Vol. 21, p. 105.

OBLIGATIONS OF THE PRIESTHOOD. Think what it means to hold keys of authority which—if exercised in wisdom and in righteousness—are bound to be respected by the Father, the Son, and the Holy Ghost! Do you honor this Priesthood? Do you respect the office and honor the key of authority that you possess in the Melchizedek Priesthood, which is after the order of the Son of God? Will you, who hold this Priesthood, profane the name of Deity? Would you be riotous, and eat and drink with the drunken, with the unbelieving and with the profane? Would you, holding that Priesthood, forget your prayers, and fail to remember the Giver of all good? Would you, holding that Priesthood, and possessing the right and authority from God to administer in the name of the Father, and of the Son, and of the Holy Ghost, violate the confidence and the love of God, the hope and desire of the Father of all of us? For, in bestowing that key and blessing upon you, he desires and expects you to magnify your calling. Would you, as an elder in the Church of Jesus Christ, dishonor your wife or your children? Would you desert the mother of your children, the wife of your bosom, the gift of God to you, which is more precious than life itself? For without the woman the man is not perfect in the Lord, no more than the woman is perfect without the man. Will you honor the Sabbath day and keep it holy? Will you observe the law of tithing and all the other requirements of the gospel? Will you carry with you at all times the spirit of prayer and the desire to do good? Will you teach your children the principles of life and salvation so that when they are eight years old they will desire baptism, of their own accord?—*Improvement Era*, Vol. 21, December, 1917, pp. 105-6.

HOW HONOR FOR THOSE WHO BEAR THE PRIESTHOOD IS BEGOTTEN. If you will honor the holy Priesthood in yourself first, you will honor it in those who preside over you, and those who administer in the various callings, throughout the Church.—*Improvement Era*, Vol. 21, December, 1917, p. 106.

ORDER OF THE PRIESTHOOD. An officer in the Church in one of the stakes of Zion asks whether a man's Priesthood may be taken from him in any other way than by excommunication. In other words, can a man's ordination to the Priesthood be made null and void, and he still be permitted to retain his membership in the Church; or must he be excommunicated before the Priesthood can be taken from him? The reply must be that only by excommunication in the appointed way can the Priesthood be taken from a person. We know of no other means provided by which a man who has had the Priesthood conferred upon him can be deprived of it. The constituted authorities of the Church may, however, after proper authorized hearing, decide that a man has forfeited his right to act in the Priesthood, and for this cause he may be silenced, and his certificate of ordination be taken from him, and thus have his right suspended to officiate in the ordinances of the gospel, or to exercise the Priesthood which has been conferred upon him. Then, if he persists in exercising his Priesthood and former calling, he may be taken to account for the insubordination and excommunicated.

Several examples have occurred in the history of the Church where men through transgression, duly proved and decided upon by the constituted authorities have been stopped from acting in the Priesthood, which is just as effectual as taking away their Priesthood would be, if it were possible; but this has taken no ordination from them, and if in such cases the transgressors should repent and make complete and satisfactory restitution, they would still hold the same Priesthood which they held before they were silenced, or stopped from acting. A person once ordained a bishop, an elder, or high priest, continues to hold the office. A bishop is still a bishop though he may remove to another ward, or for other reasons temporarily lose his calling. But in case he is wanted to act in a new office, or place, and the proper authorities call him to act, it is not necessary to re-ordain him a bishop; he would only need to be set apart for his new calling. So with other officers in the Priesthood, once having received the Priesthood, it cannot be taken from them, except by transgression so serious that they must forfeit their standing in the Church. But, as stated, their right to officiate, may be suspended or stopped. The Lord can take away the power and efficacy of their ordinations, and will do so if they transgress. No endowments or blessings in the house of the Lord, no patriarchal blessings, no ordination to the Priesthood, can be taken away, once given. To prevent a person for cause from exercising the rights and privileges of acting in the offices of the Priesthood, may be and has been done, and the person so silenced still remains a member of the Church, but this does not take away from him any Priesthood that he held.—*Improvement Era*, Vol. 11, 465-6.

PRIESTHOOD MEMBERSHIP ROLLS. First.—Each quorum should have one roll only and every person holding the Priesthood should be enrolled in the quorum having jurisdiction in the ward where his

Church membership is recorded. The practice of keeping a supplemental or inactive roll is not approved.

Second.—Recommends from one quorum to another are not required. The present arrangement for admitting members in the quorum is already published as follows:

"The certificate of ordination should be carefully preserved by the person ordained; and, whenever necessary, it should be presented to the proper authority as an evidence of his ordination. Upon this evidence he should be admitted to membership in the usual manner by the quorum having jurisdiction in the ward or stake where he resides, provided he has been accepted as a member of the ward. If he does not possess a certificate of ordination, and the recommend upon which he is received in the ward names his Priesthood and ordination, it should be accepted as evidence that he holds that office, provided there is no evidence to the contrary and provided he has been admitted as a member of the ward in full fellowship."

Third.—When a person holding the Priesthood removes from one ward to another, and is accepted as a member of the ward into which he moves, it becomes the duty of the ward clerk to notify the president of the quorum of the arrival of this person. The new member should present his certificate of ordination as evidence that he holds the Priesthood, and upon that certificate he should be presented for admission to membership in the quorum to which members of that ward holding the same Priesthood belong. It is the duty of the ward clerk to report at the next ward weekly Priesthood meeting the arrival of any person holding the Priesthood, and every such newly arrived member should be enrolled in the proper class, whether he has attended a class meeting or not.

Fourth.—When a member holding the Priesthood becomes a member of the ward, the proper quorum officer having jurisdiction should look after him and see that he becomes enrolled in the quorum.

Fifth.—It is the duty of the secretary of a High Priests' or Elders' quorum to prepare certificates of ordination, and to have them signed by the proper officers, presented to the ward clerk to be entered upon the ward record, and then delivered to the persons in whose favor they are issued. Seventies' certificates of ordination are issued by the First Council of Seventy. When a person is ordained a Seventy, by any other person than a member of the First Council, the proper quorum officers should immediately notify the First Council of Seventy, requesting a certificate of ordination to be mailed or delivered to the quorum officer, and after it has been entered on the quorum record and the ward record it should be delivered to the person in whose favor it is issued.

Sixth.—When a quorum withdraws its fellowship from one of its members, a report of the action of the quorum should be sent to the bishop of the ward.—*Improvement Era*, Vol. 19, pp. 752-753.

ALL SHOULD EXERCISE THEIR AUTHORITY. A deacon in the Church should exercise the authority of that calling in the Priesthood, and honor that position as sincerely and faithfully as a high priest or an apostle should his calling, feeling that he bears a portion of the responsibility of the kingdom of God in the world, in common with all his brethren. Every man should feel in his heart the necessity of doing his part in the great latter-day work. All should seek to be instrumental in rolling it forth. More especially is it the duty of every one who possesses any portion of the authority of the holy Priesthood to magnify and honor that calling, and nowhere can we begin to do so to better advantage than right here, within ourselves and when we have cleaned the inside of the platter, cleansed our own hearts, corrected our own lives, fixed our minds upon doing our whole duty toward God and man, we will be prepared to wield an influence for good in the family circle, in society, and in all the walks of life.— *Deseret Weekly News*, Vol. 24, p. 708.

THE LEADERS OF ISRAEL. These mighty men who sit before this stand clothed with power from Almighty God, are not self-called. They have not been chosen by man. They have not chosen themselves, but they have been called by the power of the Almighty to stand in high places in the Church of Jesus Christ of Latter-day Saints, as presidents, as fathers to the people, as counselors, as judges, and as leaders, walking in the way that the people of God should follow them into all truth and into the possession of greater light, greater power and wisdom and understanding. God bless you, my brethren. And while you stand united, as you have stood in the past, and as you have manifested your union here during this conference, so God will magnify you before your flocks and in the midst of your people, and will increase your power and your strength to do good and to accomplish his purposes, until you shall be satisfied with your labors and have exceeding great joy therein; and your people will rise up and call you blessed, they will pray for you and sustain you by their faith and good works.—Oct. C. R., 1905, p. 94.

A TESTIMONY OF JOSEPH SMITH AND HIS SUCCESSORS. I bear my

testimony to you and to the world, that Joseph Smith was raised up by the power of God to lay the foundations of this great latter-day work, to reveal the fulness of the gospel to the world in this dispensation, to restore the Priesthood of God to the world, by which men may act in the name of the Father, and of the Son, and of the Holy Ghost, and it will be accepted of God; it will be by his authority. I bear my testimony to it; I know that it is true.

I bear my testimony to the divine authority of those who have succeeded the Prophet Joseph Smith in the presidency of this Church. They were men of God. I knew them; I was intimately associated with them, and as one man may know another, through the intimate knowledge that he possesses of him, so I can bear testimony to the integrity, to the honor, to the purity of life, to the intelligence, and to the divinity of the mission and calling of Brigham, of John, of Wilford, and of Lorenzo. They were inspired of God to fill the mission to which they were called, and I know it. I thank God for that testimony and for the Spirit that prompts me and impels me towards these men, toward their mission, toward this people, toward my God and my Redeemer. I thank the Lord for it, and I pray earnestly that it may never depart from me—worlds without end.— Oct. C. R., 1910, pp. 4, 5.

GOODNESS OF THE LEADERS OF THE CHURCH. I have served from my youth up along with such men as Brigham Young, Heber C. Kimball, Willard Richards, George A. Smith, Jedediah M. Grant, Daniel H. Wells, John Taylor, George Q. Cannon, and Wilford Woodruff and his associates, and Lorenzo Snow and his associates, the members of the twelve apostles, the seventies, and the high priests in the Church of Jesus Christ of Latter-day Saints for more than sixty years; and, that my word may be heard by every stranger within the sound of my voice, I want to testify to you that better men than these have never lived within the range of my acquaintance. I can so testify because I was familiar with these men, grew up from babyhood with them, associated with them in council, in prayer and supplication, and in travel from settlement to settlement through our country here, and in crossing the plains. I have heard them in private and in public, and I bear my testimony to you that they were men of God, true men, pure men, God's noblemen; virtuous men who never were either tempted to do evil or tempted others to do wrong, men whose examples and whose lives were above reproach, except in what corrupt, wicked or ignorant men supposed they saw and presumed to denounce as wrong in them.—*April C. R., 1917, p. 6.*

DIVINE MISSIONS OF PRESIDENTS OF CHURCH. I testify to you, as I know and feel that I live and move and have my being, that the Lord raised up the boy prophet, Joseph Smith, and endowed him with divine authority, and taught him those things which were necessary for him to know that he might have power to lay the foundation of God's Church and kingdom in the earth. Joseph Smith was true to the covenants that he made with the Lord, true to his mission, and the Lord enabled him to accomplish his work, even to the sealing of his testimony with his shed blood. His testimony is now, and has been, in force among the children of men as verily as the blood of Jesus Christ is in force and a binding testimony upon all the world, and it has been from the day it was shed until now, and will continue until the winding up scene.

I bear my testimony to you my brethren and sisters, of the divinity of the mission and work that was accomplished by President Brigham Young and his associates in fleeing from the wrath that threatened in Illinois and Missouri and other places, into these peaceful vales, which was done by the will of heaven and by the guiding power of the Holy Spirit, President Young and the pioneers were enabled to lay the foundation of a commonwealth, the equal of which is scarcely to be found within the borders of our glorious land; and it was done, not by the wisdom of Brother Brigham, nor of Brother Heber C. Kimball, nor of any of their associates, grand men as they were, true servants of the living God as they were, faithful and true to their callings, grand as was their integrity to the cause of Zion—but back of them, behind them, above them and below, and all around them, was the power of God, leading and directing them, and thus consummating his purposes through their instrumentality. We give the honor to our Father in heaven and we also honor and bless the names of those great and good men whom the Lord chose to accomplish his purposes, and through whom he did accomplish his purpose without failure.

I bear my testimony to the integrity of John Taylor as one of the purest men I ever knew in my life, a man clean from head to foot, clean in body and clean in spirit, free from every vulgar thing, so common among the children of men. I know whereof I speak, for I was with him day and night, month after month, year after year, and I bear my testimony of his integrity. He was a martyr with the Prophet Joseph Smith. He suffered more than death with Joseph and Hyrum, and the Lord preserved him and honored him by calling him to take charge of his work for a season in the earth, thus exalting him to that most glorious and most responsible position that any man could be called to occupy in the Church of Jesus Christ of Latter-day Saints.

I bear my testimony to the faithfulness of Wilford Woodruff, a man in whom there was no guile, a man honest to the core, a man susceptible to the impressions of the Spirit of the Lord, a man guided by inspiration in the performance of his duty, far more than by any gift of wisdom or of judgment that he himself possessed.

I bear my testimony to the work that was accomplished by President Lorenzo Snow, although it was brief, yet some of the things which were left for him to do were absolutely necessary in order to relieve his successor and others that may arise in time to come, from mistakes and errors that had crept in before.

As to the present administration of the gospel and of the work of the Lord I have nothing to say. Let the work speak for itself, let the people and the voice of the people of the Church of Jesus Christ of Latter-day Saints say what is being done by the Lord, let it not be said by me nor by my counselors and my associates. The Lord forbid that I should ever imagine for one moment that we are of any great importance in this great work of the Lord. Others may be raised up, and the Lord can shape their minds. He can qualify them and can humble them, if need be, to fit them for the duties and responsibilities that may be required at their hands. I believe that Zion is prospering, and that as far as our spiritual life, our spiritual growth, and our faith are concerned, as well as our temporal condition, we are prosperous, and all is well in Zion today.—Oct. C. R., 1917.

THE PRESIDENTS OF THE CHURCH HAVE BEEN INSPIRED. I knew President Brigham Young, and I bear my testimony to the world that not only was Joseph Smith inspired of God and raised up to lay the foundations of this great latter-day work, but Brigham Young was raised up and sustained by the power of Almighty God to continue the mission of Joseph and to accomplish the work that he laid out during his lifetime. I have been connected with President John Taylor, and I testify that he also was a man of God. He was indeed God's mouthpiece. He was a martyr with the Prophet Joseph, for his blood was shed with Joseph's and Hyrum's, but the Lord preserved his life that he might fulfill the mission unto which he was called to preside over the Church for a season. I was intimately acquainted with President Wilford Woodruff, and I bear testimony to the mission of that gracious, good man. I have also been more or less intimate with President Snow, and I bear testimony that his work was of God.—Oct. C. R., (Special), 1901, p. 96.

WHEN TO ORGANIZE THE FIRST PRESIDENCY. After the death of the Prophet Joseph Smith, the Twelve Apostles continued as the presiding quorum of the Church for a number of years; but finally they were moved upon by the Holy Spirit to reorganize the First Presidency of the Church, with Brigham Young as president, and Heber C. Kimball and Willard Richards as his counselors. In reality this organization might have been effected within twenty-four hours after the death of the Prophet Joseph Smith, but their action was delayed, until they found by experience that the exercise of the functions of presidency and the government of the Church by twelve men at the head, was not only cumbersome but was not fully perfect in the order of the Holy Priesthood as established by the Lord. On the death of President Brigham Young, President John Taylor followed in some measure the example of his predecessor and it was some time before the Presidency of the Church was organized. The Presidency was finally organized, however, with John Taylor as president, and George Q. Cannon and myself as counselors.

At the death of President Taylor, President Woodruff hesitated and he allowed a little time to pass before the Presidency was again organized. When at last he became convinced that it was his duty, and necessary in order to carry out the purposes of the Lord, he organized the Presidency of the Church. At that time he gave a solemn injunction to his fellow servants in relation to this. He desired it understood that in all future times, when the President of the Church should die, and thereby the First Presidency become disorganized it would be the duty of the proper authorities of the Church to proceed at once, without any unnecessary delay, to reorganize the First Presidency.

As soon as the news reached us of the death of President Woodruff, who was in California at the time, President Lorenzo Snow said to me, "it will be our duty to proceed as soon as possible to reorganize the Presidency of the Church." As you are aware, after the burial of the remains of President Woodruff, he proceeded at once to do this. In this connection I may tell you another thing. President Snow said to me, "you will live to be the President of the

Church of Jesus Christ of Latter-day Saints, and when that time comes you should proceed at once and reorganize the Presidency of the Church." This was his counsel to me, and the same was given to the Twelve Apostles. In accordance with the principle and with the injunction of President Snow, within one week after his death the apostles proceeded to designate the new Presidency of the Church and we did this strictly in accordance with the pattern that the Lord has established in his Church, unanimously.

I desire to read a little from the revelation in relation to the order of the Holy Priesthood, that you may understand our views concerning adhering as nearly as we can to the holy order of government that has been established by revelation through the Prophet Joseph Smith in the Dispensation of the Fulness of Times. We cannot deny the fact that the Lord has effected one of the most perfect organizations, in this Church, that ever existed upon the earth. I do not know of any more perfect organization than exists in the Church of Jesus Christ of Latter-day Saints today. We have not always carried out strictly the order of the Priesthood; we have varied from it to some extent; but we hope in due time that, by the promptings of the Holy Spirit, we will be led into the exact channel and course that the Lord has marked out for us to pursue and adhere strictly to the order that he has established. I will read from a revelation that was given to the Prophet Joseph Smith, at Nauvoo, Hancock County, Illionis, January 19, 1841, which stands as the law of the Church in relation to the presentations of the authorities of the Holy Priesthood as they were established in the Church, and from which I feel that we have no right to depart.—Oct. C. R., (Special), 1901, pp. 70, 71. Doctrine and Covenants 124:123-145.

FIRST PRESIDENCY NOT NECESSARILY APOSTLES. We have the council of the first presidency consisting of three presiding high priests who are called of God and appointed to preside over the Church and over the Priesthood of God, and I want to say here that it does not follow and never has followed that the members of the First Presidency of the Church are necessarily to be ordained apostles. They hold by virtue of their rights as Presidents of the Church all the keys and all the authority that pertains to the Melchizedek Priesthood, which comprehends and comprises all of the appendages to that Priesthood, the lesser Priesthood, and all the offices in the Priesthood from first to last and from the least to the greatest.—April C. R., 1912.

THE PRIESTHOOD AND ITS OFFICES. In the Era for February, it

was stated that several persons who had acted as counselors in the First Presidency had never been ordained apostles. Several correspondents have objected to the statement that Sidney Rigdon, Jedediah M. Grant, Daniel H. Wells, John R. Winder, and others were not ordained apostles. We still maintain, upon lack of convincing evidence to the contrary, that none of these brethren was ever ordained an apostle. We do know positively that John R. Winder, Sidney Rigdon, William Law and Hyrum Smith, all of whom were members in the First Presidency of the Church, were never ordained apostles. But, be that as it may, however, the main point we wish to make is this, that it was not necessary that they should be so ordained apostles in order to hold the position of counselor in the First Presidency. The leading fact to be remembered is that the Priesthood is greater than any of its offices; and that any man holding the Melchizedek Priesthood may, by virtue of its possession, perform any ordinance pertaining thereto, or connected therewith, when called upon to do so by one holding the proper authority, which proper authority is vested in the President of the Church, or in any whom he may designate. Every officer in the Church is under his direction, and he is directed of God. He is also selected of the Lord to be the head of the Church, and so becomes, when the Priesthood of the Church (which includes its officers and its members), shall have so accepted and upheld him. (Doctrine and Covenants, section 107:22.) No man can justly presume to have authority to preside, merely by virtue of his Priesthood as is the case with Joseph Smith of the reorganized church, for in addition, he must be chosen and accepted by the Church. The reverse was the case with him. Such action was repudiated by the Twelve, the quorum in authority after the martyrdom, and by the whole Church. An office in the Priesthood is a calling, like apostles, high priest, seventy, elder, and derives all its authority from the Priesthood; these officers hold different callings, but the same Priesthood.

The apostolic office in its very nature, is a proselyting office. When an apostle presides, he, like the high priest, the seventy, the elder, or the bishop, presides because of the High Priesthood which has been conferred upon him; and furthermore because he has been called upon so to do by the acknowledged head of the Church. (Doctrine and Covenants, section 107:23-33.) And so with the high priest who has been called to officiate in the First Presidency, in which case he is "accounted equal" with the President of the Church in holding the keys of the Presidency (section 90:6) as long as the President remains. When he dies, the calling of his counselors ends, and the responsibility of Presidency falls upon the quorum of Twelve Apostles, because they hold the Holy Melchizedek Priesthood and are the next quorum in authority. (Doctrine and Covenants, section 107:24.) It is not the apostleship (Doctrine and Covenants section 107), but the Priesthood and the calling by proper authority which enables any person to preside. Every man holding the Holy Melchizedek Priesthood may act in any capacity and do all things that such Priesthood holds, provided he is called upon by proper authority to so officiate; but he would have no right to depart from the limitations of his office, unless he is specially called upon by one whose calling, from those over him up to the head, would clearly authorize him to give such instructions. It is always to be presumed, also, that order will be observed, and that the servants of the Lord will not depart from that order, and call upon men to do things which the law of the Priesthood and the nature of their office do not authorize, unless there is special occasion for it. The Lord says that all things are governed by law. (See Doctrine and Covenants, section 88:42.) It is not consistent, for instance, to imagine that the Lord would call upon a deacon to baptize.

Witness the calling, on February 14, 1835, of David Whitmer and Martin Harris, both high priests, by the Prophet Joseph, in conformity with prior revelation from God (See Doctrine and Covenants, section 18) to "search out the Twelve." They chose the Twelve, ordained and set them apart for their exalted callings, because they were called upon by the prophet of God who had been instructed of the Lord, and also because these men held the necessary authority of the Priesthood, which authority was exercised, in this case as it should be in all cases, upon proper calling. The Doctrine and Covenants makes it very clear that while each officer in the Church has a right to officiate in his own standing, "the Melchizedek Priesthood holds the right of presidency, and has power and authority over all the offices in the Church in all ages of the world, to administer in spiritual things." (Doctrine and Covenants, section 107:8.)

Further, in the same revelation verses 65 and 66, we are told:

"Wherefore it must needs be that one be appointed of the High Priesthood to preside over the Priesthood, and he shall be called President of the High Priesthood of the Church:

"Or in other words, the Presiding High Priest over the High Priesthood of the Church."

It is well to remember that the term "High Priesthood," as frequently used, has reference to the Melchizedek Priesthood, in contradistinction to the "lesser," or Aaronic Priesthood.—*Improvement Era*, Vol. 5, p. 549, May, 1902.

AUTHORITY OF THE PRESIDENT OF THE CHURCH. I have the right to bless. I hold the keys of the Melchizedek Priesthood and of the office and power of patriarch. It is my right to bless; for all the keys and authority and power pertaining to the government of the Church and to the Melchizedek and Aaronic Priesthood are centered in the presiding officer of the Church. There is no business nor office, within the Church, that the President of the Church may not fill, and may not do, if it is necessary, or if it is required of him to do it. He holds the office of patriarch; he holds the office of high priest and of apostle, of seventy, of elder, of bishop and of priest, teacher and deacon in the Church; all these belong to the Presidency of the Church of Jesus Christ of Latter-day Saints, and they can officiate in any and in all of these callings when occasion requires.—Oct. C. R., 1915, p. 7.

RELATION OF MEMBERS OF FIRST PRESIDENCY. I desire to make another remark or two before we close our conference. I will call your attention to the fact that the Lord in the beginning of this work revealed that there should be three high priests to preside over the High Priesthood of his Church and over the whole Church. (Doctrine and Covenants 107:22, 64, 65, 66, 67, 91 and 92.) He conferred upon them all the authority necessary to preside over all the affairs of the Church. They hold the keys of the house of God and of the ordinances of the gospel, and of every blessing which has been restored to the earth in this dispensation. This authority is vested in a presidency of three high priests. They are three presidents. The Lord himself so calls them. (Doctrine and Covenants section 107:29.) But there is one presiding president, and his counselors are presidents also. I propose that my counselors and fellow presidents in the First Presidency shall share with me in the responsibility of every act which I shall perform in this capacity. I do not propose to take the reins in my own hands to do as I please; but I propose to do as my brethren and I agree upon, and as the Spirit of the Lord manifests to us. I have always held, and do hold, and trust I always shall hold, that it is wrong for one man to exercise all the authority and power of presidency in the Church of Jesus Christ of Latter-day Saints. I dare not assume such a responsibility, and I will not, so long as I can have men like these (pointing to Presidents Winder and Lund) to stand by and counsel with me in the labors we have to perform, and in doing all those things that shall tend to the peace, advancement and happiness of the people of God and the building up of Zion. If at any time my brethren of the apostleship shall see in me a disposition to depart from this principle, or a forgetfulness on my part of this covenant that I make today before this body of Priesthood, I ask them in the name of my Father, that they will come to me, as my brethren, as counselors in the Priesthood, as watchmen on the towers of Zion, and remind me of this covenant and promise which I make to the body of the Church in general conference assembled at this time. The Lord never did intend that one man should have all power, and for that reason he has placed in his Church, presidents, apostles, high priests, seventies, elders and the various officers of the lesser Priesthood, all of which are essential in their order and place according to the authority bestowed on them. The Lord never did anything that was not essential or that was superfluous. There is a use for every branch of the Priesthood that he has established in his Church. We want every man to learn his duty, and we expect every man will do his duty as faithfully as he knows how, and carry off his portion of the responsiblity of building up Zion in the latter days.

I felt like I wanted to say that much to these my brethren who bear the holy Priesthood—men who wield influence for the salvation of souls, who set good examples before the people among whom they dwell, who teach them the right way, admonish them from sin, lead them in the path of duty, and enable them to stand firm and steadfast in the faith of the gospel, wherewith they have been made free from sin and from the grasp of Satan. God bless all Israel, is my prayer, in the name of Jesus. Amen.—Oct. C. R. (Special), 1901, p. 82.

DUTIES OF APOSTLES. The duty of the Twelve Apostles of the Church is to preach the gospel to the world, to send it to the inhabitants of the earth and to bear testimony of Jesus Christ the Son of God, as living witnesses of his divine mission. That is their special calling and they are always under the direction of the Presidency of the Church of Jesus Christ of Latter-day Saints when that presidency is intact, and there is never at the same time two equal heads in the Church—never. The Lord never ordained any such thing, nor designed it. There is always a head in the Church, and if the Presidency of the Church are removed by death or other cause, then the next head of the Church is the Twelve Apostles, until a presidency is again organized of three presiding high priests who have the right to hold the office of First Presidency over the Church; and, according to the doctrine laid down by President Wilford Woodruff, who saw the necessity for it, and that of President Lorenzo Snow, if the president should die, his counselors are then released from that presidency, and it is the duty of the Twelve Apostles to proceed at once, in the manner that has been pointed out, to see that the First Presidency is reorganized, so that there may be no deficiency in the working and order of the Priesthood in the Church.—*April C. R., 1913, pp. 4, 5.*

TESTIMONY OF THE APOSTLES. For instance these twelve disciples of Christ are supposed to be eye and ear witnesses of the divine mission of Jesus Christ. It is not permissible for them to say, I believe, simply; I have accepted it simply because I believe it. Read the revelation; the Lord informs us they must *know*, they must get the knowledge for themselves. It must be with them as if they had seen with their eyes and heard with their ears and they know the truth. That is their mission, to testify of Jesus Christ and him crucified and risen from the dead and clothed now with almighty power at the right hand of God, the Savior of the world. That is their mission, and their duty, and that is the doctrine and the truth that it is their duty to preach to the world and see that it is preached to the world. Where they can not go themselves they are to have the help of others called to their assistance, the seventies first, also the elders and the high priests. Those who hold the Melchizedek Pristhood, who are not otherwise appointed, are under their direction to preach the gospel to the world and to declare the truth—that Jesus is the Christ and that Joseph is a prophet of God, and was authorized and qualified to lay the foundation of the kingdom of God. And when I say kingdom of God I mean what I say. Christ is the King —not man. No man is king of the kingdom of God; God is the King of it, and we acknowledge him and him only as Sovereign of his Kingdom.—*April C. R., 1916, p. 6.* (Doctrine and Covenants 18:26-33.)

THE PRESIDING BISHOPRIC. Before we get through with the conference, we expect to hear some reports from the Presiding Bishopric, who are the temporal custodians of the means of the Church, and whose duty it is to account for the receipt and disbursement of these funds; and you will be surprised, perhaps, to learn how generally and universally, in the Church, the means gathered from the tithes of the people are disposed of for the benefit of all the people—and not a few.—*April C. R.*, 1912, p. 6.

WHEN TO SUBMIT QUESTIONS TO THE GENERAL AUTHORITIES. If you have a question to ask, or some problem that you are not sure you are able to solve, I would suggest to you that you figure it out yourselves and reach the very best conclusion that you can of the matter; and then, if you are still not quite satisfied with it, and you cannot get sufficient of the Spirit of the Lord to reveal to you the absolute truth, as to whether you are right or wrong, just submit to us your conclusion, and we think we can answer that a good deal easier and quicker than we can solve your questions in the way they are generally put to us.—*April C. R.*, 1910, p. 45.

NO NEED TO POINT OUT DEFECTS OF CHURCH LEADERS. I do not think it is my right or prerogative to point out the supposed defects of the Prophet Joseph Smith, or Brigham Young, or any other of the leaders of the Church. Let the Lord God Almighty judge them and speak for or against them as it may seem to him good—but not me; it is not for me, my brethren, to do this. Our enemies may have taken advantage of us, in times gone by, because of unwise things that may have been said. Some of us may now give to the world the same opportunity to speak evil against us, because of that which we say, which should not be spoken at all.—*Oct. C. R.*, 1909, pp. 124, 125.

HELP THE GENERAL AUTHORITIES. The general authorities of the Church will be presented possibly tomorrow, and if not then, the next day. We desire the brethren and sisters who come to the conference to come with their hearts full of the spirit of wisdom and of truth, and if you discern in us any lack of wisdom or of judgment, any failure in the performance of our duty, we desire that those who have superior experience and knowledge, and greater intelligence, will do us the honor and favor of coming to us individually and letting us know wherein we come short. We will give a thousand errors, if we can find them, or if they exist in us—any moment, for one truth.—*April C. R.*, 1908, p. 8.

TEMPORAL SUPPORT OF GENERAL AUTHORITIES. There is not one of the general authorities in the Church who draws one dollar from the tithes of the people for his own use. Well, you may say, how do they live? I will give you the key: The Church helped to support in its infancy the sugar industry in this country, and it has some means invested in that enterprise. The Church helped to establish the Z. C. M. I., and it has a little interest in that, and in some other institutions which pay dividends. In other words, tithing funds were invested in these institutions, which give employment to many, for which the Trustee-in-Trust holds stock certificates, which are worth more today than what was given for them; and the dividends from these investments more than pay for the support of the general authorities of the Church. So we do not use one dollar of your tithing.—Apr. C. R., 1907, pp. 7, 8.

A Blessing Upon Stake Presidencies and Other Officers. May God bless the presidents of the stakes of Zion and their counselors, and all the officers of the Church of Jesus Christ of Latter-day Saints. May he help them to be pure, holy, honest, upright men, after God's own heart, free from the sins of the world, broadminded, full of the love of truth, charity, the spirit of forgiveness, mercy and kindness, that they may be as fathers indeed in the midst of the people, and not tyrants. You, my brethren, are not called to be masters; you are called to be servants. Let those who would be great among you be the servants of all. Let us follow in the footsteps of our Master, the Lord Jesus Christ. He alone is the perfect example for mankind. He is the only infallible rule and law, way and door into everlasting life. Let us follow the Son of God. Make him our exemplar, and our guide. Imitate him. Do his work. Become like unto him, as far as it lies within our powers to become like him that was perfect and without sin.—Apr. C. R., 1907, p. 118. (Doc. and Cov. 18:21-25.)

Counsel of Stake Presidents and Bishops. Above all things let me say to the presidents of stakes and counselors and presidents of missions, and to the bishops and their counselors—let me say to you all, live exemplary lives, so that you can each say to the people: "Come and follow me, follow my example, obey my precepts; be in union with me, and follow Christ."—Oct. C. R., 1906, p. 8.

Duties of Stake Presidents. I want to say to these presidents of stakes who are present: you have my confidence, you have my love. I pray for you every day of my life, and I trust that you remember me and my brethren in your prayers. We understand the responsibilities that rest upon you in the discharge of your duties. You are fathers to the people; that great responsibility rests upon you; your labors are manifold and sometimes very difficult. We realize

the burdens that you have to bear, the patience that you have to
exercise and exhibit in the discharge of your duty, in order that you
may avoid giving offense, and that you may reconcile the people, over
whom you preside, to that which is right without using drastic
measures. We understand this, and you have our sympathy, our
fellowship, our love, and what strength you may derive from our
faith and prayers that you may preside in righteousness over your
different stakes of Zion, and that your brethren associated with you
may be united with you, and that you may pull together in that which
is right and proper for the upbuilding of Zion and the defense of the
people of God.—Oct. C. R., 1905, p. 8.

DUTY OF HIGH COUNCILS. The duty of the high councils of
the Church, when they are called to act upon questions involving
the membership or standing of members of the Church, is to find
out the truth, the facts, and then judge according to the truth and
the facts that are brought to their understanding, always tempered
with mercy, love, and kindness, and with the spirit in their souls to
save and not to destroy; our aim should be to build up, and not to tear
down. Our calling is to convey the spirit of love, truth, peace and
good will to mankind throughout the world; that war may cease;
that strife may come to an end, and that peace may prevail.—Apr.
C. R., 1915, p. 5.

DUTIES OF PATRIARCHS. We have a number of patriarchs in the
Church whose duty it is to bestow blessings upon the heads of those
who seek blessings at their hands. They are fathers. They hold the
evangelical office in the Church. It is their business and right to
bestow blessings upon the people, to make promises unto them in the
name of the Lord, as it may be given them by the inspiration of the
Holy Spirit, to comfort them in the hours of sorrow and trouble, to
strengthen their faith by the promises that shall be made to them
through the Spirit of God, and to be fathers indeed of the people,
leading them into all truth.—Oct. C. R., 1904, p. 4.

DUTIES OF HIGH PRIESTS. In addition to these organizations we
have in each stake of Zion an organization called the high priests'
quorum, to which all high priests of the Church belong, including
the presidency and the high councilors of the stake, and also the
bishops and their counselors, all the patriarchs, and all others who
have been ordained to the office of high priest in the Church, which
office is the office of presidency in the Melchizedek Priesthood, not
that every man who holds the office of high priest is a president.

Only he who is called, appointed and set apart to preside among the high priests holds the presiding authority and office.—Oct. C. R., 1904, p. 3.

DUTIES OF HIGH PRIESTS' QUORUMS. The high priests' quorums should have their regular meetings. They should meet together as often as circumstances will permit or as necessity requires, and grow and unite together. They should establish their schools of instruction and enlightenment; for it is the duty of the high priests' quorums to teach the principles of government, of union, of advancement and of growth in the kingdom of God. They are indeed the fathers of the people at large. In our high priests' quorum are numbered the presidents of stakes and their counselors, bishops and counselors, patriarchs, and all that have been ordained to the office of high priest in the Melchizedek Priesthood. All such belong to the high priests' quorum. They come under its supervision, and they should have a lively union with it, not a dead connection. They should be united with the quorum in such a way that they give it all the force that they can impart for good. They should give it their individual influence, their hearty support, their confidence, and the benefit of their advice and counsel. They should not pull apart, nor be disinterested in these matters.—Apr. C. R., 1907, p. 5.

DUTY OF HIGH PRIESTS. Every man who holds the office of high priest in the Church, or has been ordained a high priest, whether he is called to active position in the Church or not—inasmuch as he has been ordained a high priest, should feel that he is obliged—that it is his bounden duty, to set an example before the old and young worthy of emulation, and to place himself in a position to be a teacher of righteousness, not only by precept but more particularly by example—giving to the younger ones the benefit of the experience of age, and thus becoming individually a power in the midst of the community in which he dwells. Every man who has light should let that light shine, that those who see it may glorify their Father which is in heaven, and honor him who possesses the light and who causes it to shine forth for the benefit of others. In a local capacity, there is no body of priesthood in the Church who should excel, or who are expected to excel, those who are called to bear the office of high priest in the Church. From among those who hold this office are chosen the presidents of stakes and their counselors, and the high councils of the stakes of Zion, and from this office are chosen the bishops, and the bishops' counselors in every ward in Zion; and heretofore, of this office are those who have been called to take charge of our stake Mutual Improvement organizations. Those holding this office are, as a rule, men of advanced years, and varied experience, men who have filled missions abroad, who have preached the gospel to the nations of the earth, and who have had experience not only abroad but at home. Their experience and wisdom is the ripened fruit of years of labor in the Church, and they should exercise that wisdom for the benefit of all with whom they are associated.—Apr. C. R., 1908, pp. 5, 6.

PURPOSE AND DUTIES OF SEVENTIES. The seventies are called to be assistants to the twelve apostles; indeed they are apostles of the Lord Jesus Christ, subject to the direction of the Twelve, and it is their duty to respond to the call of the Twelve, under the direction of the First Presidency of the Church, to preach the gospel to every creature, to every tongue and people under the heavens, to whom they may be sent. Hence they should understand the gospel, and they should not be wholly dependent upon our auxiliary organizations for instruction, neither should they be wholly dependent upon the missionary classes in our Church schools for their knowledge of the gospel, and for their qualifications to preach that gospel to the world. They should take up the study of the gospel, the study of the scriptures and the history of the dealings of God with the people of the earth, in their own quorums, and make those quorums schools of learning and instruction, wherein they may qualify themselves for every labor and duty that may be required at their hands.—Apr. C. R., 1907, pp. 5, 6.

DUTY OF SEVENTIES. The Seventies have no responsibility of presiding. It is not the calling or duty of their office to preside. They are traveling elders, and they are to preach the gospel to the world, under the direction of the twelve apostles, who constitute the traveling high council of the Church, and who are special witnesses of Jesus Christ to all the world.—Oct. C. R., 1901, p. 72.

DUTIES OF SEVENTIES. We have also in the Church, today, I am informed, 146 quorums of seventy. These constitute a body of elders of somewhere in the neighborhood of 10,000 men, whose special duty it is to respond to the call of the apostles to preach the gospel, without purse or scrip, to all the nations of the earth. They are minute men. It is expected that they will be ready, whenever they are called, to go out in the world, or to go out to the various organizations of the Church to fulfil missions and to perform such duties as shall be required of them, in order that the work of the Lord and the work of the ministry may be upheld and sustained and carried on in the Church and throughout the world.—Oct. C. R., 1904, p. 3.

SEVENTIES' QUORUMS TO BE REPLENISHED FROM ELDERS' QUORUMS. Gather in from the elders' quorums those who have proved themselves worthy, and who have gained experience, and make seventies of them, so that the quorum of the seventies may be replenished; and the aged ones, whose physical condition will not permit them any longer to do missionary duty in the world, let them be ordained high priests and patriarchs, to bless the people and to minister at home. Gather in the strong, the vigorous, the young, the able-bodied, who have the spirit of the gospel in their hearts, to fill up the ranks of the seventies, that we may have ministers to preach the gospel to the world. They are needed. We cannot now meet the demand.—Oct. C. R., 1905, p. 96.

ELDERS TO PROCLAIM GOSPEL. I believe that the elders of Israel, and the officers of the Church, should devote themselves to the proclamation of the gospel of life everlasting, and that they should not dwell or seek to dwell upon trivial and nonsensical things, or upon personal conduct or extraneous affairs. I think they should be dignified and sincere in their spirit and utterances. I think they should be moved by the spirit of truth and of the inspiration of the gospel, and consider that it is their mission to bear record of Jesus Christ, of Joseph Smith, and of the divinity of the great latter-day work, the foundations of which Joseph Smith was instrumental in the hands of God in establishing in the latter days. I believe if our brethren will devote their thought, their minds and efforts in this direction, that they will please the Lord, they will satisfy the Saints, and they will fulfil the object of their mission better than they can possibly do by criticizing themselves or others, or dwelling on the faults and failings of men.—Oct. C. R., 1909, p. 124.

DUTIES OF ELDERS. I am not prepared to state how many elders we have in the Church; but they are very numerous. It is the duty of this body of men to be standing ministers at home; to be ready at the call of the presiding officers of the Church and the stakes, to labor in the ministry at home, and to officiate in any calling that may be required of them, whether it be to work in the temples, or to labor in the ministry at home, or whether it be to go out into the world,

along with the seventies, to preach the gospel to the world.—Oct.
C. R., 1904, p. 4.

AUTHORITY OF THE BISHOPS AND OTHER PRESIDING OFFICERS.
A bishop is the presiding officer of his ward, and where the bishop is
in the ward, his counselors and those who are members of his ward
are subject to his presidency. He cannot yield it up. He cannot give
it to another; or, if he does, he violates one of the sacred principles
of the government of the priesthood. He may direct his counselors,
the first or the second, to do his will, to carry out his wishes, to
execute his desires, or his commands; but in so doing the counselor
does not act as the bishop, but he acts under the direction of the
presiding authority. He does not act independently of the bishop,
but subordinate to the bishop, and is subject entirely to the bishop's
direction. This principle prevails, or should prevail, in the Sunday
school organization of the Church. We can commission and appoint;
that is, those who preside can call upon their aids for assistance, they
can direct them to accomplish labors, but in every instance when they
do, it is by and with and under the consent of the presiding authority,
and by his advice, but not independently. Our missions have not
always been organized strictly according to the pattern that the Lord
has given. In a great many instances the presiding elder has been
the presiding officer of the mission.

But in recent years, in many instances, it has been deemed wise,
not only to have a presiding elder in the mission, but also assistants
to the president, or counselors, that they may render him such assistance and counsel as he may need. In all these things the presiding
officer is the head, should be regarded in his place, and his place should
be held sacred in the minds of his associates. And no man possessing
a correct understanding of the spirit of the gospel and of the authority
and law of the Holy Priesthood will attempt for a moment to run
before his file leader or to do anything that is not strictly in harmony
with his wish and the authority that belongs to him. The moment
a man in a subordinate position begins to usurp the authority of his
leader, that moment he is out of his place, and proves by his conduct
that he does not comprehend his duty, that he is not acting in the
line of his calling, and is a dangerous character. He will set bad
examples, he will mislead, he will lead others into error, having fallen
into error himself; indeed, he is in error the moment he acts contrary
to and independent of the direction of his presiding officer; and if
he continues in that course he will go astray entirely, and those who

follow him will follow him astray. We all understand that principle, I think, and I would like to see my brethren and sisters who are connected with the Sunday school work observe it strictly, but in the true spirit; not with any kind of stiff formality or set ways, but in the true spirit of presidency, lovingly subject to divine authority, the authority that God has instituted that we may emulate, the example of the Son himself, who came to earth, and while he possessed majestic power to heal the sick, to restore sight to the blind, hearing to the deaf, and bring the dead to life, and to accomplish wonderful things, walking upon the waves, stilling the storms, casting out devils, and multiplying the loaves and fishes, by which he fed the multitudes of people, yet in accomplishing all this he declared, over and over again, this great principle, that he came not to do his own will, but the will of him that sent him, recognizing in every feature of his message and ministry in the world that God was at the head, and that he did nothing of himself, but only that which the Father sent him to do. Thus he was acting under the authority of his president or file leader—of him who sent him and commissioned him to accomplish the work he was sent to do. Let us follow that spirit and example and adopt that principle in our lives, then we shall never have presiding elders and officers in the Church at logger-heads with each other, contending with each other, and at cross purposes. They will always be one. They will see eye to eye, they will understand better the principles of divine government, the principles of the gospel and the promptings of the Holy Spirit.—Oct. C. R., 1905 (Sunday School), pp. 109, 110.

DUTIES OF BISHOPS. It is expected that the bishop of a ward with his counselors will understand the necessities of every member of his ward. Then they have as assistants and helpers a large corps of elders, and priests, teachers and deacons of the lesser Priesthood, who render assistance to them in the temporal as well as the spiritual affairs of the Church. It devolves upon the bishopric of the ward to look after the poor, to minister unto the sick and the afflicted, and to see that there is no want nor suffering among the people in these organized divisions of the Church. It is also the duty of these presiding officers in the Church to look after the spiritual welfare of the people, to see that they are living moral, pure and upright lives, that they are faithful in the discharge of their duties as Latter-day Saints, that they are honest in their dealings with one another, and with all the world. It is their business to see that spiritual light exists in their hearts, and that the people under their presidency and direction are living the lives of Saints, as far as it is possible for men and women, in the mortal body, beset by the weaknesses and imperfections of mankind, to be Saints.—Oct. C. R., 1904, pp. 2, 3.

BISHOPS AND LESSER PRIESTHOOD SHOULD BE ACTIVE. The bishops and the lesser priesthood should be very active and energetic. We should look after the boys who have been ordained deacons, teachers, and priests in the Church. We should find something for them to do in their calling. Let them be appointed to active labors in their several spheres. Put forward those who have not had experience to accompany those who have, and give them something to do. Let the deacons not only assist to keep the meeting houses in repair and their grounds in proper condition, but let them be set to work to look after the welfare of the widows and fatherless, the aged and the poor. Many of our young men who are idle, languishing for the want of something to do, could be made more useful in helping the poor to clean up about their homes and make them comfortable, and helping them to live in such a way that life would be pleasant to them. There is no reason why the members of the lesser priesthood should not be engaged in missions and labors of this kind.—Apr. C. R., 1908, p. 6.

DUTIES OF THE LESSER PRIESTHOOD. Then we have the lesser priesthood, who attends to the different temporal matters of the Church, consisting of priests, teachers and deacons, who labor under the direction of the bishopric in the various wards in which they dwell, for the work of the ministry, for the edifying of the body of Christ, the unifying of the people and bringing them up to the standard of righteousness that they should reach in the flesh, according to the light they possess and the ability and talent which the Lord has given them.—Oct. C. R., 1904, p. 4.

LESSER PRIESTHOOD. The bishops should take especial charge of the lesser priesthood, and train them in the duties of their callings —the priests, teachers and deacons. Our young men should be looked after. The boys, as soon as it is prudent, should be called to take part in the lesser Priesthood. If it were possible to grade them, from the deacon to the priest, and from the priest upward, through all the offices that will eventually devolve upon them, it would be one of the best things that could be done. All these things should be looked after by the presiding authorities of the Church, especially those who preside over the quorums. I will repeat what I said before, it is expected that every man on whom responsibility is placed will do his duty faithfully and be diligent in the performance thereof. —Apr. C. R., 1907, p. 6.

THE WORK OF THE BISHOPRIC. The work of the bishopric is both temporal and spiritual. The average bishop gives all his time and efforts for the betterment of the people over whom he presides. The bishop should not try to do all the work that is necessary to be done in his ward. His counselors are there to help him, and a due portion of the responsibility of the bishop of the ward should be placed upon his counselors. Neither is it wise that the bishopric of the ward should feel they are compelled to do all that is necessary to be done in their wards. They should exercise their right to call upon the priesthood to visit the people as teachers and preachers of the gospel of Jesus Christ that they may give to all as far as possible an opportunity to exercise their talents and to do good in their wards. It is sometimes advisable to give to each counselor special duties, and assign each of the counselors his proportion of the responsibilities which belong to the bishopric, each one doing some special work for which he is adapted, so that all may be active.—Oct. C. R., 1914, p. 6.

DIGNITY OF TEACHERS' CALLING. We have had called to our attention, recently, the fact that some men who are of long standing in the Church—indeed, some of them born and reared in the Church, and who are occupying prominent positions in some of the quorums of the Priesthood—when their presidents or their bishops of the wards in which they live call upon them to visit the Saints, teach the principles of the gospel and perform the duties of teachers, they coolly inform their bishops that they have graduated from that calling and refuse to act as teachers. Brother Charles W. Penrose is eighty-two years of age. I am going on seventy-six, and I believe that I am older than several of these good men who have graduated from the duties in the lesser Priesthood, and I want to tell them and you that we are not too old to act as teachers, if you will call us to do it—not one of us. There is never a time, there never will come a time to those who hold the Priesthood in the Church of Jesus Christ of Latter-day Saints, when men can say of themselves that they have done enough. So long as life lasts, and so long as we possess ability to do good, to labor for the upbuilding of Zion, and for the benefit of the human family, we ought, with willingness, to yield with alacrity to the requirements made of us to do our duty, little or great.—Apr. C. R., 1914, p. 7.

VALUE OF TEACHERS' WORK. I don't know of any duty that is
more sacred, or more necessary, if it is carried out as it should be, than
the duties of the teachers who visit the homes of the people, who
pray with them, who admonish them to virtue and honor, to unity,
to love, and to faith in and fidelity to the cause of Zion; who strive to
settle uncertainties in the minds of the people and bring them to the
standard of the knowledge that they should possess in the gospel
of Jesus Christ. May all the people open their doors, call in the
members of their families, and respect the visit of the teachers to
their homes, and join with them in striving to bring about a better
condition, if possible, in the home than ordinarily exists. If you
can advance, try to aid the teachers to help you make that advancement.—Apr. C. R., 1915, p. 140.

THE RESTORATION OF THE MELCHIZEDEK PRIESTHOOD. "No man
can be exalted unless he be independent. * * * Mankind are naturally
independent and intelligent beings, they have been created for the
express purpose of exalting themselves." The study of the subject
of the Holy or Melchizedek Priesthood, including the Aaronic, is one
of vast importance to the human family. The student of the true
science of theology will readily comprehend the necessity of its existence among men, for the reason that true theology, or the Church of
Jesus Christ, cannot exist without it. It lies at the foundation of the
Church, it is the authority by which the Church is established or
organized, built up and governed, and by which the gospel is preached,
and all the ordinances thereof designed for the salvation of mankind
are administered or solemnized. No ordinance of the gospel can be
performed acceptably to God or with efficacy to man except by its
authority and power, and certainly there is no ordinance or rite instituted by the Almighty in the great plan of redemption which is not
essential to the salvation or exaltation of his children. Therefore,
where the Melchizedek or Holy Priesthood does not exist, there can
be no true Church of Christ in its fulness. When this Priesthood
is not found among mankind they are destitute of the power of
God, and therefore of the true science of theology, or the Church
and religion of Jesus Christ who is the great High Priest and Apostle
of our salvation. While the Prophet Joseph Smith was engaged
in translating the Book of Mormon, in 1829, he and Oliver Cowdery
became animated over the truths and glorious promises unfolded
to them in their work, and desired to reach out after these blessings
before their work was done, but the Lord gently admonished them not

to be in a hurry; he said: "You must wait yet a little while, for ye are not yet ordained," but the promise was given that they should be ordained thereafter, and they should go forth and deliver the word of God unto the children of men, and he pronounced a woe upon the inhabitants of the earth if they would not then hearken unto their words.

The ordinary meaning of the word priesthood, as generally understood and applied in the world, signifies a class or body of men set apart for sacred duties, or holding the priestly office, or an order of persons composed of priests spoken of or taken collectively. This is not, however, the sense in which the words Melchizedek or Holy Priesthood, are used here. Reference is made in this article to the sacred office itself, or the principle of power which constitutes the office, and is the authority by which individuals or the several orders, or quorums, as we use the term, composing the priesthood of the Church, may legitimately act in the name of the Lord; or the moving, directing, controlling, governing or presiding agency, right and authority, which is vested in the Godhead and delegated unto man for the purpose of his instruction, initiation into the Church, spiritual and temporal guidance, government and exaltation. That is the Melchizedek Priesthood, which is without father, without mother, or descent, or beginning of days, or end of life, which the great high priest, Melchizedek, so honored and magnified in his time that it was called after his name, in honor to him and to avoid the too frequent repetition of the name of the Son of God.

This distinction between the quorums of the priesthood and the Priesthood itself should always be kept in mind in the use of the term Melchizedek or Holy Priesthood. The Holy Priesthood after the order of the Son of God was the original name given to this Priesthood. Subsequently it was called the Melchizedek Priesthood. This Priesthood was confirmed upon Adam, Abel, Seth, Enoch, Methuselah, Noah, Melchizedek, Abraham, Moses and many others, and doubtless upon many of the prophets prior to the birth of Christ, upon his chosen disciples among the Jews, before his crucifixion, and upon the Nephite disciples upon this continent, after his resurrection and ascension on high. These he made his apostles, to bear witness of him upon both hemispheres and to all the world; and doubtless the Savior conferred this Priesthood upon other disciples whom he chose from among the "other sheep" of whom he spoke to the Nephites, which were not of the folds of the Jews or of the

Nephites, whose records are yet to come forth to bear witness of him, in the due time of the Lord.

We learn from the revelations that God took Moses, and the Holy Priesthood also, out of the midst of the children of Israel. But the lesser or Aaronic Priesthood, which was confirmed upon Aaron and his seed, continued among them till the coming of Christ in the meridian of time. John, the son of Zacharias, was probably the last who held the keys of this Priesthood among the Jews. He was raised up and sent as the forerunner of Christ to prepare the way for his first coming. And he was also sent to the world in this dispensation to begin the work of preparation for Christ's second advent.

"There are in the Church two Priesthoods, namely, the Melchizedek and Aaronic, including the Levitical Priesthood. Why the first is called the Melchizedek Priesthood is because Melchizedek was such a great high priest. Before his day it was called the Holy Priesthood after the order of the Son of God." The Melchizedek Priesthood holds the keys of all the spiritual blessings of the Church, of the mysteries of the kingdom of heaven, of communion with the general assembly and Church of the first born, and the presence of God, the Father, and Jesus, the Mediator.

The Aaronic Priesthood is an appendage to the first, and holds the keys of the ministering of angels, and the outward ordinances and letter of the gospel, the baptism of repentance for the remission of sins, agreeable to the covenants and commandments.

The Melchizedek Priesthood which Christ restored to the earth, remained among men between three and four hundred years afterwards. When in consequence of transgressions, apostasy from the true order of the Priesthood and Church of Christ, the innovations of priestcraft and paganism, the true order of God was lost, the Holy Priesthood was taken from the earth, and the Church of Christ ceased to be among men, so far as we have any knowledge by revelation or from the history and records of the past.

Then were fulfilled many predictions of the prophets and apostles, contained in the word of God. Among them the word of God spoken by John, in the 12th chapter of Revelations, and the prophecy of Amos: "Behold the days come, saith the Lord God, that I will send a famine in the land, not a famine of bread, nor a thirst for water, but of hearing the words of the Lord: and they shall wander from sea to sea, and from the north even to the east, they shall run to and fro to seek the word of the Lord, and shall not find it." (Amos

8:11, 12.) The proclamation of the word of the Lord is, and always has been dependent upon the authority of the Holy Priesthood.

How could they hear without a preacher, and how shall they preach except they be sent?

The Gentiles among whom the Priesthood had been established and the gospel preached, fell away also after the example of unbelief and the manner of the Jews, or children of Israel. God who spared not the natural branches, also cut off engrafted ones, and "Mystery, Babylon the Great, the mother of harlots and abominations of the earth," was set up as foretold by the Prophet Daniel and the Apostle John. This power made war with the Saints, and overcame them, changed time and laws, "wore out the Saints of the Most High," was drunken with their blood and with the blood of the martyrs of Jesus, and destroyed the holy people. But this mystical power, in turn, is to be overcome and, in the due time of the Lord, utterly destroyed.

Before this great event shall occur must come to pass the restoration of the gospel of Christ, and the establishment of the kingdom of God again on the earth, with all the powers and blessings of the Holy Priesthood, concerning which we have the most positive assurances. The declarations of the sacred writers of the Bible and the Book of Mormon not only affirm the restoration of all things spoken of by holy prophets relative to this great event, but also that this kingdom shall no more be thrown down nor be left to another people, nor cease until the whole earth shall be filled with the brightness of its glory, with its truths, its power, might, majesty and dominion, and that the kingdom and the greatness thereof under the whole heaven will be given unto the Saints of the Most High God, and they shall possess it forever. The declaration of this truth is even now very galling to the unbelieving world, and to those who reject the truth; nevertheless the Saints will inherit the blessings, and the word of God will come to pass, however much the wicked object to it or whether we as the beginners in the great cause endure faithful to the end and realize the promise or not. This great and glorious redemption will be consummated through the power and agencies of the Holy or Melchizedek Priesthood, by means of which and the inspiration of the Holy Spirit, God has ever dealt, and will always deal, with the children of men; for this Priesthood "administereth the gospel and holdeth the key of the mysteries of the kingdom, even the key of the kingdom of God; therefore, in the ordinances thereof, the power of godliness is manifest; and without the ordinance thereof, and the authority of the Priesthood, the power of God is not manifest unto men in the flesh; for without this no man can see the face of God, even the Father and live." (*Doc. and Cov.* 84:19-22.)

The Lesser Priesthood holdeth the key of the ministering of angels and the preparatory gospel; which gospel is the gospel of repentance and of baptism, and the remission of sins, which continued "with the house of Aaron among the children of Israel until John, whom God raised up, being filled with the Holy Ghost from his mother's womb." He, John, "was baptized while he was yet in his childhood and was ordained by the angel of God at the time he was eight days old unto this power, to overthrow the kingdom of the Jews, and to make straight the way of the Lord before the face of his people, to prepare them for the coming of the Lord in whose hand is given all power." (*Doc. and Cov.* 84:26-28.)

It was the same John who appeared to Joseph Smith and Oliver Cowdery, on the fifteenth day of May, 1829, and conferred upon them the Aaronic Priesthood with all its keys and power. The ordination was in the following words:

"Upon you my fellow servants, in the name of Messiah, I confer the Priesthood of Aaron, which holds the keys of the ministering of angels, and of the gospel of repentance, and of baptism by immersion for the remission of sins; and this shall never be taken again from the earth, until the sons of Levi do offer again an offering unto the Lord in righteousness." There is nothing said here about the offices of this Priesthood. They were an after consideration. I will remark here that the Priesthood is greater than the offices which grew out of it, and are mere appendages to it, "all other authorities or offices in the Church are appendages to this Priesthood"—meaning the Melchizedek Priesthood. But there are two divisions or grand heads (not three, nor many); one is the Melchizedek Priesthood and the other is the Aaronic or Levitical Priesthood. The offices in the Priesthood are necessary appendages thereof—for the purposes of order and government, and the duties of these several offices are defined in the revelations and laws and commandments of God.

This most sacred and important event, above quoted, occurred at or near a place called Harmony, in Susquehanna county, Pennsylvania, while Joseph Smith was living there, engaged in the translation of the Book of Mormon, and Oliver Cowdery was writing for him. We have not, unfortunately, any account so definite, of the reception by Joseph and Oliver, of the Melchizedek Priesthood as we have the confirmation of the Aaronic Priesthood. But we have positive information and knowledge that they did receive this Priesthood at the hands of Peter, James and John, to whom the keys and power thereof were committed by the Lord Jesus Christ, and who were commissioned to restore it to the earth in the dispensation of the fulness of times. We cannot fix the exact date when this Priesthood was restored, but it occurred some time between the 15th of May, 1829, and the 6th of April, 1830. We can approximate to within a few months of the exact time, but no further, from any of the records of the Church, Joseph, the Prophet, designates the place where their ordination took place, in his address to the Saints (Sec. 128:20) written in 1842, as follows:

"Again what do we hear? * * * the voice of Peter, James, and John, in the wilderness between Harmony, Susquehanna county, and Colesville, Broome county, on the Susquehanna river, declaring themselves as possessing the keys of the kingdom of the dispensation of the fulness of times." And in a revelation given September, 1830, referring to Joseph and Oliver, the Lord said in reference to partaking again of the Sacrament on the earth, that "the hour cometh that I will drink of the fruit of the vine with you on the earth, and with Moroni, * * * and also with Elias, * * * and also John the son of Zacharias, * * * which John I have sent unto you, my servants, Joseph Smith, Jun., and Oliver Cowdery, to ordain you unto this first Priesthood which you have received, that you might be called and ordained even as Aaron; and also Elijah, * * * and also with Joseph and Jacob, and Isaac, and Abraham, your fathers, by whom the promises remain; and also with Michael, or Adam, the father of all, the prince of all, the ancient of days. And also with Peter, and James, and John, whom I have sent unto you, by whom I have ordained you and confirmed you to be apostles, and especial witnesses of my name, and bear the keys of your ministry, and of the same things which I revealed unto them; unto whom I have committed the keys of my kingdom, and a dispensation of the gospel for the last times; and for the fulness of times, in the which I will gather together in one all things, both which are in heaven and which are on earth." (Doc. and Cov. 27:5-13.)

A revelation given April, 1830, Sec. 20:2, 3, says: "Which commandments were given to Joseph Smith, Jun., who was called of God and ordained an apostle of Jesus Christ, to be the first elder of this Church; and to Oliver Cowdery, who was also called of God, an apostle of Jesus Christ, to be the second elder of this Church, and ordained under his hand." After the Melchizedek Priesthood was conferred upon Joseph and Oliver, by the ancient apostles, they were commanded to ordain each the other, as we see by the above quotation, and the 10th and 11th verses of Section 21 Doctrine and Covenants.

It would appear from the instructions given in the revelations, dated June, 1829, that the apostleship had been then conferred on Joseph Smith, Oliver Cowdery, and David Whitmer. If this supposition is correct, it reduces the period of uncertainty when this glorious event actually took place to a few weeks, or from the middle of May to the end of June. It is also asserted that David Whitmer supposed the event to have taken place about this time. It is evident, however, that David received the apostleship under the hands of Joseph and Oliver, and was not present when they received it under the ministration of the ancient apostles.

In the first edition of the *Compendium* under the heading of "Chronology of the most important events which have transpired in the Church of Jesus Christ of Latter-day Saints, from A. D. 1820, to 1856," we find the following brief statement: "June 6, 1831, the Melchizedek Priesthood was first given." This detached sentence conveys the idea that the Melchizedek Priesthood was not given until fourteen months after the Church was established. Many have been misled and others greatly puzzled over this statement, knowing that "elders were ordained" on the 6th day of April, 1830, a year and two months before, and that "the office of an elder comes under the Priesthood of Melchizedek."

It is a pity that greater attention is not paid to matters of history, for then such mistakes would not occur. Several errors of this character have crept into history through neglect or want of proper attention to the subjects. The passage of history from which this brief and misleading extract was taken reads as follows: "On the sixth of June (1831) the elders from the various parts of the country where they were laboring, came in; and the conference before appointed, convened in Kirtland; and the Lord displayed his power in a manner that could not be mistaken. The man of sin was revealed, and the authority of the Melchizedek Priesthood was manifested, and conferred for the first time upon several of the elders." Now, if this does not mean that on this occasion several elders received their first ordination, then it must mean that these several elders who had previously been ordained, then, for the first time, received the power or authority of their ordinations. The words "conferred for the first time upon several of the elders," would seem at first glance to mean that several were then ordained elders, but taking the complete sentence together, namely, "The man of sin was revealed, and the authority of the Melchizedek Priesthood was manifested, and conferred for the first time upon several of the elders," we naturally conclude that several who had previously been ordained elders, had not yet received the spirit, or power, or authority of their ordinations, but that now for the first time, the authority of the Priesthood having been manifested, it fell upon them. It is evident from the context that the word authority as used in this quotation means power. It reads as follows: "It was clearly evident that the Lord gave us power in proportion to the work to be done, and strength according to the race before us, and grace and help as our needs required." That several persons were ordained on that occasion is directly stated, as follows: "Great harmony prevailed; several were ordained; faith was strengthened; and humility so necessary for the blessing of God to follow prayer, characterized the Saints." One thing is perfectly clear, and that is, no reference whatever is here made to the restoration of the Melchizedek Priesthood by Peter, James and John, which great event occurred, without doubt, between May and July, 1829. However until about the time this conference was held, the term Melchizedek Priesthood was seldom or never used. The High Priesthood, or the Holy Priesthood, were the terms generally applied until then.

Thus this glorious Priesthood, which "is after the holiest order of God," has been restored to man in its plenitude and power in the present age for the "last times," and no part of it will be "taken from the earth again until the sons of Levi do offer again an offering unto the Lord in righteousness," or "until God shall gather together in one all things, both which are in heaven and which are on earth." In conclusion I will call the attention of the readers of this to Sections 5, 13, 27, 84, 107, 110 and 128 of the Doctrine and Covenants for further reflection on the subject.—Contributor, Vol. 10, 1889, pp. 307-311.

TRIBUTE TO HEBER C. KIMBALL. My first remembrance of President Heber C. Kimball goes back to the days of my childhood. He was a familiar and prominent figure in my mind in Nauvoo, Illinois, as the father of his sons, William, Heber, and David, with whom, as a little boy, I was more intimate although the two former were several years my seniors. I also recall him in those early days as the possessor of one of the best homes in the City of Nauvoo, and as the husband of "Aunt" Vilate Kimball, one of the dearest, kindest, most motherly souls who ever came within the range of my memory or acquaintance; and also as the father of Helen M. Kimball, a beautiful young woman, very much resembling her mother in appearance, and who was somewhat noted in the Smith family as being in some way related to it and who, after the death of the Prophet Joseph Smith, was married to Horace K. Whitney, and became the mother of our present poet and historian, Orson F. Whitney.

One of my most distinct recollections of President Kimball was in the winter of 1845-6, in the Nauvoo temple. My mother, and her sister, Mercy R. Thompson, were much engaged in the work going on in the temple that winter, and President Kimball was also associated with the work being done there. It was there that my father's children were sealed to their parents and President Kimball officiated.

In February, 1846, President Kimball took up the line of march, with the Twelve and the Saints who were driven out of Nauvoo, for their long journey into the wilderness, which eventually led to the occupancy of the valley of the Great Salt Lake, the settlement of Utah, by the Saints, and the fulfilment of the prophecy by Joseph Smith, that the Saints should gather to the Rocky Mountains.

The incident which more particularly specialized this departure of President Kimball to my mind, was the fact that my brother John, now the patriarch, and then a boy of about twelve years, accompanied President Kimball and family on their pilgrimage into the unknown wilderness, leaving us in Nauvoo in great fear and doubt as to whether we should ever see them again or not. This made an indelible impression upon my mind, and ever since there seemed to be inseverable ties connecting us with President Kimball and his family.

In 1848 we crossed the plains in a subdivision of President Kimball's company. He baptized me in City Creek, in 1850, where the junction of East and North Temple streets now is.

In July, 1852, while attending a meeting which was held in Salt Lake City, my mother was taken sick and went to the home of President Kimball, where she remained during her last illness; under the care of Aunt Vilate. This brought me almost constantly for months directly in contact with President Kimball and family.

It was here I became more familiar with his home life and

habits. I was greatly impressed and moved by his manner of praying in his family. I have never heard any other man pray as he did. He did not speak to the Lord as one afar off, but as if conversing with him face to face. Time and again I have been so impressed with the idea of the actual presence of God, while he was conversing with him in prayer, that I could not refrain from looking up to see if he were actually present and visible. While President Kimball was very strict in his family, he was ever kind and tender towards them.

I sometimes thought he was even kinder to me than to his own boys. I have heard him reprove them, but no word of reproof ever fell from his lips upon me. Later, through him, I was sent on my first mission. No better or kinder thing was ever done for me. It gave me four years of experience and seasoning which fixed my whole course of life, and it came just at the right time to the boy that I was.

Later I was associated with him in the Endowment House, where I served with him and under his direction for years. This brought me into the most intimate relation with him, and gave to each of us the most complete and perfect opportunity of becoming thoroughly acquainted with each other. I learned to love him with the truest love, and the many evidences of his love and confidences in me are beyond all question.

My latest recollections of him are associated with a most unusual call made upon a number of brethren in 1861, by President Brigham Young, to accompany him on a mission to Provo. Among these were Heber C. Kimball, Wilford Woodruff, Abraham O. Smoot, Elijah F. Sheets, George G. Bywater and myself. These brethren all located in Provo with President Young, and those of the number possessed of means (Presidents Young and Kimball, and Elders Smoot and Sheets) proceeded at once to build themselves homes there.

It was while President Kimball was engaged in building and preparing a place for a portion of his family in Provo, that he met with an accident from which he did not recover, and soon after, Monday, June 22, 1868, came his final summons to meet the actual presence of the gracious Father, with whom he had, in prayer, so long and truly counseled, as if face to face with him, and whom he had devotedly served to the last moment.

President Heber C. Kimball was one of God's noblemen. True

as steel to every trust. Pure as refined gold. Fearless of foes or of death. Keen of perception, full of the spirit of the prophets. Inspired of God. Valiant in the testimony of Christ; a lifelong, undeviating friend and witness of the divine calling and mission of Joseph Smith. He was called by the grace of God, ordained by living authority, and lived and died an apostle of the Lord Jesus Christ.—*Young Woman's Journal*, Vol. 20, 1909, pp. 251-252.

TRIBUTE TO ERASTUS SNOW. My earliest vivid recollection of Elder Erastus Snow was in the fall of 1848, just after my arrival in Salt Lake Valley. I had the privilege of listening to a most excellent discourse by him in the bowery at the north side of the old Pioneer fort. This discourse so impressed itself and the speaker, upon my mind, that it and he ever after held a most distinguished place in my memory. As an orator and profound reasoner, I always felt impressed that he had no superior, especially when he warmed up to his subject, and entered into his discourse with the full force and energy of his active and vigorous mind.

As a counselor, his wisdom was manifest from every point of view.

As a colonizer and builder, from the pioneer days to the completion of his work, he was equal to the foremost of his associates. In point of endurance and perseverance in whatever he engaged, he was untiring and almost inexhaustible.

As a legislator or statesman, he was the peer of any of his associates, among whom were builders of this commonwealth. One of the marked peculiarities of his character was continuity and perseverance in whatever he undertook to do, until his object was attained and his purpose accomplished. Nothing could turn him aside from the discharge of his duty. He was, without doubt, a chosen and an effective instrument in the hand of God for the accomplishment of the mission assigned him, in which he always concentrated his mind, and threw the whole force of his vigorous and noble spirit.

As the head of a numerous family, he was an example to all mankind. His friendship was always true and boundless. I esteem him as one of the great men, not only of the Church of Jesus Christ of Latter-day Saints, but of the world.—*Improvement Era*, Vol. 14, Feb., 1911, p. 280.

PURPOSE OF VISITS OF CHURCH LEADERS. We have come to see the condition and the spirit of the Latter-day Saints, and to present ourselves before them; that they may judge us by what we say and by the spirit we bring, as to whether we are in fellowship with them and with the Lord; and that they may see whether we measure up to the standards that they expect in those who stand at the head of the Church.—*Improvement Era*, Vol. 21, December, 1917, p. 98.

Chapter X

SPIRITUAL GIFTS

THE GIFT OF TONGUES. The devil himself can appear like an angel of light. False prophets and false teachers have arisen in the world. There is perhaps no gift of the Spirit of God more easily imitated by the devil than the gift of tongues. Where two men or women exercise the gift of tongues by the inspiration of the Spirit of God, there are a dozen perhaps who do it by the inspiration of the devil. Bless your souls, apostates speak in tongues, apostates prophesy, apostates claim to have marvelous manifestations. And what is that to us? The trouble is, we know so little of the truth ourselves, and we live by it so poorly, that almost any little jackanapes in the country may rise up and claim he has had a vision or some marvelous dream, and however absurd or untrue it may be, he may find believers and followers among those who profess to be Latter-day Saints.

I believe in the gifts of the Holy Spirit unto men, but I do not want the gift of tongues, except when I need it. I needed the gift of tongues once, and the Lord gave it to me. I was in a foreign land, sent to preach the gospel to a people whose language I could not understand. Then I sought earnestly for the gift of tongues, and by this gift and by study, in a hundred days after landing upon those islands I could talk to the people in their language as I now talk to you in my native tongue. This was a gift that was worthy of the gospel. There was a purpose in it. There was something in it to strengthen my faith, to encourage me and to help me in my ministry. If you have need of this gift of tongues, seek for it and God will help you in it. But I do not ask you to be very hungry for the gift of tongues, for if you are not careful the devil will deceive you in it. He can talk by the gift of tongues as well as the Lord can. Paul did not seem to care much about the gift of tongues either. He said to the Corinthians:

"I had rather speak five words with my understanding, that by my voice I might teach others also, than ten thousand words in an unknown tongue."—1 Cor. 14:19.

So far as I am concerned, if the Lord will give me ability to teach the people in my native tongue, or in their own language to the understanding of those who hear me, that will be sufficient gift

of tongues to me. Yet if the Lord gives you the gift of tongues, do
not despise it, do not reject it. For if it comes from the Spirit of
God, it will come to those who are worthy to receive it, and it is all
right. But this idea of seeking it, desiring it, when you don't pay
your tithing, when you don't pray in your families, when you don't
pay your debts, when you desecrate the Sabbath day, and when you
neglect other duties in the Church; I tell you the devil will take
advantage of you by and by, if he does not at first.—Apr. C. R., 1900,
p. 41.

THE SACRAMENT OF THE LORD'S SUPPER. The Sacrament of the
Lord's Supper is a very important and sacred ordinance; however
simple it may appear to our minds, it is one which will add to our
acceptance before God, or to our condemnation.

It was instituted by the Savior in the place of the law of sacrifice
which was given to Adam, and which continued with his children
down to the days of Christ, but which was fulfilled in his death, he
being the great sacrifice for sin, of which the sacrifices enjoined in
the law given to Adam were a similitude.

The Lord designed in the beginning to place before man the
knowledge of good and evil, and gave him a commandment to cleave
to good and abstain from evil. But if he should fail, he would give
to him the law of sacrifice and provide a Savior for him, that he might
be brought back again into the presence and favor of God and partake
of eternal life with him. This was the plan of redemption chosen
and instituted by the Almighty before man was placed on the earth.
And when man did fall by transgressing the law which was given him,
the Lord gave to him the law of sacrifice, and made it clear to his
understanding, that it was for the purpose of reminding him of that
great event that should transpire in the meridian of time, whereby
he and all his posterity might be brought forth by the power of
redemption and resurrection from the dead, and partake of eternal
life with God in his kingdom. For this reason Adam and his posterity,
from generation to generation, observed this law, and continually
looked forward to a time when there should be provided for them a
means of redemption from the fall and restoration from death to life,
for death was the penalty of the law transgressed, which man was
powerless to avert, that fiat of God being, "In the day that thou
eatest thereof, thou shalt surely die," and this penalty was to follow
upon all flesh, all being as helpless and dependent as he was in this
matter. Their only hope of redemption from the grave and the power

of death was in the Savior whom God had promised, who should suffer death, but being without sin, having himself never transgressed any law, being without blemish, pure and holy, he should have power to break the bands of death and from the grave rise to immortal life, thereby opening the way for all who should follow him in the regeneration, to come forth to life again, redeemed from the penalty of the law, and from the sin of transgression to eternal life. In anticipation, therefore, of this great sacrifice which was to be offered for Adam and his seed, they offered sacrifices more or less acceptable, and in conformity to the pattern given, in proportion to the knowledge of God and of the gospel which they had, in their faithfulness from generation to generation, to the days of Jesus.

They would take the firstlings of their flocks, the best fruits of their fields, and those things which were emblematic of purity, innocence, and perfection, symbolical of him who was without sin, and as "a lamb slain from the foundation of the world," and offer sacrifices unto God in memory of him, and the matchless and wonderful deliverance to be wrought out for them by him.

Undoubtedly the knowledge of this law and of other rites and ceremonies was carried by the posterity of Adam into all lands, and continued with them, more or less pure, to the flood, and through Noah, who was a "preacher of righteousness," to those who succeeded him, spreading out in all nations and countries, Adam and Noah being the first of their dispensations to receive them from God. What wonder, then, that we should find relics of Christianity so to speak among the heathens, and nations who know not Christ, and whose histories date back beyond the days of Moses, and even beyond the flood, independent of and apart from the records of the Bible. The ground taken by infidels, that "Christianity" sprang from the heathen, it being found that they have many rites similar to those recorded in the Bible, etc., is only a vain and foolish attempt to blind the eyes of men and dissuade them from their faith in the Redeemer of the world, and from their belief in the Scriptures of divine truth, for if the heathen have doctrines and ceremonies resembling to some extent those which are recorded in the Scriptures, it only proves, what is plain to the Saints, that these are the traditions of the fathers handed down from generation to generation, from Adam, through Noah, and that they will cleave to the children to the latest generation, though they may wander into darkness and perversion, until but a slight resemblance to their origin, which was divine, can be seen. * * *

The ordinances of the gospel have been restored in their purity. We know why the law of sacrifice was given to Adam, and how it is that relics of the gospel are found among the heathen.

When Jesus came and suffered, "the just for the unjust," he that was without sin for him that had sinned, and was subjected to the penalty of the law which the sinner had transgressed, the law of sacrifice was fulfilled, and instead thereof he gave another law, which we call the "Sacrament of the Lord's Supper," by which his life and mission, his death and resurrection, the great sacrifice he had offered for the redemption of man, should be kept in everlasting remembrance, for, said he, "this do ye * * * in remembrance of me, for as often as ye eat this bread and drink this cup, ye do shew the Lord's death till he come." Therefore this law is to us what the law of sacrifice was to those who lived prior to the first coming of the Son of Man, until he shall come again. Therefore, we must honor and keep it sacredly, for there is a penalty attached to its violation, as we shall see by reading the words of Paul (1 Cor. 11:27-30):

"Wherefore whosoever shall eat this bread, and drink this cup of the Lord, unworthily, shall be guilty of the body and blood of the Lord.

"But let a man examine himself, and so let him eat of that bread, and drink of that cup.

"For he that eateth and drinketh unworthily, eateth and drinketh damnation to himself, not discerning the Lord's body.

"For this cause many are weak and sickly among you, and many sleep."

And it is even more plainly given in the Book of Mormon, which I will read (III Nephi 18:26-29):

"And now it came to pass that when Jesus had spoken these words, he turned his eyes again upon the disciples whom he had chosen, and said unto them, behold verily, verily, I say unto you, I give unto you another commandment, and then I must go unto my Father, that I may fulfil other commandments which he hath given me. And now behold, this is the commandment which I give unto you, that ye shall not suffer any one knowingly, to partake of my flesh and blood unworthily, when ye shall minister it; for whoso eateth and drinketh my flesh and blood unworthily, eateth and drinketh damnation to his soul; therefore if ye know that a man is unworthy to eat and drink of my flesh and blood, ye shall forbid him."

These are some of the injunctions and commandments that are

given in relation to the partaking of the Lord's Supper. Now let us be careful what we do, that we may not incur the penalty affixed to the transgression of this law, remembering that the ordinances which God has given are sacred and binding, that his laws are in force, especially upon all that have covenanted with him in baptism, and upon all unto whom they come, whether they embrace them or not, as Jesus said, "This is the condemnation of the world, that light has come into the world, but ye love darkness rather than light." Therefore all men will be held accountable for the use they make of the light which they possess. For this reason we are commanded to preach the gospel unto every creature, that those who obey and are baptized may be saved, and those who reject it may be condemned.

I bear my testimony to these things. I know that Joseph Smith was and is a prophet of the living God, and President Young is also a prophet of God, and that by inspiration and revelation, and not of man. God bless you, and help us to be faithful, is my prayer in the name of Jesus. Amen.—Discourse delivered in the Thirteenth Ward Assembly Rooms, Salt Lake City, February 9, 1873, *Journal of Discourses*, Vol. 15, pp. 234-238.

ORDER OF ADMINISTERING TO THE SICK. In the matter of administering to the sick, according to the order and practice established in the Church, care should be taken to avoid unwarranted repetitions. When an administration is made, and when the blessing pronounced upon the afflicted one has been received, the ordinance should not be repeated, rather let the time be given to prayer and thanksgiving for the manifestation of divine power already granted and realized. No limit should be or can be set to the offering of prayer and the rendering of praise to the Giver of Good, for we are specially told to pray without ceasing, and no special authority of the Priesthood or standing in the Church is essential to the offering of prayer; but the actual administration by anointing with oil and by the imposition of hands by those who hold the proper office in the Priesthood is an authoritative ordinance, too sacred in its nature to be performed lightly, or to be repeated loosely when the blessing has been gained. —*Juvenile Instructor*, Vol. 38, January, 1902, p. 18.

THE USE OF A TESTIMONY. The sanctity of a true testimony should inspire a thoughtful care as to its use. That testimony is not to be forced upon everybody, nor is it to be proclaimed at large from the housetop. It is not to be voiced merely to "fill up the time" in a public meeting; far less to excuse or disguise the speaker's poverty of thought or ignorance of the truth he is called to expound.

The individual testimony is a personal possession. One cannot give his testimony to another, yet he is able to aid his earnest brother in gaining a true testimony for himself. The over-zealous missionary may be influenced by the misleading thought that the bearing of his testimony to those who have not before heard the gospel message, is to convince or condemn, as the hearers accept or reject. The elder is sent into the field to preach the gospel—the good news of its restoration to earth, showing by scriptural evidence the harmony of the new message with the predictions of earlier times; expounding the truths embodied in the first principles of the gospel; then if he bears his testimony under divine inspiration, such a testimony is as a seal attesting the genuineness of the truths he has declared, and so appealing to the receptive soul whose ears have been saluted by the heaven-sent message.

But the voicing of one's testimony, however eloquently phrased or beautifully expressed, is no fit or acceptable substitute for the needed discourse of instruction and counsel expected in a general gathering of the people. The man who professes a testimony as herein described, and who assumes that his testimony embraces all the knowledge he needs, and who therefore lives in indolence and ignorance shall surely discover his error to his own cost and loss. A gift from God, if neglected, or unworthily used, is in time withdrawn; the testimony of the truth will not remain with one who, having received, uses not the sacred gift in the cause of individual and general advancement.

Search out the truth of the written word; listen for and receive the truth declared by living prophets and teachers; enrich your minds with the best of knowledge and facts. Of those who speak in his name, the Lord requires humility, not ignorance. Intelligence is the glory of God; and no man can be saved in ignorance.

Study and strive to acquire the knowledge that leads toward, and the wisdom that shall reach, the goal of life eternal. Your testimony as to the truth of the restored gospel may operate toward salvation or condemnation as it is used or misused.—*Juvenile Instructor,* Vol. 41, August, 1906, p. 465.

PURPOSE AND PRACTICE OF TESTIMONY BEARING. The practice of bearing testimonies once a month in the Sabbath schools has become so general, and is of such far-reaching importance to the faith and happiness of our young people, that a word of caution and of encouragement may be helpful at this time. It is not the chief purpose of testimony bearing to accumulate physical evidences of the truth of the gospel. It is not so much argument and physical demonstration that are wanted as it is the cultivation of the Spirit of God within the hearts of the children.

Many of the children live in homes where there is comparatively little or no sickness, and perhaps have no opportunity whatever to witness manifestations of divine power in the healing of the sick. At testimony meetings, these children would perhaps have little to say if the idea prevailed that the testimonies of the children were to consist chiefly, if not wholly, in recounting instances of healing through the administrations of the elders.

The healing of the sick is but one of those spiritual blessings that follow those who have faith, and the blessing belongs peculiarly to the Church, but is not confined exclusively to those who are members of the Church. In Christ's day, many were healed who were strangers to his great mission, simply through their faith in him, or that the glory of God might be made manifest.

Now, the healing of the sick is simply one of the evidences; but if it were the only evidence of the divinity of this work it would be insufficient, because in the organization of the Church, the existence of apostles, the gathering, the payment of tithes and offerings, the laying on of hands, baptism, and other laws and ordinances of the gospel are equally evidence of its divine origin, and the importance of one ought not to be emphasized to the neglect of any other. The fact that all these ordinances and principles are taught and practiced by the Saints constitutes a convincing argument that the Church is now the same as it was in the days of the Master.

Testimony-bearing should have a strong educational influence upon the feelings and lives of the children, and it is intended to cultivate within them feelings of thankfulness and appreciation for the blessings they enjoy. The Spirit of God may work within the life of a child and make the child realize and know that this is the work of God. The child knows it rather because of the Spirit than because of some physical manifestation which he may have witnessed. Our testimony meetings, then, should have as one of their aims the cultivation of the children's feelings of gratitude not only toward God, but toward their parents, teachers and neighbors. It is advisable, therefore, to cultivate as far as possible their appreciation for the blessings that they enjoy.

Testimony bearing is chiefly for the benefit of those who bear the testimony, in that their gratitude and appreciation are deepened. Testimony bearing is not the accumulation of arguments or evidences solely for the satisfaction and testimony of others. Let the testimonies, then, of the young people include the training of their feelings by way of making them more appreciative and more thankful for the blessings they enjoy, and the children should be made to understand what these blessings are and how they come to them. It is an excellent way to make people helpful and thankful to others, by first making them thankful to God.—*Juvenile Instructor*, Vol. 38, April, 1903, p. 246.

THE TEMPORAL AND THE SPIRITUAL NOT SEPARATE. You must continue to bear in mind that the temporal and the spiritual are blended. They are not separate. One cannot be carried on without the other, so long as we are here in mortality. The Church of Jesus Christ of Latter-day Saints on the earth is a physical organization as well as a spiritual organization. We need practical faith—that is, we need to practice the principles of our faith. Without the practice of the principles of the gospel, we can never realize our hopes and expectations concerning the results of this great latter-day work.— Oct. C. R., 1900, p. 46.

SPIRITUAL AND TEMPORAL SALVATION. The Latter-day Saints believe not only in the gospel of spiritual salvation, but also in the gospel of temporal salvation. We have to look after the cattle and the sheep and the horses, the gardens and the farms, the irrigation canals and ditches, and other necessary things for the maintenance of ourselves and our families in the earth. In this respect this Church is different from many other denominations. We do not feel that it is possible for men to be really good and faithful Christian people unless they can also be good, faithful, honest and industrious people. Therefore, we preach the gospel of industry, the gospel of economy, the gospel of sobriety. We preach that the idler shall not eat the bread of the laborer, and that the idler is not entitled to an inheritance in Zion. We preach that those who are industrious, those who work, those who through their integrity and industry are good citizens of the kingdom of God, are better citizens of the country in which they live than those who are not so diligent in this regard.—Apr. C. R., 1904, p. 74.

THE GOSPEL DESIGNED FOR TEMPORAL BENEFITS, ALSO. The work that we are engaged in is not designed to be limited by the spiritual necessities of the people alone. It is the purpose of God in restoring the gospel and the holy Priesthood not only to benefit mankind spiritually, but also to benefit them temporally. The Lord has expressed this many times, in the word that he gave to his servant Joseph Smith, the prophet; he designed that his people should become the richest of all people. And this not only means the richest of all people in heavenly gifts—in spiritual blessings and riches, but it also means that the people of God shall be the richest of all people with regard to temporal matters. If faithful, we have a right to claim the blessings of the Lord upon the labor of our hands, our temporal labors. The farmer has a right to ask the Lord for blessings upon his farm, upon the labor that he bestows upon it. He has a right to claim the blessings of the Lord upon the animals that are necessary to the cultivation of his farm. He has a right to ask God to bless the grain that he sows and the seeds of the fruit that he plants in the soil. It is his privilege, not only to ask and claim these blessings at the hand of the Lord, but it is his right and privilege to receive blessings from God upon his labor, upon his farm, and upon all that he puts his hand unto in righteousness. It is our privilege to ask God to remove the curse from the earth, and to make it fruitful. If we will live so that we shall be entitled to his favor, and so that we may justly and righteously claim the blessings and gifts that he has promised unto his Saints, then that which we ask will be given, and we shall receive and enjoy them more abundantly. It is our privilege to ask God to bless the elements that surround us and to temper them for our good, and we know he will hear and answer the prayers of his people, according to their faith.—*Apr. C. R., 1898, pp. 9-10.*

THE SPIRIT NEEDS FOOD. Many people are inconsistent in that they study concerning the needs of the body, and observe strictly the laws of health, yet they disregard the equally urgent needs of the spirit. For the spirit, as well as the body, needs food. Some people are either ignorant or thoughtless concerning the great blessings promised to those who observe the Word of Wisdom.—*Improvement Era, Vol. 21, December, 1917, p. 103.*

CHAPTER XI

OBEDIENCE

OBEDIENCE AN ETERNAL PRINCIPLE. We have entered into the bond of that new and everlasting covenant agreeing that we would obey the commandments of God in all things whatsoever he shall command us. This is an everlasting covenant even unto the end of our days. And when is the end of our days? We may think it has reference to the end of our mortal lives; that a time will come after we have finished this probation when we can live without obedience to the commandments of God. This is a great error. We shall never see the day in time nor in eternity, when it will not be obligatory, and when it will not be a pleasure as well as a duty for us, as his children, to obey all the commandments of the Lord throughout the endless ages of eternity. It is upon this principle that we keep in touch with God, and remain in harmony with his purposes. It is only in this way that we can consummate our mission, and obtain our crown and the gift of eternal lives, which is the greatest gift of God. Can you imagine any other way?

God has established all things in their order. The house of God is a house of order, and not a house of confusion. In this house God himself is the Supreme Head, and he must be obeyed. Christ is in the image and likeness of his being, his Only Begotten Son, and he stands as our Savior and our God. We must walk in his paths, and observe his precepts to do them, or we will be cut off. Next unto God and Christ, on the earth is placed one unto whom the keys of power and the authority of the holy Priesthood are conferred, and unto whom the right of presidency is given. He is God's mouthpiece to his people, in all things pertaining to the building up of Zion and to the spiritual and temporal salvation of the people. He is as God's vicegerent; I do not hesitate to announce this truth; for it is his word, and therefore it is true. The people who have entered into covenant to keep the commandments of the Lord must hearken unto the voice of him who is placed to preside over them; and, secondarily, to those who are called to act with him as his counselors in the holy Priesthood. It takes this council of three to constitute the presiding and governing authority of the Priesthood on the earth. God the Father, God the Son, and God the Holy Ghost, constitute the Godhead and the matchless governing quorum over all the creations of the Father. Three men stand at the head of the Church on the earth. Yet there are those who call themselves Saints who hesitate not to rise up in condemnation of, and to express words of hatred and malice toward these men who stand at the head of the Church of Jesus Christ of Latter-day Saints.—Apr. C. R., 1898, pp. 68-69.

How to Rise Above the Weakness of Mortality. I would like all the Latter-day Saints to feel in their hearts that the work in which they are engaged is not only the work that God has instituted in the latter days, but that it is a work in which each individual member of the Church is deeply and vitally interested. Every man and every woman should feel a deep and abiding interest in the work of the Lord, in the growth and development of the great latter-day cause, which cause is intended for the redemption of all men from the powers of sin, from all its contaminating effects, for the redemption of man from his own weakness and ignorance, and from the grasp that Satan holds upon the world, that men may be made free; for no man is or can be made free without possessing a knowledge of the truth and obeying the same. It is only the possession and observance of the truth that can make men free, and all those who do not possess and obey it are slaves and not free men.

It is only by obedience to the laws of God that men can rise above the petty weaknesses of mortality and exercise that breadth of affection, that charity and love, that should actuate the hearts and the motives of the children of men. The gospel as it has been restored is intended to make free indeed, free to choose the good and forsake the evil, free to exercise that boldness in their choice of that which is good, by which they are convinced of right, notwithstanding the great majority of the people of the world may point at them the finger of scorn and ridicule. It requires no especial bravery on the part of men to swim with the currents of the world. When a man makes up his mind to forsake the world and its follies and sins, and identify himself with God's people, who are everywhere spoken evil of, it takes courage, manhood, independence of character, superior intelligence and a determination that is not common among men; for men shrink from that which is unpopular, from that which will not bring them praise and adulation, from that which will in any degree tarnish that which they call honor or a good name.—Oct. C. R., 1903, pp. 1, 2.

Obedience to Church Ordinances Indispensable. From re-

marks that sometimes fall from members of the Church one is led
to believe that they regard the gospel of Jesus Christ simply from
the standpoint of a code of morals; that if one lives an honest, upright
life, that is all that the gospel requires of him; that it is not necessary
to observe the rites, ceremonies and ordinances of the Church; that
the latter constitute a sort of religious trapping that has no substantial
value in the plan of life and salvation. Such a position does not
harmonize with the word of God given to this people nor with the
teachings of Christ in his day, nor is it in harmony with the universal
instinct of man to worship God.

Jesus himself attended to the ordinance of baptism; he instituted
the sacrament of the Lord's supper, and ordained its observance; and
performed other rites which he thought essential to man's salvation.
In the case of Nicodemus, he so emphasized baptism that he made
the birth of water and the Spirit essential to man's salvation.

Besides the rites and ceremonies and the moral effect they and
other means of worshiping God have upon the moral life of man,
the gospel is also a power in itself. It is a creative power which gives
man not alone dominion in the world, but the power, if he can
attain it by his faith, to ordain and create other worlds. On one
occasion Jesus commended to the disciples the value of faith as
a power when he told them that if they had faith as a grain of mustard,
they could say unto the mountain, be thou removed, and it should be
done. It is true that our faith would be greatly weakened by acts
of immorality, and it might be wholly destroyed by such acts; but faith
and morality are not convertible terms. A moral life is one of the
means by which we cultivate faith, but it is not the only means.
We may not see any moral virtue in the ordinance of baptism, in the
laying on of hands, or in any other rite or ceremony of the Church,
but our obedience to these rites and ordinances may be quite as
helpful in developing our faith as any act of charity we may perform.
Faith is always a gift of God to man, which is obtained by obedience,
as all other blessings are.

The man or woman in this Church who desires to enrich his or
her faith to the highest possible degree will desire to observe every
rite and ordinance in the Church in conformity to the law of obedience
to the will of God. In these things, and through them, man gains
a more perfect knowledge of God's purposes in the world. An enriched faith means an enlarged power, and though man may not have
in this life an occasion to exercise all the powers that come to him

through the enrichment of his faith, those powers may be exercised in their fulness in eternity, if not in time. The man or woman, therefore, among the Latter-day Saints, who does not see the necessity for the ordinances of the House of God, who does not respond to the requirements of the gospel in all its rites and ordinances, can have no proper conception of the great work which the Latter-day Saints have been called upon to perform in this age, nor can he or she enjoy the blessing that comes from the virtue of obedience to a law higher than that of man.—*Juvenile Instructor*, Vol. 38, November 1, 1903, p. 656.

OBEDIENCE BRINGS LIGHT AND FREEDOM. The gospel is very simple when we understand it properly. It is plain and easily understood. It is always right, good, uplifting, comforting and enlightening. It prompts men and women to do that which is acceptable before God, who is just, righteous, all-wise, all-good, and all-merciful.

The gospel teaches us to forgive, to overcome selfishness, covetousness; to abjure anger, wrath, faultfinding, complaining and the spirit of contention and strife. The gospel warns and forewarns the children of men against the evils which bring disunion and contention and shut out honesty and love from among the children of men; which mislead people to acts of injustice, selfishness, covetousness, wickedness and sin, things which the gospel of Jesus Christ teaches us to eschew and avoid as we would the gates of hell. There is nothing intricate or incomprehensible in the gospel of Jesus Christ to those who possess the Spirit of the Lord.

There is nothing mysterious and unaccountable in the dealings of God with his children if we can only see and understand by the spirit of truth. Jesus has given us in this life the example, the type of that which exists in greater perfection, in a purer, higher and more glorious excellence where he dwells himself. The gospel teaches us to do here just what we would be required to do in the heavens, with God and the angels, if we would listen to its teachings, and obey it, and put it into practice. There would be no covetousness in the hearts of the children of men, if they possessed the Spirit of Jesus Christ, and understood the precepts of the gospel as he taught and admonished all men to observe them.

There would be no strife, no anger, nothing of the spirit of unforgiveness, unchastity and injustice, in the hearts of the children of men, if we loved the truth and obeyed it as it was taught by the

Son of Man. With this spirit we could advance to the extreme position that we would pray for those who despitefully use us, who speak all manner of evil against us falsely, accuse us of wrongdoing, and lay plans and plots to bring us into disrepute. There would be no such desires in the hearts of the children of men, if they possessed the Spirit of the Lord Jesus Christ. There would be no contention, dishonor, nor dishonesty among neighbors nor in the communities of the people. None would take advantage of the unwary, the weak or unsuspecting; no one would seek to wrong another; but, on the contrary, we would feel like Jesus himself expressed it, "he that is greatest among you, let him be the servant of all." If we would be great among the children of men, let us show that we are willing to serve and to do good to our fellowmen, set them a right example, shield them from wrong, show them the right way, help them to avoid error and sin, and to walk in the light, as God is in the light, that they may have fellowship with him and with one another, and that the blood of Christ may indeed cleanse them from all sin.

The spirit of the gospel should teach us that if men sue us at the law, and take away our coat wrongfully and wickedly, intending to injure or degrade us, that we would rise above the spirit of contention and retribution in our own souls, and speak as Jesus spoke: "Forgive them, for they know not what they do."

My brethren and sisters, if we would build up ourselves, or ever become worthy to inherit the kingdom of God, we will do so on the principle of eternal truth. The truth is what will make us free; free from error, prejudice, selfishness, ignorance, contention, the power of the adversary of our souls, free from the power of death and hell; free to inherit the fulness of the everlasting gospel; free to have joy in our hearts for all things good and for the welfare of mankind; free to forgive those who err because of lack of judgment and understanding. But the Spirit of truth, mark you, will not tolerate and will not forgive determined, premeditated and deliberate wrong in man or woman, in the world—truth will not tolerate it. We can not forgive that kind or class of crime and wickedness. We can not, or if we do, we transgress the laws of God, for he has no sympathy with Satan, nor with him who knoweth to do good and doeth evil; who knoweth to do right but is determined to do wrong. There is no forgiveness to such without humble and most contrite repentance of sin. When one gets far enough along in the crime of wickedness and disobedience to the principles of the gospel, and in the abandonment of love for his fellowmen and for the Church of Jesus Christ, so that he will fight and lie about the Church and the truth, and seek by every power within his reach to injure and wrong them, there is no forgiveness for that man, and if he goes just far enough, there is no repentance for him either.

And how do you pray? To be heard because of many words? No; but because the Lord has said it is your duty to inquire of him; I will be inquired of, by my people; I will be asked for blessings, for my gifts, and the door will be opened to those who knock, and those who seek after the truth shall find it.

Fathers, pray with your families; bow down with them morning and at night; pray to the Lord, thank him for his goodness, mercy and Fatherly kindness, just as our earthly fathers and mothers have been extremely kind to us poor, disobedient and wayward children.

Do you pray? What do you pray for? You pray that God may recognize you, that he may hear your prayers, and that he may bless you with his Spirit, and that he may lead you into all truth and show you the right way; that he will warn you against wrong and guide you into the right path; that you may not fall astray, that you may not veer into the wrong way unto death, but that you may keep in the narrow way. You pray for your wives to have health and strength, blessed to be happy and contented, true to their children, true to their homes, true to you. The wives pray that they may also have power to overcome the weaknesses of fallen human nature, and rise to teach their children the beauty and glory of a righteous life, and that the children may be blessed to carry out in their lives the wish and desire of their parents; that they may perfect their lives here by living up to the wise teachings of the gospel. So we pray for what we need.

While in my boyhood days, when I was like some of these little boys, I used to wonder—how could the Lord hear me when I was in secret, or wherever I might be? I wondered at it! Do you wonder at it now, when you have learned something of the late discoveries made by human wisdom and human intelligence?

They have discovered that there is a principle by which communication between distant points, thousands of miles away, may take place, and one man may communicate with another through the air, his words and voice being distinctly and clearly heard. If in the midst of the Pacific ocean, a thousand or more miles from shore, I could send a message inland a thousand or more miles, and could

send it without the medium of wire, merely by the power or force of
electricity, to my home thousands of miles away, how easy, is it not,
for God to hear our prayers, who understands, and knows all things,
long before we ever thought of such wonderful inventions and who
has power over all things!

Is it any wonder that the Lord can hear you when you whisper,
even in your secret closet? Is there any doubt in your minds about it?
If man can communicate across the continent by means of a telephone
without wires—by means of human invention, by reason of the wisdom
of man, is there any one who doubts the ability of God to hear the
earnest, honest supplication of the soul? Do not doubt any more
that the Lord can hear your prayers, when, with a small instrument,
sensitive to the electric spark, you can distinctly hear the human
voice in your home received from the ocean thousands of miles away.
When you can communicate to some one in the midst of the ocean
from your home, far inland from the ocean—do not for a moment
doubt that the Lord understands all these means of communication
and that he has means of hearing and understanding your innermost,
exact thoughts. "Prayer is the soul's sincere desire, uttered or un-
expressed." It does not take many words to ask the Lord for what
we need; but we must ask in faith, confidence and trust. It will not
do to have doubts in our minds when we call upon the Lord for a
blessing. "If any of you lack wisdom, let him ask of God, that giveth
to all men liberally, and upbraideth not; and it shall be given
him. But let him ask in faith, nothing wavering. For he that wavereth is like a wave of the sea, driven with the wind and tossed. For let
not that man think that he shall receive anything of the Lord."
(James 1:5-7.)

When a little child bows down in its perfect simplicity and asks
the Father for a blessing, the Father hears the voice, and will answer
in blessings upon his head, because the child is innocent and asks
in full trust and confidence.

These are simple principles that I have sought to impress upon
your minds. They are simple, but necessary, and essential. There
is no mystery about them, there is no mystery in the birth of man
into the world, when you understand the laws of nature, which are
the laws of God—no mystery about it. There will be no more mystery
in the resurrection from the dead to life and everlasting light, than
there is in the birth of man into the world, when we understand the
truth, as we will some day, as the Lord of glory instituted it. There

is no mystery in the birth or begetting of the Son of God, nor regarding his birth into the world. It was just as natural, and as strictly in accordance with the laws of nature and of God, as the birth of any one of his children, the birth of any one of us. It was simply in accordance with truth, and law and order. Will the men of the world receive the gospel? Will they hearken to the truth? Or will they mystify the truth and seek to becloud the children of men over simple truths when they should understand them? From the middle-aged to the gray-haired man, as well as the youth, all should understand the principles of the gospel, the simple truths given for the redemption and exaltation of man.—*Granite Stake Conference,* Sunday, Nov. 25, 1917.

BLESSING FROM OBEDIENCE. Every good and perfect gift comes from the Father of Light, who is no respecter of persons and in whom there is no variableness, nor shadow of turning. To please him we must not only worship him with thanksgiving and praise, but render willing obedience to his commandments. By so doing he is bound to bestow his blessings; for it is upon this principle (obedience to law) that all blessings are predicated.—*Improvement Era,* Vol. 21, December, 1917.

Chapter XII

PRAYER

Pray Every Day. Observe that great commandment given of the Master, always to remember the Lord, to pray in the morning, and in the evening, and always remember to thank him for the blessings that you receive day by day.—Oct. C. R., 1914, p. 6.

Pray in Wisdom. My brethren and sisters, let us remember and call upon God and implore his blessings and his favor upon us. Let us do it, nevertheless, in wisdom and in righteousness, and when we pray we should call upon him in a consistent and reasonable way. We should not ask the Lord for that which is unnecessary or which would not be beneficial to us. We should ask for that which we need, and we should ask in faith, "nothing wavering, for he that wavereth," as the apostle said, "is like the wave of the sea, driven by the wind and tossed. For let not that man think that he shall receive anything of the Lord." But when we ask of God for blessings let us ask in the faith of the gospel, in that faith that he has promised to give to those who believe in him and obey his commandments.—Oct. C. R., 1914, p. 7.

Keep the Spirit of Prayer. We should carry with us the spirit of prayer throughout every duty that we have to perform in life. Why should we? One of the simple reasons that appeals to my mind with great force is that man is so utterly dependent upon God! How helpless we are without him; how little can we do without his merciful providence in our behalf! I have often been led to make the remark, that not one of us, not a human being in all the world can make even a single spear of grass grow without the help of God. We have to use his earth, we must avail ourselves of the benefit of his soil, his air and his sunshine, and the moisture that God provides, and gives to the earth, to enable us to produce even a single blade of grass; and the same applies to everything that ministers to our existence in the world. You can't raise an ear of corn or grain of wheat without God's help. You cannot produce a single thing essential to the existence of man or beast without the help of God. Then, why should we not feel dependent upon the Lord? Why should we not call upon his name? Why should we not remember him in our prayers? Why should we not love him with all our heart and mind, and strength, since he has given us life, since he has formed us in his own likeness and image, since he has placed us here that we may become like unto his Only Begotten Son and to inherit the glory, exaltation and reward provided for God's own children?—Oct. C. R., 1914, p. 6.

TRUE PRAYER. I pray you, my young brethren who are present in this vast congregation, and who are liable to be called to preach the gospel to the world, when you are called to go out, I pray that you will know how to approach God in prayer. It is not such a difficult thing to learn how to pray. It is not the words we use particularly that constitute prayer. Prayer does not consist of words, altogether. True, faithful, earnest prayer consists more in the feeling that rises from the heart and from the inward desire of our spirits to supplicate the Lord in humility and in faith, that we may receive his blessings. It matters not how simple the words may be, if our desires are genuine and we come before the Lord with a broken heart and contrite spirit to ask him for that which we need. I would like to know if there is a young man in this congregation, or anywhere else, who does not need something of the Lord. Where is there a soul upon the earth that does not need something that the Almighty can give? In the first place, all that we have comes from him. It is by his providence that we exist on the earth. It is by his kind mercy that we see and hear, that we have the power of speech, and that we possess intelligence, for as the sage of old said, "There is a spirit in man; and the inspiration of the Almighty giveth them understanding." Therefore, the very power of understanding that we possess is the gift of God. In and of ourselves we are but a lifeless lump of clay. Life, intelligence, wisdom, judgment, power to reason, all are the gifts of God to the children of men. He gives us our physical strength as well as our mental powers. Every young man should feel from the depth of his heart that he is indebted to Almighty God for his being and for every attribute that he possesses which is in likeness of the attributes of God. We should seek to magnify the attributes that we possess. We should honor God with our intelligence, with our strength, with our understanding, with our wisdom, and with all the power that we possess. We should seek to do good in the world. This is our duty; and if a young man can only feel as all men should feel, he will find that it is an easy matter for him to bow down before the Lord in humble prayer and seek unto God for the aid, comfort, and inspiration of his Holy Spirit, that he may not be left entirely to himself, nor to the wisdom and ways of the world. But as a rule, where young men have good parents to provide for them, where they have good homes and their food and raiment are sure, they feel that they are not dependent upon anybody, unless perchance they should be afflicted in some way, and then begin to realize their weakness and dependence. But I want to say to you, my young friends, that in the hour of your independence, at the moment when you feel the strongest, you should bear in mind that you are but human, the breath of life is in your nostrils, and you are destined to pass from this world through the portals of death.—Oct. C. R., 1899, pp. 69, 70.

How to Pray. My brethren and sisters, do not learn to pray with your lips only. Do not learn a prayer by heart, and say it every morning and evening. That is something I dislike very much. It is true that a great many people fall into the rut of saying over a ceremonious prayer. They begin at a certain point, and they touch at all the points along the road until they get to the winding up scene; and when they have done, I do not know whether the prayer has ascended beyond the ceiling of the room or not.—Oct. C. R., 1899, pp. 71, 72.

An Address on Prayer. I thought that a few words from the Book of Mormon might be appropriate as concluding advice and counsel, written by the prophet Moroni:

"And now, my brethren, I judge these things of you because of your peaceable walk with the children of men;

"For I remember the word of God, which saith by their works ye shall know them; for if their works be good, then they are good also.

"For behold, God hath said, A man being evil cannot do that which is good; for if he offereth a gift, or prayeth unto God, except he shall do it with real intent it profiteth him nothing.

"For behold, it is not counted unto him for righteousness.

"For behold, if a man being evil, giveth a gift, he doeth it grudgingly; wherefore it is counted unto him the same as if he had retained the gift; wherefore he is counted evil before God.

"And likewise also is it counted evil unto a man, if he shall pray, and not with real intent of heart; yea, and it profiteth him nothing; for God receiveth none such." (Moroni 7:4-9.)

Here, indeed, is a text that would give an opportunity to one moved by the proper spirit, to make a telling discourse among the Latter-day Saints—not applicable to all, but applicable to far too many.

It is not good for us to pray by rote, to kneel down and repeat the Lord's prayer continually. I think that one of the greatest follies I have ever witnessed is the foolish custom of men repeating the Lord's prayer continually without considering its meaning. The Lord gave this as a pattern to his disciples who were going out into the world to preach the gospel. It was to show them that they were not to use many words, but were to come directly to the Lord, and ask him for the things they might need, consequently one of the specific provisions in that prayer, and the example set was: "Give us this day our daily bread;" and we see people clothed with plenty, possessed of millions, perhaps, and yet, if they pray at all, they repeat simply the Lord's prayer. It thus becomes only a form; there is no power in it; neither is it acceptable, because it is not offered from the heart, nor with the understanding; and I think that it is desirable for us to look well to our words when we call upon the Lord. He hears us in secret, and can reward us openly. We do not have to cry unto him with many words. We do not have to weary him with long prayers. What we do need, and what we should do as Latter-day Saints, for our own good, is to go before him often, to witness unto him that we remember him and that we are willing to take upon us his name, keep his commandments, work righteousness; and that we desire his Spirit to help us. Then, if we are in trouble, let us go to the Lord and ask him directly and specifically to help us out of the trouble that we are in; and let the prayer come from the heart, let it not be in words that are worn into ruts in the beaten tracks of common use, without thought or feeling in the use of those words. Let us speak the simple words, expressing our need, that will appeal most truly to the Giver of every good and perfect gift. He can hear in secret; and he knows the desires of our hearts before we ask, but he has made it obligatory, and a duty that we shall call upon his name—that we shall ask that we may receive; and knock that it may be opened to us; and seek that we may find. Hence, the Lord has made it a loving duty that we should remember him, that we should witness unto him morning, noon, and night, that we do not forget the Giver of every good gift unto us.

"Wherefore, a man being evil, cannot do that which is good; neither will he give a good gift.

"For behold, a bitter fountain cannot bring forth good water; neither can a good fountain bring forth bitter water, wherefore a man being a servant of the devil, cannot follow Christ; and if he follow Christ, he cannot be a servant of the devil.

"Wherefore, all things which are good, cometh of God; and that which is evil, cometh of the devil; for the devil is an enemy unto God, and fighteth against him continually, and inviteth and enticeth to sin, and to do that which is evil continually.

"But behold, that which is of God, inviteth and enticeth to do good continually; wherefore, everything which inviteth and enticeth to do good, and to love God, and to serve him, is inspired of God.

"Wherefore take heed, my beloved brethren, that ye do not judge that which is evil to be of God, or that which is good and of God, to be of the devil.

"For behold, my brethren, it is given unto you to judge, that ye may know good from evil; and the way to judge is as plain, that ye may know with a perfect knowledge, as the daylight is from the dark night.

"For behold, the Spirit of Christ is given to every man, that they may know good from evil; wherefore I show unto you the way to judge; for everything which inviteth to do good, and to persuade to believe in Christ, is sent forth by the power and gift of Christ; wherefore ye may know with a perfect knowledge it is of God.

"But whatsoever thing persuadeth men to do evil, and believe not in Christ and deny him, and serve not God, then ye may know with a perfect knowledge it is of the devil, for after this manner doth the devil work, for he persuadeth no man to do good, no, not one; neither doth his angels; neither do they who subject themselves unto him.

"And now, my brethren, seeing that ye know the light by which ye may judge, which light is the light of Christ, see that ye do not judge wrongfully; for with that same judgment which ye judge, ye shall also be judged.

"Wherefore I beseech of you, brethren, that ye should search diligently in the light of Christ, that ye may know good from evil; and if ye will lay hold upon every good thing, and condemn it not, ye certainly will be a child of Christ." (Moroni 7:10-19.)

I think that here, in the words that I have read, are some plain fingerboards, some plain, simple guideposts; and if we, as Latter-day Saints, believing as we do in the divinity of this book which was translated by the gift and power of God, through the inspiration that came to the Prophet Joseph Smith, would read these words as be-lieving children should read, with understanding, in faith, being sure that God inspired them, and then put them into practice, I think it would not be long before we could do away with appeals to bishops' courts, and high councils, and with the present necessity for teachers' visits, to try to settle difficulties among Latter-day Saints. I believe every man would be his own judge, for he would judge righteously, because he would judge in the light of truth, in the light and justice—not selfishly, not covetously, but in the light that has come from the heavens in the latter days, through revelations from God.—*Improvement Era*, Vol. 11, August, 1908, pp. 729-732.

PRAY FOR THE AUTHORITIES. We have met together this afternoon in the capacity of a conference of this stake of Zion. We have had presented before us the stake authorities, together with the home missionaries, that we might sustain them by our vote, which means also by our faith and prayers, and to stand by them in the discharge of all the duties that devolve upon them. It is an important duty resting upon the Saints who vote to sustain the authorities of the Church, to do so not only by the lifting of the hand, the mere form, but in deed and in truth. There never should be a day pass but all the people composing the Church should lift up their voices in prayer to the Lord to sustain his servants who are placed to preside over them. Not only should they do this in behalf of the president of the stake and his counselors, but they should do it in behalf of the high council, before whom, in connection with the presidency of the stake, matters of vast importance to the members of the Church are brought from time to time for their judgment and counsel. These men should have the faith of the people to sustain them in discharge of their duties, in order that they may be strong in the Lord. These authorities are also presented before the people, so that if there is any fault in them, worthy of objection, to their acting in the positions to which they are called, the Saints who know of these objections may make them manifest, in order that such inquiry may be instituted as may be necessary to ascertain the truth, that those who are not worthy may be dropped, and only such as are worthy and faithful in the performance of their duties be sustained in these exalted positions in the Church.

We should not permit ourselves to go about from day to day with a spirit of murmuring and fault-finding in our hearts against those who are presented before us to be sustained in responsible positions. If we have anything in our hearts against any of these brethren, it is our duty, as conscientious members of the Church, first, as the Spirit may direct, to go to them alone and make known to them our feeling toward them and show them the cause of such feeling; not with a desire in our hearts to widen or increase the difficulty, but we should go to them in the spirit of reconciliation and brotherly love, in a true Christian spirit, so that if any feeling of bitterness exists within us it may be absolutely removed; and if we have cause against our brother, that we may be in a position to remedy the evil. We should seek to love one another and to sustain one another as children of God and as brothers and sisters in the cause.

The presentation of the authorities of the Church before a conference is made obligatory upon the Church. It is the command of the Lord that we shall meet together to transact the business of the Church, an important part of which is to sustain the authorities of the Church, thus renewing our covenant to uphold God's authority which he has instituted in the earth for the government of his Church. And I cannot emphasize too strongly the importance of Latter-day Saints honoring and sustaining in truth and in deed the authority of the Holy Priesthood which is called to preside. The moment a spirit enters the heart of a member to refrain from sustaining the constituted authorities of the Church, that moment he becomes possessed of a spirit which inclines to rebellion or dissension; and if he permits that spirit to take a firm root in his mind, it will eventually lead him into darkness and apostasy. It makes no difference how much we may profess to love the gospel and prize our standing in the Church, if we allow the spirit of darkness to take possession of our minds, the light and love within us will go out, and bitterness and enmity will take possession of our souls. Then, oh how dark, how bitter and wicked we may become!—*Salt Lake Stake, C. R., June 12, 1898.*

BLESSINGS FOLLOW PRAYERS. Family and secret prayers should be observed, not alone to comply with the commandment of the Lord, but because of the wonderful blessings to be gained. The Lord has said we should inquire of him.—*Improvement Era*, Vol. 21, December, 1917, p. 104.

CORRECT OUR NEGLECTS. What shall we do if we have neglected our prayers? Let us begin to pray. If we have neglected any other duty, let us seek unto the Lord for his Spirit, that we may know wherein we have erred and lost our opportunities, or let them pass by us unimproved.—*Deseret Weekly News*, Vol. 24. p. 708.

Chapter XIII

TITHING; THE POOR; INDUSTRY

Why the Law of Tithing Was Instituted. The Lord revealed to his people in the incipiency of his work a law which was more perfect than the law of tithing. It comprehended larger things, greater power, and a more speedy accomplishment of the purposes of the Lord. But the people were unprepared to live by it, and the Lord, out of mercy to the people, suspended the more perfect law, and gave the law of tithing, in order that there might be means in the storehouse of the Lord for the carrying out of the purposes he had in view; for the gathering of the poor, for the spreading of the gospel to the nations of the earth, for the maintenance of those who were required to give their constant attention, day in and day out, to the work of the Lord, and for whom it was necessary to make some provision. Without this law these things could not be done, neither could temples be built and maintained, nor the poor fed and clothed. Therefore the law of tithing is necessary for the Church, so much so that the Lord has laid great stress upon it.—*Apr. C. R.*, 1900, p. 47.

Essential Nature of the Law of Tithing. By this principle (tithing) the loyalty of the people of this Church shall be put to the test. By this principle it shall be known who is for the kingdom of God and who is against it. By this principle it shall be seen whose hearts are set on doing the will of God and keeping his commandments, thereby sanctifying the land of Zion unto God, and who are opposed to this principle and have cut themselves off from the blessings of Zion. There is a great deal of importance connected with this principle, for by it it shall be known whether we are faithful or unfaithful. In this respect it is as essential as faith in God, as repentance of sin, as baptism for the remission of sin, or as the laying on of hands for the gift of the Holy Ghost. For if a man keep all the law save one point, and he offend in that, he is a transgressor of the law, and he is not entitled to the fulness of the blessings of the gospel of Jesus Christ. But when a man keeps all the law that is revealed, according to his strength, his substance, and his ability, though what he does may be little, it is just as acceptable in the sight of God as if he were able to do a thousand times more.—*Apr. C. R.*, 1900, pp. 47, 48.

THE LAW OF TITHING A TEST. The law of tithing is a test by which the people as individuals shall be proved. Any man who fails to observe this principle shall be known as a man who is indifferent to the welfare of Zion, who neglects his duty as a member of the Church, and who does nothing toward the accomplishment of the temporal advancement of the kingdom of God. He contributes nothing, either, toward spreading the gospel to the nations of the earth, and he neglects to do that which would entitle him to receive the blessings and ordinances of the gospel.—Apr. C. R., 1900, p. 47.

THE LAW OF TITHING, THE LAW OF REVENUE. The purpose of the law of tithing is similar to that of the law of revenue which is enacted by every state, every country, and every municipality in the world, I suppose. There is no such thing as an organization of men for any purpose of importance, without provisions for carrying out its designs. The law of tithing is the law of revenue for the Church of Jesus Christ of Latter-day Saints. Without it, it would be impossible to carry on the purposes of the Lord.

TITHING. No doubt, a good deal more could be read from the scriptures in relation to this principle of tithing, which God has revealed to us in this dispensation, and which he requires at our hands, that we may sanctify, by obedience to his law, this land that it may become indeed a land of Zion unto us; and the promise is, that if we will obey the laws of God, if we will put our trust in him, if we will draw near unto him he will draw near unto us, and he will reward us with his favor and his blessing. He will rebuke the devourer, and he will cause that the earth shall be fruitful, that it shall yield in its strength to the husbandman, the tiller of the soil, and to the herder of flocks. He will increase his kine, and will prosper him upon the right hand and upon the left, and he shall have an abundance, because he puts his trust in God; he draws near unto him, and he is willing to prove him, to see whether he will not open the windows of heaven and pour out blessings upon him that he shall not have room to contain them. Let every man who has received the gospel of Jesus Christ receive this saying, and hearken to these words, for all they are worth. Some men may esteem them lightly, and those who do, will, without doubt, fail to draw near, they will neglect to prove the Lord, they will not fulfil the commandments that he has given, and they will never know that God tells the truth, and that he is able to fulfil his word and promise unto his people when they are willing to obey and keep his law. While they who appreciate these promises, who obey these laws that were given anciently, and have been renewed again in the dispensation of the fulness of times, for the blessing of the people, for the building up of Zion, for the feeding of the widow and the orphan, or the spreading of the gospel of Christ to the nations of the earth, and for the gathering of the people from the four quarters of the earth, those who hearken to these words, prize them as the truth, and apply them in their practice throughout their lives, will come to know that God is a rewarder of those who diligently serve him, and that he is able to fulfil his promises unto them.

A short time ago I met a brother—I need not call his name, for he is but one among thousands who can bear the same testimony, not only by the word of mouth but by the evidences of thrift, of prosperity, of progress and of improvement which surround him in the midst of the deserts. This season he has gathered in rich harvests, his farms having produced in abundance, while the farms of many of his neighbors are clogged with weeds, and their harvests have been only one-half or one-third what his has been. How do you account for it? I account for it in the fact that God has blessed him; and so does he, for he is an intelligent man, a man that not only labors wisely and prudently, but in the fear of God, and in the desire of his heart to obey his laws. He said to me and my companion with whom we were traveling: "God has blessed me because I have striven to keep his laws, and because I have been true to my family." He went out there upon the desert seven or eight years ago, impoverished by persecution and exile, being driven from his home and from his affairs, compelled to wander in exile for years, part of the time preaching the gospel. He returned seven or eight years ago, and settled down upon the desert. Today, out of the earth, the burning sands, he has produced beautiful homes, he has fruitful fields, which are spread out before the eyes of any man who wishes to go and look upon them. He pays his tithing, he remembers his offerings, he is obedient to the laws of God, and he is not afraid to bear testimony to his friends and neighbors that it is through obedience that God has blessed and prospered him, and made him what he is today. He is not the only one; there are others who are prospered in like manner. And I testify that it is because God has blessed him, and his soil, and his labors, that he obtained the increase, and secured the blessings for which he sought and labored. He has acted in good faith with the

Lord; the Lord has known his heart, and has blessed him accordingly, and he is prosperous today in that desert, while as to many of his neighbors—go and look for yourselves at their broad acres. They tell the story for themselves. His lands are clear from noxious weeds, because he has labored, and taken care of his lands, and because God has inspired him, and enlightened his mind. The Lord has blessed him in his basket and in his store, in his labors and in the thoughts of his mind, he has been inspired and enabled to accomplish the work that he has done: I testify that it is because of man's faith in the promise of the Lord, and his desire to obey his laws, that he is blessed and prospered of him.—Oct. C. R., 1897, pp. 35, 36.

THE WIDOW AND HER TITHING. Will you then deny the widow, because she has only a mite to bestow? Because the tenth which she proposes to give in obedience to the commandment of God is but a penny, are you going to deprive her of the privilege of having her name enrolled on the book of the law of the Lord, and of having her genealogy acknowledged and recorded in the archives of the Church? And because her name is not found there, are you going to deny her the privileges of the house of God and of the ordinances of the gospel? I think it is time the bishops understood this principle. The bishop should encourage every man, woman and child, who earns and receives a return for labor, to honor the Lord and to prove obedient to the law of God by giving the one-tenth of that which he or she receives, as the Lord requires, so that they may have their names enrolled on the book of the law of the Lord, that their genealogies may be had in the archives of the Church, and that they may be entitled to the privileges and blessings of the house of God.

I recollect most vividly a circumstance that occurred in the days of my childhood. My mother was a widow, with a large family to provide for. One spring when we opened our potato pits, she had her boys get a load of the best potatoes and she took them to the tithing office; potatoes were scarce that season. I was a little boy at the time, and drove the team. When we drove up to the steps of the tithing office, ready to unload the potatoes, one of the clerks came out and said to my mother, "Widow Smith, it's a shame that you should have to pay tithing." He said a number of other things that I remember well, but they are not necessary for me to repeat here. The first two letters of the name of that tithing clerk were William Thompson, and he chided my mother for paying her tithing, called her anything but wise or prudent; and said there were others who were strong and able to work that were supported from the tithing office. My mother turned upon him and said: "William, you ought to be ashamed of yourself. Would you deny me a blessing? If I did not pay my tithing, I should expect the Lord to withhold his blessings from me. I pay my tithing, not only because it is a law of God, but because I expect a blessing by doing it. By keeping this and other laws, I expect to prosper, and to be able to provide for my family." Though she was a widow, you may turn to the records of the Church from the beginning unto the day of her death, and you will find that she never received a farthing from the Church to help her support herself and her family; but she paid in thousands of dollars in wheat, potatoes, corn, vegetables, meat, etc. The tithes of her sheep and cattle, the tenth pound of her butter, her tenth chicken, the tenth of her eggs, the tenth pig, the tenth calf, the tenth colt—a tenth of everything she raised was paid. Here sits my brother who can bear testimony to the truth of what I say, as can others who knew her. She prospered because she obeyed the laws of God. She had abundance to sustain her family. We never lacked as much as many others did; for while we found nettle greens most acceptable when we first came to the valley; and while we enjoyed thistle roots, segoes and all that kind of thing, we were no worse off than thousands of others, and not as poor as many, for we were never without corn-meal and milk or butter, to my knowledge. Then that widow had her name recorded in the book of the law of the Lord. That widow was entitled to the privileges of the house of God. No ordinance of the gospel could be denied her, for she was obedient to the laws of God, and she would not fail in her duty, though discouraged from observing a commandment of God by one who was in an official position.

This may be said to be personal. By some it may be considered egotistical. But I do not speak of it in that light. When William Thompson told my mother that she ought not to pay tithing, I thought he was one of the finest fellows in the world. I believed every word he said. I had to work and dig and toil myself. I had to help plow the ground, plant the potatoes, hoe the potatoes, dig the potatoes, and all like duties, and then to load up a big wagon-box full of the very best we had, leaving out the poor ones, and bringing the load to the tithing office, I thought in my childish way that it looked a little hard, specially when I saw certain of my playmates and early associates of childhood, playing round, riding horses and having good times, and who scarcely ever did a lick of work in their lives, and yet were being fed from the public crib. Where are those boys today? Are they known in the Church? Are they prominent among the people of God? Are they or were they ever valiant in the testimony of Jesus Christ? Have they a clear testimony of the truth in their hearts? Are they diligent members of the Church? No; and never have been, as a rule, and most of them are dead or vanished out of sight. Well, after I received a few years of experience, I was converted, I found that my mother was right and that William Thompson was wrong. He denied the faith, apostatized, left the country, and led away as many of his family as would go with him. I do not want you to deny me the privilege of being numbered with those who have the interests of Zion at heart, and who desire to contribute their proportion to the upbuilding of Zion, and for the maintenance of the work of the Lord in the earth. It is a blessing that I enjoy, and I do not propose that anybody shall deprive me of that pleasure.—Apr. C. R., 1900, pp. 48, 49.

THE WIDOW AND TITHING. I preach that which I believe and that which I do know to be true, and I do know that if men will obey the laws of God, God will honor and bless them. I have proven it all my life through. I saw it manifested in circumstances which occurred in my childhood, and I know that God has blessed the widow and the fatherless when they have been obedient to his laws and have kept his commandments.

I can tell you the history of a widow woman, with a large family, who was more particular, if possible, to pay the Lord what belonged to him than she was to pay to her neighbors to whom she might be indebted, and she never was indebted to her neighbors, thank God, for anything that she did not pay to the last cent, because the Lord blessed her with plenty, and in her latter years she did not have to borrow of her neighbors, nor did she have to call upon the Church for support, either, but she paid thousands of dollars in products and money into the storehouse of the Lord, although she was a widow with a large family to support. I know this. I can testify of this, and that the Lord Almighty blessed her, not only in the products of her fields, but in her flocks and herds. They were not devoured. They were not destroyed. They did not lie down and die. They increased. They did not stray away; and thieves did not steal them.

One reason for that was, she had a little boy that watched them very carefully under her direction, and prompting. Her eye was upon everything, she had supervision over everything, she directed those whom she employed, and her children; and I am a witness—and here sits another witness (Patriarch John Smith)—that God, the eternal Father, blessed her and prospered her while she lived, and she was not only enabled to maintain herself and children that were left to her in poverty, in a day of trial, and when she was driven out into the wilderness, but she was able to feed scores of the poor, and to pay her tithes besides. Verily the Lord prospered her, and she was blessed.—Oct. C. R., 1897, pp. 35-37.

WHO RECEIVES CHURCH HELP SHOULD BE TITHE PAYERS. When one comes to a bishop and asks for assistance because of his or her straitened circumstances, the first thing the bishop should do is to inquire if he or she is a tithe-payer. He should know whether the name is on the book of the law of the Lord, and if not on the book, if he or she has been derelict and negligent in relation to this principle of tithing, he or she has no claim upon the bishop, neither have their children; and if, under those circumstances, the bishop assists him, it will simply be out of pure charity and not because such have any claim upon the Church. That is why the widow who receives assistance from the Church should pay her tithing, so that her name may be on the records of the Church. It is not a law that is applicable to one and not to another. If the rich may not receive blessings because their names are not on the record, then neither shall the poor receive blessings in the house of God, if their names are not recorded. So long as a poor person receives his or her support through the tithings of the people, they should be willing to observe the law themselves in order that they may be entitled to what they receive. They should show by their observance of the law that they are law-keepers and not law-breakers. Our children, as soon as they become old enough to earn means, should be taught to pay their tithing, that their names may be written in the book of the law of the Lord, so that if perchance their father die and they are left orphans, their names as well as the names of their parents, will be found upon the records and they will, as God lives, be entitled to their support and to their education. It is our duty to look after these children and see that they have an equal chance with those who are most favored with parents to look after them.—Oct. C. R., 1899, pp. 44, 45.

USE OF TITHING. I mention this simply to show that these men, whose whole time is occupied in the ministry, are only drawing their necessary support from the Church. They must have that. You would not begrudge them that. Men who are faithful, valiant, instant in season and out of season, and consequently engaged in the work of the ministry, you surely would not say that they should not have food to eat, raiment to wear, and where to lay their heads; and that is all these men get from the Church. The laborer is certainly worthy of his hire. So that your tithing is not enriching your brethren of the ministry. It is being used to keep up the ordinances of the house of God in these four temples. Thousands and thousands of dollars of it are being used in educating the youth of Zion and in maintaining the Church schools. Thousands of dollars are being expended to feed and clothe the poor, and to take care of those who are dependent upon the Church. They look to their "mother" for succor and support, and it is right and proper that the Church should provide for its own poor and indigent, feeble and helpless, so far as possible.—Apr. C. R., 1901, p. 71.

COMMERCIALISM AND TITHING. The Church is charged with commercialism. There is not the least resemblance of it, in truth. The Church is neither buying nor selling goods or chattels. It is not engaged in merchandising of any description, and never has been; and there could not well be a more false and groundless statement made against the Church than to charge it with commercialism. It is true that, unlike other churches or religious organizations, the people of this Church observe the law of tithing, which is the law of revenue of the Church. We do not pass around the hat to you, nor the collection box, for means to defray the expenses incident to carrying on of the work of the Church. You give it voluntarily. This reminds me of another falsehood that is spread abroad by our enemies, namely: That the "Mormon" people are compelled to pay tithing, that the authorities of the Church demand it of them, that it is made obligatory upon them, and is tyrannically exacted from them all the time, which is an infamous falsehood, a slander, for there is not a word or syllable of truth in it. The observance of the law of tithing is voluntary. I can pay my tithing or not, as I choose. It is a matter of choice with me, whether I will do it or not do it; but, feeling as I do, loyal to the Church, loyal to its interests, believing that it is right and just to observe the law of tithing I do observe it—on the same principle that I think it is right for me to observe the law of repentance, and of baptism, for the remission of sins. It is my pleasure to do my duty with reference to the observance of these principles, and to pay my tithing. The Lord has revealed how this means shall be cared for, and managed; namely, by the Presidency of the Church and the High Council of the Church (that is, the Twelve Apostles), and the Presiding Bishopric of the Church. I think there is wisdom in this. It is not left for one man to dispose of it, or to handle it alone, not by any means. It devolves upon at least eighteen men, men of wisdom, of faith, of ability, as these eighteen men are. I say it devolves upon them to dispose of the tithes of the people and to use them for whatever purpose in their judgment and wisdom will accomplish the most good for the Church; and because this fund of tithing is disposed of by these men whom the Lord has designated as having authority to do it, for the necessities and benefit of the Church, they call it "commercialism." What absurdity! You may just as well call their practices in passing around their contribution boxes, for collecting means with which to build their churches, with which to pay their ministers, and with which to carry on the monetary affairs of their churches, "commercialism," as for them to charge us with "commercialism," because we handle the tithing of the Church, and appropriate and use it for the benefit of the Church.—Apr. C. R., 1912, pp. 5, 6.

TITHING USED CAREFULLY AND FULL ACCOUNTS KEPT. I defy any man on earth to point his finger to a dollar that is wilfully wasted or stolen by the servants of God. The tithing books are kept as accurately and as perfectly as any books are kept in any bank. Every man who pays a dollar tithing gets his credit on the books; and if he wants to see that his credit is there he can go and see for himself. But we do not propose to open our books and show your accounts to every Tom, Dick and Harry in the land who never did pay any tithing. We do not propose to do that, if we can help it. But you Latter-day Saints who pay your tithes and your offerings, if you want to see for yourselves that you may be eye and ear witnesses, the books are open to you, and you can come and examine your accounts any business day you want.—Oct. C. R., 1905, p. 5.

BOOKS OPEN TO TITHEPAYERS. The man who complains about not knowing what is done with the tithing, in ninety-nine cases out of a hundred, is the man who has no credit on the books of the Church for paying tithing. We do not care to exhibit the books of the Church to such carpers, and to that class of people. But there is not a tithe-payer in the Church who cannot go to the Presiding Bishop's office, or to the office of the Trustee-in-Trust, if he desires, and find his account, and see to it that every dollar he has given to the Lord for tithing is credited to him. Then, if he wants to be more searching as a tithe-payer, and find out what is done with the tithing, we will set before him the whole thing, and if he has any good counsel to give us we will take it from him. But we will not—because we do not have to, and it is not the business of the world to require it—open our books to the world, unless we wish to. We are not ashamed of them. We are not afraid for them to be inspected. They are honest and straight; and there is not a man in the world who will look at them, but will say so, if he is honest himself.—Apr. C. R., 1906, pp. 6, 7.

We Should Sympathize with the Unfortunate. We too frequently see a disposition on the part of our children to make fun of the unfortunate. A poor cripple, or a poor, weak-minded person comes along, and the boys will poke fun at him, and make unbecoming remarks about him. This is entirely wrong, and such a spirit as this should never be witnessed among the children of the Latter-day Saints.—Oct. C. R., 1904, pp. 87,88.

Charity to be Accepted Only When Necessary. There is such a thing as encouraging idleness and fostering pauperism among men. Men and women ought not to be willing to receive charity unless they are compelled to do so to keep them from suffering. Every man and woman ought to possess the spirit of independence, a self-sustaining spirit, that would prompt him or her to say, when they are in need, "I am willing to give my labor in exchange for that which you give me." No man ought to be satisfied to receive, and to do nothing for it. After a man is brought down to poverty and is under the necessity of receiving aid, and his friends give it to him, he should feel that it is an obligation under which he is placed, and when the Lord should open his way he would return the gift. That is the feeling we should cultivate in our hearts, to make us a free and independent people. The cultivation of any other feeling or spirit than this is calculated to make paupers, to degrade and bring mankind down to beggary, which is a most wretched condition for men to be in. It is a bad thing for men to think the world owes them a living, and all they have to do is to beg or steal to get it. * * * I don't refer to the cripple, or to those who are enfeebled by age, because I look at them in an entirely different light; there is a necessity for them to live, and there is a necessity for us to assist such, but there is no great need in this world for men and women who are able to work and will not work.—Apr. C. R., 1898, pp. 46-48.

CEASE TO WASTE TIME; CEASE TO BE IDLE. I desire to say to this congregation at this time that I have felt very strongly of late a desire, a responsibility, I may say, resting upon me, to admonish the Latter-day Saints everywhere to cease loitering away their precious time, to cease from all idleness. It is said in the revelations that the idler in Zion shall not eat the bread of the laborer, and there is vastly too much, in some parts—not universally, but there is far too much precious time wasted by the youth of Zion, and perhaps by some that are older and more experienced and who ought to know better, in the foolish, vain and unprofitable practice of card-playing. We hear of card parties here and card parties there, and entertainments where the playing of cards is the principal amusement; and the whole evening is thus wasted. The whole precious time of those who are gathered together on occasions of this kind, aggregating many hours, absolutely wasted. If there was nothing else to be said against this practice, that alone should be sufficient to induce Latter-day Saints not to indulge in this foolish and unprofitable pastime.

Read good books. Learn to sing and to recite, and to converse upon subjects that will be of interest to your associates, and at your social gatherings, instead of wasting the time in senseless practices that lead only to mischief and sometimes to serious evil and wrongdoing; instead of doing this, seek out of the best books knowledge and understanding. Read history. Read philosophy, if you wish. Read anything that is good, that will elevate the mind and will add to your stock of knowledge, that those who associate with you may feel an interest in your pursuit of knowledge and of wisdom.—Oct. C. R., 1903, p. 98.

GOSPEL BLESSING OBTAINED BY LABOR. We can never attain to the blessings of the gospel by merely becoming acquainted with it and then sitting down and doing nothing ourselves to stem the current of evil that is preying upon us and upon the world.—Apr. C. R., 1900. p. 40.

IDLERS HAVE NO PLACE IN ZION. There should be no idlers in Zion. Even the poor who have to be assisted should be willing to do all in their power to earn their own living. Not one man or woman should be content to sit down and be fed, clothed, or housed without any exertion on his or her part to compensate for these privileges. All men and women should feel a degree of independence of character that would stimulate them to do something for a living, and not be idle; for it is written that the idler shall not eat the bread of the laborer of Zion, and he shall not have place among us. Therefore, it is necessary that we should be industrious, that we should intelligently apply our labor to something that is productive and conducive to the welfare of the human family. God help us to do this, is my prayer. Amen.—*Apr. C. R.*, 1899, p. 42; Doc. and Cov. 42:42; 68:30; 75:29.

A MESSAGE OF THE LATTER-DAY SAINTS ON BEHALF OF THE POOR. The position of the Latter-day Saints in regard to the poor is perhaps well understood by most readers of the *Era*. But there are some points which are not quite clear to a number of our friends.

God has commanded this people to remember the poor, and to give means for their support. No other community, perhaps, has proved more willing than the Latter-day Saints to obey this command. They have demonstrated this in the past and have been very willing to impart of their properties to aid the poor and unfortunate, not only in their own midst, but also those who live in other nations and other places in our own country. No call for help has ever been heard in vain by them. And this is true, notwithstanding the fact that they have often suffered from unjust oppression and great poverty, in which they have received little, if any, sympathy and no help. They have always taken care of themselves and besides have helped others.

A leading mission of the Church is to teach the gospel of Christ in the world. It has an important message to deliver, which not only includes the spiritual salvation of men, but also their temporal welfare. It not only teaches that faith is necessary, but also that works are required. Belief in Jesus is well and good, but it must be of a living kind which induces the believer to work out his own salvation, and to aid others to do the same. We do not believe in charity as a business; but rather we depend on mutual helpfulness. While the gospel message requires faith and repentance, it requires also that temporal necessities must be met. So the Lord has revealed plans for the temporal salvation of the people. For the benefit of the poor we have the fast instituted, a leading object of which among other things is to provide the poor with food and other necessities until they may help themselves. For it is clear that plans which contemplate only relieving present distress are deficient. The Church has always sought to place its members in a way to help themselves, rather than adopting the method of so many charitable institutions of providing for only present needs. When the help is withdrawn or used up, more must be provided from the same source, thus making paupers of the poor and teaching them the incorrect principle of relying upon others' help, instead of depending upon their own exertions. This plan has made the Latter-day Saints independent wherever they have settled. It has prevented a constant recurring of calls for help and established permanent conditions by which the people help themselves. Our idea of charity, therefore, is to relieve present wants and then to put the poor in a way to help themselves so that in turn they may help others. The funds are committed for distribution to wise men, generally to bishops of the Church, whose duty it is to look after the poor.

We submit the equitable fast-day plan of the Lord to the churches of the world as a wise and systematic way of providing for the poor. I say equitable because it gives an opportunity for the contribution of much or little, according to the position and standing of those who contribute; and besides, it helps both the giver and the receiver. If the churches would adopt the universal monthly fast-day, as observed by the Latter-day Saints, and devote the means saved during the day to the alleviation, blessing and benefit of the poor, and with a view to helping them to help themselves, there would soon be no poor in the land.

It would be a simple matter for people to comply with this requirement to abstain from food and drink one day each month, and to dedicate what would be consumed during that day to the poor, and as much more as they pleased. The Lord has instituted this law; it is simple and perfect, based on reason and intelligence, and would not only prove a solution to the question of providing for the poor, but it would result in good to those who observe the law. It would call attention to the sin of over-eating, place the body in subjection to the spirit, and so promote communion with the Holy Ghost, and insure a spiritual strength and power which the people of the nation so greatly need. As fasting should always be accompanied by prayer, this law would bring the people nearer to God, and divert their minds once a month at least, from the mad rush of worldly affairs and cause them to be brought into immediate contact with practical, pure and undefiled religion—to visit the fatherless and the widow, and keep themselves unspotted from the sins of the world. For religion is not in believing the commandments only, it is in doing them. I would to God that men would not only believe Jesus Christ and his teachings, but would broaden their belief to the extent of doing the things that are taught by him, and doing them in spirit.

He certainly taught fasting, prayer and helpfulness. No better start can be made than by fasting, praying to God, and sacrificing means for the poor. This law combines belief and practice, faith and works, without which neither Armenian nor Latter-day Saint, neither Jew nor Gentile, can be saved.

When appeals are made to the Latter-day Saints for aid, they are always willing to comply; but we have also our mission to perform; to preach the gospel, to establish peace, secure plenty, and promote happiness in the land; and our people have learned through the commandments of God how to take care of themselves and are trying to help others to do likewise. They are ever helping each other and it is seldom that poor are found among them who are unprovided for. They are practically independent and may become entirely so by a stricter adherence to the law of the Lord! We believe that if other communities would adopt the plans of consecration, fasting, and tithing, which the Lord has revealed to he Latter-day Saints and carry them out in spirit, with faith and works, that poverty and pauperism would be greatly reduced or entirely overcome. Opportunities would be presented so that all might obtain work and thus provide for themselves; and the other command of the Lord would be obeyed: "Thou shalt not be idle; for he that is idle shall not eat the bread nor wear the garments of the laborer."—*Improvement Era*, Vol. 10, pp. 831-833.

CHAPTER XIV

TEMPERANCE; THE SABBATH

MAN SHOULD BE MASTER OF HIS APPETITES. How humiliating it must be to a thoughtful man to feel that he is a slave to his appetites, or to an over-weening and pernicious habit, desire or passion! We believe in strict temperance. We believe in abstinence from all injurious practices, and from the use of all hurtful things. Poison, in the judgment of the physician, may be beneficial, under some conditions in life, as a momentary relief; but poison, under any circumstance, should only be used as a temporary expedient, necessary, perhaps, in our best judgment, for the time being, for the instant—for sudden and certain desired relief—but the continued use of that poison will fasten its fangs upon us, so to speak, in such a way that by and by we will find that we are overpowered by it, and we become slaves of the pernicious habit that becomes a tyrannical master over us.— *Apr. C. R.*, 1908, p. 4.

MODERATION. We may make evil of all amusements, but the Saints should not be unwise, but rather understand what the will of the Lord is, and practice moderation in all things. They should avoid excesses and cease from sin, putting far from them "the lusts of men;" and in their amusements and pastimes adopt a course that looks to the spirit as well as the letter, the intention and not the act alone, the whole and not the part, which is the meaning of moderation. In this way their conduct will be reasonable and becoming, and they shall find no trouble in understanding the will of the Lord.

Let me exhort the young people particularly, and the Saints generally, to weigh well the value of moderation in all their actions and amusements. Remember, too, that excessive feasting is not good; neither is excessive labor, but idleness and waste of precious time is infinitely worse. "Let your moderation be known to all men."—*Improvement Era*, Vol. 6, p. 857, Sept., 1903.

TEMPERANCE. We endorse any movement looking to temperance, looking to virtue, tending to purity of life and to faith in God and obedience to his laws; and we are against evil of every description; and we are, in our faith and prayers, against evil-doers—not that we would pray for evil to come upon evil-doers, but that evil-doers might

see the folly of their ways and the wickedness of their acts and repent
of them and turn away from them.—Oct. C. R., 1908, p. 8.

How to Teach Temperance. The best way to teach temperance is to keep the Word of Wisdom; and the next best is to assist
others to keep it, by removing artificial temptations from their lives.
Such temptation is the saloon, and it is time that the sentiment in
the communities where the members of the Church reside should
be declared against this soul-destroying evil.—*Juvenile Instructor*,
Vol. 46, p. 333, June, 1911.

Use of Tobacco and Strong Drinks. The use of tobacco in
its various forms and of strong drinks to some extent is also to be
lamented and deplored, especially among the youth, and this evil
should be stamped out. The people of God should set their faces
like flint against these practices, and they should see to it that their
children are taught better, and that a better example is set before
them by their parents, in order that the children may grow up without sin in these things.—Oct. C. R., 1901, p. 2.

Do Not Smoke. Teach your children not to smoke; persuade
them not to do it. Watch and look after them, and try to teach
them better, and to be courteous and kind.—Apr. C. R., 1905, p. 86.

The Saloon. No member of the Church of Jesus Christ of
Latter-day Saints can afford to do himself the dishonor, or bring
upon himself the disgrace, of crossing the threshold of a liquor saloon
or a gambling hell, or of any house of ill-fame of whatever name or
nature it may be. No Latter-day Saint, no member of the Church,
can afford it, for it is humiliating to him, it is disgraceful in him to
do it, and God will judge him according to his works.—Oct. C. R.,
1908, p. 7.

If, I say, the people observe the principles of this revelation
(Doctrine and Covenants 89), there could not exist in their midst
that most obnoxious institution known as a saloon; it can not exist
where only Latter-day Saints dwell.—Oct. C. R., 1908, p. 6.

Defeat the Liquor Interests. The liquor interests—the
enemies of the race—are again making keen efforts to restore the
former low-down conditions. In some places, we understand, enough
petitioners have already been obtained and the names filed with the
commissioners requesting an election this June. With all good people
we join in hoping that these efforts may utterly fail to restore the
saloon. This should be the desire of all Latter-day Saints, and their

prayers should be supported by their works and votes. In these elections the wives, mothers and sisters have their golden opportunity with fathers and brothers to arise and utterly crush the cursed traffic in drink for which so many have suffered in sweat, and pain, and tears.—*Improvement Era*, Vol. 16, 1912-13, p. 824.

VITALITY AND PATENT MEDICINES. Instead of flocking out to hear smooth-tongued impostors people should leave them severely alone. Instead of dosing themselves with patent medicines, they should learn to keep their bodies healthy by right living (see Doctrine and Covenants, Sec 89), by inhaling pure air, taking plenty of exercise, and bathing not only often in fresh water, but also in the sunshine with which our merciful Father has so abundantly provided us. If there are cases of sickness, as there will be notwithstanding any precaution we may take, which common sense and good nursing, or simple home remedies do not suffice to cure, let us follow the advice of the Scriptures (James 5:14-16), but if we do not believe in the elders, or in the prayer of faith saving the sick, let a reputable and faithful physician be consulted. By all means, let the quack, the traveling fakir, the cure-all nostrum, and the indiscriminate dosing with patent medicine, be abolished like so much trash.

The young man who would cope with the world, who would be full of vigor, and fresh for the battle of life, will find his strength in living according to the word of the Lord; for the promise is that all "who remember to keep and do these sayings, walking in obedience to the commandments, shall receive health in their navel, and marrow to their bones, and shall find wisdom and great treasures of knowledge, even hidden treasures; and shall run and not be weary, and shall walk and not faint; and I, the Lord, give unto them a promise, that the destroying angel shall pass by them, as the children of Israel, and not slay them."—*Improvement Era*, Vol. 5, June, 1902, p. 624.

STAMP OUT PROFANITY AND VULGARITY. We should stamp out profanity, and vulgarity, and everything of that character that exists among us; for all such things are incompatible with the gospel and inconsistent with the people of God.—*Oct. C. R.*, 1901, p. 2.

SATURDAY'S WORK. A good modern eighth commandment might read something like this: Do not so overwork and fret on Saturday as to deprive the Sabbath of the devotions and worship that belong to it as a day of rest.

In the home, Saturday is the day set apart for house cleaning, for extra cooking, for mending and all sorts of repairs that the Sabbath is thought to require. In business, Saturday is a day for picking up all lose ends, for closing up all the unfinished details of a week's work.

The consequences of our modern treatment of the last day of the week are too often manifested in an indolence and supine indifference that make our feelings and a total lack of energy almost incompatible with the spirit of worship. No worn-out man or woman, by the excessive toil of an early Saturday morning and a late Saturday night, can properly worship God in spirit and in truth.—*Juvenile Instructor*, Vol. 44, July, 1909, p. 295.

PURPOSE OF THE SABBATH. The Sabbath is a day of rest and of worship, designated and set apart by special commandment of the Lord to the Church of Jesus Christ of Latter-day Saints, and we should honor and keep it holy. We should also teach our children this principle.—Oct. C. R., 1901, pp. 1, 2.

THE MEANING OF SUNDAY. True, Sunday is a day of rest, a change from the ordinary occupations of the week, but it is more than that. It is a day of worship, a day in which the spiritual life of man may be enriched. A day of indolence, a day of physical recuperation is too often a very different thing from the God-ordained day of rest. Physical exhaustion and indolence are incompatible with a spirit of worship. A proper observance of the duties and devotions of the Sabbath day will, by its change and its spiritual life, give the best rest that men can enjoy on the Sabbath day.

Saturday evening may be wisely set apart as a time for thoughtful conversation or helpful reading as an introduction to the Sabbath day.—*Juvenile Instructor*, Vol. 44, July, 1909, p. 297.

WHAT SHALL WE DO ON THE SABBATH DAY? My belief is that it is the duty of Latter-day Saints to honor the Sabbath day and keep it holy, just as the Lord has commanded us to do. Go to the house of prayer. Listen to instructions. Bear your testimony to the truth. Drink at the fountain of knowledge and of instruction, as it may be opened for us from those who are inspired to give us instruction. When we go home, get the family together. Let us sing a few songs. Let us read a chapter or two in the Bible, or in the Book of Mormon, or in the book of Doctrine and Covenants. Let us discuss the principles of the gospel which pertain to advancement in the school of divine knowledge, and in this way occupy one day in seven. I think it would be profitable for us to do this.—M. I. A. Conference, June 11, 1916, Young Woman's Journal, Vol. 27, pp. 455-460.

NECESSITY OF SUNDAY WORSHIP. It is imperatively necessary, at all times, and especially so when our associations do not afford us the moral and spiritual support which we require for our advancement, that we go to the house of the Lord to worship and mingle with the Saints, that their moral and spiritual influence may help to correct our false impressions and restore us to that life which the duties and obligations or our conscience and true religion impose upon us.

"Good times" are often dangerous times, and social fraternity, if not of the right character, will prove more harmful than helpful. Let us, therefore, in the midst of our worldly callings and associations, not forget that paramount duty which we owe to ourselves and to our God.—Juvenile Instructor, Vol. 47, March, 1912, p. 145.

BE WISE IN ALL YOU DO. Leave these poisonous and injurious things alone; live within your means; get out of debt; and keep out of debt; do not run faster than you can go safely; be careful and cautious in what you do; advise with those who have wisdom and experience, before you leap, lest you leap into the dark; and so guard yourselves from possible evil and disadvantage, that the Lord can pour out the blessings of heaven upon you, yes, "open the windows of heaven" and pour out upon you blessings that you shall scarcely have room to contain them.—Apr. C. R., 1910, pp. 6, 7.

THE NATURE AND PURPOSE OF FASTING. The law to the Latter-day Saints, as understood by the authorities of the Church, is that food and drink are not to be partaken of for twenty-four hours, "from even to even," and that the Saints are to refrain from all bodily gratification and indulgences. Fast day being on the Sabbath, it follows, of course, that all labor is to be abstained from. In addition, the leading and principal object of the institution of the fast among the Latter-day Saints was that the poor might be provided with food and other necessities. It is, therefore, incumbent upon every Latter-day Saint to give to his bishop, on fast day, the food that he or his family would consume for the day, that it may be given to the poor for their benefit and blessing; or, in lieu of the food, that its equivalent amount, or, if the person is wealthy, a liberal donation, in money, be so reserved and dedicated to the poor.

Now, while the law requires the Saints in all the world to fast from "even to even" and to abstain both from food and drink, it can easily be seen from the Scriptures, and especially from the words of Jesus, that it is more important to obtain the true spirit of love for God and man, "purity of heart and simplicity of intention," than it is to carry out the cold letter of the law. The Lord has instituted the fast on a reasonable and intelligent basis, and none of his works are vain or unwise. His law is perfect in this as in other things. Hence, those who can are required to comply thereto; it is a duty from which they cannot escape; but let it be remembered that the observance of the fast day by abstaining twenty-four hours from food and drink is not an absolute rule, it is no iron-clad law to us, but it is left with the people as a matter of conscience, to exercise wisdom and discretion. Many are subject to weakness, others are delicate in health, and others have nursing babies; of such it should not be required to fast. Neither should parents compel their little children to fast. I have known children to cry for something to eat on fast day. In such cases, going without food will do them no good. Instead, they dread the day to come, and in place of hailing it, dislike it; while the compulsion engenders a spirit of rebellion in them, rather than a love for the Lord and their fellows. Better teach them the principle, and let them observe it when they are old enough to choose intelligently, than to so compel them.

But those should fast who can, and all classes among us should be taught to save the meals which they would eat, or their equivalent, for the poor. None are exempt from this; it is required of the Saints, old and young, in every part of the Church. It is no excuse that in some places there are no poor. In such cases the fast donation should be forwarded to the proper authorities for transmission to such stakes of Zion as may stand in need.

So shall we gain favor in the sight of God, and learn the acceptable fast before him.—*Improvement Era,* Vol. 6, December, 1903, p. 146.

KEEPING THE SABBATH HOLY. To observe the Sabbath day properly is the plain duty of every Latter-day Saint—and that includes the young men and young women and the boys and girls. It may seem strange that it should be necessary to repeat this often-asserted fact. But there appear to be some people, and sometimes whole communities, who neglect this duty, and therefore stand in need of this admonition.

What are we required to do on the Sabbath day? The revelations of the Lord to the Prophet Joseph are very plain on this subject, and these should govern us, for they are in strict harmony with the teachings of the Savior. Here are some of the simple requirements:

The Sabbath is appointed unto you to rest from your labors.

The Sabbath is a special day for you to worship, to pray, and to show zeal and ardor in your religious faith and duty—to pay devotions to the Most High.

The Sabbath is a day when you are required to offer your time and attention in worship of the Lord, whether in meeting, in the home, or wherever you may be—that is the thought that should occupy your mind.

The Sabbath day is a day when, with your brethren and sisters, you should attend the meetings of the Saints, prepared to partake of the sacrament of the Lord's supper; having first confessed your sins before the Lord and your brethren and sisters, and forgiven your fellows as you expect the Lord to forgive you.

On the Sabbath day you are to do no other thing than to prepare your food with singleness of heart, that your fasting may be perfect, and your joy may be full. This is what the Lord calls fasting and prayer.

The reason for this required course upon the Sabbath day is also plainly stated in the revelations. It is that one may more fully keep himself unspotted from the world; and to this end, also, the Saints are required to go to the house of prayer and offer up their sacraments on the Sabbath day.

Now, what is the promise to the Saints who observe the Sabbath? The Lord declares that inasmuch as they do this with cheerful hearts and countenances, the fulness of the earth is theirs: "the beasts of the field and the fowls of the air, and that which climbeth upon the trees and walketh upon the earth. Yea, and the herb, and the good things which cometh of the earth, whether for food or for raiment, or for houses, or for barns, or for orchards, or for gardens, or for vineyards." (Doctrine and Covenants 59.)

These are all made for the benefit and use of man to please the eye and to gladden the heart, to strengthen the body and to enliven the soul. All are promised to those who keep the commandments, and among the commandments is this important one, to observe properly the Sabbath day.

The Lord is not pleased with people who know these things and do them not.

Men are not resting from their labors when they plow, and plant and haul and dig. They are not resting when they linger around the home all day on Sunday, doing odd jobs that they have been too busy to do on other days.

Men are not showing zeal and ardor in their religious faith and duty when they hustle off early Sunday morning on the cars, in teams, in automobiles, to the canyons, the resorts, and to visit friends or places of amusement with their wives and children. They are not paying their devotions in this way to the Most High.

Not in seeking pleasure and recreation do they offer their time and attention in the worship of the Lord; nor can they thus rejoice in the spirit of forgiveness and worship that comes with partaking of the holy sacrament.

Boys and young men are not fasting with singleness of heart that their joy may be full when they spend the Sabbath day loafing around the village ice-cream stand or restaurant, playing games, or in buggy riding, fishing, shooting, or engaged in physical sports, excursions and outings. Such is not the course that will keep them unspotted from the world, but rather one that will deprive them of the rich promises of the Lord, giving them sorrow instead of joy, and unrest and anxiety instead of the peace that comes with works of righteousness.

Let us play and take recreation to our hearts' content during other days, but on the Sabbath let us rest, worship, go to the house of prayer, partake of the sacrament, eat our food with singleness of heart, and pay our devotions to God, that the fulness of the earth may be ours, and that we may have peace in this world and eternal life in the world to come.

"But," says one, "in our settlement we have no other day for amusement and sports, excursions and outings, ball games and races."

Then demand one.

Is it possible that parents, in the face of the promises of the Lord, will deny a day in the week when their children may have recreation; and so force them to spend the Sabbath in sports!

One prominent man, in one of the northern stakes, where ball games and other sports are said to be the rule on Sunday, asked what could be done to remedy the evil. He was told to try a half holiday on one of the week days.

"Then," he replied, "we can have no change nor remedy. Here are hundreds of acres of hay and ripening fields crying for workmen, and we cannot spare our boys for play."

The best reply to such an argument is the question: "Which is best—to let the hay go to ruin, or the boy?" Let the hay go; save the boy. He is worth more than all your material possessions. Save him in the spirit of the gospel—protect him from Sabbath breaking —by offering a little temporal sacrifice, and the Lord will keep his promise to you. Get together in your ward, unitedly select a day for play and recreation; and like faithful Saints demand that the Sabbath day, as far as you and yours are concerned, shall be devoted to the Lord our God.—*Improvement Era*, Vol. 13, 1909-10, pp. 842-844.

Do Not Rob the Sabbath Day. It is incumbent on members of the Church to so plan their work that there shall be no excuse for robbing the Lord's day of its sanctity. To this end let the boys and girls have a half holiday during the week, which may be profitably used for recreations, leaving the Sabbath for spiritual culture and worship. It is equally obligatory that we so plan our amusements that these shall not interfere with our worship. Let therefore some other night than Saturday be provided for the purpose. The Lord has commanded his people to observe the Sabbath day to keep it holy, and on that day to go to the house of prayer and offer up their sacraments in righteousness with willing hearts and penitent spirits.— *Improvement Era*, Vol. 12, 1909, p. 315.

Man Must Be Master of Himself. No man is safe unless he is master of himself; and there is no tyrant more merciless or more to be dreaded than an uncontrollable appetite or passion. We will find that if we give way to the groveling appetites of the flesh and follow them up, that the end will be invariably bitter, injurious and sorrowful, both to the individual and society. It is hurtful in example as well as in its individual effects; dangerous and hurtful to the unwary; while the denial of these appetites—the crucifixion of the flesh, so to speak—and an aspiration for something noble; whenever possible, doing good to our fellow creatures, hoping for the future, laying up treasures in heaven, where moth and rust cannot corrupt, and where thieves cannot break through and steal—all these things will bring everlasting happiness; happiness for this world and the world to come.

If there is no pleasure in the world except that which we experience in the gratification of our physical desires—eating, drinking, gay associations, and the pleasures of the world—then the enjoyments of the world are bubbles, there is nothing in them, there is no lasting benefit or happiness to be derived from them.—*Deseret Weekly News*, Vol. 33 ,1884, p. 130.

Chapter XV

MANY DUTIES OF MAN

The Object of Man's Existence. The object of our being here is to do the will of the Father as it is done in heaven, to work righteousness in the earth, to subdue wickedness and put it under our feet, to conquer sin and the adversary of our souls, to rise above the imperfections and weaknesses of poor, fallen humanity, by the inspiration of Almighty God and his power made manifest, and thus become indeed the saints and servants of the Lord in the earth.—Apr. C. R., 1902, p. 85.

We Deal With the Lord. We are dealing with our faith and consciences; you are dealing not with me, not with the Presidency of the Church, but with the Lord. I am not dealing with men respecting my tithing, my dealings are with the Lord; that is, with reference to my own conduct in the Church as a tithe-payer, and with reference to my observance of the other laws and rules of the Church; if I fail to observe the laws of the Church, I am responsible to my God, and will have to answer to him, by and by, for my neglect of duty, and I may have to answer to the Church for my fellowship. If I do my duty, according to my understanding of the requirements that the Lord has made of me, then I ought to have a conscience void of offense; I ought to have satisfaction in my soul, in the consciousness that I have simply done my duty as I understand it, and I will risk the consequences. With me it is a matter between me and the Lord; so it is with every one of us.—Apr. C. R., 1911, p. 6.

Necessity for All to Accomplish Their Missions. He that sent his Only Begotten Son into the world to accomplish the mission which he did, also sent every soul within the sound of my voice, and indeed every man and woman in the world, to accomplish a mission, and that mission cannot be accomplished by neglect; nor by indifference; nor can it be accomplished in ignorance. We must learn our duty; learn the requirements that the Lord has made at our hands, and understand the responsibilities that he has placed upon us. We should learn the obligation that we are under to God and to each other, and that we are under also to the cause of Zion, that has been restored to the earth in the latter days. These things are essential, and we cannot prosper in spiritual things, we cannot grow in knowledge and understanding, our minds cannot expand in the knowledge of God, or in wisdom, nor in the gifts of the Holy Spirit, without we devote our thoughts and our efforts toward our own betterment, toward the increase of our own wisdom, and knowledge in the things of God.

We labor day by day for the bread that perishes, and we devote but a few hours, comparatively, in seeking to obtain the bread of life. Our thoughts, in great measure, are placed upon worldly things, the things that perish, and therefore we are prone to neglect the higher duties that devolve upon us as the children of our Father, and to forget, in some measure, the greater obligations that rest upon us. It is therefore proper, and indeed it becomes the duty of those who are placed upon the towers as watchmen in Zion, to exhort the people to diligence, to prayerfulness, to humility, to a love of the truth that has been revealed to them, and to earnest devotion to the work of the Lord, which is intended for their individual salvation, and so far as they have influence upon others, the salvation of those whom they may have power to influence to move in the right direction; not that I can save any man, nor that any one man can save any other man or fit him for exaltation in the kingdom of God. This is not given to me to do for others, nor is it given to any man to be a Savior in this sense, or in this way, to his fellowman; but men can set an example; men can urge the precepts of the gospel. Men can proclaim the truth to others, and can point out the way to them in which to walk, and if they will harken to their counsel, listen to their admonitions and be led by them, they themselves will seek the path of life and they will walk in it, and obtain their exaltation for themselves. And thus the work required of us by the Lord is an individual work, it devolves upon each individual alike. No man can be saved in the kingdom of God in sin. No man will ever be forgiven of his sins by the just Judge, except he repent of his sins. No man will ever be freed from the power of death unless he is born again as the Lord Almighty has decreed, and declared to the world by the mouth of his Son in the meridian of time, and as he has declared it again in this dispensation through the Prophet Joseph Smith. Men can only be saved and exalted in the kingdom of God in righteousness, therefore we must repent of our sins, and walk in the light as Christ is in the light, that his blood may cleanse us from all sins, and that we may have fellowship with God and receive of his glory and exaltation.—Oct. C. R., 1907, p. 4.

GOD HONORS THOSE WHO HONOR HIM. Though the Lord should try me by withholding his blessings from me, and making me to drink to the very dregs the bitter cup of poverty, that should make no difference to me. The point is, what is the law of God? And if I know that law, it is my duty to obey it, though I suffer death in consequence. Many a man has gone to the stake in obedience, as he believed, to the commandments of God. Not one of the ancient disciples who were chosen of Jesus Christ, escaped martyrdom, except Judas and John. Judas betrayed the Lord, and then sacrificed his own life; and John received the promise of the Lord that he should live until He came again to the earth. All the others were put to death, some crucified, some dragged in the streets of Rome, some thrown from pinnacles, and some stoned to death. What for? For obeying the law of God and bearing testimony to that which they knew to be true. So may it be today. But let the spirit of this gospel be so imbedded in my soul that though I go through poverty, through tribulation, through persecution, or to death, let me and my house serve God and keep his laws. However, the promise is that you shall be blessed through obedience. God will honor those who honor him, and will remember those who remember him. He will uphold and sustain all those who sustain truth and are faithful to it. God help us, therefore, to be faithful to the truth, now and forever.—Apr. C. R., 1900, pp. 49, 50.

QUALIFICATIONS OF LATTER-DAY SAINTS. Now we all need patience, forbearance, forgiveness, humility, charity, love unfeigned, devotion to the truth, abhorrence of sin and wickedness, rebellion and disobedience to the requirements of the gospel. These are the qualifications requisite to Latter-day Saints and to becoming Latter-day Saints and members in good standing in the Church of Jesus Christ and heirs of God and joint heirs with Jesus Christ. No member in good standing in the Church will be drunken or riotous or profane or will take advantage of his brother or his neighbor, or will violate the principles of virtue and honor and righteousness. No member of the Church of Jesus Christ of Latter-day Saints in good standing will ever be chargeable with such offenses as these, because members will avoid these evils, and they will live above them. Then we have a mission in the world: each man, each woman, each child who has

grown to understanding or to the years of accountability, ought to be
an example to the world. They ought not only to be qualified to
preach the truth, to bear testimony of the truth, but ought to live so
that the very life they live, the very words they speak, their every
action in life will be a sermon to the unwary and to the ignorant,
teaching them goodness, purity, uprightness, faith in God and love
for the human family.—Apr. C. R., 1916, pp. 6, 7.

PERFECTION IN OUR SPHERE. I sincerely hope that the spirit of
the conference will abide with us, will go with us to our homes, and
that we will be able to continue to build on the foundations of the
gospel of the Son of God until we become perfect, even as our Father
in heaven is perfect, according to the sphere and intelligence that
we act in and possess. I do not expect that any of us will ever become
in mortality quite so perfect as God is perfect; but in the spheres in
which we are called to act, and according to the capacity and breadth
of intelligence that we possess, in our sphere, and in the existence of
the talent, the ability, and intelligence that God has given to us, we
may become as perfect in our sphere as God is perfect in his higher
and more exalted sphere. I believe that.—Apr. C. R., 1915, p. 140.

LET EVERY MAN LIVE TO BEAR CLOSEST INSPECTION. Let every
man's life be so that his character will bear the closest inspection, and
that it may be seen as an open book, so that he will have nothing to
shrink from or be ashamed of. Let all men who are elevated to
positions of trust in the Church live so that no man can point to
their faults, because they will have no faults; so that no man can
justly accuse them of wrongdoing, because they do no wrong; that
no man can point out their defects as "human" and as "weak mortals,"
because they are living up to the principles of the gospel, and are not
merely "weak human creatures," devoid of the Spirit of God and the
power to live above sin. That is the way for all men to live in the
kingdom of God.—Oct. C. R., 1906, pp. 9, 10.

NEED OF INDIVIDUAL RESPONSIBILITY. It is not safe for men or
women to conclude that because they have fulfilled carefully their
public responsibilities they have done all that is required of them.
Public requirements are changeable. Public demands vary with the
times. Sometimes they are strict and sometimes they are very lax.
Public sentiment becomes fickle and it is often indifferent to the
conduct of individuals who take license from a public indifference to
wrongdoing. Individual responsibility is more concerned with the

duties which men owe to their God whose requirements are positive and constant. When men feel that they are ever under an All-Seeing Eye, their conduct is measured in the strictest terms. They are not subject to lapses of public sentiment.

The first and highest standard of correct living is to be found in that individual responsibility which keeps men good for the truth's sake. It is not difficult for men who are true to themselves to be true to others. Men who honor God in their private lives do not need the restraint of public opinion which may not only be indifferent, but positively wrong. It is by the individual responsibilities which men feel that they are able to place themselves on the right side of all public questions. Those who neglect the inner life are dependent upon public guidance which leads them into all sorts of inconsistencies.

To walk safely and steadfastly without leaning upon the arm of flesh is the individual duty of every Latter-day Saint. Such a duty becomes a responsibility which men owe to themselves and to their God. The Saints should study their responsibilities, both public and individual, and find out, if they can, just what they are.—*Juvenile Instructor*, December, 1909, Vol. 44, p. 519.

CONQUER OURSELVES FIRST. I feel very grateful for the excellent peace and spirit which has pervaded all our meetings. It is true we are all engaged in a warfare, and all of us snould be valiant warriors in the cause in which we are engaged. Our first enemy we will find within ourselves. It is a good thing to overcome that enemy first and bring ourselves into subjection to the will of the Father, and into strict obedience to the principles of life and salvation which he has given to the world for the salvation of men. When we shall have conquered ourselves, it will be well for us to wage our war without, against false teachings, false doctrines, false customs, habits and ways, against error, unbelief, the follies of the world that are so prevalent, and against infidelity, and false science, under the name of science, and every other thing that strikes at the foundations of the principles set forth in the doctrine of Christ for the redemption of men and the salvation of their souls.—Oct. C. R., 1914, p. 128.

LET US CONQUER OURSELVES. Let us conquer ourselves, and then go to and conquer all the evil that we see around us, as far as we possibly can. And we will do it without using violence; we will do it without interfering with the agency of men or of women. We will do it by persuasion, by long-suffering, by patience, and by for-

giveness and love unfeigned, by which we will win the hearts, the
affections and the souls of the children of men to the truth as God
has revealed it to us. We will never have peace, nor justice, nor truth,
until we look to the only true fountain for it, and receive from the
fountain head.—Oct. C. R., 1906, p. 129.

CHARITY THE GREATEST PRINCIPLE. Charity, or love, is the
greatest principle in existence. If we can lend a helping hand to the
oppressed, if we can aid those who are despondent and in sorrow, if
we can uplift and ameliorate the condition of mankind, it is our
mission to do it, it is an essential part of our religion to do it.—Apr.
C. R., 1918, p. 4.

LOOK FOR GOOD; NOT FOR EVIL. Change the focus of your view,
and of your eye, from watching for evil to watching for that which
is good, that which is pure, and leading and prompting those who
err into that path which has no error in it, and that will not admit of
mistakes. Look for good in men, and where they fail to possess it,
try to build it up in them; try to increase the good in them; look for
the good; build up the good; sustain the good; and speak as little about
the evil as you possibly can. It does not do any good to magnify
evil, to publish evil, or to promulgate it by tongue or pen. There is
no good to be obtained by it. It is better to bury the evil and magnify
the good, and prompt all men to forsake evil and learn to do good;
and let our mission be to save mankind and to teach and guide in
the path of righteousness, and not to sit as judges and pass judgment
upon evil-doers, but rather to be saviors of men.—Apr. C. R., 1913, p. 8.

ESTIMATE MEN BY THEIR NOBLE DEEDS. One fruitful source of
apostasy from the Church comes from an inclination on the part of
those who apostatize to consider the small, mostly unintentionally
committed errors of its officers, rather than the broader and more
important labors which enter into their experience. Young men so
inclined turn from the infinite truth of the gospel, and the mighty
plan of salvation, the eternal purposes of God, to carp and cavil upon
the insignificant actions and the imperfect achievements of men,
judging the inspiring magnitude of the former by the disagreeable and
tiresome detail of the latter. Many of the serious annoyances of
communal life among the Saints would be obliterated entirely, if men
would search for the great and noble aspirations actuating their
neighbors, rather than for the imperfect sidelights that lay bare their
puny shortcomings. Those who wish to advance in the world will

avoid soul-destroying, mind-narrowing thoughts, and devote the days allotted to them, which it will be found are none too numerous, in studying the greater, nobler, and grander subjects that tend to build character, provide happiness, and create harmony with the mighty purposes of the Church and its founder, the Lord Jesus Christ.

Let us estimate our brethren by their best desires and noblest aspirations, not by their trifling shortcomings and failures. We estimate the majesty of the Wasatch by Monte Christo, Baldy, Observatory, the mighty Cottonwoods, Clayton, Timpanogos, and Nebo—its loftiest peaks—not by its rolling elevations or hillocky spurs, rocky ravines or trifling canyons. So also let us judge our fellows, and so the Church. It is the better way.—*Improvement Era*, March, 1902, Vol. 5, p. 388.

LET US SUSTAIN ONE ANOTHER. Let us sustain Christ, his people, and his cause of righteousness and redemption; let us sustain one another in the right, and kindly admonish one another in regard to wrongdoing, that we may be friends and saviors on Mount Zion, one for another, and that we may help the weak and strengthen them, encourage the doubtful and bring light to their right understanding as far as it is possible, that we may be instrumental in the hands of God of being saviors among men. Not that we have power to save men. We have not; but we have power to show them how they can obtain salvation through obedience to the laws of God. We can show them how to walk in order to be saved, for we have the right to do that, we have knowledge and understanding as to how to do it, and it is our privilege to teach it and to enforce it by example as well as by precept among our associates wherever we are in the world.— Oct. C. R., 1907, pp. 9, 10.

DO NOT BEAR MALICE AGAINST ONE ANOTHER. Brethren and sisters, we want you to be united. We hope and pray that you will go from this conference to your homes feeling in your hearts and from the depths of your souls to forgive one another, and never from this time forth to bear malice toward another fellow creature. I do not care whether he is a member of the Church of Jesus Christ of Latter-day Saints or not, whether he is a friend or a foe, whether he is good or bad. It is extremely hurtful for any man holding the Priesthood, and enjoying the gift of the Holy Ghost, to harbor a spirit of envy, or malice, or retaliation, or intolerance toward or against his fellowmen. We ought to say in our hearts, let God judge between me and thee, but as for me, I will forgive. I want to say to you that Latter-day Saints who harbor a feeling of unforgiveness in their souls are more guilty and more censurable than the one who has sinned against them. Go home and dismiss envy and hatred from your hearts; dismiss the feeling of unforgiveness; and cultivate in your souls that spirit of Christ which cried out upon the cross, "Father, forgive them; for they know not what they do." This is the spirit that Latter-day Saints ought to possess all the day long. The man who has that spirit in his heart and keeps it there will never have any trouble with his neighbor; he will never have any difficulties to bring before the bishop, nor high council; but he will always be at peace with himself, at peace with his neighbors, and at peace with God. It is a good thing to be at peace with God.—Oct. C. R., 1902, pp. 86, 87.

HONOR YOURSELVES AND YOUR NEIGHBORS. We admonish, we beseech our brothers and sisters, in the gospel of Jesus Christ, not only to honor themselves by a proper course of living, but also to honor and love and be charitable to their neighbors, every one of them. We admonish you not only to keep the greatest of all the commandments that has ever been given of God to man, to love the Lord your God, with all your heart, and mind, and strength, but we exhort you also to observe that second law, next unto it, to love your neighbors as yourselves; return good for evil, do not revile others because you are or may be reviled. We have no need to tear down the houses of other people (using this expression as a symbol). We are perfectly willing that they should live in the homes they have erected for themselves, and we will try to show them a better way. While we will not condemn that which they love and cherish above all other things in the world, we will endeavor to show them a better way and build them a better house, and then invite them kindly, in the spirit of Christ, of true Christianity, to enter the better dwelling. This is the principle, and I wish to impress it upon you this morning. I desire to impress, if I can, upon the minds of the parents the necessity of properly instructing and teaching their children with reference to this glorious principle, charity and love, that love for our neighbor that will enable us to cherish his rights as sacredly as we cherish our own, to defend his rights and liberties, put up the fallen bars in the fences of our neighbors that are carelessly left down, just as we would put our own bars up surrounding our own fields, in order to protect our crops from the ravages of stray animals.—Apr. C. R., 1917, p. 4.

Avoid Courts. Be reconciled to each other. Do not go to the courts of the Church nor to the courts of the land for litigation. Settle your own troubles and difficulties; and, as Bishop Hunter used to say, which is an axiom that cannot be disputed, there is only one way in which a difficulty existing between man and man can be truly settled, and that is when they get together and settle it between them. The courts cannot settle troubles between me and my brother.—Oct. C. R., 1916, pp. 6, 7.

Let Us Live Our Religion. I will say now to all of the Latter-day Saints: Let us live our religion; let us pay our tithing and be blessed; let us remember the poor and the needy, and sustain and help them; let us visit the sick and afflicted, and administer consolation unto them; let us help the weak; let us do all in our power to build up Zion, to establish righteousness in the earth, and to plant in the hearts of the people the glorious truth that Jesus is the Christ, the Redeemer of the world, that Joseph Smith is a prophet of the living God, whom the Lord raised up in these last days to restore the everlasting gospel and the power of the Holy Priesthood to the world.—Oct. C. R., 1902, p. 88.

Lel Us Be True to the Faith. We should set an example; we should be true to the faith, as Brother Stephens sings to us; true to the faith! We should be true to our covenants, true to our God, and true to one another, and to the interests of Zion, no matter what the consequences may be, no matter what may result. I can tell you that the man who is not true to Zion and to the interests of the people will be the man who will be found, by and by, left out and in a pitiable spiritual condition. The man who stays with the kingdom of God, the man who is true to this people, the man who keeps himself pure and unspotted from the world, is the man that God will accept, that God will uphold, that he will sustain, and that will prosper in the land, whether he be in the enjoyment of his liberty or be confined in prison cells, it makes no difference where he is, he will come out all right.—Oct. C. R., 1906, p. 9.

Church Duties Are Paramount. Our duties in the Church should be, I think, paramount to every other interest in the world. It is true that we are under the necessity of looking after our worldly interests. It is, of course, necessary for us to labor with our hands and our minds, in our various occupations for obtaining the necessaries of life. It is essential that the Latter-day Saints should be industrious and persevering in all the labors that devolve upon them, for it is written that "the inhabitants of Zion shall remember their labors, inasmuch as they are appointed to labor, in all faithfulness; for the idler shall be had in remembrance before the Lord." Again it is written: "Let every man be diligent in all things. And the idler shall not have place in the Church, except he repent and mend his ways." Again: "Thou shalt not be idle; for he that is idle shall not eat the bread nor wear the garments of the laborer." But in all our labors in life, in all the cares that beset us, and the temporal responsibilities that rest upon us, we should put uppermost in our thoughts, and highest in our appreciation and love, the cause of Zion, which is indeed the cause of truth and righteousness.—Oct. C. R., 1907, p. 2. See Doctrine and Covenants 42:42; 68:30; 75:29.

WE SHOULD STUDY THE GOSPEL. I believe it is good to seek knowledge out of the best books, to learn the histories of nations, to be able to comprehend the purposes of God with reference to the nations of the earth; and I believe that one of the most important things, and perhaps more important to us than studying the history of the world, is that we study and become thoroughly acquainted with the principles of the gospel, that they may be established in our hearts and souls, above all other things, to qualify us to go out into the world to preach and teach them. We may know all about the philosophy of the ages and the history of the nations of the earth; we may study the wisdom and knowledge of man and get all the information that we can acquire in a lifetime of research and study, but all of it put together will never qualify any one to become a minister of the gospel unless he has the knowledge and spirit of the first principles of the gospel of Jesus Christ.—Apr. C. R., 1915, p. 138.

ENCOURAGE SINGING. It delights my heart to see our little children learning to sing, and to see the people, our people everywhere, improving their talents as good singers. Everywhere we go among our people, we find sweet voices and talent for music. I believe that this is a manifestation to us of the purpose of the Lord in this direction toward our people, that they will excel in these things, as they should excel in every other good thing.—Apr. C. R., Sunday School, 1904, p. 81.

CULTIVATE SINGING. I can remember when I was a little boy,

hearing my father sing. I do not know how much of a singer he was, for at that time I was not capable of judging as to the quality of his singing, but the hymns he sang became familiar to me, even in the days of my childhood. I believe that I can sing them still, although I am not much of a singer. When young men go out into the world to preach the gospel, they will find it very beneficial for them to know how to sing the songs of Zion. I repeat the admonition and request made by Brother McMurrin, who has recently returned from a lengthy mission to Europe, that the young men who are eligible to preach the gospel, and who are likely to be called into the missionary field, begin at once to improve their talent to sing, and do not think it is beneath their dignity to join the choirs of the wards in which they live and learn how to sing. When we listen to this choir, under the leadership of Brother Stephens, we listen to music, and music is truth. Good music is gracious praise of God. It is delightsome to the ear, and it is one of our most acceptable methods of worshiping God. And those who sing in the choir and in all the choirs of the Saints, should sing with the spirit and with the understanding. They should not sing merely because it is a profession, or because they have a good voice; but they should sing also because they have the spirit of it, and can enter into the spirit of prayer and praise to God who gave them their sweet voices. My soul is always lifted up, and my spirit cheered and comforted, when I hear good music. I rejoice in it very much indeed.—Oct. C. R., 1899, pp. 68, 69.

BE FREE FROM DEBT. One of these subjects is, that in the time of prosperity, which we are now enjoying, it is highly proper for the Latter-day Saints to get out of debt. I have unceasingly urged this thought upon the brethren for the past year or more. Wherever I have had the opportunity of speaking, I have scarcely ever forgotten to hold out to the people the necessity—that I feel, at least—of our settling our obligations and freeing ourselves from debt in the day of prosperity. Our experience in the years that have passed must have led us to the conclusion that we have periods of prosperity, followed by periods of depression. We have now had a long period of success and prosperity, and we may expect, almost at any time, to see these conditions change and a time of depression spread over the land and over the people. I would say, in connection with this subject, that one of the best ways that I know of to pay my obligations to my brother, my neighbor, or business associate, is for me first to pay my obligations to the Lord. I can pay more of my debts to my neighbors, if I have contracted them, after I have met my honest obligations with the Lord, than I can by neglecting the latter; and you can do the same. If you desire to prosper, and to be free men and women and a free people, first meet your just obligations to God, and then meet your obligations to your fellowmen. Bishop Hunter used to put the matter in these words: "Brethren, pay your tithing and be blessed", and that is just what I mean.—*Apr. C. R., 1903, p. 2.*

What the Lord Requires of His Saints. There is a circumstance recorded in the Scriptures, that has been brought forcibly to my mind while listening to the remarks of the elders who have spoken to us during conference. A young man came to Jesus and asked what good things he should do that he might have eternal life. Jesus said unto him, "Keep the commandments." The young man asked which of them. Then Jesus enumerated to him some of the commandments that he was to keep—he should not murder, nor commit adultery, nor steal, nor bear false witness, but he should honor his father and mother, and love his neighbor as himself, etc. Said the young man, "All these I have kept from my youth up: what lack I yet?" Jesus said, "If thou wilt be perfect, go and sell that thou hast, and give to the poor, and thou shalt have treasure in heaven: and come and follow me." And we are told that he turned away sorrowful, because he had great possessions. He would not hearken to, nor obey the law of God in this matter. Not that Jesus required of the young man to go and sell all that he possessed and give it away; that is not the principle involved. The great principle involved is that which the elders of Israel are endeavoring to enforce upon the minds of the Latter-day Saints today. When the young man turned away in sorrow, Jesus said to his disciples, "A rich man shall hardly enter into the kingdom of heaven." (See Matt. 19:16-23.)

Is this because the rich man is rich? No. May not the rich man, who has the light of God in his heart, who possesses the principle and spirit of truth, and who understands the principle of God's government and law in the world, enter into the kingdom of heaven as easily, and be as acceptable there as the poor man may? Precisely. God is not a respecter of persons. The rich man may enter into the kingdom of heaven as freely as the poor, if he will bring his heart and affections into subjection to the law of God and to the principle of truth; if he will place his affections upon God, his heart upon the truth, and his soul upon the accomplishment of God's purposes, and not fix his affections and his hopes upon the things of the world. Here is the difficulty, and this was the difficulty with the young man. He had great possessions, and he preferred to rely upon his wealth rather than forsake all and follow Christ. If he had possessed the spirit of truth in his heart to have known the will of God, and to have loved the Lord with all his heart and his neighbor as himself, he would have said to the Lord, "Yea, Lord, I will do as you require, I will go and sell all that I have, and give it to the poor." If he had had it in his heart to do this, that alone might have been sufficient, and the demand would probably have stopped there; for undoubtedly the Lord did not deem it essential for him to go and give his riches away, or to sell his possessions and give the proceeds away, in order that he might be perfect, for that, in a measure, would have been improvident. Yet, if it had required all this to test him and to prove him, to see whether he loved the Lord with all his heart, mind, and strength, and his neighbor as himself, then he ought to have been willing to do it; and if he had been, he would have lacked nothing and would have received the gift of eternal life, which is the greatest gift of God, and which can be received on no other principle than the one mentioned by Jesus to the young man. If you will read the sixth lecture on faith, in the book of Doctrine and Covenants, you will learn that no man can obtain the gift of eternal life unless he is willing to sacrifice all earthly things in order to obtain it. We cannot do this so long as our affections are fixed upon the world.

It is true that we are in a measure of the earth, earthy; we belong to the world. Our affections and our souls are here; our treasures are here, and where the treasure is there the heart is. But if we will lay up our treasures in heaven; if we will wean our affections from the things of this world, and say to the Lord our God, "Father, not my will, but thine be done," then may the will of God be done on earth as it is done in heaven, and the kingdom of God in its power and glory will be established upon the earth. Sin and Satan will be bound and banished from the earth, and not until we attain to this condition of mind and faith will this be done.

Then let the Saints unite; let them hearken to the voices of the servants of God that are sounded in their ears; let them hearken to their counsels and give heed to the truth; let them seek their own salvation, for, so far as I am concerned, I am so selfish that I am seeking after my salvation, and I know that I can find it only in obedience to the laws of God, in keeping the commandments, in performing works of righteousness, following in the footsteps of our file leader, Jesus the Exemplar and the Head of all. He is the Way of life, he is the Light of the world, he is the Door by which we must enter, in order that we may have a place with him in the celestial kingdom of God.—*Journal of Discourses*, Vol. 18, 1877, pp. 133-135.

CULTIVATE GRATITUDE. We are almost daily put under obligations to one another, especially to friends and acquaintances, and the sense of obligation creates within us feelings of thankfulness and appreciation which we call gratitude. The spirit of gratitude is always pleasant and satisfying because it carries with it a sense of helpfulness to others; it begets love and friendship, and engenders divine influence. Gratitude is said to be the memory of the heart.

And where there is an absence of gratitude, either to God or man, there is the presence of vanity and the spirit of self-sufficiency. Speaking of Israel, Paul says: "Because that, when they knew God, they glorified him not as God, neither were thankful; but became vain in their imaginations, and their foolish heart was darkened."—(Rom. 1:21)

Thomas Gibbons expresses in verse most beautifully the idea of ingratitude:

"That man may last, but never lives,
Who much receives, but nothing gives;
Whom none can love, whom none can thank,
Creation's blot, creation's blank."

Naturally people feel grateful to those who have done them a kindness, and the feeling of gratitude is generally a sufficient compensation for those who have done a kind and unselfish act. But when one does a favor for another, and behind that favor is the secret and selfish intent that the gratitude which is awakened by the favor shall become a debt which the receiver at some time and in some way must repay to the selfish needs of the one who bestowed the favor, then gratitude becomes a debt which it is expected will be paid.

An act of apparent kindness can never result in good when it is intended to put any man under obligations that deprive him of his freedom to act. That is the characteristic of a politician. It is buying up one's freedom, and such a bargain is worse upon the man who seeks to make it than Shylock's contract for a pound of flesh.

When we win the friendship of others, because that friendship is helpful and encouraging to us, and because we need it for our happiness in life, gratitude of others toward us has a beautiful and lasting charm. That is the gratitude which Saints enjoy.

It is always safer and better to enjoy the gratitude which we feel to others than to set store upon the gratitude which we think others should have toward us. The grateful man sees so much in the world to be thankful for, and with him the good outweighs the evil. Love overpowers jealousy, and light drives darkness out of his life. Pride destroys our gratitude and sets up selfishness in its place. How much happier we are in the presence of a grateful and loving soul, and how careful we should be to cultivate, through the medium of a prayerful life, a thankful attitude toward God and man!—*Juvenile Instructor*, Vol. 38, April, 1903, pp. 242, 243.

BACKBITING. In a letter recently received by me, the following request and question were submitted for my opinion: "I would like you to define backbiting. There seems to be a difference of opinion respecting the meaning of the term. Some claim that so long as you speak the truth about a person, it is not backbiting, no matter what you say or how you say it. Would it not be better, if we knew a person had faults, to go to him privately and labor with him, than to go to others and speak of his faults?"

Nothing could be farther from the spirit and genius of the gospel than to suppose that we are always justified in speaking the truth about a person, however harmful the truth to him may be. The gospel teaches us the fundamental principles of repentance, and we have no right to discredit a man in the estimation of his fellowmen when he has truly repented and God has forgiven him. We are constantly beset by temptation, and often say and do things of which we immediately repent, and no doubt, if our repentance is genuine, it is always acceptable to our Heavenly Father. After he has accepted the contrition of the human heart and forgiven men their trespasses, it is dangerous for us to hold up their evil deeds for the contempt of the world.

As a rule, it is not necessary to be constantly offering advice to those who in our judgment are possessed of some fault. In the first place, our judgments may be in error, and in the second place, we may be dealing with a man who is strongly imbued with the spirit of repentance, and who, conscious of his weakness, is constantly struggling to overcome it. The utmost care, therefore, should be observed in all our language that implies a reproach of others. As a general rule, backbiting is better determined by the spirit and purpose that actuate us in speaking of things we consider faults in others than in the words themselves. A man or woman who possesses the Spirit of God will soon detect in his or her own feelings the spirit of backbiting, as that spirit is present in the remarks that are made concerning others. The question of backbiting, therefore, is probably best determined by the ancient rule that, "the letter killeth but the spirit giveth life."— *Juvenile Instructor*, October 15, 1904, Vol. 39, p. 625.

Do Not Inflict Wounds, But Heal Wounds. Almost anyone can inflict a wound. It may be made by a word, a slight, or by general conduct. But the healing of a wound is an art not acquired by practice alone, but by the loving tenderness that comes from universal good will and a sympathetic interest in the welfare and happiness of others. If people were always as ready to administer kindness as they are indifferent to the pain of others—if they were as patient to heal as they are quick to wound—many an unkind word would never be spoken, many a slight would be avoided. The art of healing is really one of the highest qualities and attributes of man; it is a characteristic of a great and noble soul; the sure indication of generous impulse.

In the discipline of the home, of the school, and social life, the infliction of wounds may be unavoidable, if they be not an actual necessity; but wounds should never be left open to fester—they should be bound up and cared for until they are healed. Perhaps the most perfect ideal in the art of healing is the mother whose tender and gracious love asserts itself in taking away the sting of a deserved or undeserved punishment. How her love heals every wound! How quick her caresses bind up and soothe! The example of her life is the wisdom which love teaches. In the school, children may suffer humiliation into which their wayward or careless conduct has brought them, and their punishment may be just; but their wounds the teacher should never leave unhealed. Nature wounds us when we violate her laws; but nature has her antiseptic methods of treating and healing every wound. The wise teacher has his also.

The cultivation of kindly thoughts and sentiments towards others is always helpful in the art of healing. It is sometimes helpful to lift ourselves out of our own shells in which, by our surroundings and habits of thought, we are incrusted, and place ourselves in the positions which others occupy in life. Constant consideration for the welfare and happiness of others, is every day imposed upon us by the divine injunction, "Thou shalt love thy neighbor as thyself."

The test, then, of our soul's greatness is rather to be sought in our ability to comfort and console, our ability to help others, rather than in our ability to help ourselves and crowd others down in the struggle of life. If the reader will stop a moment to reflect upon the healing qualities of Christ's life, he will understand that Christ was a Master in the art of healing, not alone of the wounds he made, but of self-inflicted wounds, and the wounds that others made. What a comfort his life is to those in sorrow! How instinctively our thoughts turn to him! How prone we are to go to him for consolation! He is truly the great Healer of the afflictions of others.—*Juvenile Instructor,* March, 1903, Vol. 38, pp. 178, 179.

USE GOOD LANGUAGE. Language, like thought, makes its impression and is recalled by the memory in a way that may be unpleasant if not harmful to those who have been compelled to listen to unseemly words. Thoughts that in themselves are not proper may be exalted or debased by the language used to express them. If inelegant expressions should be eschewed, what shall be said of profanity?—*Juvenile Instructor,* May 1, 1906, Vol. 41, p. 272.

DO NOT DESTROY LIFE WANTONLY. I have just a few words to say in addition to those that have already been said, in relation to shedding blood and to the destruction of life. I think that every soul should be impressed by the sentiments that have been expressed here this evening by all who have spoken, and not less with reference to the killing of our innocent birds, natives of our country, who live upon the vermin that are indeed enemies to the farmer and to mankind. It is not only wicked to destroy them, it is abominable, in my opinion. I think that this principle should extend, not only to the bird life, but to the life of all animals. When I visited, a few years ago, the Yellowstone National Park, and saw in the streams and the beautiful lakes, birds swimming quite fearless of man, allowing passers-by to approach them as closely almost as tame birds, and apprehending no fear of them, and when I saw droves of beautiful deer herding along the side of the road, as fearless of the presence of men as any domestic animal it filled my heart with a degree of peace and joy that seemed to be almost a foretaste of that period hoped for when there shall be none to hurt and none to molest in all the land, especially among all the inhabitants of Zion. These same birds, if they were to visit other regions, inhabited by man, would, on account of their tameness, doubtless become more easily a prey to the gunner. The same may be said of those beautiful creatures—the deer and antelope. If they should wander out of the park, beyond the protection that is established there for these animals, they would become, of course, an easy prey to those who were seeking their lives. I never could see why a man should be imbued with a blood-thirsty desire to kill and destroy animal life. I have known men—and they still exist among us—who enjoy what is, to them, the "sport" of hunting birds and slaying them by the hundreds, and who will come in after a day's sport, boasting of how many harmless birds they have had the skill to slaughter, and day after day, during the season when it is lawful for men to hunt and kill (the birds having had a season of protection and not apprehending danger) go out by scores or hundreds, and you may hear their guns early in the morning on the day of the opening, as if great armies had met in battle; and the terrible work of slaughtering the innocent birds goes on.

I do not believe any man should kill animals or birds unless he needs them for food, and then he should not kill innocent little birds that are not intended for food for man. I think it is wicked for men to thirst in their souls to kill almost everything which possesses animal life. It is wrong, and I have been surprised at prominent men whom I have seen whose very souls seemed to be athirst for the shedding of animal blood. They go off hunting deer, antelope, elk, anything they can find, and what for? "Just for the fun of it!" Not that they are hungry and need the flesh of their prey, but just because they love to shoot and to destroy life. I am a firm believer, with reference to these things, in the simple words of one of the poets:

"Take not away the life you cannot give,
For all things have an equal right to live."

—*Juvenile Instructor*, April, 1913, Vol. 48, pp. 308-309.

COMMENCEMENT ADDRESS. The point which seems the most perspicuous, and which will appear with greatest force to your minds, no doubt, on this occasion, is that it should have a speedy ending. Not so, however, with the efforts of those students who graduate with honors from this college, today. Before them lies a strange, meandering, endless path, by them as yet untrodden, however well beaten by the weary feet of pilgrims who have passed over to the great beyond. This path is fraught with all there is in life, of good or ill to them. They are entering upon the great problem of life, and each will be compelled to solve that problem for himself. The problem of death—which is spiritual midnight—the unenlightened soul—will solve itself. As the stream flows naturally down the slope to the dead waters of our inland sea, so is the common trend of the natural man down to the dark valley of the shadows of death. He needs to make no effort to reach this goal; by lazily floating on the tide of common events, he will reach it all too soon. But, to the fountain of life, to the summit of existence, to the fulness of moral, religious and intellectual manhood, the finger board of truth points eternally up the stream. To reach this glorious fountain, to scale this magnificent height, one must work; he must stem the current, must climb the hill—must climb and work and persevere. Thus he will succeed.

It is a very important thing to make a commencement in life. It is no less important to make that commencement upon a sound and proper footing. A man going to the summit of Twin Peaks, which tower towards the heavens on the southeast of us, will have a long, weary journey before he reaches his destination. Although not far away at first, if he starts off toward the northwest, the longer he continues in that direction the further he goes from his objective point. True, he may circumscribe the earth and, if he keep the proper bearing, will come back to the point at last. But eternity is a wondrous globe to circumnavigate, and we will find it to our advantage not to undertake the feat when we can so easily avoid it by commencing as we should. Error is a worthless and an injurious thing. To avoid it should always be our careful study. Mistakes, if they are indeed mistakes, are never fortunate, and may be extremely painful and hard to rectify. But the sooner rectified the better. It is braver and more honorable to promptly disavow and fly from error, no matter what the present seeming cost, or to frankly acknowledge a mistake, and apologize for it, and thus get rid of it, than to crouch beneath the burden, which is moral cowardice.

The students now graduating from this school in the branches of education which they have taken, are ready to commence the application of the knowledge they have acquired to the practical duties of life. You may apply this knowledge to the development of the natural resources and prosperity of our country, or to the betterment of the social problems of the times in which you live, or you may apply it to the further intellectual development of yourselves and others. That which you have gained by study and the assistance of your teachers should be wisely used by you as an aid to the attainment of other and greater knowledge.

Whatever may be your course in the future, or your choice of occupation, always remember the grand scriptural injunction: "Whatsoever thy hand findeth to do, do it with thy might; for there is no work, nor device, nor knowledge, nor wisdom, in the grave, whither thou goest." (Ec. 9:10.) This scripture applies directly to the temporal life and death, and only to them. Whatever is worth doing at all, should be well and faithfully and thoroughly done. The failures occurring in the legitimate pursuits of life, resulting solely from the unprofitableness thereof, are few and far between. The vast majority of failures are the results of neglect, or of want of careful attention, or of ignorance, or of dishonesty on the part of the applicants, and not of the business itself.

Carefully select your occupation with a view to your qualifications or adaptability therefor; let it be worthy of the noblest ambition and purest desire, and then engage in it in earnest, put your heart into it, and your mind upon it, with due consideration to other essential things, until you succeed. All extremes should be avoided. To fix the heart and mind upon a single object, however good, and close the eyes to all else in life, may make an expert, a bigot, or a crank, but never a wise and broad-minded man. It is foolish to become too much absorbed in material things. Labor and relaxation should go hand in hand, and pure and undefiled religion will lighten every burden you have to bear, and help to sweeten the bitter draught of many a sorrowing soul. The proper admixture of labor and leisure will not only promote the highest mental capabilities, but also the most perfect physical conditions.

Man is a dual being. He is spiritual and he is physical. The latter is dependent upon the former for intelligence and life. The body without the spirit is dead, but the spirit is an immortal and an independent principle and being. It is the more important part, yet man bestows more thought and labor upon the body, as a rule, than upon the better part. Neither should be neglected, least of all, the spiritual. This is truth, and it is the truth that makes man free. By it they stand, without it they fall.

The great Teacher of the world has said, "If ye continue in my word, then are ye my disciples indeed; and ye shall know the truth, and the truth shall make you free." (John 8:31-2.) Again: "And truth is knowledge of things as they are, and as they were, and as they are to come." (Doc. and Cov. 93:24.)

This knowledge of truth, combined with proper regard for it, and its faithful observance, constitutes true education. The mere stuffing of the mind with a knowledge of facts is not education. The mind must not only posses a knowledge of truth, but the soul must revere it, cherish it, love it as a priceless gem; and this human life must be guided and shaped by it in order to fulfil its destiny. The mind should not only be charged with intelligence, but the soul should be filled with admiration and desire for pure intelligence which comes of a knowledge of the truth. The truth can only make him free who hath it, and will continue in it. And the word of God is truth, and it will endure forever.

Educate yourself not only for time, but also for eternity. The latter of the two is the more important. Therefore, when we shall have completed the studies of time, and enter upon the commencement ceremonies of the great hereafter, we will find our work is not finished, but just begun, we may then say with the poet:

> "Lay this aside—say not your work is done,
> No need of love or goodness ever dies,
> But in the lives of others—multiplies,
> Say it has just begun."

In conclusion permit me to repeat a portion of the first psalm: "Blessed is the man that walketh not in the counsel of the ungodly, nor standeth in the way of sinners, nor sitteth in the seat of the scornful. But his delight is in the law of the Lord; and in his law doth he meditate day and night. And he shall be like a tree planted by the rivers of water, that bringeth forth his fruit in his season; his leaf also shall not wither; and whatsoever he doeth shall prosper. The ungodly are not so; but are like the chaff which the wind driveth away."—Contributor, Vol. 16, pp. 569-571. Delivered at the commencement exercises of the Latter-day Saints College, Salt Lake City, June 5, 1895.

OUR MAIN PURPOSE OF LIFE. The important consideration is not how long we can live but how well we can learn the lesson of life, and discharge our duties and obligations to God and to one another. One of the main purposes of our existence is that we might conform to the image and likeness of him who sojourned in the flesh without blemish—immaculate, pure, and spotless! Christ came not only to atone for the sins of the world, but to set an example before all men and to establish the standard of God's perfection, of God's law, and of obedience to the Father.—*Improvement Era*, Vol. 21, p. 104, December, 1917.

HOW TO LOVE YOUR NEIGHBOR. Love your neighbor as yourself? How are you to do it? If your neighbor is in danger, protect him to the utmost of your power. If you see your neighbor's property in danger of injury, protect his property as you would your own, as far as it lies in your power: If your neighbor's boy or girl is going astray, go directly to your neighbor, in the spirit of love, and help him to reclaim his child. How are we to love our neighbor as we love ourselves. It is the simplest thing in the world; but too many people are selfish and narrow and not given to that breadth of feeling which reaches out and considers the benefit and welfare of their neighbors; and they narrow themselves down to their own peculiar and particular benefit and blessing and well being, and feel it to say: "O, let my neighbor take care of himself." That is not the spirit that should characterize a Latter-day Saint.—*Improvement Era*, Vol. 21, pp. 103, 104, December, 1917.

QUESTION OF CHURCH LEADERS. We have come to ask you if you are in strict accord with the two great commandments: "Thou shalt love the Lord thy God with all thy heart, and with all thy soul, and with all thy mind, * * * and thy neighbor as thyself."—*Improvement Era*, Vol. 21, p. 98, December, 1917; Matt. 22: 34-40.

THE SIN OF INGRATITUDE. And I believe that one of the greatest sins of which the inhabitants of the earth are guilty today is the sin of ingratitude, the want of acknowledgement, on their part, of God and his right to govern and control. We see a man raised up with extraordinary gifts, or with great intelligence, and he is instrumental in developing some great principle. He and the world ascribe his great genius and wisdom to himself. He attributes his success to his own energies, labor and mental capacity. He does not acknowledge the hand of God in anything connected with his success, but ignores him altogether and takes the honor to himself; this will apply to almost all the world. In all the great modern discoveries in science, in the arts, in mechanics, and in all material advancement of the age, the world says, "We have done it." The individual says, "I have done it," and he gives no honor or credit to God. Now, I read in the revelations through Joseph Smith, the prophet, that because of this, God is not pleased with the inhabitants of the earth but is angry with them because they will not acknowledge his hand in all things.—*Deseret Weekly News*, 1884, Vol. 33, p. 130; Doc. and Cov. 59: 21.

PITY FOR ENEMIES. I assure you I feel grateful for the love, the prayers and the support of friends, and I earnestly desire to merit their confidence. Personally I have no enemies. My enemies are not mine, they are his whom I am trying to serve! The devil does not care much about me. I am insignificant, but he hates the *Priesthood*, which is after the order of the Son of God! I love my friends, and I pity my enemies.—Letter to Elder Joseph E. Taylor, Nov. 16, 1917.—*Life of Joseph F. Smith* p. 351.

CHAPTER XVI.

MARRIAGE, THE HOME AND THE FAMILY

NECESSITY OF MARRIAGE. The house of the Lord is a house of order and not a house of confusion; and that means that the man is not without the woman in the Lord, neither is the woman without the man in the Lord; and that no man can be saved and exalted in the kingdom of God without the woman, and no woman can reach the perfection and exaltation in the kingdom of God alone. That is what it means. God instituted marriage in the beginning. He made man in his own image and likeness, male and female, and in their creation it was designed that they should be united together in sacred bonds of marriage, and one is not perfect without the other. Furthermore, it means that there is no union for time and eternity that can be perfected outside of the law of God, and the order of his house. Men may desire it, they may go through the form of it, in this life, but it will be of no effect except it be done and sanctioned by divine authority, in the name of the Father and of the Son and of the Holy Ghost.—Apr. C. R., 1913, pp. 118-119.

MARRIAGE, GOD-ORDAINED AND SANCTIONED. "And again, I say unto you, that whoso forbiddeth to marry is not ordained of God, for marriage is ordained of God unto men." (Doc. and Cov. 49:15)

I desire to emphasize this. I want the young men of Zion to realize that this institution of marriage is not a man-made institution. It is of God. It is honorable, and no man who is of marriageable age is living his religion who remains single. It is not simply devised for the convenience alone of man, to suit his own notions, and his own ideas; to marry and then divorce, to adopt and then to discard, just as he pleases. There are great consequences connected with it, consequences which reach beyond this present time, into all eternity, for thereby souls are begotten into the world, and men and women obtain their being in the world. Marriage is the preserver of the human race. Without it, the purposes of God would be frustrated; virtue would be destroyed to give place to vice and corruption, and the earth would be void and empty.

Neither are the relationships that exist, or should exist, between parents and children, and between children and parents, of an ephemeral nature, nor of a temporal character. They are of eternal consequence, reaching beyond the veil, in spite of all that we can do. The man, and the woman who are the agents, in the providence of God, to bring living souls into the world, are made before God and the heavens, as responsible for these acts as is God himself responsible for the works of his own hands, and for the revelation of his own wisdom. The man and the woman who engage in this ordinance of matrimony are engaging in something that is of such far-reaching character, and is of such vast importance, that thereby hangs life and death, and eternal increase. Thereupon depends eternal happiness, or eternal misery. For this reason, God has guarded this sacred institution by the most severe penalties, and has declared that whosoever is untrue to the marriage relation, whosoever is guilty of adultery, shall be put to death. This is scriptual law, though it is not practiced today, because modern civilization does not recognize the laws of God in relation to the moral status of mankind. The Lord commanded, "Whosoever sheddeth innocent blood, by man shall his blood be shed." Thereby God has given the law. Life is an important thing. No man has any right to take life, unless God commanded it. The law of God as to violation of the marriage covenant is just as strict, and is on a parallel with law against murder notwithstanding the former is not carried out. * * *

Now, every young person throughout the Church should understand this very thoroughly. The Church authorities and the teachers of our associations should inculcate the sacredness, and teach the duty of marriage, as it has been revealed in the latter days to us. There should be a reform in the Church in this regard, and a sentiment created in favor of honorable marriage, and that would prevent any young man, or any young woman, who is a member of the Church, from marrying except by that authority which is sanctioned of God. And no man holding the Priesthood who is worthy and of age should remain unmarried. They should also teach that the law of chastity is one of the most vital importance, both to children, and to men and to women. It is a vitally important principle to the children of God in all their lives, from the cradle to the grave. God has fixed dreadful penalties against the transgression of his law of chastity, of virtue, of purity. When the law of God shall be in force among men, they will be cut off who are not absolutely pure and unsoiled and spotless—both men and women. We expect the women to be pure, we expect them to be spotless and without blemish, and it is as necessary and important for man to be pure and virtuous as for woman; indeed, no woman would ever be other than pure if men were so. The gospel of Jesus Christ is the law of love, and love of God with the whole heart and mind is the greatest commandment, and the next is like unto it: love thy neighbor as thyself. This also should be remembered in the marriage relation, for, while it is said that the desires of the woman shall be to her husband, and he shall rule over her, it is intended that that rule shall be in love and not in tyranny. God never rules tyrannically, except when men so corrupt themselves that they are unfit to live. Then, and under such conditions, it is the story of all his dealings with mankind, that he sends judgment upon them and wipes them out and destroys them.—*Improvement Era*, July,1902, pp. 713-17.

RIGHTEOUSNESS AND NECESSITY OF MARRIAGE. Many people imagine that there is something sinful in marriage; there is an apostate tradition to that effect. This is a false and very harmful idea. On the contrary, God not only commends but he commands marriage. While man was yet immortal, before sin had entered the world, our heavenly Father himself performed the first marriage. He united our first parents in the bonds of holy matrimony, and commanded them to be fruitful and multiply and replenish the earth. This command he has never changed, abrogated or annulled; but it has continued in force throughout all the generations of mankind.

Without marriage the purposes of God would be frustrated, so far as this world is concerned, for there would be none, to obey his other commands.

There appears to be a something beyond and above the reasons apparent to the human mind why chastity brings strength and power to the peoples of the earth, but it is so.

Today a flood of iniquity is overwhelming the civilized world. One great reason therefor is the neglect of marriage; it has lost its sanctity in the eyes of the great majority. It is at best a civil contract, but more often an accident or a whim, or a means of gratifying the passions. And when the sacredness of the covenant is ignored or lost sight of, then a disregard of the marriage vows, under the present moral training of the masses, is a mere triviality, a trifling indiscretion.

The neglect of marriage, this tendency to postpone its responsibilities until middle life, that so perniciously affects Christendom, is being felt in the midst of the Saints.

Certainly we are not in favor of the very early marriages that prevailed a few centuries ago.

But what we wish to impress upon the Saints is that the legitimate union of the sexes is a law of God, that to be blessed of him, we must honor that law; that if we do not do so the mere fact that we are called by his name will not save us from the evils that neglect of this law entails, that indeed we are only his people when we observe his law; that when we do not do so we may expect the same unfortunate results to come upon us as flow to the rest of humanity from the same causes.

We believe that every man holding the holy Priesthood should be married, with the very few exceptions of those who through infirmities of mind or body are not fit for marriage. Every man is a worse man in proportion as he is unfit for the married state. We hold that no man who is marriageable is fully living his religion who remains unmarried. He is doing a wrong to himself by retarding his progress, by narrowing his experiences, and to society by the undesirable example that he sets to others, as well as he, himself, being a dangerous factor in the community.

We say to our young people, get married, and marry aright. Marry in the faith, and let the ceremony be performed in the place God has appointed. Live so that you may be worthy of this blessing. If, however, obstacles, not at present removable, prevent this most perfect form of marriage, have your bishop perform the ceremony, and then, at the earliest possible moment, go to the temple. But do not marry those out of the Church, as such unions almost invariably lead to unhappiness and quarrels and often finally to separation. Besides, they are not pleasing in the sight of heaven. The believer and unbeliever should not be yoked together, for sooner or later, in time or in eternity, they must be divided again.

And now we desire with holy zeal to emphasize the enormity of sexual sins. Though often regarded as insignificant by those not knowing the will of God, they are, in his eyes an abomination, and if we are to remain his favored people they must be shunned as the gates of hell. The evil results of these sins are so patent in vice, crime, misery and disease that it would appear that all, young and old, must perceive and sense them. They are destroying the world. If we are to be preserved we must abhor them, shun them, not practice the least of them, for they weaken and enervate, they kill man spiritually, they make him unfit for the company of the righteous and the presence of God.—*Juvenile Instructor,* Vol. 37, p. 400, July 1, 1902.

MALE AND FEMALE ENTER HEAVEN. No man will ever enter there until he has consummated his mission; for we have come here to be comformed to the likeness of God. He made us in the beginning in his own image and in his own likeness, and he made us male and female. We never could be in the image of God if we were not both male and female. Read the Scriptures, and you will see it for yourselves as God has made it. He has made us in his own form and likeness, and here we are male and female, parents and children. And we must become more and more like him—more like him in love, in charity, in forgiveness, in patience, long-suffering and forbearance, in purity of thought and action, intelligence, and in all respects, that we may be worthy of exaltation in his presence. It is for this that we have come to the earth. This is the work that we have to perform. God has shown us the way and given us the means by which we may consummate and fill our mission upon this earth and perfect our destiny; for we are destined and foreordained to become like God, and unless we do become like him we will never be permitted to dwell with him. When we become like him you will find that we will be presented before him in the form in which we were created, male and female. The woman will not go there alone, and the man will not go there alone, and claim exaltation. They may attain a degree of salvation alone, but when they are exalted they will be exalted according to the law of the celestial kingdom. They cannot be exalted in any other way, neither the living nor the dead. It is well for us to learn something about why we build temples, and why we administer in them for the dead as well as for the living. We do this that we may become like unto him, and dwell with him eternally; that we may become sons of God, heirs of God and joint heirs with Jesus Christ.—*Tabernacle Sermon,* June 12, 1898.

MARRIAGE TO REPLENISH THE EARTH. Those who have taken upon themselves the responsibility of wedded life should see to it that they do not abuse the course of nature; that they do not destroy the principle of life within them, nor violate any of the commandments of God. The command which he gave in the beginning to multiply and replenish the earth is still in force upon the children of men. Possibly no greater sin could be committed by the people who have embraced this gospel than to prevent or to destroy life in the manner indicated. We are born into the world that we may have life, and we live that we may have a fulness of joy, and if we will obtain a fulness of joy, we must obey the law of our creation and the law by which we may obtain the consummation of our righteous hopes and desires—life eternal.—*Apr. C. R.,* 1900, p. 40.

ETERNAL MARRIAGE. Why did he teach us the principle of eternal union of man and wife? Because God knew that we were his children here, to remain his children forever and ever, and that we were just as truly individuals, and that our individuality was as identical as that of the Son of God, and would therefore continue, worlds without end, so that the man receiving his wife by the power of God, for time and for all eternity, would have the right to claim her and she to claim her husband, in the world to come. Neither would be changed, except from mortality to immortality; neither would be other than himself or herself, but they will have their identity in the world to come precisely as they exercise their individuality and enjoy their identity here. God has revealed this principle, and it has its bearings upon the evidence that we possess of the actual, literal resurrection of the body, just as it is and as the prophets have declared it in the Book of Mormon.—*Apr. C. R.,* 1912, pp. 136-137; Mosiah 15:20-23; 16:7-11; Alma 40.

ETERNITY OF THE FAMILY ORGANIZATIONS. Our associations (family) are not exclusively intended for this life, for time, as we distinguish it from eternity. We live for time and for eternity. We form associations and relations for time and all eternity. Our affections and our desires are found fitted and prepared to endure not only throughout the temporal or mortal life, but through all eternity. Who are there besides the Latter-day Saints who contemplate the thought that beyond the grave we will continue in the family organization? the father, the mother, the children recognizing each other in the relations which they owe to each other and in which they stand to each other? this family organization being a unit in the great and perfect organization of God's work, and all destined to continue throughout time and eternity?

We are living for eternity and not merely for the moment. Death does not part us from one another, if we have entered into sacred relationships with each other by virtue of the authority that God has revealed to the children of men. Our relationships are formed for eternity. We are immortal beings, and we are looking forward to the growth that is to be attained in an exalted life after we have proved ourselves faithful and true to the covenants that we have entered into here, and then we will receive a fulness of joy. A man and woman who have embraced the gospel of Jesus Christ and who have begun life together, should be able by their power, example and influence to cause their children to emulate them in lives of virtue, honor, and in integrity to the kingdom of God which will redound to their own interest and salvation. No one can advise my children with greater earnestness and solicitude for their happiness and salvation than I can myself. Nobody has more interest in the welfare of my own children than I have. I cannot be satisfied without them. They are part of me. They are mine; God has given them to me, and I want them to be humble and submissive to the requirements of the gospel. I want them to do right, and to be right in every particular, so that they will be worthy of the distinction that the Lord has given them in being numbered among his covenant people who are choice above all other people, because they have made sacrifice for their own salvation in the truth. Speaking of the fashions of the world, I do not care to say very much on the subject, but I do think that we live in an age the very trend of which is to vice and wickedness. I believe that to a very large extent the fashions of the day, and especially the fashions of women, have a tendency to evil and not to virtue or modesty, and I deplore that evident fact, for you see it on every hand. Young men want to get homes that are palatial, that are fine in all their appointments, and as modern as anybody else's before they will get married. I think it is a mistake. I think that young men and young women, too, should be willing, even at this day, and in the present condition of things, to enter the sacred bonds of marriage together and fight their way together to success, meet their obstacles and their difficulties, and cleave together to success, and cooperate in their temporal affairs, so that they shall succeed. Then they will learn to love one another better, and will be more united throughout their lives, and the Lord will bless them more abundantly. I regret, I think it is a crying evil, that there should exist a sentiment or a feeling among any members of the Church to curtail the birth of their children. I think that is a crime wherever it occurs, where husband and wife are in possession of health and vigor and are free from impurities that would be entailed upon their posterity. I believe that where people undertake to curtail or prevent the birth of their children that they are going to reap disappointment by and by. I have no hesitancy in saying that I believe this is one of the greatest crimes of the world today, this evil practice.—*Relief Society Magazine*, Vol, 4, June, 1917, p. 314 *et seq.*

IMPORTANCE OF MARRIAGE WITHIN THE CHURCH. I may be pardoned, since it is pretty well known everywhere, I believe, that I speak my mind if I speak at all, if I say to you, Mormon, Jew, and Gentile, believer and unbeliever, present in this congregation, I would rather take one of my children to the grave than I would see him turn away from this Gospel. I would rather take my children to the cemetery, and see them buried in innocence, than I would see them corrupted by the ways of the world. I would rather go myself to the grave than to be associated with a wife outside of the bonds of the new and everlasting covenant. Now, I hold it just so sacred; but some members of the Church do not so regard the matter. Some people feel that it does not make very much difference whether a girl marries a man in the Church, full of the faith of the Gospel, or an unbeliever. Some of our young people have married outside of the Church; but very few of those who have done it have failed to come to grief. I would like to see Latter-day Saint men marry Latter-day Saint women; and Methodists marry Methodists, Catholics marry Catholics, and Presbyterians marry Presbyterians, and so on to the limit. Let them keep within the pale of their own faith and church. There is nothing that I can think of, in a religious way, that would grieve me more intensely than to see one of my boys marry an unbelieving girl, or one of my girls marry an unbelieving man. While I live, and they will hearken to my voice, you can depend upon it, none of them will ever do it, and I would to God that every father in Israel saw it just as I do, and would carry it out just as I intend to do.—*October Conference, 1909.*

NO MARRIAGE IN HEAVEN. Why did Jesus teach the doctrine that there was no marrying nor giving in marriage in the other world? Why did he teach the doctrine that marriage was instituted by the Father and designed to be accomplished in this life? Why did he rebuke those who sought to entrap him when they brought to him the example of the fulfilment of the law of Moses, for Moses wrote the law that God gave him, that if a man married in Israel and died without issue, it was the duty of his brother to take his widow and raise up seed unto his brother; and when seven of these brothers—(which is doubtless a problem that these men put to the Savior in order to entrap him if they could)—had taken her, to whom should she belong in the resurrection, since they all had her? Jesus declared to them, "Ye do err, not knowing the Scriptures, nor the power of God." They did not understand the principle of sealing for time and for all eternity; that what God hath joined together neither man nor death can put asunder. (Matt. 19: 6.) They had wandered from that principle. It had fallen into disuse among them; they had ceased to understand it; and consequently they did not comprehend the truth; but Christ did. She could only be the wife in eternity of the man to whom she was united by the power of God for eternity, as well as for time; and Christ understood the principle, but he did not cast his pearls before the swine that tempted him.—*Apr. C. R.* 1912, p. 136.

PLURAL MARRIAGE FORBIDDEN. Official Statement—"Inasmuch as there are numerous reports in circulation that plural marriages have been entered into contrary to the official declaration of President Woodruff, of September 26, 1890, commonly called the Manifesto, which was issued by President Woodruff and adopted by the Church at its general conference, October 6, 1890, which forbade any marriages violative of the law of the land; I Joseph F. Smith, President of the Church of Jesus Christ of Latter-day Saints, hereby affirm and declare that no such marriages have been solemnized with the sanction, consent or knowledge of the Church of Jesus Christ of Latter-day Saints, and I hereby announce that all such marriages are prohibited, and if any officer or member of the Church shall assume to solemnize or enter into any such marriage he will be deemed in transgression against the Church and will be liable to be dealt with according to the rules and regulations thereof, and excommunicated therefrom.

"Joseph F. Smith,

"President of the Church of Jesus Christ of Latter-day Saints."

—*Apr. C. R.,* 1904, p. 75.

FURTHER STATEMENT. We have announced in previous conferences, as it was announced by President Woodruff, as it was announced by President Snow, and as it was reannounced by me and my brethren and confirmed by the Church of Jesus Christ of Latter-day Saints, plural marriages have ceased in the Church. There isn't a man today in this Church or anywhere else, outside of it, who has authority to solemnize a plural marriage—not one! There is no man or woman in the Church of Jesus Christ of Latter-day Saints who is authorized to contract a plural marriage. It is not permitted, and we have been endeavoring to the utmost of our ability to prevent men from being led by some designing person into an unfortunate condition that is forbidden by the conferences, and by the voice of the Church, a condition that has to some extent, at least, brought reproach upon the people. I want to say that we have been doing all in our power to prevent it or to stop it; and in order that we might do this, we have been seeking, to our utmost, to find the men who have been the agents and the cause of leading people into it. We find it very difficult to trace them but when we do find them, and can prove it upon them, we will deal with them as we have dealt with others that we have been able to find.—Apr. C. R., 1911, p. 8.

MARRIAGE AND LARGE FAMILIES DESIRABLE. Bachelorhood and small families carry to the superficial mind the idea that they are desirable because they bring with them the minimum of responsibility. The spirit that shirks responsibility shirks labor. Idleness and pleasure take the place of industry and strenuous effort. The love of pleasure and of an easy life in turn make demands upon young men who refuse to look upon marriage and its consequent family enlargement as a sacred duty. The real fault lies with the young men. The license of the age leads them from paths of duty and responsibility to the pitfalls of a pleasure-loving world. Their sisters are the victims of neglect and of a great social and family wrong.

Women would marry if they could, and would accept cheerfully the responsibilities of family life. This loss to the home is a loss the nation must feel, as years go on. Time will vindicate the laws of God and the truth that individual human happiness is found in duty and not in pleasure and freedom from care.

The spirit of the world is contagious. We cannot live in the midst of such social conditions without suffering from the effects of their allurements. Our young people will be tempted to follow the example of the world about them. There is already a strong tendency to make sport of the obligations to marry. Pretexts of ambition are set up as an excuse to postpone marriage till some special object is attained. Some of our leading young men desire to complete first a course of study at home or abroad. Being natural leaders in society their example is dangerous and the excuse is one of questionable propriety. It were better far that many such young men never went to college than that the excuse of college life be made the reason for postponing marriage beyond the proper age.— *Juvenile Instructor*, Vol. 40, pp. 240, 241, April 15, 1905.

BE TRUE TO YOUR WIVES AND CHILDREN. And oh! my brethren, be true to your families, be true to your wives and children. Teach them the way of life. Do not allow them to get so far from you that they will become oblivious to you or to any principle of honor, purity or truth. Teach your children so that they cannot commit sin without violating their conscience, teach them the truth, that they may not depart from it. Bring them up in the way they should go, and when they get old they will not depart from it. If you will keep your boys close to your heart, within the clasp of your arms; if you will make them to feel that you love them, that you are their parents, that they are your children, and keep them near to you, they will not go very far from you, and they will not commit any very great sin. But it is when you turn them out of the home, turn them out of your affection—out into the darkness of the night into the society of the depraved or degraded; it is when they become tiresome to you, or you are tired of their innocent noise and prattle at home, and you say, "Go off somewhere else,"—it is this sort of treatment of your children that drives them from you, and helps to make criminals and infidels of them. You cannot afford to do this. How would I feel to enter into the kingdom of God—(if such a thing were possible) and see one of my children outside among the sorcerers, the whoremongers, and those who love and make a lie, and that because I have neglected my duty toward him or have not kept a proper restraint upon him? Do you think I shall be exalted in the kingdom of my God with this stain and blot upon my soul? I tell you, No! No man can get there until he atones for such crime as this—for it is a crime in the sight of God and man for a father to carelessly or wilfully neglect his children. This is my sentiment. Take care of your children. They are the hope of Israel, and upon them will rest, by and by, responsibility of the bearing of the kingdom of God in the earth. The Lord bless them and keep them in the path of righteousness. I humbly pray, in the name of Jesus. Amen.—Apr. C. R., 1902, p. 87.

RESPECT THE RIGHTS OF OTHERS. I sincerely hope that we shall succeed in impressing upon the minds of the rising generation a sincere regard, not only for themselves, to keep themselves pure and unspotted from the world, but a sincere regard for the rights and privileges of others. Our children should be taught to respect not only their fathers and their mothers, and their brothers and sisters, but they should be taught to respect all mankind, and especially should they be instructed and taught and brought up to honor the aged and the infirm, the unfortunate and the poor, the needy, and those who lack the sympathies of mankind.

We too frequently see a disposition on the part of our children to make fun of the unfortunate. A poor cripple, or a poor weak-minded person comes along, and the boys will poke fun at him, and make unbecoming remarks about him. This is entirely wrong, and such a spirit as this should never be witnessed among the children of the Latter-day Saints. They ought to be taught better at home. They should be thoroughly taught better than this in our Sunday schools, and in all the schools, so far as that is concerned, that our children attend. Our children should be taught to venerate that which is holy, that which is sacred. They should venerate the name of God. They should hold in sacred veneration the name of the Son of God. They should not take Their holy names in vain; and they should also be taught to respect and venerate the temples of God, the places of worship of their fathers and mothers. Our children should be taught also that they have rights in the house of the Lord equal to their parents and equal to their neighbors or anybody else. It always pains me to see our little ones disturbed in this right. I witnessed a little circumstance in our meeting this afternoon in the aisle; a little child was sitting by its mother on a seat. Somebody came along and took the little child off its seat, and occupied the seat himself, leaving the child to stand. I want to say to you, my brethren and sisters, that that act sent a pang to my heart. I would not, for anything in the shape of remuneration of a wordly character, grieve the heart of a little child in the house of God, lest an impression should be left upon its mind that would make the house of worship a distasteful place, and it would prefer not to come within its walls, than to come and be offended.—*Juvenile Instructor*, Vol. 39, p. 657, Semi-Annual S. S. Conference, October 9, 1904.

MUTUAL TREATMENT OF HUSBAND, WIFE AND CHILDREN. Parents, in the first place, whether they do it or not, should love and respect each other, and treat each other with respectful decorum and kindly regard, all the time. The husband should treat his wife with the utmost courtesy and respect. The husband should never insult her; he should never speak slightly of her, but should always hold her in the highest esteem in the home, in the presence of their children. We do not always do it, perhaps; some of us, perhaps, do not do it at all. But nevertheless it is true that we ought to do it. The wife, also should treat the husband with the greatest respect and courtesy. Her words to him should not be keen and cutting and sarcastic. She should not pass slurs or insinuations at him. She should not nag him. She should not try to arouse his anger or make things unpleasant about the home. The wife should be a joy to her husband, and she should live and conduct herself at home so the home will be the most joyous, the most blessed place on earth to her husband. This should be the condition of the husband, wife, the father and the mother, within the sacred precinct of that holy place, the home. Then it will be easy for the parents to instill into the hearts of their children not only love for their fathers and their mothers, not only respect and courtesy towards their parents, but love and courtesy and deference between the children at home. The little brothers will respect their little sisters. The little boys will respect one another. The little girls will respect one another and the girls and boys will respect one another, and treat one another with that love, that deference and respect that should be observed in the home on the part of the little children. Then it will be easy for the Sunday school teacher to continue the training of the child under the hallowed influence of the Sabbath school; and the child will be tractable and easily led, because the foundation of a correct education has been laid in the heart and mind of the child at home. The teacher can then help the little children, brought up under these proper influences, to render respect and courtesy to all men and especially to the unfortunate, the aged and the infirm.—*Apr. C. R.,* 1905, pp. 84-85.

WE SHOULD BE EXAMPLES TO OUR FAMILIES. When I think of our mothers, the mothers of our children, and realize that under the inspiration of the gospel they live virtuous, pure honorable lives, true to their husbands, true to their children, true to their convictions of the gospel, oh, how my soul goes out in pure love for them how noble and how God-given, how choice, how desirable and how indispensable they are to the accomplishment of God's purposes and the fulfilment of his decrees! My brethren, can you mistreat your wives, the mothers of your children? Can you help treating them with love and kindness? Can you help trying to make their lives as comfortable and happy as possible, lightening their burdens to the utmost of your ability, making life pleasant for them and for their children in their homes? How can you help it? How can any one help feeling an intense interest in the mother of his children, and also in his children? If we possess the Spirit of God, we can not do otherwise. It is only when men depart from the right spirit, when they digress from their duty, that they will neglect or dishonor any soul that is committed to their care. They are bound to honor their wives and children. Intelligent men, men of business, men of affairs, men who are involved constantly in the labors of life, and have to devote their energies and thought to their labors and duties, may not enjoy as many comforts with their families as they would like, but if they have the Spirit of the Lord with them in the performance of their temporal duties, they will never neglect the mothers of their children, nor their children. They will not fail to teach them the principles of life and set before them a proper example. Don't do anything yourselves that you would have to say to your boy, "Don't do it." Live so that you can say, "My son, do as I do, follow me, emulate my example." That is the way fathers should live, every one of us; and it is a shame, a weakening, shameful thing for any member of the Church to pursue a course that he knows is not right, and that he would rather his children should not follow.—Apr. C.R., 1915, pp.6-7.

THE TRUEST GREATNESS. After all, to do well those things which God ordained to be the common lot of all man-kind, is the truest greatness. To be a successful father or a successful mother is greater than to be a successful general or a successful statesman. One is universal and eternal greatness, the other is ephemeral. It is true that such secondary greatness may be added to that which we style commonplace; but when such secondary greatness is not added to that which is fundamental, it is merely an empty honor, and fades away from the common and universal good in life, even though it may find a place in the desultory pages of history. Our first care, after all, brings us back to that beautiful admonition of our Savior: "Seek ye first the kingdom of God, and his righteousness; and all these things shall be added unto you." (Matt. 6:33.)

We should never be discouraged in those daily tasks which God has ordained to the common lot of man. Each day's labor should be undertaken in a joyous spirit and with the thought and conviction that our happiness and eternal welfare depend upon doing well that which we ought to do, that which God has made it our duty to do. Many are unhappy because they imagine that they should be doing something unusual or something phenomenal. Some people would rather be the blossom of a tree and be admiringly seen than be an enduring part of the tree and live the commonplace life of the tree's existence.

Let us not be trying to substitute an artificial life for the true one. He is truly happy who can see and appreciate the beauty with which God has adorned the commonplace things of life.—*Juvenile Instructor,* Vol. 40, pp. 752-3 Dec. 15, 1905.

PARENTS RESPONSIBLE FOR THEIR CHILDREN. The parents in Zion will be held responsible for the acts of their children, not only until they become eight years old, but, perhaps, throughout all the lives of their children, provided they have neglected their duty to their children while they were under their care and guidance and the parents were responsible for them.—*Apr. C. R.,* 1910, p. 6.

FALSE CONFIDENCE. God forbid that there should be any of us so unwisely indulgent, so thoughtless and so shallow in our affection for our children that we dare not check them in a wayward course, in wrong-doing and in their foolish love for the things of the world more than for the things of righteousness, for fear of offending them. I want to say this: Some people have grown to possess such unlimited confidence in their children that they do not believe it possible for them to be led astray or do wrong. They do not believe they could do wrong, because they have such confidence in them. The result is, they turn them loose, morning, noon, and night, to attend all kinds of entertainments and amusements, often in company with those whom they know not and do not understand. Some of our children are so innocent that they do not suspect evil, and therefore, they are off their guard and trapped into evil. I do not like, and it is not pleasant for me, to throw chips, so to speak, for I do not know what may come to me in the future. I do not know what sorrows may await me, in my children or in their children. I cannot tell what the future may bring forth; but I would feel today as though my life has been, in part, a failure if, at this moment, any one of my children had thrown off their allegiance to their father or to their mother and taken the bits in their own teeth, so to speak, to do as they please in the world without regard to their parents.—*October Conference,* 1909—*Life of Joseph F. Smith* p. 404.

THE FATHER THE PRESIDING AUTHORITY OF THE FAMILY. There is no higher authority in matters relating to the family organization, and especially when that organization is presided over by one holding the higher Priesthood, than that of the father. The authority is time honored, and among the people of God in all dispensations it has been highly respected and often emphasized by the teachings of the prophets who were inspired of God. The patriarchal order is of divine origin and will continue throughout time and eternity. There is, then, a particular reason why men, women and children should understand this order and this authority in the households of the people of God, and seek to make it what God intended it to be, a qualification and preparation for the highest exaltation of his children. In the home the presiding authority is always vested in the father, and in all home affairs and family matters there is no other authority paramount. To illustrate this principle, a single incident will perhaps suffice. It sometimes happens that the elders are called in to administer to the members of a family. Among these elders there may be presidents of stakes, apostles, or even members of the first presidency of the Church. It is not proper under these circumstances for the father to stand back and expect the elders to direct the administration of this important ordinance. The father is there. It is his right and it is his duty to preside. He should select the one who is to administer the oil, and the one who is to be mouth in prayer, and he should not feel that because there are present presiding authorities in the Church that he is therefore divested of his rights to direct the administration of that blessing of the gospel in his home. (If the father be absent, the mother should request the presiding authority present to take charge.) The father presides at the table, at prayer, and gives general directions relating to his family life whoever may be present. Wives and children should be taught to feel that the patriarchal order in the kingdom of God has been established for a wise and beneficent purpose, and should sustain the head of the household and encourage him in the discharge of his duties, and do all in their power to aid him in the exercise of the rights and privileges which God has bestowed upon the head of the home. This patriarchal order has its divine spirit and purpose, and those who disregard it under one pretext or another are out of harmony with the spirit of God's laws as they are ordained for recognition in the home. It is not merely a question of who is perhaps the best qualified. Neither is it wholly a question of who is living the most worthy life. It is a question largely of law and order, and its importance is seen often from the fact that the authority remains and is respected long after a man is really unworthy to exercise it.

This authority carries with it a responsibility and a grave one, as well as its rights and privileges, and men can not be too exemplary in their lives, nor fit themselves too carefully to live in harmony with this important and God-ordained rule of conduct in the family organization. Upon this authority certain promises and blessings are predicated, and those who observe and respect this authority have certain claims on divine favor which they cannot have except they respect and observe the laws that God has established for the regulation and authority of the home. "Honor thy father and thy mother: that thy days may be long upon the land which the Lord thy God giveth thee," was a fundamental law to ancient Israel, and is binding upon every member of the Church today, for the law is eternal.

The necessity, then, of organizing the patriarchal order and authority of the home rests upon principle as well as upon the person who holds that authority, and among the Latter-day Saints family discipline, founded upon the law of the patriarchs, should be carefully cultivated, and fathers will then be able to remove many of the difficulties that now weaken their position in the home, through unworthy children.

The principles here set forth are of more importance than many parents have heretofore attached to them, and the unfortunate position today in the homes of many of the elders of Israel is directly traceable to a want of appreciation of their truthfulness.—*Juvenile Instructor*, Vol. 37, p. 148. March 1, 1902.

DUTIES OF FATHERS. May the fathers in Israel live as they should live; treat their wives as they should treat them; make their homes as comfortable as they possibly can; lighten the burden upon their companions as much as possible; set a proper example before their children; teach them to meet with them in prayer, morning and night, and whenever they sit down to partake of food, to acknowledge the mercy of God in giving them the food that they eat and the raiment that they wear, and acknowledge the hand of God in all things. This is our duty, and if we do not do it the Lord will be displeased, for he has said so. He is only pleased with those who acknowledge his hand in all things. —Oct. C. R., 1909, p. 9; Doc. and Cov. 59: 7, 21.

MOTHERHOOD THE FOUNDATION OF HOME AND NATION. Motherhood lies at the foundation of happiness in the home, and of prosperity in the nation. God has laid upon men and women very sacred obligations with respect to motherhood, and they are obligations that cannot be disregarded without invoking divine displeasure. In I Timothy 2:13-15, we are told that "Adam was first formed, then

Eve. And Adam was not deceived, but the woman being deceived was in the transgression. Notwithstanding she shall be saved in childbearing, if they continue in faith and charity and holiness with sobriety." Can she be saved without child-bearing? She indeed takes an awful risk if she wilfully disregards what is a pronounced requirement of God. How shall she plead her innocence when she is not innocent? How shall she excuse her guilt when it is fastened upon her?

The question of parental obligation in the matter of children is not generally denied. A failure to fulfill the obligation, however, is too frequently excused.

"Children," we are told, "are a heritage of the Lord;" they are also, the Psalmist tells us, "his reward." If children are cut off from their birthright, how shall the Lord be rewarded? They are not a source of weakness and poverty to family life, for they bring with them certain divine blessings that make for the prosperity of the home and the nation. "As arrows are in the hand of a mighty man; so are children of the youth. Happy is the man that hath his quiver full of them: they shall not be ashamed, but they shall speak with the enemies in the gate." (Psalms 127:4, 5)

What answer shall men and women make in excuse of conduct which contravenes the commandments of God? Those whose hearts are in touch with God's most sacred laws will make great sacrifices honestly to fulfil them.

There has, however, of late arisen a condition in our social life that is working against the divine requirements of motherhood. Men and women plead the enormous increase in the cost of child-bearing. The requirements for motherhood in matters of doctor's fees, nurses' bills and hospital charges, are so great as to discourage men and women of slender means. The burden of such expenses is certainly becoming great, and if they are likely to stand directly in the way of God's requirement, something should be done either to remove them or mitigate them, and some means should be provided that will protect the family and the nation against destruction. It is a problem well worthy the attention of our law-makers, who appropriate generously in matters that are insignificant when compared with the health, wealth and physical prosperity of the nation that encourages the birth of children. —*Juvenile Instructor*, Vol. 50, pp. 290, 291, May, 1915.

HUSBAND'S SUCCESS DEPENDENT UPON WIFE'S FITNESS. There is no organization or government in the world so perfectly planned for the education of men and women to executive responsibilities as is the Church of Jesus Christ of Latter-day Saints. Government in the home and in the Church constitutes an important part in the lives of the people, and the government in the home is the basis of all successful government in church or state. In the home the mother is the principal disciplinarian in early child life, and her influence and discipline determine in a great measure the ability of her children to assume in manhood and womanhood the larger governments in church and state.

In addition, however, to home government, women often stand with their husbands in responsible places and share in some measure the success or failure which characterizes their husbands' administration of affairs. In selecting men to occupy responsible positions in the Church, it not infrequently happens that a useful and competent man is barred from consideration because of the deplorable want of fitness in the wife, and though a wife may not always bar a husband's opportunities, she may, nevertheless, prove a great hindrance to him in the discharge of the duties that belong to his office. If our sisters could only realize how helpful they might be to their husbands who hold responsible positions in the Church, and if they would only take pride and pleasure in their husbands' administration of affairs, the conduct of men in public office would in many instances be very greatly improved.

The word and the law of God are as important for women who would reach wise conclusions as they are for men; and women should study and consider the problems of this great latter-day work from the standpoint of God's revelations, and as they may be actuated by his Spirit, which it is their right to receive through the medium of sincere and heartfelt prayer. A woman without heartfelt devotion for the things of God is not prepared to stand at her husband's side and enjoy his confidence in the graver responsibilities that devolve upon him in the government of the Church. Husbands are justified in withholding their confidence from and in refusing to be influenced by wives whose worldly ambitions and want of appreciation of divine things lead them to contend for personal advantages and selfish gains. Wives of leaders should have a generous feeling for all that relates to the affairs over which their husbands preside. Such women should not be exclusive in their social relations, and should avoid the evils that frequently come from yielding to the influence and views of a small coterie that may have selfish aims and personal advantages to serve.—*Juvenile Instructor*, Vol. 38, pp. 371, 372, 1903.

DUTY OF PARENTS. It is the duty of Latter-day Saints to teach their children the truth, to bring them up in the way they should go, to teach them the first principles of the gospel, the necessity of baptism for the remission of sins, and for membership in the Church of Christ; teaching them the necessity of receiving the gift of the Holy Ghost by the laying on of hands, which will lead them into all truth, and which will reveal to them things that have passed and things which are to come, and show to them more clearly those things which are present with them, that they may comprehend the truth, and that they may walk in the light as Christ is in the light; that they may have fellowship with him and that his blood may cleanse them from all sin.—*Apr. C. R.*, 1912, p. 135.

BLESSING AND NAMING INFANTS. In accordance with the rule of the Church, children born to members of the Church are taken to the monthly fast meetings in the several wards, and are there blessed and named by or under the direction of the bishopric. It is usual on such an occasion for the bishop to call upon the father of the child, if he is present, and if he be an elder in good standing, to take part with the bishopric in the ordinance. This is in every way proper for the blessing so pronounced is in the nature of a father's blessing. Record of the ordinance so performed in the ward meeting is made by the ward clerk.

However, a father holding the higher Priesthood, may desire to bless and name his child at home, perhaps at an earlier date than would be convenient or possible for mother and babe to attend a fast meeting in the ward. Many elders desire to perform this ordinance within the circle of their own families on or about the eighth day of the child's life. This also is proper, for the father, if he is worthy of his Priesthood, has certain rights and authority within his family, comparable to those of the bishop with relation to the ward. Too often amongst us the head of the family, though he holds the higher Priesthood, fails to magnify his calling as the spiritual head of his household. It would be better if every elder who is a father rose to the dignity of his position, and officiated in his holy office within his family organization. He may call to his aid any others who are worthy holders of the requisite authority in the Priesthood, but it is his privilege to stand as the head of his household, and to perform the ordinances pertaining to his family. The question arises,

and has recently been presented in specific form, if an elder performs
the ordinances of naming and blessing his own child at home, is it
necessary that the ordinance be repeated in the ward meeting? We
answer, No. The father's blessing is authoritative, proper, and sufficient; but every such case must be promptly reported to the bishop
of the ward, who will direct the clerk to make full and proper record
of the matter, entering the name of the child, with date of birth
and blessing, and all data as to parentage, etc., on the books of the
ward. It is the duty of the teachers and priests in their house to
house visitations among the people to see that all such reports are
fully and promptly made.

The repetition of the ordinance of naming and blessing children
tends to diminish our regard for the authority and sanctity attending
the father's blessing within the household.

But let it not be forgotten that if the child be not blessed and
named by due authority at home it should be taken to the fast meeting
of the ward on the earliest possible occasion, there to receive the
blessing and to have its name duly entered on the books of the
Church.—*Juvenile Instructor*, Vol. 38, January, 1903.

WATCH YOUR CHILDREN. Some people have grown to possess
such unlimited confidence in their children that they do not believe
it possible for them to be led astray or to do wrong. They do not
believe they could do wrong, because they have such confidence in
them. The result is they turn them loose, morning, noon and night,
to attend all kinds of entertainments and amusement, often in company with those whom they know not and do not understand. Some
of our children are so innocent that they do not suspect evil, and,
therefore, they are off their guard and are trapped into evil.—Oct. C.
R., 1909, p. 4.

DUTY TO TEACH CHILDREN. Another great and important duty
devolving upon this people is to teach their children, from their cradle
until they become men and women, every principle of the gospel,
and endeavor, as far as it lies in the power of the parents, to instil
into their hearts a love for God, the truth, virtue, honesty, honor
and integrity to everything that is good. That is important for all
men and women who stand at the head of a family in the household
of faith. Teach your children the love of God, teach them to love
the principles of the gospel of Jesus Christ. Teach them to love
their fellowmen, and especially to love their fellow members in the
Church that they may be true to their fellowship with the people

of God. Teach them to honor the Priesthood, to honor the authority that God has bestowed upon his Church for the proper government of his Church.—Apr. C. R., 1915, pp. 4, 5.

WHAT TO TEACH YOUR CHILDREN. We are a Christian people, we believe in the Lord Jesus Christ, and we feel that it is our duty to acknowledge him as our Savior and Redeemer. Teach it to your children. Teach them that the Prophet Joseph Smith had restored to him the Priesthood that was held by Peter and James and John, who were ordained under the hands of the Savior himself. Teach them that Joseph Smith, the prophet, when only a boy, was chosen and called of God to lay the foundations of the Church of Christ in the world, to restore the holy Priesthood, and the ordinances of the gospel, which are necessary to qualify men to enter into the kingdom of heaven. Teach your children to respect their neighbors. Teach your children to respect their bishops and the teachers that come to their homes to teach them. Teach your children to respect old age, gray hairs, and feeble frames. Teach them to venerate and to hold in honorable remembrance their parents, and to help all those who are helpless and needy. Teach your children, as you have been taught yourselves, to honor the Priesthood which you hold, the Priesthood which we hold as elders in Israel. Teach your children to honor themselves, teach your children to honor the principle of presidency by which organizations are held intact and by which strength and power for the well-being and happiness and upbuilding of the people are preserved. Teach your children that when they go to school they should honor their teachers in that which is true and honest, in that which is manly and womanly, and worth while; and also teach them to avoid the bad examples of their teachers out of school, and the bad principles of men and women who are sometimes teachers in schools. Teach your children to honor the law of God and the law of the state and the law of our country. Teach them to respect and hold in honor those who are chosen by the people to stand at their head and execute justice and administer the law. Teach them to be loyal to their country, loyal to righteousness and uprightness and honor, and thereby they will grow up to be men and women choice above all the men and women of the world.—Apr. C. R., 1917, pp. 5, 6.

WHAT CHILDREN SHOULD BE TAUGHT. I pray you, my brethren and sisters, who have children in Zion, and upon whom rests the greater responsibility, teach them the principles of the gospel, teach them to have faith in the Lord Jesus Christ, and in baptism for the remission of sins when they shall reach the age of eight years. They must be taught in the principles of the gospel of Jesus Christ by their parents, or the blood of the children will be upon the skirts of those parents. It seems to me so plain a duty and so necessary for them to see to it that their children avail themselves of the opportunities that are afforded them in having them taught and instructed in these principles in the Sunday schools that are established in the Church and conducted Sunday after Sunday for the benefit of their children. I should feel contemptible, I was going to say, in my own mind, in my own feelings, if I had children who were neglected by their parents in regard to these matters. Our little ones are only too anxious to go to Sunday school, no matter what may occur, whether it rains or is cold or pleasant, or what not; whether they are sick or well, they cannot be kept from the Sunday school unless there is great cause for it.—Apr. C. R., 1903, p. 81.

TRAINING OF CHILDREN AT HOME AND IN SUNDAY SCHOOL. It does not need argument to convince our minds that our children will be just about what we make them. They are born without knowledge or understanding—the most helpless creatures of the animal creation born into the world. The little one begins to learn after it is born, and all that it knows greatly depends upon its environment, the influences under which it is brought up, the kindness with which it is treated, the noble examples shown it, the hallowed influences of father and mother, or otherwise, over its infant mind. And it will be largely what its environment and its parents and teachers make it.

The child of the lowest of our native tribes born in a wigwam and the child born in luxury start out almost equal, so far as the possibilities of learning are concerned. A great deal depends upon the influence under which it is brought up. You will observe that the most potent influence over the mind of a child to persuade it to learn, to progress, or to accomplish anything, is the influence of love. More can be accomplished for good by unfeigned love, in bringing up a child, than by any other influence that can be brought to bear upon it. A child that cannot be conquered by the lash, or subdued by violence, may be controlled in an instant by unfeigned affection and sympathy. I know that is true; and this principle obtains in every condition of life.

The Sunday school teacher should govern the children, not by passion, by bitter words or scolding, but by affection and by winning their confidence. If a teacher gets the confidence of a child it is not impossible to accomplish every desired good with that child.

I would have it understood that I believe that the greatest law and commandment of God is to love the Lord our God with all our mind, might and strength, and our neighbors as ourselves, and if this principle is observed at home the brothers and sisters will love one another; they will be kind and helpful to one another, showing forth the principle of kindness and being solicitous for one another's good. Under these circumstances the home comes nearer being a heaven on earth, and children brought up under these influences will never forget them, and though they may be in trying places, their memories will revert to the homes where they enjoyed such hallowed influences, and their better natures will assert themselves no matter what the trials or temptations may be.

Brethren and sisters of the Sunday school, I implore you to teach and control by the spirit of love and forbearance until you can conquer. If children are defiant and difficult to control, be patient with them until you can conquer by love, and you will have gained their souls, and you can then mould their characters as you please.

Sometimes children do not like their teachers, and the teachers are impatient with the children, and complain of them as being very uncouth, uncontrollable and bad. The children in their turn tell their parents how they despise their teachers, and say they don't want to go to school any more because the teacher is so cross. I have heard of these things and know them to be true. On the other hand, if children say to father and mother, "We think we have the best teacher in the world, in our Sunday school," or, "We have the best teacher in our district school that ever lived," it proves that those teachers have won the affections of the children, and the little ones are as clay in the hands of the potter to be moulded in any shape desired. This is the position you teachers should occupy, and if you get their affections this will be the report the children will make regarding you.—*Oct. C. R.,* 1902, pp. 92, 93.

TEACH CHILDREN THE GOSPEL. It is the duty of parents to teach their children the principles of the gospel and to be sober-minded and industrious in their youth. They should be impressed from the cradle to the time they leave the parental roof to make homes and assume the duties of life for themselves, that there is a seed time and harvest, and as man sows, so shall he reap. The sowing of bad habits in youth will bring forth nothing better than vice, and the sowing of the seeds of indolence will result invariably in poverty and lack of stability in old age. Evil begets evil, and good will bring forth good.

I have heard people say, "We pass this way but once, and we might as well have a good time and make the most of it while life lasts." This is in keeping with the prediction in the Book of Mormon: "And there shall be many which shall say, Eat, drink, and be merry, for tomorrow we die; and it shall be well with us. * * * Yea, and there shall be many which shall teach after this manner, false, and vain, and foolish doctrines, and shall be puffed up in their hearts, and shall seek deep to hide their counsels from the Lord; and their works shall be in the dark." (II Nephi 28:7-9)

Let the parents in Zion give their children something to do that they may be taught the arts of industry, and equipped to carry responsibility when it is thrust upon them. Train them in some useful vocation that their living may be assured when they commence in life for themselves. Remember, the Lord has said that "the idler shall not eat the bread of the laborer," but all in Zion should be industrious. Neither should they be given to loud laughter, light and foolish speeches, worldly pride and lustful desires, for these are not only unbecoming, but grievous sins in the sight of the Lord. And, we read that the wages of sin is death, and death is banishment from the Spirit and presence of the Lord.

And above all else, let us train our children in the principles of the gospel of our Savior, that they may become familiar with the truth and walk in the light which it sheds forth to all those who will receive it. "He that seeketh me early," the Lord has said, "shall find me, and shall not be forsaken." It behooves us, therefore, to commence in early life to travel in the straight and narrow path which leads to eternal salvation.—Juvenile Instructor, Vol. 52, pp. 19, 20, January, 1917; Rom. 6:23; Prov. 8:17.

TEACH CHILDREN THE STORY OF JESUS' DEATH. Should the little children of the kindergarten be taught the events leading up to and culminating in the death of our Savior? It is a principle widely accepted that it is not desirable to teach these little ones those things that are horrifying to childish natures. And what may be said of children is equally true in all stages of student life. But death is not an unmixed horror. With it are associated some of the profoundest and most important truths of human life. Although painful in the extreme to those who must suffer the departure of dear ones, death is one of the grandest blessings in divine economy; and we think children should be taught something of its true meaning as early in life as possible.

We are born that we may put on mortality, that is, that we may clothe our spirits with a body. Such a blessing is the first step toward an immortal body, and the second step is death. Death lies along the road of eternal progress; and though hard to bear, no one who believes in the gospel of Jesus Christ, and especially in the resurrection, would have it otherwise. Children should be taught early in life that death is really a necessity as well as a blessing, and that we would not and could not be satisfied and supremely happy without it. Upon the crucifixion and the resurrection of Jesus, one of the grandest principles of the gospel depends. If children were taught this early in life, death would not have the horrifying influence that it does have over many childish minds.

Children are sure to be brought into some acquaintanceship with the incident of death, even during the kindergarten period; and it would be a great relief to the puzzled and perplexed conditions of their minds if some intelligent statements of the reason for death were made to them. No explanation of death to a child's mind can anywhere be found that is more simple and convincing than is the death of our Master, connected as it is and ever must be with the glorious resurrection.—*Juvenile Instructor*, Vol. 40, p. 336, June 1, 1905.

WISE GIVING TO CHILDREN. It is very gratifying to parents to be able to respond to the desires of their children, but it is undoubtedly a cruelty to a child to give it everything it asks for. Children may wisely be denied things which even in themselves are harmless. Our pleasures depend often more upon the qualities of our desires than upon the gratification. A child may be ladened with gifts which afford him little or no pleasure, simply because he has no desire for them. The education then of our desires is one of far-reaching importance to our happiness in life; and when we learn that there is an education of our intellects and we are set about that education with prudence and wisdom, we shall do much to increase not only our happiness but also our usefulness in the world.

God's ways of educating our desires are, of course, always the most perfect, and if those who have it in their power to educate and direct the desires of children would imitate his prudence, the chil-

dren would be much more fortunate in combating the difficulties
that beset men everywhere in the struggle for existence. And what
is God's way? Everywhere in nature we are taught the lessons of
patience and waiting. We want things a long time before we get
them, and the fact that we wanted them a long time makes them all
the more precious when they come. In nature we have our seed-
time and harvest; and if children were taught that the desires that
they sow may be reaped by and by through patience and labor, they
will learn to appreciate whenever a long-looked-for goal has been
reached. Nature resists us and keeps admonishing us to wait; indeed,
we are compelled to wait.

A man has a much greater capacity to enjoy that for which he
has labored for a number of years than one who has a similar object
given to him. It is, therefore, most unfortunate for children when
their parents greatly weaken or almost wholly destroy the children's
capacity for the enjoyment of some of the most wholesome pleasures
of life. The child who has everything he wants and when he wants
it is really to be pitied, for he has no ability to enjoy it. There may
be a hundred times more pleasure in a dollar piece for one child than
for another.

Our desires are the strongest motives which incite us to energy
and which make us productive and creative in life. If they are weak,
our creations are likely to be puny and worthless. Money that a boy
works for has a value upon his life and an actual purchasing power
greatly in excess of the money that has been given to him. And what
is true of boys is in a large measure true of girls. The girl who earns
something, who works persistently and patiently that she may have
money she can call her own has a capacity for enjoying the objects
of her desires greatly in excess of the girl who never learned to earn
a dollar. She also knows and appreciates the value of a dollar more
than the girl who never had to wait until she earned it. It is a mistake
for parents to suppose that a daughter ought never to be required
to earn anything. Every effort by which we seek the fulfilment
of our desires gives strength and character to manhood and womanhood. The man who builds a house has vastly more enjoyment in its
occupation than the man who has had a house given to him.

It is just as wrong systematically to give a child everything he
desires as to deny the child everything. When indulgent parents
fancy that they are adding to the pleasure of their children's lives
by giving to them whatever they wish, such parents are in fact

destroying the capacity of their children to enjoy the gratification of desires weakened and perverted by over-indulgence. The ability to give to children wisely is indeed a rare attainment, and is acquired only by a thoughtful and prudent exercise of the highest sense of duty which parents can feel for their children. Duty is always preferable to indulgence.—*Juvenile Instructor*, p. 400, July 1, 1903.

DO NOT PLACE CHILDREN UNDER PLEDGES. We believe it is questionable wisdom to put children under a pledge of any kind. We ourselves do not put our children under pledges, and we see no reason why we should permit others to do it. Instructions can be given to children warning them against the use of strong drinks and tobacco just as well without their being pledged as by placing that responsibility upon them. No man or set of people should be permitted to call our children together for the purpose of joining a temperance society, without they first obtain the consent of the parents or guardians of those children; and we take it for granted that no such consent would be given. We also take it for granted that boards of education could not consistently, without such permission, allow such a thing to be done in the public schools.

It should be understood that we, the Latter-day Saints, teach temperance and morality as part of our religion, and that we ourselves are competent to do this kind of work among our own children without the aid of outside temperance societies.—*Juvenile Instructor*, Vol. 37, p. 720, Dec. 1, 1902.

CHILDREN HAVE EQUAL RIGHTS WITH ELDERS IN THE HOUSE OF THE LORD. Our children should be taught also that they have rights in the house of the Lord equal to their parents and equal to their neighbors or anybody else.—Oct. C. R., 1904, p. 88.

DON'T MORTGAGE YOUR HOUSES. My brethren, see to it that you do not put a mortgage upon the roof that covers the heads of your wives and your children. Don't do it. Don't plaster your farms with mortgages, because it is from your farms that you reap your food, and the means to provide your raiment and your other necessaries of life. Keep your possessions free from debt. Get out of debt as fast as you can, and keep out of debt, for that is the way in which the promise of God will be fulfilled to the people of his Church, that they will become the richest of all people in the world. But this will not happen while you mortgage your homes and your farms, or run into debt beyond your ability to meet your obligations; and thus, perhaps, your name and credit be dishonored because you over-reached yourselves. "Never reach further than you can gather," is a good motto.—*Apr. C. R., 1915, p. 11.*

No Substitute for the Home. The growing tendency throughout the country to abandon the home for the hotel and for the nomadic life with its ever-shifting and restless spirit, manifests itself here and there among the Latter-day Saints. A word of warning at this time may not be inappropriate to those who imagine that there is some charm as well as benefit in moving about the world in quest of pleasure and novelties that come from changing frequently one's habitation.

There is no substitute for the home. Its foundation is as ancient as the world, and its mission has been ordained of God from the earliest times. From Abraham sprang two ancient races represented in Isaac and Ishmael. The one built stable homes, and prized its land as a divine inheritance. The other became children of the desert, and as restless as its ever-shifting sands upon which their tents were pitched. From that day to the present, the home has been the chief characteristic of superior over inferior nations. The home then is more than a habitation, it is an institution which stands for stability and love in individuals as well as in nations.

There can be no genuine happiness separate and apart from the home, and every effort made to sanctify and preserve its influence is uplifting to those who toil and sacrifice for its establishment. Men and women often seek to substitute some other life for that of the home; they would make themselves believe that the home means restraint; that the highest liberty is the fullest opportunity to move about at will. There is no happiness without service, and there is no service greater than that which converts the home into a divine institution, and which promotes and preserves family life.

Those who shirk home responsibilities are wanting in an important element of social well-being. They may indulge themselves in social pleasures, but their pleasures are superficial and result in disappointment later in life. The occupations of men sometimes call them from their homes; but the thought of home-coming is always an inspiration to well doing and devotion. When women abandon the home and its duties, the case is a more deplorable one. The evil effects are not confined to the mother alone. The children are robbed of a sacred right, and their love is bereft of its rallying place around the hearthstone. The strongest attachments of childhood are those that cluster about the home, and the dearest memories of old age

are those that call up the associations of youth and its happy surroundings.

The disposition among the Saints to be moving about ought to
be discouraged. If communities must swarm, let the young go, and
let the old homes be transmitted from generation to generation,
and let the home be erected with the thought that it is to be a family
abiding place from one generation to another, that it is to be a
monument to its founder and an inheritance of all that is sacred and
dear in home life. Let it be the Mecca to which an ever-increasing
posterity may make its pilgrimage. The home, a stable and pure
home, is the highest guaranty of social stability and permanence in
government.

A Latter-day Saint who has no ambition to establish a home and
give it permanency has not a full conception of a sacred duty the
gospel imposes upon him. It may be necessary at times to change
our abode; but a change should never be made for light or trivial
reasons, nor to satisfy a restless spirit. Whenever homes are built
the thought of permanency should always be present. Many of the
Saints live in parts of the country that are less productive than others,
that possess few natural attractions, yet they cherish their homes
and their surroundings, and the more substantial men and women
of such communities are the last to abandon them. There is no
substitute in wealth or in ambition for the home. Its influence is
a prime necessity for man's happiness and well-being.—*Juvenile Instructor*, Vol. 38, pp. 145, 146, March 1, 1903.

WORSHIP IN THE HOME. We have in the gospel the truth. If
that is the case, and I bear my testimony that so it is, then it is worth
our every effort to understand the truth, each for himself, and to
impart it in spirit and practice to our chlidren. Far too many risk
their children's spiritual guidance to chance, or to others rather
than to themselves, and think that organizations suffice for religious
training. Our temporal bodies would soon become emaciated, if we
fed them only once a week, or twice, as some of us are in the habit
of feeding our spiritual and religious bodies. Our material concerns
would be less thriving, if we looked after them only two hours a
week, as some people seem to do with their spiritual affairs, especially
if we in addition contented ourselves, as some do in religious matters,
to let others look after them.

No; on the other hand, this should be done every day, and in the
home, by precept, teaching and example. Brethren, there is too

little religious devotion, love and fear of God, in the home; too much worldliness, selfishness, indifference and lack of reverence in the family, or these never would exist so abundantly on the outside. Then, the home is what needs reforming. Try today, and tomorrow, to make a change in your home by praying twice a day with your family; call on your children and your wife to pray with you. Ask a blessing upon every meal you eat. Spend ten minutes in reading a chapter from the words of the Lord in the Bible, the Book of Mormon, the Doctrine and Covenants, before you retire, or before you go to your daily toil. Feed your spiritual selves at home, as well as in public places. Let love, and peace, and the Spirit of the Lord, kindness, charity, sacrifice for others, abound in your families. Banish harsh words, envyings, hatreds, evil speaking, obscene language and innuendo, blasphemy, and let the Spirit of God take possession of your hearts. Teach to your children these things, in spirit and power, sustained and strengthened by personal practice. Let them see that you are earnest, and practice what you preach. Do not let your children out to specialists in these things, but teach them by your own precept and example, by your own fireside. Be a specialist yourself in the truth. Let our meetings, schools and organizations, instead of being our only or leading teachers, be supplements to our teachings and training in the home. Not one child in a hundred would go astray, if the home environment, example and training, were in harmony with the truth in the gospel of Christ, as revealed and taught to the Latter-day Saints. Fathers and mothers, you are largely to blame for the infidelity and indifference of your children. You can remedy the evil by earnest worship, example, training and discipline, in the home.—*Improvement Era*, Vol. 7, Dec., 1904, p. 135.

THE BASIS OF A TRUE HOME. A home is not a home in the eye of the gospel, unless there dwell perfect confidence and love between the husband and the wife. Home is a place of order, love, union, rest, confidence, and absolute trust; where the breath of suspicion of infidelity can not enter; where the woman and the man each have implicit confidence in each other's honor and virtue.— *Second Sunday School Convention.*

THE IDEAL HOME. What then is an ideal home—model home, such as it should be the ambition of the Latter-day Saints to build; such as a young man starting out in life should wish to erect for himself? And the answer came to me: It is one in which all worldly considerations are secondary. One in which the father is devoted to the family with which God has blessed him, counting them of first importance, and in which they in turn permit him to live in their hearts. One in which there is confidence, union, love, sacred devotion between father and mother and children and parents. One in which the mother takes every pleasure in her children, supported by the father—all being moral, pure, God-fearing. As the tree is judged by its fruit, so also do we judge the home by the children. In the ideal home true parents rear loving, thoughtful children, loyal to the death, to father and mother and home! In it there is the religious spirit, for both parents and children have faith in God, and their practices are in conformity with that faith; the members are free from the vices and contaminations of the world, are pure in morals, having upright hearts beyond bribes and temptations, ranging high in the exalted standards of manhood and womanhood. Peace, order, and contentment reign in the hearts of the inmates—let them be rich or poor, in things material. There are no vain regrets; no expressions of discontent against father, from the boys and girls, in which they complain: "If we only had this or that, or were like this family or that, or could do like so and so!"—complaints that have caused fathers many uncertain steps, dim eyes, restless nights, and untold anxiety. In their place is the loving thoughtfulness to mother and father by which the boys and girls work with a will and a determination to carry some of the burden that the parents have staggered under these many years. There is the kiss for mother, the caress for father, the thought that they have sacrificed their own hopes and ambitions, their strength, even life itself to their children—there is gratitude in payment for all that has been given them!

In the ideal home the soul is not starved, neither are the growth and expansion of the finer sentiments paralyzed for the coarse and sensual pleasures. The main aim is not to heap up material wealth, which generally draws further and further from the true, the ideal, the spiritual life; but it is rather to create soul-wealth, consciousness of noble achievement, an outflow of love and helpfulness.

It is not costly paintings, tapestries, priceless bric-a-brac, various ornaments, costly furniture, fields, herds, houses and lands which constitute the ideal home, nor yet the social enjoyments and ease so tenaciously sought by many; but it is rather beauty of soul, cultivated, loving, faithful, true spirits; hands that help and hearts that sympa-thize; love that seeks not its own, thoughts and acts that touch our lives to finer issues—these lie at the foundation of the ideal home. —*Improvement Era*, Vol. 8, 1904-05, pp. 385-388.

FOUNDATION OF ALL GOOD IN HOME. The very foundation of the kingdom of God, of righteousness, of progress, of development, of eternal life and eternal increase in the kingdom of God, is laid in the divinely ordained home; and there should be no difficulty in holding in the highest reverence and exalted thought, the home, if it can be built upon the principles of purity, of true affection, of righteousness and justice. The man and his wife who have perfect confidence in each other, and who determine to follow the laws of God in their lives and fulfil the measure of their mission in the earth, would not be, and could never be, contented without the home. Their hearts, their feelings, their minds, their desires would naturally trend toward the building of a home and family and of a kingdom of their own; to the laying of the foundation of eternal increase and power, glory, exaltation and dominion, worlds without end.—*Juvenile Instructor*, Vol. 51, p. 739.

SECURE HOMES. In my judgment it would be prudence and wisdom for the young people to secure lands near the homes of their parents and near the body of the Church, where they can have the advantage of Sunday schools and the gatherings of the Saints, and in so doing they will be building for themselves, instead of permitting the stranger to come in and take the lands—strangers with whom in many instances we would not affiliate. We all know there are classes who come in here who up to date have not proved desirable neighbors to affiliate with, and it is just as well for our own young people to stay in the land of their birth and build them homes. I will say that we do not approve of the disposition of some to go afar off where life, property and liberty are not safe. We wish them to remain together, so that if it is necessary or desirable that the Saints should colonize, they might do it in order.

I do not want to be understood as saying or thinking that one little state is big enough to contain all the young people, and I think it is wisdom and necessary for the Latter-day Saints to take every advantage in this respect that is possible. I think our young people should get homes in Utah, Idaho, Wyoming and Colorado—in our own state and in adjoining states—in blessed America, under this grand and glorious government where life and property, and the liberties of men are safe and protected, where mob violence and revolutionary spirit do not stalk forth as in some countries of the world.

Another thing. In the old times an effort was made to co-operate and combine together and establish home industries for the production of the things that were needful for consumption of the people and to produce a revenue as well. Today we have allowed the home industry spirit to perish almost from amongst us, and we do not witness the same loyalty among the people to those things which are produced at home that there should be. There are too many people who would rather patronize some "cheap John" and buy shoddy goods, just because they can get them a few pence cheaper, than to sustain home industry, and get all wool and a yard wide. We should not encourage foreign capital to the exclusion of our own, and patronize foreign labor against our own, but we should build up our home institutions.—*From a Sermon, given in Logan, April 7, 1910.*

OWN YOUR HOMES. It was early the rule among the Latter-day Saints to have the lands so divided that every family could have a spot of ground which could be called theirs; and it has been the proud boast of this people that among them were more home owners than among any other people of like numbers. This condition had a good tendency, and whatever men said of us, the home among this people was a first consideration. It is this love of home that has made the Saints famous as colonizers, builders of settlements, and redeemers of the deserts. But in the cities there appears now to be coming into vogue the idea that renting is the thing. Of course, it may be necessary as a temporary makeshift, but no young couple should ever settle down with the idea that such a condition, as far as they are concerned, shall be permanent. Every young man should have an ambition to possess his own home. It is better for him, for his family, for society, for the state, and for the Church. Nothing so engenders stability, strength, power, patriotism, fidelity to country and to God as the owning of a home—a spot of earth that you and your children can call yours. And besides, there are so many tender virtues that grow with such ownership that the government of a family is made doubly easy thereby.

Let us continue, as a people, to be unlike the world in this regard. I hope the Saints will ever be a home owning people, and never become roamers, roomers and renters. We should no more follow the prevailing notions in this than in some other things. The people of Zion have a higher destiny than being led by the nose, as it were.

by the prevailing whims. We do not purpose being led by evil tendencies, but rather glory in being leaders ourselves in all that makes for the welfare and happiness of the home, the advancement of the Church, the prosperity of the state.—*Improvement Era*, Aug., 1904, Vol. 7, p. 796.

DO NOT MORTGAGE YOUR HOMES. Whenever a panic comes, or there is severe financial depression because of monetary conditions, the people have before them a painful object lesson on the evils of mortgaging, especially of their homes and places of business.

Men owe it to their wives and children to be prudent and conservative when business considerations touch the home, and it is doubtful whether they really have a moral right to expose helpless wives and children to the mercies of the money lender. The evils are too abundantly manifest to permit of mortgaging homes that should be sacred to the needs of those who are dependent upon them.

The Latter-day Saints have often been warned and are now earnestly admonished not to hazard their homes, and with them their wives and children, upon the altar of financial speculations.

What was taught in the early days of our history in this intermountain region is equally true today, and it is the duty of every Latter-day Saint, so far as it is possible, to own his home, to possess an earthly inheritance. It has been our pride that among the people of all the world nowhere can a greater percentage be found of those who have title to the homes in which they live. Instead of declining year by year in the total number of homes owned by the Latter-day Saints of Salt Lake City, and other large cities, there should be an increase. The matter of the Saints possessing title to their homes is something more than a question of whether it pays best to rent or to own. It is a question of vital importance to our future position, and relative strength in a land to which by every rule of equity and prudence we are entitled. There is a virtue and an assurance and a certainty in the ownership of one's home that are never felt by those who are shifting from place to place without any landed possession. The influence upon child life that comes from the possession and ownership of the family home is of itself a sufficient reason to guard it against the repeated evils of mortgaging. The Latter-day Saints owe it to themselves and they owe it to their God to be steadfast in the possession of the lands to which they hold titles, either by purchase or settlement. The evil of mortgaging homes to eastern firms, to men and companies who have no other motive than to secure their pound of flesh, is growing among the people, and especially among those in the larger cities. Against such evils the people have in the past been abundantly warned. If necessity compels the husband to place a mortgage upon the home, let it come, if possible, through a friend and not through those who may be the enemies of the people. If the Latter-day Saints will give heed to the prudent admonitions and lessons of the past, they will hesitate in the presence of the alluring temptations which are now everywhere held out, to mortgage their homes, their places of business, the canals, and the farms, for the means with which to speculate and grow rich. It is to be hoped, therefore, that where the Saints have mortgages upon their homes they will be persistent in their endeavors to remove them, and they are advised to keep intact and beyond menace the titles to their lands.

The admonitions here given are directed especially to those disposed to mortgage for the purpose of speculation, and not to those who may find it necessary through building societies or otherwise to secure homes by monthly or other periodical payments. The latter practice may lead to economic habits, while speculations too frequently create a spirit of extravagance.—*Juvenile Instructor*, Vol. 36, pp. 722-723.

EVILS OF MORTGAGING. What a blessed condition would result in Zion if the evil of going into debt, of mortgaging the home, could be made very clear to every Latter-day Saint, young and old! Well, indeed, would it be if some of the burdens of the mortgage and its accompanying sorrows, could be felt and understood by every man who has in contemplation the pawning of his home and land for money—that he might comprehend its slavery and terror—as thoroughly prior to the deed as he is sure to feel it after. In that event, he might be warned in time to avoid the fatal step, and awake as from a horrid dream to rejoice in his deliverance. With few exceptions mortgages on private property end in disaster to the giver. * * * What should we think of men who would jeopardize the position and place of the people of Zion! The land of Zion is an inheritance, and every man who mortgages his part of that inheritance places in jeopardy the land, thus not only disinheriting himself, but committing a crime against the whole community and the intelligence and wisdom that should characterize every true Latter-day Saint. The result of such action is appalling, and its contemplation something fearful to every lover of the people of God, the more so when one possesses a knowledge of how widespread is the evil.

Mortgaging, then, looked upon in its true light, is not only a private burden and detriment, in which a man's family is thrown out of house and home, and his own abilities, happiness and talents are destroyed or sadly diminished, but it is positively a public crime in a community like ours. Disposing of inheritances in Zion partakes of the nature of such action as individuals pulling up and selling for money the gold bricks from the streets of the Celestial City. It is intolerable, when looked upon in the right light! The old proverb: "Who goes a borrowing goes a sorrowing," and "Lying rides on debt's back," should appeal directly to every man who contemplates mortgaging. But if personal appeal is not strong enough, let him remember that his home or farm is likely to go for half of its value to satisfy his debt, and that his family who depend upon him will be left without adequate shelter and support. But if neither reason is strong enough to hold him back, let him remember Zion and his inheritance therein, and let her cause cry aloud to him to bring him to a realizing sense of the triple crime that he is about to commit, in order that his hand may be stayed, and he saved the humiliation, worry, anxiety and sorrow that must inevitably overtake him, unless he repent.—*Improvement Era*, Dec., 1901, Vol. 5, p. 147.

OUR FIRST DUTY TO OUR HOUSEHOLD. I want to tell you that we will be honest with you; we feel that it is the first duty of Latter-day Saints to take care of themselves and of their poor; and then, if we can extend it to others, and as wide and as far as we can extend charity and assistance to others that are not members of the Church, we feel that it is our duty to do it. But first look after the members of our own household. The man who will not provide for his own house, as one of old has said, is worse than an infidel.—*Apr. C. R.*, 1915, p. 10.

UNCHASTITY, A DOMINANT EVIL. The character of a community or a nation is the sum of the individual qualities of its component members. To say so is to voice at once an ordinary platitude and an axiom of profound import. The stability of a material structure depends upon the integrity of its several parts and the maintenance of a proper correlation of the units in harmony with the laws of forces. The same may be said of institutions, systems, and organizations in general.

Not alone is it fundamentally proper and in strict accord with both the spirit and the letter of the Divine Word, but absolutely essential to the stability of the social order that the marriage relation shall be defined and regulated by secular law. Parties to the marriage contract must be definitely invested with the responsibilities of the status they assume; and for fidelity to their obligations they are answerable to each other, to society, and to their God.

Sexual union is lawful in wedlock, and if participated in with right intent is honorable and sanctifying. But without the bonds of marriage, sexual indulgence is a debasing sin, abominable in the sight of Deity.

Infidelity to marriage vows is a fruitful source of divorce, with its long train of attendant evils, not the least of which are the shame and dishonor inflicted on unfortunate though innocent children. The dreadful effects of adultery cannot be confined to the erring participants. Whether openly known or partly concealed under the cloak of guilty secrecy, the results are potent in evil influence. The immortal spirits that come to earth to tabernacle in bodies of flesh have the right to be well born, through parents who are free from the contamination of sexual vice.

It is a deplorable fact that society persists in holding women to stricter account than men in the matter of sexual offense. What shadow of excuse, not to speak of justification, can be found for this outrageous and cowardly discrimination? Can moral defilement be any the less filthy and pestilential in man than in woman? Is a male leper less to be shunned for fear of contagion than a woman similarly stricken?

So far as woman sins it is inevitable that she shall suffer, for retribution is sure, whether it be immediate or deferred. But in so far as man's injustice inflicts upon her the consequence of his offenses, he stands convicted of multiple guilt. And man is largely responsible for the sins against decency and virtue, the burden of which is too often fastened upon the weaker participant in the crime. The frightful prevalence of prostitution, and the tolerance and even condonation with which the foul traffic is treated by so-called civilized society, are black blots on the pages of current history. * * *

Like many bodily diseases, sexual crime drags with itself a train of other ills. As the physical effects of drunkenness entail the deterioration of tissue, and disturbance of vital functions, and so render the body receptive to any distemper to which it may be exposed, and at the same time lower the powers of resistance even to fatal deficiency, so does unchastity expose the soul to divers spiritual maladies, and rob it of both resistance and recuperative ability. The adulterous generation of Christ's day were deaf to the voice of truth, and through their diseased state of mind and heart, sought after signs and preferred empty fable to the message of salvation.

We accept without reservation or qualification the affirmation of Deity, through an ancient Nephite prophet: "For I, the Lord God, delight in the chastity of women. And whoredoms are an abomination before me; thus saith the Lord of Hosts." (Jacob 2:28.)

We hold that sexual sin is second only to the shedding of innocent blood in the category of personal crimes; and that the adulterer shall have no part in the exaltation of the blessed.

We proclaim as the word of the Lord:

"Thou shalt not commit adultery."

"He that looketh on a woman to lust after her, or if any shall commit adultery in their hearts, they shall not have the Spirit, but shall deny the faith."—*Improvement Era*, June, 1918, Vol. 20, p. 738; Doc. and Cov. 63:16.

DEGREES OF SEXUAL SIN. There are said to be more shades of green than of any other color, so also we are of the opinion there are more grades or degrees of sin associated with the improper relationship of the sexes than of any other wrongdoing of which we have knowledge. They all involve a grave offense—the sin against chastity, but in numerous instances this sin is intensified by the breaking of sacred covenants, to which is sometimes added deceit, intimidation or actual violence.

Much as all these sins are to be denounced and deplored, we can ourselves see a difference both in intent and consequence between the offense of a young couple who, being betrothed, in an unguarded moment, without premeditation fall into sin, and that of the man, who having entered into holy places and made sacred covenants, plots to rob the wife of his neighbor of her virtue either by cunning or force and accomplish his vile intent.

Not only is there a difference in these wrongs, judging from the standpoint of intent, but also from that of the consequences. In the first instance the young couple who have transgressed can make partial amends by sincere repentance and by marrying. One reparation, however, they cannot make. They cannot restore the respect that they previously held for each other; and too often as a consequence of this loss of confidence their married life is clouded or embittered by the fear that each has for the other, having once sinned, may do so again. In the other case, others are most disastrously involved, families are broken up, misery is forced upon innocent parties, society is affected, doubt is thrown upon the paternity of children, and from the standpoint of gospel ordinances, the question of descent is clouded and pedigrees become worthless; altogether, wrongs are committed both to the living and the dead, as well as to the yet unborn, which it is out of the power of the offenders to repair or make right.

Sometimes an argument is advanced to limit the provisions of the law of God, as given in the book of Doctrine and Covenants, both with regard to punishment and to forgiveness to those who have entered the House of the Lord and received their endowments. This is not possible, as so many of these provisions were given in revelations published several years before the Saints were permitted to receive these holy ordinances, indeed, before any temple was built. The law as given, we believe to be general, applying to all the Saints. But undoubtedly when, in addition to the actual offense against the laws of chastity, covenants are broken, then the punishment for the double offense will, either in this life or that which is to come, be correspondingly greater and more severe.—*Juvenile Instructor*, Nov. 15, 1902, Vol. 37, p. 688.

PURITY. There is something in man, an essential part of his mind, which recalls the events of the past, and the words that we have spoken on various occasions. Words which we spoke in our childhood we can readily bring to mind. Words that we heard others speak in our infancy, we can recall, though we may be advanced in years. We recall words that were spoken in our youth and in our early manhood, as well as words that were spoken yesterday. May I say to you that in reality a man cannot forget anything? He may have a lapse of memory; he may not be able to recall at the moment a thing that he knows, or words that he has spoken; he may not have the power at his will to call up these events and words; but let God Almighty touch the mainspring of the memory, and awaken recollection, and you will find then that you have not even forgotten a single idle word that you have spoken. I believe the word of God to be true, and therefore, I warn the youth of Zion, as well as those who are advanced in years, to beware of saying wicked things, of speaking evil, and taking in vain the name of sacred things and sacred beings. Guard your words, that you may not offend even man, much less offend God.

We believe that God lives, and that he is a judge of the quick and the dead. We believe that his eye is upon the world, and that he beholds his groveling, erring and weak children upon this earth. We believe that we are here by his design, and not by choice; that we are here to fulfil a destiny, and not to fulfil a whim, or for the gratification of mortal lusts. We believe that we are immortal beings. We believe in the resurrection of the dead, and that as Jesus came forth from the grave to everlasting life, his Spirit and body uniting again never more to be separated, so has he opened the way for every son and daughter of Adam, whether living or dead, to come forth from the grave to a newness of life, to become immortal souls, body and spirit, united, never to be severed any more. We raise our voices against prostitution, and against all forms of immorality. We are not here to practice immorality of any kind. Above all things, sexual immorality is most heinous in the sight of God. It is on a par with murder itself, and God Almighty fixed the penalty of the murderer at death: "Whoso sheddeth man's blood, by man shall his blood be shed." Furthermore, he said that whosoever committed adultery should be put to death. Therefore, we raise our voices against sexual immorality, and against all manner of obscenity.

Then, we say to you who have repented of your sins, who have been buried with Christ in baptism, who have been raised from the liquid grave to newness of life, born of the water and of the Spirit, and who have been made the children of the Father, heirs of God and joint heirs with Jesus Christ—we say to you, if you will observe the laws of God, and cease to do evil, cease to be obscene, cease to be immoral, sexually or otherwise, cease to be profane, cease to be infidel, and have faith in God, believe in the truth and receive it, and be honest before God and man, that you will be set up on high, and God will put you at the head, just as sure as you observe these commandments. Whoso will keep the commandments of God, no matter whether it be you or any other people, they will rise and not fall, they will lead and not follow, they will go upward and not downward. God will exalt them and magnify them before the nations of the earth, and he will set the seal of his approval upon them, will name them as his own. This is my testimony to you.— *Improvement Era*, Vol. 6, p. 501, May, 1903.

Three Threatening Dangers. There are at least three dangers

that threaten the Church within, and the authorities need to awaken to the fact that the people should be warned unceasingly against them. As I see these, they are flattery of prominent men in the world, false educational ideas, and sexual impurity.

But the third subject mentioned—personal purity, is perhaps of greater importance than either of the other two. We believe in one standard of morality for men and women. If purity of life is neglected, all other dangers set in upon us like the rivers of waters when the flood gates are opened.—*Improvement Era*, Vol. 17, No. 5, p. 476. March, 1914.

THE GOSPEL THE GREATEST THING. One of the most important duties devolving upon the Latter-day Saints is the proper training and rearing of their children in the faith of the gospel. The gospel is the greatest thing in all the world. There is nothing to compare with it. The possessions of this earth are of no consequence when compared with the blessings of the gospel. Naked we came into the world, and naked we will go out of the world, so far as earthly things are concerned; for we must leave them behind; but the eternal possessions which are ours through obedience to the gospel of Jesus Christ do not perish—the ties that God has created between me and those whom he has given to me, and the divine authority which I enjoy through the holy Priesthood, these are mine throughout all eternity. No power but sin, the transgression of the laws of God, can take them from me. All these things are mine, even after I leave this probation.—*Improvement Era*, Vol. 21, pp. 102, 103, December, 1917.

DUTY OF HUSBAND TO WIFE. If there is any man who ought to merit the curse of Almighty God it is the man who neglects the mother of his child, the wife of his bosom, the one who has made sacrifice of her very life, over and over again for him and his children. That is, of course, assuming that the wife is a pure and faithful mother and wife.—*Improvement Era*, Vol. 21, p. 105, December, 1917.

WIVES AND HUSBANDS IN ETERNITY. We expect to have our wives and husbands in eternity. We expect our children will acknowledge us as their fathers and mothers in eternity. I expect this: I look for nothing else. Without it I could not be happy. The thought or belief that I should be denied this privilege hereafter would make me miserable from this moment. I never could be happy again without the hope that I shall enjoy the society of my wives and children in eternity. If I had not this hope, I should be of all men most unhappy; "for if in this life only we have hope in Christ, we are of all men most miserable." All who have tasted of the influence of the Spirit of God, and have had awakened within them a hope of eternal life, cannot be happy unless they continue to drink of that fountain until they are satisfied, and it is the only fountain at which they can drink and be satisfied.—*Deseret Weekly News,* Vol. 33, p. 131, 1884.

IMPORTANCE OF FILIAL AFFECTION. Do not add to their burdens by neglect, by extravagance or by misconduct. Rather suffer that your right hand be cut off, or your eye plucked out than that you would bring sorrow or anguish to your parents because of your neglect of filial affection to them. So children, remember your parents. After they have nurtured you through the tender years of your infancy and childhood, after they have fed and clothed and educated you, after having given you a bed to rest upon and done all in their power for your good, don't you neglect them when they become feeble and are bowed down with the weight of their years. Don't you leave them, but settle down near them, and do all in your power to minister to their comfort and well-being.—*Improvement Era,* Vol. 21, p. 105, December, 1917.

FAMILY GOVERNMENT BY LOVE. I learned in my childhood, as most children, probably, have learned, more or less at least, that no love in all the world can equal the love of a true mother.

I did not think in those days, and still I am at a loss to know, how it would be possible for anyone to love her children more truly than did my mother. I have felt sometimes, how could even the Father love his children more than my mother loved her children? It was life to me; it was strength; it was encouragement; it was love that begat love or liking in myself. I knew she loved me with all her heart. She loved her children with all her soul. She would toil and labor and sacrifice herself day and night, for the temporal comforts and blessings that she could meagerly give, through the results of her own labors, to her children. There was no sacrifice of self—of her own time, of her leisure or pleasure, or opportunities for rest—that was considered for a moment, when it was compared with her duty and her love to her children.

When I was fifteen years of age, and called to go to a foreign country to preach the gospel—or to learn how, and to learn it for myself—the strongest anchor that was fixed in my life, and that helped to hold my ambition and my desire steady, to bring me upon a level and keep me straight, was that love which I knew she had for me who bore me into the world.

Only a little boy, not matured at all in judgment, without the advantage of education, thrown in the midst of the greatest allurements and temptations that it was possible for any boy or any man to be subjected to—and yet, whenever these temptations became most alluring and most tempting to me, the first thought that arose in my soul was this: Remember the love of your mother. Remember how she strove for your welfare. Remember how willing she was to sacrifice her life for your good. Remember what she taught you in your childhood and how she insisted upon your reading the New Testament—the only book, except a few little school books, that we had in the family, or that was within reach of us at that time. This feeling toward my mother became a defense, a barrier between me and temptation, so that I could turn aside from temptation and sin by the help of the Lord and the love begotten in my soul, toward her whom I knew loved me more than anybody else in all the world, and more than any other living being could love me.

A wife may love her husband, but it is different to that of the love of mother to her child. The true mother, the mother who has the fear of God and the love of truth in her soul, would never hide from danger or evil and leave her child exposed to it. But as natural as it is for the sparks to fly upward, as natural as it is to breathe the breath of life, if there were danger coming to her child, she would step between the child and that danger; she would defend her child to the uttermost. Her life would be nothing in the balance, in comparison with the life of her child. That is the love of true motherhood for children.

Her love for her husband would be different, for if danger should come to him, as natural as it would be for her to step between her child and danger, instead, her disposition would be to step behind her husband for protection, and that is the difference between the love of mother for children and the love of wife for husband—there is a great difference between the two.

I have learned to place a high estimate upon the love of mother. I have often said, and will repeat it, that the love of a true mother comes nearer being like the love of God than any other kind of love. The father may love his children, too; and next to the love that the mother feels for her child, unquestionably and rightfully, too, comes the love that the father feels for his child. But, as it has been illustrated here by Brother Edward H. Anderson, the love of the, father is of a different character, or degree, to the love of the mother for her child; illustrated by the fact he related here of having the privilege of working with his boy, having him in his presence, becoming more intimate with him, learning his characteristics more clearly; becoming more familiar and more closely related to him; the result of which was that his love for his boy increased, and the love of the boy increased for his father, for the same reason, merely because of that closer association. So the child learns to love his mother best, as a rule, when the mother is good, wise, prudent, and intelligent, because the child is with her more, they are more familiar with each other and understand each other better.

Now, this is the thought that I desire to express: Fathers, if you wish your children to be taught in the principles of the gospel, if you wish them to love the truth and understand it, if you wish them to be obedient to and united with you, love them! and prove to them that you do love them by your every word or act to them. For your own sake, for the love that should exist between you and your boys— however wayward they might be, or one or the other might be, when you speak or talk to them, do it not in anger, do it not harshly, in a condemning spirit. Speak to them kindly; get them down and weep with them if necessary and get them to shed tears with you if possible. Soften their hearts; get them to feel tenderly toward you. Use no lash and no violence, but argue, or rather reason—approach them with reason, with persuasion and love unfeigned. With these means, if you cannot gain your boys and your girls, they will prove to be reprobate to you; and there will be no means left in the world by which you can win them to yourselves. But, get them to feel as you feel, have interest in the things in which you take interest, to love the gospel as you love it, to love one another as you love them; to love their parents as the parents love the children. You can't do it any other way. You can't do it by unkindness; you cannot do it by driving; our children are like we are; we couldn't be driven; we can't be driven now. We are like some other animals that we know of in the world. You can coax them; you can lead them, by holding out inducements to them, and by speaking kindly to them, but you can't drive them; they won't be driven. We won't be driven. Men are not in the habit of being driven; they are not made that way.

This is not the way that God intended, in the beginning, to deal with his children—by force. It is all free love, free grace. The poet expressed it in these words:

"Know this, that every soul is free,
To choose his life and what he'll be;
For this eternal truth is given,
That God will force no man to heaven."

You can't force your boys, nor your girls into heaven. You may force them to hell, by using harsh means in the efforts to make them good, when you yourselves are not as good as you should be. The man that will be angry at his boy, and try to correct him while he is in anger, is in the greatest fault; he is more to be pitied and more to be condemned than the child who has done wrong. You can only correct your children by love, in kindness, by love unfeigned, by persuasion, and reason.

When I was a child, somewhat a wayward, disobedient little boy—not that I was wilfully disobedient, but I would forget what I ought to do; I would go off with playful boys and be absent when I should have been at home, and I would forget to do things I was asked to do. Then I would go home, feel guilty, know that I was guilty, that I had neglected my duty and that I deserved punishment.

On one occasion I had done something that was not just right, and my mother said to me: "Now, Joseph, if you do that again I shall have to whip you." Well, time went on, and by and by, I forgot it, and I did something similar again; and this is the one thing that I admired more, perhaps, than any secondary thing in her; it was that when she made a promise she kept it. She never made a promise, that I know of, that she did not keep.

Well, I was called to account. She said: "Now, I told you. You knew that if you did this I would have to whip you, for I said I would. I must do it. I do not want to do it. It hurts me worse than it does you, but I must whip you."

Well, she had a little rawhide, already there, and while she was talking or reasoning with me, showing me how much I deserved it and how painful it was to her, to inflict the punishment I deserved, I had only one thought and that was: "For goodness' sake whip me; do not reason with me," for I felt the lash of her just criticism and admonition a thousand fold worse than I did the switch. I felt as if, when she laid the lash on me, I had at least partly paid my debt and had answered for my wrong doing. Her reasoning cut me down into the quick; it made me feel sorry to the very core!

I could have endured a hundred lashes with the rawhide better than I could endure a ten-minutes' talk in which I felt and was made to feel that the punishment inflicted upon me was painful to her that I loved—punishment upon my own mother!—Extracts from an address given at a "Home Evening" meeting in Granite Stake, 1909. *Improvement Era,* Vol. 13, pp. 276-280.

THE HOME AND THE CHILD. But what are we doing in our homes to train our children; what to enlighten them? What to encourage them to make home their place of amusement, and a place where they may invite their friends for study or entertainment? Have we good books, games, music, and well-lighted, well-ventilated, warm rooms for their convenience and pleasure? Do we take personal interest in them and in their affairs? Are we providing them with the physical knowledge, the mental food, the healthful exercise, and the spiritual purification, that will enable them to become pure and robust in body, intelligent and honorable citizens, faithful and loyal Latter-day Saints?

We frequently neglect giving them any information concerning their bodily well-being. In our cities we appear to be providing our young people too much mental exercise, and no physical diversion and work, while in our country settlements, we seem to be overburdening them with bodily labor, and in many cases doing little or nothing for their mental development and recreation. Hence, in the one case they seek forbidden places and pleasure, on account of too much mental exercise; and in another, because of too little.

Now then, are we studying their wants as we do our business, and our farms and our animals? Are we looking after them, and if necessary bringing them in from the street when absent, and providing them in our homes with what they lack? Or are we to a great extent neglecting these things in the home and home training, and considering our children of secondary value to horses and cattle and lands?

These are important points for consideration, and fathers and mothers should honestly study them, and as honestly answer them to their own satisfaction. We may well invest means in the home for the comfort, convenience, entertainment and training of our children. We may well give our sons and daughters some time for recreation and diversion, and some provision in the home for satisfying their longing for legitimate physical and mental recreation, to which every child is entitled, and which he will seek in the street or in objectionable places, if it is not provided in the home. In addition to this, and supplementary to the training in the home, it is to be hoped that our organizations will as soon as possible provide every arrangement for legitimate entertainment and recreation, physical and intellectual, that will tend to attract our young people, and hold them interested, loyal and contented within the pale of our own influence and organizations. —*Improvement Era*, Vol. 11, pp. 302-303, 1907-1908.

CHAPTER XVII

AMUSEMENTS AND FASHIONS

YOUTH SHOULD LOOK FORWARD. Our youth should not be left to spend their time almost entirely in the mad whirl of pleasure and amusement, without a thought of advancing years with the attendant bodily ailments and physical infirmities which are bound to come. They should be given to understand that what are generally considered as the pleasures of youth are on the wing, and will soon pass, leaving in their rear only sad remembrances of wasted opportunities that cannot be recalled. They should not be permitted to waste their time and their parents' substance in frivolous pastime and riotous living, which can only result in vicious or evil habits being formed. —*Juvenile Instructor*, Vol. 52, January, 1917, p. 19.

PROPER AMUSEMENTS. Our amusements should be characterized by their wholesome social environments. We should have proper regard to the character of those with whom we associate in places of amusement; and we should be governed by a high sense of responsibility to our parents, to our friends and to the Church. We should know that the pleasures which we enjoy are such as have upon them the stamp of divine approval. They should be endorsed by our parents and by our religious associates, and by those true principles which should always regulate our intercourse with one another in Church membership. Amusements which, in themselves, and in commendable social surroundings, may be proper and wholesome, should be avoided unless associates are unquestionable and the places are reputable and are conducted under proper restraints.

There are limits in our recreations beyond which we cannot safely go. They should be guarded in character and curtailed in frequency to avoid excess. They should not occupy all, nor even the greater part of our time; indeed, they should be made incidental to the duties and obligations of life, and never be made a controlling motive or factor in our hopes and ambitions. There are so many dangers lurking in those amusements, and the fascination for them which take hold upon the lives of our young people, sometimes to the very possession of them, that they should be carefully guarded and warned against the temptations and evils that are likely to ensnare them, to their destruction.—*Juvenile Instructor*, Vol. 49, June, 1914, pp. 380, 381.

PROPER CHARACTER OF AMUSEMENTS. The character and variety of our amusements have so much to do with the welfare and character of our young people that they should be guarded with the utmost jealousy for the preservation of the morals and stamina of the youth of Zion.

In the first place they should not be excessive; and young people should be discouraged from giving themselves up to the spirit and frivolity of excessive mirth. No Latter-day Saint needs to be told that two or three dances a week for his children are out of all sense or reason. Too frequent dances are not only injurious to stability of character, but they are highly detrimental to good health; and wherever possible other amusements than the ball rooom should be introduced into the lives of our young people. They should be trained to appreciate more and more amusements of a social and intellectual character. Home parties, concerts that develop the talents of youth, and public amusements that bring together both young and old, are preferable to the excessive practice of dancing.

In the second place, our amusements should be consistent with our religious spirit of fraternity and religious devotion. In too many instances the ball room is devoid of our supplication for Divine protection. Our dancing should be, as far as possible, under the supervision of some Church organization, and we should be scrupulously careful to open the dance by prayer. * * * The question of amusements is one of such far-reaching importance to the welfare of the Saints that the presiding authorities of every ward should give it their most careful attention and consideration.

In the third place, our amusements should interfere as little as possible with the work of the school-room. It is very desirable that the early education of our young people should be carried on with as little interruption as possible, and frequent dances during the school season are detrimental both to the body and to the mind.

Lastly, it is to be feared that in many homes, parents abandon all regulation respecting the amusement of their children, and set them adrift to find their fun wherever and whenever they can. Parents should never lose control of the amusements of their children during their tender years, and should be scrupulously careful about the companionship of their young people in places of amusements.—*Juvenile Instructor*, Vol. 39, March 1, 1904, pp. 144, 145.

SOCIAL DUTIES. The city people have become accustomed to living near neighbors for years without associating together. There are instances where good people, well acquainted in business and upon the street, have lived neighbors for twenty-five or more years, and yet not invited each other to their homes, to take dinner together, nor to have a social hour or evening. They live so near each other that they can almost shake hands, from door to door, yet never call, nor associate together; they are perfectly exclusive. That is not a wise nor a good way, especially when, as Latter-day Saints, we should be looking after the welfare of mankind, by preaching the gospel in word and in deed. Would it not be much better if we arranged a little dinner, or invited our neighbor to come and join us in a little social, to become acquainted and make him feel we are not strangers to him, nor he to us? And let us remember the definition which Christ sanctioned of neighbor, as well as the requirement: He that showeth mercy unto me is my neighbor, and the commandment is: Thou shalt love thy neighbor as thyself.

I hope we shall do better. But there is really little sociability among us, and there is an exclusiveness that is not in keeping with the warmth of the gospel. We do not think enough of each other; we do not care for each other; we take little or no notice of each other; and, finally, we pass each other on the street without the slightest recognition. We scarcely bow to a brother, unless we are really intimate with him. That is not the spirit that belongs to "Mormonism." It is contrary to that friendship and sociability that ought to characterize Latter-day Saints. I believe in the broadest, most charitable, the kindest and most loving spirit that it is possible for broadminded and big-souled men to exercise or to possess; and that this spirit ought to be the spirit possessed and diffused by the Saints everywhere.

Let us, then, gather in the honest in heart, and treat them and one another with the spirit of warmth and love characteristic of the gospel. Then talk about the unfortunate, the drunken, the weak, the erring! Do not shun them, either. They ought to be saved as well as everybody else; and, if it is possible, let us save them, too, as well as the worthy, the good and the pure. Let us save the sinner, and bring him to a knowledge of the truth, if possible.

Our Mutual Improvement Associations are invited to make a specialty of this social work; the bishops should lend their aid to the officers in selecting and setting apart capable and experienced missionaries, as well as ward teachers, who should devote their energies, among the people. The indifferent youth, as well as the stranger and the friendless in our midst, should be made welcome at our gatherings, and be induced to feel at home among the people of God. And then, let it be remembered, every family, every person, has a duty in this line. Because men or women are not ward or association officers is no good reason why they should be exempt from the common social amenities of life, nor why they should not be subject to doing good temporally, spiritually and socially.—*Improvement Era*, Vol. 7, October, 1904, p. 957.

THE DANGER OF PLEASURE HUNTING. In order that a young man may make up his mind what course in life to take he must pay some thought on where he is going in the long run; what shall be the condition he would like to enjoy through life, and particularly the end towards which he would like to work. Otherwise it will be hard for him to steer his actions from day to day towards the goal of his ambition.

Calmly viewing the hundreds of sayings to be found in good books, and hearing also the experiences and warnings of many more wise men who live in our time and settlements, who are exemplary shepherds of the people in our many Church organizations, and who are constantly giving warning against excessive pleasure-seeking, the thoughtful young man must confess that pleasure is not the goal that he would seek—that the man would seek who desires to make the best out of life.

The wise man is, therefore, going to steer his course away from the living death of pleasure-seeking. He is not going into bondage or debt to buy automobiles and other costly equipages to keep pace with the rush of fashionable pleasure-seeking, in this respect. He is not going to borrow money to satisfy the popular craze for traveling in Europe or in our own country, with no purpose in view but pleasure. He is not going to grow nervous and gray in a struggle for means that his wife and daughter, for mere pleasure, may spend the summer at costly, fashionable resorts, or in distant lands. It is true that there are many in our community who do not appear to be wise, and who are doing just these and other foolish acts for so-called pleasure.

The result of this hunt for pleasure and excitement and for keeping pace with what only the very wealthy can but ought not to do, is that many are forced to undertake all kinds of illegitimate schemes to obtain money to gratify the tendency. Hence the growth of financial immorality. Many underhanded methods are adopted to obtain means, and even cheating and lying and deceiving friends and neighbors are frequently resorted to in order that money may be obtained to gratify the inordinate desire for pleasure. The story is told of one good lady who got flour at her grocer's on credit, and sold it for cash at a bargain to get money to go pleasure-seeking. Thus the morals are corrupted. This applies to rich and poor alike.

You men who are sensible fathers, is this course worth while?

Young men who have a goal in sight, is this the course to take to fit your purpose and to get the best results out of life?

Without discussing wealth and fame, shall we not call a halt in this pleasure craze, and go about the legitimate business of true Latter-day Saints, which is to desire and strive to be of some use in the world? Shall we not instead do something to increase the genuine joy and welfare and virtue of mankind as well as our own by helping to bear the burdens under which the toilers are groaning, by rendering loving, devoted and unselfish service to our fellow men?—*Improvement Era*, Vol. 12, July, 1909, p. 744.

HARMFUL EFFECTS OF BAD BOOKS. It would be difficult to estimate the harmful influences upon the thoughts, feelings, and actions of the young, brought about by the practice of reading dime novels. Books constitute a sort of companionship to everyone who reads, and they create within the heart feelings either for good or for bad. It sometimes happens that parents are very careful about the company which their children keep and are very indifferent about the books they read. In the end the reading of a bad book will bring about evil associates.

It is not only the boy who reads this strange, weird and unnatural exciting literature who is affected by its influence, but in time he influences others. This literature becomes the mother of all sorts of evil suggestions that ripen into evil practices and bring about an unnatural and debased feeling which is ever crowding out the good in the human heart and giving place to the bad. It was Shelley who said that "strange thoughts beget strange deeds," and when our children are reading books that are creating strange and unusual and undesirable thoughts in their minds we need not be surprised to learn that they have committed some unusual, some strange, or unnatural act. It is in the thoughts and feelings that we have to combat the evils and temptations of the world, and the purification of our thoughts and feelings should be made the special effort of every father and mother. Fuller once wrote, "It seems my soul is like a filthy pond where fish die soon and frogs live long." It is remarkable how easy it is to learn sin and how hard it is to forget it.

A story is told of an English officer in India, who one day went to the book shelf to take down a book. As he reached his hand up over the volume his finger was bitten by an adder. After a few hours the finger began to swell. Later on the swelling went into his arm, and finally the whole body was affected, and in a few days the officer was dead. There are adders concealed in many a cheap and trashy book, and they are always common in dime novels. Their effects upon our souls are poisonous, and in time they are sure to produce a moral and spiritual death. * * * The influence of these novels is all the more dangerous because the feelings and thoughts which they engender in the heart and mind are more or less hidden and the evil consequences of such reading frequently does not manifest itself until some overt and horrible act is the result of months and sometimes years of imagination and wonderment. Let the Saints beware of the books that enter their homes, for their influences may be as poisonous and deadly as the adder which brought death to the English officer in India.—*Juvenile Instructor*, May 1, 1902, Vol. 37, p. 275.

PROPER READING. There is altogether too much novel reading of that class of novels which teaches nothing useful, and only tends to the excitement of the emotions. Excessive novel reading we all know is detrimental to the intellectual development of those who engage in it, and the wise and those who seek advancement might well give more time to useful, educational works—books that would enlighten the reader on history, biography, religion, and other important subjects which all well-informed people are expected to understand.

Many of our young people, and some older ones, too, are not familiar with their own religion nor with the beautiful and striking doctrines of the gospel with which it is so laden. This class devote more time to reading useless or sensational books than they do to the study and contemplation of works that would familiarize them with the principles of the gospel. If they were better informed in this line, and understood the saving doctrines and every-day questions of their religion, more than they do, they would not be trapped by false teachings, false leaders, and advocates of cults that are false.

They would not be misled as some of them are.—*Improvement Era,* May, 1909, Vol. 12, p. 561.

RAFFLING AND GAMBLING. Is it proper to raffle property for the benefit of missionaries? No; raffling is a game of chance, and hence leads to gambling; for that reason, if for no other, it should not be encouraged among the young men of the Church. President Young declared raffling to be a modified name of gambling; said that "as Latter-day Saints we cannot afford to sacrifice moral principles to financial gain," and advised the sisters through the *Woman's Exponent* not to raffle. President Lorenzo Snow endorsed and approved of these sentiments; and I have often expressed my unqualified disapproval of raffling; the General Sunday School Board have declared against it; and finally the state law makes it unlawful to raffle with dice; and if it is unlawful with dice, in principle, is it not just as injurious with any other device? With all these objections, should it not be clear to anyone that raffling horses, quilts, bicycles and other property is not sanctioned by the moral law nor approved by the general Church authorities? But it continues just the same, and if you do not believe in it, you should refuse to patronize it, so helping the cause. Now, how shall we aid the missionary who wishes to sell a horse, or what not? Let everybody give a dollar, and let the donors decide by vote to what worthy man, not of their number, the horse shall be given. No chance about that—it is pure decision, and it helps the people who wish to buy chances solely for the benefit of the missionary to discourage the gambling propensities of their natures. However, here is an additional thought: The element of chance enters very largely into everything we undertake, and it should be remembered that the spirit in which we do things decides very largely whether we are gambling or are entering into legitimate business enterprises.—*Improvement Era,* Vol. 6, February, 1903, p. 308.

GAMES OF CHANCE. *To Whom It May Concern:* Among the vices of the present age gambling is very generally condemned. Gambling under its true name is forbidden by law, and is discountenanced by the self-respecting elements of society. Nevertheless, in numerous guises the demon of chance is welcomed in the home, in fashionable clubs, and at entertainments for worthy charities, even within the precincts of sacred edifices. Devises for raising money by appealing to the gambling instinct are common accessories at church socials, ward fairs, and the like.

Whatever may be the condition elsewhere, this custom is not to be sanctioned within this Church; and any organization allowing such is in opposition to the counsel and instruction of the general authorities of the Church.

Without attempting to specify or particularize the many objectionable forms given to this evil practice amongst us, we say again to the people that no kind of chance game, guessing contest, or raffling device can be approved in any entertainment under the auspices of our Church organizations.

The desire to get something of value for little or nothing is pernicious; and any proceeding that strengthens that desire is an effective aid to the gambling spirit, which has proved a veritable demon of destruction to thousands. Risking a dime in the hope of winning a dollar in any game of chance is a species of gambling.

Let it not be thought that raffling articles of value, offering prizes to the winners in guessing-contests, the use of machines of chance, or any other device of the kind is to be allowed or excused because the money so obtained is to be used for a good purpose. The Church is not to be supported in any degree by means obtained through gambling.

Let the attention of stake and ward officers, and those in charge of auxiliary organizations of the Church be directed to what has been written on this subject and to this present reminder. An article over the signature of the President of the Church was published in the *Juvenile Instructor*, October 1, 1902 (Volume 37, p. 592), in which were given citations from earlier instruction and advice to the people on this subject. For convenience, part of that article is repeated here. In reply to a question as to whether raffling and games of chance are justifiable when the purposes to be accomplished are good, this was said: "We say emphatically, No. Raffle is only a modified name of gamble."

President Young once said to Sister Eliza R. Snow: "Tell the sisters not to raffle. If the mothers raffle, the children will gamble. Raffling is gambling." Then it is added: "Some say, What shall we do? We have quilts on hand—we cannot sell them, and we need means to supply our treasury, which we can obtain by raffling for the benefit of the poor. Rather let the quilts rot on the shelves than adopt the old adage, 'The end will sanctify the means.' As Latter-day Saints, we cannot afford to sacrifice moral principle to financial gain."

—*Improvement Era*, December, 1908, Vol. 12, p. 143.

THE EVIL OF CARDS. But, you say, we must have recreation; what shall we do? Turn to domestic enterprises, and to the gaining of useful knowledge of the gospel. Let the love of reading good and useful books be implanted in the hearts of the young, let them be trained to take pleasure and recreation in history, travel, biography, conversation and classic story. Then there are innocent games, music, songs, and literary recreation. What would you think of the man who would argue for whisky and beer as a common beverage because it is necessary for people to drink? He is perhaps little worse than the man who would place cards in the hands of my children— whereby they would foster the spirit of chance and gambling leading down to destruction—because they must have recreation. I would call the first a vicious enemy, and refer him to water to drink; and the latter an evil spirit in the guise of innocence, and refer him to recreation containing no germs of spiritual disease leading to the devil!

Let our evenings be devoted to innocent amusements in the home, and let all chance games be banished from our families, and only recreation indulged in that is free from gambling and the gambling spirit. And let excessive card-playing, and the person who strolls about among neighbors at all hours of the night and day encouraging this evil, be put far from us. Just as sure as we encourage this evil it will bring other grievous troubles in its wake, and those who indulge excessively will lose the spirit of the gospel, and go to temporal and spiritual ruin.

Young people in their recreations should strive to form a love for that which will not be injurious. It is not true that only that recreation can be enjoyed that is detrimental to the body and spirit. We should train ourselves to find pleasure in that which invigorates, not stupefies and destroys the body; that which leads upward and not down; that which brightens, not dulls and stunts the intellect; that which elevates and exalts the spirit, not that clogs and depresses it. So shall we please the Lord, enhance our own enjoyment, and save ourselves and our children from impending sins, at the root of which, like the evil genius, lurks the spirit of cards and gaming. —*Improvement Era*, Vol. 14, June, 1911, pp. 735-8.

WASTING TIME WITH CARDS. It is no uncommon thing for women, young and middle-aged, to spend whole afternoons, and many of them, evenings as well, in playing cards, thus wasting hours and days of precious time in this useless and unprofitable way. Yet those same people, when approached, declare they have no time to spend as teachers in the Sabbath schools, and no time to attend either Sunday schools or meetings. Their church duties are neglected for lack of time, yet they spend hours, day after day, at cards. They have thereby encouraged and become possessed of a spirit of indolence, and their minds are filled with the vile drunkenness, hallucination, charm and fascination, that take possession of the habitual card-player to the exclusion of all spiritual and religious feeling. Such a spirit detracts from all sacred thought and sentiment. These players at length do not quite know whether they are Jews, Gentiles, or Saints, and they do not care a fig.

While a simple game of cards in itself may be harmless, it is a fact that by immoderate repetition it ends in an infatuation for chance schemes, in habits of excess, in waste of precious time, in dulling and stupor of the mind, and in the complete destruction of religious feeling. These are serious results, evils that should and must be avoided by the Latter-day Saints. Then again, there is the grave danger that lurks in persistent card playing, which begets the spirit of gambling, of speculation and that awakens the dangerous desire to get something for nothing.—*Improvement Era*, Vol. 6, August, 1903, p. 779.

CARD PLAYING. One's character may be determined in some measure by the quality of one's amusements. Men and women of industrious, business-like, and thoughtful habits care little for frivolous pastimes, for pleasures that are sought for their own sake. It is not easy to imagine that leading men in the Church would find any pleasure that was either inspiring or helpful at the card table; indeed the announcement that a president of a stake, bishop of a ward, or other leading official of the Church was fond of card playing would be a shock to every sense of propriety even among young people who are not seriously inclined to the duties and responsibilities of life. Such a practice would be looked upon as incompatible with the duties and responsibilities of a religious life. Even business men, as a rule, are distrustful of business associates whose inclinations engage them in frequent card playing.

But it may be said that the same objections do not hold good in respect to young people who do not take life so seriously; but the evil is that young people who indulge in the frivolous and vicious pastime of card playing are never likely to take life seriously unless they forsake such questionable pleasures early in life. It is the serious and thoughtful man and woman who are most likely to assume the higher and nobler responsibilities of life, and their tastes and pleasures are never satisfied by means of a deck of cards.

Card playing is an excessive pleasure; it is intoxicating and, there-fore, in the nature of a vice. It is generally the companion of the cigarette and the wine glass, and the latter lead to the poolroom and gambling hall. Few men and women indulge in the dangerous pastime of the card table without compromising their business affairs and the higher responsibilities of life. Tell me what amusements you like best and whether your amusements have become a ruling passion in your life, and I will tell you what you are. Few indulge frequently in card playing in whose lives it does not become a ruling passion.

Cards are the most perfect and common instrumentalities of the gambler that have been devised, and the companionship of cards, unlike the companionship of most other games, is that of the gam-bling den and the saloon. But cards do not stand alone in their enticement to evil. Any game that ultimately leads to questionable society, because it is the chief pleasure of such society, should be excluded from the home. There are innocent games enough to satisfy the required pleasures of the home without encouraging card playing. —Juvenile Instructor, Vol. 38, September 1, 1903, p. 529.

Stop Card Playing. I am told that the prevalence of card parties in the homes of the Latter-day Saints is much greater than is supposed by those whom society people never think of inviting to make the card table the source of an evening's pastime. The presiding authorities are not invited to the card parties, and, as a rule, are not permitted to witness them, simply because those who give such parties feel that a deck of cards in the hands of a faithful servant of God is a satire upon religion.

I have heard that some who are called to officiate in holy or-dinances have, when absent from the House of the Lord, or when tardy in arriving, excused themselves because of the time occupied in giving or attending a card party. Those who thus indulge are not fit to administer in sacred ordinances. They are no more worthy than others who violate good morals in any respect. They should be excused.

I am told that young people offer as an excuse for such question-able pastime the accusation that cards are played in the homes of certain leading men in the Church. Bishops, however, ought never to be deterred in their efforts to suppress the evil by counter complaints of this kind. The bishop has the same right to inquire, through the means of his teachers, into the pleasures of the homes of the highest authorities of the Church as he has into those of its most humble members. If it be true that card playing is prevalent in the Church, the bishops are charged with the responsibility for the evil and it is their duty to see that it is abolished, or that men and women who encourage it be brought to account before their brethren and sisters for the pernicious example they are setting before the youth of Zion. Certainly no bishop can report his ward in good condition where such a practice prevails.

Presidents of stakes are not without their responsibility in this matter, and at the general priesthood meetings of the stakes they should make searching inquiry of the bishops concerning card parties in the homes of the Saints. It is an easy matter for every bishop to know through the medium of the ward teachers, whether there are any practices in the homes of the people inconsistent with the mission of "Mormonism," and card playing is certainly inconsistent with that mission. No man who is addicted to card playing should be called to act as a ward teacher, such men cannot be consistent advocates of that which they do not themselves practice.

The card table has been the scene of too many quarrels, the birthplace of too many hatreds, the occasion of too many murders to admit one word of justification for the lying, cheating spirit which it too often engenders in the hearts of its devotees.

My frequent and emphatic expressions on this subject are the result of the alarm I have felt over the well founded reports that have come to me concerning the prevalence of card playing in the homes of some who profess to be Latter-day Saints. Upon every officer in the Church reponsible in any way for the dangers of the card table is placed, and placed heavily, the duty of doing all that he or she possibly can in prayerful and earnest manner to eradicate the evil. Let us be fully conscious of the old adage which says that "The devil likes to souse whatever is wet," and stop card playing in the home before it reaches the gambler's table.—*Juvenile Instructor,* Vol. 38, Sept. 15, 1903, p. 561.

PERNICIOUS NATURE OF CARD PLAYING. Card playing is a game of chance, and because it is a game of chance it has its tricks. It encourages tricks; its devotees measure their success at the table by their ability through devious and dark ways to win. It creates a spirit of cunning and devises hidden and secret means, and cheating at cards is almost synonymous with playing at cards.

Again, cards have a bad reputation and they are the known companions of bad men. If no other reason existed for shunning the card table, its reputation alone should serve as a warning. It may be conceded that superb skill is often acquired in this game of chance, but this skill itself endangers the moral qualities of the possessor and leads him on to questionable practices.

Such games as checkers and chess are games more of fixed rules, whose application are open and freer from cunning devices. Such games do not intoxicate like cards and other games of chance.—*Juvenile Instructor*, Vol. 38, October 1, 1903, p. 591.

CARDS IN THE HOME. But if cards are played in the home and under the eye of an anxious and loving parent, what harm can come from it all? is asked. Most vices in the beginning take on attractive and innocent appearing garbs, and a careful examination of the career of many an unfortunate man will reveal the first step of his misfortune in some "innocent pastime" whose vice rarely manifests itself in its infancy. There are different spirits in the world and the gambling spirit is one of them, and cards have been from time immemorial the most common and universal means of gratifying that spirit. An "innocent game of cards" is the innocent companion of an innocent glass of wine and the playmate of tricksters.

Again, all amusements become pernicious when pursued excessively. No game in the world has been played a thousandth part of the time, aye all the games in the world have not consumed a thousandth part of the time, that cards have taken. The game itself leads to excessiveness; it is the enemy of industry; it is the foe of economy and the boon companion of the Sabbath-breaker. The best possible excuse that any one can render for playing cards is that there is a possible escape from the dangers to which it leads; and the best explanation that people can give for such a vice is the adventurous spirit of man that delights in that which is hazardous to his physical and moral safety.—*Juvenile Instructor*, Vol. 38, Oct. 1, 1903, p. 593.

EVIL FASHIONS. In my sight the present-day fashions are abominable, suggestive of evil, calculated to arouse base passion and lust, and to engender lasciviousness, in the hearts of those who follow the fashions, and of those who tolerate them. Why? Because women are imitating the very customs of a class of women who have resorted to that means to aid them to sell their souls. It is infamous, and I hope the daughters of Zion will not descend to these pernicious ways, customs and fashions, for they are demoralizing and damnable in their effect.—Oct. C. R., 1913, p. 8.

I do not want to be burdensome to this vast congregation by talking too long, but I have another thought that weighs upon my mind, and this is not in relation to men, but is with respect to the women, and more particularly with regard to the manner in which they dress. Never, perhaps, at least within the period of my life—and I have lived in the world nearly seventy-five years—never, I say, within the period of my life and experience have I seen such obscene, uncleanly, impure, and suggestive fashions of women's dress as I see today. Some of them are abominable. I lift my voice against these audacious practices and these infamous fashions, and I pray that you who have daughters in Zion will save them, if you can, from following these obscene fashions, that if followed, will destroy the last vestige of true womanly modesty, and reduce them to the level of the courtesans of the streets of Paris, from whence these debasing fashions come.—October Conference, 1913. *Life of Joseph F. Smith*, p. 405.

IMPROPER FASHIONS. Please set the example before your sisters that God would have them follow. When we teach people to observe the laws of God and to honor the gifts that are bestowed upon them in the covenants of the gospel of Jesus Christ, we don't want you teachers to go out and set an example before your sisters that will destroy their faith in our teachings. I hope you will take that to heart, for it has a meaning to it. I am talking to the teachers among the sisters. We hear it reported, from time to time, that some of the teachers that are sent out among our sisters not only do not set the example that they ought to set, but they set the example they should not set for our sisters; they teach them by example to break the word of wisdom, rather than to keep it. They teach them to mutilate their garments, rather than to keep them holy and undefiled, by setting the example before them, and we can tell you the names if you want to know. I am not scolding; I don't want it to be understood that I am finding fault. I am only telling a solemn truth, and I am sorry that I have it to say, but I want it to be distinctly understood. We see some of our good sisters coming here to the temple occasionally decorated in the latest and most ridiculous fashions that ever disgraced the human form divine. They do not seem to realize that they are coming to the house of God, and we have to forbid them entrance, or find fault with them, and they go away grieved and say sometimes, "We don't want to go there any more." Why? Because they come unprepared, like the man who was found at the feast without the wedding garment, who also had to be turned out. (Matt. 22:1-14) We have to turn them out occasionally, because they will not hearken to the counsel that has been given to them.—Oct. C. R., 1914, p. 130.

EXCLUSIVE CLUBS AMONG CHURCH MEMBERS. There is no need of exclusive clubs among the Latter-day Saints. The many auxiliary organizations should be made to supply every legitimate public, and social amusement of the young people, and, in addition to the regular Church and quorum meetings, should meet every religious and ethical educational need of our community.—Improvement Era, Vol. 12, February, 1909, p. 313.

A LESSON FOR THE BOYS. Self-respect requires, among other things, that one shall behave like a true gentleman, in a house of worship. No self-respecting person will go to a house devoted to the service of God to whisper, gossip and visit; rather, it is one's duty to put on self-restraint, to give one's undivided attention to the speaker, and concentrate the mind upon his words that his thoughts may be grasped to one's benefit and profit.

Among the strong helps to gain self-respect are personal purity and proper thoughts which are the bases of all proper action. I wish that all young men could appreciate the value there is in this practice, and in giving their youthful days to the service of the Lord. Growth, development, progress, self-respect, the esteem and admiration of men naturally follow such a course in youth. The Savior set a striking example in this matter, and was early about his Father's business. He did not leave it until his older years, but even as early as twelve he had developed so far in this line that he was able to teach men of wisdom and doctors of knowledge in the temple. Samuel, the prophet, had so prepared himself by a pure, self-respecting childhood that he was perfectly attuned to the whisperings of God. The shepherd youth David was chosen above his older brethren to serve in high places in the Master's cause. Other great characters in history were also selected early in life; and the best men in all ages gave their young manhood to the service of God who honored them abundantly with commendation and approval. In more modern times the Lord chose Joseph Smith in early youth to be the founder of the new and glorious dispensation of the gospel. Brigham Young was but a youth when he determined to devote his life to the Church; John Taylor,

Wilford Woodruff, and in fact all the early founders of the Church devoted their youth and manhood to the cause of Zion. You may look around today, and who are the leaders among the people but those who early and zealously devoted themselves to the faith? And you may foretell who are to be the leaders by observing the boys who show self-respect and purity and who are earnest in all good works. The Lord will not choose men from any other class of his people and exalt them into prominence. The opposite course, waiting to serve the Lord until the wild oats of youth are sown, is reprehensible. There is always something lacking in the man who spends his youth in wickedness and sin, and then turns to righteousness in later years. Of course, the Lord honors his repentance, and it is better far that a man should late turn from evil than to continue in sin all his days, but the fact is clear that the best part of his life and strength is wasted, and there remains only poor, broken service to offer the Lord. There are regrets and heartburnings in repenting late in life from the follies and sins of youth, but there are consolation and rich reward in serving the Lord in the vigorous days of early manhood.

Self-respect, deference for sacred things, and personal purity are the beginnings and the essence of wisdom. The doctrines of the gospel, the Church restraint, are like school-masters to keep us in the line of duty. If it were not for these schoolmasters, we would perish and be overcome by the evil about us. We see men who have freed themselves from Church restraint and from the precious doctrines of the gospel, who perish about us every day! They boast of freedom, but are the slaves of sin.

Let me admonish you to permit the gospel schoolmaster to teach you self-respect and to keep you pure and free from secret sins that bring not only physical punishment, but sure spiritual death. You cannot hide the penalty which God has affixed to them—a penalty often worse than death. It is the loss of self-respect, it is physical debility, it is insanity, indifference to all powers that are good and noble—all these follow in the wake of the sinner in secret, and of the unchaste. Unchastity, furthermore, not only fixes its penalty on the one who transgresses, but reaches out unerring punishment to the third and fourth generation, making not only the transgressor a wreck, but mayhap involving scores of people in his direct line of relationship, disrupting family ties, breaking the hearts of parents, and causing a black stream of sorrow to overwhelm their lives.

Such a seeming simple thing, then, as proper conduct in a house of worship leads to good results in many respects. Good conduct leads to self-respect, which creates purity of thought and action. Pure thought and noble action lead to a desire to serve God in the strength of manhood and to become subservient to the schoolmasters, Church restraint, and the doctrines of the gospel of Christ.—*Improvement Era*, Vol. 9, 1905-6, pp. 337-339.

Chapter XVIII

LOVE YOUR ENEMIES

WE ARE NOT DISCOURAGED. We are not disheartened, we are not discouraged, we are not faint-hearted. We believe in the Lord and we know that he is mighty to save, thta he has guided the destinies of this people from the first moment until the present, and that it is not in consequence of the wisdom of men that we have escaped the plots, schemes and machinations of our enemies, and that we have been permitted to live and grow in the land, to become what we are, but it is through the wisdom, mercy and blessing of Him who rules the destinies not only of men but of nations. We owe all to God; we extend our thankfulness and gratitude to him for the manifestations of his love and care and protection.—Oct, C. R., 1906, p. 2.

I FORGIVE ALL MEN. I feel in my heart to forgive all men in the broad sense that God requires of me to forgive all men, and I desire to love my neighbor as myself; and to this extent I bear no malice toward any of the children of my Father. But there are enemies to the work of the Lord, as there were enemies to the Son of God. There are those who speak only evil of the Latter-day Saints. There are those—and they abound largely in our midst—who will shut their eyes to every virtue and to every good thing connected with this latter-day work, and will pour out floods of falsehood and misrepresentation against the people of God. I forgive them for this. I leave them in the hands of the just Judge. Let him deal with them as seemeth him good, but they are not and cannot become my bosom companions. I cannot condescend to that. While I would not harm a hair of their heads, while I would not throw a straw in their path, to hinder them from turning from the error of their way to the light of truth; I would as soon think of taking a centipede or a scorpion, or any poisonous reptile, and putting it into my bosom, as I would think of becoming a companion or an associate of such men.

These are my sentiments, and I believe that they are correct. If you can throw yourself in the way of the sinner to stop him in his downward course, and become an instrument in the hand of the Lord of turning him from the way of vice, iniquity, or crime, into the way of righteousness and uprightness, you are justified, and that

is demanded of you. You should do this. If you can save a sinner
from his wickedness, turn the wicked from the course of death that
he is pursuing, to the way of life and salvation, you will save a soul
from death, and you will have been an instrument in the hand of
the Lord of turning the sinner unto righteousness, for which you will
receive your reward. Some of our good Latter-day Saints have become
so exceedingly good (?) that they cannot tell the difference between
a Saint of God, an honest man, and a son of Beelzebub, who
has yielded himself absolutely to sin and wickedness. And they call
that liberality, broadness of mind, exceeding love. I do not want to
become so blinded with love for my enemies that I cannot discern
between light and darkness, between truth and error, between good
and evil, but I hope to live so that I shall have sufficient light in me
to discern between error and truth, and to cast my lot on the side
of truth and not on the side of error and darkness. The Lord bless
the Latter-day Saints. If I am too narrow with reference to these
matters, I hope that the wisdom of my brethren and the Spirit of
Light from the Lord may broaden my soul.—Oct. C. R., 1907, pp. 5, 6.

WE LEAVE OUR ENEMIES IN GOD'S HANDS. We thank God for
his mercies and blessings; and I do not know but what we owe in
small degree gratitude to those who have bitterly opposed the work
of the Lord; for in all their opposings and bitter strife against our
people, the Lord has developed his power and wisdom, and has
brought his people more fully into the knowledge and favor of the
intelligent people of the earth. Through the very means used by
those who have opposed the work of God, he has brought out good
for Zion. Yet it is written, and I believe it is true, that although it
must needs be that offenses come, woe unto them by whom they
come; but they are in the hands of the Lord as we are. We bring
no railing accusation against them. We are willing to leave them in
the hands of the Almighty to deal with them as seemeth him good.
Our business is to work righteousness in the earth, to seek for the
development of a knowledge of God's will and of God's ways, and
of his great and glorious truths which he has revealed through the
instrumentality of Joseph, the prophet, not only for the salvation of
the living but for the redemption and salvation of the dead.—Apr.
C. R., 1908, p. 2.

LEAVE RESULTS IN GOD'S HANDS. God will deal with them in
his own time and in his own way, and we only need to do our duty,
keep the faith ourselves, to work righteousness in the world ourselves,

and leave the results in the hands of him who overruleth all things for the good of those who love him and keep his commandments.—Apr. C. R., 1905, p. 6.

OUR DEBT TO OUR ENEMIES. I was going to say that we did not owe anything to our enemies; that was the first thought that sprang into my mind, but I will hold that back. I think we owe something to our enemies, too, for the advancement of the cause of Zion, for up to date everything that has been done to thwart the purposes of God and to frustrate his designs has been overruled for the good of Zion and for the spread of truth. And that will continue to be the case until the end, for they are fighting God's work, and not mine nor that of any other man.—Oct. C. R., 1906, p. 2.

A PRAYER FOR OUR ENEMIES. Let the Lord God have mercy upon those who seek to hurt the cause of Zion. O God, pity the misguided, the erring, the foolish, the unwise. Put thy Spirit in their hearts, turn them from the error of their ways and from their follies, and bring them back into the way of righteousness and into thy favor. I ask mercy for my enemies—those who lie about me and slander me, and who speak all manner of evil against me falsely. In return, I beseech God my heavenly Father to have mercy upon them; for those who do it, not knowing what they are doing, are only misguided, and those who are doing it with their eyes open certainly need, most of all, the mercy, compassion and pity of God. May God pity them. May he have mercy upon them. I would not harm a hair of their heads, for all I am worth in the world. I would not throw a block in their way to prosperity. No; and I beseech my brethren that they keep hands off the enemies of our people and those who are paving their own road to destruction and will not repent, who are sinning with their eyes open, who know that they are transgressing the laws of God and vilifying and lying against the servants of the Lord. Have mercy upon them. Do not touch them; for that is just what they would like. Let them alone. Let them go. Give them the liberty of speech they want. Let them tell their own story, and write their own doom. We can afford it. They do not hurt us, and if it affords them any amusement, I am sure they are welcome to it.—Oct. C. R., 1905, p. 95.

THE GOLDEN RULE. We need mercy; then let us be merciful. We need charity; let us be charitable. We need forgiveness; let us forgive. Let us do unto others what we would that they should do unto us. Let us welcome the new year and dedicate to it our best efforts, our loyal service, our love and fellowship, and our supplication for the welfare and happiness of all mankind.—*Juvenile Instructor*, Vol. 46, January, 1911, p. 16.

WHY THE WORLD DOES NOT LOVE US. "If ye were of the world, the world would love its own; but because ye are not of the world, but I have chosen you out of the world, therefore the world hateth you." (John 15:19) The followers of Jesus were his chosen people, and because they were chosen by him, the world hated them. The Jews were the chosen people of God, and because they were his chosen people the world hated them. Nowhere in the world today is the word Jew wholly disassociated with the feeling of contempt. The feelings may differ greatly in degree, but they are all of one kind. The word "Mormon," or Latter-day Saint, is everywhere likewise associated with feelings of contempt. Contempt is the heritage of a chosen people. Ought we therefore to court the contempt of the world? By no means. On the other hand, we should not be discouraged because it comes to us unsought. Some of our friends— mostly in the Church, some few out of it—would lift us out of the contempt of the world, and keep us out of it, if we would simply be governed by their counsels. The truth is, we are not strangers to hatred; and the contempt of the world has been our lot so much that we have no reason to be discouraged when it comes, even in violent forms. The danger lies not so much in our own peculiarity as in the disposition of many of our people to court popularity at all costs, as if it were something devoutly to be wished for. There is too often a timid submission before the indignation storms that occasionally sweep over the country.—*Juvenile Instructor*, Vol. 39, August, 1904, p. 464.

LOVE ONE ANOTHER. Let us, brethren, love one another, and exercise patience and forbearance, avoiding judgment, except when called upon to render it, and then tempering the law with a father's love. The Latter-day Saints must be promoters of both law and religion, as exemplified in the justice and mercy of God.—*Improvement Era*, Vol. 6, 1903, p. 550.

KEEP ALOOF FROM THE WICKED. We should keep ourselves aloof from the wicked; the dividing line should be distinctly drawn between God and Belial, between Christ and the world, between truth and error, and between right and wrong. We ought to cleave to the right, to the good, to the truth, and forsake the evil.—*Deseret Weekly News*, Vol. 31, 1882, p. 674.

THE ENEMIES TO FEAR. For my part I do not fear the influence of our enemies from without, as I fear that of those from within. An open and avowed enemy, whom we may see and meet in an open field, is far less to be feared than a lurking, deceitful, treacherous enemy hidden within us, such as are many of the weaknesses of our fallen human nature, which are too often allowed to go unchecked, beclouding our minds, leading away our affections from God and his truth, until they sap the very foundations of our faith and debase us beyond the possibility or hope of redemption, either in this world or that to come. These are the enemies that we all have to battle with, they are the greatest that we have to contend with in the world, and the most difficult to conquer. They are the fruits of ignorance, generally arising out of unrebuked sin and evil in our own hearts. The labor that is upon us is to subdue our passions, conquer our inward foes, and see that our hearts are right in the sight of the Lord, that there is nothing calculated to grieve his Spirit and lead us away from the path of duty.

CHAPTER XIX

EDUCATION AND INDUSTRIAL PURSUITS

WE ARE EVER LEARNING. We are not "ever learning and never coming to a knowledge of the truth." On the contrary, we are ever learning and are ever drawing nearer to a proper comprehension of the truth, the duty and the responsibility that devolve upon members of the Church who are called to responsible positions in it. Not only does this apply to those members who are called to act in responsible positions, but it applies to those who may be termed "lay members," if we may use such a term with reference to members of the Church of Jesus Christ of Latter-day Saints.

Who is there, under the circumstances that exist around us, that is not growing? Who is there of us that is not learning something day by day? Who is there of us that is not gaining experience as we pass along, and are attending to the duties of membership in the Church, and to the duties of citizens of our state, and citizens of our great and glorious nation? It seems to me that it would be a very sad comment upon the Church of Jesus Christ of Latter-day Saints and her people to suppose for a moment that we are at a standstill, that we have ceased to grow, ceased to improve and to advance in the scale of intelligence, and in the faithful performance of duty in every condition in which we are placed as a people and as members of the Church of Christ.—Oct. C. R., 1915, p. 2.

ADDRESS ON IGNORANCE. The subject which has been dwelt upon is a broad one: "What can be done to stem the tide of evil that is sweeping through the land?" I apprehend that one of the greatest evils existing, that is "sweeping through the land," is that of ignorance, coupled with indifference. I presume that if the ignorant were not so indifferent to these facts and to their condition they might be prompted to learn more than they do. The trouble with men and women is that they too frequently close their eyes to the facts that exist around them, and it seems to be very difficult for many of the people to learn and adapt to their lives those simple truths that should be in fact the household words and precepts of every Latter-day Saint, and of every home of a Latter-day Saint. How shall we stem the tide of this evil, this indifference, this consequent ignorance? It appears to me that the only way to do it is to wake up and become interested, or to interest ourselves in those things which are so important and necessary to the happiness and well-being of the children of men, especially that which is so needful for the happiness and well-being of ourselves individually.

It isn't all that is necessary, to learn the truth or to cease to be ignorant. Following that comes the application of the understanding and knowledge that we gain, to those works and things that are needful for our protection and for the protection of our children, our neighbors, our homes, our happiness.

I see occasionally, as I walk out in the evening, crowds of little girls and boys who seem to me from their appearance as not yet having reached their teens, little boys and little girls perhaps from ten to fourteen, and perhaps some of them older, in defiance of the curfew law, playing in the streets, loitering together in shady nooks, in alleys, in the recesses about their homes or the homes of somebody else. This I apprehend is an evil, a very serious evil. How will you stem it? How can it be prevented?—M. I. A. Conference, 1910; Young Woman's Journal, Vol. 21, pp. 403-406.

THE VALUE OF PRACTICAL EDUCATION. I have often thought of the undesirableness of the young men of our community seeking for light employments, and lucrative positions, without regard to manual and mechanical skill, and knowledge and ability in agriculture.

None can deny that there is too great a tendency among the young men, especially in our larger cities, to seek the lighter employments. Politics, law, medicine, trade, clerking, banking, are needful and good in their place, but we need builders, mechanics, farmers, and men who can use their powers to produce something for the use of man.

Salaried positions, in which little responsibility is required, are well enough for young men who are making a beginning, but it should be the ambition of all to get out and take upon themselves responsibility, and to become independent, by themselves becoming producers, and skilful workers.

If life is valuable in comparison with the experience we obtain, every youth will increase the worth of his life in proportion to the new obstacles that he is able to conquer. In a routine, there are no difficulties to encounter; neither is there profit to the mind or body in the sameness of dependent positions. But let the man who would grow and develop, go forth into the practical and productive ways of life. These will lead to broadmindedness and independence, while the other road ends in narrowness and dependence.

And here, also, a word to parents who have daughters. Are you fitting them for the practical duties of mother and wife, that they may in due time go out and make homes what they should be? Or are you training your daughters to play the lady by making them accomplished in flourishes, and expert in ostentatious embellishments? Is mother doing all the work? If you say yes to the last two questions, you are not doing your full duty to your child. For, while accomplishment and polished grace, attainments in music and art, and a knowledge of the sciences, are good and useful in their place, it is not intended that these shall replace the common labors of life. Where children are so trained, their parents have done them a positive injustice, of which both the children and the parents may live to be ashamed.

While we are educating our children in all that may be termed the beautiful in science and art, we should not fail to insist that they shall learn to do practical things, and that they do not despise the common labors of life. Any other course toward them is an injustice to the boys and girls, as well as to ourselves and the community in general.

I believe the morals of the people will improve as skill in workmanship and productive labors is acquired. Parents, too, will find it easier to govern and control their children, if these are trained in useful manual labor. We shall not then witness the sad spectacle of young men loafing about our cities hunting for some easy place that just suits their notions of work, which, if they can not find, they will not labor at all, but go without in idleness. Mischief and devilment, frequently so common because the hands are unemployed, will decrease and better order will prevail.

Thus, while not decrying education in the aesthetic sense, I think it is a serious duty devolving upon parents and those who have educational matters in hand to provide a supplemental if not a coordinate course in practical labor for every boy and girl, which shall make them proficient in handiwork, and enable them to expend their powers in the production of something for the material use and benefit of man.—*Improvement Era*, Vol. 6, January, 1903, p. 229.

PRACTICAL EDUCATION ADVOCATED. I desire again to say that I would be pleased to see more of our young men learning trades instead of trying to learn professions, such as the profession of law, or of medicine, or other professions. I would rather a man would become a good mechanic, a good builder, a good machinist, a good surveyor, a good farmer, a good blacksmith, or a good artisan of any kind than to see him follow these other kinds of professions. We need, however, those who are capable of teaching in the schools, and I would like to see a greater interest manifested by our young men and women in normal training, that they might become proficient teachers and look forward to following this profession, because it is a most important one, and great results will follow the faithful performance of the duties and labors of those who are engaged in it. I would like to see the giving of proper instruction to those who are seeking education, as well as the creating of facilities in our midst for all who desire not only the common branches of education, but the higher branches, that they may obtain these privileges and benefits at home instead of being compelled to go abroad to complete their education.

Some of our friends took very grievous offense at what I said in respect to some of these things last April, I believe. I was sorry to hear what they said in relation to this. Why, bless your soul, the counsel that I gave last April in relation to these matters was in the interest of all parties and of all professions. I did not speak a disrespectful word of any profession. I simply advised, and I still advise, the young men of Zion to become artisans rather than to become lawyers. I repeat it; and yet I would to God that every intelligent man among the Latter-day Saints was able to read law and to be his own lawyer. I wish that every young man could and would study and become familiar with the laws of his state and with the laws of his nation and with the laws of other nations. You cannot learn too much in these directions; but I think there are too many trying to be lawyers, for the good of that profession. They are eating one another up, to some extent. Not long ago a young man who had studied law and hung out his shingle here, after waiting for business, trying to stir up business for some length of time, came so near starving himself and family that he came and wanted to know what to do. He could not make a living in the profession of law. I asked him if he knew how to do anything else. He said yes, he was a good printer. Well, then, I said, abandon the profession of law and take up the profession of printing; do something that you can do and that you can make a living at. If he had any practice at all in law, my counsel to him, if he obeyed it—and he did—would have been a benefit to those who remained in the profession. There are some men, most honorable, most genuine, and most intelligent, who are following the profession of the law. I wish I could say that much of all.

Then, my brethren and sisters, get out of debt. My young friends, learn to become skilful in the arts and in mechanics and in something that will be material, useful in building up the commonwealth where we live and where all our interests are centered.—Oct. C. R., 1903, pp. 5, 6.

BOYS SHOULD BE TAUGHT THE ARTS OF INDUSTRY. One of the things that I think is very necessary is that we should teach our boys mechanism, teach them the arts of industry, and not allow our sons to grow up with the idea that there is nothing honorable in labor, except it be in the professions of law, or in some other light, practically unproductive, and I was going to say, unremunerative employment, but I know of scarcely any employment more remunerative than is the practice of law to those, at least, who are proficient. But what do they do to build up the country? What do they produce to benefit the world? There may be a few of them who have farms; there may be a few of them who have manufactories; there may be a few of them who may be interested and engaged in other productive labor, something that will build up the country and the people and establish permanence, stability and prosperity in the land; but the vast majority of them are leeches upon the body politic and are worthless as to the building up of any community. There are a good many of our boys who feel that they could not be farmers, and that the pursuit of farming and stock-raising is beneath their dignity. There are some who think it is menial and low for them to engage in building enterprises as masons, carpenters, or builders in general.

There are but a few of our boys who take to the hammer and to the anvil and to those pursuits of labor that are essential to the permanence of any community in the world and that are necessary to build up the country.

I say that we are remiss and slack in relation to these things, that we are not instilling them sufficiently in the minds of our children, and that we are not giving them the opportunity that they should enjoy of learning how to produce from the earth and the materials that are on the face of it or in the bowels of it, that which is necessary for the advancement and prosperity of mankind. Some of us have the idea that it is degrading for our daughters to learn how to cook, how to keep house, or to make a dress, apron or bonnet, if necessary. No; daughters in families that are blessed with plenty of means are taught to play the piano, to sing, to go out in society and spend their time in idle, useless pleasure, instead of being taught how to be economical, industrious and frugal, and how to become good housewives. That is degrading! I would like to say to this congregation, and to the world, that if I possessed millions of dollars I would not be satisfied or content in my mind unless my boys knew how to do something that would bring them in a living, how to handle a pitchfork, or to run a mowing machine or reaper, or how to plow the ground and sow the seed; nor would I be satisfied if my daughters did not know how to keep a house. I would be ashamed of my children if they did not know something of these things.

We need manual training schools instead of so much book-learning and the stuffing of fairy tales and fables which are contained in many of our school books of today. If we would devote more money and time, more energy and attention to teaching our children manual labor in our schools than we do, it would be a better thing for the rising generation.

There are many subjects of this character, in addition to the principles of the gospel of eternal truth and the plan of life and salvation, that can be dwelt upon with profit by those who may speak to us.—*Apr. C. R.*, 1903, pp. 2, 3.

MANUAL TRAINING AND AGRICULTURE. We want to make these valleys of the mountains teem with the products of our own labor, and skill, and intelligence. I believe it to be suicidal for us to patronize those who are at a distance from us, when we should and could go to work and organize our labor and produce everything at home; we might thereby give employment to everybody at home, develop the intelligence and the skill of our children, instead of letting them hunt after these fancy occupations that so many young people desire above manual labor. The schools of the Latter-day Saints and some of the state schools are beginning to introduce manual labor. Some of our boys are learning how to make tables, chairs, sofas, book-cases, bureaus and all that sort of thing—all good as far as it goes; but if we want a mason to lay brick, we have to look mostly to some man who has come from England or Germany, or from somewhere else, to lay our brick. Why? Because our boys do not like to lay brick. If we want a good blacksmith, we must hunt up some foreigner who has learned the trade in his mother country, and who has come here with a knowledge of blacksmithing; we must find such a man before we can get blacksmithing done, because boys do not like to be black-smiths. They don't like even to be farmers; they would rather be lawyers or doctors than to be farmers. This is the case with too many of our boys, and it is a great mistake. I hope the time will come when the children of the Latter-day Saints will learn that all labor that is necessary for the happiness of themselves and of their neighbors, or of mankind in general, is honorable; and that no man is degrading himself because he can lay brick, or carry on carpentry or blacksmith-ing, or any kind of mechanism, no matter what it is, but that all these things are honorable, and are necessary for the welfare of man and for the building up of the commonwealth.—Oct. C. R., 1909, p. 8.

AGRICULTURE AND MECHANIC ARTS IN CHURCH SCHOOLS. We have sought to encourage in our Church schools the establishment of departments of mechanic arts and manual training; and, so far as I know, everything possible is being done, at least in the principal schools, for the training of our youth, not only in the regular me-chanic arts, but also in the art of agriculture. An agricultural course has recently been started in the Brigham Young University, and one of our most proficient scientists has been called to take charge of the class. I am happy to say that some of our oldest farmers are delighted with the information that they have obtained by attending this class. I heard a brother who had been farming for many years say that he had always been under the impression that when a man could not do anything else, all he had to do was to turn his attention to the plow and cultivate the soil, for anybody could be a farmer, but he had found out since attending this class that it required intelligence and intelligent application to be a good farmer, as well as to be a good artisan. In connection with this I may state a circumstance that came under my own observation years ago. A certain brother had lived upon his farm for some fourteen or fifteen years. He had cultivated it every year the best he could, but it had become so impoverished that he could not make a living off it any longer, and he became so disgusted with the country, especially with his farm, that he concluded, if he could only trade the farm off for a team and wagon that would take him out of the country, he would be glad to go. By and by, his man came along, and he sold his farm for a team and wagon, in which he put his wife and children and moved to some other country. The purchaser took possession of this worn-out farm, and within three years, by intelligent operation, he was able to gather from that farm forty bushels of wheat to the acre, and other products in proportion. The nutriment of the soil had been exhausted, and it needed resuscitation; so he went to work, gave it the nourishment it required, and reaped a bountiful harvest as a result of his wisdom. There are too many of our farmers who think it does not need any skill to be a farmer; but this good brother in Provo, to whom I alluded, found it did. So we are teaching agriculture in our schools, as well as the mechanic arts. The Brigham Young College is putting up a building now wherein are to be taught all sorts of industries; where our youth will be able to learn carpentry, blacksmithing, domestic arts, and other trades that will be useful to them. Yet we find it a drag to induce anybody possessed of means to contribute very largely to it. Some of our wealthiest men felt they were doing their utmost when they donated perhaps a hundred dollars towards a building that will cost eight or ten thousand dollars, if not more.—Apr. C. R., 1906, pp. 5, 6.

WE SHOULD STUDY AGRICULTURE. In connection with this matter, I think it is wisdom for us, as agriculturists, to study agriculture and to become able to produce out of an acre of ground as much as the "heathen Chinee," or as much as any other people can produce from the same ground. I do not see why we cannot learn to cultivate the soil as intelligently and as profitably as any other class of people in the world; and yet it is a well known fact that up to the present we have not devoted that attention, care, thoughtfulness, or that intelligence to agriculture in our country that we should have done and that we are now learning to do, by the aid of schools where men who desire to follow agriculture may learn the nature of the soil and all the other conditions necessary to produce the largest results for their labor.—Apr. C. R., 1910, p. 4.

DIGNITY OF AGRICULTURE. I believe there is no labor on earth more essential to the well-being of a community or more honorable than the labor which is necessary to produce food from mother earth. It is one of the most noble occupations. And next to it is the tending of the flocks of sheep and cattle. This is another noble occupation, if it is only carried on properly and righteously. These are the foundation of the prosperity of every community in the world. When the farming community is prosperous, when the Lord blesses the earth and makes it fruitful, then the blacksmith, the carpenter, and those who follow other pursuits, will also be prosperous. But when the earth refuses to yield of its strength for the good of mankind, then all other business is stagnant and will languish. Therefore, let us till the earth;

let us cultivate the soil; let us produce our own living out of the earth, by the blessing of God, as far as we possibly can, always keeping in mind that we have entered into solemn covenant with God, which is an eternal covenant, and from which he cannot depart or be moved, and in which we can only fail by ourselves transgressing that new and everlasting covenant and turning away from it.—*Apr. C. R.,* 1898, p. 70.

ENCOURAGE FORESTRY. Professor Fernow, of the Department of Forestry, at Washington, declares that at the present rate of consumption our supply of timber suitable for manufactured lumber will not last thirty years. If it were true that our lumber supply was likely to be exhausted within the next hundred years, it would still be a matter of alarming concern to the people of this country. The use of lumber is not the only serious question involved. Our trees aid the precipitation of moisture and store it away for its gradual distribution during the hot summer months.

The time is not distant in Utah when people will be compelled to grow their own lumber, just as they grow other products of the farm. What would we do without Oregon and the Sierras of Nevada? Oregon timber may now be very plentiful and rainfall ample, but some day the Oregonians will demand a cessation of their forest destruction.

It is the business of presiding authorities in the stakes and wards of the Church to study thoughtfully and to forward the interests of the people. It is to be hoped that these authorities will look into the matter of establishing the forestry industry, and see if something can be done in their sections of the country to inaugurate the planting of trees on private estates for the supply of lumber in years to come. It would be commendable in the highest degree to the Latter-day Saints if they would set apart here and there a small acreage of their land to tree culture. If this matter is taken up in priesthood meetings and some united action agreed upon, future disaster may be averted.

The Latter-day Saints ought not to be governed by purely selfish motives in the use of their landed inheritances. The number among us who have converted a single acre of our farms into forestry must be extremely small, and yet it is a duty which we owe to ourselves and to those who have the right to rely upon us to give this matter our earnest consideration. The cultivation of timber lands will in time be remunerative; but we are so accustomed to look for immediate returns that we insist upon an early harvest for all that we do. The policy of living for today is not only destructive of our material interests, but it begets a selfishness harmful to religion and discreditable to patriotism.

No ward or branch of the Church can long remain free from a public interest without endangering its spiritual life and the spirit of progress. Public interests are necessary to protect us against the elements of social and material decay. Evidences of the truth of these principles are abundantly manifest in those communities where public spirit has been wanting and public improvements have not been undertaken for years. The wise and active president of a stake or bishop of a ward will not fail to appreciate the value of a public spirit and a united effort in the accomplishment of some necessary and commendable public undertaking; and if there is not something immediately at hand, he will look about to discover, if he can, a means for calling out in a united and patriotic way the energies of the people. We here therefore suggest that one of the public duties which every Latter-day Saint owes to the Church and to his country is the extension of valuable timber forests upon both private lands and public domains.—*Juvenile Instructor*, Vol. 38, August 1, 1903, p. 466.

YOUNG WOMEN SHOULD HAVE PRACTICAL PREPARATION FOR LIFE.

I, too, think it is very important that young women should early form some design, some definite purpose in life. Let that resolve be a noble one, a good one; something with a view of benefiting others as well as one's self. Perhaps your sphere may be in the household; if so, let every member feel that you are indispensable to the comfort of home, by your good works and your love and patience. You may be a stay and a comfort and a help to your mother, though you may not be called to herculean tasks or heroic sacrifices. Fix in your minds noble thoughts, cultivate elevated themes, let your aims and aspirations be high. Be in a certain degree independent; to the degree of usefulness, helpfulness and self-reliance, though no human beings can be said truly to be independent of their fellow beings, and there is no one reckless enough to deny our utter dependence on our heavenly Father. Seek to be educated in the highest meaning of the term; get the most possible service out of your time, your body and brains, and let all your efforts be directed into honorable channels, that no effort shall be wasted, and no labor result in loss or evil.

Seek the very best society; be kind, polite, agreeable, seeking to learn whatever is good, and comprehend the duties of life that you may be a blessing to all those with whom you associate, making the very most and best of your lot in life. * * *

It does not matter how wealthy the Latter-day Saints become; so long as they are worthy of that name they will teach their sons and daughters the dignity of labor and how grand it is to be practical in the duties and responsibilities of life. One of the speakers during the general conference remarked that if his children could not cultivate but one set of faculties, rather than theoretical, he would choose practical labor. It is very important to the welfare, usefulness, happiness, and comfort of our daughters (in view of certain circumstances) that they learn some branch of industry that could be turned to practical account in the way of making a living, should circumstances require it. Mothers should see to it that their daughters do this, and that when she is no longer by them, they may be capable of providing themselves with the necessaries of life.

There are people fond of saying that women are the weaker vessels. I don't believe it. Physically, they may be; but spiritually, morally, religiously and in faith, what man can match a woman who is really convinced? Daniel had faith to sustain him in the lion's den, but women have seen their sons torn limb from limb, and endured every torture satanic cruelty could invent because they believed. They are always more willing to make sacrifices, and are the peers of men in stability, Godliness, morality and faith. I can not understand how a man can be unkind to any woman, much less to the wife of his bosom, and the mother of his children, and I am told that there are those who are absolutely brutal, but they are unworthy the name of men. I believe that most women are very devoted to their children, desiring for them most ardently all that is good, and I loathe with every fibre of my soul the son who turns against the mother who gave him birth. I cannot tolerate the young lady who appears well in society at the expense of the comfort of her mother at home. Do not fear to divide the burdens, and to do all in your power to brighten the lot of your mother, and you will find blessings that are never discovered in the path of selfishness.

And I exhort you young sisters to sustain those who are placed over you, to improve all your opportunities, and refrain from evil; and, mark me, you will attain to a high standard of character and the honors of life, and become potent factors in forming your communities. Maintain your dignity, integrity, and virtue at the sacrifice of life. Take this course, and although you may be ignorant of many things, you will be esteemed as of the noblest types of womanhood. With such virtues for her adornment, no man could help loving such a young lady.—*Young Woman's Journal*, Vol. 3, 1891-1892, pp. 142-144.

OBJECT OF CHURCH SCHOOLS. The object, I may say almost the only purpose, for the maintenance of Church schools is that true religion and undefiled before God the Father, may be inculcated in the minds and hearts of our children while they are getting an education, to enable the heart, the soul and the spirit of our children to develop with proper teaching, in connection with the secular training that they receive in schools.—*Oct. C. R.*, 1915, p. 4.

VALUE OF CHURCH SCHOOLS. In my opinion the Church schools are laying the foundation for great usefulness among the people of God, and they should be sustained by the people and by the Church. The Church is sustaining them, and as we acquire more means and become more free from obligations which have been resting upon the Church for years, we will be more free-handed to administer to the needs of our Church schools, as well as other requirements of that nature.—*Apr. C. R.*, 1906, p. 6.

PURPOSE OF CHURCH SCHOOLS. The purpose of our Church schools is the harmonious development of our young people in all that relates to their future well-being and progress; and eternal progress can be enjoyed only when the principles of eternal life are associated with their daily existence. Whatever hinders upward progression deadens the sensibilities and real enjoyments of this world's life. And education that has for its highest ideals the pursuit of worldly ambitions is wanting in that free and unrestrained flow of the spirit which makes for higher freedom and a more wholesome life. As we ripen in years and in experience, our spiritual lives have more and more to do with our real happiness. Our thoughts are more frequently turned inward as we contemplate the approaching end of this life and the unfolding of the greater life to come.—*Juvenile Instructor*, Vol. 47, November, 1912, p. 630.

THE CHURCH AMPLE FOR ALL NECESSARY ORGANIZATION. The Church is provided with so many priesthood organizations that only these can be recognized therein. No outside organization is necessary. There is no call for individuals to organize clubs, or special gatherings in social, educational, or national capacity, in order to express wishes or desires for reforms that can always be expressed in the organizations that already exist in the Church. There is enough to do in the general ward organizations, under Church control, to fill requirements, to satisfy all righteous ambitions, and to develop the latent talent of the people. It is neither proper nor necessary to establish further public organizations under individual leadership, unsanctioned by the Church authorities. If further public organizations are required, they will be founded by proper authority, when it can be proved that there is indeed any need for them. Such separate action leads to clannishness, conflict and disunion, and is not pleasing in the sight of God.—*Improvement Era*, Vol. 6, Dec., 1902, p. 150.

DEVELOP FACULTIES IN CHURCH ORGANIZATIONS. Where men are ambitious to show their ability and fitness as leaders, teachers, organizers, champions of a righteous cause, or saviors of men, let them develop these qualities in the many suitable organizations now existing in the Church, which are waiting, yea, often crying aloud, for men with just such superior ability. This course, pursued with the right spirit, will do good, and meet the blessings of the Lord, while the other, by playing upon their pride of nationality, their natural desire to conquer, and their sectional clannishness, will lead to schisms among the people that will finally cause them to lose the spirit of the gospel.—*Improvement Era*, Vol. 6, Dec., 1902, p. 151.

THE FOUNDATION OF PROSPERITY. The very foundation of all real prosperity is home industry and home manufacture. This lies at the foundation of the prosperity of every permanently prosperous community. It is the source of wealth. I think, therefore, we ought to encourage home manufacture and every home industry. We ought to co-operate together, if there is any kind of business in which there is a profit, let us co-operate together and let us have the benefit of that profit among ourselves instead of giving it to strangers.— *Deseret Weekly News*, Vol. 33, 1884, p. 446.

THE OBJECT OF CO-OPERATION. Co-operation is a principle that President Young was very much concerned about, and that he endeavored, with his brethren, to impress upon the minds of the people throughout the land. Under his administration our co-operative institutions were established, and by his efforts, many of the people, especially in the southern part of Utah and in Arizona, became united together in organizations that were called "The United Order." The object was co-operation, that the principle of union in labor as well as in faith might be developed to its fullest extent in the midst of the Saints.—*Deseret Weekly News*, Vol. 33, 1884, p. 466.

CHAPTER XX

MISSIONARIES

How Missionaries Are Called. No person but the President of the Church has the authority to call missionaries to preach the gospel; others may suggest or recommend, but they do so to him, and he issues the call. We draw attention to this fact as it occasionally happens that some brother is spoken to about going on a mission by one of the general authorities, by the president of the stake or by his bishop, and he at once goes to work and begins to prepare to leave, sometimes going so far as to rent his farm, sell his belongings or lease his property. Then, when no date is appointed for his departure and no field of labor assigned him, he feels disappointed and aggrieved.—*Juvenile Instructor*, Vol. 37, February, 1902, p. 82.

Requirements of Prospective Missionaries. In accordance with the present regulations of the First Presidency, brethren are not now sent on missions who have not themselves a testimony of the truth of the work of the Lord. It is deemed inconsistent to send men out into the world to promise to others through obedience to the gospel that which they have not themselves received. Neither is it considered proper to send men out to reform them. Let them first reform at home if they have not been strictly keeping the commandments of God. This applies to the Word of Wisdom as well as to all other laws of heaven. No objection is offered to men being called who in earlier years may have been rough or wayward, if in later years they have lived a godly life and brought forth the precious fruits of repentance. Neither should men be sent who are not in good health; a sickly elder is able to do but little good himself and often impedes the work of his companion; and, too frequently, has to be sent home after a short absence entailing suffering on himself and expense to the people or the Church.—*Juvenile Instructor*, Vol. 37, February, 1902, p. 82.

The Kind of Men Wanted for Missionaries. We do not want boys that have been in saloons, that have been in houses of ill-fame, that have been gamblers, that have been drunkards, that have been infamous in their lives—we do not want such to go into the ministry of this holy gospel to represent the Son of the living God and the power of redemption to the world. We want young men who have been born or adopted in the covenant, who have been reared in purity, who have kept themselves unspotted from the world, and can go into the nations of the earth and say to men, "Follow me, as I follow Christ." Then we would like to have them know how to sing, and to pray. We expect them to be honest, virtuous, and faithful unto death to their covenants, to their brethren, to their wives, to their fathers and mothers, to their brothers and sisters, to themselves and to God. Where you get men like this to preach the gospel to the world, whether they know much to begin with or not, the Lord will put his Spirit into their hearts, and he will crown them with intelligence and power to save the souls of men. For the germ of life is in them. It has not been vitiated or corrupted; it has not been driven away from them.—*Oct. C. R.*, 1899, pp. 72-3.

NECESSARY QUALIFICATIONS OF MISSIONARIES. Another thing—one of the indispensable qualifications of the elders who go out into the world to preach is humility, meekness and love unfeigned, for the well-being and the salvation of the human family, and the desire to establish peace and righteousness in the earth among men. We can not preach the gospel of Christ without this spirit of humility, meekness, faith in God and reliance upon his promises and word to us. You may learn all the wisdom of men, but that will not qualify you to do these things like the humble, guiding influence of the Spirit of God will. "Pride goeth before destruction, and an haughty spirit before a fall."

It is necessary for the elders who go out into the world to preach to study the spirit of the gospel, which is the spirit of humility, the spirit of meekness and of true devotion to whatever purpose you set your hand or your mind to do. If it is to preach the gospel, we should devote ourselves to the duties of that ministry, and we ought to strive with the utmost of our ability to qualify ourselves to perform that specific labor, and the way to do it is to live so that the spirit of God will have communion and be present with us to direct us in every moment and hour of our ministry, night and day.—*Apr. C. R.*, 1915, p. 138.

FURTHER QUALIFICATIONS OF MISSIONARIES. There are many excellent men but very few really good missionaries. The characteristics of a good missionary are: A man who has sociability—whose friendship is permanent and sparkling—who can ingratiate himself into the confidence and favor of men who are in darkness. This cannot be done offhand. You must get acquainted with a man, learn him and gain his confidence and make him feel and know that your only desire is to do him good and bless him; then you can tell him your message, and give him the good things you have for him, kindly and lovingly. Therefore, in selecting missionaries, choose such as have sociability, who have friendship and not enmity towards men; and if you have not any such in your ward, train and qualify some young men for this work. Some men can never make good missionaries, and you should not select such. In the very first place, a missionary should have in himself the testimony of the Spirit of God—the witness of the Holy Ghost. If he has not this, he has nothing to give. Men are not converted by eloquence or oratory; they are convinced when they are satisfied that you have the truth and the Spirit of God.—*Improvement Era*, also *Digest of Instructions*, Y. M. M. I. A., 1904.

WHAT MISSIONARIES SHOULD TEACH. Our elders are instructed here, and they are taught from their childhood up, that they are not to go out and make war upon the religious organizations of the world when they are called to go out to preach the gospel of Jesus Christ, but to go and bear with them the message which has been given to us through the instrumentality of the Prophet Joseph, in this latter dispensation, whereby men may learn the truth, if they will. They are sent out to offer the olive branch of peace to the world, to offer the knowledge that God has spoken from the heavens once more to his children upon the earth; that God has in his mercy restored again to the world the fulness of the gospel of his Only Begotten Son, in the flesh, that God has revealed and restored to mankind the divine power and authority from himself, whereby they are enabled and authorized to perform the ordinances of the gospel of Jesus Christ necessary for their salvation; and their performance of these ordinances must of necessity be acceptable unto God who has given to them the authority to perform them in his name. Our elders are sent out to preach repentance of sin, to preach righteousness, to preach to the world the gospel of life, of fellowship, and of friendship among mankind, to teach men and women to do that which is right in the sight of God and in the presence of all men, to teach them the fact that God has organized his Church, a Church of which he, himself, is the author and the founder—not Joseph Smith, nor President Brigham Young, not the Twelve Apostles, that have been chosen in this dispensation—to them does not belong the honor of establish-

ing the Church. God is its author, God is its founder, and we are
sent out, and we send out our elders, to make this proclamation to
the world, and leave it to their own judgment and discretion as to
whether they will investigate it, learn the truth for themselves, and
accept it, or whether they will reject it. We do not make war upon
them; if they do not receive it, we do not contend with them; if
they fail to benefit themselves by receiving the message that we give
to them for their own good, we only pity. Our sympathy goes out
to those who will not receive the truth and who will not walk in the
light when the light shines before them; not hatred, not enmity,
not the spirit of condemnation; it is our duty to leave condemnation
in the hands of Almighty God. He is the only real, true, righteous,
impartial judge, and we leave judgment in his hands. It is not our
business to proclaim calamities, judgments, destruction, and the wrath
of God upon men, if they will not receive the truth. Let them
read the word of God, as recorded in the New and the Old Testa-
ments; and, if they will receive it, let them read the word that has
been restored through the gift and power of God to Joseph the
prophet, as contained in the Doctrine and Covenants and in the
Book of Mormon. Let them read these things, and they will learn
here, themselves, the promises that God has made to those who will
not hearken when they hear the truth, but will close their ears
and their eyes against the light. We need not repeat these things
and try to impose upon the feelings and judgments of men by
threatening them or by warning them against the dangers and evils
that may come upon the ungodly, the disobedient, the unthankful,
and those who will not yield to the truth. They will learn it soon
enough, if we do not mention it to them at all.—Apr. C. R., 1915,
pp. 3-4.

WHAT AND HOW TO TEACH. The question often arises in the
minds of young men who find themselves in the mission field,
"What shall I say?" And another follows closely upon it, "How
shall I say it?" To those who go out in earnestness and who have
made a partial study of the principles of the gospel at home, the
first question will soon be solved even if they have failed to make the
very best use of their time and opportunities in our schools, associations, and religious meetings. They will soon find attraction in the
principles of truth, and as they find time, by close application, become
familiar with the teachings set forth in the gospel of Jesus Christ, as
revealed to and taught by the Latter-day Saints. But the second

question, involving the best method of delivering the message which the missionary has gone out to proclaim, that is not always so readily solved. And yet, the success or failure of a mission largely depends upon the false or accurate solution of this problem.

While no specific rule may be given, experience has taught that the simplest way is the best. Having learned the principles of the gospel, through a prayerful spirit and by careful study, these should be presented to men in humility, in the simplest forms of speech, without presumption or arrogance and in the spirit of the mission of Christ. This cannot be done if a young missionary waste his effort in a vain-glorious attempt to become a noisy orator. This is the point I wish to impress upon the elders, and to advise that all oratorical effort be confined to appropriate times and places. The mission field is not the place for such effort. The gospel is not successfully taught by ostentatious display of words and argument, but rather is expressed by modest and rational statements of its simple truth, uttered in a way that will touch the heart and appeal, as well, to reason and sound sense.

It isn't the rounded period, but the thought which it contains that is of value; nor is it the faultless sentence so much as the spirit accompanying the speaker that awakens life and light in the soul. The spirit must first be with the missionary, if he shall succeed in awakening its response in his hearers; and this is true whether the words be spoken in conversation, face to face, or in public gatherings. The spirit will not manifest itself in the person who devotes his time to deliver what he has to say in pompous words or with display of oratory. He hopes to please artificially, and not effectively through the heart.

It is, therefore, of great importance that the gospel should be preached in the simplest and most intelligible way. This does not mean that the language should not be choice, nor that all the refinement possible should not be employed, but that there should be no affectation, nothing "put on." There is enough in the gospel to occupy our earnest time and language, without devoting our time to artificial effects. By earnestness and simplicity the missionary will not only establish himself in the truth, but his testimony will convince others. He will also learn to stand for himself with God as his helper; he will touch the hearts of the people and will have the pleasure of seeing them come to an understanding of his message. The spirit of the gospel will shine forth from his soul and others will partake of his light and rejoice therein. The other course will be ineffectual, serving no useful purpose, either to the missionary himself or to those who hear him, but rather leading to vanity, emptiness and futility.

In the mission field, as in our daily lives, it is best to be natural, rational—neither given to exaggeration of spiritual gifts nor to destructive affectation in act or language. It is best to develop simplicity of speech, earnestness of manner, humility of spirit, and a feeling of love for our fellows, thereby cultivating that well-balanced common sense in our lives that shall command the respect and admiration of the honest in heart, and insure the continual presence and aid of the Spirit of God.

NOT ALL MEN READY TO ACCEPT THE GOSPEL. I was struck by a remark made by one of the brethren with respect to the many people who saw and heard the Prophet Joseph Smith and yet didn't believe that he was a prophet of God, or a man raised up by the Almighty to lay the foundations of this great latter-day work. It was said that the Lord had not revealed it unto them. Now, I do not dispute that statement, nor call it in question; but it occurred to me that there are thousands of men who have heard the voices of the inspired servants of God, unto whom the Almighty has borne record of the truth, and yet they have not believed it. It is my opinion that the Lord bears record to the testimonies of his servants unto those who hear those testimonies, and it is left with them whether or not they will harden their hearts against the truth and not listen to it, and abide the consequences. I believe the Spirit of the Almighty God is upon most of the elders who go out into the world to proclaim the gospel. I believe their words are accompanied by the testimony of the Spirit of God. But all men are not open to receive the witness and the testimony of the Spirit. And the responsibility will rest with them. Yet it may be possible the Lord withholds his Spirit from some, for a wise purpose in him, that their eyes are not opened to see and their minds not quickened to comprehend the word of truth. As a rule, however, it is my opinion that all men who are seeking after the truth and are willing to receive it, will also receive the witness of the Spirit which accompanies the words and testimonies of the servants of the Lord; while those whose hearts are hardened against the truth and will not receive it when it is borne record of to them, will remain ignorant and without a comprehension of the gospel. I believe there are tens of thousands of people who have heard the truth and have been pricked in their hearts, but they are seeking every refuge they possibly can to hide themselves from their convictions of the truth. It is among this class that you will find the enemies of the cause of Zion. They are opposing the truth in order to hide themselves from their convictions of the truth. There are men, possibly within the sound of my voice—certainly within the limits of this city—who have read our books, who have listened to the discourses of the elders, and who are familiar with the doctrines of the Church; but they will not acknowledge—openly, at least—the truth of this gospel and the divinity of this work. Well, the responsibility rests with them. God will judge them and deal with them in his own way and time. Many of them, through their efforts to bring reproach upon the cause of Zion, are awakening the attention of people in the world to "Mormonism," and thus unwittingly advancing the cause of Zion, while they know it not. I thank God my Father that he brings good out of the evil designed against his people by their enemies. And he will continue to do this. The clouds may gather over our heads, and, as in the past, it may seem impossible for us to penetrate them; yet there can be no clouds so dark, so gloomy or so heavy, but God will roll them away in his own time and will bring good out of threatening evil. He has done it in the past, he will do it in the future; for it is his work, not the work of man.—*Apr. C. R.,* 1899, pp. 40-41.

OUR PEOPLE GENEROUS TO MISSIONARIES. I believe I can confidently say that the Latter-day Saints, as a rule, are among the most hospitable, generous and kindhearted people that can be found upon the earth. Not long ago one of our elders returned from a mission in the South. There had been a question raised in his mind as to whether the Latter-day Saints in Zion would be as open-handed, as hospitable, as kindhearted and as willing to receive and entertain a stranger as were the people of the South, and he determined to put the matter to the test. The story of his visits to some of our people here is published in the *Improvement Era,* No. 6, Vol. 1, p. 399. I cannot give it to you in detail, but will only attempt a brief outline. Representing himself as a minister of the gospel from the state of Tennessee, traveling without purse or scrip, as the elders of the Church of Jesus Christ of Latter-day Saints were generally doing, he called upon Brother B. Y. Hampton, of the Hampton House, and asked for entertainment without charge. Bro. Hampton readily consented to take care of him. He next called at the Temple

Barber Shop, with a similar representation, and asked for a "shave and shingle," on the same terms, which was readily complied with, and he was asked to "come again." He next called upon Brother Henry Dinwoodey, and presenting himself as before, asked for means to pay his fare on the railroad, going north, whereupon Brother Dinwoodey handed him out the money. Needing a mainspring in his watch, he called upon Brothers John Daynes & Son, and introduced himself as before, and they cheerfully repaired his watch. He then called upon Thomas G. Webber, of Z. C. M. I., and in the same guise asked for a pair of shoes, which Col. Webber generously gave him. Having a tooth which needed filling, he called at the dental parlors of Dr. Fred Clawson, whom he convinced, after some difficulty, that he was not an old friend and school mate, but really a minister of the gospel from Tennessee, having a similar name; the doctor readily consented to filling his tooth without money or price. Thus it was proven that the Latter-day Saints were as generous, as kindhearted, as ready to help the stranger of another religion, as were the good people of the Southern States, and for that matter of any other country. Having put these people to the test, in other words, having weighed them in the balance and found them not wanting in each case, he fully explained his motive and who he was, to their mutual delight. And when the elder returned their gifts or declined to receive the favors granted him without proper remuneration in each case, as I understand, the brethren insisted that what they had done was in good faith on their part, and he was welcome to the same, believing that an elder who had spent two years and upwards on a mission, laboring without purse or scrip, would be likely to stand almost as much in need of such help as would the strange minister whom he had personated.—Apr. C. R., 1898, pp. 46-7.

ADVICE TO MISSIONARIES. The missionary labor accomplished by the Church of Jesus Christ of Latter-day Saints is a subject of growing comment and marvel among people of the world who come to learn of its extent and results. This feeling of wonder is blended with admiration in the minds of those who study the details of our missionary system, and who are able to appreciate the self-sacrifice, enduring faith, and God-fearing reliance by which the missionaries of the Church are distinguished. The fact that those of our people who go forth on missions do so at their own expense, unsalaried, indeed, without hope of pecuniary reward, spending years away from home—usually years of early manhood—the years that are regarded as most valuable in shaping the individual's course and position in life —this fact, indeed, may well arouse the surprise and admiration of the world.

Many of our devoted missionaries are valiantly striving to do their best, and to make their best better, day by day; great is and greater yet shall be their reward. Others are lacking in energy and effort; their work is done, if at all, in a half-spirited way, and their thoughts are ever running ahead to the time of their release and return.

To those of the first class the days are all too short and the months too few for the exalted labors in which they find such genuine satisfaction and happiness. To the others the days drag and the weeks are burdensome.

The individual elder is left largely to the guidance of the spirit of his calling, with which he should be imbued. If he fail to cultivate that spirit, which is the spirit of energy and application, he will soon become torpid, indolent and unhappy. Every missionary should strive to devote part of each day to study and prayerful thought on the principles of the gospel and the theology of the Church. He should read and reflect and pray. True, we are opposed to the preparing of set sermons to be delivered with the thought of oratorical effect and rhetorical display; yet when an elder arises to address a congregation at home or abroad, he should be thoroughly prepared for his sermon. His mind should be well stored with thoughts worth uttering, worth hearing, worth remembering; then the spirit of inspiration will bring forth the truths of which his auditors are in need, and give to his words the ring of authority.

Brethren—you to whom these words of admonition apply, for your own sakes, if not for the sake of those whose welfare is your charge—beware of indolence and neglect. The adversary is only too eager to take advantage of your apathy, and you may lose the very testimony of which you have been sent to bear record before the world.

We would recommend to conference presidents and other presiding officers in the various branches of the Church, that where possible, they have the elders in their charge follow regularly and systematically a study of the standard works and other approved publications of the Church, thus more fully equipping themselves as teachers to the world.

There is little excuse for the idle man in any walk of life; work is abundant for every one who will labor; but least of all is there excuse or palliation in the case of a listless or idle missionary pretending to be busy in the service of his Lord.

It is to be earnestly recommended that elders abroad on missions, as indeed Latter-day Saints in general, avoid contentious argument and debate regarding doctrinal subjects. The truth of the gospel does not depend for its demonstration on heated discussion; the message of truth is most effectively delivered when expressed in words of simplicity and sympathy.

The history of our missionary work already written proves the futility of public debate and argument between our elders and their opponents; and this in spite of the fact that in the great majority of such undertakings the forensic victory has been won by our representatives. A testimony of the truth is more than a mere assent of the mind, it is a conviction of the heart, a knowledge that fills the whole soul of its recipient.

Missionaries are sent forth to preach and teach the first principles of the gospel, Christ and him crucified, and practically nothing more in the way of theological doctrine. They are not commissioned to expound their own views on intricate questions of theology, nor to mystify their hearers with a show of profound learning. Teachers they are and must be, if they meet in any degree the responsibilities of their high calling; but they should teach as nearly as they can after the manner of the Master—seeking to lead by love for their fellows, by simple explanation and persuasion; not trying to convince by force.

Brethren, leave these themes of profitless discussion alone; keep closely to the teachings of the revealed word, as made plain in the standard works of the Church and through the utterances of the living prophets; and let not a difference of views on abstruse matters of doctrine absorb your attention, lest thereby you become estranged from one another and separated from the Spirit of the Lord.

The standard works of the Church and other approved writings should be carefully studied and commented on by the brethren; every Latter-day Saint, and particularly every elder in the field, should seek to become learned in the gospel; but let it not be forgotten that to understand the inspired writings aright the reader must himself have the spirit of inspiration; and this spirit will never impel one to hostile discussion or wordy contests.

Seek first the Kingdom of God and his righteousness, and all else that is desirable, including the knowledge for which you yearn, shall be given unto you.—*Juvenile Instructor*, Vol. 38, October 15, 1903, p. 624.

WORDS TO MISSIONARIES. This is a great labor; one of incalculable worth and benefit in Zion. In order to succeed, you must be on the Lord's side; you must have the co-operation of the Spirit of God. You must feel the importance of your mission, and that mission is to vitalize those who are charged with the responsibility and care of the young men of Israel. Your duty to teach them how to do their work effectively, and how best to accomplish the salvation of the young. Therefore, you must possess the spirit of the mission in your hearts; and, in order to do that, you must be prayerful and humble. Be genial and kind so that you may cope with all difficulties. Be not discouraged, but press on until all obstacles yield to your efforts.

MISSIONARIES AND THE WORD OF WISDOM. Young men cannot hope to be successful missionaries who violate the Word of Wisdom. Its observance is necessary to the spiritual fervor and assurance which carry conviction to the hearts of those who receive the words of the elders. The absolute necessity of the observance of the Word of Wisdom in the missionary field makes it desirable that all who violate this important law to the people, reform before they can hope to accomplish anything helpful to others, either by precept or example.

There is no thoughtful Latter-day Saint who does not look forward with some pleasure to the time when his son will be called on a mission. No greater honor can come to a home than a call to represent the work of the Lord among the nations; yet parents are too frequently indifferent about the preparation their sons receive prior to the call to fill a mission. Fundamental in that preparation is the observance of the Word of Wisdom. So important do I esteem this subject that at a recent conference in the Beaver stake I was led to speak upon it at considerable length. The extracts that follow from that discourse should be of interest and deep concern to every reader of the *Juvenile Instructor:*

"Now, I do wish with all my heart—not because I say it, but because it is written in the word of the Lord—that you would give heed to this Word of Wisdom. It was given unto us 'not by commandment'; but by the word of President Brigham Young, it was made a commandment unto the Saints. It is written here for our guidance, for our happiness and advancement in every principle that pertains to the kingdom of God, in time and throughout eternity, and I pray you to observe it. It will do you good; it will ennoble your souls; it will free your thoughts and your hearts from the spirit of destruction; it will make you feel like God, who sustains even the sparrow, that it does not fall to the ground without his notice; it will bring you nearer to the similitude of the Son of God, the Savior of the world, who healed the sick, who made the lame to leap for joy, who restored hearing to the deaf and sight to the blind, who distributed peace, joy, and comfort to all with whom he came in contact, and who cured and destroyed nothing, save it was the barren fig tree, and that was to show forth his power more than anything else:

" 'And all saints who remember to keep and do these sayings, walking in obedience to the commandments, shall receive health in their navel, and marrow to their bones.

" 'And shall find wisdom and great treasures of knowledge, even hidden treasures;

" 'And shall run and not be weary, and shall walk and not faint;

" 'And I, the Lord, give unto them a promise, that the destroying angel shall pass by them, as the children of Israel, and not slay them.' (Doc. and Cov. 89:18-21.)

"Are these glorious promises not sufficient to induce us to observe this Word of Wisdom? Is there not something here that is worthy our attention? Are not 'great treasures' of knowledge, even 'hidden treasures,' something to be desired? But when I see men and women addicting themselves to the use of tea and coffee, or strong drinks, or tobacco in any form, I say to myself, here are men and women who do not appreciate the promise God has made unto them. They trample it under their feet, and treat it as a thing of naught. They despise the word of God, and go contrary to it in their actions. Then when affliction overtakes them, they are almost ready to curse God, because he will not hear their prayers, and they are left to endure sickness and pain.

"And among the least things that we should do is to keep the Word of Wisdom. Brethren and sisters, do not be so weak! I recollect a circumstance that occurred three years ago in a party that I was traveling with. There were one or two who persisted in having their tea and coffee at every place they stopped. I preached the Word of Wisdom right along; but they said, 'What does it matter? Here is So-and-so, who drinks tea and coffee.' Thus the act of one woman or one man nullified not only all that I or my brethren said in relation to it, but also the word of God itself. I said at one time, 'Oh, yes, you say it is a good thing to drink a little tea or coffee, but the Lord says it is not. Which shall I follow?' The Lord says that if we will observe the Word of Wisdom we shall have access to great treasures of knowledge, and hidden treasures; we shall run and not be weary, we shall walk and not faint; and the destroying angel shall pass us by, as he did the children of Israel, and not slay us. But the class of men of whom I speak say, in effect, 'We don't care what the Lord says or promises, we will drink tea and coffee anyhow.' Such people will set a bad example, no matter what others say or what God has said. They will take the bits in their own mouths, and do as they please, regardless of the effect upon the Saints. I say, out upon such practices! If I could not travel with the people of God and observe the laws of God, I would quit traveling. But if the Lord will give me strength to keep his word, so that I can teach it conscientiously, from the heart as well as from the lips, I will visit you, and labor with you, and plead with you. I will pray for you and earnestly beseech you, my brethren and sisters, especially the young men of Zion, to cease practicing these forbidden things, and observe the laws of God, so that you can run and not be weary, walk and not faint, and have access to great treasures of knowledge, hidden treasures, and every blessing that the Lord has promised through obedience."—*Juvenile Instructor*, Vol. 37, December, 1902, p. 721.

CAUTION TO MISSIONARIES. I am sorry to say it, but if these two boys, recently drowned, had kept away from those rivers, where they had no special duty, or calling, they would not have been drowned as they were. I would like it to be understood by the presidents of missions, and by the elders, that are out in the world, that it is not a good thing, neither is it at all wise for our elders to go out on excursions, on dangerous lakes, on streams, or bodies of water, just for fun. They would better keep away. The Lord will protect them in the discharge of their duty; and if they are more careful of their health, there will not be so many of them become a prey to disease. We know of some incidents that were the cause of the death of some of our brethren who have passed away in the mission field. They lacked caution. They did not exercise the best wisdom and judgment. They went too far for their strength and were not as careful of themselves as they ought to have been. I do not speak this to blame these brethren. I have not the least doubt but they have done according to the best wisdom they possessed; but there is such a thing as overdoing. A man may fast and pray till he kills himself, and there isn't any necessity for it; nor wisdom in it. I say to my brethren, when they are fasting, and praying for the sick, and for those who need faith and prayer, do not go beyond what is wise and prudent in fasting and prayer. The Lord can hear a simple prayer offered in faith, in half a dozen words, and he will recognize fasting that may not continue more than twenty-four hours, just as readily and as effectually as he will answer a prayer of a thousand words and fasting for a month. Now, remember it. I have in mind elders now on missions, anxious to excel their associates. Each wants to get most "red marks" of credit, and so he will exert himself beyond his strength; and it is unwise to do it. The Lord will accept that which is enough, with a good deal more pleasure and satisfaction than that which is too much and unnecessary. It is good to be earnest, good to be diligent, to persevere, and to be faithful all the time, but we may go to extremes in these things, when we do not need to. The Word of Wisdom dictates that when we become weary we should stop and rest. When we are threatened with exhaustion through over exertion, wisdom would caution us to wait, to stop; not to take a stimulant to urge us on to greater extremes, but go where we can retire and rest and recuperate according to the laws of nature. That is the best way to do.

Now, I do not blame my dear brethren who have met with death abroad; yet, I wish that they could and would have escaped it.—Oct. C. R., 1912, pp. 134-135.

HEALTH OF MISSIONARIES TO BE GUARDED. Presidents of all the missions are under strict instructions from the Presidency of the Church to guard carefully the health of the elders who are laboring under their direction. These presidents of missions are also under instructions to send home any and all elders whose health or whose other circumstances may make it necessary for them to return.—Oct. C. R., 1904, p. 41.

MISSIONARIES IN ILL HEALTH. I would like to exhort the elders who are upon missions, and those who shall go upon missions in the future, not to allow the thoughts to enter their hearts that they will be criticized or be made to suffer in their character or their standing in the Church because their health will not permit them to fulfil a two or three years' mission abroad. We would like them rather to feel in themselves a wholesome aversion to coming home without having filled an honorable mission, when their health and other conditions will permit them to do so; and if they have any reluctance about coming home at all, before completing their missions, it should be based upon this principle.—Oct. C. R., 1904, p. 42.

CARE OF RETURNED MISSIONARIES. It is also a good thing for the bishops in all the wards to look after their returned missionaries. It is a pity that after so many of our boys who go abroad and fill good missions return home, they should be apparently dropped or ignored by the presiding authorities of the Church and be permitted to drift away again into carelessness and indifference, and eventually, perhaps, to wander entirely away from their Church duties. They should be kept in the harness, they should be made active in the work of the ministry, in some way, that they may better keep the spirit of the gospel in their minds and in their hearts and be useful at home as well as abroad.

There is no question as to the fact that missionary service is required and is as necessary in Zion, or here at home, as it is abroad. Many people seem to be careless with reference to the proper training of their children. We see too many boys that are falling into very careless, if not into pernicious, ways and habits. Every missionary boy who returns from his mission full of faith and good desire should take it upon himself to become a savior as far as possible of his young and less experienced associates at home. When a returned missionary sees a boy falling into bad ways and is becoming accustomed to bad habits, he should feel that it is his duty to take hold of him, in connection with the presiding authorities of the stake or of the ward in which he lives, and exercise all the power and influence he can for the salvation of that erring young man who has not the experience that our elders abroad have had, and thus become a means of saving many and of establishing them more firmly in the truth.—Oct. C. R., 1914, pp. 4-5.

WORK FOR RETURNED MISSIONARIES. Returned missionaries ought to be in demand where brave hearts, strong minds and willing hands are wanted. The genius of the gospel is not that of negative goodness—mere absence of what is bad; it stands for aggressive energy well directed, for positive goodness—in short, for work.

We hear much of men who are specially gifted, of geniuses in the world's affairs; and many of us force ourselves to think that we are capable of little and therefore may as well take life easy, since we do not belong to that favored class. True, not all are endowed with the same gifts, nor is every one imbued with the strength of a giant;

yet every son and every daughter of God has received some talent, and each will be held to strict account for the use or misuse to which it is put. The spirit of genius is the spirit of hard work, plodding toil, whole-souled devotion to the labor of the day.

Let no one think that any honorable labor is beneath him; harbor no dislike for the work of the hands, but let the mind direct them in skill and energy. The example set by our late beloved President Wilford Woodruff has often been cited abroad, and held up for the admiration and emulation of those who are not of us; it is that of most of the leading men of our Church. Even in his old age he did his share of physical toil, and rejoiced in his ability to "hoe his row" and hold his own with his grandchildren on the farm.

"My son, be up and doing, and the Lord will be with thee."—*Juvenile Instructor*, Vol. 38, p. 689.

DUTY OF A PERSON CALLED ON A MISSION. When a man is called to go on a mission, and a field of labor is assigned to him, he should, I think, say in his heart, "Not my will be done, but thine, O Lord."—*Deseret Weekly News*, Vol. 33, 1884, p. 226.

CHAPTER XXI

FALSE TEACHINGS

THE DEVIL'S KNOWLEDGE. The devil knows the Father much better than we. Lucifer, the son of the morning, knows Jesus Christ, the Son of God, much better than we; but in him it is not and will not redound to eternal life; for knowing, he yet rebels; knowing, he is yet disobedient; he will not receive the truth; he will not abide in the truth; hence he is perdition, and there is no salvation for him. The same doctrine applies to me and to you and all the sons and daughters of God who have judgment and knowledge and are able to reason between cause and effect, and determine the right from the wrong, and the good from the evil, and who are capable of seeing the light and distinguishing it from the darkness. Then this is the gospel of Jesus Christ, to know the only true and living God and his Son whom he has sent into the world, which knowledge comes through obedience to all his commandments, faith, repentance of sin, baptism by immersion for the remission of sins, the gift of the Holy Ghost by the laying on of hands by divine authority, and not by the will of man.—*Apr. C. R., 1916, p. 4.*

THE ENEMY OF TRUTH ALWAYS ARRAYED AGAINST THIS WORK. From the day that the Prophet Joseph Smith first declared his vision until now, the enemy of all righteousness, the enemy of truth, of virtue, of honor, uprightness, and purity of life, the enemy of the only true God, the enemy to direct revelation from God and to the inspirations that come from the heavens to man has been arrayed against this work.—*Apr. C. R., 1909, p. 4.*

WHY THE TRUTH IS HATED. Why should men be embittered against you because of this, because of your belief in Joseph Smith? Why should they become your enemies because you declare your faith in a new revelation from the Father and from the Son to mankind for their guidance? Why should they? Let me tell you why: for the very same reason precisely that the embittered and unbelieving Pharisees and hypocrites of the Savior's time persecuted the Redeemer of earth, for the very reason that they later put to death the disciples of Jesus Christ, whom he ordained as apostles and as special witnesses of himself, who bore testimony of him and of the gospel to all the nations of the earth. They put them to death one by one, some of

them in the most cruel manner, simply because they preached Jesus
Christ, and him crucified and risen from the dead, and ascended into
heaven, and sitting with all glory and power and majesty and might
at the right hand of his Father, God. The world felt injured by it.
Why? Because it laid the ax at the root of the tree of error, of superstition, and of tradition, of lack of faith, and unbelief. It laid the
ax at the root of the tree of wickedness, in the world, and of ignorance
of God and his principles, and the plan of life and salvation, and the
world hated the disciples, because of it, and they hated the Son of
God because of it, and they crucified him. They hated the disciples
because of it, and they put them to death. That is why they hate
you, for the same reason; that is, those who do hate you, those who
have exercised their power, their will and their thoughts or minds
sufficiently to be imbued with the spirit of persecution and hatred
against the light and the truth.—Oct. C. R., 1911, p. 5.

ONLY THOSE WHO DENY THE FAITH CONTEND. You find the
spirit of contention only among apostates and those who have denied
the faith, those who have turned away from the truth and have
become enemies to God and his work. There you will find the spirit
of contention, the spirit of strife. There you will find them wanting
to "argue the question," and to dispute with you all the time. Their
food, their meat, and their drink is contention which is abominable
in the sight of the Lord. We do not contend. We are not contentious, for if we were we would grieve the Spirit of the Lord from us,
just as apostates do and have always done.—Apr. C. R., 1908, p. 7.

BEWARE OF FALSE TEACHERS. I know that this is the work of
God, and he is carrying it on. The honor of triumph over error, sin
and injustice will belong to God and not to you or me, or any other
man. Some men there will be who would limit the power of God
to the power of men, and we have some of these among us and they
have been among our school teachers. They would have you disbelieve the inspired accounts of the Scriptures, that the winds and
the waves are subject to the power of God; and believe the claim of
the Savior to cast out devils, raise the dead, or perform miraculous
things, such as cleansing the leper, is only a myth. They would make
you believe that God and his Son Jesus Christ did not appear in
person to Joseph Smith, that this was simply a myth, but we know
better; the testimony of the Spirit has testified that this is the truth.
And I say, beware of men who come to you with heresies that things
come by laws of nature of themselves, and that God is without power.

I am thankful that men who make such claims are few in number in the world, and I hope they will become fewer still.—*Logan Journal,* April 7, 1914.

WHERE TO EXPECT FALSE DOCTRINE. Among the Latter-day Saints, the preaching of false doctrines disguised as truths of the gospel, may be expected from people of two classes, and practically from these only; they are:

First—The hopelessly ignorant, whose lack of intelligence is due to their indolence and sloth, who make but feeble effort, if indeed any at all, to better themselves by reading and study; those who are afflicted with a dread disease that may develop into an incurable malady—laziness.

Second—The proud and self-vaunting ones, who read by the lamp of their own conceit; who interpret by rules of their own contriving; who have become a law unto themselves, and so pose as the sole judges of their own doings. More dangerously ignorant than the first.

Beware of the lazy and the proud; their infection in each case is contagious; better for them and for all when they are compelled to display the yellow flag of warning, that the clean and uninfected may be protected.—*Juvenile Instructor,* Vol. 41, p. 178.

KNOWLEDGE OF SIN UNNECESSARY. It has been very wisely said that "the knowledge of sin tempteth to its commission."

It has been said that now and then the morbid curiosity of a missionary leads him into questionable places, and the only excuse he has for visiting these dens of vice is that he would like to see the shady side of life in some of our great cities that he may know thereof for himself. He wants to see "Paris by night" in order that he may know something of the actual life of vast numbers of his fellowmen. Such knowledge can have no beneficial effect upon the thoughts or feelings of the missionary who seeks it. It does not strengthen him in the duties of his calling. It is a peculiar sort of knowledge that is enticing to the feelings and imaginations, and tends in some measure to degrade the soul.

It is not necessary that our young people should know of the wickedness carried on in any place. Such knowledge is not elevating, and it is quite likely that more than one young man can trace the first step of his downfall to a curiosity which led him into questionable places. Let the young men of Zion, whether they be on missions or whether they be at home, shun all dens of infamy. It is not necessary that they should know what is going on in such places. No man is better or stronger for such knowledge. Let them remember that "the knowledge of sin tempteth to its commission," and then avoid those temptations that in time to come may threaten their virtue and their standing in the Church of Christ.—*Juvenile Instructor*, Vol. 37, May, 1902, p. 304.

RETREAT FROM EVIL. Sometimes in life, we are brought face to face with an enemy whose evil ways are beyond our power of combat, a victory over which cannot be hoped for. There is only one escape from moral annihilation and that is in retreat. The man with accumulated and unforgiven wrong behind him may find all retreat cut off and his condition in the world hopeless; and he who recklessly cuts off every opportunity of retreat by the neglected evils of the past is most unfortunate.

The daily practice, then, of seeking divine mercy and forgiveness as we go along, gives us power to escape evils, that can be overcome only by a safe retreat from them.—*Juvenile Instructor*, Vol. 44, August, 1909, p. 339.

THE LAW OF RECOMPENSE. Let me impress it upon you that one never can hold quite the same relation to a law of God which he has transgressed, as if one has lived in conformity with its requirements. It is unreasonable to expect it, and contrary to the laws of nature to conclude that you can. If a person has determined that sin can easily be wiped out, and hence, that he will enjoy unlawful pleasures in youth, repenting in later life, with an idea in his mind that repentance will blot out completely the results of his sin and debauchery, and place him on a level with his fellow who has kept in virtue the commandments, from the beginning—time will wake him up to his serious and great mistake. He may and will be forgiven, if he repent; the blood of Christ will make him free, and will wash him clean, though his sins be as scarlet; but all this will not return to him any loss sustained, nor place him on an equal footing with his neighbor who has kept the commandments of the better law. Nor will it place him in the position where he would have been, had he not committed wrong. He has lost something which can never be regained, notwithstanding the perfection, the loving mercy, the kindness and forgiveness of the Lord God.—*Improvement Era*, Vol. 7, January, 1904, p. 225.

SYMPATHY WITH CRIMINALS. There is a deplorable tendency among the people of this nation to sympathize with murderers, bank defaulters, evil adventurers, and a hundred other classes of criminals who are at large or who have been arrested or convicted for breaking the law. Such a tendency is not alone manifest among the people of the various states and territories of our nation, it is also apparent among the Latter-day Saints. This sympathy for criminals is entirely abnormal, and has a tendency to lower and destroy the moral sentiment of any people who indulge in it. For a Latter-day Saint to sympathize either with crime or with criminals, is a burning shame, and it is high time that the teachers of the community should stem such tendency and inculcate a sentiment that would make it extremely abhorrent to commit crime. Young men may please God by thinking right, by acting right, by shunning, as they would destruction, not only every crime, but the spirit either to see or sympathize with the criminal, or to hear or read the details of his damnable acts. It is an old saying, that we are what we think; then, to be a good Latter-day Saint it is necessary to think pure thoughts, to imbibe pure ideas, and to let the mind dwell continually upon the noble things, and the good deeds, and the exalted thoughts of life, discarding all sympathy or interest for crime and criminals, and all thought of evil. The man or woman who will resort to the court room, who will visit criminals with flowers, who will read and constantly discuss every detail of crime, should be condemned, frowned upon, and their actions should be made detestable in the eyes of the pure in heart. When a murderer is condemned, he should be detested, dropped, and forgotten; and so also should criminals of other classes who sin grievously against law and the commandments of God.—*Improvement Era*, Vol. 5, August, 1902, p. 803.

THE CRIME OF WITCHCRAFT AND OTHER SUPERSTITIONS. After all the horrors, persecutions, and cruelties that have been brought about by the senseless belief in witchcraft, it seems strange in this age of enlightenment that men or women, especially those who have received the gospel, can be found anywhere who believe in such a pernicious superstition. The Bible and history alike conclusively brand this superstition as a child of evil. In ancient times, God required the Israelites to drive the Canaanites from their land, and witchcraft was one of the crimes which he laid at the door of the Canaanites, and for which they were adjudged unworthy of the land which they possessed.

Witchcraft has not infrequently been the last resort of the evil doer. Men bereft of the Spirit of God, when the voice of the Lord has ceased to warn them, have frequently resorted to witchcraft, in the endeavor to learn that which Heaven withheld; and the people of God from very early days to the present have been troubled with superstitious and evil-minded persons who have resorted to divination and kindred devices for selfish purposes, and scheming designs. In the middle ages it rested like a nightmare upon all Christendom.

Let it not be forgotten that the evil one has great power in the earth, and that by every possible means he seeks to darken the minds of men, and then offers them falsehood and deception in the guise of truth. Satan is a skilful imitator, and as genuine gospel truth is given the world in ever-increasing abundance, so he spreads the counterfeit coin of false doctrine. Beware of his spurious currency, it will purchase for you nothing but disappointment, misery and spiritual death. The "father of lies" he has been called, and such an adept has he become, through the ages of practice in his nefarious work, that were it possible he would deceive the very elect.

Those who turn to soothsayers and wizards for their information are invariably weakening their faith. When men began to forget the God of their fathers who had declared himself in Eden and subsequently to the later patriarchs, they accepted the devil's substitute and made for themselves gods of wood and stone. It was thus that the abominations of idolatry had their origin.

The gifts of the Spirit and the powers of the holy Priesthood are of God, they are given for the blessing of the people, for their encouragement, and for the strengthening of their faith. This Satan knows full well, therefore he seeks by imitation-miracles to blind and deceive the children of God. Remember what the magicians of Egypt accomplished in their efforts to deceive Pharaoh as to the divinity of the mission of Moses and Aaron. John the Revelator saw in vision the miracle-working power of the evil one. Note his words. "And I beheld another beast coming up out of the earth; * * * and he doeth great wonders, so that he maketh fire come down from heaven on the earth in the sight of men. And deceiveth them that dwell on the earth, by the means of those miracles," etc. (Rev. 13:11-14.) Further, John saw three unclean spirits whom he describes as "the spirits of devils, working miracles." (Rev. 16:13-14.)

That the power to work wonders may come from an evil source is declared by Christ in his prophecy regarding the great judgment: "Many will say to me in that day, Lord, Lord, have we not prophesied in thy name? and in thy name have cast out devils? and in thy name done many wonderful works? And then will I profess unto them, I never knew you; depart from me, ye that work iniquity." (Matt. 7:22-23.)

The danger and power for evil in witchcraft is not so much in the witchcraft itself as in the foolish credulence that superstitious people give to the claims made in its behalf. It is outrageous to believe that the devil can hurt or injure an innocent man or woman, especially if they are members of the Church of Christ—without that man or woman has faith that he or she can be harmed by such an influence and by such means. If they entertain such an idea, then they are liable to succumb to their own superstitions. There is no power in witchcraft itself, only as it is believed in and accepted.—*Juvenile Instructor*, Vol. 37, p. 560.

SUPERSTITIOUS PRACTICES. It is needless to assert that to those who are intelligent, and not bound by old notions and superstitions, there is no truth in what people call witchcraft. Men and women who come under the influence of a belief therein are bewitched by their own foolishness, and are led astray by pretenders and mischief-makers who "peep and mutter." It is really astonishing that there should be any to believe in these absurdities. No man or woman who enjoys the Spirit of God and the influence and power of the holy Priesthood can believe in these superstitious notions, and those who do, will lose, indeed have lost, the influence of the Spirit of God and of the Priesthood, and are become subject to the witchery of Satan, who is constantly striving to draw away the Saints from the true way, if not by the dissemination of such nonsense, then by other insidious methods.

One individual can not place an affliction upon another in the way that these soothsayers would have the people believe. It is a trick of Satan to deceive men and women, and to draw them away from the Church and from the influence of the Spirit of God, and the power of his holy Priesthood, that they may be destroyed. These peepstone-men and women are inspired by the devil, and are the real witches, if any such there be. Witchcraft, and all kindred evils, are solely the creations of the superstitious imaginations of men and women who are steeped in ignorance, and derive their power over people from the devil, and those who submit to this influence are deceived by him. Unless they repent, they will be destroyed. There is absolutely no possibility for a person who enjoys the Holy Spirit of God even to believe that such influences can have any effect upon him. The enjoyment of the Holy Spirit is absolute proof against all influences of evil; you never can obtain that Spirit by seeking diviners, and men and women who "peep and mutter." That is obtained by imposition of hands by the servants of God, and retained by right living. If you have lost it, repent and return to God, and for your salvation's sake and for the sake of your children, avoid the emissaries of Satan who "peep and mutter" and who would lead you down to darkness and death.

It is impossible for anyone possessing the spirit of the gospel and having the power of the holy Priesthood to believe in or be influenced by any power of necromancy.—*Improvement Era*, Vol. 5, September, 1902, pp. 896-899.

THE MESSIAH CRAZE. Your communication has been received. In response, I send you a few of my reflections on the subject of the so-called "Messiah craze" among the Lamanites.

Just what these manifestations have been is a matter of some doubt, in my mind, not as to their evident purpose, judging from the many newspaper reports of the main features of the manifestations so much talked about, for it seems clear that the purpose or object thereof has been to awaken in the benighted minds of these degenerate people a belief and faith in and ultimately a knowledge of a crucified and risen Redeemer, and the righteous precepts which he taught.

That God will manifest his purposes to the Lamanites in his own time and way there can be no doubt in the minds of those who believe in the divine origin of the Book of Mormon—for in that book this fact is made unmistakably clear, but just how he will do so in every particular, and just what agencies he will use to bring about his purposes in this regard, may be matters of conjecture beyond what has actually been revealed. One of the agencies, we know, will be the Book of Mormon itself. Through the medium of the holy Priesthood, which has been restored to the earth in these latter times, God will also operate to accomplish his will. So far, however, but little of good has been effected through either of these channels, on account of the extremely benighted condition of the minds, and the wild nomadic habits of the red men. And for many other sufficient reasons they have not been susceptible to the impressions of the Holy Spirit, nor capable of rising to the comprehension of its power.

The time had not come, and is not yet come, for them to

receive the message and the work bequeathed them by their fathers, as designed of God—but the time will come, and may be nearer at hand than many anticipate. That these supernatural manifestations, if they indeed are such, indicate the beginning of that time may without inconsistency be believed. To suppose that the work will be accomplished in a day—or in any very brief period—would be folly. God has not heretofore worked, nor will he be likely to so work among this remnant of his people. Their fall and degradation came slowly, by degrees, and in like manner will their redemption, doubtless, come to pass. Yet he will cut his work short in righteousness, and it behooves the Saints always to be ready.

That the Lord will hasten their enlightenment by means of dreams, visions, and heavenly manifestations, when the time shall come, and that holy messengers may appear to them from time to time, and that among them shall yet be inspired men of God raised up as teachers to instruct them in the truth, we cannot doubt, for these things have been promised in the last times both in the Book of Mormon and in the Bible, and also in the revelations to Joseph Smith the prophet. But all these things will come to pass as God has determined, in his own time and way. And blessed will he be who shall be worthy to bear the message of good tidings and the offering of peace, the word of God and the means of redemption to the seed of Joseph, to whom the promises are made, and woe to him who shall despise and scoff in the day of God's power.

With reference to who the personage is (one or more) who is claimed by the Lamanites to have visited them, there appears to me to be room for grave doubts. From all the reports I have seen upon this subject, it is not at all conclusive to my mind that he was indeed the Messiah. Upon this point we must consider the sources of our information; it has come to us second handed, through interpreters and writers whose knowledge of the Lamanitish tongues may or may not be very imperfect, who have absolutely no knowledge of the ancient history of the race, and of the purposes and promises of God concerning them. That they know the scriptural account of Jesus, the Son of God, his crucifixion, resurrection, and ascension on high, with the promise to come again in like manner as he ascended, and this only, we need not question, but knowing only this and nothing more respecting this matter, they might easily be misled by the reports coming from persons far removed from the actual witnesses.

And yet a Latter-day Saint, who knows something of the

history of those people and of the promises made to them by their
forefathers, hearing the same story, would conclude that perhaps
one or more of the three Nephite disciples who tarried, whose mission
was to minister to the remnants of their own race, had made an
appearance to Porcupine and perhaps to many others, and taught
them Jesus and him crucified and risen from the dead, and that he
was soon to come again in power and great glory to avenge them of
their wrongs upon the wicked and restore them to their lands and
to the knowledge of their fathers and of the Son of God.

This would be a very natural conclusion and not at all inconsistent with the established principles of the gospel and our knowledge
of the manner of God's dealings with the children of men. While
it is more than likely that Christ might send messengers to the
Lamanites to prepare the way for his coming in the fulness of time,
it is highly improbable that Christ himself would appear to a people
so utterly unprepared to receive and comprehend him.

True, the Father and the Son appeared to the boy Joseph in the
beginning of this dispensation, but he was a chosen instrument from
eternity to open up the last dispensation of the gospel, and God had
prepared a chosen band to join him in that work. But Moroni, Peter,
James and John, and divers other messengers were sent to open the
way and prepare the foundations of this great work and restore the
records of the ancient people of this continent to the world. The
foundations of that work having been laid, the authority of God
established, the order of the Priesthood and the laws of the Church
revealed, shall we look for these things to be ignored, or for the
knowledge of God to come through the appointed channels?

While they will come in harmony with revealed and established
truth, and not in conflict therewith, nor in conflict with the order of
heaven which exists on the earth, the object to be attained by such
manifestations as the Lamanites claim to have had, admitting the
same to be true and from God, can be no other than to begin the
preparation of the Lamanites to receive a correct knowledge of God
and of their fathers, and of the holy gospel already revealed and
established among men, that they might believe, obey and be saved
thereby.

Far be it from me to wish to close the channels of communication
between the Savior of the world himself and the remnants of Lehi.
No one can be more free to admit his perfect right and power to visit
whom he pleases, at his pleasure, for the channels of communication

between God and man cannot be cut off nor closed by man, nor ever will be while God has a purpose to accomplish by revealing himself. But that we may not be deceived, led into error, tossed to and fro by every wind of doctrine, the foolish vagaries or the cunning craftiness of men, or follow the false cry of, Lo, here is Christ, or there, God has instituted the true order of communication between himself and man, and has established it in his Church, and to this truth all mankind will do well to take heed, lest they be deceived. That which is in harmony with this is of God, that which is contrary to it is from beneath. It is in perfect harmony with the order of heaven for ministering spirits or messengers from God or Christ to visit the Lamanites or any other people, as Cornelius of old was visited, and as Christ visited Saul, and for the same purposes.—Letter to Editor of *Young Woman's Journal* in answer to question regarding reported visitations to Indians. *Young Woman's Journal*, Vol. 2, 1890-1891, pp. 268-271.

ONE MIGHTY AND STRONG. In conclusion we would say that the Latter-day Saints by this time should be so well settled in the conviction that God has established his Church in the earth for the last time, to remain, and no more to be thrown down or destroyed; and that God's house is a house of order, of law, of regularity, that erratic disturbers of that order of men of restless temperament, who, through ignorance and egotism, become vain babblers, yet make great pretensions to prophetic powers and other spiritual graces and gifts, ought not to have any influence with them, nor ought the Saints to be disturbed in their spirit by such characters and their theories. The Church of Christ is with the Saints. It has committed to it the law of God for its own government and perpetuation. It possesses every means for the correction of every wrong or abuse or error which may from time to time arise, and that without anarchy, or even revolution; it can do it by process of evolution—by development, by an increase of knowledge, wisdom, patience and charity.

The presiding quorums of the Church will always be composed of such men, they will be chosen in such manner, that the Saints can be assured that solid wisdom, righteousness, and conscientious adherence to duty, will characterize the policy of those who are entrusted with the administration of the affairs of the Church. While, from time to time, as the work of the Lord may have need of their services, men of exceptional talents and abilities will develop among the people of God; and without disorder or eruption or excitement

they will be called of the Lord through the appointed agencies of the
Priesthood and Church authority, to positions that will afford them
opportunity for service.   They will be accepted by the Saints in the
regular order, appointed by the law of the Church, just as Edward
Partridge was called and accepted, and just as the "one mighty and
strong" will be called and accepted when the time comes for his
services.

JOSEPH F. SMITH,
JOHN R. WINDER,
ANTHON H. LUND,
First Presidency.

—Improvement Era, Vol. 10, 1906-1907, pp. 929-943.

CHAPTER XXII

AUXILIARY ORGANIZATIONS

DEFINITIONS OF AUXILIARY ORGANIZATIONS. I have in mind our auxiliary organizations; what are they? Helps to the standard organizations of the Church. They are not independent. I want to say to the Young Men's and Young Ladies' Mutual Improvement Associations, and to the Relief Society, and to the Primaries, and to the Sunday Schools, and Religion classes, and all the rest of the organizations in the Church, that not one of them is independent of the Priesthood of the Son of God, not any of them can exist a moment in the acceptance of the Lord when they withdraw from the voice and from the counsel of those who hold the Priesthood and preside over them. They are subject to the powers and authority of the Church, and they are not independent of them; nor can they exercise any rights in their organizations independently of the Priesthood and of the Church.—Apr. C. R., 1913, p. 7.

PLACE OF AUXILIARY ORGANIZATIONS IN THE CHURCH. It is sometimes argued that the auxiliary organizations of the Church are not councils of the Priesthood. This is admitted, but, on the other hand, the boards—general, stake and ward—are composed of men holding the Priesthood and, though being called to be an officer in an auxiliary organization confers no additional office in the Priesthood, it takes none away—the brother still remains a high priest, seventy, or elder as before. Furthermore, the officers of these organizations are duly presented at the general or local conferences, as the case may be, and are there sustained by the vote of the people, and by that vote, these organizations become recognized institutions of the Church, and as such the officers should be respected in their callings and given recognition and support in the performances of their duties in all that relates to the bodies which they represent.

The principles laid down in the foregoing relating to the Sunday Schools apply equally to all auxiliary organizations of the Church.—Juvenile Instructor, Vol. 39, January 1, 1904, pp. 17-18.

RELATION BETWEEN AUTHORITIES OF WARD AND AUXILIARY ORGANIZATIONS. Questions are frequently asked touching the relationship that should exist between the presiding authorities of a ward and the authorities of an auxiliary organization, such, for example, as the superintendent of the Sunday School. The organizations of the Church are intended to promote harmony, and if understood there is no reason why discord should arise between the bishop and those called upon to act in the auxiliary organizations. The question is often asked, for instance, who should select and install a superintendent of a Sunday School, or what step should be taken in cases where the superintendent of a school for any reason whatever vacates his office. The first step in case the superintendent vacates his office is for his first or second assistant, as the case may be, to request the secretary of the school either to notify or remind the bishop of the ward of the vacancy, and at the same time notify the stake superintendent of Sunday Schools; and this notice or reminder should be given to the bishop and stake superintendent at the earliest possible convenience in order that all unnecessary delays may be avoided. The second step in such cases is the selection of the proper officer or officers to fill the vacancy or vacancies. It is, of course, within the authority of the bishop of a ward to select and install the superintendent of the Sunday School in his ward, but bishops of wards should not take such a step without the co-operation of the stake superintendent. This last named officer represents the presidency of the stake in carrying on the work of this auxiliary organization of the Church. The stake presidency holds the stake superintendent responsible in a large measure for the character of the man and the progress of the work of the Sunday Schools throughout the stake, and the bishop therefore who proceeds to select and install the ward superintendent without the approval or knowledge of the stake superintendent, does not show proper respect for him or for the stake president, who is entitled to be represented in the selection of a ward superintendent. On the other hand, a stake superintendent is not authorized to organize the superintendency of a Sunday School without consulting the bishop of the ward, with whom it is his duty to be in complete harmony. There is wisdom, as well as order, in the mutual recognition of these stake and ward authorities. In the first place, the superintendent, by reason of his experience in Sunday School work, and his knowledge of the special qualifications required, may be, from his point of view, well qualified to make suitable recommendations. On the other hand, the bishop is, or at any rate should be, more familiar than any one else with the character and daily lives of the members of his ward. After satisfying the special requirements made by a stake superintendent there may be wanting in the proposed ward superintendent some indispensable character-istics, or there may be some unworthiness known only to the bishop. If the stake superintendent, therefore, and the bishop of the ward approach each other in a spirit of harmony and mutual helpfulness, there is no reason why they may not be united in nearly every instance upon the most suitable man. Should a case arise in which the bishop and stake superintendent find themselves unable to agree, or both wish to defer to the judgment of some higher authority, the proper step to take is to submit the matter to the president of the stake for his judgment or decision, as the case may be. When such an agree-ment has been arrived at, it is the duty of the bishop to install the new superintendent in his office.

In connection with the subject here touched upon a question has also arisen respecting the propriety of a bishop presiding over a Sunday School when the superintendent is present. If I were bishop I should recognize with scrupulous care all the presiding officers in my ward and should think it discourteous to them to assume the duties to which they had been called. There are without doubt instances where the bishops can with propriety offer suggestions that will be helpful to the superintendent without the least humiliation to him; and there may be extreme cases in which the bishop would be justified in assuming the control of a school but it should not be the rule. On the other hand if I were a school superintendent I would show the greatest deference to the bishop whenever he was present and aim as far as possible to satisfy his wishes and make the school all he could desire it should be.—*Juvenile Instructor*, Vol. 39, January, 1904, pp. 16-17.

PURPOSE AND DUTIES OF RELIEF SOCIETY. A word or two in relation to the Relief Society. This is an organization that was established by the Prophet Joseph Smith. It is, therefore, the oldest auxiliary organization of the Church, and it is of the first importance. It has not only to deal with the necessities of the poor, the sick and the needy, but a part of its duty—and the larger part, too—is to look after the spiritual welfare and salvation of the mothers and daughters of Zion; to see that none is neglected, but that all are guarded against misfortune, calamity, the powers of darkness, and the evils that threaten them in the world. It is the duty of the Relief Societies to look after the spiritual welfare of themselves and of all the female members of the Church. It is their duty to collect means from those who have in abundance, and to distribute it wisely unto those in need. It is a part of their duty to see that there are those capable of being nurses as well as teachers and exemplars in Zion, and that they have an opportunity to become thoroughly prepared for this great labor and responsibility. I have heard of a disposition on the part of some of our sisters to become a law unto themselves in relation to these things. I would like to say that it is expected of the Relief Society, especially the general authorities of that great organization, that they will have a watchcare over all its organizations among the women of Zion. They stand at the head of all such; they ought to stand at the head, and they should magnify their calling, and see to it that error is not permitted to creep in, that cabals are not formed, that secret combinations may not get a foothold, to mislead the sisters. They should see to it that the other organizations of women in the Church correspond and are in harmony with their organizations. Why should this be? In order that the women of Zion may be united, that their interests may be in common, and not conflicting or segregated, and that the purpose of this organization may be realized and the organization itself be effective for good in every part of the Church throughout the world, wherever the gospel is preached. We realize that it is impossible for men or women possessing physical weaknesses on account of age or infirmities, to meet every requirement; but we expect every man and woman entrusted with responsibility in the Church to do their duty to the utmost of their ability. That we look for; that we pray for; for that we labor to the best of the ability and strength we possess.—*Apr. C. R.*, 1906, pp. 3-4.

OBJECTS OF THE RELIEF SOCIETY. Furthermore, I desire to commend the work of the Relief Society, an organization that was effected by the Prophet Joseph Smith. The objects of this organization are manifold. It is not designed to look only after the poor and the needy as to their bodily necessities, but it is also intended to look after the spiritual, mental and moral welfare of the mothers and daughters in Zion, and all who are engaged or interested in female work. I commend the Relief Societies to the bishops, and say, be friendly to these organizations, because they are auxiliary organizations and a great help to the bishops.—*Oct. C. R.*, 1902, p. 88 .

DUTIES AND PURPOSE OF THE RELIEF SOCIETY. I will speak of the Relief Society as one great organization in the Church, organized by the Prophet Joseph Smith, whose duty it is to look after the interests of all the women of Zion and of all the women that may come under their supervision and care, irrespective of religion, color or condition. I expect to see the day when this organization will be one of the most perfect, most efficient and effective organizations for good in the Church but that day will be when we shall have women who are not only imbued with the spirit of the gospel of Jesus Christ, and with the testimony of Christ in their hearts, but also with youth, vigor and intelligence to enable them to discharge the great duties and responsibilities that rest upon them. Today it is too much the case that our young, vigorous, intelligent women feel that only the aged should be connected with the Relief Society. This is a mistake. We want the young women, the intelligent women, women of faith, of courage and of purity to be associated with the Relief Societies of the various stakes and wards of Zion. We want them to take hold of this work with vigor, with intelligence and unitedly, for the building up of Zion and the instruction of women in their duties—domestic duties, public duties, and every duty that may devolve upon them. —Apr. C. R., 1907, p. 6.

THE RELIEF SOCIETY. I can say the same with reference to the first and most important auxiliary organization of the Church, that of the Relief Society. They have been doing the best they could; but now we have suggested a complete organization of that society, that is, the general authorities of that organization; and we trust that from this time forth, they will be able to begin with renewed energy, judgment and wisdom, the performance of the duties that devolve upon them, even those who are called to take the oversight of this great work in Zion, the Relief Society organization.—Apr. C. R., 1911, p. 7.

OBJECT OF SUNDAY SCHOOLS AND CHURCH SCHOOLS. The object of our Sunday Schools and the object of our Church schools, the great, the paramount object, is to teach our children the truth, teach them to be honorable, pure-minded, virtuous, honest and upright, and enable them, by our advice and counsel and by our guardianship over them, until they reach the years of accountability, to become the honorable of the earth, the good and the pure among mankind, the virtuous and the upright, and those who shall be worthy to enter the house of God and not be ashamed of themselves in the presence of angels, if they should come to visit them.—Apr. C. R., 1903, p. 82.

THE TEACHER ESSENTIAL IN SUNDAY SCHOOL WORK. One of the essentials to a good Sunday School is to have good, pure-minded, intelligent, noble, true and faithful teachers. If you will have a child develop to what he should be, he that teaches the child should be developed to what he ought to be, and until he is developed in intelligence, in faith, in works of righteousness, in purity of heart and mind and spirit, he is not in a very good position to elevate others to it.— *Oct. C. R.*, 1903, p. 99.

THE FIRST QUALIFICATION OF A SUNDAY SCHOOL TEACHER. The first qualification of a teacher in our Sunday Schools is that he be heart and soul a Latter-day Saint. He must believe in and unreservedly accept the doctrines of the Church, otherwise his teachings will be subversive of the very purpose for which these schools are maintained.

It is a self-evident truth, that no one can give what he does not possess, and the teacher who is lacking a testimony of the gospel can never inspire such testimony in his pupils.

The measure of personal liberty allowed by our liberal Church organization in the matter of giving instruction is great but such liberty must not be degraded into a license to teach as the doctrines of the Church what is but the personal belief of the individual. A teacher finding himself a non-believer in any of the principles or tenets of the Church, will, if he be truly honorable, voluntarily ask release from his position. No one can in righteousness be asked to teach what he does not believe and accept as the truth, nor will one who is sincere in his convictions attempt to do so; still less will any teacher who loves the truth dishonor his position by employing its opportunities to inculcate personal views not in harmony with the teachings of the Church.—*Juvenile Instructor*, Vol. 49, April 1, 1914, p. 210.

THE PRINCIPLE OF SABBATH SCHOOL TEACHING. There is one point that has rested upon my mind in relation to the Sabbath Schools, and it is this: I think there is nothing in the Sunday School work more necessary or essential than that all the teachers of the Sunday Schools should win the love and the confidence of their pupils. I believe that greater good can be done in the Sunday Schools by the teachers where they have the absolute affection and confidence of their pupils than under any other conditions. You may teach them, you may drill them in concert, and you may have them commit to memory, and labor in every other way that you possibly can to accomplish the good that you desire with your children, but in nothing, in my opinion, can you succeed so well as when you possess their undivided love and confidence. If a child thinks a teacher is harsh with him or her, or unkind toward him, or does not feel a real, genuine love for him, if he feels that the teacher is not taking a real interest in him as one who loves him, he can never be led to possess the right spirit; but when he feels that the teacher loves him, is trying to do him good and to teach him that which will be for his everlasting welfare, then the teacher has an influence over the child, that when he studies he will study with a purpose and with an earnest desire to be benefited and to please the teacher; because he knows and feels in his little heart that the teacher loves him and is seeking to do him good. I have entertained this sentiment from the beginning, in relation to the instruction of the little children. It is a principle that obtains at the home as well as in the Sunday School. If you can only convince your children that you love them, that your soul goes out to them for their good, that you are their truest friend, they, in turn, will place confidence in you and will love you and seek to do your bidding and to carry out your wishes with your love. But if you are selfish, unkindly to them, and if they are not confident that they have your entire affection, they will be selfish, and will not care whether they please you or carry out your wishes or not, and the result will be that they will grow wayward, thoughtless and careless, and although you may drill them, like a parrot, to repeat verses and to speak in concert, and all that sort of thing, they will do it mechanically, without affection, and without its having that effect upon their souls that you desire it should have.—*Apr. C. R.*, 1902, pp. 97-98.

THE STAKE SUNDAY SCHOOL BOARD. As the General Sunday School Union Board represents the First Presidency of the Church and constitutes, under the direction of the Presidency and Council of the Twelve, the highest authority in the Church on Sunday School matters, so the Stake Board, under the direction of the Stake Presidency and General Sunday School Board, represents the highest authority in Sunday School work in the stake. If it were not so, there would be no unity.—*Juvenile Instructor*, Vol. 43, August, 1908, p. 310.

THE IMPORTANCE OF M. I. A. WORK. I want to say a few words to the Mutual Improvement Associations. You young men and young women, officers of the Mutual Improvement Associations, I implore you to go from this conference and do your duty. Look after the wayward, the disobedient, the thoughtless, and the indifferent. It is necessary that they should be guarded and looked after. As it has been expressed here, time and again, it is better for us to save our own boys who are being misled at home, than it is for us to go out into the world and spend years of time and endless means in order to gather in a few people from the world, while some of our own boys and girls need redemption as much as they; besides, these people of the world are so full of the traditions and superstitions of their fathers when they gather to Zion that it is difficult, if not impossible, for them entirely to overcome these traditions and get down to a full comprehension of the gospel and a complete reception of the truth. Yet a soul saved out in the world is as precious in the sight of God as a soul saved at home. But we have work to do right at home, at our own doors; and it will not do for us to neglect the work necessary to be done at our own thresholds, and then go out into the world to do work that is no more necessary. Let us do our duty everywhere.—Oct. C. R., 1902, p. 87.

THE FIELD OF THE YOUNG MEN'S MUTUAL IMPROVEMENT ASSOCIATION. The systematic work now being done by the quorums of priesthood provides our young men with the necessary teachings in formal theology and trains them in the duties that pertain to their callings in the Priesthood.

There is, however, a strong need among the young men of the Church to have an organization and meetings which they themselves conduct; in which they may learn to preside over public assemblies to obtain a practice necessary to express themselves before the public; and to enjoy themselves in studying and practicing civil, social, scientific, religious and educational affairs.

The Young Men's Mutual Improvement Associations, therefore, should be strengthened and their efficiency increased in order to offset and counteract the tendency now so prevalent to establish private clubs, secret and social organizations, and select educational societies.

They may be made to cover all these requirements, and it will be a wise policy to grant them the fullest liberty, consistent with the order and policy of the Church, in the selection of their officers, management and conduct of their associations.

It is of vital importance that not only the young men of our Church but also the regularly constituted stake and ward officers thereof shall have a clear understanding as to the place and privileges which the Mutual Improvement Associations hold among the Latter-day Saints, in order to promote harmony, union of purpose, and the best interests of all concerned.

To define this field and to give an understanding to our young people and all concerned, we deem it expedient that a declaration should be made at this our June conference, that there is as great opportunity now as ever before for these organizations, and that increased activity in other departments should cause no abatement of effort or efficiency in our associations; but rather that renewed effort should be put forth by the Improvement workers, and that every facility should be afforded them by stake and ward authorities to accomplish their glorious mission among the youth of Zion.

The field to be occupied is religious, social and educational. The religious work is not to be formally theological in its nature, but rather to be confined to the limits outlined by President Brigham Young, when the organizations were first established: "Let the key-note of your work be the establishment in the youth of an individual testimony of the truth and magnitude of the great Latter-day work; and the development of the gifts within them." In other words, to obtain a testimony of the truth, and to learn to declare and express that testimony; and to develop all noble gifts within them.

The social includes control of various public and private amuse-ments; musical, dramatic and other entertainments and festivals; field sports, athletic tournaments, excursions and other varieties of social gatherings.

The educational should include regular class work in ethics and practical religion, literature, science, history, biography, art, music, civil government—supplemented by debates, oratorical and musical contests, lectures, essays, writing for publication, reading and speaking under the auspices of the organization, and if necessary carried on in departments under instructors capable of specializing in their particu-lar lines.

We have directed the General Board to appoint committees to have in charge, under the direction of the whole Board, these various lines, who have a thorough knowledge of the work, and who are in sympathy with our young men.

These committees may be sub-divided or added to as the wisdom of the Board or the exigencies of the work may demand; and like organizations may be instituted in the various stakes and wards, as far as practicable or necessary. At the meetings of the Board reports from these committees will be asked for and given as a regular order of business.

We believe that this course will promote the welfare of all and a good feeling among our young people, and prevent their seeking other organizations and interests to which to devote their time and attention.

There is no mental, social or physical excellence or enjoyment that the Church does not foster and desire to promote among the young men of our community, and its purpose in sustaining the Mutual Improvement Associations and charging them with the care of our young men is to answer every desire of this nature and to provide among ourselves the gratification of every legitimate ambition and impulse to excel in these fields without having to seek opportunities elsewhere.

From the presiding priesthood of the Church in the stakes of Zion, and in the wards and missions, we therefore ask, in behalf of our young men, sympathy and support, to sustain and uphold the Young Men's Mutual Improvement Associations in the field of usefulness herein briefly outlined, and to provide them with places of meeting and amusement.

We ask that the associations be permitted to select men of education and ability for class and special teachers, who are suitable, agreeable and capable, and who are in love with the young people and in full sympathy with them and their views.

Granting them the fullest liberty consistent with the order and policy of the Church will encourage them in the faith, and they will not be a whit less amenable to the Church authorities, but rather will grow more enthusiastic in every way for the promotion of the work of the Lord. The Young Men's Mutual Improvement Associations have been from the first in very deed helps to the priesthood, and in behalf of its members we pledge ourselves and them to continue in this line in the future; being certain that no trust or added responsibility imposed upon our young people will be violated, but they will prove loyal to the authorities and the work of the Lord.

Respectfully,

JOESPH F. SMITH,
HEBER J. GRANT,
B. H. ROBERTS,
General Superintendency.

The foregoing Declaration of the Place and Privileges of the Young Men's Mutual Improvement Association was read and adopted at the Annual Conference, June 5, 1909.—*Improvement Era*, Vol. 12, August, 1909, p. 819.

PURPOSE OF MUTUAL IMPROVEMENT ASSOCIATIONS. Our work is

in one sense primary work, and yet it reaches beyond primary grades. The first and great object of the organization of the Mutual Improvement Associations as auxiliary organizations of the Priesthood in the Church was to become instrumental in bringing the youth of Zion to a knowledge of the truth, and in guiding them into the straight and narrow path. We have found that there is in some degree a feeling of shyness and of fear that seizes the minds of some of our youth when the organizations of the Priesthood are mentioned. Some of the children grow up more or less indifferent, more or less afraid of the responsibilities involved in the performances of the Church duties. They are like colts that need training, and it is difficult sometimes to reach them. But through these auxiliary organizations we have been able to reach out a guiding hand, and to exert an influence for good over many of our young men and women, whom it would have been difficult to reach by the organizations of the Priesthood. So far, these organizations have accomplished a most excellent primary work; for this is in the sense of a primary work, and I do not know but the necessity of our organizations will continue as long as we have children growing up amongst us who are shy of the Priesthood, and who are afraid of assuming the duties and responsibilities that belong to the Church.

Then we have instituted class work, have written manuals, and have given out subjects for study and improvement by all those who are connected with these organizations which have been intended to lead them along into greater experiences and better understanding of the principles of the gospel of Jesus Christ. For, after all, this is the great and grand object of these organizations.

The fact is, my brethren and sisters and friends, that the gospel of Christ is the biggest thing in the world. Very few of us, probably, comprehend its greatness. The way we are situated in life, engaged day in and day out, week in and week out, year in and year out, in the daily vocations of life; struggling to earn bread for our necessities, and the necessities of those who are dependent upon us, struggling to build homes for ourselves and our children; struggling to collect the elements of the earth and subdue them, and to bring them into subjection to our will; working, toiling, striving day by day in temporal things, in the cares and thoughts of the world, we are inclined to give very little thought, very little reflection to the more important things, those things which shall endure after mortality shall come to an end. And the most of mankind have come to the conclusion, judging them by their acts, and their walk and conversation in life, that the greatest thing in the world is to obtain wealth. And then, having obtained wealth and the things that wealth produces, or will bring to them, they feel that the rest of life and the responsibilities of it are very trifling and unimportant, and they leave their religion to their priests, if they have any religion at all. And the great majority of the world today, I believe, that is, on our hemisphere, are becoming very indifferent toward religion of any kind. The cheaper it can be found or obtained by them the better they like it; the less exertion required of them to be members of a church organization the better it suits them. The less care they are required to give to religion the better they like it; and if they can find something that will bring solace and ease and relaxation to an overburdened conscience for having committed crime in the thought that men possess power to forgive sin, that suits them about as well as anything else, and a little better. Hence we can see where the world is drifting today as far as religion is concerned. If they can get it cheap, if it does not cause them any exertion, they do not mind having just a little of it. But this is not the case with Latter-day Saints. Nor is it the case with a living religion. For I want to tell you that the religion of Christ is not a Sunday religion; it is not a momentary religion; it is a religion that never ends; and it requires duties of its devotees on Monday, Tuesday, Wednesday and all of the days of the week just as sincerely, just as strongly, as it does on the Sabbath day. And I would not give the ashes of a rye straw, for a Sunday religion, or for a religion that is manufactured by men, whether by priests or laymen. My religion is the religion of God. It is the religion of Jesus Christ, otherwise it would be absolutely worthless to me, and it would be worthless to all other men, so far as religion is concerned. If it is not in my soul, if I had not received it in my heart, or if I did not believe it with all my might, mind and strength and be it, live it, and keep it secure in my heart all the days of my life—week days as well as days of rest, in secret as well as in public, at home and abroad, everywhere the same; then the religion of Christ, the religion of well doing, the religion of righteousness, the religion of purity, the religion of kindliness, faith, salvation from temporal sins, and salvation and exaltation in the kingdom of our God—my religion would not be the gospel of the Son of God to me. This is "Mormonism;" and that is the kind of religion we want to teach to our children. We must receive it ourselves and teach it from our hearts to their hearts and from our affections to their affections, and we can then inspire them because of our own faith and our own faithfulness and convictions of the Church.

These organizations of young men and women are intended to help the wayward, giddy and wild; to work with those who are at large in the world, who are not subject to any organization at all; to gather them in; hunt them up, and get hold of them by love, by kindness, by the spirit of salvation, the spirit to bring them to a knowledge of the truth, that they may find the way of life and walk in it; that they may have light everlasting within themselves through the Spirit of God.

All truth cometh from the Lord. He is the fountain of truth; or in other words, he is the everlasting spring of life and truth, and from him cometh all knowledge, all wisdom, all virtue and all power. When I read books that are scattered broadcast through the world, throwing discredit upon words and teachings and doctrines of the Lord Jesus Christ, saying that some of the ideas Jesus uttered, truths that he promulgated, have been enunciated before by the ancient philosophers among the heathen nations of the world, I want to tell you that there is not a heathen philosopher that ever lived in all the world from the beginning, that had a truth or enunciated a principle of God's truth that did not receive it from the fountain head, from God himself. God knew the truth before any heathen philosopher. No man has received intelligence but has had to come to the Fountain Head. He may not have known it, may not have realized the source of his knowledge, but it came from God. God taught the first truth that was ever taught to man. The Lord has bestowed his truth upon the earth from generation to generation and he has visited the people in various ways, from age to age, according to the nearness with which he could draw them to himself. He has raised up philosophers among them, teachers of men, to set the example, and to develop the mind and understanding of the human race in all nations of the world. God did it, but the world do not give credit to God, but give it to men, to heathen philosophers. They give credit to them. I give it to God. And I tell you God knew the truth before they did, and through revelation they got it. If they received light at all they had it from God, just as Columbus got it from the Lord. What inspired Columbus with the spirit of unrest, the spirit of longing, with an intense desire that he could not overcome, to seek out this western hemisphere? Brethren and sisters, I acknowledge God's hand in it. It was inspiration that seized Columbus, and he was moved by it. But men do not acknowledge God's hand in it. In the Book of Mormon, we learn it was God's Spirit working upon him. The Lord moved upon Columbus and he could not restrain the influence that was upon him until he had accomplished the work. The same may be said of any intelligent man that has enlightened humanity, from the earliest ages down to the present time.

Let me say to you, my fellow workers in the cause of Zion, do not forget to acknowledge the hand of God in all things. He told the Jews that he had other sheep that were not of that fold, and that he must visit them. He did visit them. He came to the sheep of the fold occupying this continent, dwelling here unknown to the Jews, and he revealed the principles of the gospel to them. And when he visited them, he said, "Ye are they of whom I said, Other sheep I have which are not of this fold; them also I must bring, and they shall hear my voice; and there shall be one fold, and one shepherd." (III Nephi 15:21.)

Read in the Doctrine and Covenants of a parable in which the kingdom of God is likened unto a man with twelve servants working in his field, each having his portion called an allotment. The Lord visited the first and taught him the truth and cheered him up by his presence and voice and counsel; then he visited the second, then the third and so on until the twelfth, each in his time, each in his season, each according to his necessities. (Doctrine and Covenants 88:51-63.)

And so it has been with God from the foundation of the world. He has visited all nations, kindred, tongues, and people, and yet the truth has not been revealed to the world in its fulness, and men have not been called to do the work that Christ was called to do; nor the work that Abraham was called to do; nor that which Noah was appointed to do; nor that appointed to the twelve apostles to preach his name and proclaim his gospel to the world. They were called like Columbus to do work God required them to do. Later God revealed the power of steam to Watt, just as he has inspired every other philosopher and scientist and great man of the world. I acknowledge the hand of God in it. I give God the honor, the glory; and I know that it is in accordance with his purpose that he has inspired these things to be brought to pass. I believe that Mohammed was an inspired man and the Lord raised him up to do the work he did.

I believe God raised up Joseph Smith to lay the foundation of the gospel of Christ in the dispensation of the fulness of times; that it will remain and no more be broken up; but will continue until God's promises are accomplished in the world and Christ shall come and reign, whose right it is to reign in the midst of the earth. This is what I believe about it, and the Lord's hand was in the raising up of Joseph Smith to accomplish the work.

Joseph Smith was called to do this work; and he did it. He has been an instrument in the hands of God by giving each of us the power to obtain knowledge for ourselves through the mercy and love of God, and to become teachers of it to the world; teachers not only to our children, but to nations that are in darkness and know not the truth. And it is a living, daily religion, an hourly religion. It requires us to do right today, this hour, this week, this month and this year; and so on from year to year, to live our religion—which is the religion of Jesus Christ—of righteousness, of truth, of mercy, of love, forgiveness, kindness, union and peace on earth and good will to man and all the world. This is our mission.

May the Lord bless you, my brethren and sisters, and my fellow workers in the cause of Zion, is my prayer.—*Young Woman's Journal,* Vol. 18, 1907, pp. 312-315.

THE FOUNTAIN OF TRUTH. We hear frequently of men who throw discredit on the doctrine of Jesus Christ, our Savior and Redeemer, because some of the principles, doctrines, and philosophy which he taught are said to have been spoken before his day by heathen philosophers.

A variety of examples are sometimes quoted to show that Zoroaster and other ancient philosophers made known truths, and that the Old Testament, the Avesta, and other writings, contain sentiments, which were repeated, perhaps in slightly different form, by the Son of God. He taught nothing new, they say, and so they incline to belittle his mission, and accuse him of plagiarizing the truth.

It is conceded by a number of competent students that the ideals which have grown from the doctrines of Christ are a direct development of what is found in the teachings of the Old Testament, particularly in the Psalms and in the second part of Isaiah. But, on the other hand, it is just as certain that these ideals received a finish and an enrichment, by the touch of the Savior, vastly beyond and above what they possessed before, and also they are placed on deeper and firmer foundations. This, let it be said to begin with, is because they were his before they were ever uttered by man.

Even in the five distinctive and characteristic topics generally considered by commentators original in the teachings of Jesus, we find little if anything new, except the enlargement. These are named as the Fatherhood of God; subjects or members of the Kingdom; the Messiah; the Holy Ghost; and the Tri-Unity of God.

But the idea of the Fatherhood of God was not unknown either to the Pagans or to Israel. Zeus from the time of Homer had borne the name "Father of gods and men." But, both in Jewish and Pagan literature, the idea was superficial and meant little more than "originator" (Genesis 1:26); and in the old Jewish scripture God is more particularly called the Father of his people, Israel. (Deut. 14:1; Isaiah 63:6) But in the teachings of Christ there is a fuller embodiment of revelation in the word Father, and the application which he makes of the Fatherhood of God invests his life with supreme tenderness and beauty. As an example: In the old scriptures, we are told, "Like as a father pitieth his children, so the Lord pitieth them that fear him;" (Psalms 103:13), but by the interpretation of Jesus, the love of God as Father extends beyond these limitations even to those who are unthankful and evil: "But I say unto you, love your enemies, bless them that curse you, do good to them that hate you, and pray for them which despitefully use you, and persecute you; that ye may be the children of our Father which is in heaven; for he maketh his sun to rise on the evil and on the good, and sendeth rain on the just and the unjust." (Matt. 5:45.) "But love ye your enemies, and do good, and lend, hoping for nothing again; and your reward shall be great, and ye shall be the children of the Highest; for he is kind unto the unthankful and to the evil." (Luke 6:35.)

And so with other doctrines of Christ; while perhaps not new, they were enriched by the addition of fuller, broader, more loving conceptions of God and his purposes; in which compulsion was eliminated, and lowly service, love, and self-sacrifice were substituted and made the true forces of an acceptable life. Even the answer to the lawyer's question, often called the eleventh commandment, "Master, which is the great commandment in the law?" had been given to the children of Israel, (Lev. 19:18) over two thousand years before its perfected meaning was impressed upon the learned Pharisee. (Matt. 22:34, 40.)

But what of all this? Are we therefore to discredit the teachings of the Savior? Verily no. Let it be remembered that Christ was with the Father from the beginning, that the gospel of truth and light existed from the beginning, and is from everlasting to everlasting. The Father, Son, and Holy Ghost, as one God, are the fountain of truth. From this fountain all the ancient learned philosophers have received their inspiration and wisdom—from it they have received all their knowledge. If we find truth in broken fragments through the ages, it may be set down as an incontrovertible fact that it originated at the fountain, and was given to philosophers, inventors, patriots, reformers, and prophets by the inspiration of God. It came from him through his Son Jesus Christ and the Holy Ghost, in the first place, and from no other source. It is eternal.

Christ, therefore, being the fountain of truth, is no imitator. He taught the truth first; it was his before it was given to man. When he came to the earth he not only proclaimed new thought, but repeated some of the everlasting principles which had been heretofore only partly understood and enunciated by the wisest of men. And in so doing he enlarged in every instance upon the wisdom which they had originally received from him, because of his superior abilities and wisdom, and his association with the Father and the Holy Ghost. He did not imitate men. They made known in their imperfect way what the inspiration of Jesus Christ had taught them, for they obtained their enlightenment first from him. He taught the gospel to Adam, and made known his truths to Abraham and the prophets. He was the inspirer of the ancient philosophers, Pagan or Israelite, as well as of the great characters of more modern times. Columbus, in discovery; Washington, in the struggle for freedom; Lincoln, in emancipation and union; Bacon, in philosophy; Franklin, in statesmanship and diplomacy; Stephenson, in steam; Watts, in song; Edison, in electricity; and Joseph Smith, in theology and religion, found the source of their wisdom and the marvelous truths which they advocated, in Jesus Christ.

Calvin, Luther, Melanchthon, and all the reformers, were inspired in thoughts, words, and actions to accomplish what they did for the amelioration, liberty and advancement of the human race. They paved the way for the more perfect gospel of truth to come. Their inspiration, as with that of the ancients, came from the Father, his Son, Jesus Christ, and the Holy Ghost, the one true and living God. This may also truthfully be said concerning the Revolutionary fathers of this nation, and all who have in the ages past contributed to the progress of civil and religious freedom. There is no light or truth which did not come to them first from him. Men are mere repeaters of what he has taught them. He has voiced no thought originating with man. The teachings of Jesus did not begin with his incarnation; for, like truth, he is eternal. He not only inspired the ancients, from the beginning, but when he came to earth he reiterated eternal, original truth, and added gloriously to the revelations men had uttered. When he returned to the Father, he still took, and does take, an interest in his children and people, by revealing to them new truths, and by inspiring their actions; and, as men grow in the knowledge of God, they shall become more and more like him unto the perfect day, when his knowledge shall cover the earth as the waters cover the deep.

It is folly, therefore, to discredit the Savior on the grounds that he has uttered nothing new; for, with the Father and the Spirit, he is the author of that which persists—the truth—that which has been, that which is, and that which will continue forever.—*Improvement Era,* Vol. 10, 1907, pp. 627-30.

TEACHERS MUST BELIEVE IN JESUS CHRIST. Any man who will question the divinity of the mission of the Lord Jesus Christ, or will deny the so-called miracles of the scriptures, is unfit to be a teacher of Latter-day Saint children.—*Improvement Era,* Vol. 21, December, 1917, p. 104.

Chapter XXIII

POLITICAL GOVERNMENT

THE TEN COMMANDMENTS. I believe with all my soul in the gospel of Jesus Christ, and in the law of God, and I do not think any honest and intelligent man or woman could help but believe in the justice, the righteousness and the purity of the laws that God wrote upon the tablets of stone. These principles that I propose to read to you are the foundation and basic principles of the Constitution of our country, and are eternal, enduring forevermore, and cannot be changed nor ignored with impunity:

"And God spake all these words, saying, I am the Lord thy God, which have brought thee out of the land of Egypt, out of the house of bondage. Thou shalt have no other gods before me."

That is what it means now, and what it meant to the Latter-day Saints, and what the Latter-day Saints understood it to mean, when they embraced the gospel of Jesus Christ.

"Thou shalt have no other gods before me." He is the Father of our spirits, the Father of our Lord and Savior Jesus Christ, who is our God; and we shall not have any other before him.

"Thou shalt not make unto thee any graven image, or any likeness of anything that is in heaven above, or that is in the earth beneath, or that is in the water under the earth:

"Thou shalt not bow down thyself to them, nor serve them: for I the Lord thy God am a jealous God, visiting the iniquity of the fathers upon the children unto the third and fourth generation of them that hate me; and showing mercy unto thousands of them that love me, and keep my commandments." (Exodus 20:1-6.)

Infidels will say to you: "How unjust, how unmerciful, how un-Godlike it is to visit the iniquities of the parents upon the children to the third and fourth generation of them that hate God." How do you see it? This way: and it is strictly in accordance with God's law. The infidel will impart infidelity to his children if he can. The whoremonger will not raise a pure, righteous posterity. He will impart seeds of disease and misery, if not of death and destruction, upon his offspring, which will continue upon his children and descend to his children's children to the third and fourth generation. It is perfectly natural that the children should inherit from their fathers, and if they sow the seeds of corruption, crime and loathsome disease, their children will reap the fruits thereof. Not in accordance with God's wishes, for his wish is that men will not sin and therefore will not transmit the consequences of their sin to their children, but that they will keep his commandments, and be free from sin and from entailing the effects of sin upon their offspring; but inasmuch as men will not hearken unto the Lord, but will become a law unto themselves, and will commit sin, they will justly reap the consequences of their own iniquity, and will naturally impart its fruits to their children to the third and fourth generation. The laws of nature are the laws of God who is just; it is not God that inflicts these penalties, they are the effects of disobedience to his law. The results of men's own acts follow them.

"Thou shalt not take the name of the Lord thy God in vain; for the Lord will not hold him guiltless that taketh his name in vain."

This is an eternal principle; it is not one that we may obey today and disobey tomorrow, or that we may espouse today as a part of our faith, and abandon tomorrow with impunity. It is a principle that is inherent in the plan of life and salvation, for the regeneration of mankind.

"Remember the Sabbath day, to keep it holy. Six days shalt thou labor, and do all thy work; but the seventh day is the Sabbath of the Lord thy God: in it thou shalt not do any work, thou, nor thy son, nor thy daughter, thy manservant, nor thy maid-servant, nor thy cattle, nor thy stranger that is within thy gates," etc.

That is: Thou shalt honor the Sabbath day and keep it holy. Do we do it? Is it necessary to do it? It is absolutely necessary to do so in order that we may be in harmony with God's law and commandments; and whenever we transgress that law or that commandment we are guilty of transgressing the law of God. And what will be the result, if we continue? Our children will follow in our footsteps; they will dishonor the command of God to keep one day holy in seven; and will lose the spirit of obedience to the laws of God and his requirements, just as the father will lose it if he continues to violate the commandments.

"Honor thy father and thy mother: that thy days may be long upon the land which the Lord thy God giveth thee."

When will we ever outgrow that command? When can we set it aside? When shall we reach the time that we can dishonor our father and mother? Never! It is an eternal principle, and I am sorry to say—not sorry for the Japs and for the Chinese—these heathen nations, as we have been in the habit of calling them—I am not sorry for them, but for the comparison with them. Those heathen nations set the civilized Christian world an example in the honor they bestow upon their parents, and yet this Christian people and nation and all the Christian nations of the earth, who have the word of the Lord, and the counsels of the Son of God for their guidance, are not leading out in setting an example of obedience, as they should, to this great commandment of the Lord, "Honor thy father and thy mother: that thy days may be long in the land which the Lord thy God giveth thee."

Again, "Thou shalt not kill." That is a command of God. It is irrevocable, unless he revokes it; you and I can't revoke it; we must not transgress it; it is binding upon us, we should not take away the life we cannot restore or give back. It is an eternal, unchangeable law.

"Thou shalt not commit adultery." Just as unchangeable! just as eternal! for the adulterer hath no place in the kingdom of God, nor can he attain to an exaltation there.

"Thou shalt not steal."

"Thou shalt not bear false witness against thy neighbor."

"Thou shalt not covet thy neighbor's house, thou shalt not covet thy neighbor's wife, nor his man-servant, nor his maid-servant, nor his ox, nor his ass, nor anything that is thy neighbor's." (Exodus 20:7-17.)

"Thou shalt not covet." We may say we are thankful that the Lord has blessed our neighbor above that which he has blessed us. We may be thankful that the Lord has given to our neighbor greater wisdom and ability to honestly gather to himself. But we should not covet it. We should not be envious, because we are commanded not to be.

Now, these are the commandments of God, the principles contained in these commandments of the great Eternal are the principles that underly the Constitution of our country, and all just laws. Joseph Smith, the prophet, was inspired to affirm and ratify this truth, and he further predicted that the time would come, when the Constitution of our country would hang as it were by a thread, and that the Latter-day Saints, above all other people in the world, would come to the rescue of that great and glorious palladium of our liberty. We cannot brook the thought of it being torn into shreds, or destroyed, or trampled under foot and ignored by men. We cannot tolerate the sentiment, at one time expressed, by a man high in authority in the nation. He said: "The constitution be damned; the popular senti-ment of the people is the constitution!" That is the sentiment of anarchism, and has spread to a certain extent, and is spreading over "the land of liberty and the home of the brave." We do not tolerate it. Latter-day Saints cannot tolerate such a spirit as this. It is anarchy. It means destruction. It is the spirit of mobocracy, and the Lord knows we have suffered enough from mobocracy, and we do not want any more of it. Our people from Mexico are suffering from the effects of that same spirit. We do not want any more of it, and we cannot afford to yield to that spirit or contribute to it in the least degree. We should stand with a front like flint against every spirit or species of contempt or disrespect for the constitution of our country and the constitutional laws of our land.—Oct. C. R., 1912, pp. 8-11.

THE LAWS OF GOD AND THE LAWS OF THE LAND. Nearly all the brethren who have spoken at this conference have referred to the cir-cumstances in which we, as a people, are now placed; and it would seem unnecessary for me to make any further reference to this all-prevailing subject with which the people generally are more or less familiar, and in which we necessarily are considerably interested. But while the brethren who have spoken have merely referred to some of the sayings of the Prophet Joseph, and to items in the revelations through him, to the Church, I feel impressed to read in the hearing of the congregation one or two passages from the revelations previously referred to. I will, therefore, call the attention of the congregation to a verse or two in the revelation given in 1831, which will be found on page 219 of the Doctrine and Covenants:

"Let no man break the laws of the land, for he that keepeth the laws of God hath no need to break the laws of the land:

"Wherefore, be subject to the powers that be, until He reigns whose right it is to reign, and subdues all enemies under his feet.

"Behold, the laws which ye have received from my hand are the laws of the Church, and in this light ye shall hold them forth. Behold here is wisdom." (Doc. and Cov. 58:21-23.)

The following I quote from a revelation given in December, 1833, page 357:

"According to the laws and the constitution of the people which I have suffered to be established, and should be maintained for the rights and protection of all flesh, according to just and holy principles,

"That every man may act in doctrine and principle pertaining to futurity, according to the moral agency which I have given unto him, that every man may be accountable for his own sins in the day of judgment.

"Therefore, it is not right that any man should be in bondage one to another.

"And for this purpose have I established the constitution of this land, by the hands of wise men whom I raised up unto this very purpose, and redeemed the land by the shedding of blood." (Doc. and Cov. 101:77-80.)

Again, in a revelation on page 342:

"And now, verily I say unto you concerning the laws of the land, it is my will that my people shall observe to do all things whatsoever I command them;

"And that law of the land which is constitutional, supporting that principle of freedom in maintaining rights and privileges, belongs to all mankind, and is justifiable before me;

"Therefore, I, the Lord, justify you, and your brethren of my Church, in befriending that law which is the constitutional law of the land;

"And as pertaining to law of man, whatsoever is more or less than these, cometh of evil.

"I, the Lord God, make you free, therefore ye are free indeed; and the law also maketh you free;

"Nevertheless, when the wicked rule, the people mourn,

"Wherefore, honest men, and wise men should be sought for diligently, and good men and wise men ye should observe to uphold; otherwise whatsoever is less than these cometh of evil.

"And I give unto you a commandment, that ye shall forsake all evil and cleave unto all good, that ye shall live by every word which proceedeth forth out of the mouth of God;

"For he will give unto the faithful line upon line, precept upon precept; and I will try you and prove you herewith;

"And whoso layeth down his life in my cause, for my name's sake, shall find it again, even life eternal:

"Therefore be not afraid of your enemies, for I have decreed in my heart, saith the Lord, that I will prove you in all things, whether you will abide in my covenant, even unto death, that you may be found worthy;

"For if ye will not abide in my covenant, ye are not worthy of me." (Doc. and Cov. 98:4-15.)

This, as I understand it, is the law of God to the Church of Jesus Christ of Latter-day Saints in all the world. And the requirements here made of us must be obeyed, and practically carried out in our lives, in order that we may secure the fulfilment of the promises which God has made to the people of Zion. And it is further written, that inasmuch as ye will do the things which I command you, thus saith the Lord, then am I bound; otherwise there is no promise. We can therefore only expect that the promises are made and will apply to us when we do the things which we are commanded. (Doc. and Cov. 82:10; 101:7; 124:47-49.)

We are told here that no man need break the laws of the land who will keep the laws of God. But this is further defined by the passage which I read afterwards—the law of the land, which all have no need to break, is that law which is the constitutional law of the land, and that is as God himself has defined it. And whatsoever is more or less than this cometh of evil. Now, it seems to me that this makes this matter so clear that it is not possible for any man who professes to be a member of the Church of Jesus Christ of Latter-day Saints to make any mistake, or to be in doubt as to the course he should pursue under the command of God in relation to the observance of the laws of the land. I maintain that the Church of Jesus Christ of Latter-day Saints has ever been faithful to the constitutional laws of our country. I maintain, also, that I have a right to this opinion, as an American citizen, as one who was not only born on American soil, but who descended from parents who for generations were born in America. I have a right to interpret the law in this manner, and to form my own conclusions and express my opinions thereon, regardless of the opinions of other men.

I ask myself, What law have you broken? What constitutional law have you not observed? I am bound not only by allegiance to the government of the United States but by the actual command of God Almighty, to observe and obey every constitutional law of the land, and without hesitancy I declare to this congregation that I have never violated nor transgressed any law, I am not amenable to any penalties of the law, because I have endeavored from my youth up to be a law-abiding citizen, and not only so, but to be a peacemaker, a preacher of righteousness, and not only to preach righteousness by word, but by example. What, therefore, have I to fear? The Lord Almighty requires this people to observe the laws of the land, to be subject to "the powers that be," so far as they abide by the fundamental principles of good government, but he will hold them responsible if they will pass unconstitutional measures and frame unjust and proscriptive laws, as did Nebuchadnezzar and Darius, in relation to the three Hebrew children and Daniel. If lawmakers have a mind to violate their oath, break their covenants and their faith with the people, and depart from the provisions of the constitution, where is the law, human or divine, which binds me, as an individual, to outwardly and openly proclaim my acceptance of their acts? * * *

I wish to enter here my avowal that the people called Latter-day Saints, as has been often repeated from this stand, are the most law-abiding, the most peaceable, long-suffering and patient people that can today be found within the confines of this republic, and perhaps anywhere else upon the face of the earth; and we intend to continue to be law-abiding so far as the constitutional law of the land is concerned; and we expect to meet the consequences of our obedience to the laws and commandments of God, like men. These are my sentiments briefly expressed, upon this subject.

No NATIONALITIES IN THE CHURCH. In speaking of nationalities, we all understand or should that in the Church of Jesus Christ of Latter-day Saints there is neither Scandinavian, nor Swiss, nor German, nor Russian, nor British nor any other nationality. We have become brothers in the household of faith, and we should treat the people from these nations that are at war with each other, with due kindness and consideration. It is nothing but natural that people who are born in a land, though they may have emigrated from it, who have left their kindred there, many of them, that they will naturally have a tender feeling toward their fatherland. But the Latter-day Saints who have come from England and from France and from Germany and Scandinavia and Holland, into this country, no matter what their country may be involved in, it is not our business to distinguish them in any way by criticism or by complaint toward them, or by condemnation, because of the place where they were born. They could not help where they were born, and they have come here to be Latter-day Saints, not to be Germans, nor to be Scandinavians, nor to be English, nor French, nor to belong to any other country in the world. They have come here to be members of the Church of Jesus Christ of Latter-day Saints, and good and true citizens of the United States, and of the several states in which they live, and of other places throughout the world, where Latter-day Saints are building homes for themselves.—Apr. C. R., 1917, p. 11.

LATTER-DAY SAINTS LOYAL TO THE UNITED STATES. We must always bear in mind that we are not only citizens of the kingdom of God, but we are citizens of the United States and of the states in which we dwell. We have ever been loyal both to our state and nation, as well as to the Church of God, and we defy the world to prove to the contrary. We have been willing to fight our country's battles, to defend her honor, to uphold and sustain her good name, and we propose to continue in this loyalty to our nation and to our people unto the end.—Apr. C. R., 1905, p. 46.

LOYALTY TO THE CONSTITUTION OF THE UNITED STATES. And I hope with all my soul that the members of the Church of Jesus Christ of Latter-day Saints will be loyal in their very hearts and souls, to the principles of the constitution of our country. From them we have derived the liberty that we enjoy. They have been the means of guaranteeing to the foreigner that has come within our gates, and to the native born, and to all the citizens of this country, the freedom and liberty that we possess. We cannot go back upon such principles as these. We may go back upon those who fail to execute the law as they should. We may be dissatisfied with the decision of judges and may desire to have them removed out of their places. But the law provides ways and means for all these things to be done under the constitution of our country, and it is better for us to abide the evils that we have than to fly to greater evils that we know not what the results will be.—Apr. C. R., 1912, p. 8.

PROUD OF THE UNITED STATES. I feel proud of the nation of which we are a part, because I am convinced in my own mind that there is not another nation upon the face of the globe where the Lord Almighty could have established his Church with so little difficulty and opposition as he has done here in the United States. This was a free country, and religious toleration was the sentiment of the people of the land. It was the asylum for the oppressed. All the people of the world were invited here to make homes of freedom for themselves, and under these tolerant circumstances the Lord was able to establish his Church, and has been able to maintain it and preserve it up to this time, that it has grown and spread, until it has become respectable—not only by its members, not only by the few years of age that it possesses, but respectable because of its intelligence, respectable because of its honesty, its purity, union and industry, and for all its virtues.—Apr. C. R., 1905, p. 6.

ORIGIN AND DESTINY OF THE UNITED STATES: LOYALTY OF THE

LATTER-DAY SAINTS. This great American nation the Almighty raised up by the power of his omnipotent hand, that it might be possible in the latter days for the kingdom of God to be established in the earth. If the Lord had not prepared the way by laying the foundations of this glorious nation, it would have been impossible (under the stringent laws and bigotry of the monarchical governments of the world) to have laid the foundations for the coming of his great kingdom. The Lord has done this. His hand has been over this nation, and it is his purpose and design to enlarge it, make it glorious above all others, and to give it dominion, and power over the earth, to the end that those who are kept in bondage and serfdom may be brought to the enjoyment of the fullest freedom and liberty of conscience possible for intelligent men to exercise in the earth. The Church of Jesus Christ of Latter-day Saints will be a strong supporter of the nation of which we are a part, in the accomplishment of this grand purpose. There are no more loyal people to their country on God's earth today than are the Latter-day Saints to this country. There are no better, purer or more honorable citizens of the United States to be found than are found within the pale of the Church of Jesus Christ of Latter-day Saints. I testify to this, and I know whereof I speak. We never have been enemies to our nation. We have always been true to it. Though we have been persecuted, we have said, We will put our trust in thee. We have been driven and maligned, not by the nation, but by insidious, wicked, unprincipled, hypocritical, lying, deceitful goats in sheep's clothing, who are jealous and constantly raising a hue and cry against the covenant people of God. Our government would have befriended us, protected us, preserved our rights and liberties, and would have defended us in the enjoyment of our possessions, if it had not been for these infernal hounds who are enemies to morality and to the truth. If there be anything despicable, if there be anything that can never, no, never, enter into the kingdom of God, it is a wilful liar; and if we have not been lied about, maligned and misrepresented of late, then I do not know what lying is. Well, let the falsifiers go on and lie. Some people are evidently doomed to lie. President Woodruff used to say there were some people in his day who were born to lie, and they were true to their missions. There are some of these born liars still with us and still true to their mission. They cannot, it would seem, tell the truth; they often do not when it would be for their best good. So let them go on and lie as much as they desire But let us do right, keep the laws of

God, and the laws of man, honor our membership in the kingdom of God, our citizenship in the state of Utah, and our broader citizenship in the nation of which we are a part, and then God will sustain and preserve us, and we will continue to grow as we have done from the beginning, only our future growth will be accelerated and be far greater than it has been in the past. These slanders and falsehoods that are circulated abroad with the view of bringing the ire of the nation upon us will, by and by, be swept away, and because of these misrepresentations the truth will be brought out clearer and plainer to the world. Thus the word of the Lord will be verified, that they cannot do anything against, but for, the kingdom of God. This is the Lord's work, it is not man's, and he will make it triumphant. He is spreading it abroad, and giving it deep root in the earth, that its branches may grow and spread, and its fruit be seen throughout the length and breadth of the land.—*Apr. C. R.*, 1903, pp. 73-74.

SAINTS TO SERVE GOD. The Latter-day Saints are in the midst of these mountains for the express purpose of serving Almighty God. We have not come here to serve ourselves, nor to serve the world. We are here because we have believed in the gospel that has been restored in the latter day through the Prophet Joseph Smith. We are here because we believe that God Amighty has organized his Church and has restored the fulness of the gospel and holy Priesthood. We are here because we have received the testimony of the Spirit of God that the course which we have pursued in this regard is right and acceptable in the sight of the Lord. We are here because we have come in obedience to the command of the Almighty.— *Oct. C. R.*, 1899, p. 43.

GUIDED BY GOD TO THE WEST. On somewhat parallel lines our people might go back in memory to Ohio and to Missouri and to Illinois, and recall incidents and conditions that existed in those early days by which our people were harassed, mobbed, persecuted, hated and driven away from their possessions in Ohio, Missouri and Illinois. It was hard for our people in those times, and under the conditions that then existed, to see where God in his providence designed good for his people in permitting these conditions to exist. But who today will dispute the fact that, although we were compelled to leave Ohio, Missouri, and Illinois, against our will, our wishes, our interests temporally, as was supposed,—it was for our ultimate good? Who of us will now contend that the overruling Providence which brought us to this place made a mistake? None of us! When we look back to it we see clearly, beyond any possible doubt, that the hand of God was in it. And while it was necessary for us to be moved from our footholds on the soil that our fathers had obtained from the government of the United States, and from old settlers, and while we were compelled to do it against our supposed interests—we now see it has resulted in the greatest blessing possible to us and the Church.

What could we have done in Ohio? What room was there for growth and development for the Church of Jesus Christ of Latter-day Saints in Caldwell county, or in Jackson county, or in Clay county, Missouri? Where was the chance for this Church to spread abroad, grow, and obtain a foothold in the earth, as we possess it today, in the state of Illinois—a populous state, her lands occupied by older inhabitants who were uncongenial and unfriendly? They had no faith in our good intentions, nor in the divinity of our cause. They feared us, because the Saints were progressive. The spirit of growth, development, and of advancement characterized the life and labors and existence of communities of Latter-day Saints, as it has with our people in Mexico.—Oct. C. R., 1912, p. 6.

TRUE PATRIOTISM. Patriotism should be sought for and will be found in right living, not in high sounding phrases or words. True patriotism is part of the solemn obligation that belongs both to the nation and to the individual and to the home. Our nation's reputation should be guarded as sacredly as our family's good name. That reputation should be defended by every citizen, and our children should be taught to defend their country's honor under all circumstances. A truly patriotic spirit in the individual begets a public interest and sympathy which should be commensurate with our nation's greatness. To be a true citizen of a great country takes nothing from, but adds to, individual greatness. While a great and good people necessarily adds greatness and goodness to national life, the nation's greatness reacts upon its citizens and adds honor to them, and insures their welfare and happiness. Loyal citizens will probably be the last to complain of the faults and failures of our national administrators. They would rather conceal those evils which exist, and try to persuade themselves that they are only temporary and may and will in time be corrected. It is none the less a patriotic duty to guard our nation whenever and wherever we can against those changeable and revolutionary tendencies which are destructive of a nation's weal and permanence.—*Juvenile Instructor*, Vol 47, July, 1912, pp. 388-389.

IMPORTANCE OF NATIONAL PATRIOTISM. Our national welfare should always be a theme deeply rooted in our minds and exemplified in our individual lives, and the desire for our nation's good should be stronger than political party adherence. The nation's welfare means the welfare of every one of its citizens. To be a worthy and a prosperous nation, it must possess those qualities which belong to individual virtues. The attitude of our country toward other nations should always be honest and above suspicion, and every good citizen should be jealous of our nation's reputation both at home and abroad. National patriotism is, therefore, something more than mere expression of willingness to fight, if need be.—*Juvenile Instructor*, Vol. 47, July, 1912, p. 389.

THE CHURCH NOT PARTISAN. The Church of Jesus Christ of Latter-day Saints is no partisan Church. It is not a sect. It is THE CHURCH OF JESUS CHRIST OF LATTER-DAY SAINTS. It is the only one today existing in the world that can and does legitimately bear the name of Jesus Christ and his divine authority. I make this declaration in all simplicity and honesty before you and before all the world, bitter as the truth may seem to those who are opposed and who have no reason for that opposition. It is nevertheless true and will remain true until he who has a right to rule among the nations of the earth and among the individual children of God throughout the world shall come and take the reins of government and receive the bride that shall be prepared for the coming of the Bridegroom.— *Improvement Era*, Vol. 20, May, 1918, p. 639. See also *Gospel Doctrine*, pp. 169-170.

THE CHURCH LOYAL. All churches claim to be divinely appointed and place God above country, and any man who renders true homage to God can not break the law, for he lives above it. No man can be a good Latter-day Saint and not be true to the best interests and general welfare of his country. After all these years, it is folly to say that the Church is antagonistic to the national government. The part which our people took in the Mexican and Spanish-American wars should be enough to eternally brand such statements false. The allegiance claimed from its members by the Church does not prevent a member from being a loyal citizen of the nation. It rather aids him; fidelity to the Church enables a man better to entertain patriotic allegiance to his nation and country. There is nothing required of a Latter-day Saint that can in any way be construed to militate against loyalty to the nation, and for that reason Senator Smoot is under no obligations to the Church that can come in conflict with his fealty to country. It is plain that the campaign of the ministers is unjustified.—*Improvement Era, Vol.* 7, March, 1904, p. 382.

LATTER-DAY SAINTS ARE GOOD CITIZENS. A good Latter-day Saint is a good citizen in every way. I desire to say to the young men of our community: be exemplary Latter-day Saints, and let nothing deter you from aspiring to the greatest positions which our nation has to offer. Having secured a place, let your virtue, your integrity, your honesty, your ability, your religious teachings, implanted in your heart at the knees of your devoted "Mormon" mothers, "so shine before men, that they may see your good works, and glorify your Father which is in heaven."—*Improvement Era, Vol.* 6, April, 1903, p. 469.

CHURCH NOT RESPONSIBLE FOR POLITICAL PARTIES. The Church of Christ is not responsible for the actions of either of the political parties, in any sense, or form. If it were, they would stop their quarreling and contending, and the bitterness and animosity they exhibit towards one another would cease. If we had anything to do with them, we would stop their wrangling, and we would have peace in their ranks. The fact that they quarrel as they do is proof positive we have nothing to do with them.—*Apr. C. R.,* 1899, p. 41.

THE CHURCH NOT IN POLITICS. The Church does not engage in politics; its members belong to the political parties at their own pleasure—to the Republicans, the Democrats, or to no party at all. They are not asked, much less required, to vote this way or that—a requirement made by the Protestant ministers of their members against the Saints. But they cannot justly be denied their rights as citizens, and there is no reason why they should be, for, on the average, they are as loyal, as sober, as well educated, as honest, as industrious, as virtuous, as moral, as thrifty, and as worthy in every other respect as any people in the nation or on the earth, for that matter. I think that they are just a little better in these respects than most other communities or individuals.

To the young men who may be disheartened by false attacks upon the Saints, and to the missionaries in the world, who are driven and persecuted, I wish to say: have no fear; slacken not your labors for the truth; live as becometh Saints. You are in the right way, and the Lord will not let your efforts fail. This Church stands in no danger from opposition and persecution from without. There is more to fear in carelessness, sin and indifference, from within; more danger that the individual will fail in doing right and in conforming his life to the revealed doctrines of our Lord and Savior Jesus Christ. If we do the right, all will be well, the God of our fathers will sustain us, and every opposition will tend only to the further spread of the knowledge of truth.—*Improvement Era*, Vol. 6, June, 1903, p. 625.

SHUN THE SPIRIT OF MOB VIOLENCE. Nobody in the world deplores more than do the Latter-day Saints the prevalence and brutality of mob violence. If mob violence in this country did not have its origin in the drivings and persecutions of the Latter-day Saints, it is certain that no class of people in this country have suffered more and longer from the lawlessness of the mob than have the Latter-day Saints. For more than half a century the "Mormons" have been the victims of lawless mob violence against which very little has been said, for the chief reason that the victims had been so long pursued by hatred and prejudice that the world had been taught to withdraw all its sympathy from them. Whipping, driving, and shooting "Mormon" elders in the South called forth no anxiety and little objection upon the part of the press; and the "Mormon" elder, pure and upright in his life, has received less sympathy and protest in his favor than the negro ravisher who deserved, perhaps, the punishment, however inexcusable the method of executing it.

The Latter-day Saints in Utah, and everywhere, are earnestly and prayerfully admonished to shun as a sacred religious duty the spirit of mob violence. It is better to be patient and endure deprivations of human rights than to violate the institutions of our country, and to substitute violence for law and order. If the reign of the mob extends its hideous rule over this country as rapidly in the future as it has done in the past, it may reach communities where the Saints live before they are aware of its presence. It is not only the duty of every Latter-day Saint, therefore, to refrain from the violent and unlawful conduct of bodies of men bent upon human destruction, but to exercise his influence and power to restrain others from imbuing their hands in the blood of their fellow men.—*Juvenile Instructor*, Vol. 38, September, 1903, p. 564.

THE DANGER OF MOBS. One of the greatest menaces to our country is that of the combination of men into irresponsible, reckless mobs, wild with prejudice, hatred and fanaticism, led by men of ambition, or passion, or hatred. There is no other thing in the world that I can conceive of so absolutely obnoxious to God and good men as a combination of men and women filled with the spirit of mobocracy. Men combining together to stop or shut off the food supply from the mouth of the honest laborer to starve the man that is willing to work, and the wife and the children who are dependent upon him, because he is not willing to join a mob, is one of the most infamous perils and menaces to the people of our country today. I do not care who they are, or what name they go by. They are a menace to the peace of the world.—Oct. C. R., 1911, p. 122.

THE BASIS OF LABOR UNIONS. If we are to have labor organizations among us, and there is no good reason why our young men might not be so organized, they should be formed on a sensible basis, and officered by men who have their families and all their interests around them. The spirit of good-will and brotherhood, such as we have in the gospel of Christ, should characterize their conduct and organizations. For be it known, the religious note is and should remain the dominant note of our character and of all our actions.

While there is no reason why workmen should not join together for their own mutual protection and benefit, there is every reason why in so doing they should regard the rights of their fellows, be jealous of the protection of property, and eliminate from their methods of warfare, boycotts, sympathetic strikes, and the walking delegate.—*Improvement Era*, Vol. 6, August, 1903, p. 182.

LABOR UNIONS. Labor unions will find that the same eternal law of justice applies to unions that applies to individuals, that fair dealing and rational conduct must be maintained if financial misfortunes are averted. Where there are Latter-day Saints in unions they should assume a conservative attitude and never arouse men's prejudices by inflaming their passions. There can be no objections to a firm and persistent contention for the right of labor, if the contention is maintained in the spirit of reason and fairness. Above all things, the Latter-day Saints should hold sacred the life and liberty of their fellow-men, as also their rights of property and maintain inviolate every right to which humanity is entitled.

The unions are forcing our people into an inconsistent and dangerous attitude when they compel Latter-day Saints within the union to make war upon their brethren who are without the union, and thereby denying the most sacred and God-given rights of one class of Saints that another class may gain some advantage over a third person, their employer. Such conduct is destructive of the liberty which every man is entitled to enjoy, and will lead in the end to the spirit of contention and apostasy.

It is not easy to see how the Latter-day Saints can endorse the methods of modern labor unions. As a people we have suffered too much from irrational class prejudice and class hatred to participate in violent and unjust agitations. No one denies the rights of laborers to unite in demanding a just share of the prosperity of our country, provided the union is governed by the same spirit that should actuate men who profess the guidance of a Christian conscience.

In the present status of capital and labor there should be mutual interests; and at the same time workmen should realize that there is a limit to the pressure which capital can endure by the demands made upon it. Competition has always given some measure of relief to the laborer by the demands of capital for human service, and men should not therefore abandon themselves to the supposed power of arbitrary demands which labor unions are now making in many cases upon their employers. The contention for the recognition of unions is often a very indefinite factor, for no one seems to know just what that recognition means now, or what it is to mean in the future. If recognition means the exclusive right of any class of men to gain a livelihood by their work, then recognition should be persistently and forcefully resisted.

The Latter-day Saints, whether in the unions or out of them, know very well whether individual or united demands are arbitrary and unjust, and they will lose nothing by a manly refusal to violate their sense of justice.—*Juvenile Instructor*, Vol. 38, June, 1903, p. 370.

CAUSE OF WAR. The condition of the world today presents a spectacle that is deplorable, so far as it relates to the religious convictions, faith and power of the inhabitants of the earth. Here we have nations arrayed against nations, and yet in every one of these nations are so-called Christian peoples professing to worship the same God, professing to possess belief in the same divine Redeemer, many of them professing to be teachers of God's word, and ministers of life and salvation to the children of men, and yet these nations are divided one against the other, and each is praying to his God for wrath upon and victory over his enemies and for his own preservation. Would it be possible, could it be possible, for this condition to exist if the people of the world possessed really the true knowledge of the gospel of Jesus Christ? And if they really possessed the Spirit of the living God—could this condition exist? No; it could not exist, but war would cease, and contention and strife would be at an end. And not only the spirit of war would not exist, but the spirit of contention and strife that now exists among the nations of the earth, which is the primal element of war, would cease to be. We know that the spirit of strife and contention exists to an alarming extent among all the people of the world. Why does it exist? Because they are not one with God, nor with Christ. They have not entered into the true fold, and the result is they do not possess the spirit of the true Shepherd sufficiently to govern and control their acts in the ways of peace and righteousness. Thus they contend and strive one against another, and at last nation rises up against nation in fulfilment of the predictions of the prophets of God that war should be poured out upon all nations. I don't want you to think I believe that God has designed or willed that war should come among the people of the world, that the nations of the world should be divided against one another in war, and engaged in the destruction of each? God did not design or cause this. It is deplorable to the heavens that such a condition should exist among men, but the conditions do exist, and men precipitate war and destruction upon themselves because of their wickedness, and that because they will not abide in God's truth, walk in his love, and seek to establish and maintain peace instead of strife and contention in the world.—Oct. C. R., 1914, p. 8.

ATTITUDE TOWARDS WAR. We do not want war. We do not want to see our nation go to war. We would like to see it the arbiter of peace for all nations. We would like to see the government of the United States true to the constitution, an instrument inspired by the spirit of wisdom from God. We want to see the benignity, the honor, the glory and the good name, and the mighty influence for peace of this nation, extended abroad, not only over Hawaii and the Philippines, but over the islands of the sea east and west of us. We want to see the power, the influence for good, for elevating mankind, and for the establishment of righteous principles spread out over these poor, helpless peoples of the world, establishing peace, good will and intelligence among them, that they may grow to be equal, if possible, to the enlightened nations of the world.—Oct. C. R., 1912, p. 7.

WE WANT PEACE. We want peace in the world. We want love and good will to exist throughout the earth, and among all the people of the world; but there never can come to the world that spirit of peace and love that should exist, until mankind will receive God's truth and God's message unto them, and acknowledge his power and authority which is divine, and never found in the wisdom only of men.—Oct. C. R., 1914, p. 7.

WHEN PEACE SHALL COME. We will never have peace until we have truth. We will never be able to establish peace on earth and good will until we have drunk at the fountain of righteousness and eternal truth, as God has revealed it to man.—Oct. C. R., 1914, p. 129.

PEACE ON EARTH, GOOD WILL TO MEN. We certainly live in troublesome times; and, notwithstanding the peace that pervades our own land, we are not without our troubles at home. There is, among us today, I am sorry to say, the germ of the spirit that has prompted, very largely, the conditions that exist in Europe today—internal unrest, dissatisfaction, discontent, internal contention over political, labor and religious matters, and almost every subject that affects society at this time. And the very germ that has prompted the terrible results that we see in the nations of Europe, is at work among us here today. We need not forget it, nor ignore it, either.

There is just one power, and one only, that can prevent war among the nations of the earth, and that is true religion and undefiled before God, the Father. Nothing else will accomplish it. It is a very common expression today that there is good in all religions. So there is; but there is not sufficient good in the denominations of the world to prevent war, nor to prevent contention, strife, division and hatred of one another.

And, put all the good doctrines, in all the denominations of the world, together, and they do not constitute sufficient good to prevent the evils that exist in the world. Why? Because the denominations lack the essential knowledge of God's revelation and truth, and the enjoyment of that spirit which comes from God that leadeth unto all truth, and that inspires men to do good and not evil, to love and not to hate, to forgive and not to bear malice, to be kind and generous and not to be unkind and contracted.

So, I repeat, there is but one remedy that can prevent men from going to war, when they feel disposed to do it, and that is the Spirit of God, which inspires to love, and not to hatred, which leads unto all truth, and not unto error, which inclines the children of God to pay deference to him and to his laws and to esteem them as above all other things in the world.

The Lord has told us that these wars would come. We have not been ignorant that they were pending, and that they were likely to burst out upon the nations of the earth at any time. We have been looking for the fulfilment of the words of the Lord that they would come. Why? Because the Lord wanted it? No; not by any means. Was it because the Lord predestined it, or designed it, in any degree? No, not at all. Why? It was for the reason that men did not hearken unto the Lord God, and he foreknew the results that would follow, because of men, and because of the nations of the earth; and therefore he was able to predict what would befall them, and came upon them in consequence of their own acts, and not because he has willed it upon them, for they are but suffering and reaping the results of their own actions.

Well, my sisters, "peace on earth, and good will to men," is our slogan. That is our principle. That is the principle of the gospel of Jesus Christ. And while I think it is wrong, wickedly wrong, to force war upon any nation, or upon any people, I believe it is righteous and just for every people to defend their own lives and their own liberties, and their own homes, with the last drop of their blood. I believe it is right, and I believe that the Lord will sustain any people in defending their own liberty to worship God according to the dictates of their conscience, any people trying to preserve their wives and their children from the ravages of the war. But we do not want to be brought into the necessity of having to defend ourselves.

If the condition of the world appears to you as it does to me, at the present time it seems to me that you have within your hearts and minds one of the strongest evidences that has ever been brought to your understanding, of the truth of the declaration which God gave to the world through Joseph Smith, that "they draw near to me with their lips, but their hearts are far from me; they teach for doctrines the commandments of men: having a form of godliness, but they deny the power thereof," and have it not. (*History of the Church*, Vol. 1, p. 6.) In Germany, at this time, Protestants and Catholics are praying to God for victory over their foes. In France and England and in Russia and in Belgium, and Austria, and in all other countries, that are at war with one another, they are praying. Protestants and Catholics together for victory. The Allies are praying for victory, to the same God, supposed to be, for these are called Christian nations, and they are members of the same churches, worshiping in the same forms of religion and yet they are calling upon God one against another, to defend them against their enemies, and to strengthen their arms to destroy their foes. What does it prove? It proves what God said. They have not his Spirit; they have not his power to guide them. They are not in possession of his truth; and, therefore, the very conditions that exist are the results of this unbelief in the truth; and this worship of men and organizations and powers of men is divested of the power of God.

Now, my sisters, I am speaking from my point of view, and my point of view is that Christ was divinely appointed and sent into the world to relieve mankind of sin through repentance; to relieve mankind from the death which came upon them by the sin of the first man. I believe it with all my soul. I believe that Joseph Smith was raised up by Almighty God to renew the spirit, power and plan of God's Church, of Christ's gospel and holy Priesthood. I believe it with all my soul, or I would not be here. I therefore stand upon this principle, that the truth is in the gospel of Jesus Christ, that the power of redemption, the power of peace, the power for good will, love, charity and forgiveness, and the power for fellowship with God, abides in the gospel of Jesus Christ and in obedience to it on the part of the people. I therefore admit, and not only admit but claim, that there is nothing greater on earth, nor in heaven, than the truth of God's gospel which he has devised and restored for the salvation and the redemption of the world. And it is through that that peace will come to the children of men, and it will not come to the world in any other way. The nations cannot possess it without they come to God, from whom they are to receive the spirit of union and the spirit of love. And those organizations in the world, created with a view to combining men, possess in them so many of the elements of self-destruction that they cannot exist long, as they are, and under the influences which hold them together today. I can tell you that there is no combination formed by men that will prosper and continue to endure, unless it is based upon the principles of truth, righteousness, and justice toward all. When a man comes to me and says: "You must be my servant, you must obey me, or conform to my plan, or we will starve you to death," I don't care how many elements of goodness there are in the organization that will exclude me from a right to worship God according to the dictates of my conscience, or that would prevent me from laboring in honest labor to earn my bread, it possesses the elements of decay and destruction, and it cannot last, for it is wrong, absolutely wrong.

In the gospel is the light of freedom. Men worship God according to the dictates of their own conscience. We can not compel you to obey the principles of the gospel at all.

That is the principle of the gospel of Jesus Christ. But these man-made organizations will force you to do as they will, or they will damn you and destroy you; and therein lies the elements of self-destruction in themselves, because they can only last for a time.—*Relief Society Magazine*, Vol. 2, No. 1, 1914, p. 13.

THE KEY TO PEACE. There is only one thing that can bring peace into the world. It is the adoption of the gospel of Jesus Christ, rightly understood, obeyed and practiced by rulers and people alike. It is being preached in power to all nations, kindreds, tongues and peoples of the world, by the Latter-day Saints, and the day is not far distant when its message of salvation shall sink deep into the hearts of the common people, who, in sincerity and earnestness, when the time comes, will not only surely register their judgment against a false Christianity, but against war and the makers of war as crimes against the human race. For years it has been held that peace comes only by preparation for war; the present conflict should prove that peace comes only by preparing for peace, through training the people in righteousness and justice, and selecting rulers who respect the righteous will of the people.

Not long hence and the voice of the people shall be obeyed, and the true gospel of peace shall dominate the hearts of the mighty. It will then be impossible for war lords to have power over the life and death of millions of men as they now have, to decree the ruin of commerce, industry, and growing fields, or to cause untold mental agony and human misery like plague and pestilence to prevail over the nations. It looks much as if, after the devastation of wars, as promised in the scriptures, (and who shall say that it may not follow this war?) the self-constituted monarchs must give way to rulers chosen by the people, who shall be guided by the doctrines of love and peace as taught in the gospel of our Lord. There will then be instituted a new social order in which the welfare of all shall be uppermost, and all shall be permitted to live in the utmost liberty and happiness.—*Improvement Era*, Vol. 17, No. 11, September, 1914, p. 1074.

GOD STRIVES WITH WARRING NATIONS. Would the nations of the earth that are at war with each other be at war as they are, if the Spirit of God Almighty had pervaded their souls and moved and actuated them in their designs? No; not at all. Worldly ambition, pride, and the love of power, determination on the part of rulers to prevail over their competitors in the national games of life, wickedness at heart, desire for power, for worldly greatness, have led the nations of the earth to quarrel with one another and have brought them to war and self-destruction. I presume there is not a nation in the world today that is not tainted with this evil more or less. It may be possible, perhaps to trace the cause of the evil, or the greatest part of it, to some particular nation of the earth; but I do not know. This I do believe, with all my heart, that the hand of God is striving with certain nations of the earth to preserve and protect human liberty, freedom to worship him according to the dictates of conscience, freedom and the inalienable right of men to organize national governments in the earth, to choose for themselves their own leaders; men whom they may select as standards of honor, of virtue and truth, men of wisdom, understanding and integrity; men who have at heart the well being of the people who choose them to govern, to enact and execute the laws in righteousness. I believe that the Lord's hand is over the nations of the world today, to bring about this rule and this reign of liberty and righteousness among the nations of the earth. He has some hard material to work with, too. He is working with men who never prayed, men who have never known God, nor Jesus Christ whom he has sent into the world, and whom to know is life eternal. God is dealing with nations of infidels, men who fear not God, and love not the truth, men who have no respect for virtue or purity of life. God is dealing with men who are full of pride and ambition; and he will find it difficult, I fear, to control them and lead them directly in the course that he would have them pursue to accomplish his purposes; but he is striving to uplift. God is striving to bless, to benefit, to happify, to ameliorate the condition of his children in the world, to give them freedom from ignorance and a knowledge of him, to learn of his ways and to walk in his paths, that they may have his Spirit to be with them always, to lead them into all truth. —*Improvement Era*, Vol. 20, July, 1917, p. 823.

CONDUCT OF THE BOYS IN THE ARMY. Therefore, when our boys and our maturer men are invited and chosen, selected and called, to go out to help to protect and defend these principles, we hope and pray, and we certainly have some reason to believe, that there will be some, at least, from amidst the great family of mankind in the world, who will have some affinity with the Spirit of God and at least some desire, some inclination, to hearken to the whisperings of the still small voice of the Spirit, that leadeth to peace and happiness, to the well-being and the uplifting of mankind in the world and to life eternal. When a Latter-day Saint, a man born, perhaps, and reared under the bond of the New and Everlasting Covenant of the gospel, enlists in the army of the United States, in the National Guard, which has been recommended here by President Penrose to you—and which I confirm and emphasize, because I think the citizens of the state should be united together, and the cities and the state should stand together and should have sympathy and fellowship for each other, more than they could expect to derive from those of other states and places, who are strangers and foreigners to them—that when our boys, thus born, are called into the army of the United States, I hope and pray that they will carry with them the Spirit of God, not the spirit of bloodshed, of adultery, of wickedness, but the spirit of righteousness, the spirit which leads to do good, to build up, to benefit the world, and not to destroy and shed blood.

Remember the passage of scripture that was quoted here by President Lund, as related in the Book of Mormon, concerning the pure young men that abjured war and the shedding of blood, lived pure and innocent, free from the contaminating thought of strife, of anger, or wickedness in their hearts; but when necessity required, and they were called to go out to defend their lives, and the lives of their fathers and mothers, and their homes, they went—not to destroy but to defend, not to shed blood but rather to save the blood of the innocent and of the unoffending, and the peace-lovers of mankind.

Will those men who go out from Utah, from the Church of Jesus Christ of Latter-day Saints, forget their prayers? Will they forget God? Will they forget the teachings that they have received from their parents at home? Will they forget the principles of the gospel of Jesus Christ and the covenants that they have made in the waters of baptism, and in sacred places? Or will they go out as men, in every sense—pure men, high-minded men, honest men, virtuous men, men of God? That is what I am anxious about.

I want to see the hand of God made manifest in the acts of the men that go out from the ranks of the Church of Jesus Christ and from the state of Utah, to help to defend the principles of liberty and sound government for the human family. I want to see them so live that they can be in communion with the Lord, in their camps, and in their secret places, and that in the midst of battle they can say: "Father, my life and my spirit are in thine hand!"

I want to see the boys that go away from here in this cause, go feeling just as our missionaries do when sent out into the world.

carrying with them the spirit a good mother feels when she parts with her boy, on the morning of his departure for his mission. She embraces him with all the mother's love in her soul!

I know how the mother feels for her boy when he goes away from home on a mission, where he will be in the midst of strangers, without friends, trying to preach the gospel to the world. She says to him: "My boy, I have taught you the principles of the gospel. I have taught you to pray to God, at my knees, from the time you were a child until you have reached manhood. I have taught you virtue. I have taught you honor. I have taught you to stand for the Truth, and to honor your father and your mother in the world, and by so doing honor the fathers and the mothers, and the daughters of all men, wherever you go. Never in your life think of defiling any man's wife, or daughter, any more than you would think of defiling your mother or your sister! Go out into the world from your home clean. Keep yourself pure and unspotted from the world, and you will be immune from sin, and God will protect you. You will be in his hands. Then, if anything should happen that would cost you your life, you will lay it down in the service of humanity, and of God. You would lay down your life pure and undefiled. Your spirit would ascend from that tenement of clay inhabited in this world, into the glorious presence of God, undefiled, uncontaminated, pure and clean as the spirit of a child just born into the world. Thus you would be acceptable to God, ready to receive your crown of glory and everlasting reward."

So I would say, "My boy, my son, and your son, when you go out to face the disasters that are now afflicting the world, go out as you do on a mission, be just as good and pure and true in the army of the United States as you are in the army of the elders of Israel who are preaching the gospel of love and peace to the world. Then, if you unavoidably fall prey to the bullet of the enemy you will go pure as you have lived; you will be worthy of your reward; you will have proved yourself a hero, and not only a hero, but a valiant servant of the living God, worthy of his acceptation and of admission into the loving presence of the Father!"

It is in such things as this that we can see the hand of God. If our boys will only go out into the world this way, carrying with them the spirit of the gospel and the behavior of true Latter-day Saints, no matter what may befall them in life, they will endure with the best. They will be able to endure as much as anybody else can possibly endure of fatigue or of suffering, if necessary, and when they are brought to the test they will stand it! Because they have no fear of death! They will be free from fear of the consequences of their own lives. They will have no need to dread death, for they have done their work; they have kept the faith, they are pure in heart, and they are worthy to see God!

I have some feelings in these matters, for I have boys of my own, and I love my sons. They have grown up with me. They are mine! The Lord gave them to me. I expect to claim them, in the relationship of father and sons that exists between us, throughout all eternities that will come. I would rather see my sons shot down by the enemies of God and humanity, by those who are inimical to the freedom of the children of men, while defending the cause of Righteousness and Truth, a thousand times rather, than to see them die the vile death of sinners and of transgressors of the laws of God. While death in battle might be instantaneous, or it might linger, perhaps, to one whose cause is just it would be honorable; but the death that is caused by the transgression of the laws of God, by the poison and sting of sin, is to be dreaded worse, a thousand times, than to die sinless in defending the cause of Truth.

I don't want to see one of my boys lose the faith of the gospel of Jesus Christ. I don't want to see one of them deny Christ, the Son of the living God, the Savior of the world. I do not want one of them to turn his back upon the divine mission of the Prophet Joseph Smith whose blood courses in their veins. I would rather see them perish in defending a cause of righteousness, a thousand times, while they are firm in the faith, than I would see them live to deny that faith and the God that gave them life! That is where I stand with reference to the matters that are facing us at this moment!—*Improvement Era*, Vol. 20, July, 1917, p. 824, *June C. R.*

MESSAGE TO THE BOYS IN WAR SERVICE. Our country is at war. This regrettable condition has been forced upon us by enemies of representative government and individual freedom. Despotism is endeavoring to gain the ascendency and to establish its might in the earth. Many of our young men who have been reared in the Church, and taught the principles of the gospel in the Sabbath Schools and other organizations of the Church, have been called to the colors in defense of our liberties and the liberty and freedom of the world. In all probability they will be sent to the front before many months have passed, to take their places in the trenches in the European battlefields and engage in this appalling conflict, the like of which the world has never seen until this day.

We most sincerely hope that our young men will prove loyal to their country and stand honorably in its defense and prove themselves worthy in every respect as defenders of those principles for which our government was born and for which it still exists.

In going forth to war these young men are liable to be confronted with danger far greater than that which they might expect from the bullets of the enemy. There are many evils that usually follow in the wake of marshaled armies equipped for and engaged in war, far worse than honorable death which may come in the conflict of battle. It matters not so much when our young men are called, or where they may go, but it does matter much to their parents, friends and associates in the truth, and above all to themselves, how they go. They have been trained all their lives as members of the Church to keep themselves pure and unspotted from the sins of the world, to respect the rights of others, to be obedient to righteous principles, to remember that virtue is one of the greatest gifts from God. Moreover, that they should respect the virtue of others and rather die a thousand times than defile themselves by committing deadly sin. We want them to go forth clean, both in thought and action, with faith in the principles of the gospel and the redeeming grace of our Lord and Savior. We would have them remember that only by living clean and faithful lives can they hope to attain the salvation promised through the shedding of the blood of our Redeemer.

If they will go forth in this manner, fit companions for the Spirit of the Lord, free from sin, and trusting in the Lord, then whatever befalls them they will know that they have found favor in the sight of God. Should death overtake them while thus engaged in the discharge of duty in defense of their country, they need have no fear, for their salvation is assured. Moreover, under conditions such as these they will have a better claim to the blessings of the Almighty and, like the two thousand young men of Helaman's army, they will be more likely to receive the protecting care of the Lord.

Let them go in the spirit of truth and righteousness; the spirit which will direct them to save rather than destroy; which leads to do good rather than to commit evil; with love in their hearts for their fellow men, prepared to teach all mankind the saving principles of the gospel. And, should they be required, in the defense of the principles for which they go, to shed the blood of any among the contending forces, it shall not be a sin, and the blood of their enemies shall not be required at their hands.

We will have no fear for those who will be true to the covenants they have made in the waters of baptism and observe to keep the commandments of God. If they die, they shall die unto the Lord and shall stand before him spotless and void of offense. And should they return unharmed, we will give to our Father in heaven the credit for his protecting care over them while in the discharge of perilous duty. While they are away the prayers of the Saints will ascend in their behalf for their protection, and we sincerely hope their prayers will not be without avail, and surely they will avail if our boys will continue to be worthy of the mercies of the Lord.—*Juvenile Instructor*, August, 1917, p. 404, Vol. 52.

Chapter XXIV

ETERNAL LIFE AND SALVATION

Eternal Life and Salvation. Every man born into the world will die. It matters not who he is, nor where he is, whether his birth be among the rich and the noble, or among the lowly and poor in the world, his days are numbered with the Lord, and in due time he will reach the end. We should think of this. Not that we should go about with heavy hearts or with downcast countenances; not at all. I rejoice that I am born to live, to die, and to live again. I thank God for this intelligence. It gives me joy and peace that the world cannot give, neither can the world take it away. God has revealed this to me, in the gospel of Jesus Christ. I know it to be true. Therefore, I have nothing to be sad over, nothing to make me sorrowful. All that I have to do with in the world is calculated to buoy me up, to give me joy and peace, hope and consolation in this present life, and a glorious hope of salvation and exaltation in the presence of my God in the world to come. I have no reason to mourn, not even at death. It is true, I am weak enough to weep at the death of my friends and kindred. I may shed tears when I see the grief of others. I have sympathy in my soul for the children of men. I can weep with them when they weep; I can rejoice with them when they rejoice; but I have no cause to mourn, nor to be sad because death comes into the world. I am speaking now of the temporal death, the death of the body. All fear of this death has been removed from the Latter-day Saints. They have no dread of the temporal death, because they know that as death came upon them by the transgression of Adam, so by the righteousness of Jesus Christ shall life come unto them, and though they die, they shall live again. Possessing this knowledge, they have joy even in death, for they know that they shall rise again and shall meet again beyond the grave. They know that the spirit dies not at all; that it passes through no change, except the change from imprisonment in this mortal clay to freedom and to the sphere in which it acted before it came to this earth. We are begotten in the similitude of Christ himself. We dwelt with the Father and with the Son in the beginning, as the sons and daughters of God; and at the time appointed, we came to this earth to take upon ourselves tabernacles, that we might become conformed to the

likeness and image of Jesus Christ and become like him; that we might
have a tabernacle, that we might pass through death as he has passed
through death, that we might rise again from the dead as he has
risen from the dead. As he was the first fruits of the resurrection
of the dead, so shall we be the second fruits of the resurrection from
the dead; for as he came forth, so shall we come forth. What is there,
therefore, to be sad about? What is there to make us heavy of heart
or sorrowful in this matter? Nothing at all. Sorrowful, indeed, to
think that we shall live forever! Is there any cause for sorrow
to know that we shall rise from the dead, and possess the same
tabernacle that we have here in mortality? Is there cause for sorrow
in this great, glorious gospel truth that has been revealed to us in
this dispensation? Certainly there can be no sorrow connected with
a thought like this. There must be only joy connected with this
knowledge—the joy that springs from the ten thousand feelings
and affections of the human soul; the joy that we feel in association
with brethren, with wives and children, with fathers and mothers,
with brothers and sisters. All these joyous thoughts spring up in our
souls at the thought of death and the resurrection. Wherein should
we be sad or sorrowful? On the contrary, it is cause for joy unspeakable, and for pure happiness. I cannot express the joy I feel at the
thought of meeting my father, and my precious mother, who gave
me birth in the midst of persecution and poverty, who bore me in
her arms and was patient, forbearing, tender and true during all
my helpless moments in the world. The thought of meeting her,
who can express the joy? The thought of meeting my children who
have preceded me beyond the veil, and of meeting my kindred and
my friends, what happiness it affords! For I know that I shall meet
them there. God has shown me that this is true. He has made it
clear to me, in answer to my prayer and devotion, as he has made
it clear to the understanding of all men who have sought diligently
to know him.—Oct. C. R., 1899, pp. 70-71.

CLOSE RELATION OF THE NEXT LIFE. I feel sure that the Prophet
Joseph Smith and his associates, who, under the guidance and inspiration of the Almighty, and by his power, began this latter-day
work, would rejoice and do rejoice,—I was going to say if they were
permitted to look down upon the scene that I behold in this tabernacle; but I believe they do have the privilege of looking down upon
us just as the all-seeing eye of God beholds every part of his handiwork. For I believe that those who have been chosen in this dispen-

sation and in former dispensations, to lay the foundation of God's work in the midst of the children of men, for their salvation and exaltation, will not be deprived in the spirit world from looking down upon the results of their own labors, efforts and mission assigned them by the wisdom and purpose of God, to help to redeem and to reclaim the children of the Father from their sins. So I feel quite confident that the eye of Joseph, the prophet, and of the martyrs of this dispensation, and of Brigham, and John, and Wilford, and those faithful men who were associated with them in their ministry upon the earth, are carefully guarding the interests of the kingdom of God in which they labored and for which they strove during their mortal lives. I believe they are as deeply interested in our welfare today, if not with greater capacity, with far more interest, behind the veil, than they were in the flesh. I believe they know more; I believe their minds have expanded beyond their comprehension in mortal life, and their interests are enlarged and expanded in the works of the Lord to which they gave their lives and their best service. Although some may feel and think that it is a little extreme to take this view, yet I believe that it is true; and I have a feeling in my heart that I stand in the presence not only of the Father and of the Son, but in the presence of those whom God commissioned, raised up, and inspired, to lay the foundations of the work in which we are engaged. Accompanying that sense of feeling, I am impressed with the thought that I would not this moment say or do one thing that would be taken as unwise or imprudent, or that would give offense to any of my former associates and co-laborers in the work of the Lord.

I would not like to say one thing, or express a thought, that would grieve the heart of Joseph, or of Brigham, or of John, or of Wilford, or of Lorenzo, or of any of their faithful associates in the ministry. Sometimes the Lord expands our vision from this point of view and this side of the veil, that we feel and seem to realize that we can look beyond the thin veil which separates us from that other sphere. If we can see, by the enlightening influence of the Spirit of God and through the words that have been spoken by the holy prophets of God, beyond the veil that separates us from the spirit world, surely those who have passed beyond, can see more clearly through the veil back here to us than it is possible for us to see to them from our sphere of action. I believe we move and have our being in the presence of heavenly messengers and of heavenly beings. We are not separated from them. We begin to realize more and more fully, as we become acquainted with the principles of the gospel, as they have been revealed anew in this dispensation, that we are closely related to our kindred, to our ancestors, to our friends and associates and co-laborers who have preceded us into the spirit world. We cannot forget them; we do not cease to love them; we always hold them in our hearts, in memory, and thus we are associated and united to them by ties that we cannot break, that we cannot dissolve or free ourselves from. If this is the case with us in our finite condition, surrounded by our mortal weaknesses, shortsightedness, lack of inspiration and wisdom, from time to time, how much more certain it is, and reasonable and consistent, to believe that those who have been faithful, who have gone beyond, are still engaged in the work for the salvation of the souls of men, in the opening of the prison doors to them that are bound and proclaiming liberty to the captives, who can see us better than we can see them—that they know us better than we know them. They have advanced; we are advancing; we are growing as they have grown; we are reaching the goal that they have attained unto; and therefore, I claim that we live in their presence, they see us, they are solicitous for our welfare, they love us now more than ever. For now they see the dangers that beset us; they can comprehend better than ever before, the weaknesses that are liable to mislead us into dark and forbidden paths. They see the temptations and the evils that beset us in life, and the proneness of mortal beings to yield to temptation and to wrong doing; hence their solicitude for us and their love for us and their desire for our well being must be greater than that which we feel for ourselves. I thank God for the feeling that I possess and enjoy, and for the realization that I have that I stand, not only in the presence of Almighty God, my Maker and Father, but in the presence of his Only Begotten Son in the flesh, the Savior of the world; and I stand in the presence of Peter and James (and perhaps the eyes of John are also upon us and we know it not) and that I stand also in the presence of Joseph, and Hyrum, and Brigham and John, and those who have been valiant in the testimony of Jesus Christ and faithful to their mission in the world, who have gone before. When I go, I want to have the privilege of meeting them with the consciousness that I have followed their example, that I have carried out the mission in which they were engaged, as they would have it carried out; that I have been as faithful in the discharge of duty, committed to me and required at my hand, as they were faithful in their time, and that when I meet them, I shall meet them as I met them here, in love, in harmony, in unison, and in perfect confidence that I have done my duty as they have done theirs.

I hope you will forgive me for my emotion. You would have peculiar emotions, would you not, if you felt that you stood in the presence of your Father, in the very presence of Almighty God, in the very presence of the Son of God and of holy angels? You would feel rather emotional, rather sensitive. I feel it to the very depths of my soul this moment. So I hope you will forgive me, if I exhibit some of my real feelings.—Apr. C. R., 1916, pp. 2-4.

CONDITION IN A FUTURE LIFE. Some people dream, you know, and think, and teach that all the glory they ever expect to have in the world to come is to sit in the light and glory of the Son of God, and sing praises and songs of joy and gratitude all their immortal lives. We do not believe in any such things. We believe that every man will have his work to do in the other world, just as surely as he had it to do here, and a greater work than he can do here. We believe that we are on the road of advancement, of development in knowledge, in understanding, and in every good thing, and that we will continue to grow, advance, and develop throughout the eternities that are before us. That is what we believe.—Apr. C. R., 1912, p. 8.

SPIRITUAL DEATH. But I want to speak a word or two in relation to another death, which is a more terrible death than that of the body. When Adam, our first parent, partook of the forbidden fruit, transgressed the law of God, and became subject unto Satan, he was banished from the presence of God, and was thrust out into outer spiritual darkness. This was the first death. Yet living, he was dead —dead to God, dead to light and truth, dead spiritually; cast out from the presence of God; communication between the Father and the Son was cut off. He was as absolutely thrust out from the presence of God as was Satan and the hosts that followed him. That was spiritual death. But the Lord said that he would not suffer Adam nor his posterity to come to the temporal death until they should have the means by which they might be redeemed from the first death, which is spiritual. Therefore angels were sent unto Adam, who taught him the gospel, and revealed to him the principle by which he could be redeemed from the first death, and be brought back from banishment and outer darkness into the marvelous light of the gospel. He was taught faith, repentance, and baptism for the remission of sins, in the name of Jesus Christ, who should come in the meridian of time and take away the sin of the world, and was thus given a chance to be redeemed from the spiritual death before he should die the temporal death.

Now, all the world today, I am sorry to say, with the exception of a handful of people who have obeyed the new and everlasting covenant, are suffering this spiritual death. They are cast out from the presence of God. They are without God, without gospel truth, and without the power of redemption; for they know not God nor his gospel. In order that they may be redeemed and saved from the spiritual death which has spread over the world like a pall, they must repent of their sins, and be baptized by one having authority, for the remission of their sins, that they may be born of God. That is why we want these young men to go out into the world to preach the gospel. While they themselves understand but little, perhaps, the germ of life is in them. They have been born again, they have received the gift of the Holy Ghost, and they have the authority of the holy Priesthood, by which they can administer in the name of the Father, and of the Son, and of the Holy Ghost. Though they may know but little in the beginning, they can learn, and as they learn they can preach, and as they have opportunity they can baptize for the remission of sins. Therefore, we want them to do their duty at home. We want them above all things to be pure in heart.—Oct. C. R., 1899, p. 72.

THE UNPARDONABLE SIN. Now, if Judas really had known God's power, and had partaken thereof, and did actually "deny the truth" and "defy" that power, "having denied the Holy Spirit after he had received it," and also "denied the Only Begotten," after God had "revealed him" unto him, then there can be no doubt that he "will die the second death."

That Judas did partake of all this knowledge—that these great truths had been revealed to him—that he had received the Holy Spirit by the gift of God, and was therefore qualified to commit the unpardonable sin, is not at all clear to me. To my mind it strongly appears that not one of the disciples possessed sufficient light, knowledge nor wisdom, at the time of the crucifixion, for either exaltation or condemnation; for it was afterward that their minds were opened to understand the scriptures, and that they were endowed with power from on high; without which they were only children in knowledge, in comparison to what they afterwards become under the influence of the Spirit.

Saul, of Tarsus, possessing extraordinary intelligence and learning, brought up at the feet of Gamaliel, taught according to the perfect manner of the law, persecuted the Saints unto death, binding and delivering unto prisons both men and women; and when the blood of the Martyr Stephen was shed, Saul stood by keeping the raiment of those who slew him, and consented unto his death. And "he made havoc of the Church, entering into every house, and haling men and women committed them to prison. And when they were put to death, he gave his voice against them, and he "punished them oft in every synagogue, and compelled them to blaspheme; and being exceedingly mad against them, persecuted them even unto strange cities," and yet this man committed no unpardonable sin, because he knew not the Holy Ghost (Acts 8:3; 9:1; 22:4; 26:10, 11); while, for the crime of adultery with Bathsheba, and for ordering Uriah to be put in the front of battle in a time of war, where he was slain by the enemy, the Priesthood, and the kingdom were taken from David, the man after God's own heart, and his soul was thrust into hell. Why? Because "the Holy Ghost spake by the mouth of David"—or, in other words, David possessed the gift of the Holy Ghost, and had power to speak by the light thereof. But even David, though guilty of adultery and murder of Uriah, obtained the promise that his soul should not be left in hell, which means, as I understand it, that even he shall escape the second death.

While suspended upon the cross, in the agonies of death, as he was about to yield up his spirit, our gracious, glorious Savior breathed this memorable and merciful prayer: "Father, forgive them; for they know not what they do." (Luke 23:34.)

No man can sin against light until he has it; nor against the Holy Ghost, until after he has received it by the gift of God through the appointed channel or way. To sin against the Holy Ghost, the Spirit of Truth, the Comforter, the Witness of the Father and the Son, wilfully denying him and defying him, after having received him, constitutes this sin. Did Judas possess this light, this witness, this Comforter, this baptism of fire and the Holy Ghost, this endowment from on high? If he did, he received it before the betrayal, and therefore before the other eleven apostles. And if this be so, you may say, "he is a son of perdition without hope." But if he was destitute of this glorious gift and outpouring of the Spirit, by which the witness came to the eleven, and their minds were opened to see and know the truth, and they were able to testify of him, then what constituted the unpardonable sin of this poor, erring creature, who rose no higher in the scale of intelligence, honor or ambition than to betray the Lord of glory for thirty pieces of silver?

But not knowing that Judas did commit the unpardonable sin; nor that he was a "son of perdition without hope" who will die the second death, nor what knowledge he possessed by which he was able to commit so great a sin, I prefer, until I know better, to take the merciful view that he may be numbered among those for whom the blessed Master prayed, "Father, forgive them; for they know not what they do."—*Improvement Era*, Vol. 21, June, 1918, p. 732.

THE RESURRECTION. Speaking of the resurrection, the subject on which so much has been said during this conference, and appropriately said, too—we distinctly believe that Jesus Christ himself is the true, and only true type of the resurrection of men from death unto life. We believe there is no other form of resurrection from death to life; that as he rose, and as he preserved his identity, even to the scars of the wounds in his hands and feet and side, that he could prove himself to those that were skeptical of the possibility of rising from the dead, that he was indeed himself, the Lord crucified, buried in the tomb, and raised again from death to life, so it will be with you and with every son and daughter of Adam, born into the world. You will not lose your identity any more than Christ did. You will be brought forth from death to life again, just as surely as Christ was brought forth from death to life again, just as surely as those who ministered to the Prophet Joseph Smith had been raised from death to life—therefore, in the same manner in which Christ has been raised, so will life, and the resurrection from death to life again, come upon all who have descended from our first parents. The death that came into the world by Adam's transgression has been conquered, and its terror vanquished by the power and righteousness of the Son of God. He came to redeem man from the temporal death, and also to save him from spiritual death if he will repent of his sins, and will believe on the name of Christ, follow his example, and obey his laws.—*Apr. C. R.*, 1912, pp. 135-136.

NATURE OF MINISTERING ANGELS. We are told by the Prophet Joseph Smith, that "there are no angels who minister to this earth but those who do belong or have belonged to it." Hence, when messengers are sent to minister to the inhabitants of this earth, they are not strangers, but from the ranks of our kindred, friends, and fellow-beings and fellow-servants. The ancient prophets who died were those who came to visit their fellow creatures upon the earth. They came to Abraham, to Isaac, and to Jacob; it was such beings—holy beings if you please—who waited upon the Savior and administered to him on the Mount. The angel that visited John, when an exile, and unfolded to his vision future events in the history of man upon the earth, was one who had been here, who had toiled and suffered in common with the people of God; for you remember that John, after his eyes had beheld the glories of the great future, was about to fall down and worship him, but was peremptorily forbidden to do so. "See thou do it not; for I am thy fellow-servant, and of thy brethren the prophets, and of them which keep the sayings of this book; worship God." (Rev. 22:9) Jesus has visited the people of this earth from time to time. He visited and showed himself in his spiritual body to the brother of Jared, touching certain stones with his finger, that the brother of Jared had fashioned out of the rock, making them to give light to him and his people in the barges in which they crossed the waters of the great deep to come to this land. He visited others at various times before and after he tabernacled in the flesh. It was Jesus who created this earth, it therefore is his inheritance, and he had a perfect right to come and minister to inhabitants of this earth. He came in the meridian of time and tabernacled in the flesh, some 33 years among men, introducing and teaching the fulness of the gospel, and calling upon all men to follow in his footsteps; to do the same thing that he himself did, that they might be worthy to inherit with him the same glory. After he suffered the death of the body, he appeared, not only to his disciples and others on the eastern continent, but to the inhabitants of this continent, and he ministered unto them as he did to the people in the land of Palestine. In like manner our fathers and mothers, brothers, sisters and friends who have passed away from this earth, having been faithful, and worthy to enjoy these rights and privileges, may have a mission given them to visit their relatives and friends upon the earth again, bringing from the divine Presence messages of love, of warning, or reproof and instruction, to those whom they had learned to love in the flesh. And so it is with Sister Cannon. She can return and visit her friends, provided it be in accordance with the wisdom of the Almighty. There are laws to which they who are in the Paradise of God must be subject, as well as laws to which we are subject. It is our duty to make ourselves acquainted with those laws, that we may know how to live in harmony with his will while we dwell in the flesh, that we may be entitled to come forth in the morning of the first resurrection, clothed with glory, immortality and eternal lives, and be permitted to sit down at the right hand of God, in the kingdom of heaven. And except we become acquainted with those laws, and live in harmony with them, we need not expect to enjoy these privileges; Joseph Smith, Hyrum Smith, Brigham Young, Heber C. Kimball, Jedediah M. Grant, David Patten, Joseph Smith, Sen., and all those noble men who took an active part in the establishment of this work, and who died true and faithful to their trust, have the right and privilege, and possess the keys and power, to minister to the people of God in the flesh who live now, as much so and on the same principle as the ancient servants of God had the right to return to the earth and minister to the Saints of God in their day.

These are correct principles. There is no question about that in my mind. It is according to the Scriptures; it is according to the revelation of God to the Prophet Joseph Smith; and it is a subject upon which we may dwell with pleasure and perhaps profit to ourselves, provided we have the Spirit of God to direct us.—Discourse delivered at the funeral services of Elizabeth H. Cannon, Fourteenth Ward assembly rooms, Salt Lake City, January 29, 1882, *Journal of Discourses*, Vol. 22, pp. 350-353.

REDEMPTION BEYOND THE GRAVE. "But woe unto him that has the law given; yea, that has all the commandments of God, like unto us, and that transgresseth them, and that wasteth the days of his probation, for awful is his state." (II Nephi 9:27-38; see also Alma 11:40, 41.)

Now, it is evident that such as these have no chance for redemption, no matter what may be done for them in hope or by faith, for they will have sinned against life and knowledge, and are, therefore, worthy of damnation. It is nowhere revealed that such as these will ever be forgiven, although we are informed that all of God's judgments are not given unto men.

There is no other means of salvation revealed or given to the children of men except that offered by the Son of God, and those who reject this, whether before or after they have received it in part, cannot be saved, because they rejected the means of their redemption and salvation. Not so with those to whom Christ went to deliver the gospel when his body lay in the tomb; they were disobedient to the message of Noah, which was a warning to them to repent or they should be destroyed by a flood. We are not told to what extent the gospel of Christ, in its fulness, was proclaimed to them, but are left to suppose that the message of Noah was not the fulness of the gospel, but a cry of repentance from sin that they might escape de-struction by the flood. They hardened their hearts against Noah's message, and would not receive it, and were punished for this disobedience in their destruction by the flood; thus in part paying the penalties for their disobedience; but not having received the light they could not be condemned as those spoken of in II Nephi 9, who had all the commandments of God given unto them.

Therefore, Jesus went with his message to their spirits in prison and proclaimed liberty and deliverance to them through their obedience in the spirit world, that the work might be done for them in the flesh, and they be judged according to men in the flesh, and live according to God in the spirit. So there is no conflict in these scriptures. Of course, there is a difference between those who receive the light of the gospel and the testimony of Jesus Christ and after-wards rebel against that light and reject it, thereby putting Christ to an open shame and crucifying him, and those who are referred to by Alma: "Therefore the wicked remain as though there had been no redemption made." These are not under as great a condemnation as those who have received it and rejected it; but so long as they remain unrepentant and wicked, there is no redemption for them any more than for others; but it is possible that these may repent in the spirit world.

In relation to the deliverance of spirits from their prison house, of course, we believe that can only be done after the gospel has been preached to them in the spirit, and they have accepted the same, and the work necessary to their redemption by the living be done for them. That this work may be hastened so that all who believe, in the spirit world, may receive the benefit of deliverance, it is revealed that the great work of the Millennium shall be the work in the temples for the redemption of the dead; and then we hope to enjoy the benefits of revelation through the Urim and Thummim, or by such means as the Lord may reveal concerning those for whom the work shall be done, so that we may not work by chance, or by faith alone, without knowledge, but with the actual knowledge revealed unto us. It stands to reason that, while the gospel may be preached unto all, the good and the bad, or rather to those who would repent and to those who would not repent in the spirit world, the same as it is here, redemption will only come to those who repent and obey. There is, no doubt, great leniency given to people who are anxious to do the work for their dead, and in some instances, very unworthy people may have the work done for them; it does not follow, however, that they will receive any benefit therefrom, and the correct thing is to do the work only for those of whom we have the testimony that they will receive it. However, we are disposed to give the benefit of the doubt to the dead, as it is better to do the work for many who are unworthy than to neglect one who is worthy. Now, we know in part and see in part, but steadfastly look forward to the time when that which is perfect will come. We are left largely to our own agency here, to exercise our own intelligence and to receive all the light that is revealed so far as we are capable of receiving it, and only those who seek the light, and desire it, are likely to find it.—*Improvement Era*, Vol. 5, December, 1901, pp. 145-147.

NATURE OF DEATH. God has given laws to govern all his works, and especially has he given laws to govern his people, who are his sons and daughters. We have come to sojourn in the flesh, to obtain tabernacles for our immortal spirits; or, in other words, we have come for the purpose of accomplishing a work like that which was accomplished by the Lord Jesus Christ. The object of our earthly existence is that we may have a fulness of joy, and that we may become the sons and daughters of God, in the fullest sense of the word, being heirs of God and joint heirs with Jesus Christ, to be kings and priests unto God, to inherit glory, dominion, exaltation, thrones and every power and attribute developed and possessed by our Heavenly Father. This is the object of our being on this earth. In order to attain unto this exalted position, it is necessary that we go through this mortal experience, or probation, by which we may prove ourselves worthy, through the aid of our elder brother Jesus. The spirit without the body is not perfect. It is not capacitated, without the body, to possess a fulness of the glory of God, and therefore it cannot, without the body, fulfil its destiny. We are foreordained to become conformed to the likeness of the Lord Jesus Christ; and in order that we may become like unto him, we must follow in his footsteps, even until we sanctify ourselves by the law of truth and righteousness. This is the law of the celestial kingdom, and when we die, its power will bring us forth in the morning of the first resurrection, clothed with glory, immortality and eternal lives. Unless we do keep the law that God has given unto us in the flesh, which we have the privilege of receiving and understanding, we cannot be quickened by its glory, neither can we receive the fulness thereof, and the exaltation of the celestial kingdom.

"There is a law, irrevocably decreed in heaven before the foundations of the world, upon which all blessings are predicated; and when we obtain any blessing from God, it is by obedience to that law upon which it is predicated."—(Doctrine and Covenants 130:20.)

We must, therefore, learn the laws of heaven, which are the laws of the gospel, live and obey them with all our hearts, and in faith abide in them, perfecting ourselves thereby, in order to receive the fulness of the glory of that kingdom. * * *

While we are in mortality we are clogged, and we see as through a glass darkly, we see only in part, and it is difficult for us to comprehend the smallest things with which we are associated. But when we put on immortality, our condition will be very different, for we ascend into an enlarged sphere; although we shall not become perfect immediately after our departure from the body, for the spirit without the body is not perfect, and the body without the spirit is dead. The disembodied spirit during the interval of the death of the body and its resurrection from the grave is not perfect, hence it is not prepared to enter into the exaltation of the celestial kingdom; but it has the privilege of soaring in the midst of immortal beings, and of enjoying, to a certain extent, the presence of God, not the fulness of his glory, not the fulness of the reward which we are seeking and which we are destined to receive, if found faithful to the law of the celestial kingdom, but only in part.

The righteous spirit that departs from this earth is assigned its place in the Paradise of God; it has its privileges and honors which are in point of excellency, far above and beyond human comprehension; and in this sphere of action, enjoying this partial reward for its righteous conduct on the earth, it continues its labors, and in this respect is very different from the state of the body from which it is released. For while the body sleeps and decays, the spirit receives a new birth; to it the portals of life are opened. It is born again into the presence of God. The spirit of our beloved sister in taking its departure from this world is born again into the spirit world, returning there from the mission it has been performing in this state of probation, having been absent a few years from father, mother, kindred, friends, neighbors, and from all that was dear; it has returned nearer to the home-circle, to old associations and scenes, much in the same way as a man who comes home from a foreign mission, to join again his family and friends and enjoy the pleasures and comforts of home.

This is the condition of her whose remains now lie before us, and of every one who has been faithful to virtue and purity, while traveling here below; but more especially of those who while here had the privilege of obeying the gospel, and who lived true and faithful to its covenants. Instead of continuing here among the things of time, surrounded as we are with the weaknesses of a fallen world, and subject to earthly cares and sorrows, they are freed from them to enter a state of joy, glory and exaltation; not a fulness of any one of them, but to await the morning of the resurrection of the just, to come forth from the grave to redeem the body, and to be reunited with it and thus become a living soul, an immortal being, never more to die. Having accomplished its work, having gone through its earthly probation, and having fulfilled its mission here below, it is then prepared for the knowledge and glory and exaltation of the celestial kingdom. This Jesus did; and he is our forerunner, he is our exemplar. The path which he marked out we have to walk, if we ever expect to dwell and be crowned with him in his kingdom. We must obey and put our trust in him, knowing that he is the Savior of the world.

What reason have we to mourn? None, except that we are deprived for a few days of the society of one whom we love. And if we prove faithful while in the flesh we will soon follow, and be glad that we had the privilege of passing through mortality, and that we lived in a day in which the fulness of the everlasting gospel was preached, through which we will be exalted, for there is no exaltation except through obedience to law. Every blessing, privilege, glory, or exaltation is obtained only through obedience to the law upon which the same is promised. If we will abide the law, we shall receive the reward; but we can receive it on no other ground. Then let us rejoice in the truth, in the restoration of the Priesthood—that power delegated to man, by virtue of which the Lord sanctions in the heavens what man does upon the earth. The Lord has taught us the ordinances of the gospel by which we may perfect our exaltation in his kingdom. We are not living as the heathen, without law; that which is necessary for our exaltation has been revealed. Our duty, therefore, is to obey the laws; then we shall receive our reward, no matter whether we are cut down in childhood, in manhood, or old age; it is all the same, so long as we are living up to the light we possess we shall not be shorn of any blessing, nor deprived of any privilege; for there is a time after this mortal life, and there is a way provided by which we may fulfil the measure of our creation and destiny, and accomplish the whole great work that we have been sent to do, although it may reach far into the future before we fully accomplish it.

Jesus had not finished his work when his body was slain, neither did he finish it after his resurrection from the dead; although he had accomplished the purpose for which he then came to the earth, he had not fulfilled all his work. And when will he? Not until he has redeemed and saved every son and daughter of our father Adam that have been or ever will be born upon this earth to the end of time, except the sons of perdition. That is his mission. We will not finish our work until we have saved ourselves, and then not until we shall have saved all depending upon us; for we are to become saviors upon Mount Zion, as well as Christ. We are called to this mission. The dead are not perfect without us, neither are we without them. We have a mission to perform for and in their behalf; we have a certain work to do in order to liberate those who, because of their ignorance and the unfavorable circumstances in which they were placed while here, are unprepared for eternal life; we have to open the door for them, by performing ordinances which they cannot perform for themselves, and which are essential to their release from the "prison-house," to come forth and live according to God in the spirit, and be judged according to men in the flesh.

The Prophet Joseph Smith has said that this is one of the most important duties that devolves upon the Latter-day Saints. And why? Because this is the dispensation of the fulness of times, which will usher in the millennial reign, and in which all things spoken by the mouths of holy prophets, since the world began, must be fulfilled, and all things united, both which are in heaven and in the earth. We have that work to do; or, at least all we can of it, leaving the balance to our children, in whose hearts we should instill the importance of this work; rearing them in the love of the truth and in the knowledge of these principles, so that when we pass away, having done all we can do, they will then take up the labor and continue it until it is consummated.

May the Lord bless this bereaved family and comfort them in their deprivation. Those who die in the Lord shall not taste of death. When Adam partook of the forbidden fruit he was cast out from the presence of God into outer darkness; that is, he was shut out from the presence of his glory and the privilege of his society, which was spiritual death. This was the first death; this indeed was death; for he was shut out from the presence of God; and ever since, Adam's posterity have been suffering the penalty of this spiritual death, which is banishment from his presence and the society of holy beings. This first death will also be the second death. Now we look upon the mortal remains of our departed sister; her immortal part has gone. Where? Into outer darkness?—banished from the presence of God? No, but born again into his presence, restored, or born from death to life, to immortality and to joy in his presence. This is not death, then; and this is true in relation to all Saints who die in the Lord and the covenant of the gospel. They return from the midst of death to life, where death has no power.

There is no death except to those who die in sin, without the sure and steadfast hope of the resurrection of the just. There is no death where we continue in the knowledge of the truth and have hope of a glorious resurrection. Life and immortality are brought to light through the gospel; hence, there is no death here; here is a peaceful slumber, a quiet rest for a little season, and then she will come forth again to enjoy this tabernacle. If there is anything lacking in regard to ordinances pertaining to the House of the Lord, which may have been omitted or not reached, those requirements can be attended to for her. Here are her father and mother, her brothers and sisters; they know the ordinances necessary to be performed in order to secure every benefit and blessing that it was possible for her to have received in the flesh. These ordinances have been revealed unto us for this very purpose, that we might be born into the light from the midst of this darkness—from death into life.

We live, then; we do not die; we do not anticipate death but we anticipate life, immortality, glory, exaltation, and to be quickened by the glory of the celestial kingdom, and receive of the same even a fulness. This is our destiny; this is the exalted position to which we may attain and there is no power that can deprive or rob us of it, if we prove faithful and true to the covenant of the gospel.—Funeral sermon preached over the remains of Emma Wells, Salt Lake City, April 11, 1878.—*Journal of Discourses*, Vol. 19, 1878, pp. 258-265.

THE RESURRECTION. Guided by the Spirit of the Lord Jesus by faith in God, in the testimony of his prophets and in the scriptures, I accept the doctrine of the resurrection with all my heart, and rejoice at its confirmation in nature with the awakening of each returning spring. The Spirit of God testifies to me, and has revealed to me, to my complete personal satisfaction, that there is life after death, and that the body which we lay down here will be reunited with our spirit, to become a perfect soul, capable of receiving a fulness of joy in the presence of God.—*Improvement Era*, Vol. 16, 1912-1913, pp. 508-510.

THE RESURRECTION. It is true, all of us are clothed with mortality, but our spirits existed long before they took upon them this tabernacle that we now inhabit. When this body dies, the spirit does not die. The spirit is an immortal being, and when separated from the body takes its flight to the place prepared for it, and there awaits the resurrection of the body, when the spirit will return again and re-occupy this tabernacle which it occupied in this world.

This great and glorious principle of the resurrection is no longer a theory, as some think, but it is an accomplished fact which has been demonstrated beyond all successful contradiction, doubt or controversy. Job, who lived before the resurrection of Christ, possessing the spirit of prophecy, looked forward to the time of the resurrection. He comprehended the fact. He understood the principles and knew the power and design of God to bring it to pass, and predicted its accomplishment. He declares: "I know that my Redeemer liveth, and that he shall stand at the latter day upon the earth." He further says, "And though after my skin worms destroy this body, yet in my flesh shall I see God." (Job 19:25-26) He looked forward to something not yet done, something which had never been done in this world before his day. It was not accomplished till long after his time. Having received the spirit of the gospel and of revelation, he was enabled to look down into unborn time and see his body which had moulded and crumbled into dust, raised from the dead. What he saw by the eye of faith has become actual history unto us, and we possess not only the history of the fact but a knowledge by the testimony of the Holy Ghost of its truth. We are not therefore situated as Job was; we live in the latter times which are pregnant with grand and glorious events, among the greatest of which is this glorious principle of the resurrection of the dead, which is no longer a mere prediction, a cherished hope, or a prophetic promise, but a reality; for long before our day it has actually been accomplished. Christ himself burst the barriers of the tomb, conquered death and the grave and came forth "the first fruits of them that slept." But, says one, how can we know that Jesus was put to death or resurrected? We have plenty of evidence to show that Jesus was crucified and resurrected. We have the testimony of his disciples, and they produce irrefutable evidence that they did see him crucified, and witnessed the wounds of the nails and spear which he received on the cross. They also testify that his body was laid away in a sepulchre wherein no man had lain, and they rolled a great stone to the door and departed.

Now the chief priests and Pharisees were not satisfied with the crucifixion and burial of our Lord and Savior; they remembered that while living he had said that after three days he would rise again, so they established a strong guard to protect the sepulchre, and set a seal upon the stone, lest his disciples should come by night and steal away the body and say unto the people, "He is risen from the dead," and thus perpetuate a fraud upon the world.

Lo and behold! by this act those unbelieving guards became actual witnesses to the fact that a heavenly personage came and rolled away the stone and that Jesus came forth. The disciples witness and testify to the resurrection, and their testimony can not be impeached. It therefore stands good, and is true and faithful.

But is this the only evidence we have to depend on? Have we nothing but the testimony of the ancient disciples to rest our hopes upon? Thank God we have more. And the additional evidence which we possess enables us to become witnesses to the truth of the testimony of the ancient disciples. We go to the Book of Mormon; it testifies of the death and resurrection of Jesus Christ in plain and unmistakable terms; we may go to the book of Doctrine and Covenants containing the revelations of this dispensation, and we shall find clear and well defined evidence there. We have the testimony of the Prophet Joseph Smith, the testimony of Oliver Cowdery, and the testimony of Sidney Rigdon, that they saw the Lord Jesus—the same that was crucified in Jerusalem—and that he revealed himself unto them. Joseph and Sidney testify to it as follows:

"We, Joseph Smith, Jr., and Sidney Rigdon, being in the Spirit on the sixteenth of February, in the year of our Lord, one thousand eight hundred and thirty-two, by the power of the Spirit our eyes were opened and our understandings were enlightened, so as to see and understand the things of God—even those things which were from the beginning before the world was, which were ordained of the Father, through his Only Begotten Son, who was in the bosom of the Father, even from the beginning, of whom we bear record, and the record which we bear is the fulness of the gospel of Jesus Christ, who is the Son, whom we saw and with whom we conversed in the heavenly vision." (Doc. and Cov. 76: 11-14)

They were called to be special witnesses of Jesus Christ and his death and resurrection.

We have also the testimony of the ancient disciples who lived on this continent of the crucifixion and resurrection. You will find their testimony recorded in the Book of Mormon. The disciples who lived upon this continent knew what transpired at Jerusalem; the Lord showed them these things. After his resurrection he manifested himself to his disciples on this continent, and showed them the wounds he had received on Calvary. They were convinced that Jesus was the Christ and the Redeemer of the world. They beheld him in the flesh and they bear witness of it, and their testimony is true. We have the testimony of many witnesses. We have the testimony of eleven special witnesses to the divine origin of the Book of Mormon, which book testifies of Christ's resurrection, containing as it does the records of the ancient prophets and disciples of Christ on this continent, thus confirming their testimonies.

Is this all the evidence we have? No. Joseph Smith boldly declared to the world that if mankind would sincerely repent of their sins and be baptized by authority, they should not only receive a remission of their sins, but, by the laying on of hands, they should receive the Holy Ghost, and should know of the doctrine for themselves. Thus all who obey the law and abide in the truth become witnesses of this and other equally great and precious truths. Today there are thousands of Latter-day Saints living in Utah and throughout the world who have attained to the possession of these things, both men and women. If we witness by our acts, and from our hearts, our determination to carry out the mind and will of the Lord, we shall have this double assurance of a glorious resurrection, and be able to say as the Prophet Job said—his was a glorious declaration— "For I know that my Redeemer liveth, and that he shall [again] stand at the latter day upon the earth: and though after my skin worms destroy this body, yet in my flesh shall I see God: whom I shall see for myself, and mine eyes shall behold, and not another; though my reins be consumed within me." (Job 19:25-27) Thousands have received this testimony and can witness unto God and testify from their hearts that they know these things.

I bear my testimony, and surely it is of as much force and effect, if it be true, as the testimony of Job, the testimonies of the disciples of Jerusalem, the disciples on this continent, of Joseph Smith, or any other man who told the truth. All are of equal force and binding on the world. If no man had ever testified to these things upon the face of the globe, I want to say as a servant of God, independent of the testimonies of all men and of every book that has been written, that I have received the witness of the Spirit in my own heart, and I testify before God, angels and men, without fear of the consequences, that I know that my Redeemer lives, and I shall see him face to face, and stand with him in my resurrected body upon this earth, if I am faithful; for God has revealed this unto me. I have received the witness, and I bear my testimony, and my testimony is true.

The testimony of the Latter-day Saints is in addition to and consonant with that of the disciples of Jesus Christ who lived at Jerusalem, those who lived on this continent, the Prophet Joseph, Oliver, Sidney, and others, of our crucified and risen Redeemer, because they received it not of them, but by the same Spirit by which they received it. No man ever received this testimony unless the Spirit of God revealed it unto him.

We will see Brother Urie again. Sister Urie will meet him on the other side of the grave. The spirit and the body will be reunited. We shall see each other in the flesh, in the same tabernacles that we have here while in mortality. Our tabernacles will be brought forth as they are laid down, although there will be a restoration effected; every organ, every limb that has been maimed, every deformity caused by accident or in any other way, will be restored and put right. Every limb and joint shall be restored to its proper frame. We will know each other and enjoy each other's society throughout the endless ages of eternity, if we keep the law of God. It is for us to remain true and faithful and keep our covenants, and to train our children up in the paths of holiness, virtue and truth, in the principles of the gospel, that we may with them be prepared to enjoy the perfect and eternal day.—Discourse delivered at the funeral services of James Urie, Sixteenth ward, Salt Lake City, February 3, 1883.—*Journal of Discourses*, Vol. 24, pp. 75-82.

ON THE RESURRECTION. I believe that as Christ arose from the dead, so shall all the faithful arise. We shall all see one another again. I know that Jesus is the Christ, that after his death and burial he arose from the dead, and became the first fruits of the resurrection. To all believers, and to the Latter-day Saints especially, there is sweet comfort in this knowledge, and in the thought that through obedience to the ordinances and principles of the gospel, which Christ, our Savior, taught and enjoined upon the people and his disciples, men shall be born again, redeemed from sin, arise from the grave, and like Jesus return into the presence of the Father. Death is not the end. When we, sorrowing, lay away our loved ones in the grave, we have an assurance based upon the life, words and resurrection of Christ, that we shall again meet and shake hands and associate with them in a better life, where sorrow and trouble are ended, and where there is to be no more parting.

This knowledge is one of the greatest incentives that we have to live right in this life, to pass through mortality, doing and feeling and accomplishing good. The spirits of all men, as soon as they depart from this mortal body, whether they are good or evil, we are told in the Book of Mormon, are taken home to that God who gave them life, where there is a separation, a partial judgment, and the spirits of those who are righteous are received into a state of happiness which is called paradise, a state of rest, a state of peace, where they expand in wisdom, where they have respite from all their troubles, and where care and sorrow do not annoy. The wicked, on the contrary, have no part nor portion in the Spirit of the Lord, and they are cast into outer darkness, being led captive, because of their own iniquity, by the evil one. And in this space between death and the resurrection of the body, the two classes of souls remain, in happiness or in misery, until the time which is appointed of God that the dead shall come forth and be reunited both spirit and body, and be brought to stand before God, and be judged according to their works. This is the final judgment.

Where a man has obeyed the principles of the gospel, used his influence for good, injured no soul, loved righteousness, and despised wrong doing, laying down his body to the rest of the righteous in the grave, I feel and know that, in addition to the spirit's promised state of peace and rest in paradise, there will be a glorious reunion of body and spirit, a bright awakening for him in the resurrection, and a future beyond, full of happiness. When this time shall come, none but God knoweth, but we do know that all men shall come forth from the dead.

Now, I know these statements to be true; I know them to be true by the thrill of the inspiration of God which fills my entire being with this knowledge. To me they are consistent with God's wisdom and with his holy purposes. We have the testimony of Christ, the testimony of the prophets, the whisperings of the Holy Spirit, and with these evidences, I cannot help but believe, and know that there is a resurrection of the dead, a literal, actual resurrection of the body. I cannot believe that a wise and merciful God would create a man like our friend and brother, upright, honorable, honest in all his dealings and in his life, only to live a few years, then to pass away forever, to be known no more. As Jesus arose from the dead so will he, and all the innocent and righteous, arise. The elements which compose this temporal body will not perish, will not cease to exist, but in the day of the resurrection these elements will come together again, bone to bone, and flesh to flesh. The body will come forth as it is laid to rest, for there is no growth nor development in the grave. As it is laid down, so will it arise, and changes to perfection will come by the law of restitution.—*Improvement Era*, Vol. 7, June, 1914, p. 619.

RESURRECTION AND FINAL JUDGMENT. When the spirit leaves the body, it returns, says the prophet, immediately to God, to be assigned to its place, either to associate with the good and the noble ones who have lived in the paradise of God, or to be confined in the "prison-house" to await the resurrection of the body from the grave. Therefore we know that Brother Clayton has gone to God, gone to receive the partial judgment of the Almighty which pertains to the period intervening between the death of the body and the resurrection of the body, or the separation of the spirit from the body and their uniting together again. This judgment is passed upon the spirit alone. But there will come a time which will be after the resurrection, when the body and spirit shall be reunited, when the final judgment will be passed on every man. This is in accordance with the vision of John the Revelator:

"And I saw the dead, small and great, stand before God; and the books were opened: and another book was opened, which is the book of life: and the dead were judged out of those things which were written in the books, according to their works.

"And the sea gave up the dead which were in it; and death and hell delivered up the dead which were in them: * * * and death and hell were cast into the lake of fire. This is the second death.

"And whosoever was not found written in the book of life was cast into the lake of fire." (Rev. 20:12-15)

That is the final judgment, which we will all receive after we have performed this our earthly mission.

The Savior did not finish his work when he expired on the cross, when he cried out, "It is finished." He, in using those words, had no reference to his great mission to the earth, but merely to the agonies which he suffered. The Christian world, I know, say he alluded to the great work of redemption. This, however, is a great mistake, and is indicative of the extent of their knowledge of the plan of life and salvation. I say, he referred merely to the agonies of death, and the sufferings he felt for the wickedness of men who would go so far as to crucify their Redeemer. It was this feeling, and this alone, that prompted him to cry out in the agony of his soul, "It is finished," and then he expired.

But his work was not completed; it was in fact only begun. If he had stopped here, instead of his being the Savior of the world, he, as well as all mankind, would have perished irredeemably, never to have come forth out of the grave; for it was designed from the beginning that he should be the first fruits of them that slept; it was part of the great plan that he should burst the bands of death and gain the victory over the grave. If, therefore, his mission had ceased when he gave up the ghost, the world would have slumbered in the dust in interminable death, never to have risen to live again. It was but a small part of the mission of the Savior that was performed when he suffered death; it was indeed the lesser part; the greater had yet to be done.

It was in his resurrection from the tomb, in his coming forth from death unto life, in uniting again the spirit and the body that he might become a living soul; and when this was done, then he was prepared to return to the Father. And all this was in strict accordance with the great plan of salvation. For even Christ himself, though without sin, was required to observe the outward ordinance of baptism, in order to fulfil all righteousness.

So, after his resurrection from the dead he could return to the Father, there to receive the welcome plaudit, Well done; you have done your work, you have accomplished your mission, you have wrought out salvation for all the children of Adam; you have redeemed all men from the grave; and through their obedience to the ordinances of the gospel which you have established, they can also be redeemed from the spiritual death, again to be brought back into our presence, to partake of glory, exaltation and eternal life with us.

And so it will be when we come forth out of the grave, when the trump shall sound, and these our bodies shall rise and our spirits shall enter into them again, and they shall become living souls, no more to be dissolved or separated, but to become inseparable, immortal, eternal.

Then we shall stand before the bar of God to be judged. So says the Bible, so says the Book of Mormon, and so say the revelations which have come direct to us through the Prophet Joseph Smith. And then those who have not been subject and obedient to the celestial law will not be quickened by the celestial glory. And those who have not been subject and obedient to the terrestrial law will not be quickened by the terrestrial glory. And those who have not been subject and obedient to the telestial law, will not be quickened by a telestial glory; but they will have a kingdom without glory.

The sons of perdition, men who once were in possession of the light and truth, but who turned away from them and denied the Lord, putting him to an open shame, as did the Jews when they crucified him and said, "His blood be on us, and on our children;" men who consent, against light and knowledge, to the shedding of innocent blood, it will be said unto them, "Depart from me, ye cursed." (Matt. 25:41) I never knew you; depart into the second death, even banishment from the presence of God for ever and ever, where the worm dieth not and the fire is not quenched, from whence there is no redemption, neither in time nor in eternity. Herein is the difference between the second and the first death wherein man became spiritually dead; for from the first death he may be redeemed by the blood of Christ, through obedience to the laws and ordinances of the gospel, but from the second, there is no redemption at all.

We read in the book of Doctrine and Covenants, that the devil tempted Adam, and he partook of the forbidden fruit, and transgressed the commandment, wherein he became subject to the will of the devil because he yielded unto temptation, and because of this transgression he became "spiritually dead, which is the first death, even that same death, which is the last death, which is spiritual, which shall be pronounced upon the wicked when I shall say—Depart, ye cursed!" (Doc. and Cov. 29:41.)

But who will receive such punishment? Only those who deserve it, those who commit the unpardonable sin.

Then there is the banishment of the transgressor (not the sons of perdition) into the prison-house, a place of punishment, with no exaltation, no increase, no dominion, no power, whose inhabitants after their redemption may become servants of them that have obeyed the laws of God and kept the faith. That will be the punishment of such as reject the truth, but sin not unto death.—Discourse delivered at funeral of William Clayton, in the Seventeenth Ward meeting-house, Salt Lake City, December 7, 1879.—*Journal of Discourses,* Vol. 21, 1881, pp. 9-13.

CONDITION OF CHILDREN IN HEAVEN. If we have received the testimony of the spirit of truth in our souls we know that all is well with our little children who pass away, that we could not, if we would, better their condition; and least of all would it better their condition if we could call them back here, for the reason that so long as man is in the world, clothed with mortality, surrounded by the evils that are in the world, he runs chances and is subject to risks, and there are responsibilities resting upon him which may prove fatal to his future prosperity, happiness and exaltation. It is only those who are thoroughly and firmly grounded in the truth, who are established in the principles of life, that will be able to certainly claim the reward of the faithful, and an exaltation in the presence of the Father. As soon as any man turns away from the truth that binds him to God, that moment he is in danger, and may fall.

But, with little children who are taken away in infancy and innocence before they have reached the years of accountability, and are not capable of committing sin, the gospel reveals to us the fact that they are redeemed, and Satan has no power over them. Neither has death any power over them. They are redeemed by the blood of Christ, and they are saved just as surely as death has come into the world through the fall of our first parents. It is further written that Satan has no power over men or women, except that power which he gains over them in this world. In other words, none of the children of the Father who are redeemed through obedience, faith, repentance, and baptism for the remission of sins, and who live in that redeemed condition, and die in that condition are subject to Satan. Therefore he has no power over them. They are absolutely beyond his reach, just as little children are who die without sin. To my mind this is a consolation and a glorious truth that my soul delights in. I am grateful to my heavenly Father that he has revealed it unto me, for it affords a consolation that nothing else can give, and it brings a joy to my spirit that nothing can take away, except the consciousness on my part of having sinned and transgressed against light and knowledge which I may have possessed.

Under these circumstances, our beloved friends who are now deprived of their little one, have great cause for joy and rejoicing, even in the midst of the deep sorrow that they feel at the loss of their little one for a time. They know he is all right; they have the assurance that their little one has passed away without sin. Such children are in the bosom of the Father. They will inherit their glory and their exaltation, and they will not be deprived of the blessings that belong to them; for, in the economy of heaven, and in the wisdom of the Father, who doeth all things well, those who are cut down as little children are without any responsibility for their taking off, they, themselves, not having the intelligence and wisdom to take care of themselves and to understand the laws of life; and, in the wisdom and mercy and economy of God our Heavenly Father, all that could have been obtained and enjoyed by them if they had been permitted to live in the flesh will be provided for them hereafter. They will lose nothing by being taken away from us in this way.

This is a consolation to me. Joseph Smith, the prophet, was the promulgator under God of these principles. He was in touch with the heavens. God revealed himself unto him, and made known unto him the principles that lie before us, and which are comprised in the everlasting gospel. Joseph Smith declared that the mother who laid down her little child, being deprived of the privilege, the joy, and the satisfaction of bringing it up to manhood or womanhood in this world, would, after the resurrection, have all the joy, satisfaction and pleasure, and even more than it would have been possible to have had in mortality, in seeing her child grow to the full measure of the stature of its spirit. If this be true, and I believe it, what a consolation it is. Jesus Christ was the Son of God before he came into the world, yet he came as an infant, grew and developed into manhood, and when his spirit departed from its tabernacle it went to proclaim the gospel to the spirits which were imprisoned, possessing all the intelligence, powers and faculties which it had in the flesh, except the possession of the body, wherein he became absolutely like unto God. And so I believe it is with all men that come into the world. Every spirit that comes to this earth to take upon it a tabernacle is a son or a daughter of God, and possesses all the intelligence and all the attributes that any son or daughter can enjoy, either in the spirit world, or in this world, except that in the spirit, and separated from the body, they lacked just the tabernacle of being like God the Father. It is said that God is a spirit, and they who worship him must worship him in spirit and in truth. But he is a spirit possessing the tabernacle of flesh and bones, as tangible as a man's and therefore to be like God and

Jesus all men must have a body. It matters not whether these tabernacles mature in this world, or have to wait and mature in the world
to come, according to the word of the Prophet Joseph Smith, the body
will develop, either in time or in eternity, to the full stature of the
spirit, and when the mother is deprived of the pleasure and joy of
rearing her babe to manhood or to womanhood in this life, through
the hand of death, that privilege will be renewed to her hereafter, and
she will enjoy it to a fuller fruition than it would be possible for her
to do here. When she does it there, it will be with the certain knowledge that the results will be without failure; whereas here, the results
are unknown until after we have passed the test.

With these thoughts in my mind, I take consolation in the fact
that I shall meet my children who have passed behind the veil; I have
lost a number, and I have felt all that a parent can feel, I think, in the
loss of my children. I have felt it keenly, for I love children, and I
am particularly fond of the little ones, but I feel thankful to God for
the knowledge of these principles, because now I have every confidence in his word and in his promise that I will possess in the future
all that belongs to me, and my joy will be full. I will not be deprived
of any privilege or any blessing that I am worthy of and that may be
properly entrusted to me. But every gift, and every blessing that it
is possible for me to become worthy of I shall possess, either in time
or in eternity, and it will not matter, so that I acknowledge the hand
of God in all these things, and say in my heart, "The Lord giveth
and the Lord taketh away, blessed be the name of the Lord." This is
the way we should feel with regard to our children, or our relatives,
or friends, or whatever vicissitudes we may be called to pass through.

Now, the beauty of this to me is that I know these things, that I
am satisfied of them, and so long as I possess the spirit of truth I have
no fear that any doubt or uncertainty will ever enter my mind in
regard to these principles. There is only one course that I might
pursue which would bring about mistrust and fear, trembling and
doubt, in relation to these things. And that would be for me to deny
the truth and cut myself loose from the guiding influences of the Holy
Spirit, for I do know that so long as a man is under the guiding influence of the Spirit of God he never can deny these truths which God
has revealed to him, and in that condition he is not subject to the
power of Satan. It is only when he transgresses the law of God, and
dismisses these principles from his thoughts, that he becomes subject
to the powers of evil, that his mind becomes darkened, and he begins

to doubt and fear. But, let a man have the Spirit of God in his heart, that Spirit which reveals the things of God unto men, and makes them to know the truth as God himself knows it, he never can doubt those things which God has revealed. Therefore, I rejoice in these truths, for I know they are true.

I know that Brother Heber and his companion, if they are faithful to the light they possess and to the covenants that they have entered into before the Lord, will just as assuredly inherit the joy and the possession and the glory of this little one that has now departed, as that they see its little form lying here before them this moment. Everyone who has the spirit of truth in his soul must feel this to be true.— Remarks at the funeral of Daniel Wells Grant, child of Heber J. Grant, and Emily Wells Grant, in family residence, Salt Lake City, March 12, 1895.—Young Woman's Journal, Vol. 6, pp. 369-374.

STATUS OF CHILDREN IN THE RESURRECTION. The spirits of our children are immortal before they come to us, and their spirits, after bodily death, are like they were before they came. They are as they would have appeared if they had lived in the flesh, to grow to maturity, or to develop their physical bodies to the full stature of their spirits. If you see one of your children that has passed away it may appear to you in the form in which you would recognize it, the form of childhood; but if it came to you as a messenger bearing some important truth, it would perhaps come as the spirit of Bishop Edward Hunter's son (who died when a little child) came to him, in the stature of full-grown manhood, and revealed himself to his father, and said: "I am your son."

Bishop Hunter did not understand it. He went to my father and said: "Hyrum, what does that mean? I buried my son when he was only a little boy, but he has come to me as a full-grown man— a noble, glorious, young man, and declared himself my son. What does it mean?"

Father (Hyrum Smith, the Patriarch) told him that the Spirit of Jesus Christ was full-grown before he was born into the world; and so our children were full-grown and possessed their full stature in the spirit, before they entered mortality, the same stature that they will possess after they have passed away from mortality, and as they will also appear after the resurrection, when they shall have completed their mission.

Joseph Smith taught the doctrine that the infant child that was laid away in death would come up in the resurrection as a child; and, pointing to the mother of a lifeless child, he said to her: "You will have the joy, the pleasure, and satisfaction of nurturing this child, after its resurrection, until it reaches the full stature of its spirit." There is restitution, there is growth, there is development, after the resurrection from death. I love this truth. It speaks volumes of happiness, of joy and gratitude to my soul. Thank the Lord he has revealed these principles to us.

In 1854, I met with my aunt, the wife of my uncle, Don Carlos Smith, who was the mother of that little girl that Joseph Smith, the Prophet, was speaking about when he told the mother that she should have the joy, the pleasure, and the satisfaction of rearing that child, after the resurrection, until it reached the full stature of its spirit; and that it would be a far greater joy than she could possibly have in mortality, because she would be free from the sorrow and fear and disabilities of mortal life, and she would know more than she could know in this life. I met that widow, the mother of that child, and she told me this circumstance and bore testimony to me that this was what the Prophet Joseph Smith said when he was speaking at the funeral of her little daughter.

One day I was conversing with a brother-in-law of mine, Lorin Walker, who married my oldest sister. In the course of the conversation he happened to mention that he was present at the funeral of my cousin Sophronia, and that he heard the Prophet Joseph Smith declare the very words that Aunt Agnes had told me.

I said to him, "Lorin, what did the Prophet say?" and he repeated, as nearly as he could remember, what the Prophet Joseph said in relation to little children. The body remains undeveloped in the grave, but the spirit returns to God who gave it. Afterwards, in the resurrection, the spirit and body will be reunited; the body will develop and grow to the full stature of the spirit; and the resurrected soul will go on to perfection. So I had the statement of two witnesses who heard this doctrine announced by the Prophet Joseph Smith, the source of intelligence.

Eventually I was in conversation with Sister M. Isabella Horne. She began to relate to me the circumstance of her being present at the funeral that I refer to, when Joseph spoke of the death of little children, their resurrection, as little children, and of the glory, and honor, and joy, and happiness the mother would have in rearing her little children in the resurrection to the full stature of their spirits.

"Well," she said, "I heard Joseph say that. I was at that funeral." Sister Isabella Horne told me this.

Then I said to her: "Why haven't you spoken about it before? How is it you have kept it to yourself all these long years? Why haven't you let the Church know something about this declaration of the Prophet?"

She replied: "I did not know whether it was my duty to do so, or whether it would be proper or not."

I said: "Who else was there?"

"My husband was there."

"Does he remember it?"

"Yes, he remembers it."

"Well, will you and Brother Horne give me an affidavit in writing, stating the fact, and let it be sworn to?"

She said, "With the greatest of pleasure."

So I have the testimony in affidavit form of Brother and Sister Horne, in addition to the testimony of my aunt, and the testimony of my brother-in-law, in relation to the Prophet Joseph's remarks at that funeral.

Just a little while later, to my joy and satisfaction, the first man I ever heard mention it in public was Franklin D. Richards; and when he spoke of it, I felt in my soul: the truth has come out. The truth will prevail. It is mighty, and it will live; for there is no power that can destroy it. Presidents Woodruff and Cannon approved of the doctrine and after that I preached it.

It is a good thing for us not to attempt to advance new doctrine, or new and advanced thought in relation to principles and doctrines pertaining to, or presumed to pertain to, the gospel of Jesus Christ, without weighing it carefully, with the experience of years, before we attempt to make a doctrinal test and to advance it to the people of the Lord. There is so much simple truth, necessary to be understood, that has been revealed to us in the gospel that it is extreme folly in us to attempt to go beyond the truth that has been revealed, until we have mastered and can comprehend the truth that we have. There is a great deal within our reach that we have not yet mastered.—*Improvement Era*, Vol. 21, May, 1918, pp. 567-573.

ADDRESS AT FUNERAL SERVICES OF MARY A. FREEZE. There does not seem to be much left to be said. I endorse heartily and fully every kindly sentiment that I have heard expressed here this afternoon with reference to our departed sister. I have known her, as a worker

in the Church, for a goodly number of years, and have had the pleasure
of frequently meeting her in the various capacities in which she has
labored in the Church, and in every instance I have been more and
more impressed with the pure character and spirit of the woman.
There was a calmness about her appearance, her conversation, and her
conduct that seemed to indicate a well-matured character and a well-
established principle of life. Nothing that I have ever perceived in
her has appeared flighty, unsettled, or unstable, but in everything, her
life indicated a life of stability, of reliability and fidelity to the Lord
and to his covenants.

After hearing the many good things that have been said (yet, as
Brother Joseph E. Taylor has remarked, "not half has been told") in
relation to the good life and labors of our dear sister, it makes my mind
revert to the blessed hopes that are inspired in our souls by and through
our faith in the gospel of our Lord Jesus Christ—the hope that that
gospel inspired in our souls that we are following in the footsteps
of our Redeemer and that every man and woman following in his
footsteps will become like him, will enjoy the blessed privileges which
he enjoyed, will pass through the varied ordeals through which he
passed, and will eventually land at the same goal and will be blessed
with the same privileges, and power and glory, and exaltation that he,
himself, vindicated, proved and fulfilled in his life and death and
resurrection from death to life again. I cannot conceive of any more
desirable thing than is vouchsafed to us in the gospel of Jesus Christ—
that though we die, yet we shall live again, and though we die and
dissolve into the native elements of which our tabernacles are composed, yet these elements will again be restored to each other and be
reorganized, and we will become again living souls just as the Savior
did before us; and his having done so has made it possible for all the
rest of us. What can there be more joyous to think of than the fact
that Brother Freeze, who loved his wife and whom she loved, to whom
he was true and who was true to him all her days of association with
him as wife and mother, will have the privilege of coming up on the
morning of the first resurrection clothed with immortality and eternal
life, and resume the relationship that existed between them in
this life, the relationship of husband and wife, father and mother, parents to their children, having laid the foundation for eternal
glory and eternal exaltation in the kingdom of God! Life without
this hope would seem to me in vain. And yet there is nothing that
I have ever discovered in the world, except the gospel of Jesus Christ,

that gives this assurance. Nothing has ever pointed it out in a tangible way except the gospel of Jesus Christ. Jesus Christ has laid this foundation, has taught this principle and this truth, and has uttered that memorable sentiment that, "He that believeth in me, though he were dead, yet shall he live; and whosoever liveth and believeth in me shall never die." (John 11:25, 26.)

Now, to me this explains the sentiment expressed by Brother Joseph E. Taylor, when he said he did not feel the presence of death when he went to visit her. Do you feel the presence of death here? He did not feel it then. Just prior to the departure of her spirit, there was no element of death there. The element of dissolution—the separation of the spiritual from the temporal, of the immortal from the mortal was visible, but in the presence of the Spirit of the Lord, and with the hope inspired in the gospel of the Son of God, that "he that believeth in me, though he were dead, yet shall he live; and whosoever liveth and believeth in me shall never die," and in the knowledge of the fact that every provision the Lord has given by which we may be prepared to enjoy the fulness of these blessings has been observed and entered into, believed and followed by this good woman, what reason could there be, under such circumstances, for thoughts of death? It was not death, but a change from mortality to immortality, from death, in fact, to life everlasting.

Now, I believe that if ever a soul in the world is entitled to the enjoyment or realization of that saying of the Son of God this good woman is entitled to it; for I believe, according to her knowledge, she was true to every principle by which she might fulfil the intent of it and by which she may receive the verification of it in the world to come.

I do not feel that it would be proper or necessary for me to occupy very much time, but while the brethren and sisters were speaking, the thought naturally passed through my mind—what will be her occupation in the world to come? What will she do there? We are told that she will not be idle. She could not be idle. In God's plans, there is no such thing as idleness. God is not pleased with the thought of idleness. He is not idle, and there is no such thing as inertia in the providences and in the purposes of God. We are either growing and advancing, or are retrograding. We are not stationary. We must grow. The principles of everlasting growth and development tend to glory, to exaltation, to happiness, and to a fulness of joy. What has she been doing? She has been working in the temple, among other things. She has been working, also, as a minister of life among young women of the Church of Jesus Christ of Latter-day Saints. She has labored diligently and earnestly in trying to persuade the daughters of Zion to come to a knowledge of the truth as she possessed it. She seemed to be thoroughly established in it. I have never discovered the least symptom of any dubiety in her mind in reference to the gospel of Jesus Christ. She has been laboring to bring others of the daughters of Zion to the same standard of knowledge, faith and understanding of the principles of the gospel of Christ that she herself possessed, a ministering angel and a mother in Israel, seeking the salvation of other daughters and other mothers in Israel. What can you conceive of grander than a calling like that? Then, as I said, she has been at work in the temple. What for? Administering ordinances that God has revealed are essential to the salvation of the living and their preparation for greater exaltation and glory here and hereafter, and also for the redemption of the dead. What can you think of greater than this? To my mind, there isn't anything so great and so glorious in this world as to labor for the salvation of the living and for the redemption of the dead. We read of the Savior going to preach the gospel to the spirits in prison, when his body lay in the tomb. That was a part of the great mission he had to perform. He was sent not only to preach the gospel to those dwelling in mortality, but he was foreordained and anointed of God to open the doors of the prison house to those in bondage and to proclaim his gospel to them.

I have always believed, and still do believe with all my soul, that such men as Peter and James and the twelve disciples chosen by the Savior in his time, have been engaged all the centuries that have passed since their martyrdom for the testimony of Jesus Christ, in proclaiming liberty to the captives in the spirit world and in opening their prison doors. I do not believe that they could be employed in any greater work. Their special calling and anointing of the Lord himself was to save the world, to proclaim liberty to the captives, and the opening of the prison doors to those who were bound in chains of darkness, superstition, and ignorance. I believe that the disciples who have passed away in this dispensation—Joseph, the Prophet, and his brother Hyrum, and Brigham, and Heber, and Willard, and Daniel and John, and Wilford and all the rest of the prophets who have lived in this dispensation, and who have been intimately associated with the work of redemption and the other ordinances of the gospel of the Son of God in this world, are preaching that same gospel that they lived and preached here, to those who are in darkness in the spirit world and who had not the knowledge before they went. The gospel must be preached to them. We are not perfect without them—they cannot be perfect without us.

Now, among all these millions of spirits that have lived on the earth and have passed away, from generation to generation, since the beginning of the world, without the knowledge of the gospel—among them you may count that at least one-half are women. Who is going to preach the gospel to the women? Who is going to carry the testimony of Jesus Christ to the hearts of the women who have passed away without a knowledge of the gospel? Well, to my mind, it is a simple thing. These good sisters who have been set apart, ordained to the work, called to it, authorized by the authority of the holy Priesthood to minister for their sex, in the House of God for the living and for the dead, will be fully authorized and empowered to preach the gospel and minister to the women while the elders and prophets are preaching it to the men. The things we experience here are typical of the things of God and the life beyond us. There is a great similarity between God's purposes as manifested here and his purposes as carried out in his presence and kingdom. Those who are authorized to preach the gospel here and are appointed here to do that work will not be idle after they have passed away, but will continue to exercise the rights that they obtained here under the Priesthood of the Son of God to minister for the salvation of those who have died without a knowledge of the truth. Some of you will understand when I tell you that some of these good women who have passed beyond have actually been anointed queens and priestesses unto God and unto their husbands, to continue their work and to be the mothers of spirits in the world to come. The world does not understand this —they cannot receive it—they do not know what it means, and it is sometimes hard for those who ought to be thoroughly imbued with the spirit of the gospel—even for some of us, to comprehend, but it is true.

Now, may the Lord bless Brother Freeze. As Sister Martha Tingey has said, Sister Freeze could never have done the work she has done if it had not been for his seconding her in her efforts. He consented to her partially neglecting her home duties in order to labor in a broader field for the salvation of others. But just here let me say a word to you mothers. Oh, mothers, salvation, mercy, life everlasting begin at home. "What profiteth it a man, though he gain the whole world and lose his own soul?" What would it profit me, though I should go out into the world and win strangers to the fold of God and lose my own children? Oh! God, let me not lose my own. I can not afford to lose mine, whom God has given to me and whom I am responsible for before the Lord, and who are dependent upon me for guidance, for instruction, for proper influence. Father, do not permit me to lose interest in my own, in trying to save others. Charity begins at home. Life everlasting should begin at home. I should feel very badly to be made to realize, by and by, that through my neglect of home, while trying to save others, I have lost my own. I do not want that. The Lord help me to save my own, so far as one can help another. I realize I cannot save anybody, but I can teach them how to be saved. I can set an example before my children how they can be saved, and it is my duty to do that first. I owe it more to them than to anybody else in the world. Then, when I have accomplished the work I should do in my own home circle, let me extend my power for good abroad just as far as I can.

My brethren and sisters, I know as I know I live that Joseph Smith was and is and ever will be the instrument chosen of God the eternal Father to lay the foundation of the Church of Jesus Christ of Latter-day Saints, and to establish the kingdom of God on earth, never more to be thrown down. I bear testimony to you. I know as I know I live that every doctrine that he taught is calculated to build up, to ennoble, to enlarge the soul, to establish peace and righteousness in the hearts of the children of men, and lead them up to God, and not away from him. I know it as I know I live. It is true, and I thank God that, like my dear sister here, whose earthly remains only now are with us, he has made me to believe it and to accept of it without recourse. I believe it with all my heart, just as I believe I live, and as I believe my own mother and father. Let us all strive for this belief, and if we will, we shall have joy and satisfaction, and we shall enter into God's rest, right here, in this world. For he that entereth in God's rest here will never more be disturbed by the hallucinations of sin and wickedness, and the enemies of truth will have no power over him.

That God will help us to reach that point is my prayer, and may the blessings of the Lord attend the family of Sister and Brother Freeze and their children, that not one of them will ever take a course that will bring sorrow to their beloved and sainted mother. That has been one of the stimulants of my life, one of the things that has made me strive to do good. I would not grieve my blessed mother, if I knew it, for anything in the world. There is nothing between me and the heavens that would compensate for doing something that would grieve or hurt my mother. Why? Because she loved me, she would have died for me over and over again, if such were possible, only to have saved me. Why should I grieve, why should I disappoint her? Why should I take a course contrary to her own life and her life's teachings to me, for she taught me honor, and virtue, and truth, and integrity to the kingdom of God, and she taught me not only by precept but by example. I would not grieve her for the world. Boys and girls, do not do anything to grieve your mother. You know she was a Latter-day Saint, you know she was true to her convictions. Be as true as she was, and, as the Lord lives, you will be exalted with your mother, and will have a fulness of joy, which, may God grant, is my prayer in the name of Jesus. Amen.—*Young Woman's Journal*, Vol. 23, 1911, pp. 128-132.

THE RESURRECTION. Now I am going to take the liberty of reading a little scripture to you, and then, as I go along, express my belief and conviction in relation to what we believe as Latter-day Saints with reference to the resurrection from the dead. I shall not take the pains or time to go into the subject in detail, for there are a great many scriptures that can be brought to bear upon the subject, scattered through the New Testament, in the declaration of the Son of God; but I will content myself by reading the description of his resurrection. We all know that he was lifted upon the cross; that he was pierced in the side, and that his life blood flowed from the body; and that he groaned upon the cross and gave up the spirit; that his body was taken from the cross, embalmed and wrapped in clean linen and laid in a new sepulchre wherein the body of no man had ever been laid. And then, remembering the remark that he was to lay down his body and take it up again, the claim that he made that that temple was to be destroyed but that it would be raised up the third day, that he was going to lay down his life and take it up again, the chief priests went to the chief authorities and demanded that a great stone be placed at the mouth of the sepulchre and that a seal be placed upon it, and that also a guard should be placed there, lest his disciples should come at night and take away the body and impose upon the public the claim that he had risen from the dead. And so a cordon of soldiers were placed to guard the tomb, and a great stone was placed at the mouth of the sepulchre, and a seal was placed upon it according to the history given in the scriptures of it, so that it would be absolutely impossible for the disciples of Christ to perpetrate a deception upon the world by clandestinely stealing and taking away the body of Christ and then proclaiming to the world that his body had been raised from the dead. Sometimes even the enemies of the truth and those who are seeking to destroy it become the unwitting means of verifying truth and of putting it beyond possibility of a doubt; for if they had not taken this precaution themselves, and if their guard had not been placed at the tomb to guard the sepulchre to see that no fraud could be perpetrated, then they could easily have gone out to the world and said, "Why, his disciples came and took the body away; they slipped in and stole it at night." But they closed their own mouths in a vain attempt to destroy the effects of his resurrection from the dead upon the minds of the people and upon the history of the world.

Thomas, one of the Twelve, called Didymus, was not with them when Jesus came, after his resurrection. "The other disciples therefore said unto him, We have seen the Lord. But he said unto them, Except I shall see in his hands the print of the nails, and put my finger into the print of the nails, and thrust my hand into his side, I will not believe." (John 20:25.)

We have a great many Didymuses in our day and generation, but we hope that there are none of them here, but the other class Jesus named.

"And after eight days again his disciples were within, and Thomas with them: then came Jesus, the doors being shut, and stood in the midst, and said, Peace be unto you. Then saith he to Thomas, Reach hither thy finger, and behold my hands; and reach hither thy hand, and thrust it into my side: and be not faithless, but believing. And Thomas answered and said unto him, My Lord and my God. Jesus saith unto him, Thomas, because thou hast seen me, thou hast believed: blessed are they that have not seen, and yet have believed." (John 20:26-29)

The disciple who wrote this, the beloved disciple, the personal witness himself, he who ran to the sepulchre and who outran Peter and came to it first, and looked into it, and who afterwards went into it after Peter, he who has written these words, says further: "And many other signs truly did Jesus in the presence of his disciples, which are not written in this book: but these are written, that ye might believe that Jesus is the Christ, the Son of God; and that believing ye might have life through his name." (John 20:30, 31)

Now what I want to call to your minds is, emphatically, the undeniable and unequivocal and direct description of the body, the resurrected body of the Lord Jesus Christ, given in this narrative of his resurrection and appearance to his disciples, which dissipates all imagination or thought that the death of the body and the departure of the spirit from the body is the resurrection of the dead. Does it not? Christ is the Son of God, and his disciples bear faithful record of the truth as they witnessed it—as they declare they did witness it; for they declare that they saw it with their eyes, heard it with their ears, were pricked in their hearts, and they examined the wounds with their own hands, to see and feel that he was indeed the same individual, the same person, the same body that was crucified, bearing the same marks that were inflicted upon the body while it was extended upon the cross—all this must go to show to you that the resurrection of Christ was the resurrection of himself, and not his spirit. Before I proceed further, there is another scripture that I will read to you, from the 24th chapter of Luke:

"And, behold, two of them went that same day to a village called Emmaus, which was from Jerusalem about three-score furlongs. And they talked together of all these things which had happened. And it came to pass, that, while they communed together and reasoned, Jesus himself drew near, and went with them. But their eyes were holden that they should not know him." (Luke 24:13-16)

And he journeyed and talked with them on the way, and unfolded the scriptures unto them, but they did not know that it was he. They did not personally know that it was Christ resurrected.

"And it came to pass, as he sat at meat with them, he took bread, and blessed it, and brake, and gave to them."

Now this is not the testimony of John. This is the testimony of Luke, another of the disciples of Christ.

"And their eyes were opened, and they knew him; and he vanished out of their sight. And they said one to another, Did not our heart burn within us, while he talked with us by the way, and while he opened to us the scriptures? And they rose up the same hour, and returned to Jerusalem, and found the eleven gathered together, and them that were with them, saying, The Lord is risen indeed, and hath appeared to Simon. And they told what things were done in the way, and how he was known of them in breaking of bread. And as they thus spake, Jesus himself stood in the midst of them, and saith unto them, Peace be unto you. But they were terrified and affrighted, and supposed that they had seen a spirit. And he said unto them, Why are ye troubled? and why do thoughts arise in your hearts? Behold my hands and my feet, that it is I myself: handle me, and see; for a spirit hath not flesh and bones as ye see me have. And when he had thus spoken, he shewed them his hands and his feet. And while they yet believed not for joy, and wondered, he said unto them, Have ye here any meat? And they gave him a piece of broiled fish, and of an honeycomb. And he took it, and did eat before them. And he said unto them, These are the words which I spake unto you, while I was yet with you, that all things must be fulfilled, which were written in the law of Moses, and in the prophets, and in the psalms, concerning me." (Luke 24:30-44)

Now, shall we accept the scriptural definition of the resurrection of the body? Shall we accept Christ's manifestation in his own person resurrected from the dead? Or shall we take the Rev. Mr. Phillip's opinion of it, that the death of the body and the separation of the spirit from it is the resurrection of the dead? Which do you choose?

Joseph the Prophet declared in the Book of Doctrine and Covenants (Sec. 130:22) that the Father has a body of flesh and bones as tangible as man's, and the Son of God has a body of flesh and bones, as he himself has declared that he has, and is not a mere spirit, but is a risen being, a resurrected soul. And the Holy Ghost is a personage of spirit, but not a personage of bones and flesh, as are the Father and the Son. Consequently, the Holy Spirit, or the Holy Ghost, may be conferred upon men, and he may dwell with them for a while, or he may continue to dwell with them in accordance with their worthiness, and he may depart from them at his will.

Now I am going to read a little from the Book of Mormon, a book of scripture that was translated by the gift and power of God, for the voice of God declared to the three witnesses that it had been translated by the gift and power of God and that it was true. The three witnesses declared and testified to its truth, and eight other witnesses, besides the Prophet Joseph, declared that they beheld the plates and handled them, and saw the engravings on them, and that they do know that Joseph Smith did have the plates from which the Book of Mormon was translated. And it is one of the greatest puzzles to scientists that they are discovering in the path of ancient civilization of this continent evidences and proofs of the divinity of the Book of Mormon, that they cannot dispute or gainsay. And their wonder is, how Joseph Smith, a man unlearned in history, in theology, in science, a man without book learning, practically, could ever so closely hit upon facts that are now being discovered by explorers and scientists throughout this historical country, that the Book of Mormon covers, and they say it is perplexing to them. It is astonishing to them that three men could testify, as the three witnesses to the Book of Mormon have testified, and that the eight other witnesses could testify as they have done, and yet not one of them ever repudiate his testimony. They cannot understand and they cannot account for it upon any scientific principle. If it was a fraud, and these men were deceived or led into a trap, and did it by sophistry or with a purpose of deceiving the world, surely some one or more of them would have risen to the truth before they died and have divulged the fraud. But no, not one of them did. They apostatized from Joseph, but they did not deny the divinity of the Book of Mormon. They remained faithful and true to their testimony to that. True, they declared that Joseph Smith had gone astray, that the Church had gone astray, just like all other apostates have declared. You never saw apostates anywhere who would admit that they were wrong; but they always claim that they are right, and the Church is wrong. So it was with Oliver Cowdery until he repented and returned to the Church.

So it was with David Whitmer until the day of his death. He believed that Joseph had been led astray, first, into receiving the Melchizedek Priesthood as well as the Aaronic Priesthood. That he received the Aaronic Priesthood and was ordained under the hand of John the Baptist he admitted and believed, but he denied any ordination under the hands of Peter, James, and John to the Melchizedek Priesthood, and consequently he went to work and organized a church and a presidency after the order of the Aaronic Priesthood. But never, up to the time of his death, did he deny his testimony as one of the three witnesses, and in his dying words he declared that his testimony contained in this book is true.

So did Oliver Cowdery. He came back into the Church after saying many bad things and after wandering about for a while, and confessed his follies and his wrong, and claimed that if he could only be permitted to come back a lay member in the Church it would be all that he could ask, or would ask for. He felt that he was unworthy of anything better or greater, and he was permitted to come back and be baptized.

Martin Harris also came back and was baptized into the Church, and died with his testimony on his lips, for not one of them ever repudiated his testimony.

Furthermore, not one of the eight witnesses ever did, either. Neither did the Prophet Joseph. So, here you have a record, the witnesses of which remain unimpeached and whose integrity no power beneath the kingdom of God can impeach, for they told the truth, and they abode in the truth which they told until they died in the flesh.

Now, one of the ancient disciples or prophets who lived upon this continent, who was inspired of God and who delivered this message to the world afterwards that was engraven upon plates of gold, and preserved and handed down and revealed in this dispensation of the world, has something precious to say upon this subject. This is not from Jerusalem. This is not a message that was delivered to the disciples of Christ in Jerusalem; but this is a message that was delivered by a prophet who lived upon this continent; and here are his words:

"And he shall come into the world to redeem his people; [for this was before the coming of Christ to redeem his people] and he shall take upon him the transgression of those who believe on his name; and these are they that shall have eternal life, and salvation cometh to none else."

Now let me say here: "He shall come into the world, and he shall take upon him the transgressions of those who believe on his name."

And those who believe will do the works that he commands. No man that will believe in truth will ever refuse to do what is required. And these are they that believe, that shall have eternal life, and salvation cometh to none else.

"Therefore, the wicked remain as though there had been no redemption made, except it be the loosing of the bands of death; for behold, the day cometh that all shall rise from the dead and stand before God, and be judged according to their works. Now, there is a death which is called a temporal death; and the death of Christ shall loose the bands of this temporal death, that all shall be raised from this temporal death; the spirit and the body shall be reunited again in its perfect form; both limb and joint shall be restored to its proper frame, even as we now are at this time; and we shall be brought to stand before God, knowing even as we know now, and have a bright recollection of all our guilt. Now this restoration shall come to all, both old and young, both bond and free, both male and female, both the wicked and the righteous; and even there shall not so much as a hair of their heads be lost; but all things shall be restored to its perfect frame, as it is now, or in the body, and shall be brought and be arraigned before the bar of Christ the Son, and God the Father, and the Holy Spirit, which is one eternal God, to be judged according to their works, whether they be good or whether they be evil. Now, behold, I have spoken unto you concerning the death of the mortal body, and also concerning the resurrection of the mortal body. [Not the resurrection of the spirit, but the resurrection of the mortal body.] I say unto you that this mortal body is raised to an immortal body; that is from death; even from the first death unto life, that they can die no more; their spirits uniting with their bodies, never to be divided; thus the whole becoming spiritual and immortal, that they can no more see corruption." (Alma 11:40-45)

Now that is the doctrine of the Latter-day Saints. That is the resurrection of Jesus Christ, and, as he is the first fruits of the resurrection from the dead, as he was raised up, so will he raise up all the children of his Father upon whom the curse of Adam came. For as by one man came temporal death upon all men, so by the righteousness of Christ all shall come to life, through the resurrection from the dead upon all men; whether they be good or whether they be evil, whether they be black or white, bond or free, learned or unlearned, or whether they be young or old, it matters not. The death that came by the fall of our first parents is eradicated by the resurrection of the Son of God, and you and I cannot help it.—*Journal of Discourses*, October 26, 1867.

WORK FOR THE DEAD. The work for our dead, which the Prophet Joseph laid upon us with more than ordinary injunction, instructing us that we should look after those of our kinfolk and our ancestors who have died without the knowledge of the gospel, should not be neglected. We should avail ourselves of those sacred and potent ordinances of the gospel which have been revealed as essential to the happiness, salvation and redemption of those who have lived in this world when they could not learn the gospel and have died without the knowledge of it, and are now waiting for us, their children, who are living in an age when these ordinances can be performed, to do the work necessary for their release from the prison-house. Through our efforts in their behalf their chains of bondage will fall from them, and the darkness surrounding them will clear away, that light may shine upon them and they shall hear in the spirit world of the work

that has been done for them by their children here, and will rejoice
with you in your performance of these duties.—Oct. C. R., 1916, p. 6.

TEMPLE ORDINANCES UNCHANGED. We are engaged in temple
work. We have built four temples in this land, and we built two
temples in the eastern country before we came here. During the
lifetime of the Prophet Joseph Smith one of the two was built and
dedicated, and the foundation of the other was laid and the walls had
well progressed when he was martyred. It was finished by the efforts
of the people under the most trying circumstances, and in poverty,
and was dedicated unto the Lord. The ordinances of the house of
God were administered therein as they had been taught to the leading
authorities of the Church by the Prophet Joseph Smith himself. The
same gospel, the same ordinances, the same authority and blessings,
that were administered by the Prophet Joseph Smith and taught by
him to his associates are now being enjoyed by and taught to the
Latter-day Saints in the four temples that have been built in these
valleys of the mountains. When you hear anybody say that we have
changed the ordinances, that we have transgressed the laws, or have
broken the everlasting covenants which were entered into under the
personal administration of the Prophet Joseph Smith, tell them for
me, tell them for President Snow, for President Cannon, and for all
those who are living today who received blessings and ordinances under
the hands of the Prophet Joseph Smith, that they are in error. The
same gospel prevails today, and the same ordinances are administered
today, both for the living and for the dead, that were administered by
the Prophet himself, and delivered by him to the Church.—Oct. C. R.,
1900, pp. 46, 47.

CARE AND NEED OF TEMPLES. We feel that an effort should be
made to preserve the temples of God, those houses that have been
erected for the purpose of administering the ordinances of the gospel
therein, for the living and the dead. We desire that these buildings
shall be preserved and kept in repair and in a wholesome condition,
so that the Spirit of the Lord may dwell in them, and that those
who minister therein may feel the presence and influence of his
Spirit. We also feel that when the time shall come and our hands
shall be free from the obligations that now rest upon us, other places
should be prepared for the convenience of the Latter-day Saints in
more distant stakes, in order that those who are living at great dis-
tances from the center may have the privilege of receiving the ordinances of the gospel without being put to the great expense and

loss of time that is necessary now in journeying from 500 to 1,000 miles in order to reach the houses of God. We hope to see the day when we shall have temples built in the various parts of the land where they are needed for the convenience of the people; for we realize that one of the greatest responsibilities that rests upon the people of God today is that their hearts shall be turned unto their fathers, and that they shall do the work that is necessary to be done for them in order that they may be joined together fitly in the bond of the New and Everlasting Covenant from generation to generation. For the Lord has said, through the Prophet, that this is one of the greatest responsibilities devolving upon us in this latter day.—Oct. C. R., 1902, pp. 2, 3.

PREACHING THE GOSPEL IN THE SPIRIT WORLD. Never has there been a name brought to the intelligence of the human race since the foundation of the world that has cost so much, that has accomplished so much, that has been revered and honored so much as the name of Jesus Christ, once so hated, and persecuted, and then crucified. The day will come, and it is not far distant either, when the name of the Prophet Joseph Smith will be coupled with the name of Jesus Christ of Nazareth, the Son of God, as his representative, as his agent whom he chose, ordained and set apart to lay anew the foundations of the Church of Jesus Christ, possessing all the powers of the gospel, all the rites and privileges, the authority of the holy Priesthood and every principle necessary to fit and qualify both the living and the dead to inherit eternal life and to attain to exaltation in the kingdom of God. The day will come when you and I will not be the only ones who will believe this, by a great deal, but there will be millions living and dead who will proclaim this truth. This gospel revealed to the Prophet Joseph is already being preached to the spirits in prison, to those who have passed away from this stage of action into the spirit world without the knowledge of the gospel. Joseph Smith is preaching that gospel to them. So is Hyrum Smith. So is Brigham Young, and so are all the faithful apostles that lived in this dispensation under the administration of the Prophet Joseph. They are there, having carried with them from here the holy Priesthood that they received under authority, and which was conferred upon them in the flesh; they are preaching the gospel to the spirits in prison; for Christ, when his body lay in the tomb, went to proclaim liberty to the captives and opened the prison doors to them that were bound. Not only are these engaged in that work but hundreds and thousands of others; the elders that have died in the mission field have not finished their missions, but they are continuing them in the spirit world. Possibly the Lord saw it necessary or proper to call them hence as he did. I am not going to question that thought, in the least, nor dispute it. I leave it in the hand of God, for I believe that all these things will be overruled for good, for the Lord will suffer nothing to come to his people in the world that he will not overrule eventually for their greater good.—M. I. A. Conference, June 5, 1910; *Young Woman's Journal*, Vol. 21, pp. 456-460.

VISION OF THE REDEMPTION OF THE DEAD. On the third of October, in the year nineteen hundred and eighteen, I sat in my room pondering over the Scriptures and reflecting upon the great atoning sacrifice that was made by the Son of God for the redemption of the world, and the great and wonderful love made manifest by the Father and the Son in the coming of the Redeemer into the world, that through his Atonement and by obedience to the principles of the gospel, mankind might be saved.

While I was thus engaged, my mind reverted to the writings of the Apostle Peter to the primitive saints scattered abroad throughout Pontus, Galatia, Cappadocia, and other parts of Asia where the gospel had been preached after the crucifixion of the Lord. I opened the Bible and read the third and fourth chapters of the first epistle of Peter, and as I read I was greatly impressed, more than I had ever been before, with the following passages:

"For Christ also hath once suffered for sins, the just for the unjust, that he might bring us to God, being put to death in the flesh, but quickened by the Spirit:

"By which also he went and preached unto the spirits in prison;

"Which sometime were disobedient, when once the longsuffering of God waited in the days of Noah, while the ark was a preparing, wherein few, that is, eight souls were saved by water." (I Peter 3:18-20)

"For, for this cause was the gospel preached also to them that are dead, that they might be judged according to men in the flesh, but live according to God in the spirit." (I Peter 4:6)

As I pondered over these things which are written, the eyes of my understanding were opened, and the Spirit of the Lord rested upon me, and I saw the hosts of the dead, both small and great. And there were gathered together in one place an innumerable company of the spirits of the just, who had been faithful in the testimony of Jesus while they lived in mortality, and who had offered sacrifice in the similitude of the great sacrifice of the Son of God, and had suffered tribulation in their Redeemer's name. All these had departed the mortal life, firm in the hope of a glorious resurrection, through the grace of God the Father and his Only Begotten Son, Jesus Christ.

I beheld that they were filled with joy and gladness, and were rejoicing together because the day of their deliverance was at hand. They were assembled awaiting the advent of the Son of God into the spirit world, to declare their redemption from the bands of death. Their sleeping dust was to be restored unto its perfect frame, bone to his bone, and the sinews and the flesh upon them, the spirit and the body to be united never again to be divided, that they might receive a fulness of joy.

While this vast multitude waited and conversed, rejoicing in the hour of their deliverance from the chains of death, the Son of God appeared, declaring liberty to the captives who had been faithful, and there he preached to them the everlasting gospel, the doctrine of the resurrection and the redemption of mankind from the fall, and from individual sins on conditions of repentance. But unto the wicked he did not go, and among the ungodly and tho unrepentant who had defiled themselves while in the flesh, his voice was not raised, neither did the rebellious who rejected the testimonies and the warnings of the ancient prophets behold his presence, nor look upon his face. Where these were, darkness reigned, but among the righteous there was peace, and the saints rejoiced in their redemption, and bowed the knee and acknowledged the Son of God as their Redeemer and Deliverer from death and the chains of hell. Their countenances shone and the radiance from the presence of the Lord rested upon them and they sang praises unto his holy Name.

I marveled, for I understood that the Savior spent about three years in his ministry among the Jews and those of the house of Israel, endeavoring to teach them the everlasting gospel and call them unto repentance; and yet, notwithstanding his mighty works and miracles and proclamation of the truth in great power and authority, there were but few who hearkened to his voice and rejoiced in his presence and received salvation at his hands. But his ministry among those who were dead was limited to the brief time intervening between the crucifixion and his resurrection; and I wondered at the words of Peter wherein he said that the Son of God preached unto the spirits in prison who sometime were disobedient, when once the longsuffering of God waited in the days of Noah, and how it was possible for him to preach to those spirits and perform the necessary labor among them in so short a time.

And as I wondered, my eyes were opened, and my understanding quickened, and I perceived that the Lord went not in person among the wicked and the disobedient who had rejected the truth, to teach them; but behold, from among the righteous he organized his forces and appointed messengers, clothed with power and authority, and commissioned them to go forth and carry the light of the gospel to them that were in darkness, even to all the spirits of men. And thus was the gospel preached to the dead. And the chosen messengers went forth to declare the acceptable day of the Lord, and proclaim liberty to the captives who were bound; even unto all who would repent of their sins and receive the gospel. Thus was the gospel preached to those who had died in their sins, without a knowledge of the truth, or in transgression, having rejected the prophets. These were taught faith in God, repentance from sin, vicarious baptism for the remission of sins, the gift of the Holy Ghost by the laying on of hands, and all other principles of the gospel that were necessary for them to know in order to qualify themselves that they might be judged according to men in the flesh, but live according to God in the spirit.

And so it was made known among the dead, both small and great, the unrighteous as well as the faithful, that redemption had been wrought through the sacrifice of the Son of God upon the cross. Thus was it made known that our Redeemer spent his time during his sojourn in the world of spirits, instructing and preparing the faithful spirits of the prophets who had testified of him in the flesh, that they might carry the message of redemption unto all the dead unto whom he could not go personally because of their rebellion and transgression, that they through the ministration of his servants might also hear his words.

Among the great and mighty ones who were assembled in this vast congregation of the righteous, were Father Adam, the Ancient of Days and father of all, and our glorious Mother Eve, with many of her faithful daughters who had lived through the ages and worshiped the true and living God. Abel, the first martyr, was there, and his brother Seth, one of the mighty ones, who was in the express image of his father Adam. Noah, who gave warning of the flood; Shem, the great High Priest; Abraham, the father of the faithful; Isaac, Jacob, and Moses, the great law-giver of Israel; Isaiah, who declared by prophecy that the Redeemer was anointed to bind up the broken hearted, to proclaim liberty to the captives, and the opening of the prison to them that were bound, were also there.

Moreover, Ezekiel, who was shown in vision the great valley of dry bones which were to be clothed upon with flesh to come forth again in the resurrection of the dead, living souls; Daniel, who foresaw and foretold the establishment of the kingdom of God in the latter days, never again to be destroyed nor given to other people; Elias, who was with Moses on the Mount of Transfiguration; Malachi, the prophet who testified of the coming of Elijah—of whom also Moroni spake to the Prophet Joseph Smith—declaring that he should come before the ushering in of the great and dreadful day of the Lord, were also there. The prophet Elijah was to plant in the hearts of the children the promises made to their fathers, foreshadowing the great work to be done in the temples of the Lord in the Dispensation of the Fulness of Times, for the redemption of the dead and the sealing of the children to their parents, lest the whole earth be smitten with a curse and utterly wasted at his coming.

All these and many more, even the prophets who dwelt among the Nephites and testified of the coming of the Son of God, mingled in the vast assembly and waited for their deliverance, for the dead had looked upon the long absence of their spirits from their bodies as a bondage. These the Lord taught, and gave them power to come forth, after his resurrection from the dead, to enter into his Father's kingdom, there to be crowned with immortality and eternal life, and continue thenceforth their labors as had been promised by the Lord, and be partakers of all blessings which were held in reserve for them that love him.

The Prophet Joseph Smith, and my father, Hyrum Smith, Brigham Young, John Taylor, Wilford Woodruff, and other choice spirits who were reserved to come forth in the fulness of times to take part in laying the foundations of the great Latter-day work, including the building of the temples and the performance of ordinances therein for the redemption of the dead, were also in the spirit world. I observed that they were also among the noble and great ones who were chosen in the beginning to be rulers in the Church of God. Even before they were born, they, with many others, received their first lessons in the world of spirits, and were prepared to come forth in the due time of the Lord to labor in his vineyard for the salvation of the souls of men.

I beheld that the faithful elders of this dispensation, when they depart from mortal life, continue their labors in the preaching of the gospel of repentance and redemption, through the sacrifice of the Only Begotten Son of God, among those who are in darkness and under the bondage of sin in the great world of the spirits of the dead. The dead who repent will be redeemed, through obedience to the ordinances of the house of God, and after they have paid the penalty of their transgressions, and are washed clean, shall receive a reward according to their works, for they are heirs of salvation.

Thus was the vision of the redemption of the dead revealed to me, and I bear record, and I know that this record is true, through the blessing of our Lord and Savior, Jesus Christ, even so. Amen. —*Joseph F. Smith.*

This *Vision of the Redemption of the Dead* was submitted October 31, 1918, to the Counselors in the First Presidency, the Council of the Twelve and the Patriarch, and by them unanimously accepted.—*Improvement Era,* Vol. 22, December, 1918, pp. 166-170.

Moderation in Burial Displays. A good friend who is often called upon to attend to the proprieties on behalf of the dead, calls attention in a letter to the indulgence of extravagance in the laying away of our departed friends and relatives. She believes that the Lord is not pleased with the profusion of flowers, the expensive dress, and even with the ornaments of gold in the form of rings and other jewelry used in decorating the dead.

We certainly recommend moderation and wisdom in the use of flowers, the hire of carriages, and the purchase of caskets. In the old scriptures we have numerous examples of simplicity in burials. While we are not called upon literally to follow these, they should be a lesson to us to avoid ostentations, and to attend to these matters with only such displays and preparations as will show due respect for the departed, and proper consideration for the living.

Relating to dress, the Latter-day Saints burial clothes are all sufficient for our day. Anything more is unnecessary, which good, common sense would clearly suggest; while the burial of jewelry with the dead can serve no good purpose. It savors of vanity, and might prove a temptation to grave robbers,—a naturally horrible thought. In like manner with carriages and caskets, only the necessary and modest should be used.—*Improvement Era,* Vol. 12, December, 1908, p. 145.

Who Cannot be Reached by the Gospel? And he that believes, is baptized, and receives the light and testimony of Jesus Christ, and walks well for a season, receiving the fulness of the blessings of the gospel in this world, and afterwards turns wholly unto sin, violating his covenants, he will be among those whom the gospel can never reach in the spirit world; and all such go beyond its saving power, they will taste the second death, and be banished from the presence of God eternally.—Oct. C. R., Deseret Weekly News, Vol 24, 1875, p. 708.

MEN CANNOT BE SAVED IN WICKEDNESS. We have a few people among us who are so wrapped up in and so devoted to some of their kindred who have been guilty of every species of abomination and wickedness in the world, that, the moment they are dead they will come and ask for permission to go into the house of God to perform the ordinances of the gospel for their redemption. I do not blame them for their affection for their dead, nor do I blame them for the desire in their heart to do something for their salvation, but I do not admire their wisdom, nor can I agree witth their conception of right and justice. You cannot take a murderer, a suicide, an adulterer, a liar, or one who was or is thoroughly abominable in his life, here, and simply by the performance of an ordinance of the gospel, cleanse him from sin and usher him into the presence of God. God has not instituted a plan of that kind, and it cannot be done.—Life of Joseph F. Smith, p. 399.

PRINCIPLE OF BAPTISM FOR THE DEAD. Here will come in the principles of baptism for the dead, and of proxy and heirships, as revealed through the Prophet Joseph Smith, that they may receive a salvation and an exaltation, I will not say a fulness of blessing and glory, but a reward according to their merits and the righteousness and mercy of God, even as it will be with you and with me. But there is this difference between us and the antediluvians—they rejected the gospel, consequently they received not the truth nor the testimony of Jesus Christ; therefore they did not sin against a fulness of light, while we have received the fulness of the gospel; are admitted to the testimony of Jesus Christ, and a knowledge of the living and true God, whose will it is also our privilege to know, that we may do it. Now if we sin, we sin against the light and knowledge, and peradventure we may become guilty of the blood of Jesus Christ, for which sin there is no forgiveness, neither in this world nor in the world to come.—Oct. C. R., Deseret Weekly News, Vol. 24, 1875, p. 708.

Chapter XXV

JOSEPH SMITH THE PROPHET

THE REALITY OF JOSEPH'S VISION. Our critics say it was an apparition that the Prophet Joseph saw, but he did not say so. He said the personages who appeared to him were real men, and there is nothing more improbable in his statement than in the recital in the Bible of the conception and birth of Christ, and of John the Baptist. To us has come the account of the birth, life and work of Christ, and there is nothing in the narrative to cause us to believe it more readily than that story of the Prophet Joseph Smith. Christ walked and talked and counseled with his friends when he came down from heaven over 1900 years ago. Is there any reason why he could not come again, why he should not visit this earth once more and talk with men today? If there is I should be glad to hear it.

The thing I want to impress upon you is that God is real, a person of flesh and bones, the same as you are and I am. Christ is the same, but the Holy Ghost is a person of spirit.

If Joseph Smith's teachings were untrue, then those of the Great Nazarene fall to the ground, for they are one and the same. You can't philosophize the truths of the gospel away, nor explain them by saying the prophet was a victim of apparitions, for they are real, tangible facts behind which stand a great mass of proof as good as has ever been offered to substantiate any statement. It is a comfort, a blessing, a delight to me, and I pray that it may ever be so to you.— Logan Journal, March 14, 1911.

SERVICE OF JOSEPH SMITH. Our faith in Jesus Christ lies at the foundation of our religion, the foundation of our hope for remission of sins, and for exaltation after death, and for the resurrection from death to everlasting life. Our faith in the doctrines that have been restored through the instrumentality of the Prophet Joseph Smith confirms and strengthens us and establishes beyond a question or doubt, our faith and belief in the divine mission of the Son of God. Joseph Smith was the instrument chosen of God and endowed with his authority to restore the holy Priesthood, the power of God to bind on earth and in heaven,—the power of the Priesthood by which men may perform ordinances of the gospel of Jesus Christ for the salvation of mankind. Through Joseph Smith the gospel of repentance, baptism in water for the remission of sins, the baptism of the Holy Ghost and by fire have been restored, and the knowledge that Jesus is the Christ, the Only Begotten Son of God, is made manifest through the spirit of truth. We are obligated to this humble servant that the Lord chose to lay the foundation of this work for the ordinances of the gospel of the Son of God, then and still unknown to the world, by which we may become united together as families, as kindreds, under the bonds of the new and everlasting covenant, for time and for all eternity. We are obligated to the Prophet Joseph Smith, as an instrument in the hand of the Lord, for the knowledge that we possess of the work which is necessary to be done in the house of God, for the salvation of the living and the redemption of the dead, and for the eternal union of souls who are united in this life by the power of God, under the bond of the everlasting covenant. We are indebted, or obligated at least, to the Prophet Joseph Smith, as the instrument in the hands of God, for the knowledge we now possess that a man cannot be exalted into the presence of God and the full enjoyment of his glory, alone. It was not designed for the man to be alone, for the man is not without the woman, neither the woman without the man, in the Lord.—Oct. C. R., 1916, p. 3.

JOSEPH SMITH'S NAME WILL NEVER PERISH. God lives, and Jesus is the Christ, the Savior of the world. Joseph Smith is a prophet of God—living, not dead; for his name will never perish. The angel that visited him and declared God's message unto him, told him that his name should be held for good and for evil throughout the world. This prediction was made in the days of his youth, before the Church was organized, and before there was any prospect of that which has since been accomplished. The declaration was made, notwithstanding it then seemed an absolute impossibility; but from the day it was spoken until this moment, and from now on until the winding-up scene, the name of Joseph Smith, the prophet of the nineteenth century, has been, is being, and will be heralded abroad to the nations of the earth, and will be held in honor or contempt by the people of the world. But the honor in which it is now held by a few will by and by be increased that his name shall be held in reverence and honor among the children of men as universally as the name of the Son of God is held today; for he did and is doing the work of the Master. He laid the foundations in this dispensation for the restoration of the principles that were taught by the Son of God, who for these principles lived, and taught, and died, and rose from the dead.

Therefore I say, as the name of the Son of God shall be held in reverence and honor, and in the faith and love of men, so will the name of Joseph Smith eventually be held among the children of men, gaining prestige, increasing in honor and commanding respect and reverence, until the world shall say that he was a servant and Prophet of God. The Lord God Omnipotent reigneth. Peace on earth, good will to men, is the proclamation that Joseph the Prophet made, and that is the same as his Master, the Lord Jesus Christ, made to the world. That is the mission we are trying to fulfil, and the proclamation we are seeking to make to the world today. It is the mission that these young men have been chosen to proclaim, and be witnesses of to the nations of the earth. It is their duty to see to it that this proclamation and this gospel of peace and good will shall be sent to every nation, and kindred, and tongue, and people, under the whole heavens. God bless Israel, is my earnest prayer in the name of Jesus. Amen.—Oct. C. R., 1907, pp. 125-126.

THE PROPHET JOSEPH SMITH. Brother Woodruff, in the course of his remarks, made the assertion that Joseph Smith was the greatest prophet that has ever lived, of whom we have any knowledge, save and except Jesus Christ himself. The world would say that he was an impostor; and the Lord said that his name should be had for good and for evil among all the nations of the earth; and this much, at least, so far as his name has become known, has been fulfilled. This prediction was made through the Prophet Joseph Smith himself, when he was an obscure youth, and when there was but little prospect of his name ever becoming known beyond the village where he lived. It was at an early period of his life, and at the beginning of the work that this prophecy or revelation was given, and it has been truly verified. Today there is not another man, perhaps, who has figured in religion, whose name is so wide-spread among the nations, as that of Joseph Smith. In connection with the work of which he was the instrument in the hands of God of laying the foundation, his name is spoken of in nearly every civilized nation upon the globe, for good or for evil. Where it is spoken of for good, it is by those who have had the privilege of hearing the gospel which has come to the earth through him, and who have been sufficiently honest and humble to receive the same. They speak of him with a knowledge which they have received by the inspiration of the Holy Spirit, through obedience to the principles which he taught, as a prophet and as an inspired man. They speak to his praise, to his honor, and they hold his name in honorable remembrance. They revere him, and they love him, as they love no other man, because they know he was the chosen instrument in the hands of the Almighty in restoring the gospel of life and salvation unto them, of opening their understandings of the future, of lifting the veil of eternity, as it were, from before their eyes. Those who have received the principles which he promulgated know they pertain not only to their own salvation, happiness and peace, spiritual and temporal, but to the welfare, happiness, salvation and exaltation of their kindred who have died without a knowledge of the truth.

The work in which Joseph Smith was engaged was not confined to this life alone, but it pertains as well to the life to come, and to the life that has been. In other words, it relates to those who have lived upon the earth, to those who are living and to those who shall come after us. It is not something which relates to man only while he tabernacles in the flesh, but to the whole human family from eternity to eternity. Consequently, as I have said, Joseph Smith is held in reverence, his name is honored; tens of thousands of people thank God in their hearts, and from the depths of their souls, for the knowledge the Lord has restored to the earth through him, and therefore they speak well of him and bear testimony of his worth. And this is not confined to a village, nor to a state, nor to a nation, but extends to every nation, kindred, tongue and people where the gospel, up to the present, has been preached—in America, Great Britain, Europe, Africa, Australia, New Zealand and upon the islands of the sea. And the Book of Mormon, which Joseph Smith was the instrument in the hands of God in bringing forth to this generation, has been translated into the German, French, Danish, Swedish, Welsh, Hawaiian, Hindustani, Spanish, and Dutch languages, and this book will be translated into other languages, for according to the predictions it contains, and according to the promises of the Lord through Joseph Smith it is to be sent unto every nation, and kindred, and people under the whole heavens, until all the sons and daughters of Adam shall have the privilege of hearing the gospel as it has been restored to the earth in the dispensation of the fulness of times.

The world presume that we have not received a knowledge of the truth. Those who are in ignorance in regard to the character, life, and labors of Joseph Smith, who have never read his revelations or studied or investigated his claims to divine authority, and are ignorant of his mission, revile him, sneer at his name, and ridicule his claims to prophetic inspiration, and called him an impostor in his day, except a few who hearkened to his instruction, and believed his testimony. The great majority of mankind then living who knew of Christ, deemed him an impostor, and considered him worthy to be put to death; precisely the same feeling existed towards Joseph Smith.

* * * *

Let us return to the Prophet Joseph Smith. He was accused of nearly everything that was vile, by his enemies, who, as is well known by the Latter-day Saints, were generally entirely ignorant of his true character and mission. What did Joseph Smith do? Was human blood found upon his hands? No, verily no. He was innocent. Was he a slanderer and vilifier? No, verily, he was not. Did he wrongfully and unjustly accuse men of wickedness? No, he did not. Did he institute an order of things that has proved injurious to the human family? Let the people who have become acquainted with his doctrines, and with the institutions which he established upon the earth, and his own life's labor, answer.

He was born December 23, 1805, in the state of Vermont. His parents were American citizens, as had been their ancestors for generations. In the spring of 1820, he received the first supernatural or heavenly manifestation. He was then fourteen years of age. Ordinarily we do not expect a very great deal from a boy who is only fourteen years of age, and it is not likely that a boy of that tender age could have become very vicious or wicked, especially when he was born and reared on a farm, apart from the corrupting vices of great cities, and free from contact with the debasing influence of vile associations. It is not likely that he spent many idle moments during the working years of his life, up to fourteen years of age; for his father had to labor for his living and earn it from the soil by the labor of his hands, being a poor man with a large family to support.

In 1820, as I have said, Joseph Smith received a revelation in which he claimed that God had declared that he was about to restore the ancient gospel in its purity, and many other glorious things. In consequence of this, Joseph Smith became very notorious in the neighborhood where he resided, and people began to regard him with a great deal of suspicion. He was at once called an impostor, and a few years later he was styled by his enemies, "old Joe Smith." His fame became known throughout the United States. He was called a "money digger," and many other contemptuous things. If you will look at his history, and at the character of his parents, and surroundings, and consider the object of his life, you can discover how much consistency there was in the charges brought against him. All this was done to injure him. He was neither old nor a "money digger," nor an impostor, nor in any manner deserving of the epithets which they applied to him. He had never injured anybody, nor robbed anybody—he never did anything for which he could be punished by the laws under which he lived.

When he was between 17 and 18 years of age, he received another heavenly manifestation, and some great and glorious things were revealed to him, and for four years subsequently he received visits from a heavenly messenger. He did not claim he was in communication with wicked men or demons from the lower regions. He claimed he was in communication with Moroni, one of the ancient prophets who lived upon this continent. He was a good man when he lived here, and it is not likely that he had become wicked since he went away. This personage, he claimed, revealed to him the mind and will of the Lord, and showed him the character of the great work that he, in the hands of God was to be instrumental in establishing in the earth when the time should come. This was the labor that was performed by the angel Moroni, during the four years intervening between 1823 and 1827. In 1827 he received from the hands of the angel Moroni, the gold plates from which this book (Book of Mormon) was translated by him through the inspiration of the Almighty, and the gift and power of God unto him. I heard it read when I was a child. I have read it many times since, and I have asked myself, scores of times, have you ever discovered one precept, doctrine, or command, within the lids of that book, that is calculated to injure anybody, to do harm to the world, or that is in contradiction to the word of God as contained in the Bible? And the answer invariably came, No, not one solitary thing, every precept, doctrine, word of advice, prophecy, and indeed every word contained within the lids of that book, relating to the great plan of human redemption and salvation, are calculated to make bad men good and good men better.

Did Joseph Smith during the three years intervening between 1827 and 1830, while he was laboring with his hands for a scanty subsistence, dodging his enemies, and trying to evade the grasp of those who sought to destroy him and prevent the accomplishment of his mission, struggling all the while against untold obstacles and depressing embarrassments to complete the translation of this book, have much chance of becoming wicked or corrupt? I do not think he had. When he had finished translating the Book of Mormon he was still only a boy, yet in producing this book he developed historical facts, prophecies, revelations, predictions, testimonies and doctrines, precepts and principles that are beyond the power and wisdom of the learned world to duplicate or refute. Joseph Smith was an unlearned youth, so far as the learning of the world is concerned. He was taught by the angel Moroni. He received his education from above, from God Almighty, and not from man-made institutions; but to charge him with being ignorant would be both unjust and false; no man or combination of men possessed greater intelligence than he, nor could the combined wisdom and cunning of the age produce an equivalent for what he did. He was not ignorant, for he was taught by him from whom all intelligence flows. He possessed a knowledge of God and of his law, and of eternity, and mankind have been trying, with all their learning, wisdom and power—and not content with that, they have tried with the sword and cannon—to extirpate from the earth the superstructure which Joseph Smith, by the power of God, erected; but they have signally failed, and will yet be overwhelmed by their efforts to destroy it.

Again, the world say that Joseph Smith was an indolent person. The Church of Jesus Christ of Latter-day Saints was organized April 6, 1830. Joseph Smith was martyred in Carthage, Illinois, on the 27th day of June, 1844—fourteen years after the organization of the Church. What did he accomplish in these fourteen years? He opened up communication with the heavens in his youth. He brought forth the Book of Mormon, which contains the fulness of the gospel; and the revelations contained in the Book of Doctrine and Covenants; restored the holy Priesthood unto man; established and organized the Church of Jesus Christ of Latter-day Saints, an organization which has no parallel in all the world, and which all the cunning and wisdom of men for ages has failed to discover or produce and never could have done. He founded colonies in the states of New York, Ohio, Missouri and Illinois, and pointed the way for the gathering of the Saints into the Rocky Mountains; sent the gospel into Europe and to the islands of the sea; founded the town of Kirtland, Ohio, and there built a temple that cost scores of thousands of dollars; he founded the city of Nauvoo in the midst of persecution; gathered into Nauvoo and vicinity some 20,000 people, and commenced the building of the temple there, which when completed cost one million dollars; and in doing all this he had to contend against the prejudices of the age, against relentless persecution, mobocracy, and vile calumny and slander, that were heaped upon him from all quarters without stint or measure. In a word, he did more in from fourteen to twenty years for the salvation of man than any other man, save Jesus only, who ever lived, and yet he was accused by his enemies of being an indolent and worthless man!

Where shall we go to find another man who has accomplished a one-thousandth part of the good that Joseph Smith accomplished? Shall we go to the Rev. Mr. Beecher, or Talmage, or any other of the great preachers of the day? What have they done for the world, with all their boasted intelligence, influence, wealth, and the popular voice of the world in their favor! Joseph Smith had none of their advantages, if these are advantages. And yet, no man in the nineteenth century, except Joseph Smith, has discovered to the world a ray of light upon the keys and power of the holy Priesthood, or the ordinances of the gospel, either for the living or the dead. Through Joseph Smith, God has revealed many things which were kept hidden from the foundation of the world in fulfilment of the prophets—and at no time since Enoch walked the earth has the Church of God been organized as perfectly as it is today, not excepting the dispensation of Jesus and his disciples,—or, if it was, we have no record of it. And this is strictly in keeping with the objects and character of this great latter-day work, destined to consummate the great purposes and designs of God concerning the dispensation of the fulness of times.

The principle of baptism for the redemption of the dead, with the ordinances appertaining thereto, for the complete salvation and exaltation of those who have died without the gospel, as revealed through Joseph Smith, is alone worth more than all the dogmas of the so-called Christian world combined.

Joseph Smith is accused of being a false prophet. It is, however, beyond the power of the world to prove that he was a false prophet. They may so charge him, but you who have received the testimony of Jesus Christ, by the spirit of prophecy, through his administrations, are my witnesses that they have not the power to prove him false, and that is why they are so vexed about it. In my humble opinion many of our enemies know that they lie before God, angels and men, when they make this charge, and they would only be too glad to produce proof to sustain their accusations, but they cannot. Joseph Smith was a true prophet of God. He lived and died a true prophet, and his words and works will yet demonstrate the divinity of his mission to millions of the inhabitants of this globe. Perhaps not so many that are now living, for they have in a great measure rejected the gospel, and the testimony which the elders of this Church have borne to them; but their children after them, and generations to come, will receive with delight the name of the Prophet Joseph Smith, and the gospel which their fathers rejected. Amen.—Discourse delivered in Assembly Hall, Salt Lake City, Oct. 29, 1882. *Journal of Discourses*, Vol. 24, 1884, pp. 8-16.

PREDICTION OF JOSEPH SMITH FULFILLED. As the time remaining is so short, I think I could not do better than devote it to continuing the subject dwelt upon by Brother Cannon.

The Doctrine and Covenants, as well as the Book of Mormon, contains indisputable evidence of the divine calling and mission of Joseph Smith. For instance, I will refer the congregation to the revelation given December 25, 1832, in relation to the great war of the Rebellion, with which all are more or less familiar. (Doctrine and Covenants 87) A portion of that revelation has been literally fulfilled, even to the very place indicated in the prediction where the war should commence; which, as was therein stated, was to terminate in the death and misery of many souls.

Again, in the revelation given in March, 1831, to Parley P. Pratt and Lemon Copley, the following remarkable prediction is found:

"But before the great day of the Lord shall come, Jacob shall flourish in the wilderness, and the Lamanites shall blossom as the rose. Zion shall flourish upon the hills and rejoice upon the mountains, and shall be assembled together unto the place which I have appointed." (Doctrine and Covenants, 49:24, 25)

Who, let me ask, unless he was inspired of the Lord, speaking by the gift and power of God, at that remote period of the Church's history, when our numbers were few, when we had no influence, name or standing in the world—who, I would ask, under the circumstances in which we were placed when this prediction was made, could have uttered such words unless God inspired him? Zion is, indeed, flourishing on the hills, and it is rejoicing on the mountains, and we who compose it are gathering and assembling together unto the place appointed. I now ask this congregation if they cannot see that this prediction (which was made many years before the idea prevailed at all among this people that we should ever migrate and gather out to these mountain valleys) has been and is being literally fulfilled? If there were no other prophecy uttered by Joseph Smith, fulfillment of which could be pointed to, this alone would be sufficient to entitle him to the claim of being a true prophet.

Again, in the revelation given February, 1834, this remarkable promise and prophecy is found:

"Verily I say unto you, I have decreed a decree which my people shall realize, inasmuch as they hearken from this very hour, unto the counsel which I, the Lord their God, shall give unto them. Behold they shall, for I have decreed it, begin to prevail against mine enemies from this very hour, and by hearkening to observe all the words which I, the Lord their God, shall speak unto them, they shall never cease to prevail until the kingdoms of the world are subdued under my feet, and the earth is given unto the Saints, to possess it for ever and ever." (Doctrine and Covenants 103:5-7)

Is there a person within the sound of my voice, or anywhere else upon the face of the wide earth, who can say that this promise has failed, that this prediction is not founded in truth, that so far it has not been fulfilled? I stand before this vast congregation, and am at the defiance of any human being to say that this was not pronounced by the spirit of truth, by the inspiration of the Almighty, for it has been fulfilled, and is being fulfilled, and that, too, in the face of opposition of the most deadly character; and what remains will be fulfilled literally and completely. And it is the fear in the heart of Satan that this will be the case that causes him to stir up his emissaries to oppose the kingdom of God and seek, if possible, to destroy this great and glorious work. For it is a living fact, a fact that fills the hearts of the righteous and God-fearing with unspeakable joy, and the hearts of the wicked and ungodly with consternation and jealous fear, that this work of God, this work of redemption and salvation in which we are engaged, is moving forward and is destined to continue in its onward march until the kingdoms of the world shall be subdued and brought under the law of Almighty God. And that this will come to pass, I can assure you, the enemy of all righteousness comprehends as well as we do. Yes, he knows that this will eventually be the case, better than many who profess to have received the Holy Spirit in their hearts; and, therefore, he is diligently seeking to stir up the hearts of the wicked to fight against the Saints of God, until they are discomfited, and Zion is free.

These predictions concerning the triumph of the cause of God over the wicked who contend against them, were uttered by Joseph Smith in his youth, in the early rise of the Church when, to all human appearance, their fulfillment was absolutely impossible. At that time there were but few who could believe, that dared to believe the truth of these predictions. The few, comparatively, that did believe when they heard, were those whose minds had been enlightened by the Holy Spirit of Promise and who, therefore, were prepared to receive them. As these predictions have been fulfilled, so those not yet fulfilled will come to pass in the due time of the Lord; and as this latter-day work has so far grown and assumed force and power in the earth, so it will continue to do, and there is no power beneath the celestial kingdom that can prevent its growth, or the consummation of all that has been predicted concerning it.—Apr. C. R., *Journal of Discourses*, Vol. 25, 1884, pp. 97-101.

Joseph Smith the Boy. To me there is a sweet fascination in the contemplation of his childhood and youth. I love to contemplate the innocence and the artless simplicity of his boyhood. It bears record that he was honest, that he was led by the Spirit of God to perform his wonderful mission. How could a child at his age be impelled by other than honest motives in the accomplishment of his high and holy calling? What he did he was led to do by the inspiration and guidance of his Heavenly Father, of this I feel assured.

He was much like other children; his play was like that of his companions; his thoughts, like those of most children, were innocent, and consequently he was incapable of the knavery and connivance that his enemies declared he practiced. Though poor, his parents were honest and good; they delighted in the truth, and it was their honest desire to live according to the best light within them. Love and good will to all found expression in their hearts and actions, and their children were imbued with like sentiments. They were firm believers in God, and trusted in his watchcare over his children. They had frequently received manifestations of his loving kindness, in dreams, visions, and inspirations, and God had healed their little ones, in answer to prayer, when they were nigh unto death. It was in such an atmosphere that the boy was reared. Joseph was a remarkably quiet and well-disposed child who gave his parents little or no trouble. As early as the age of eight, he gave proof that besides being thoughtful, easily governed, and of sweet and loving disposition, he possessed the foundation principles of good character—filial affection, patience, endurance, courage.

Concerning his spiritual manifestations, is it reasonable to suppose that there could have been premeditated deceit on the part of the boy, and such a boy, in his simple statement of what he saw and heard? No; neither could the answer which the heavenly messenger gave to him, have been composed in the child's own mind. Joseph Smith's testimony concerning his heavenly manifestation, in later life, was as simple, straight-forward, plain, and true, as it had been in childhood; the fidelity, courage, and love implanted in and character- istic of his life in boyhood neither faltered nor changed with maturity. His wisdom came in revelations of God to him.

One marked illustration of his character was his love for children. He never saw a child but he desired to take it up and bless it and many he did so bless, taking them in his arms and upon his knee. I have myself sat upon his knee. He was so fond of children that he would go far out of his way to speak to a little one, which is to me a striking characteristic of true manhood. He had a like true love for the human race. I know, and have known from my childhood, that he was a prophet of God, and I believe in his divine mission with all my heart; and in the authenticity and inspiration of the revelations which he received, and the Book of Mormon which he was instrumental in bringing forth.—*Improvement Era*, Vol 21, December, 1917, p. 167.

Joseph Smith, a Restorer. I think it is wrong to count Joseph the Prophet one who fought old forms, in the sense that he established new principles and doctrines. He fought existing religious forms, it is true, but he merely became the means, in God's providence, to restore the old truths of the everlasting gospel of Jesus Christ, the plan of salvation, which is older than the human race. It is true, also, that his teachings were new to the people of his day because they had apostatized from the truth—but the principles of the gospel are the oldest truths in existence. They were new to Joseph's gen- eration, as they are in part to ours, because men had gone astray, been cast adrift, shifted hither and thither by every new wind of doctrine which cunning men—so-called progressives—had advanced. This made the Prophet Joseph a restorer, not a destroyer, of old truths. And this does not justify us in discarding the simple, fundamental principles of the gospel and running after modern doctrinal fads and notions.—*Improvement Era*, Vol. 15, June, 1912, p. 737.

Plural Wives of Joseph Smith, the Prophet. I can positively state, on indisputable evidence, that Joseph Smith was the author, un- der God, of the revelation on plural marriage. On this subject, we have the affidavit of William Clayton, private secretary of Joseph

Smith, that he wrote the revelation as it was given through the lips of the prophet and that he himself sealed to Joseph Smith as a plural wife, Lucy Walker, at Joseph Smith's own residence, on May 1, 1843. This lady is still living, in Salt Lake City, and is willing to testify at any moment to this fact. Following are some of the names of young ladies who were sealed to the Prophet Joseph Smith in Nauvoo, as testified to under oath by themselves—this during the lifetime of the prophet: Eliza R. Snow, Sarah Ann Whitney, Helen Mar Kimball, Fanny Young (sister to Brigham Young), and Rhoda Richards (sister to Willard Richards who was with the prophet at his martyrdom in Carthage jail). All these noble women have testified, under oath, giving names and dates, that they were sealed during his lifetime, to the Prophet Joseph Smith. These facts have been published in Jenson's *Historical Record*, and in the *Deseret News*, in years past; and I know, by the established and virtuous character of these noble women, that their testimonies are true.

A careful reading of the revelation on plural marriage should convince any honest man that it was never written by Brigham Young, as it contains references to Joseph Smith himself, and his family, which would be utterly nonsensical and useless if written by President Young. The fact is, we have the affidavit of Joseph C. Kingsbury, certifying that he copied the original manuscript of the revelation within three days after the date on which it was written. I knew Joseph C. Kingsbury well. Furthermore, the revelation was read by Hyrum Smith to a majority of the members of the High Council, in Nauvoo, at about the time it was given, to which fact we have the sworn statements of the members of the High Council.—*Improvement Era*, Vol. 5, October, 1902, p. 988.

WHAT DOES THE MARTYRDOM OF JOSEPH AND HYRUM TEACH US? What does the martyrdom teach us? The great lesson that "where a testament is there must also of necessity be the death of the testator" (Heb. 9:16) to make it of force. Moreover, that the blood of martyrs is indeed the seed of the Church. The Lord permitted the sacrifice, that the testimony of those virtuous and righteous men should stand as a witness against a perverse and unrighteous world. Then, again, they were examples of the wonderful love of which the Redeemer speaks: "Greater love hath no man than this, that a man lay down his life for his friends." (John 15:13) This wonderful love they manifested to the Saints and to the world; for both realized and expressed their conviction, before starting on the journey to Carthage, that they were going to their death. They might have escaped; in fact, had but a few days before made the start for the Rocky Mountains, but were recalled by the groundless fears of false friends who made the accusation that they were fleeing from dangers that were equally as great towards the peace and happiness of the members of the Church as they could possibly be towards themselves. Satan said to Job: "All that a man hath will he give for his life." Of the true servant, and where perfect love abides, that is not true! Joseph and Hyrum Smith returned and calmly went to their death, feeling that their lives were of no value to themselves if unvalued by their friends, or if they were needed as a sacrifice for the protection of their worthy followers. Their courage, their faith, their love for the people were without bounds, and they gave all that they had for their people. Such devotion and love left no doubt in the minds of those who enjoyed the companionship of the Holy Spirit that these good men and true were indeed the authorized servants of the Lord.

This martyrdom has always been an inspiration to the people of the Lord. It has helped them in their individual trials; has given them courage to pursue a course in righteousness and to know and to live the truth, and must ever be held in sacred memory by the Latter-day Saints who have learned the great truths that God revealed through his servant Joseph Smith.—*Juvenile Instructor*, Vol. 51, June, 1916, p. 381.

DIVINE AUTHORITY OF JOSEPH SMITH AND HIS SUCCESSORS. I bear my testimony to you and to the world that Joseph Smith was raised up by the power of God to lay the foundations of this great latter-day work, to reveal the fulness of the gospel to the world in this dispensation, to restore the Priesthood of God to the world, by which men may act in the name of the Father and of the Son and of the Holy Ghost, and it will be accepted of God; it will be by his authority. I bear my testimony to it; I know that it is true.

I bear my testimony to the divine authority of those who have succeeded the Prophet Joseph Smith in the presidency of the Church. They were men of God; I knew them; I was intimately associated with them and as one man may know another, through the intimate knowledge that he possesses of him, so I can bear testimony to the integrity, to the honor, to the purity of life, to the intelligence, and to the divinity of the mission and calling of Brigham, of John, of Wilford and of Lorenzo. They were inspired of God to fill the missions to which they were called, and I know it. I thank God for that testimony, and for the spirit that prompts me and impels me toward these men, toward their mission, toward this people, toward my God and my Redeemer. I thank the Lord for it, and I pray earnestly that it may never depart from me—worlds without end.—*Improvement Era*, Vol. 14, Nov., 1910, p. 74.

God's Guiding Hand Seen in Church History. In connection with this thought it may be proper, consistent and timely, for me to remark that each individual member of the Church assembled here this morning is a free man or a free woman, possessing to the utmost degree all the qualifications and characteristics of freedom, independent with reference to individual action and choice, of every other man and of every other woman present. This being a fact, which is a fact, the unanimity exhibited on the part of the audience, with reference to the actions that have been taken, vindicate the belief and the assertion which I make, that the members of this congregation are certainly in harmony with the will of the Father. They are united; they see eye to eye; their sympathy is with one another and with the cause they represent. Their hearts are in the work in which they are engaged, and that because of their choice, because they have fully weighed all matters connected with their standing in the Church, and with regard to the course which they have taken today; they have, voluntarily, without coercion, without compulsion, without any restraint, except the restraint of their own consciences, shown that they see eye to eye, that they are one and are therefore entitled to be acknowledged of the Master as his own and as of him. I believe that there is not a freer, more independent nor a more intelligent people to be found anywhere in the world, who are more independent in choosing the course which they pursue, in the work that they perform and in everything that they have to do with, than the Latter-day Saints.

There is not a member of the Church of Jesus Christ of Latter-day Saints, in good standing, anywhere in all the world today that is not such by reason of his independence of character, by reason of his intelligence, wisdom and ability to judge between right and wrong and between good and evil. There is not a member of the Church of Jesus Christ anywhere, in good standing, living a proper life, that would not hold up his hand against evil, against wrong, against sin, against the transgression of the laws of God, against unrighteousness or vice of any kind, with as much freedom and independence and with as firm determination as any other man or woman in the world.

I am thankful to have the privilege, this moment, of expressing this my view and firm belief and my knowledge of the real character of the Latter-day Saints throughout the world. And, when I say Latter-day Saints, I mean members of the Church of Jesus Christ of Latter-day Saints founded by God, through the instrumentality and agency of the Prophet Joseph Smith, who was chosen of God and ordained and qualified and authorized to lay the foundations of the Church of Jesus Christ, never more to be destroyed nor left to other people, never more to cease but to continue until the purposes of God shall ripen and be accomplished for the salvation of the children of men and for the redemption of the living, and of the dead who have died without a knowledge of the plan of life and salvation. In stating this I state results of my experience in associations with such men as those who laid the foundations of the Church of Jesus Christ, from the Prophet Joseph Smith down to this moment.

As a child I knew the Prophet Joseph Smith. As a child I have listened to him preach the gospel that God had committed to his charge and care. As a child I was familiar in his home, in his household, as I was familiar under my own father's roof. I have retained the witness of the Spirit that I was imbued with, as a child, and that I received from my sainted mother, the firm belief that Joseph Smith was a prophet of God; that he was inspired as no other man in his generation, or for centuries before, had been inspired; that he had been chosen of God to lay the foundations of God's Kingdom as well as of God's Church; that by the power of God he was enabled to bring forth the record of the ancient inhabitants of this continent, to revive and to reveal to the world the doctrine of Jesus Christ, not only as he taught it in the midst of the Jews, in Judea, but as he also taught it, and it was also recorded, in greater simplicity and plainness upon this continent, among the descendants of Lehi. As a child I was impressed, deeply, with the thought, and firmly with the belief, in my soul that the revelations that had been given to and through Joseph the Prophet, as contained in this book, the Book of Doctrine and Covenants, were the word of God, as were the words of the ancient disciples when they bore record of the Father and of the Son. That impression made upon me in my childhood has followed through all the vicissitudes of more than sixty years of actual and practical experience in the mission field, throughout the nations of the world, and at home in the midst of the authorized servants of God, who officiated in the name of the Father and of the Son to propagate, to build up, and to push forward the work inaugurated by the instrumentality of the boy Joseph Smith.

In my childhood, too, I was instructed to believe in the divinity of the mission of Jesus Christ. I was taught by my mother, a Saint indeed—that Jesus Christ is the Son of God; that he was indeed no other than the Only Begotten of God in the flesh, and that, therefore, no other than God the eternal Father is his Father and the author of his existence in the world. I was taught it from my father, from the Prophet Joseph Smith, through my mother who embraced the gospel because she believed in the testimony of Joseph Smith, and she believed in the honor, integrity and truthfulness of her husband; and all my boyhood days and all my years in the world I have clung to that belief; indeed, I have never had any serious dubiety in my mind, even in childhood; and when I could only imperfectly understand things with reference to the divinity of the mission of the Son of God, I accepted it as being true in the sense in which only it can be true; for in no other than the literal sense, as it is described in the scriptures of divine truth and in the testimonies of the prophets, can it be true that Jesus Christ is the Son of God. I believe it. I have believed it all my life; but I owe to the Prophet Joseph Smith the fixed and unalterable confirmation of that belief, until it has come to be, in my soul, a knowledge of the truth; and in so far as I have continued in the word of the Lord, I believe, I have been led to know the truth. I believe that I possess that freedom that comes from a knowledge of the truth, which teaches all men righteousness, virtue, honor, faith, charity, forgiveness, mercy, longsuffering patience and devotion to that which is good, and abstinence from that which is evil.

"The truth will make you free." Free from what? From error, free from doubt, and uncertainty, free from unbelief, free from the powers of darkness, free from the possibility of being tempted beyond your strength; but to resist error and to shun even the appearance of sin. This truth makes a man a Latter-day Saint. This knowledge of the truth makes you free to worship God and to love him with all your heart and mind and strength, and to do the next best thing—to love your neighbor as nearly as you possibly can as you love yourselves.

The truth that I have received teaches me that Joseph Smith was a prophet of God, teaches me to accept without recourse, other than the full and free acceptance of that truth, that God Almighty, the Father of Jesus Christ, the Father of our spirits, the maker of heaven and earth, condescended to come down to this our mother earth, in person, in company with his beloved Son, and show themselves to Joseph Smith. I believe it. The truth has made me feel that this must be true. It cannot be error, for the Lord God Almighty could never build the structure that he has built upon the testimony of the Prophet Joseph Smith, if it had been founded in error or untruth. This people never could have combined and adhered together, never could have been united, never could have seen eye to eye, never could have been one, in order that they might be acknowledged of God as his own, if we had been building upon error. If our foundations were laid in untruth and unrighteousness this could not be. But the Lord is at the bottom of this. Joseph Smith was not at the foundation of it. He was not responsible, only so far as he was obedient to the will of the Father. God is responsible for this work. The Lord Almighty has made the promises concerning this work, not Joseph Smith, not Hyrum Smith. No other man has made true promises with reference to the future of Zion and to the building up of the kingdom of God in the earth, except God inspired him to do it. Not of himself has man ever done anything of that kind. The Lord is at the bottom; the Lord is at the top; the Lord is all the way through this work, and every fibre of it is in his keeping and is moved by his magic power and by the inspiration of his Holy Spirit. That is my testimony to you.

I believe in the divinity of Jesus Christ, because more than ever I come nearer the possession of the actual knowledge that Jesus is the Christ, the Son of the living God, through the testimony of Joseph Smith contained in this book, the Doctrine and Covenants, that he saw Him, that he heard Him, that he received instructions from Him, that he obeyed those instructions, and that he today stands before the world as the last great, actual, living, witness of the divinity of Christ's mission and His power to redeem man from the temporal death and also from the second death which will follow man's own sins, through disobedience to the ordinances of the gospel of Jesus Christ. Thank God for Joseph Smith. I believe in his mission, having accepted this great truth and his narration of it.

The greatest event that has ever occurred in the world, since the resurrection of the Son of God from the tomb and his ascension on high, was the coming of the Father and of the Son to that boy Joseph Smith, to prepare the way for the laying of the foundation of his kingdom—not the kingdom of man—never more to cease nor to be overturned. Having accepted this truth, I find it easy to accept of every other truth that he enunciated and declared during his mission of fourteen years in the world. He never taught a doctrine that was not true. He never practiced a doctrine that he was not commanded to practice. He never advocated error. He was not deceived. He saw; he heard; he did as he was commanded to do; and, therefore, God is responsible for the work accomplished by Joseph Smith—not Joseph Smith. The Lord is responsible for it, and not man.

I am happy to express to this audience my knowledge of the successors of Joseph Smith. They reared me, in part, so to speak. In other words, with them I journeyed across the deserts, by the side of my ox-team, following President Brigham Young and his associates to these barren wastes, barren as they were when we first entered this valley. I believed in him then, and I know him now! I believed in his associates, and I know them now; for I lived with them; I slept with them; I traveled with them; I heard them preach and teach and exhort, and I saw their wisdom which was not the wisdom of man but the wisdom of Almighty God. When President Young set his foot down here, upon this desert spot, it was in the midst of persuasion, prayers and petitions on the part of some Latter-day Saints who had gone forward and landed upon the coast of California, that beautiful, rich country, semi-tropical, abounding in resources that no inland country would possess, inviting and appealing for settlers at that time, and just such settlers as President Brigham Young could have taken there—honest people, people who were firm in their faith, who were established in the knowledge of truth and righteousness, and in the testimony of Jesus Christ, which is the spirit of prophecy, and in the testimony of Joseph Smith which was a confirmation of the spirit of Christ and of his mission.

These people pleaded with President Young: "Come with us," they said, "and go to the coast. Go where roses bloom all the year round, where the fragrance of flowers scents the air, from May until May; where beauty reigns; where the elements of wealth are to be found, and only need to be developed. Come with us."

"No," said President Young, "we will remain here, and we will make the desert blossom like the rose. We will fulfil the Scriptures by remaining here."

I heard him tell one of the Battalion boys who came back from California with a little buckskin sack of gold nuggets, and who shook them in the face of President Young, and said to him: "Look what we could get if we were to go to California! The land is full of gold;"

but President Young pointed his finger (I was there and saw and heard it), and he said: "Brother ——, you may go to California, if you will. Those who want to go there can go, but we will remain here; and I want to tell you that those who remain here and obey counsel, in a few years will be able to buy out every one of you who go to California—ten-fold over."

(Bishop George Romney: "That is true; I know the man.")

Why, bless your soul, what did President Young know about Utah, at that early day? We did not know that there was even a lump of coal in existence in the land. I myself passed the first fall and winter after our entrance into this valley hauling wood out of Mill Creek canyon and Parley's canyon; and during that fall and winter I hauled forty loads of wood with my oxen and wagon out of these canyons. Every load I cut and hauled diminished the supply of wood for fuel for the future; and I said to myself: What will we do when the wood is all gone? How will we live here when we can't get any more fuel, for it is rapidly going? I followed that pursuit until it took me three days in the mountains with my ox-team and wagon, to get a load of wood for winter fuel; and what were we to do? Yet President Young said, "This is the place."

Well, ordinarily, our judgment and our faith would have been tried, in the decision of the president, if we had not implicit confidence in him. If we had not known that he was the mouthpiece of God, that he was the real and legitimate successor of the Prophet Joseph Smith in the Presidency of the Church of Jesus Christ of Latter-day Saints, we would have doubted his wisdom and we would have faltered in our faith in his promise and word; but no, we believed him, and we stayed; and so far as I am concerned, I am here yet; and I propose to remain here as long as the Lord wants me to stay. And what has developed?

Our good friends from the east used to come out here in the early days, and upbraid us. They said: "Why, it is the fulfilment of the curse of God upon you. You have been driven away from the rich lands of Illinois and Missouri into a desert, into a salt land."

I said: "Yes, we have salt enough here to save the world, thank God, and we may find use for it by and by."

Well, before the wood gave out entirely in the mountains, we discovered coal up here in Summit county, and then we began to discover it all along the mountains here, and we kept on discovering it, until at last we have learned that we have coal enough in Utah to furnish fuel for the whole world for a hundred years, if they want to come and get it. We have it right here, any amount of it; and they haven't got that in California; they come up here to get their coal.

We have discovered that this country was really the gold-mine country of the world; that here abounded silver as well as gold in greater abundance than in California. We have discovered now that some of our mountains here are practically made of copper, and men are hewing copper out of the mountains by millions of tons, so to speak, and coining it in the way of business into money; and thank the Lord, we do not have to go to Liverpool for the salt we use in making butter. We have it right here, just as good and pure as the best they can fetch from England or anywhere else in the world; and this salt land has proven to be a boon, a consolation and a blessing beyond all power of description.

When the army came out here, in 1858, we wanted some bullets to go out and meet General Johnston and his forces that were coming in—not to kill them; we did not want the bullets to kill them; we just wanted the bullets to scare them with. Some of the boys went out here into the mountains with a pick and shovel, and they dug up lead, impregnated somewhat with silver. They brought it in, improvised a little furnace and ran out a few tons of lead. I had the honor of being associated with that little company of men, and I brought home with me some thirty or forty pounds of lead that we just quarried out of the hill with a pick and shovel.

When I rode up to the office here, to report to President Young my return from my mission over three years, the army was approaching, and he said to me: "Well, Joseph, have you got a horse?"

I said, "Yes, sir."

"Have you got a gun?"

I said, "Yes, sir."

"Have you got any ammunition?"

I said, "No, sir."

"Well," he said, "you report to Brother Rockwood, at the commissary office, and he will furnish you with ammunition, and you take your gun and go out to the front."

So I went home and sat up all that night, running bullets out of my mountain lead; reported the next day to Brother Rockwood, received a chunk of Mother Gadbury's cheese and some crackers, and started on my horse, with a brother-in-law, for the front. I spent part of the winter of 1858, and all of the spring and a portion of the summer of 1859, guarding Uncle Sam's troops; and we never hurt one of them, not one. We never molested a single individual of them; but we hedged up their way, and they camped out at Fort Bridger all winter long, and we sent them salt to save them; and they rejected it, because they were afraid there was something in the salt, more than the savor of it. But I assure you the salt was pure and good.

Now, just before that time, I was a farmer. I had to plow my land and farm it, but I did not have a spear of grass or hay to feed my team, and how was I going to do my spring work? This valley produced mighty little hay at that time. I hitched up my team, my brother and I, and we drove sixty miles to the north and bought a couple of loads of wild grass hay, and carted that hay down sixty miles to feed our teams in order to plow our land. I used to think, how in the world are we going to live in Utah without feed for our teams. Just then the Lord sent a handful of alfalfa seed into this valley, and Christopher Layton planted it, watered it, and it matured; and from that little beginning, Utah can now produce a richer crop of hay than Illinois or Missouri can do. So the hay question was settled, and the coal question was settled. Then the question of producing food from the land. Why, it was a marvel. One good man cultivated his little farm for thirty years, without a change, and raised from fifty to sixty bushels of wheat per acre each year on his farm, during that entire period. So the soil is rich, and everything is favorable for Zion here where President Young determined that he would stay; if we had not stayed here, it is clear we would have been overwhelmed and swallowed up by the multitudes who rushed to California.

Now, my brethren and sisters, I know whereof I speak with reference to these matters, for I have come down through every atom of it, at least from the expulsion from the city of Nauvoo; in February, 1846, I stood upon the bank of the river and saw President Young and the Twelve apostles, and as many of the people of Nauvoo as had teams or could possibly migrate, cross the Mississippi river on the ice. The river froze within a day or two, because of heavy frost, which enabled them to cross as they did, and thus the first real marvel and manifestation of the mercy and the power of God was manifest, in making a roadway across the Mississippi a mile wide at that place by which our people could go on their journey to the West. I saw them go. My brother was with them, and I wondered if I would ever see him again. We remained there in Nauvoo until September, 1846, when the city was besieged, at the mouth of the cannon and musket, and my mother and her family were compelled to take all that they could move out of the house—their bedding, their clothing, the little food they possessed, leaving the furniture and everything else standing in the house, and fled across the river, where we camped without tent or shelter until the war was over. The city was conquered, and the poor people that were left there were compelled to seek shelter somewhere else. From that moment on, I have been in the conflict. I have seen it and experienced it all the way through; and I am satisfied with my experience.

I bear record to you of the divinity of the work in which you are engaged, and I bear record to you and testify that it has been the power of God, not that of President Young or of his associates, that has kept the people together and united them. By that power you have been able to come here this morning and with one united voice, and uplifted hands, sustain in the positions to which they have been chosen the men who have been called and appointed and ordained by virtue of authority from God, to preside over you and teach you things that are good to be taught and good to be known and observed, which will bring life and salvation to those who will hearken and be obedient.

The Lord bless you; the Lord bless the pure in heart throughout the world. May the Lord have mercy upon the suffering nations that are afflicted by this terrible calamity of war. May he save the poor and the needy and the honorable among the children of men, to come eventually to a knowledge of his truth, that they may be saved in his kingdom.

Much could be said. Joseph Smith taught the building of temples. I can scarcely quit. Joseph Smith was the instrument in the hand of God in revealing the ordinances of the house of God that are essential to the salvation of the living and the dead. Joseph Smith taught these principles, and his brethren to whom he taught them have carried out his views. They have put his doctrine to the test. They have obeyed his counsel, and they have honored him and his mission and sustained him as man has never been sustained by any other people under God's heavens. So we will continue to sustain Joseph the prophet, and his work that he has accomplished among the children of men, and we will abide in the truth forever, by the help of God. Even so. Amen.—*Sermon*, Salt Lake Assembly Hall, July 8, 1917.

Chapter XXVI

PERSONAL TESTIMONIES AND BLESSINGS

A Testimony. I declare unto you in all candor, and in all earnestness of soul, that I believe with all my heart in the divine mission of Joseph Smith, the Prophet, that I am convinced in every fiber of my being that God raised him up to restore to the earth the gospel of Christ, which is indeed the power of God unto salvation. I testify to you that Joseph Smith was instrumental in the hand of the Lord in restoring God's truth to the world, and also the holy Priesthood, which is his authority delegated unto man. I know this is true, and I testify of it to you. To me it is all-in-all; it is my life, it is my light; it is my hope, and my joy; it gives me the only assurance that I have for exaltation, for my resurrection from death, with those whom I have loved and cherished in this life, and with whom my lot has been cast in this world—honorable men, pure, humble men, who were obedient unto God and his commands, who were not ashamed of the gospel of Christ, nor of their convictions or knowledge of the truth of the gospel; men who were made of the stuff of which martyrs are made, and who were willing at any moment to lay down their lives for Christ's sake, and for the gospel, if need be, which they had received with the testimony of the Holy Spirit in their hearts. I want to be reunited with these men when I shall have finished my course here. When my mission is done here, I hope to go beyond into the spirit world where they dwell, and be reunited with them. It is this gospel of the Son of God that gives me the hope that I have of this consummation, and of the realization of my desire in this direction. I have staked all on this gospel, and I have not done it in vain. I know in whom I trust. I know that my Redeemer lives, and that he shall stand upon the earth in the latter days, and, as Job has expressed it, "Though after my skin worms destroy this body, yet in my flesh shall I see God."—Oct. C. R., 1907, pp. 4, 5.

This is God's Work—A Testimony. My brethren and sisters, I desire to bear my testimony to you; for I have received an assurance which has taken possession of my whole being. It has sunk deep into my heart; it fills every fiber of my soul; so that I feel to say before this people, and would be pleased to have the privilege of saying it before the whole world, that God has revealed unto me that Jesus is the Christ, the Son of the living God, the Redeemer of the world: that

Joseph Smith is, was, and always will be a prophet of God, ordained and chosen to stand at the head of the dispensation of the fulness of times, the keys of which were given to him, and he will hold them until the winding up scene—keys which will unlock the door into the kingdom of God to every man who is worthy to enter and which will close that door against every soul that will not obey the law of God. I know, as I live, that this is true, and I bear my testimony to its truth. If it were the last word I should ever say on earth, I would glory before God my Father that I possess this knowledge in my soul, which I declare unto you as I would the simplest truths of heaven. I know that this is the kingdom of God, and that God is at the helm. He presides over his people. He presides over the president of this Church, and has done so from the Prophet Joseph down to the Prophet Lorenzo, and he will continue to preside over the leaders of this Church until the winding-up scene. He will not suffer it to be given to another people, nor to be left to men. He will hold the reins in his own hands; for he has stretched out his arm to do this work, and he will do it, and have the honor of it. At the same time God will honor and magnify his servants in the sight of the people. He will sustain them in righteousness. He will lift them on high, exalt them into his presence, and they will partake of his glory forever and ever.

It is the Lord's work, and I plead with you not to forget it. I implore you not to disbelieve it; for it is true. All that the Lord said concerning this latter-day work will come to pass. The world cannot prevent it. The blind that will not see, the deaf that will not hear, cannot prevent the work from going on. They may throw blocks before the wheels, they may ridicule, they may malign, they may stir up the spirit of persecution and bitterness against the Saints, they may do all in their power to deceive the people and lead them astray; but God is at the helm, and he will lead his people to victory. Men and women may be deceived by the craftiness of the adversary and by the spirit of darkness that is in the world; they may be deceived with Christian Science, with hypnotism, with animal magnetism, with mesmerism, with spiritualism, and with all the other man-made and demon-stimulated isms which exist in the world; but the elect of God shall see and know the truth. They will not be blind, because they will see; they will not be deaf, because they will hear; and they will walk in the light, as God is in the light, that they may have fellowship with Jesus Christ and that his blood may cleanse them from all their sins.

May God help us to realize this. May he deliver us from secret combinations, and from the snares that are set to entrap our feet and to win our affections from the kingdom of God. I repeat what I have said scores of times, the kingdom of God is good enough for me. This organization of the Church of Jesus Christ of Latter-day Saints meets all my wants, and I have no need to fly to organizations that are gotten up by men for the purpose of making money. I pray God that his kingdom may be sufficient for you, that you may abide in the truth, and not be led away by those deceptive spirits that have gone forth in the world to lead men astray.

Spiritualism started in the United States about the time that Joseph Smith received his visions from the heavens. What more natural than that Lucifer should begin revealing himself to men in his cunning way, in order to deceive them and to distract their minds from the truth that God was revealing? And he has kept it up pretty well ever since. May God bless Israel, and preserve us in the truth. May he bless our president, prolong his years, and continue unto him the strength of body and mind that he possesses this day, and even more vigor as the years roll by. May the Lord have mercy upon our beloved brother, President Cannon, who is absent from us, and return him once more to his home, and to the bosom of the Church, if he has not willed otherwise. This is my humble prayer, in the name of Jesus. Amen.—Apr. C. R., 1901, pp. 72, 73.

A TESTIMONY. There is no salvation but in the way God has pointed out. There is no hope of everlasting life but through obedience to the law that has been affixed by the Father of life, "with whom there is no variableness, neither shadow of turning"; and there is no other way by which we may obtain that light and exaltation. Those matters are beyond peradventure, beyond all doubt in my mind; I know them to be true. Therefore, I bear my testimony to you, my brethren and sisters, that the Lord God Omnipotent reigneth, that he lives and that his Son lives, even he who died for the sins of the world, and that he arose from the dead; that he sits upon the right hand of the Father; that all power is given unto him; that we are directed to call upon God in the name of Jesus Christ. We are told that we should remember him in our homes, keep his holy name fresh in our minds, and revere him in our hearts; we should call upon him from time to time, from day to day; and, in fact, every moment of our lives we should live so that the desires of our hearts will be a prayer unto God for righteousness, for truth, and for the salvation of the human family. Let us guard ourselves so that there may not come into our souls a single drop of bitterness, by which our whole being might be corroded and poisoned with anger, with hatred, envy and malice, or any sort of evil. We should be free from all these evil things, that we may be filled with the love of God, the love of truth, the love of our fellow-men, that we may seek to do good unto all men all the days of our lives, and above all things be true to our covenants in the gospel of Jesus Christ.—Apr. C. R., 1909, p. 6.

THE PLEDGE OF MY LIFE. I feel happy, this morning, in having the privilege to say to you that in the days of my childhood and early youth, I made a pledge with God and with his people that I would be true to them. In looking over the experiences of my life, I cannot now discern, and do not remember a circumstance, since the beginning of my experience in the world, where I have felt, for a moment, to slacken or relax in the pledge and promise that I made to God and to the Latter-day Saints, in my youth. And if there is a man, or a woman, in the world that can point out to me an instance, in all my life, where I have been untrue to my pledge, or promise, or covenant, I shall be glad to receive that information from that man or woman. As an elder in Israel I tried to be true to that calling; I tried to my utmost to honor and magnify that calling. When I became a seventy, I felt in my heart to be true to that calling, and I strove, with all the intelligence and fervor of my soul, to be true to it. I have no knowledge nor recollection of any act of mine, or any circumstance in my life where I proved untrue or unfaithful to these callings in the Priesthood of the Son of God. Later in my life, when I was called to act as an apostle, and was ordained an apostle, and set apart to be one of the Twelve, I strove to honor that calling, to be true to it, and to my brethren, to the household of faith, and to the covenants and obligations involved in receiving this holy Priesthood which is after the order of the Son of God. I am not aware that I ever violated one of my obligations or pledges in these callings to which I have been called. I have sought to be true and faithful to all these things. I have endeavored to be true to my family; and if ever I have violated one pledge or promise, or neglected one obligation that rests upon me in these relationships, I do not know it. And when I have made pledges to the people of God, or to the world, if ever I have violated those pledges I do not know it. Furthermore, I do not believe there is a man living who does know it, who can truthfully testify that I ever did violate those pledges.

I stand before you today, my brethren and sisters and friends, on the ground that I have tried to be true to God, to the utmost of my knowledge and ability; that I have tried to be true to my people, to the utmost of my knowledge and ability; and I have been true to the world in every pledge and promise that I have made to the world, notwithstanding there have been men who have shown a disposition to make it appear that I was a hypocrite, that I was two-faced; that I was one thing to the world and another thing in secret. I want it distinctly understood that those who have conveyed such an idea as this to mankind have been wilfully injuring me, wronging me, and falsifying me and my character before the people, and I want it distinctly understood those things must stop. They must stop at least among men who profess to be members of the Church of Jesus Christ of Latter-day Saints. I can endure to be maligned and persecuted by my enemies, who are also enemies of the Kingdom of God, but I do not want to be maligned and belied by men who profess to be members of the Church of Jesus Christ of Latter-day Saints, neither intentionally nor otherwise. Now, I trust that you understand clearly what I mean. I do not know how I can make it much plainer or clearer, with the knowledge that I have of language. Then, I repeat, as the Lord has helped me in the past to be true to my covenants, that I have entered into with him and with you, with my brethren, and with the Church of Jesus Christ of Latter-day Saints, so by his help and by his blessing I propose to be true throughout the future of my life, whether I am permitted to live long or short; it matters not to me. While I live, I hope to be a true man, an honest man, a man who can face all mankind and, at last, who can stand before God, the Judge of the quick and the dead, and not quail for what I have done in the world.—Oct. C. R., 1910, pp. 2, 3.

A BLESSING. I bless you with all my soul, because you love the truth, and you manifest it. There is nothing in God's world that draws men and women so near to my heart as that they love the truth and that they love God, that they love the cause of Zion and are devoted to the interests of the Church. This endears men and women to my heart; I love them when they love this work and when they show their interest in it. It lifts my soul to heaven and fills it with joy unspeakable.—Oct. C. R., 1908, p. 97.

A TESTIMONY. My brethren and sisters, I know that my Redeemer lives. I know, as I know I live, that in person he has visited man in our time and day, and that we are not now dependent alone on the history of the past for the knowledge that we possess, of which record is borne by the Spirit of God, shed abroad in the hearts of all who enter into the covenant of the gospel of Christ. But we have the renewed and later witness and manifestation of heavenly visions and of the visitation of God the Father and Christ the Son to this their footstool; and they have in person declared their entity, their being, and they have manifested their glory. They have stretched forth their hands to accomplish their work—the work of God, and not the work of man—and while those who have been faithful shall be crowned with glory and honor in the presence of God, the honor and the glory, the credit and the praise, for the continuance and for the advancement and growth of the kingdom of God in the earth, will be due to the Father and the Son and the Holy Spirit, whose power and whose agency, whose influence and purpose, have been behind the work of God every moment since it was first given to man. It is by his power that it has grown and continued, and has become what it is, and it will continue to grow and spread, until it shall fill the earth with the glory of God, and with the knowledge of the Father and of the Son, whom to know is life eternal. This is my testimony to you, my brethren and sisters, and I bear witness of it in the name of the Lord Jesus Christ. Amen.—*Improvement Era,* Vol. 12, September, 1909, p. 914.

I Know that My Redeemer Lives. I know that my Redeemer lives. We have all the testimony and all the evidence of this great and glorious truth that the world has, that is, all that the so-called Christian world possesses; and in addition to all that they have, we have the testimony of the inhabitants of this western continent, to whom the Savior appeared and delivered his gospel, the same as he delivered it to the Jews. In addition to all this new testimony, and the testimony of the holy scriptures from the Jews, we have the testimony of the modern prophet, Joseph Smith, who saw the Father and the Son, and who has borne record of them to the world, whose testimony was sealed with his blood and is in force upon the world today. We have the testimony of others, who witnessed the presence of the Son of God in the Kirtland temple, when he appeared to them there, and the testimony of Joseph, and of Sidney Rigdon, who declared that they were the last witnesss of Jesus Christ. Therefore I say again, I know that my Redeemer lives; for in the mouths of these witnesses this truth has been established in my mind.

Besides these testimonies, I have received the witness of the

Spirit of God in my own heart, which exceeds all other evidences, for it bears record to me, to my very soul, of the existence of my Redeemer, Jesus Christ. I know that he lives, and that in the last day he shall stand upon the earth, that he shall come to the people who shall be prepared for him, as a bride is prepared for the Bridegroom when he shall come. I believe in the divine mission of the Prophet Joseph Smith, and I have every evidence that I need—at least enough to convince me, of the divinity of his mission.

I am proud to say that I have accepted, and have tried to keep and honor, every word that has proceeded from the mouth of God through him. As it is written, "Man shall not live by bread alone, but by every word that proceedeth out of the mouth of God," no one will dare to accuse me of side-tracking from or refusing to obey any doctrine taught by or revealed through the Prophet Joseph Smith. —*Improvement Era*, Vol. 14, 1910, p. 73.

Testimony. Now, there are many other things, but I cannot tell them all to you. I begin to feel that I am getting to be an old man, or rather a young man in an old body. I think I am just about as young as I ever was in my life in spirit. I love the truth today more than I ever did before, because I see it more clearly, I understand it better from day to day by the promptings and inspiration of the Spirit of the Lord that is vouchsafed to me; but my body gets tired, and I want to tell you, sometimes my poor old heart quivers considerably.—*Oct. C. R.*, 1917, pp. 6, 7.

PRESIDENT JOSEPH F. SMITH

An Appreciation

President Joseph Fielding Smith, sixth and beloved President of the Church of Jesus Christ of Latter-day Saints, has without question seen longer service in the Church than has any other living man. For sixty-five years he has been in the active ministry, under a great variety of callings; for fifty-one years he has held the apostolic calling; since 1867 he has been one of the general authorities of the Church; during seventeen years he has been President of the Church. No other man is so beloved in the Church. To advertise that President Smith will be at a meeting is to warn the people that standing room will be at a premium. His words are accepted as of inspired authority; his acts as of an honest man, tried long and severely in the crucible of life.

The confidence of the people in their President, Prophet, Seer and Revelator, has not come alone from the exalted positions he has so long occupied. The Latter-day Saints have been gathered from all corners of the earth, and from all walks, after they had become convinced that the gospel as restored through the Prophet Joseph Smith is of certain truth. Intelligence rules in the earthly Zion. The leaders of the people are subjected to searching consideration by the people, and the confidence given them is in proportion to their deserts. It is, therefore, a noble tribute to the worthiness of the man Joseph F. Smith that he is the synonym for all that the people respect and hold dear.

Surely, this man who presides over the Church, and whose life is an open book, has been prepared for his labor. If weakness were in him he would have had ample opportunity to fall. From his birth, the spirit of the great latter-day work has hovered over him; and with every passing year he has been immersed in the history of the Church.

When he was born, in Far West, on November 13, 1838, apostasy, jealousy, persecution and the beckoning hands of untruth were shaking the Church. The Church did not fall, but the hearts of the faithful were sorely tried, and even the baby, Joseph F., must have assimilated some of the solemnity of those days when the Church was being purified for its future work. It was a preparation of noble

extent to sit, in those early years, on the knees of his patriarch father
or of his prophet uncle, even though the wide import of their conversation was not understood by the boy. It was a training in steely
strength, even for the child, to witness the homecoming of the bodies
of his murdered father and uncle. For such robbery of the dearest
in life the human breast naturally and instinctively clamors for
revenge. Yet, the whole life of the boy, grown to manhood, has been
that of forgiving and loving, so that all may be made to see the truth.
Who knows at what cost the man within has been conquered? The
Church has suffered such unjust yet persistent opposition from the
beginning that one wonders that it retains its gentle love for all the
children of men.

It was splendid preparation for the man who was to be in God's
harness all the years of a long life to witness the exodus of Nauvoo.
Home and lands, household property and trinkets of sentiment—all
had to be left behind. The driven people were in the desert with their
God, and lo! their faith waxed strong. It was during the exodus that
President Smith learned lessons of faith that never have been forgotten.
Their cattle were lost and their hope was gone, but the praying mother,
in communion with the Source of Truth, arose and went directly
to the place where the oxen had strayed. Though only eight years
old, the boy drove an ox team across Iowa.

"In 1848, when nine years old, I drove a four-ox team across the
plains to Salt Lake City," writes President Smith, in an album of a
friend. That was training for the boy! From the days of that
blistering, dusty journey there was no relapse to a longing for the easy
things of life. After the arrival in the valley came the toilsome
conquest of Widow Smith's farm. The father was gone and the
children were young. Our President, from his own life, can understand the lot of the widow and the fatherless.

Then the mother died. The strong spirit and wise mind could
no longer guide the boy. The father had been murdered in cold
blood because he was fearless in the cause of truth; the mother had
died from the strain and sorrow of a life tossed in the furious storm of
those days; no material wealth was his. Thus stood the fourteen-year-
old boy who was to become the leader of his people. Men are shorn
of earthly support that they may grow strong in Godly ways!

The training had been severe, but of infinite value. When the
boy was only fifteen years old he was called to go on a mission to
the Sandwich Islands. By the labor of his hands he worked his way

to California; by more labor, earned his passage to the islands. To object or to question was not possible for one who had survived his training. During that first mission the spirit of the work came upon him. In sermon, by visit, through his quiet influence, he led men and women into the way of everlasting truth. By the power of the Priesthood he held, he healed the sick, drove out evil spirits, and brought peace to the souls of those who were heavy laden.

After nearly five years he was allowed to return home. Again he had to work his way. At last he was again with the body of his people in Salt Lake City, but penniless. The Lord does not always reward in gold and silver. He was not permitted to remain home long, for mission succeeded mission. From the Sandwich Islands he was called to England for three years; then from England again to the Sandwich Islands. To preach the gospel without purse and scrip became the order of his life.

Joseph F. Smith's ceaseless devotion to the gospel did not escape the notice of the watchful, keen-eyed leader, Brigham Young, who loved with a mighty love the memory of the martyrs Joseph and Hyrum Smith. It was a joy to the Prophet Brigham Young to find one of the blood of the martyrs giving himself to the cause for which they died. In various ways did President Young test the materials of which Joseph F. Smith was made. However, the long and hard training of boyhood and the insistent discipline in the mission field had not been in vain. President Young found him loyal to his family, his country, his Church and his God. Not even his bitterest enemy will deny that President Smith is loyal.

After some years, on July 1, 1866, a beautiful and solemn day, President Brigham Young ordained Joseph F. Smith to the apostleship. A year later, in October, 1867, he was admitted to the quorum of the Twelve. If there can be any talk in the Church of Christ of earning a position, Joseph F. Smith had earned his place in the apostolic quorum, by his purity, his intelligence, his integrity and his activity in behalf of the Church. Moreover, the people of the Church delight to honor the blood of the Prophet who was God's instrument in the mighty work of the restoration of the gospel. Welcome was he, when he entered upon his work as one of the general authorities of the Church.

As a member of the quorum of the Twelve, Joseph F. Smith showed the same activity that had so emphatically characterized his former labors. From settlement to settlement he traveled, to counsel, to preach and to take active part in the building of the West, which was yet in its swaddling clothes of conquest. Vigorous were his words wherever he went. Without doubt was his faith. His testimony of the gospel was as the highest knowledge. He was then as now a fearless champion of truth.

At the time Apostle Smith assumed a place among the general authorities of the Church, Utah conditions were rapidly changing. Many non-members of the Church, who had come in to share in the bounties of the desert made to blossom by the Saints, could not content themselves with their rich material harvest, but must needs take up arms against the Church. When the leaders of the Church were charged with disloyalty to the country, when their motives were painted as those of devils, when the whole system of "Mormon" faith was branded as the rottenest immorality, the people who remembered the days of Carthage and Nauvoo had difficulty to keep down the cry of vengeance. Across the weary desert they had trailed, leaving many by the way; in the sweat of their brows they had won the wilderness to their use, and all this that they might serve unmolested their holy God, in a worship founded on purity and truth. It was then that the clear-visioned, clear-thinking leaders raised their voices in protest against further injustice. Apostle Smith, a man of deep affections, had fought away from himself the desire for revenge for the beastly murder of his manly father; but, being a man of strength, he could not submit indifferently to the new injustice that was proposed. The Fighting Apostle they called him, as he hurled back the untruths about "Mormonism," and his relentless watchfulness became a deterrent power among those who planned evil for a good and peaceful people.

A fighting apostle he has always been—fighting for the cause of truth. Yet, Joseph F. Smith is temperamentally a man of peace. Gentle and kind are his ways. A gentleman, is the instinctive appellation bestowed upon him by all who meet him. In character, voice and manner he is the dignified peace maker. Nevertheless, his loyalty is such, and his convictions are so firmly established, that evil may not be spoken about truth without arousing the lion within him. To measure the ground; to give the foe full place and warning, to try strength according to the laws of decency, but never to give quarter to evil or untruth or injustice—that is the method of Joseph F. Smith.

In time, the years of toil wore upon President Brigham Young, who asked that more counselors, to act as assistants, be given him.

Among those whom he chose for this purpose was Joseph F. Smith. This indicated that during his apostolic career he had not forfeited the confidence of the president which he had won earlier in his life. When, at length, the great founder of Utah passed away, and the first presidency was again reorganized, the abilities and character of Apostle Smith made him, under God's inspiration, a counselor to President John Taylor. Under the administrations of Presidents Taylor, Woodruff, and Snow, for twenty-one years, President Smith remained as a counselor in the first presidency, until at length, in the providence of God, he became the president of the Church.

The vast gathering in the great Tabernacle, November 10, 1901, will ever be remembered by those present. The priesthood of the Church were seated according to their offices in the Priesthood. One by one the quorums arose, elders, seventies, high priests and the others, and voted to sustain the appointment of Joseph Fielding Smith to the Presidency. In his vigorous, later manhood, his eye clear, his voice distinct, his spirit compelling, he was vividly the greatest among the thousands of able men, the flower of a vigorous people, who had assembled there that day.

The day was the fulfilment of prophecy, for, many years before, his attainment of the exalted position of the Presidency had been predicted with the voice of authority.

Of the administration of the affairs of the Church under Joseph F. Smith's presidency nothing need be said—for we live in it and know its eloquent message. The stakes at home, the missions in Europe and in the islands of the sea, have been visited by the President in his official capacity. Prosperity, good will, spiritual power and growth, overshadow the Church. The stakes of Zion have been increased, the wards multiplied, hundreds of beautiful meeting-houses have been constructed, the priesthood has risen to a fuller recognition of its place in the Church, the temples have become crowded, new temples are being built, new converts have been added in mighty numbers, and in a thousand other ways has the Church prospered; and above all, in the face of a most bitter persecution, which has been heralded throughout the world, the faith of the people has increased until it is nigh unto impregnable. If any doubt all this, let him journey over the Church, then visit one of the general conferences of the Church. There is faith in Israel!

Not only long but varied has been the experience of this great man who presides over the Church. True to the genius of "Mormonism," he has been closely identified with all the affairs of the community in which he has lived. For seven successive terms he was a member of the Utah legislature. When the Johnston army pantomime was in progress, President Smith joined the militia and assisted in making preparations to protect the homes of the people. He has helped to locate settlements and to find ways for bringing water upon the thirsting land. He has encouraged all legitimate business and, as far as time has permitted, has taken part in it. From his earliest life he has managed his farm, and even today, with his sons, has built one of the most modern livestock farms in the West, as an example to others.

Education, guided in schools, was largely denied him, but educated is President Smith. He has read widely, spoken with many men of many minds, and has thought deeply. Of broad and generous sympathies with everything that is noble and good, he has acquired a culture, which none dares question. Schools, the public press, the theater, music and the fine arts have been encouraged by him. As a most illuminating sidelight upon his wisdom is the fact that if not all of a family can be educated, he insists that the girls must be given the first chance, for they are the mothers and makers of men.

To those who do not know President Smith, it must seem strange that the honors that have almost overwhelmed him have all come unsought. President Smith is a modest man. Like all truly great men he is not immersed in thoughts of his own greatness. Rather does he admiringly place the power he observes in other men above his own. Nevertheless, and most naturally, position after position involving trust has come to him, though he has never sought one. Those who must find flaws in the Church point out that President men he is not immersed in thoughts of his own greatness. Rather those who find fault with this condition will not realize that men who can be absolutely trusted to guard the affairs of others as they would their own, are everywhere sought after. President Smith's demonstrated integrity has brought many offices which no doubt he would gladly relinquish to others. But "Mormon," Jew, and Gentile know that as far as President Smith can control things, only honor and justice and simple honesty will prevail wherever he is found.

During the Smoot investigations it seemed as if the whole United States was arrayed against the relatively few people who, during half a century, had given themselves to the conquest of the Great American Desert. The charges filed against this people, if sustained, would make

the "Mormon" people unfit to dwell in the "land of the free and the
home of the brave." To face the investigating Committee on Privileges and Elections, composed of the best minds of the Senate of
the United States Congress, many were subpoenaed. The first witness was President Smith. Fortunately, the hearing is preserved and
printed so that all may read it. Matching mind and will and heart
and sense against the great ones of the land, President Smith was
easily their compeer. Read it. Who has ever heard of that hearing
used as a campaign document against "Mormons"? When Joseph
F. Smith's history is written, his mighty contest with the most authoritative body in the land will make his figure stand out in noble
relief. Among the men of earth, high or low, President Smith is
never at a disadvantage.

Those who had even slight acquaintance with President Smith
were not surprised at the evidence of his power among men. In all
his public work he is masterful. He is endowed with high physical
attractiveness, his musical voice is compelling, his language chaste and
correct, and his thoughts appeal to the intellect as well as to the emotions. Those who have seen him before the ten thousand, at the great
Tabernacle in Salt Lake City, have no fear that he may not be measured with the men he meets.

Perhaps the best evidence of the high intellect of President
Smith is shown in his clear understanding and explanation of the
principles of the gospel. Men often sink to oblivion in quagmires of
theological vagueness. In matters of theological doctrine the President
is lucid as the noon-day light. Some few years ago, certain men,
loving to conjecture the improbable, insisted on knowing what would
happen if all the men holding the Priesthood were to die, save one
elder. At one of the great conferences (general), before ten thousand
assembled Saints, President Smith, in one-half dozen sentences cleared
up the whole subject. It would be the privilege and duty of the one
remaining elder to organize again the whole Church with apostles,
prophets, etc., according to the revelation! The powers and purpose
and duty of the Priesthood were thus driven into the understandings
of the people, as they never had been before. His sermons abound
in such clarifying statements, backed by a simple, unfailing faith that
looks for simplicity rather than mystery in the things of God.

Perhaps enough has been said. The man of whom we write is
tender and gentle, and withal does not love much praise. To him
and his families many children have been born. To them he is loyal

with all his power, for he well knows that loyalty, with all other virtues, begins at home. Over his families he watches with tender solicitude. They in turn love him with an invariable love. It is common knowledge that when the children were young, his rest was not easy if he had not seen the little ones properly tucked away for the night. The same father-heart beats for the people whose accepted leader he is. The hearts of the people ache over the long hours he spends in the office working out the affairs of the Church, especially now that he is no longer as young as he once was. But, he is not to be dissuaded. He must see his people tucked away for the night, before his heart will be at peace. So works love! and who shall say him nay, whose care from boyhood has been the welfare of his people?

"Has this man no faults?" asks the green-eyed critic. To be sure he has, for he is mortal. But, this writing is not to show his faults; and indeed, the writer does not know them, any more than he knows the full virtue of this man who for eighty long years has lived his life openly among his people, and who is the freest from adverse criticism in his community. Men are not measured by their faults, but by their worthy deeds and qualities. In the scales of eternal justice the main requirement is that our virtues outweigh our failings. Curiously enough, the only current criticism of President Smith, among those who oppose him, is that he is too loyal to his people, his friends, his convictions. Is not that the eternal cry of the enemy who reaches out for deserters? In every manly quality, friend and foe agree that he reaches above the majority of men.

Sure is our President of his reward. For him God will richly provide. Our question may rather be, has he had during the earth's journey, his full measure of reward? Have we done our full duty? For the cause of the Church he was bereft of father and mother. In the service of the Church he has been unable to use his splendid talents for the gathering of wealth—in our day he might justly be called a poor man. The ease of life has been denied him, for almost daily he has been "under orders." Above all, as a leader in Israel, the calumny and hatred of the Church have been heaped upon him. Only a few years ago, when past his prime, the most heartless persecution to which any member of the Church has been submitted was his. For several years an influential newspaper, standing at that time for the persecution of the Church, by means fair or foul, printed daily vile cartoons of President Smith and equally vile editorials about him and his work. Every indignity conceivable to the human mind was offered him because he was the embodiment of the Church.

Should the question be put to him, he would answer that he has had a rich reward. Perhaps he feels, let it be hoped he does, the outpouring of loving thoughts from the people whenever his name is mentioned. He has been blessed to serve. That is also a great reward for effort. His life has been crowned with the assurance, from all, that his work has been well done. That is the most satisfying reward.

May his health be preserved and his life be lengthened out. There is much work yet to be done, and men do not frequently rise to the fulness of his measure! At the beginning of his eighty-first year, the people give loving greetings and good wishes and heartfelt gratitude to Joseph F. Smith, President of the Church of Jesus Christ of Latter-day Saints.—Dr. John A. Widtsoe, 1918; also in *Improvement Era*, Vol. 18, November, 1914, pp. 38-45.

REMINISCENCES

The *Era* has asked me to write a few remembrances of incidents connected with my personal association with the late President Joseph F. Smith, while they are yet fresh in memory, and it is a pleasure to comply.

The first time I ever remember seeing Joseph F. Smith was in the then little village of Wellsville, in the year 1867. He was twenty-eight years of age, and had recently been chosen one of the twelve apostles. President Brigham Young and company were making a tour of the northern settlements, and the new apostle, Joseph F. Smith, was among the number. I heard him preach in the old meetinghouse at Wellsville, and I remarked at the time what a fine specimen of young manhood he was—strong, powerful, with a beautiful voice, so full of sympathy and affection, so appealing in its tone, that he impressed me, although I was a youth of but eighteen. He was a handsome man.

At that time I was clerking in a little store owned by Father Ira Ames, one of the old Kirtland veterans of the Church. Apostle George A. Smith was one of that company and he was entertained at Brother Ames' home, where I also lived. I recall that at the dinner table, Father Ames asked George A. who of the Smiths this young man Joseph F. was.

George A. replied that he was Hyrum's son; his mother, Mary Fielding Smith.

Brother Ames remarked that he looked like a likely young fellow, and George A. replied in about these words:

"Yes, I think he will be all right. His father and mother left him when he was a child, and we have been looking after him to try and help him along. We first sent him to school, but it was not long before he licked the schoolmaster, and could not go to school. Then we sent him on a mission, and he did pretty well at that. I think he will make good as an apostle."

Some years ago I related this incident to President Smith, and he told me that the reason he had trouble with the schoolmaster was that the schoolmaster had a leather strap with which he used to chastise the children. He was a rather hard-hearted schoolmaster, one of the olden type that believed in inflicting bodily punishment.

President Smith said: "My little sister was called up (Aunt

Martha, now living in Provo) to be punished. I saw the school master bring out the leather strap, and he told the child to hold out her hand. I could not stand for that. I just spoke up loudly and said, 'Don't whip her with that,' and at that he came at me and was going to whip me, and instead of him whipping me, I licked him good and plenty."

At the time of this incident, Joseph F. (for, by that name he was affectionately called) was about fifteen years of age. But he was a strong, powerful youth, and his big heart could not tolerate such punishment, especially if it bordered on the cruel, to be inflicted upon a little child.

Another incident which I have heard him relate which shows his courage and integrity, occurred when he was returning from his mission to the Sandwich Islands, in the fall of 1857. He came home by way of Los Angeles, by what was called the Southern Route. In that year Johnston's Army was on the move for Utah, and naturally enough there was much excitement and bitterness of feeling concerning the "Mormons." In southern California, just after the little train of wagons had traveled only a short distance and made their camp, several anti-"Mormon" toughs rode into the camp on horseback, cursing and swearing and threatening what they would do to the "Mormons." Joseph F. was a little distance from the camp gathering wood for the fire, but he saw that the few members of his own party had cautiously gone into the brush down the creek, out of sight. When he saw that, he told me, the thought came into his mind, "Shall I run from these fellows? Why should I fear them?" With that he marched up with his arm full of wood to the campfire where one of the ruffians, still with his pistol in his hand, shouting and cursing about the "Mormons," in a loud voice said to Joseph F.:

"Are you a 'Mormon'?"

And the answer came straight, "Yes, siree; dyed in the wool; true blue, through and through."

At that the ruffian grasped him by the hand and said:

"Well, you are the —— —— pleasantest man I ever met! Shake, young fellow, I am glad to see a man that stands up for his convictions."

These incidents show the inherent bravery, courage, integrity of the man, and also tenderness and pity for the little helpless sister. These are the qualities upon which great men are builded.

In the spring of 1877, I was called to accompany President

Smith on a mission to Europe. I was called by him to labor in the business affairs of the Liverpool office, and from that time until the day of his death, I think I have enjoyed his personal confidence more than any man living. When I look back on it all now, I can see what a treasure, a blessing, a favor from the Almighty it has been to me.

During the last eleven years, especially, I have traveled with him almost constantly whenever he has gone from home. I have been with him on three different trips to Europe, including the first missionary trip above mentioned, and on four trips to the Sandwich Islands. Everywhere, on all occasions, I have found him the same great, brave, true-hearted, noble and magnificent leader, so simple and unaffected, so entirely democratic and unassuming.

He was always careful with his expenditures, too. He abhorred debt, and no man have I ever known who was so prompt to pay an obligation to the last penny. He could not rest until the Church was out of debt, and though hundreds of schemes, and many of them extra good schemes, too, were presented to him, which no doubt would have meant an increase of wealth for the Church, yet he resolutely set his face against debt; and would not, under any conditions or circumstances, involve the Church in that way. Neither would he himself become involved in debt in his own individual affairs, but he stuck persistently to the old motto, "Pay as you go."

Many of the older people now alive can recall that forty years ago, or even less, he was considered a radical, and many a one of that time shook his head and said, "What will become of things if that fiery radical ever becomes president of the Church?" But from the time he was made president of the Church, and even before that time, he became one of the most tolerant of men, tolerant of others' opinions; and while he would denounce sin with such righteous wrath as you would seldom see in any man, yet for the poor sinner he had compassion and pity, and even forgiveness, if sincere repentance were shown. None more ready than he to forgive and forget.

One touching little incident I recall which occurred on our first trip to the Sandwich Islands. As we landed at the wharf in Honolulu, the native Saints were out in great numbers with their wreaths of leis, beautiful flowers of every variety and hue. We were loaded with them, he, of course, more than anyone else. The noted Hawaiian band was there playing welcome, as it often does to incoming steamship companies. But on this occasion the band had been instructed by the Mayor to go up to the "Mormon" meetinghouse and there play selections during the festivities which the natives had arranged for. It was a beautiful sight to see the deep-seated love, the even tearful affection, that these people had for him. In the midst of it all I noticed a poor, old, blind woman, tottering under the weight of about ninety years, being led in. She had a few choice bananas in her hand. It was her all—her offering. She was calling, "Iosepa, Iosepa." Instantly, when he saw her, he ran to her and clasped her in his arms, hugged her, and kissed her over and over again, patting her on the head saying, "Mama, Mama, my dear old Mama."

And with tears streaming down his cheeks he turned to me and said, "Charlie, she nursed me when I was a boy, sick and without anyone to care for me. She took me in and was a mother to me."

Oh, it was touching—it was pathetic. It was beautiful to see the great, noble soul in loving, tender remembrance of kindness extended to him, more than fifty years before; and the poor old soul who had brought her love offering—a few bananas—it was all she had —to put into the hand of her loved Iosepa!

On these ocean trips there was much spare time, and we often whiled away an hour or two playing checkers. He could play a good game of checkers, much better than I. In fact, he could beat me four times out of five, but once in a while, when I played more cautiously, and no doubt when he was more careless, I could beat him. If he was beating me right along and I made an awkward move, and could see instantly that I had moved the wrong checker, he would allow me to draw it back if I noticed it immediately; but on the other hand, if I had beaten him for a game or two and should put my finger on a checker to draw it back, even though it were on the instant, he would call out with force enough, and that positive way of his, "No you don't, you leave it right there." It is in these little incidents that we show the human side of our natures.

He loved sport—manly sport. He was a natural athlete; and in his youth at foot-racing, jumping, wrestling, which were among the primitive sports of primitive days, he was a match for anyone. In later years I had induced him to take up with the ancient and royal Scottish game of golf. He got so that he could play a very good game, excellent indeed for a man of his years. But on one occasion, down at Santa Monica, when we were playing, we were up within about one hundred feet of the flag at the hole we were making for. A light stroke should have driven the ball nearer the flag, but the inclination to look up as one tries to hit the ball got the best of him, and the consequence was he topped the ball and it rolled only a couple of feet or so. He bent over for the next stroke, and the one thing which all golfers most fear, and the hardest to overcome, is that habit of looking up or taking the eye off the ball just as you go to strike. This he did, the second time, when he topped it again and it moved but a few feet further. The third time he went up to it and hit it a whack that sent it rolling one hundred feet beyond the flag. His son, Wesley, who was playing with us, called out, "Why, papa, what did you do that for? You knew it would roll away down there in the ditch!" The President straightened up and said, with a smile, "Well, I was mad at it!" I have laughed hundreds of times at that, "I was mad at it."

Of course, we agreed well together, otherwise we would not have been companionable during all these years. But sometimes I could not fully agree with him on some matters that we discussed. I recall one night we were on shipboard returning from Europe, in 1906. It was a bright, moonlight night, and we stood there leaning over the railing enjoying the smooth sea and balmy summer night air. The Smoot investigation, which had just occurred a little while before and which had stirred up so much controversy throughout the land, was fresh in our minds, and we were talking of it. I took the position that it would be unwise for Reed Smoot to be re-elected to the United States Senate. I was conscientious in my objection, and I had mar-shaled all the facts, arguments, and logic that I could; and I was well informed, I thought, on the subject, and had presented them to him in as clear and yet in as adroit a manner as I possibly could. It would take too much space here to go over the arguments, but it seemed to me that I had the best of it. I could see he began to listen with some little impatience, and yet he let me have my say, but he answered in tones and in a way that I shall never forget. Bringing his fist down with some force on the railing between us, he said, in the most forceful and positive manner:

"If ever the Spirit of the Lord has manifested to me anything clear and plain and positive, it is this, that Reed Smoot should remain in the United States Senate. He can do more good there than he can anywhere else."

Of course, I did not contend further with him, but accepted from that hour his view of the case and made it mine, too. Twelve years have passed since that time, and looking back on it now, I cannot help but think how marvelously and splendidly the inspiration of the Almighty has been vindicated, while my arguments, facts and logic have all fallen to the ground.

During the last six or eight years, hundreds of prominent people, Democrats as well as Republicans, passing through Salt Lake City, even Secretary McAdoo, himself, among them, have stated to President Smith that Utah had a great big man in the United States Senate in the person of Senator Reed Smoot. President Smith's judgment, or rather his inspiration in this matter, has been vindicated to the last degree.

As a preacher of righteousness, who could compare with him? He was the greatest that I ever heard—strong, powerful, clear, appealing. It was marvelous how the words of living light and fire flowed from him. He was a born preacher, and yet he did not set himself up to be such. He never thought highly of his own good qualities. Rather, he was simple, plain and unaffected to the last degree; and yet, there was dignity with it all which enabled anyone and everyone to say: "He is a man among men!" I ask, as preacher, leader, teacher, husband, father, citizen and man, who among our mighty ones can be likened unto him?

He loved a good story and a good joke. There was a good laugh in him always. He had no patience with vile stories, but there was a fine vein of humor in him, and could relate incidents of his early life and entertain the crowd about him as few men ever could.

He was the most methodical in all his work of any person I ever knew. Every letter that he received had to be indorsed by him with the date and any other information, and all carefully filed away. He could not stand for disorder. Everything in connection with his work was orderly. He could pack his suitcase or a trunk and line out and smooth every piece of clothing in it so it would hold more and be better packed than if anybody else had done it. His clothes, too, were always clean. Most men as they grow old are likely to have their clothes more or less spotted through dropping food on their clothing. But not so with him. To his last day his clothes were as clean and as well taken care of as if he had been a young man of thirty.

He was a most strenuous worker and never considered saving himself at all. You could go up to his little office in the Beehive most any night when he was well, and find him writing letters or attending to some other work. Perhaps some dear old soul had written him a personal letter, and he would work into the night answering it with his own hand. Indeed, he over-worked himself and no doubt injured his strong constitution.

He was careless about eating—careless as to what he ate and when he ate. His living was exceedingly simple and plain. He rarely got to bed before midnight, and the consequence was he did not get sufficient sleep and rest.

He was very fond of music and loved to sing the songs of Zion.

His love for little children was unbounded. During the trip we took last year down through the southern settlements to St. George and return, when the troops of little children were paraded before him, it was beautiful to see how he adored these little ones. It was my duty to try and get the company started, to make time to the next settlement where the crowds would be waiting for us, but it was a difficult task to pull him away from the little children. He wanted to shake hands with and talk to every one of them.

Once in a while someone would come up to him and say, "President Smith, I believe I am a kinsman of yours." I knew then that we were good for another ten minutes' delay, for that great heart of his, that went out to every kinsman as well as to the little children, could not be torn away quickly from anyone claiming kinship with him.

I have visited at his home when one of his children was down sick. I have seen him come home from his work at night tired, as he naturally would be, and yet he would walk the floor for hours with that little one in his arms, petting it and loving it, encouraging it in every way with such tenderness and such a soul of pity and love as not one mother in a thousand would show.

While he was a hard-headed, successful business man, yet very few in this dispensation have been more gifted with spiritual insight than he. As we were returning from an eastern trip, some years ago, on the train just east of Green River, I saw him go out to the end of the car on the platform, and immediately return and hesitate a moment, and then sit down in the seat just ahead of me. He had just taken his seat when something went wrong with the train. A broken rail had been the means of ditching the engine and had thrown most of the cars off the track. In the sleeper we were shaken up pretty badly, but our car remained on the track.

The President immediately said to me that he had gone on the platform when he heard a voice saying, "Go in and sit down."

He came in, and I noticed him stand a moment, and he seemed to hesitate, but he sat down.

He said further that as he came in and stood in the aisle he thought, "Oh, pshaw, perhaps it is only my imagination;" when he heard the voice again, "Sit down," and he immediately took his seat, and the result was as I have stated.

He, no doubt, would have been very seriously injured had he remained on the platform of that car, as the cars were all jammed up together pretty badly. He said, "I have heard that voice a good many times in my life, and I have always profited by obeying it."

On another occasion, at a function which was held in the palatial home of Mr. and Mrs. A. W. McCune, he made an extended talk to the gathering. He then said that when a certain brother who had been called to a responsible position in the Church was chosen for that position, he himself had never heard this spiritual voice more plainly and more clearly telling him what to do, than in this naming of the individual who was to be called for that certain office.

He lived in close communion with the Spirit of the Lord, and his life was so exemplary and chaste that the Lord could easily manifest himself to his servant. Truly he could say, "Speak, Lord, for thy servant heareth." Not every servant can hear when He speaks. But the heart of President Smith was attuned to the Celestial melodies—he could hear, and did hear.

What shall I say of the grand and glorious work that he has done in rearing the large and splendid family that he leaves behind? What a noble work for any man! Indeed no man without great nobility of soul could have accomplished it. Is not this bringing up a good family, and a large family of good citizens, good men and women, good for the Church, for the State, and for the Nation? Is not this, I say, about the most God-like piece of work that a man can do in this world? The thinking mind, who goes into this question deep enough, will see that here is the work, not only of a man, of a great man, but of a God in embryo. The whole Church can take pride in the vindication of this great principle which he had so successfully wrought out. No ordinary man could accomplish that. Happy the wife who can call him husband. Happy and blessed indeed the children who call him father. Never was man more moral and chaste and virtuous to the last fiber of his being than he. Against all forms or thoughts of licentiousness, he was set, and as immovable as a mountain. "Blessed are the pure in heart," and as he was the very purest—he shall see God.

It is written that a truly great man is known by the number of beings he loves and blesses, and by the number of beings who love and bless him. Judged by that standard alone, where is his equal to be found in all this world!

I can say of Joseph F. Smith as Carlyle said of Luther, that he was truly a great man, "great in intellect, in courage, in affection, and in integrity. Great, not as a hewn obelisk, but as an Alpine mountain." No heart ever beat truer to every principle of manhood and righteousness and justice and mercy than his; that great heart, encased in his magnificent frame, made him the biggest, the bravest, the tenderest, the purest and best of all men who walked the earth in his time!

> "His life was gentle, and the elements
> So mix'd in him, that Nature might stand up
> And say to all the world, 'This was a Man!'"

—*Charles W. Nibley*, Presiding Bishop of the Church, *Improvement Era*, Vol. 22, January, 1919, pp. 191-198.

A BIOGRAPHICAL SKETCH

It was John Locke, the great characteristic English philosopher, who, at the age of thirty, wrote:

"I no sooner perceived myself in the world, but I found myself in a storm which has lasted hitherto."

To Joseph F. Smith, who is among the greatest and most unique and notable individualities of that peculiar people, the Latter-day Saints, this sentence of Locke's is especially applicable. Only, his was enveloped in storm before he could perceive. He is the son of Hyrum Smith, the second patriarch of the Church, and brother of the Prophet Joseph. His mother was Mary Fielding, of English origin, a woman of bright and strong mind and of excellent business administrative qualities.

It was during the Missouri troubles. Governor Boggs had issued his order to exterminate the "Mormons." On the first day of November, 1838, through the heartless treachery of Colonel Hinkle, Joseph and Hyrum and several other leaders of the people were betrayed into the hands of an armed mob under General Clark. They were to be taken prisoners, and confined in jail, and perhaps shot. On the following day, these betrayed leaders were given a few moments to bid farewell to their families. Under a strong guard of militia mobocrats, Hyrum was marched to his home in Far West, and, at the point of the bayonet, with oaths and curses, was ordered to take his last farewell of his wife; for his "doom was sealed" and he was told that he would never see her again. Imagine such a shock to his companion! It would have overpowered and come near ending the life of an ordinary person. But with the natural strength of her mind, coupled with the sustaining care of God, she was upheld in this fiery trial with its added miseries to follow. It was on the 13th day of the same month of November, 1838, in the midst of plunderings, and scenes of severest hardships and persecution, that she gave birth to her first-born, who was named Joseph Fielding Smith. In the cold of the following January, leaving four little ones, under the care of her sister, Mercy R.—children of her husband by a former wife, then dead—she journeyed in a wagon with her infant to Liberty Jail in Clay county, where the husband and father was confined, without trial or conviction, his sole offense being that he was a "Mormon." She was permitted to visit him in jail, but was later compelled to continue her flight from Missouri with her children, to seek shelter in Illinois.

Such were the stormy environments of birth, and such was the first pilgrimage of the infant Joseph who has since compassed the earth and the islands of the sea, promulgating and defending the principles for which his father endured imprisonment and later martyrdom, and for which his mother suffered untold persecution and distress.

Joseph's early years were spent amidst the agitations which culminated in the martyrdom of his uncle and his father on the memorable 27th day of June, 1844. After the abandonment of the city by the Twelve, and when the majority of the Saints had been driven from Nauvoo, in September, 1846, his mother fled from the city and camped on the west side of the Mississippi River, among the trees on its banks, without wagon or tent, during the bombardment of the city by the mob. Having later succeeded in making exchanges of property in Illinois for teams and an outfit, she set out for Winter Quarters, on the Missouri River. Joseph, a lad of only about eight years, drove a yoke of oxen and a wagon most of the distance through the state of Iowa to Winter Quarters, and his other occupation, after leaving Nauvoo, was principally that of herd boy.

On these western plains he drank in the freedom of the spirit of the West, and developed that physical strength which, notwithstanding his later sedentary occupation, is still observable in his robust, erect and muscular form.

He is a lover of strength and a believer in work. "Labor is the key to the true happiness of the physical and spiritual being. If a man possesses millions, his children should still be taught how to labor with their hands; boys and girls should receive a home training which will fit them to cope with the practical, daily affairs of family life, even where the conditions are such that they may not have to do this work themselves; they will then know how to guide and direct others," said he, in a recent conversation with the writer.

The great and overpowering desire of all the Saints was to obtain means to gather to the Valley. For this purpose various kinds of labor were sought in Iowa and neighboring states, from farming to school teaching. In the fall of 1847, he drove a team for his mother to St. Joseph for the purpose of securing provisions to make the coveted journey to the Salt Lake Valley, in the spring following. The trip was successfully made.

It was in the fall of that year, while tending his mother's cattle near Winter Quarters, that he experienced one of the most exciting incidents of his life. The cattle were their only hope of means for immigration to the Valley. This fact was deeply impressed upon the boy, so that he came to view them as a precious heritage, as well as a priceless charge given to him as a herd boy. He understood the responsibility; and that is much, for neither Joseph, the boy, nor Joseph, the man, was ever known to shirk a duty or prove recreant to a responsibility.

One morning, in company with Alden and Thomas Burdick, he set out upon the usual duties of the day. The cattle were feeding in the valley some distance from the settlement, which valley was reached in two ways, one over a "bench" or plateau, the other through a ravine or small canyon. The boys each had a horse. Joseph's was a bay mare, swifter than the others. Alden suggested that Thomas and Joseph go the short route to the left, over the "bench," and he would go up the canyon to the right, so that they would meet in the valley from the two directions. The suggestion was gladly adopted, and the two set out with youthful frolic, and soon arrived at the upper end of the valley, where the cattle could be seen feeding by a stream which divided it in the center and wound down the canyon from the direction of the settlement. Having the day before them, they amused themselves with "running" their horses, and, later, in "jumping" them over a little gully in the upper part of the valley. As they were engaged in this amusement, suddenly a band of twenty or thirty Indians came into view around a point in the lower end of the valley, some distance below the cattle. Thomas first saw them, and frantically yelled, "Indians," at the same time turning his horse for the "bench" to ride for home. Joseph started to follow, but the thought came to his mind, "My cattle, I must save my cattle!" From that moment, only this thought filled his mind; everything else was blank and dark. He headed his horse for the Indians, to get around the herd before the reds should reach it. One Indian, naked like the others, having only a cloth around the loins, passed him, flying to catch Thomas. Joseph reached the head of the herd, and succeeded in turning the cattle up the ravine just as the Indians approached. His efforts, coupled with the rush and yells of the Indians, stampeded the herd, followed by Joseph, who by keeping his horse on the "dead" run, succeeded for some time in keeping between the herd and the Indians. Here was a picture! the boy, the cattle, the Indians, headed on the run for the settlement! Finally the reds cut him away from the herd, whereupon he turned, going down stream a distance, then circling around the ravine to the right, to reach the cattle from the other side. He had not gone far in that direction when other Indians were seen. They started for him, overtaking him as he emerged from the valley. He still spurred his horse, going at full speed, and while thus riding, two of the naked reds closed up beside him in the wild race, and took him, while the horses were going at full speed, one by the left arm and the other by the right leg, and lifted him from the saddle, for a moment holding him in the air, then suddenly dropping him to the ground.

Undoubtedly he would have been scalped but for the timely appearance of a company of men going to the hay fields, on the opposite side of the ravine, which scared the thieving Indians away, they having obtained both the boys' horses for their pains. In the meantime Thomas had given the alarm. Two relief companies were formed in the settlement, one a posse of horsemen under Hosea Stout, who went up the canyon and found the cattle with Alden Burdick (the pursuing Indians having abandoned the chase from fright), while the other took the "bench" route, and discovered Joseph, who with them spent the day in a fruitless search for the Indians and the cattle supposed to have been stolen. "I remember, on my way home," says Joseph, "how I sat down and wept for my cattle, and how the thought of meeting mother, who could not now go to the Valley, wrung my soul with anguish." But happily, his bravery and fidelity to trust, which are indissolubly interwoven with his character as a man, had saved the herd.

Leaving Winter Quarters in the spring of 1848, they reached the Salt Lake Valley on September 23, Joseph driving two yoke of oxen with a heavily loaded wagon the whole distance. He performed all the duties of a day watchman, herdsman and teamster, with other requirements imposed upon the men. Arriving in Salt Lake City, he again had charge of the herds, interchanging with such labors as plowing, canyon work, harvesting and fencing. During this whole time he never lost an animal entrusted to his care, this notwithstanding the numerous large wolves abounding in the country.

His education was obtained from his mother who early taught him, in the tent, in the camp, on the prairie, to read from the Bible. He has had no other, save that sterner education gathered from the practical pages of life. But his opportunities in later years have not

gone unused, and there are few college-bred men who delight more
in books than Joseph. He is, too, a fair judge of the manner and
matter of books. His leisure for reading is limited, owing to his
constant employment in the affairs of the Church; but he loves to
read books of history, philosophy, science; and has specially delighted
in such authors as Seiss and Samuel Smiles, who may be said to be
his favorites. He is fond of music, of which, though not a judge, he
is a great lover, especially enjoying the music of the human voice.

In 1852 his mother died, leaving him an orphan at the age of
fourteen. When fifteen years of age, he, with other young men, was
called on his first mission to the Sandwich Islands. The incidents
of the journey to the coast by horses, his work in the mountains at
a shingle mill for means to proceed, and the embarkment and journey
on the Vaquero for the islands, are sufficient for a long chapter in
themselves; while his labors in the Maui conference, under President
F. A. Hammond, his efforts to learn the language in the district of
Kula, his attack of sickness, the most severe of his life, caused by the
Panama fever, and his other labors and varied, trying experiences while
there, would fill a volume. He says, "Of the many gifts of the Spirit
which were manifest through my administration, next to my acquire-
ments of the language, the most prominent was perhaps the gift of
healing, and by the power of God the casting out of evil spirits, which
frequently occurred."

One incident shows how the Lord is with his servants: Joseph
was studying the language, being alone with a native family in Wail-
uku. One night, while he sat by a dismal light poring over his books
in one corner of the room where dwelt a native and his wife, the
woman was suddenly possessed; she arose and looking toward Joseph
made the most fearful noises and gestures, accompanied by terrible
physical contortions. Her husband came on his bended knees and
crouched beside him, frightened to trembling. The fear that our
young missionary felt under those circumstances was something
indescribable, but presently it all left him, and he stood up facing the
maniac woman, exclaiming: "In the name of the Lord Jesus Christ,
I rebuke you." Like a flash, the woman fell to the floor like one dead.
The husband went to ascertain if she were alive, and pronounced her
dead. Then he returned, and set up a perfect howl, which Joseph
likewise rebuked. What should Joseph do? His first impression
was to get away from the horrid surrounding, but upon reflection
he decided that such action would not be wise. His feelings were

indescribable, but having rebuked the evil, it was subdued, peace was restored, and he proceeded again with his studies. These are the class of experiences that bring a lone missionary, young as he was, close to the Lord.

After his release, and while returning from the mission in Hawaii, this incident occurred: At Honolulu he went on board the barque *Yankee*, on October 6, 1857, and with a company of elders landed in San Francisco, about the end of the month. With Edward Partridge, he went down the coast to Santa Cruz County, Cal., and from thence with a company of Saints, under Captain Charles W. Wandell, southward to the Mojave river, where he and others left the company and made a visit to San Bernardino on their way to the Salt Lake Valley. It must be said that the feeling against the "Mormons," first, on account of the exaggerated reports of the Mountain Meadows massacre, and secondly, because of the coming of Johnston's army to Utah, was exceedingly bitter on the coast. As an illustration: While they were in Los Angeles, a man, William Wall by name, came near being hung because he had confessed he was a "Mormon." A mob of men had passed sentence on him, and had prepared every detail to hang him. It was only through the wise counsel of a man among them, whose better judgment prevailed, that he was not hung. This man pointed out to the mob that here was a man who had not been near Utah when the massacre took place, a man who had no sympathy with it, who could in no way be counted as a criminal. Why should he suffer? And so Wall was finally discharged and given time to get out of the country. It was under such conditions, and such prevailing sentiment, that President Smith, then a lad of nineteen, found himself on his journey home, and on his trip to San Bernardino.

With another man, and a mail carrier, he took passage in a mail wagon. They traveled all night, and at daylight stopped near a ranch for breakfast. The passenger and the mail carrier began to prepare breakfast, while Joseph went a short distance from camp to look after the horses. Just while the carrier was frying eggs, a wagon load of drunken men from Monte came in view, on their road to San Bernardino to kill the "Mormons," as they boasted.

The oaths and foul language which they uttered, between their shooting, and the swinging of their pistols, were almost indescribable and unendurable. Only the West in its palmiest frontier days could produce anything like its equal. They were all cursing the "Mormons," and uttering boasts of what they would do when they met them. They got out at the ranch, and one of them, tumbling around, caught sight of the mail wagon, and made his way towards it. The passenger and the mail carrier, fearing for their safety, had retired behind the chaparral, leaving all the baggage and supplies, including the frying eggs, exposed and unprotected.

Just as the drunken man approached, President Smith came in view on his way to the camp, too late to hide, for he had been seen. The ruffian was swinging his weapon, and uttering the most blood-curdling oaths and threats ever heard against the "Mormons." "I dared not run," says President Smith, "though I trembled for fear which I dared not show. I therefore walked right up to the camp fire and arrived there just a minute or two before the drunken desperado, who came directly toward me, and, swinging his revolver in my face, with an oath cried out: 'Are you a —— —— —— 'Mormon?' "

President Smith looked him straight in the eyes, and answered with emphasis: "Yes, siree; dyed in the wool; true blue, through and through."

The desperado's arms both dropped by his sides, as if paralyzed, his pistol in one hand, and he said in a subdued and maudlin voice, offering his hand: "Well, you are the —— —— pleasantest man I ever met! Shake. I am glad to see a fellow stand for his convictions." Then he turned and made his way to the ranch house. Later in the day, on seeing President Smith, he only pulled his slouch hat over his eyes, and said not a word.

In 1858, Joseph F. Smith joined the militia which intercepted Johnston's army, serving until the close of hostilities, under Colonel Thomas Callister. He was later chaplain of Colonel Heber C. Kimball's regiment, with the rank of captain. He took part in many Indian expeditions, and was in every sense a minute man in the Utah militia.

In the spring of 1860, though only about 22 years of age, he was sent on a mission to Great Britain. As he had no money, he and his cousin Samuel H. B. Smith, each drove a four-mule team over the plains to Winter Quarters to pay their way. It happened that the owners of these teams were rank apostates, so that when the young men arrived at their destination, it was very well known that they were Latter-day Saints. They were moneyless, and decided finally to go to Des Moines where they tried without success to get something to do. They hunted for work in the harvest fields, but found no one who wished to employ them. The feeling was still bitter against the "Mormons" in this region, for it was only about fourteen years since the remnant of the Saints had been driven from Nauvoo. One day they met a man who asked them who they were, and where they were going, and having been told that they were going to England on a mission, the man stated that he had a sister in England whom he wished to emigrate, and asked that they take the money with them for her emigration. He stated that they might use it as they saw fit; provided on arrival they would let his sister have the money to pay her passage to America. They agreed to this, and immediately went on their way to Burlington where they took a steamer for Nauvoo; but when they got on board they learned that the steamer would not land at that place, as they had been told; and they also heard the most bitter imprecations against the Latter-day Saints, uttered in the most profane and indecent language.

Landing at Montrose, where the boat took on freight, the feeling was still more bitter. The Saints were cursed, and boasts were made of what evil would befall any "Mormon" who would dare to make his appearance. Getting on board the skiff next morning, which was to carry them over to Nauvoo, the young men found that the spirit of the mob was just as bitter as ever, but it was not known here that they were "Mormons." Several men asked them who they were, and their replies were evasive. Finally, a Catholic priest came to them and asked where they were from. "Oh! from the West," was the reply.

"How far West?"

"From the Rocky Mountains."

But the priest finally pinned them down by asking, "Are you 'Mormon' elders from Utah?"

President Smith says that under those circumstances, for a moment, never had temptation to deny the truth come to him with stronger force, but it was only for a moment. He answered, "Yes, sir, we are 'Mormon' missionaries on our way to England."

The reply seemed to satisfy the priest; and, contrary to expectations, it did not in the least increase the imprecations of the passengers. When they landed at Nauvoo, they went directly to the Mansion House, and, strange to say, the Catholic priest also stayed there. If they had not truthfully answered the queries on the boat, he would have found them out here, to their shame.

"I had never felt happier," says President Smith, "than when I saw the minister there, and knew that we had told him the truth about our mission."

On this mission he served nearly three years, returning in the summer of 1863; it was during these years that the intimacy between President George Q. Cannon, who presided over the mission, and Joseph F. Smith began; friendship and love for each other were engendered, which have since grown stronger through the intimate careers of two beautiful lives. On his return, President Young proposed at a Priesthood meeting that Joseph and his cousin, Samuel, each be given a present of $1,000 to begin life with. President Smith realized in the neighborhood of $75 in provisions and merchandise, but mostly a legacy of much annoyance from certain people who entertained the current thought that he had thus obtained a small fortune. With the exception of the cost of his passage and stage fare home, which was sent him by his aunt, Mercy R. Thompson, amounting to about $100, he paid his own expenses throughout, as he had done on previous missions.

President Smith has been too busy with his work to make money, and his temporal affairs are a strong testimony to his exclusive devotion to the public good.

He had only been at home a short time, when, in the early spring of 1864, he was called to accompany Ezra T. Benson and Lorenzo Snow on a second mission to the Sandwich Islands to regulate the affairs of that mission, which had been greatly disarranged by the well-known, shrewd and covetous actions of Walter M. Gibson. In this mission he acted as principal interpreter for the apostles. After Gibson was excommunicated from the Church, Joseph was left in charge of the mission, with W. W. Cluff and Alma L. Smith as his fellow-laborers. It was many months after Gibson had been cut off before his people left his jurisdiction and returned to the standard of the Church. Among the works accomplished by Joseph and his associates on this mission was the selection of the Laie plantation as a gathering place for the Saints, which was afterwards on their recommendation, purchased by a committee sent for that purpose by President Young, and which has proven a valuable possession for the mission, and for the Church in a general way. Joseph and his aids returned in the winter of 1864-1865.

It was while on this mission that the drowning incident occurred, mentioned in Whitney's sketch of President Lorenzo Snow. President

Smith's part in the affair has never been fully told. The ship upon which they arrived lay anchored in the channel in which the sea was nearly always rough. A breakwater had been built, under shelter of which the natives skilfully steered their boats ashore. There was much danger, however, in approaching it. When it was proposed that the party should land in the ship's unwieldy freight-boat, President Smith strongly opposed the proposition, telling the brethren that at the breakwater there was great danger of capsizing, the boat being a clumsy old tub, unfit for such a load. He refused to go ashore, and tried to prevail upon the others to abandon the attempt until a better boat could be obtained. He offered to go ashore alone, and to return with a safer boat to land the party. So persistent, however, were some of the brethren, that he was chided for his waywardness, and one of the apostles even told him: "Young man, you would better obey counsel." But he reiterated his impression of danger, refusing positively to land in that boat, and again offering to go alone for a better boat. But the brethren persisted, whereupon he asked that they leave their satchels with their clothes and valuables on the anchored ship with him, and that he be permitted to stay. This they reluctantly consented to do, and set out for land.

Joseph stood upon the ship and saw them depart, filled with the greatest apprehension for their safety. When the party reached the breakwater, he saw one of the great waves suddenly overturn the boat, dropping the company into twenty or thirty feet of water. A boat came out from shore, manned with natives, who set to work to gather them up, and obtained all but President Snow, when the boat which picked them up started for land. It was then that Elder W. W. Cluff demanded that they return for Brother Snow, who would otherwise have been abandoned and left for drowned. He was found and dragged into the boat for dead, his life being thus saved by Brother Cluff. All this time, Joseph stood in the greatest agony as a witness, helpless, on the deck of the ship. His first information of his companions' fate came from some passing natives who replied to his inquiry that one of the men (Brother Snow) was dead. But through the blessings of God and self-effort it was, fortunately, not quite so serious, his life having been restored.

Joseph had saved himself and the satchels, and he has always considered that while the brethren fatefully said of the incident: "It was to be," that a prevention in this case would have been much better than a cure. The incident illustrates two predominating traits in his character: When he is convinced of the truth, he is not afraid to express himself in its favor to any man on earth. When he does express himself, it is often with such earnestness and vigor that there is danger of his giving offense.

On his return home, he labored in the Church historian's office for a number of years; also as clerk in the endowment house, succeeding Elder John V. Long in that capacity; being in charge, after the death of President Young, until it was closed. He had been ordained an apostle under the hands of President Young, on July 1, 1866, and on the 8th of October, 1867, he was appointed to fill a vacancy in the quorum of the Twelve Apostles. In the year following, he was sent with Elder Wilford Woodruff of the Council of the Twelve and Elder A. O. Smoot to Utah county. Here he served one term in the Provo city council.

On February 28, 1874, he went on his second mission to England, where he presided over the European mission, returning in 1875, after the death of President George A. Smith. On his return he was appointed to preside over the Davis stake, until the spring of 1877, when he left on his third British mission, having first witnessed the dedication of the first temple in the Rocky Mountains, at St. George, April, 1877. He arrived in Liverpool, May 27, and was joined a short time afterwards by Elder Orson Pratt, who had been sent to publish new editions of the Book of Mormon and the Doctrine and Covenants. When news arrived of the death of President Young, they were released, and returned home, arriving in Salt Lake City, September 27.

In August of the following year, he was sent with Elder Orson Pratt on a short eastern mission, visiting noted places in the history of the Church in Missouri, Ohio, New York and Illinois. It was on this trip that they had their famous interview with David Whitmer. When the First Presidency was organized, in October, 1880, he was chosen second counselor to President John Taylor, who died July 25, 1887. He was chosen to the same position in the Presidency under President Woodruff; and holds it at present under President Snow.

It would require too much space to name his various civil positions held in Salt Lake City, and in the legislature of the territory, where he served the people long and faithfully. All my readers are familiar with the work of his recent years; it is like an open book to the whole people.

So he has been constantly in the service of the public, and by his straightforward course has won the love, confidence and esteem of the whole community. He is a friend of the people, is easily approached, a wise counselor, a man of broad views, and contrary to first impressions, is a man whose sympathies are easily aroused. He is a reflex of the best character of the "Mormon" people—inured to hardships, patient in trial, God-fearing, self-sacrificing, full of love for the human race, powerful in moral, mental and physical strength.

President Joseph F. Smith has an imposing physical appearance. Now completing his 62nd year, he is tall, erect, well-knit and symmetrical in build. He has a prominent nose and features. When speaking, he throws his full, clear, brown eyes wide open on the listener who may readily perceive from their penetrating glimpse the wonderful mental power of the tall forehead above. His large head is crowned with an abundant growth of hair, in his early years dark, but now, like his full beard, tinged with a liberal sprinkling of gray. In conversation, one is forcibly impressed with the sudden changes in appearance of his countenance, under the different influences of his mind; now intensely present, with an enthusiastic and childlike interest in immediate subjects and surroundings; now absent, the nobility of his features, set in that earnest, almost stern, majesty of expression so characteristic of his portraits—so indicative of the severity of the conditions and environments of his early life.

As a public speaker, his leading trait is an intense earnestness. He impresses the hearer with his message more from the sincerity and simplicity of its delivery, and the honest earnestness of his manner, than from any learned exhibition of oratory or studied display of logic. He touches the hearts of the people with the simple eloquence of one who is himself convinced of the truth presented. He is a pillar of strength in the Church, thoroughly imbued with the truths of the gospel, and the divine origin of God's great latter-day work. His whole life and testimony are an inspiration to the young.

I said to him: "You knew Joseph, the prophet; you are old in the work of the Church; what is your testimony to the youth of Zion concerning these things?" And he replied slowly and deliberately:

"I was acquainted with the Prophet Joseph in my youth. I was familiar in his home, with his boys and with his family. I have sat on his knee, I have heard him preach, distinctly remembering being present in the council with my father and the Prophet Joseph Smith and others. From my childhood to youth I believed him to be a

Prophet of God. From my youth until the present I have not believed that he was a Prophet, for I have known that he was. In other words, my knowledge has superceded my belief. I remember seeing him dressed in military uniform at the head of the Nauvoo Legion. I saw him when he crossed the river, returning, from his intended western trip into the Rocky Mountains, to go to his martyrdom, and I saw his lifeless body together with that of my father after they were murdered in Cathage jail; and still have the most palpable remembrance of the gloom and sorrow of those dreadful days. I believe in the divine mission of the prophets of the nineteenth century with all my heart, and in the authenticity of the Book of Mormon and the inspiration of the book of Doctrine and Covenants, and hope to be faithful to God and man and not false to myself, to the end of my days."—*Edward H. Anderson, in Lives of Our Leaders, and Juvenile Instructor, 1901.*

LAST OF THE OLD SCHOOL OF VETERAN LEADERS

Surrounded by members of his family, President Joseph F. Smith peacefully closed his active life upon earth, on Tuesday morning, at 4:50 o'clock, November 19, 1918, at his home, the Beehive House, Salt Lake City, Utah. His noble work on earth is ended. He served the people of the Church in almost every useful private and public capacity all his life. He mounted, round by round, on the ladder of experience, as herd boy, pioneer, teacher, missionary, legislator, counselor; and for the past seventeen wonderful years was leader and mouthpiece of the Church of Jesus Christ of Latter-day Saints.

President Smith's administration began October 17, 1901, when he was chosen by the Twelve and set apart as President of the Church of Jesus Christ of Latter-day Saints, the choice being ratified by a special conference and solemn assembly of the Priesthood, on Sunday, November 10, 1901. Hence, for a few days more than seventeen years, he stood at the head of God's "marvelous work and a wonder," upon the earth. His leadership was characterized by a steady growth of the people in both spiritual and temporal affairs. Much of their progress was stimulated by his forethought and consideration, by his inspiration from the Lord freely granted to the people, and by his ability to gather men about him who willingly co-operated with him for the advancement and progress of the Church, the state and the community. In both religion and business, he was conservative, staunch, firm, and yet progressive—a leader beloved and respected by all. Every Church worker among his nearest associates, as well as in the stakes of Zion, and in the far flung missions of the world, fairly loved and admired him, and so did the members of the Church.

As editor of the *Improvement Era* and the *Juvenile Instructor*, and general superintendent of the Sunday Schools and Young Men's Mutual Improvement Associations, he was a stimulating power, a fountain of wisdom to his associates. Had he devoted himself to literary work, his success in that line would have been quite as marked as in public discourse and leadership.

He showed great tenderness and love for his large and honorable family. In his last address to his children, November 10, 1918, his heart's dearest sentiments were expressed to them in these words: "When I look around me, and see my boys and my girls whom the Lord has given to me,—and I have succeeded, with His help, to make

them tolerably comfortable, and at least respectable in the world—
I have reached the treasure of my life, the whole substance that makes
life worth living."

He was ever anxious for the welfare of the young people, as well
as the old, and every good effort for their advancement was sanctioned
and supported by him. Even in the midst of the cares, burdens and
anxieties of his active life weighing heavily upon him, he was never
known to be too busy to give counsel, experience, testimony, helpful
ideas, sympathetic consideration to workers or members of the Church
who called upon him. His courtesy to all was proverbial.

The passing of President Joseph F. Smith marks an epoch in the
history of the Church. He was the last of the old school of veteran
leaders who pioneered and founded our commonwealth. The patience
with which he bore the arduous labors of his life, fully, bravely, and
cheerfully, will be a lasting inspiration to all who knew him. The
story of his achievements for the Church, in spiritual and temporal
affairs, during his long administration, would make a volume of
thrilling interest. His mortal lips are sealed in death, but his spirit
lives forever. Beloved by all, the noble workman has gone to his
rest, having done his full duty for the advancement of the "marvelous work and a wonder," established of the Lord, which must ever
continue upon its triumphant march.—*Edward H. Anderson,*
May, 1919.

ADDENDA

CONFERRING THE PRIESTHOOD. To prevent disputes over this subject that may arise over the procedure presented on page 136, we draw attention to the fact that until recently, from the days of the Prophet Joseph Smith, ordinations to the Priesthood were directly to the office therein for which the recipient was chosen and appointed, in form substantially as follows:

As to the Melchizedek Priesthood—"By authority (or in the authority) of the Holy Priesthood and by the laying on of hands, I (or we) ordain you an Elder, (or Seventy, or High Priest, or Patriarch, or Apostle, as the case may be), in the Church of Jesus Christ of Latter-day Saints, and confer upon you all the rights, powers, keys and authority pertaining to this office and calling in the Holy Melchizedek Priesthood, in the name of the Lord Jesus Christ, Amen."

As to the Lesser Priesthood—"By (or in) the authority of the Holy Priesthood I (or we) lay my (or our) hands upon your head and ordain you a Deacon (or other office in the Lesser Priesthood) in the Church of Jesus Christ of Latter-day Saints, and confer upon you all the rights, powers and authority pertaining to this office and calling in the Aaronic Priesthood, in the name of the Lord Jesus Christ, Amen."

In reference to the form of procedure mentioned on page 136, and that set forth in this addendum as adopted by the leading authorities of the Church from the beginning, our beloved and departed President, Joseph F. Smith, when questioned concerning them, decided, as of record, "It is a distinction without a difference," and "either will do."

Persons, therefore, who have been ordained in either way hold the right to officiate in all the duties of their respective offices in the Priesthood.

HEBER J. GRANT,
ANTHON H. LUND,
CHARLES W. PENROSE,
First Presidency.

A DREAM. (Recorded by President Joseph F. Smith, April 7, 1918.) I did have a dream one time. To me it was a literal thing; it was a reality.

I was very much oppressed, once, on a mission. I was almost naked and entirely friendless, except the friendship of a poor, benighted, degraded people. I felt as if I was so debased in my condition of poverty, lack of intelligence and knowledge, just a boy, that I hardly dared look a white man in the face.

While in that condition I dreamed that I was on a journey, and I was impressed that I ought to hurry—hurry with all my might, for fear I might be too late. I rushed on my way as fast as I possibly could, and I was only conscious of having just a little bundle, a handkerchief with a small bundle wrapped in it. I did not realize just what it was, when I was hurrying as fast as I could; but finally I came to a wonderful mansion, if it could be called a mansion. It seemed too large, too great to have been made by hand, but I thought I knew that was my destination. As I passed towards it, as fast as I could, I saw a notice, "Bath." I turned aside quickly and went into the bath and washed myself clean. I opened up this little bundle that I had, and there was a pair of white, clean garments, a thing I had not seen for a long time, because the people I was with did not think very much of making things exceedingly clean. But my garments were clean, and I put them on. Then I rushed to what appeared to be a great opening, or door. I knocked and the door opened, and the man who stood there was the Prophet Joseph Smith. He looked at me a little reprovingly, and the first words he said: "Joseph, you are late." Yet I took confidence and said:

"Yes, but I am clean—I am clean!"

He clasped my hand and drew me in, then closed the great door. I felt his hand just as tangible as I ever felt the hand of man. I knew him, and when I entered I saw my father, and Brigham and Heber, and Willard, and other good men that I had known, standing in a row. I looked as if it were across this valley, and it seemed to be filled with a vast multitude of people, but on the stage were all the people that I had known. My mother was there, and she sat with a child in her lap; and I could name over as many as I remember of their names, who sat there, who seemed to be among the chosen, among the exalted.

The Prophet said to me, "Joseph," then pointing to my mother, he said: "Bring me that child."

I went to my mother and picked up the child, and thought it was a fine baby boy. I carried it to the Prophet, and as I handed it to him I purposely thrust my hands up against his breast. I felt the

warmth—I was alone on a mat, away up in the mountains of Hawaii—
no one was with me. But in this vision I pressed my hand up against
the Prophet, and I saw a smile cross his countenance. I handed him
the child and stepped back. President Young stepped around two
steps, my father one step, and they formed a triangle. Then Joseph
blessed that baby, and when he finished blessing it they stepped back
in line; that is, Brigham and father stepped back in line. Joseph
handed me the baby, wanted me to come and take the baby again;
and this time I was determined to test whether this was a dream or
a reality. I wanted to know what it meant. So I purposely thrust
myself up against the Prophet. I felt the warmth of his stomach.
He smiled at me, as if he comprehended my purpose. He delivered
the child to me and I returned it to my mother, laid it on her lap.

When I awoke that morning I was a man, although only a boy.
There was not anything in the world that I feared. I could meet
any man or woman or child and look them in the face, feeling in my
soul that I was a man every whit. That vision, that manifestation
and witness that I enjoyed at that time has made me what I am, if I
am anything that is good, or clean, or upright before the Lord, if
there is anything good in me. That has helped me out in every trial
and through every difficulty.

Now, I suppose that is only a dream? To me it is a reality. There
never could be anything more real to me. I felt the hand of Joseph
Smith. I felt the warmth of his stomach, when I put my hand against
him. I saw the smile upon his face. I did my duty as he required
me to do it, and when I woke up I felt as if I had been lifted out of a
slum, out of a despair, out of the wretched condition that I was in;
and naked as I was, or as nearly as I was, I was not afraid of any white
man nor of anyone else, and I have not been very much afraid of
anybody else since that time. I know that that was a reality, to show
me my duty, to teach me something, and to impress upon me something that I cannot forget. I hope it never can be banished from
my mind.

INDEX